Blackburn Aircraft

since 1909

The Beverley, with 162 ft span and 135,000 lb maximum weight, was Blackburn's largest
aeroplane. (*de Havilland*)

Blackburn
Aircraft
since 1909

A J Jackson

PUTNAM

By the same author

AVRO AIRCRAFT SINCE 1908

BRITISH CIVIL AIRCRAFT 1919–1972

DE HAVILLAND AIRCRAFT SINCE 1915

Printed and bound in Great Britain for
PUTNAM, an imprint of
Conway Maritime Press Ltd
24 Bride Lane, Fleet Street
London EC4Y 8DR
by The University Printing House, Oxford

British Library Cataloguing in Publication Data
Jackson, A. J. (Aubrey Joseph)
Blackburn aircraft since 1909. — 2nd ed. (Rev)
1. Blackburn aeroplanes, to 1988
I. Title
629.133'34
ISBN 0–85177–830–5

Set in Monotype Plantin

First published 1968
New edition 1989

IN TRIBUTE TO
Robert Blackburn 1885–1955
Pioneer Yorkshire aviator
and specialist in the construction
of aircraft for the Fleet

Contents

Foreword

The author's interest in Blackburn aircraft can be traced to a day in the summer of 1928 when the Master of Sempill flew sedately overhead the parental homestead in the Bluebird seaplane G-EBSW as he followed the Thames, passed Southend and disappeared round the coast in the direction of Felixstowe on the first leg of his round-Britain flight. In the following year this interest was renewed and stimulated when an enlightened physics master (the late M. F. Finn, M.Sc.) conducted a Southend High School sixth form group to the Olympia Aero Show in London where young hopefuls were able to feast their eyes on the beautiful metal Lincock, the hull of the great Nile flying-boat, and the Bluebird IV prototype in which Sqn Ldr Slatter had recently flown to the Cape. Although unsuccessful when lots were drawn for occupation of the passenger's seat during a detailed description of the machine by Blackburn's representative, close contact with the Bluebird and the men responsible for it sparked off an interest in light aeroplanes which revived in 1933 when the Southend Flying Club acquired the elderly wooden Bluebird G-AABE, resplendent in its manufacturer's black and red house colours.

The soft whirring 'phut-phut' of the Genet radial as this machine took off from the grass patch in the centre of the pony track at Rochford (just north of the present Southend Airport and now built over) and its easy, if modest, progress through the local atmosphere created an ambition to learn to fly which was eventually fulfilled many years later at the nearby Flying School. Unquestionably it is to 'BE and the hours, often days, spent gazing enviously at her that the writer owes many years of pleasure as pilot of a wide variety of light aeroplanes. The silver shape of the one remaining B-2, starlike against dark trees as it passed underneath, a couple of thousand feet or so below, while it was en route from Brough to Old Warden one day in the summer of 1966, revived regrets that these did not, after all, include a Blackburn type.

From among the considerable collection of Bluebirds assembled at Heston to celebrate the return of the Hon Mrs Victor Bruce from her World Flight in February 1931, it was possible to contemplate—from a respectful distance—many important Blackburn personalities including the great 'R.B.' himself, and, a few months later, at the same spot, to witness 'Dasher' Blake at his aerobatic best in the wooden Lincock. There was also at this time a new register of civil aircraft—Britain's first such publication—produced jointly by aircraft designer W. O. Manning and R. L. 'Mossie' Preston, then secretary of the Household Brigade Flying Club. In it one read of such unheard-of types as the Blackburn Kangaroo, Dart and Velos, and furthermore one had a friend who had ventured into the Far North (as it seemed in those days), reached Brough and had actually witnessed these wonders.

Such delights were not normally for southerners, but one memorable day in May 1933 the writer was at last privileged to see a Velos in flight when Ian Parker hove slowly into sight at Heston in the ex-Reserve School G-AAAW, but little was seen or heard of the Fleet Air Arm's Darts, Ripons and Baffins since most of their working lives were spent at sea with the carriers. Occasionally there were a few on the flight line at Gosport, once a year Hendon bowed to the throbbing majesty of the Iris and Perth flying-boats and in recent times Firebrands and Buccaneers have appeared in numbers at SBAC Shows and Royal Navy open days but, by and large, Blackburn military types have always been as elusive and as little publicized as the Silent Service for which they were built.

For this reason the completion of certain sections of this book has only been possible with a great deal of assistance from those who built, flew and repaired them, coupled with long and painstaking research among such records as still exist. Through the good offices of Sqn Ldr L. A. Jackson of the Shuttleworth Trust the author was fortunate in securing an introduction to the veteran R. W. Kenworthy, test pilot at Roundhay Park and Brough from 1916 to 1925, and flew down to visit him at Camberley. As the Auster threaded its way through the complicated levels east of Farnborough the unhesitating reply to an R/T call to Blackbushe made it evident that 'Ken' was waiting on the tarmac and not much impressed by those late on ETA. Nevertheless we were regaled with a wealth of quite extraordinary anecdotes and shown many rare photographs while Mrs Kenworthy dispensed generous hospitality, and the book is the richer for their scrutiny and criticism of the earlier chapters.

Later when Hawker Siddeley Aviation Ltd made available all surviving Blackburn documents, drawings and photographs, the author received the same cordial reception at Brough from Sales and Publicity Manager Mr M. G. K. Byrne and Mr Eric Barker of the Administrative Department as he had had at Camberley. Without their quite unprecedented co-operation and enthusiasm and that of a long serving member of the company, Mr B. J. Watson, the book could hardly have been written.

During two marathon and unforgettable visits to Brough it was yet possible to sense some of the atmosphere of the 'old days'. Admittedly the towering black 1916 North Sea Hangar and 'A' Shed were turning out Buccaneers and wings for the VTOL Harrier and the wooden slipways were in ruins, but the Middle Whitton light vessel still rolled to the Humber swell and a few nights' stay in the old world surroundings of The Buccaneer were sufficient to bring to mind the legend of how the site was chosen. Formerly the Station Hotel, it was one of the two local hostelries 'discovered' in 1916 by Mark Swann one of whose contemporaries, Mr Harry Goodyear, made the author so welcome at his home in Wetherby and contributed significantly to the pre-1914 chapters. Over at Yeadon Capt A. R. Carvell of Yorkshire Flying Services Ltd displayed and described with equal enthusiasm that hallowed relic, the Kangaroo airscrew.

Grateful acknowledgement is also made to the generous assistance given by F. H. Smith and A. W. L. Nayler, past and present librarians of the Royal Aeronautical Society; J. H. Blake, Editor of *British Light Aviation*; G. W. B. Lacey, Deputy Keeper at the Science Museum; K. M. Molson, lately Curator at the Canadian National Aviation Museum, Ottawa; D. Dorrell, Editor of *Air Pictorial*; the Editorial staff of *Flight International* and Miss A. Tilbury of their photographic department; F. G. Swanborough, Editor of *Flying Review International*; J. W. R. Taylor, Editor of *Jane's All the World's Aircraft*; the Editor and staff of *Lloyd's List and Shipping Gazette*; Hal Andrews, Editor of *Naval Aviation News*, Washington, DC; P. W. Moss, compiler of *Impressments Log*; P. W. Brooks, Beagle Aircraft Ltd; C. D. Long, de Havilland Aircraft of Canada Ltd; the Journals of the Canadian, Australian and New Zealand Air Historical Societies; *Air-Britain Digest*; M. C. Richards, Japanese specialist to Air-Britain; and the staffs of the Airworthiness Department of the Board of Trade, the Air Historical Branch of the Ministry of Defence, and the Imperial War Museum photographic section.

Among the author's collaborators of long standing have been Odd Arnesen, J. A. Bagley, C. H. Barnes, C. A. Nepean Bishop, J. M. Bruce, P. T. Capon, H. F. Cowley, P. A. Jackson, P. Jarrett, G. S. Leslie, D. E. Roberts and Bruce Robertson, whose contributions, advice and criticisms have so greatly enriched this book. Coupled with theirs are the names of P. Amos, Capt W. B. Axford, RN (Ret'd.), P. M. Bowers, M. J. F. Bowyer, T. Coxall, J. D. Gillies, P. L. Gray, John Hopton, G. A. Jenks, P. R. Keating, H. Kofoed, G. C. Kohn, Flt Lt T. Mason, J. McNulty, J. D. Oughton, L. J. Sarjeant, John Stroud, Eino Ritaranta, E. Taylor and D. P. Woodhall.

Last, but by no means least, the author acknowledges the debt owed to his wife for the long hours spent at the typewriter and for providing unlimited quantities of the national beverage when spirits flagged; and to L. E. Bradford for the immense care taken with the general arrangement drawings.

Leigh-on-Sea, Essex   A.J.J.
September 1968

Sadly A. J. Jackson is no longer with us to update his work: he died in October 1982. Main changes in this revised edition are the continuation of the section on the Buccaneer and the inclusion of an appendix covering the work of the Brough factory, now part of British Aerospace, up to 1988—for which J. D. R. Rawlings has provided much help.

Byfleet, August 1988   David Dorrell

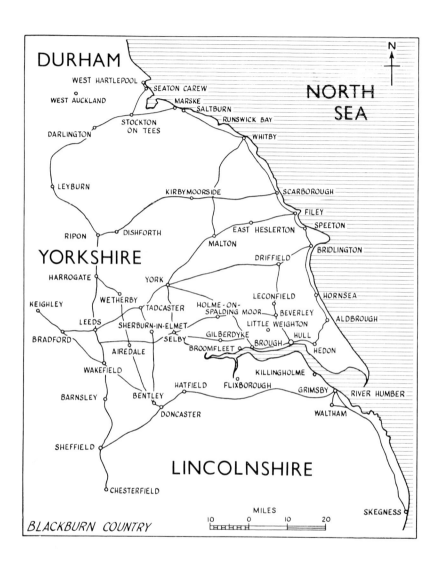

BLACKBURN COUNTRY

The main gates of the Blackburn factory at Brough prior to the merger with Hawker Siddeley Aviation Ltd. (*Flight Photo 17177S.*)

History of the Company

Blackburn Beginnings

Robert Blackburn, born on 26 March 1885, was a son of George W. Blackburn, works manager of Thomas Green and Sons Ltd, the well-known Leeds firm of steam-roller and lawn-mower manufacturers. He was educated at Leeds Modern School, soon showed outstanding scholarship, gained an honours degree in engineering under Prof Goodman at Leeds University in the early years of the century, and in 1906, at the age of 21, was made AMICE. He was then put to work in his father's drawing office where his first job (as he confided years later to Prof Collar) was to design a reduction gear for a Green road-roller. He did a very neat job and stressed all the gears for inertia loads, but father, looking over his shoulder, said, 'Nonsense, boy, the teeth should be ten times that size.' Robert rechecked his calculations and insisted that the design was sound whereupon George Blackburn took the drawing away and ordered the gears to be cut to an established practical standard dating from half a century earlier.

Realizing that clashes between his academic training and current engineering practice were inevitable, he left the firm and travelled to Germany, Belgium and France for further study, but it was the stay in France which affected his entire future. At a dinner given in Hull in 1930 to commemorate the twenty-first anniversary of his first attempt at flight, he recalled that while working for an engineering firm in Rouen in 1908 he used to ask for the

1

Friday or Saturday off in order to go to Le Mans to see Wilbur Wright flying his primitive biplane or to watch the early experiments of Latham, Blériot, Farman and other French pioneers at a small Army manoeuvre ground at Issy near Paris.

These worthies so fired the young Blackburn imagination that he determined to build an aeroplane of his own and, to avoid being 'fired' for continuously overstaying week-end leave, resigned in order to live in Paris where, in a top-floor room, he began drawings for his first monoplane. Later, when his parents arrived unexpectedly, he succeeded in persuading them to accompany him to the first Paris Aero Show and to allow him to remain in the French capital until his designs were finished.

When he returned to Leeds later in 1908, however, permission to build the machine in the Green works was refused, partly because it would have interfered with production but mainly because Blackburn senior had not spent a great deal of money on his son's technical training in order that he might build aeroplanes. Robert therefore left Greens for good but was rather more fortunate than most of his contemporary experimenters for, it is said, his father relented to the extent of giving him a measure of financial backing and assisted in setting up a small workshop of some 5–6,000 sq ft floor area beneath a clothing factory in Benson Street, Leeds—a building since demolished to make room for the road from Sheepscar to Regent Street. Harry Goodyear, one of Green's apprentices, was also detailed to go along and assist.

Robert Blackburn, OBE, AMICE, FRAeS, MIME, chairman and joint managing director of Blackburn Aircraft Ltd, photographed in 1939. (*Flight Photo 17182S.*)

2

Robert Blackburn's three-roomed bungalow on Filey Cliffs in 1911.

The monoplane was completed quite quickly and in April 1909 Blackburn took it in a horse-drawn furniture removal van to the stretch of sands between Marske and Saltburn and began attempts to make it fly. Even at this early stage he was assisting other experimenters by specializing in the manufacture of wooden airscrews in the Benson Street workshop at 35 shillings per foot of diameter and, early in 1910, put an advertisement in the technical press offering to build complete aeroplanes 'with either hand or patented automatic control' at a price of £700.

Eventually on 24 May 1910 he broke his First Monoplane without having flown in the true sense of the word and returned once more to Leeds. Harry Goodyear's suggestion that he should now go back to Greens and get on with some real work was countered by a request that he stay on and assist in the construction of a second and more conventional aeroplane. Its design was undoubtedly influenced by what Robert Blackburn had seen in France a year or so earlier, for the aircraft bore a marked external resemblance to M. Levavasseur's Antoinette monoplane, even to the small twin triangular rudders, one above and one below the elevator. These eventually became an identifying feature of many pre-1914 Blackburn aircraft. Never idle, Blackburn also made known his readiness to build aeroplanes to customers' own designs, describing himself as Blackburn Aeroplanes of 18 Spencer Place, Leeds, and offering his Second Monoplane (later known as the Light Type Monoplane to distinguish it from its predecessor) for sale at £500.

It did not sell but was tried out on a three-mile stretch of sand on the Yorkshire coast at Filey where, following an advertisement in the magazine *Flight* for 22 October 1910, he had moved into a hangar and an adjoining furnished bungalow at Low Cliffs belonging to J. W. F. Tranmer of Scarborough at a weekly rental of 10 shillings each. Adjacent to the hangar was a concrete slipway 12 ft wide down which his machine could be winched to the beach 60 yd below when the weather was suitable for flying.

These facilities were shared with Tranmer's Northern Automobile Co Ltd which had formally opened the 'aerodrome' on 25 July 1910 and used Blériot monoplanes which were overhauled, if not entirely constructed, by Blackburn in Leeds. In the following year he certainly built at least one Blériot to the order of R. T. Weiss, a pupil at the Blackburn Flying School at Filey, who overturned it there during fast taxying runs on 14 May 1911.

The famous bungalow, with modern additions, is still to be seen at Filey, but a few lumps of broken concrete are all that now remain of the slipway. The hangar, dismantled many years ago so that a second bungalow might be built on its concrete base, was re-erected in the local village where, in 1944, it was still in use as an engineering shop.

Not long after reaching Filey, the Second Monoplane attracted the attention of Bentfield C. Hucks who had accumulated a great deal of experience during more than a year with Claude Grahame-White at Hendon and in America (but who was not yet a certificated pilot). Somehow he persuaded Blackburn to let him try to fly it, succeeded, taught himself to fly on it and went on to become an extremely able and skilful pilot.

Early test pilots—*Left:* B. C. Hucks 1910–12. *Right:* R. W. Kenworthy 1917–25.

Due no doubt to vague and inconsistent data given in the company's 1911 catalogue (and faithfully but mistakenly reproduced again and again in various publications for more than 50 years), this aeroplane has been confused with Blackburn's third design called the Mercury, nine of which were built in 1911–12. Although similar in appearance, the Second Monoplane was smaller and boasted only two undercarriage wheels. No further proof of separate identity is needed if it is remembered that in March 1911, while the newly completed first Mercury was on the Blackburn stand at the Olympia Aero Show, the Second Monoplane was under repair at Filey following B. C. Hucks' accident of 8 March (see page 58).

Without question the many successful flights by his Second Monoplane

An early private owner—M. G. Christie, DSc (*front seat*) and his pilot Harold Blackburn in the Type I monoplane before the decking was fitted (*see page* 6).

established Robert Blackburn as one of the foremost British designers of the day but, like his famous contemporary A. V. Roe, he flew no more as a pilot and devoted himself entirely to the constructional side of the business, the test flying being done by Hucks. This happy partnership proved fruitful for both men, the one ably demonstrating the products of the other, and of course their friend Isaacson's engine also shared their modest successes and was built under contract in small numbers for Blackburn's next type, as well as for A. V. Roe and other experimenters, by Manning Wardle and Co. This concern also built locomotives, and its premises (known as the Boyne Engine Works) adjoined those of Isaacson's employers, the Hunslet Engine Co, both occupying part of the old Railway Foundry Estate at Hunslet, Leeds.

The next venture, in the early part of 1911, was the construction of a larger two-seater called the Mercury which necessitated a move into larger premises Blackburn had acquired off Balm Road, Leeds, and which were, in fact, disused Midland Railway stables. It was now clear that he intended to make a serious business of aviation for he now called himself The Blackburn Aeroplane Co, a styling first used publicly over his stand at the Olympia Aero

Old retainers who joined Robert Blackburn in the very beginning and served the company for a lifetime. *Left to right:* Mark Swann, Arthur Mason, Harry Goodyear and George Watson.

5

One of the Blackburn Mercury monoplanes being manhandled down the slipway to Filey beach in 1911.

Show, and engaged two new assistants, Mark Swann and George Watson who, with Harry Goodyear, were still with the company 30 years later.

During the next couple of years several Mercury variants were built at Balm Road including two with steel-tube fuselages—the first in Britain—at a time when popular interest in aviation was being stimulated all over Yorkshire by the enterprise and enthusiasm of a Leeds businessman, Stuart A. Hirst.

The Blackburn Flying School at Filey prospered, usually with three machines in service under a succession of instructors, namely B. C. Hucks, Hubert Oxley and Jack Brereton. After the School moved to Hendon in September 1912 it was managed by Harold Blackburn (no relation of Robert) but, when it closed in mid-1913, he left to become personal pilot to M. G. Christie for whom Balm Road had built a new two-seat monoplane (80 hp Gnome) for demonstration and cross-country flying. This was a development of the single-seater built earlier in the year for Cyril Foggin, and which is preserved in flying condition to this day by the Shuttleworth Trust. In later years Harold Blackburn, then Wing Commander RAF, became officer commanding the Aircraft and Armament Experimental Establishment, Martlesham Heath, from September 1924 to November 1928 and therefore responsible for evaluating several Blackburn prototypes. During the same period M. G. Christie was British Air Attaché in Washington with the rank of Group Captain.

During the whole of 1913 and part of 1914 Christie's Blackburn Type I was flown from parks, fields and beaches and, although it did not receive as much national publicity as it might have done at Hendon, it aroused tremendous interest in aviation all over Yorkshire and Lancashire. It was picketed

6

in the open for months at a time without detriment and by the end of 1913 alone had flown approximately 1,800 miles and carried 120 passengers.

The Formation of the Company

In May 1914 the Farnborough-designed B.E.2c was adopted as standard equipment for both the RFC and RNAS, and the Blackburn company became one of the several sub-contractors when an initial order for 12 was received from the Admiralty. Up to that time the company had been financed by Robert Blackburn personally but, faced with series production and the need to maintain larger premises, he formed a limited company, formally registered in June 1914 as The Blackburn Aeroplane and Motor Co Ltd with a capital of £20,000 in £1 shares 'to acquire the business of an aeroplane designer and constructor carried on by R. Blackburn as the Blackburn Aeroplane Co'. First directors were Robert Blackburn and J. E. Jackson with Stuart A. Hirst, the well known local flying enthusiast and patron, as chairman and Stephen Blakeney, for years an engineer on the London and North Western Railway, as works manager.

They had already taken possession of Olympia, a disused roller-skating rink in Roundhay Road, Leeds, and had erected their first biplane, the Blackburn Type L seaplane there. It was followed by larger and larger batches of B.E.2cs. They also built two of Harris Booth's A.D. Scouts, and developed the Sopwith Cuckoo torpedo-bomber and the Sopwith Baby seaplane which they built in quantity for the Admiralty, as well as the T.B., Triplane, G.P. and White Falcon prototypes of their own design. Although these Government contracts gave financial stability to the firm, Robert Blackburn was more interested in developing his private venture seaplanes and by 1916 felt that the time had come to establish a base equipped to handle these machines. In consequence Mark Swann was despatched to select a suitable site, which he soon discovered beside the River Humber adjacent to the main Leeds–Hull railway line at the village of Brough where there was space for an aerodrome, easy access to the river for marine aircraft and, according to

The entrance to the Olympia Works, Leeds, as it was in 1915.

legend, a couple of country pubs (the Ferry Inn and the Station Hotel) the excellence of whose beer was a deciding factor in the subsequent negotiations. An experimental section was set up quickly at the recommended spot and the first hangar and slipway completed in time for the erection and flight trials of the second G.P. seaplane later in 1916.

The establishment had no sooner been completed than the Government commandeered it as a base for No. 2 Marine Acceptance Depot and built what later became known as 'A' Shed and the Flight Shed (or North Sea Hangar). It was first used for the final erection of Short 184 seaplanes built by the Phoenix Dynamo Manufacturing Co Ltd and brought there, from 1916 onwards, from Bradford for launching. These were followed by the Phoenix-built prototype P.5 Cork flying-boat N86 which was launched on 7 August 1918.

B.E.2cs continued to flow from the Olympia works, which became the firm's Head Office and remained so for close on 30 years, but continual modernization and extension resulted in the systematic replacement of the exquisite maple skating floor by concrete. With commendable foresight an exceptionally well-equipped machine shop was also set up and Blackburns eventually became main contractors for the thousands of A.G.S. standard parts needed by the industry.

Sopwith Cuckoo production was centred at Sherburn-in-Elmet, an aerodrome 12 miles east of Leeds, but the Sopwith Baby seaplanes were constructed at Olympia and test flown from the Humber at Brough by R. W. Kenworthy, successor to test pilot Rowland Ding, killed during a B.E.2c test flight at Roundhay Park, Leeds, 12 May 1917. The big twin-engined Kangaroos, landplane version of the G.P. seaplane and first pure Blackburn type to secure a production contract, were also built at Leeds and the components transported to Brough for erection. After test flight they were merely taxied over to the Acceptance Depot pending issue to No. 246 Squadron at Seaton Carew which was successful in bombing a German U-boat with one of them in August 1918.

The Lean Years

Even before the cessation of hostilities Robert Blackburn was thinking ahead to the time when aeroplanes would play an important part in postwar society and clearly foresaw the parallel growth of commercial and private flying. With characteristic energy and enthusiasm he put these ideas into practical effect when he embarked on air transport operations in 1919 with converted wartime Kangaroos and built the small Sidecar two-seat light aeroplane suitable for private ownership. The premature end of both these pioneer ventures, brought about by the deteriorating economic situation, would have driven a lesser man out of aviation altogether.

Although the postwar slump killed the little Sidecar monoplane and brought about the collapse of Blackburn's aspirations in the field of commercial air transport and it was abundantly clear that the firm's whole future

Left: Maj F. A. Bumpus, BSc, ARCS, WhSc, FRAeS, designer, chief engineer and joint managing director with Robert Blackburn 1919–51. *Right:* Maj J. D. Rennie, FRAeS, ARTC, AMICE, chief seaplane designer 1923–46. (*BAe.*)

was in jeopardy, the company somehow managed to keep its large and well-equipped Leeds factory going on the small but unceasing demand for nuts, bolts, turnbuckles and other small fittings known in the aircraft industry as A.G.S. parts and on the production of bodies for cars, motor coaches and (at a later date) trolley-buses. They even designed and constructed a Blackburn car with boat-built body as well as an airscrew-driven sledge for the 1921 Shackleton–Rowett South Polar Expedition. This sledge was powered by one of the classic three-cylinder fan Anzani engines which probably came from one of the pre-war Filey Blériot monoplanes.

A patent Alula high-lift wing was constructed of wood and fabric in 1920 to the designs of A. A. Holle of the Commercial Aeroplane Wing Syndicate Ltd and taken to Sherburn-in-Elmet to be strut-braced to a D.H.6 fuselage. The resulting monoplane was registered G-EAWG* and a crude form of flap was incorporated, but results were not encouraging and Blackburns were commissioned to build two further wings. These were of thicker section for cantilever mounting and were planked overall with thin mahogany. One went to Sherburn for trials on the D.H.6 which had been re-engined for the experiment with a 200 hp Bentley B.R.2 rotary and was flown successfully by Capt Clinch on 2 January 1921. The other was fitted to the Martinsyde Semiquaver G-EAPX† which Blackburn's test pilot R. W. Kenworthy flew at Northolt on 27 August that year, the take-off speed being 110 mph!

When things seemed at their worst, the Air Ministry published a requirement for a new torpedo-carrying, deck-landing aeroplane, and Robert Blackburn, with unshakeable optimism, took a bold step which was to prove the turning point in the fortunes of the company. Collaborating closely with D.

---

* See the author's *De Havilland Aircraft since 1915*, page 91.
† See the author's *British Civil Aircraft 1919–1972*, volume 3, page 31.

Napier and Son Ltd of Acton, who provided one of their 450 hp Napier Lion twelve-cylinder water-cooled engines, he decided to meet this specification with a private venture machine which would be superior in every way to the earlier and unsuccessful Blackburd.

This prototype, called the Swift, was built in five months to the designs of Maj F. A. Bumpus, the Air Board's resident representative at Leeds during the construction of the G.P. seaplane and Kangaroo landplanes, who had stayed on after the war to become chief designer and joint managing director with Robert Blackburn. His assistant chief designer was G. E. Petty (who himself eventually became chief designer in 1937), and the first drawing office was simply a large wooden packing case of the type used for shipping B.E.2cs as deck cargo. It housed the entire staff of four, most of whom were bundled out when Maj Bumpus wanted to use the telephone.

By July 1920 the Swift was sufficiently complete for exhibition at the Olympia show, and secured much needed foreign orders in the following year. With the assistance of his brothers, Norman and Charles (Spencer, a third brother, favoured the motor trade), Robert Blackburn established original systems of manufacture and was awarded Air Ministry contracts for its quantity production as the Dart. This was a modified version for the Fleet Air Arm which sired a whole family of deck-landing biplanes, firmly established the Blackburn company as specialists in naval aircraft construction and kept the works fully employed until the outbreak of the next World War in 1939.

When Roundhay Park reverted to its former status as a public open space, the main Blackburn works in Leeds was deprived of adjacent aerodrome facilities, which meant that all the Swifts, Darts, Blackburns, Velos, the two enormous Cubaroos and other aircraft of the period, had to travel the road to

The erecting shop at Brough in 1925, with work in progress on the second civil Dart trainer, G-EBKG, the first Kangaroo dual conversion, G-EAIU, and the second Cubaroo, N167.

Brough some 40 miles distant for erection and flight. Robert Blackburn therefore decided that the time had come to close down the Olympia works and to concentrate all the firm's activities at Brough.

The transfer was inevitably a slow process and, though first mooted in 1925, did not gather real momentum until 1928 when an extensive building programme was pushed through at the aerodrome to enable the Head Office and the more important works departments to make the move early in 1929. The Inspection Department, machine, airscrew and wing assembly shops had to remain in Leeds, however, until a new boiler house was built at Brough in 1932 to provide sufficient power to run them.

Acute problems were created for 1,000 Leeds employees compelled to commute daily by rail to join the 500 at Brough. In the course of time they were either housed locally or replaced by local labour, so that eventually the little half-timbered works manager's house, 'Pantiles', at Brough, containing all that was left of Olympia's famous maple flooring, was the only remaining link with the old works. Dwarfed by factory buildings, the house is still in use 40 years later as the Hawker Siddeley Pensions Department.

A flying club formed by Blackburn employees in April 1923 to operate a D.H.6, which the company was going to house at Brough free of charge, failed to get started.

Marine Operations

To design and build a Schneider Trophy winner was every aircraft manufacturer's dream in the 1920s, since there was no surer way of raising the company's prestige in world markets. The point was not lost on Robert Blackburn or his directors so that when Great Britain became host country for the 1923 contest, they are said to have debated whether to pay a dividend to shareholders or enter for the competition. Inevitably they chose the latter course and Blackburn's long association with waterborne aircraft, which had ended with the cancellation of the N.1B single-seat flying-boat in 1918, was renewed in 1923 when that flying-boat's hull was used as a basis for their Schneider challenger.

Convinced that flying-boats had a military and commercial future, they also secured the services of Maj J. D. Rennie who joined the firm later that year as float and hull designer.

This able engineer had spent most of the war at Felixstowe as chief technical officer to Cdr John Porte. It was he who had been primarily responsible for engineering work on Porte's Felixstowe-built F-type flying-boats.

In January 1924, soon after Rennie's arrival, the Air Ministry awarded a contract to Blackburn's subsidiary, the North Sea Aerial and General Transport Co Ltd, for the establishment of an RAF Reserve School at Brough equipped for training seaplane as well as landplane pilots. Rennie's wooden floats for the School's Dart and Velos trainers, and later for the Blackburn I and Ripon I prototypes, were among the best in the world for clean running, ease of unsticking and smooth alighting. Then in the same year he was given

11

Wheeling out Robert Blackburn's ancient Antoinette monoplane to give
scale effect to the Cubaroo during the Press visit to Brough on 21 August 1924.

the challenging task of designing first wooden, then metal, hulls and floats for
the projected Iris flying-boats.

In designing the massive wing assemblies for these boats, Maj Bumpus was
able to draw on the experience of building large aircraft structures which had
been gained with the giant Blackburn Cubaroo landplanes. In this connection
it is interesting to recall an echo of the past that was dragged out of the Flight
Shed and photographed alongside the first Cubaroo during the Press demonstration on 21 August 1924. This was a dismantled Antoinette monoplane
complete with 50 hp Levavasseur V-8 steam-cooled engine: the actual
machine brought to England by Hubert Latham for the Blackpool Flying
Meeting in October 1910 and flown at Brooklands in 1911. Robert Blackburn
found it in a garage at Colwyn Bay in 1916 and bought it for £60 purely for the
memories it revived of his early days in Paris and for its similarity to his own
prewar Mercury monoplanes. By 1924 it was in a very bad state of repair
and in June 1926 was despatched on loan, incomplete and in damaged condition, to the Science Museum, South Kensington, where it was fitted with new
aluminium condenser tubes and placed on public exhibition. Its condition
has much improved over the years by careful dusting and polishing, and a new
brass petrol tank was made and fitted by Marconi apprentices in 1950, but,
even today, the wing covering does not extend more than 6 ft from the wing
root. In 1955 Robert Blackburn agreed to present the machine to the Museum
and the descriptive label permanently displays his name as donor.

The Seaplane Base

The first results of Rennie's work were, of course, not seen on the River
Humber until 1925 but Blackburn's unique North British seaplane base was

not entirely idle, being used in 1924 as a staging post by two foreign-sponsored westbound trans-Atlantic flights.

First to arrive were the three famous US Army Douglas D-WC World Cruisers *Chicago, Boston* and *New Orleans,* flown respectively by Lts Lowell Smith, Leigh Wade and Eric Nelson, survivors of four which had left Seattle on 6 April 1924 to circumnavigate the world from east to west. They were long-range models of the DT-2 torpedo biplane, the developed version of the DT-1 which had been selected for US Navy use after competitive trials with the Blackburn Swift F and other European types in 1922. The World Cruisers arrived at Croydon from Le Bourget on 16 July 1924 and next day flew in formation to Brough where the Blackburn company gave them a complete overhaul, installed new 400 hp Liberty 12 engines, repaired the radiators and fitted wooden floats which had been delivered from America some weeks earlier. They were launched and test flown from the Humber on 28 July and two days later left for Kirkwall, Orkney, en route for Iceland. *Boston* was sunk by gunfire after a forced alighting off the Faroes on 3 August but the others arrived in the USA on 28 September after a 27,553-mile flight lasting 175 days. *Chicago* is preserved in the Smithsonian Institution, Washington, DC, 23–1232 *New Orleans* is in the museum at Wright-Patterson Air Force Base, Dayton, Ohio, and clay pipes autographed by the crews hang in the bar of the Ferry Inn, Brough, to this day.

Italy's Signore Antonio Locatelli, the other user of Brough's facilities, was not so fortunate. He arrived from Rotterdam via Lowestoft and Cromer with three crew on 4 August 1924 in the Dornier Wal flying-boat I-DEOB powered by two 360 hp Rolls-Royce Eagle engines and was guest of Robert

John Grierson in his Gipsy Moth seaplane G-AAJP *Rouge et Noir* on suitably-inscribed Blackburn floats at Brough before the start of his flight to Iceland, 27 July 1933. (*Topical Press Photo.*)

Local colour—*Top:* The Middle Whitton light vessel photographed from Blackburn's slipway in October 1925 with the prototype Velos (float undercarriage No. 11) touching down. *Bottom:* The famous traction engine, which acted as a mobile winch for launching and retrieving all the early Blackburn flying-boats, officiating at the launch of the Sydney, October 1934.

Blackburn while his aircraft was worked on by Rolls-Royce engineers as it lay on the mud alongside the east slipway. He left for Iceland via Kirkwall in the wake of the World Cruisers on 9 August, and took off from Reykjavik, Iceland, accompanied by two of the American World Cruisers en route to Greenland on 21 August. Shortage of fuel and deteriorating weather eventually forced the Wal down on the sea but the crew was picked up by a US cruiser which located it 125 miles east of Cape Farewell, Greenland, on 24 August. At Locatelli's request the aircraft was sunk by gunfire.

Some years later long-distance pilot John Grierson also used Brough as starting point for a westward flight by the northern route in his Gipsy Moth G-AAJP *Rouge et Noir*. He flew it to Brough to be fitted with a Blackburn float undercarriage★ and made a 5½ hour nonstop flight to Scapa Flow on 4 August 1933 en route to the Faroes and Iceland where the flight was abandoned when the aircraft was damaged by heavy seas.

★ See the author's *De Havilland Aircraft since 1915*, pages 234–236.

Eventually the long awaited Blackburn aircraft emerged one at a time from the great sheds and in the period 1927–32 a total of ten large Iris, Sydney and Perth flying-boats made dignified first flights at Brough. They were always of considerable interest to local residents who used to line the river bank to watch the stately giants towed sideways out of the flight shed and lowered slowly down the slipway at the end of a cable attached to a fussing, steam enshrouded traction engine which acted as a brake.

Brough had been chosen in 1916 because it was situated at the bend of the river, for in theory seaplanes and flying-boats could then take-off in any wind direction or state of the tide. G. E. Petty revealed, in his Fifth Sir George Cayley Memorial Lecture before the Brough Branch of the Royal Aeronautical Society in Hull on 12 November 1958, that it was not as ideal a site as had been hoped. Tidal conditions not only dictated the time of day at which a boat might be launched but often made beaching so difficult that it was frequently left moored out. Even then care had to be taken to see that it was clear of the deep water shipping lane which lay close inshore between the company's slipways and the Middle Whitton light vessel only a few cables' lengths away. In Petty's opinion flying-boat development would have been easier if better operating conditions had enabled prototype testing to go ahead smoothly at Brough. As it was, teething troubles were often corrected only after the boats had reached Felixstowe or Mount Batten.

Nor was the site completely satisfactory as an aerodrome since it was beset by the Humber's own particular brand of sea mist, known locally as a 'Fret', which could sweep up the river very quickly, cover the ground up to a height of 100 ft and make landing impossible.

Left: G. E. Petty, FRAeS, assistant designer 1918–37, chief designer 1937–51. (*BAe.*) *Right:* Wg Cdr A. G. Loton, AFC, for 20 years chief flying instructor at the Brough Reserve School. (*BAe.*)

15

The Brough works, looking west, with the River Humber beyond, as it was on 10 January 1934. (*Flight Photo 13797.*)

Landplanes

Parallel with its programme of flying-boat development and additional to the series production of torpedo-bombers for the Fleet Air Arm, the Blackburn design team under Maj Bumpus also produced a number of exploratory naval prototypes such as the Airedale, Sprat, Nautilus and Beagle. None of this work brought the company much publicity since it was mostly for the Silent Service, and Blackburn types, being designed to meet very difficult specifications which demanded deck-landing capability by aeroplanes stressed for float and catapult operation, lacked the glamour of some land-based machines.

Following a long-term study of contemporary single-seat fighters, however, Blackburns had come to the conclusion that growing complexity and weight was restricting manoeuvrability. Thus in 1927, as a relief from normal work, the design staff was told to go ahead and create the smallest and most manoeuvrable biplane fighter that could be built round the 240 hp Armstrong Siddeley Lynx air-cooled radial engine. Military equipment was cut to bare essentials and the result was the delightful little Lincock whose performances in the hands of G. E. Lowdell, A. M. Blake, Flt Lt R. L. R. Atcherley and others was almost unbelievable. In practice it was found that the penalty of low power was low maximum speed and for this reason the Lincock impressed neither the RAF nor the RCAF but, although something of a financial failure, it did serve to keep the name of Blackburn in the public eye both in the United Kingdom and overseas.

Ten years earlier the company had converted a number of wartime Kangaroos for commercial purposes but did not build a purely civil transport aircraft until 1929 when it was awarded an Air Ministry contract for comparative performance measurements of a near-identical biplane and monoplane. Close links with Saunders-Roe Ltd of Cowes, Isle of Wight, who had built

16

the Blackburn Bluebird IV under sub-contract in 1929–30, led in 1931 to the appearance of the all-metal, four-seat Blackburn Segrave, a development of the Segrave Meteor originally built at Cowes in wood. The third and last of the type was used in developing the Duncanson tubular metal spar employed in the construction of the larger 200 mph H.S.T.10 transport, first Blackburn aircraft equipped with a retractable undercarriage. Unfortunately it came too late and, though nearly complete, was abandoned in 1938 to make way for urgent military construction demanded by the growing menace of war.

The only evidence of the company's interest in rotary wing aircraft was a brief announcement in December 1934 that Robert Blackburn had undertaken to build the Asboth helicopter in the United Kingdom and that Flt Lt Nicholas Comper would be consulting engineer. The scheme stemmed from a promising test flight at Budapest in 1930 by Capt R. N. Liptrot, of the Air Ministry, in a prototype with contra-rotating co-axial rotors built by the Austrian inventor Oskar Asboth. The German firm of Henschel also acquired licence rights and went on to make the design a success; but none were ever constructed at Brough.

Expansion

The success of a Cirrus-engined Bluebird in the 1931 King's Cup race led to such close liaison between Blackburns and the Cirrus Hermes Engineering Co Ltd that in February 1934 their works was transferred from Croydon to Brough and Robert Blackburn became chairman. This move, coupled with the manufacture of large numbers of Shark torpedo aircraft as Blackburn's share of the country's rearmament programme, created a demand for additional factory space which was met by enlarging existing premises at Brough and by re-opening and extending the old Olympia works in Leeds.

In anticipation of even larger contracts then under negotiation, Blackburns next decided to consolidate all its interests into one company and formed Blackburn Aircraft Ltd. Registered on 2 April 1936 with a share capital of £630,000, it took over the assets of The Blackburn Aeroplane and Motor Co Ltd and the North Sea Aerial and General Transport Co Ltd, Robert Blackburn continuing as chairman and managing director, with Maj F. A. Bumpus as chief engineer, Maj J. D. Rennie as chief seaplane designer and Capt N. W. G. Blackburn, H. C. Bevan, R. R. Rhodes, Sqn Ldr J. L. N. Bennett-Baggs and E. Hudson as directors.

Their first important move was to come to an agreement with the famous Scottish shipbuilding firm of William Denny and Bros Ltd of Dumbarton for the establishment of a new aircraft factory on the banks of the Clyde. Sir Maurice Denny then joined the Board of Blackburn Aircraft Ltd and by 1937 a new works with over 300,000 sq ft of floor space had been completed on land owned by Denny and lying to the east of their shipyard. This enabled Blackburns to transfer their entire flying-boat section from Brough and also to set up a Shark repair organization away from the main production line, the entire

Test pilots—*Left:* Sqn Ldr J. L. N. Bennett-Baggs, also a director of the company 1931–50. *Right:* Flt Lt A. M. 'Dasher' Blake, chief test pilot 1927–37. (*Flight Photos 15258, 15259.*)

works being in charge of Maj F. A. Bumpus who was assisted by H. J. Stieger, inventor of the Monospar wing and formerly chief designer of General Aircraft Ltd, Feltham. The works manager was A. T. S. Groombridge.

One of the first tasks undertaken at Dumbarton was the construction of Maj Rennie's revolutionary new Blackburn B-20 retractable-hull flying-boat, flown off the waters of the Clyde by chief test pilot Henry Bailey in April 1940.

In the same year Blackburn Aircraft Ltd completely absorbed the Cirrus Hermes Engineering Co Ltd but retained the Cirrus technical director C. S. Napier as chief engineer in charge of design in the engine section and housed his private Hendy 302 G-AAVT at Brough. He produced the four-cylinder 90 hp Cirrus Minor 1, first of a new range of light air-cooled engines, and had already test flown it in the Blackburn Bluebird IV test bed B-10 in 1936. A larger development, the 150 hp Cirrus Major 1, was flown by him in the company's Percival Gull G-ADOE in 1938.

In that year, when the last of the Shark biplanes was coming off the line at Brough and first examples of the new Skua monoplane were already flying, Blackburns completed the second stage of their break with tradition. The first, two years previously, had seen the disappearance of the old company names. Now, with the production of the Navy's first modern all-metal, retractable undercarriage cantilever monoplane, they said goodbye for ever to the biplanes with which they had been associated for so long.

Test flying of this new generation of aircraft was the responsibility of Flt Lt A. M. Blake, AFC, who had been chief test pilot ever since his engagement in November 1927 to take over from H. V. Worrall and fly Charles Blackburn on a round-Britain tour in the Blackburn Bluebird G-EBTA. Thereafter he flew all the firm's products, and there is no doubt that his

18

ability as a pilot, his calm attention to detail and outstanding memory for facts and figures were of the greatest service to the firm for almost ten years. During this time he was assisted by various Reserve School instructors, and by Sqn Ldr J. L. N. Bennett-Baggs who joined the firm in 1931 and combined test flying with his duties as director and sales manager until forced to give up by ill health.

While Shark production test flying was in full swing, Reserve School instructor Flt Lt H. Bailey, AMICE, AFRAeS, was appointed assistant test pilot, becoming chief test pilot after Blake's death at his home in Hull on 16 October 1937. In the following year, when Skua production was given highest priority, Bailey led a team of test pilots which included the former Brough and Hanworth instructor Flt Lt H. J. Wilson (later Grp Capt Wilson, CBE, AFC, holder of the world's air speed record at 606 mph in 1945), and Flg Off B. R. Rolfe, chief test pilot at the Blackburn-managed Greek National Aircraft Factory from 1921 to 1929, both of whom rejoined Blackburns on 1 June 1938.

Skua production test pilots 1938—*Left to right:* H. J. Wilson, Wg Cdr R. J. M. de St Leger (Service liasion officer), H. Bailey, B. R. Rolfe. (*Flight Photo 16670S.*)

Their labours were not in vain for on 25 September 1939, only 22 days after the outbreak of war, a Skua from the aircraft carrier *Ark Royal* shot down a Dornier Do 18 flying-boat off Heligoland and became the first British aeroplane to destroy an enemy aircraft in the 1939–45 war. A few months later, on 10 April 1940, the effectiveness of dive bombing was demonstrated impressively when Skuas flew from the Orkneys to Norway to bomb and sink the 6,000-ton enemy cruiser *Königsberg* in the narrow confines of Bergen Harbour. Officialdom, unconvinced, ordered no more dive-bombers, but the enemy continued to perfect and develop the technique with its famous Ju 87s and other aircraft and wrought havoc among Allied forces for the rest of the war.

The Skua's unsuccessful sister aircraft, the Roc turret fighter, was subcontracted to Boulton Paul Ltd just before the war and built at Wolverhampton because Blackburns themselves had received substantial contracts for the Botha and needed every inch of factory space. By 1939 the Botha was in full production both at Brough and Dumbarton and served for a few

Robert Blackburn with his brothers Charles (*left*) and Norman, photographed by the side of a production Skua in 1938. (*BAe.*)

months over the North Sea with No. 608 Squadron, but teething troubles, coupled with the collapse of France in 1940, rendered obsolete such a short-range general-purpose torpedo-bomber and, although built in larger numbers than any other Blackburn aircraft, it was used principally as a trainer for bomber crews.

The 1939–45 War

At the outbreak of war in 1939 the all-metal monocoque Shark and its rival, the steel-tube and fabric Fairey Swordfish, were both in squadron service but, due to a shortage of light alloys, war production was concentrated on the Swordfish. By way of compensation, however, Blackburns received contracts for the major share of Swordfish production for which a new factory was built at Sherburn-in-Elmet. There the machines were assembled from components supplied by the Olympia works and by a well organized group of sub-contractors. The works manager was T. Bancroft, R. W. Kenworthy's flight engineer on the Kangaroos back in 1919 and former chief engineer of the company's flying schools at Brough and Hanworth. The first Blackburn-produced Swordfish—or Blackfish as they were called—left the factory in December 1939 and the firm eventually produced a total of 1,700, peak production reaching 60 per month.

Even before the Botha contracts were terminated, Brough was turned over to building 635 Fairey Barracudas for the Navy, and Dumbarton to the construction of 250 Short Sunderland flying-boats. New Blackburn designs were also worked on, the Firebrand single-seat fighter/torpedo-bomber at Brough and the B-20 retractable-hull flying-boat at Dumbarton. These designs were linked in 1944 when a mock-up of a Firebrand with the retractable hull was constructed at Brough during an investigation into means of operating fighters among the islands of the Pacific.

Less well-known Blackburn contributions to the war effort were the repair of damaged aircraft and the modification of American naval types, such as

20

Martlets, Avengers, Corsairs and Hellcats, to suit British operational requirements. At first this work was done entirely in the United Kingdom, but from 1942 the company played a leading part in running the British Modification Centre in the United States which, by the summer of 1944, was producing 400 fully modified operational aircraft per month.

The Postwar Years

Following the pattern of 1918, the end of the war forced Blackburns into a period of retrenchment, the Leeds and Sherburn factories were closed and all aircraft and engine work concentrated at Brough. With reluctance, all work on marine projects was brought to an end and Maj J. D. Rennie, the chief seaplane designer, resigned in May 1946 after 23 years with the firm.

Following a precedent set nearly 30 years earlier, the factory was kept going on non-aeronautical production ranging from light alloy roof trusses to the huge parabolic reflectors used for the London–Birmingham television link, as well as a variety of humble domestic articles. The manufacture of the Bean range of agricultural implements was also undertaken, under contract from their designer, by a specially formed subsidiary known as The Humberside Agricultural Products Co Ltd. At the same time the Dumbarton enterprise was reconstituted as a subsidiary company and from 6 October 1947 was known as Blackburn (Dumbarton) Ltd. It was kept going thereafter on the

Blackburn B-46 Firebrand T.F. Mk 5s of No. 813 Squadron on the deck of *Implacable* in 1949.

construction of prefabricated aluminium bungalows to help relieve the housing shortage.

Meanwhile the aviation section at Brough was busy with the development and production of Cirrus engines and with building Firebrands for the post-war Navy. Test flying was initially in the hands of Flt Lt A. C. R. Thompson but Gp Capt C. G. P. Flood took over in May 1947. He left the firm in March 1948 and was succeeded by ex Royal Navy pilot P. G. Lawrence, Blackburn's experimental test pilot since 1945 who had been awarded the MBE for his part in deck landing trials with the Firebrand T.F.Mk.4 and who won the Air League Challenge Trophy in a Firebrand at Elmdon in 1949 before leaving to join Glosters. He shared development flying of the Blackburn B-48 with G. F. Bullen, a Firebrand and Prentice production test pilot with the firm from 1947 until he left in 1949 to join Hawkers.

F. F. Crocombe, H. 'Tim' Wood and D. G. Brade, designer, pilot and co-pilot respectively of the Universal Freighter, after the first flight, 20 June 1950.

Blackburn and General Aircraft Ltd

At the end of 1948, as a result of under-employment at Brough, Blackburn's interests were amalgamated with those of General Aircraft Ltd whose factory at Feltham, Middlesex, adjoined the Blackburn-owned Hanworth Aerodrome, prewar home of their B-2 equipped flying school. With effect from 1 January 1949, all General Aircraft's contracts, designs and subsidiary companies, as well as manufacturing rights of the firm's Megator marine and industrial pumps, were taken over by a new organization registered on 23 February as Blackburn and General Aircraft Ltd. H. 'Tim' Wood and F. F. Crocombe, formerly chief test pilot and chief designer, respectively, of General Aircraft Ltd, were appointed to similar positions in the combined company.

The scene was now set for the production of the Beverley heavy freighter which was to serve the RAF all over the world during a full decade, 1958–67. The delivery of all 47 Beverleys on schedule was one of the most remarkable feats of production time-keeping ever achieved in the industry, despite the extra problems posed by the sheer physical size of the aircraft. They were

WF320, prototype Universal Freighter and forerunner of the Beverley, flying over Beverley Minster, ten miles north-east of Brough.

solved as a result of skilled planning by the company's works director W. A. Hargreaves who used a scale model of the final assembly shop in order to study methods of moving large aircraft components in a confined space.

G. E. Petty, who had been 33 years with the firm and chief designer of

Blackburn Aircraft Ltd since Maj Bumpus left for Dumbarton in 1937, relinquished his position in 1951 and, F. F. Crocombe having left to join Boulton Paul Ltd, B. P. Laight was appointed chief designer to Blackburn and General Aircraft Ltd in July 1952, assisted by W. W. Greenfield and C. W. Prower.

Cautious expansion which began again at this time was not without historical significance, for in 1951 the company took over Thomas Green and Son Ltd, the Leeds firm which had been so closely connected with Robert Blackburn's pioneer efforts 40 years previously. To the Green range of rollers and mowers were added the products of the Humberside Agricultural Products Co Ltd, which then moved to Leeds to form Green's Agricultural Division.

In October 1952 the Blackburn Engine Division, which had supplied hundreds of Cirrus piston engines for postwar civil and military light aeroplanes, acquired exclusive licence rights for the development, manufacture and sale of the French Turbomeca gas-turbine engines. Sales manager for the new enterprise was Grp Capt H. J. Wilson, former Blackburn Skua test pilot, who rejoined the company in March 1953. Later still, when additional machining capacity became an urgent necessity for the Beverley programme in 1955, Jowett Cars Ltd was taken over, restyled Jowett Engineering Ltd, and its premises used as extra aircraft factory space while maintaining a spares service for Jowett car owners.

Left to right: P. G. Lawrence, G. R. I. 'Sailor' Parker and D. J. Whitehead.

Work went ahead during these years on contracts for de Havilland Chipmunk mainplanes, wing-tip tanks for Venom night-fighters and complete Percival Prentice and Boulton Paul Balliol trainers for the Ministry of Supply. The unlucky Y.B.1, first turbine-powered aircraft of Blackburn manufacture, also made its appearance as well as the experimental H.P.88 jet prototype for Handley Page Ltd. The H.P.88, which is described on page 522, made a valuable contribution to the British deterrent bomber force and consisted of a Supermarine Attacker fuselage mated to a scale model of the crescent-shaped wing intended for the Handley Page Victor.

Dumbarton was also active on a smaller scale. The manufacture of com-

The 1912 Blackburn Monoplane and a production Buccaneer S. Mk 1, XN924, at Holme-on-Spalding Moor, 16 April 1962.

ponents for aluminium houses went on unabated, but later the company recommenced aircraft work and built mainplanes for de Havilland Vampire jet fighters, the first of which left the factory on 14 May 1952. This work continued until 1954 when the manufacture of Beverley freighter components began.

The Buccaneer

In the evening of his life Robert Blackburn received many marks of esteem in recognition of his unswerving devotion to aviation. On 31 March 1950 he was made Honorary Fellow of the Royal Aeronautical Society and three years later, on 28 January 1953, his portrait in oils by Bernard Adams was presented to the Royal Aero Club, but a heart condition was causing much concern and after actively controlling the company for over 40 years he was at last compelled, on doctor's advice, to transfer much of his responsibility to younger shoulders. He moved into semi-retirement in Devonshire but continued as chairman of the company and when, in that capacity, he addressed the annual general meeting on 25 August 1955 it was to hint at a 'challenging aircraft development contract' being placed with the company which was to renew its link with the Navy, broken in 1950 when the Y.B.1 was abandoned.

The new aircraft was, of course, the Buccaneer twin-jet low-level strike aircraft, then very secret, but Robert Blackburn's wish that he might live to see it fly was not fulfilled. After meeting a large number of friends at the Farnborough SBAC Show, he returned to Devonshire and died, at the age of 70, while out fishing on 10 September 1955, penultimate day of the Show.

After his death the chairmanship was taken over by Eric Turner who, in turn, was succeeded by A. F. Jopling in 1959 when a further re-organization took place and three separate companies—Blackburn Aircraft Ltd, Blackburn Engines Ltd and Blackburn Electronics Ltd—were formed.

Work on the Buccaneer was now well advanced but the length of the runway at the factory airfield at Brough was insufficient and the company was compelled to move all development flying to the old wartime aerodrome at Holme-on-Spalding Moor, some 15 miles to the north west. Finished aircraft were towed, with wings folded, the whole distance on their own wheels, to be

25

The Buccaneer production line at Brough with engines and rotating weapons bays positioned ready for installation.

flown by a team consisting of chief test pilot D. J. Whitehead (who had succeeded H. 'Tim' Wood when he retired in April 1959), G. R. I. 'Sailor' Parker, J. G. 'Bobby' Burns, Lt Cdr E. R. Anson (on loan from the Navy and who later flew Buccaneers as a member of No. 700Z Flight and as CO of No. 801 Squadron), R. J. Chandler, P. Millett and D. Lockspeiser.

For realistic landings the main 6,000 ft runway at Holme-on-Spalding Moor was equipped with two sets of naval type arrester gear and a mirror landing aid, but the actual test flying was done to the north and north-east in order to avoid neighbouring RAF fighter airfields and the airways traffic proceeding along airway Green Two. All low-level sorties were made in the designated low flying areas in Lincolnshire.

Few of these activities were seen by Blackburn's labour force, but in a small ceremony on 12 September 1962 the name of the Station Hotel at Brough—one of the two local hostelries which had slaked the thirst of Mark Swann nearly 50 years earlier—was renamed the Buccaneer as a permanent reminder of their contribution to the nation's modern striking force.

Soon afterwards Blackburn Aircraft Ltd became a member company of the Hawker Siddeley Group and in May 1963 its styling was changed to Hawker Siddeley Aviation Ltd, Hawker Blackburn Division. Obviously such a clumsy title could not last and it was not long before internal re-organization of the Hawker Siddeley Group succeeded in obliterating the historic name of Blackburn altogether. Details of the work undertaken at Brough up to 1988 appear in Appendix F.

The North Sea Aerial and
General Transport Co Ltd

No history of the Blackburn company would be complete without reference to its operating subsidiary, the North Sea Aerial and General Transport Co Ltd, so often mentioned in this book and whose affairs were linked so closely with those of the parent company.

Formed on 23 April 1919 as the North Sea Aerial Navigation Co Ltd, its primary task was to run commercial services from the Soldiers' Field, Roundhay Park, Leeds, with converted Blackburn Kangaroos, and its first recorded movement took place on 10 May that year when R. W. Kenworthy flew a load of freight from Gosport to Leeds via the London terminal aerodrome, Hounslow Heath. An account of the North Sea company's fruitless efforts to make money on the pioneer 400 mile Leeds–Amsterdam route is given in the chapter on the Kangaroo, but nevertheless it remained in being to make what it could at the most lucrative form of postwar aviation—joyriding.

Maj R. M. S. Veale, who managed this side of the business, obtained two brand new Humber-built war surplus Avro 504K biplanes with 130 hp Clerget rotary engines, sent R. W. Kenworthy and a pilot named Clinch to collect them from the RAF depot at Aintree and had them modified to carry two passengers behind the pilot. Certificated on 2 August 1919 as G-EAGV and 'GW respectively, they gave pleasure flights to hundreds of people at towns and villages all over Lincolnshire, Yorkshire and County Durham. Clinch flew one at Scarborough Racecourse for two months before being recalled to Brough, and plans were laid for an air taxi service to serve Scarborough, Middlesborough, Stockton, Darlington, Harrogate and Brough, but in the summer of 1920 both Avros were damaged beyond repair in accidents. G-EAGW, in particular, ended its career as a crumpled heap in a field at Scarborough after a difficult forced landing by R. W. Kenworthy.

The RAF Reserve School, Brough

The North Sea Aerial Navigation Co Ltd was spared the painful effect that the postwar slump had on most joyriding concerns but it was without aircraft and, to keep the company going, Robert Blackburn made it responsible for organizing the Blackburn company's not inconsiderable road transport operations which included communications between the Leeds and Brough factories and ferrying the fleets of buses and coaches for which Blackburns had built bodies. Because of these activities the company styling was changed to the North Sea Aerial and General Transport Co Ltd at the end of 1920, but no flying was done on its own account until some years later when the Air Ministry decided to sub-contract RAF Reserve training to civilian operators.

The four firms chosen were the de Havilland Aircraft Co Ltd at Stag Lane, Edgware, whose contract was signed on 1 April 1923; the Bristol Aeroplane Co Ltd which opened its school at Filton on 15 May; William Beardmore and

Co Ltd who began instruction at Renfrew on 23 July; and lastly the North Sea Aerial and General Transport Co Ltd whose contract was signed in January 1924. From the date of its opening in the following May until 1939 the Brough Reserve School was managed by Robert Blackburn's brother, Capt Norman Blackburn, with T. Bancroft as chief engineer and Sqn Ldr A. G. Loton, AFC, as chief flying instructor.

All the Reserve Schools used primary as well as advanced trainers, and the initial equipment at Brough consisted of three Avro 548A two-seat dual control biplanes G-EBIT, 'IU and 'IV, built to order by A. V. Roe and Co Ltd at Hamble and fitted with 120 hp Airdisco vee-8 air-cooled engines driving four-bladed wooden airscrews. There Brough's similarity to the other Schools ended because the advanced trainers which came into service from 1925 onwards were the three Dart two-seat seaplanes G-EBKF, 'KG and 'KH (see page 154), and the Kangaroo dual conversions *Bonzo*, *Felix the Cat*, *Wilfred*, *Pip* and *Squeak*, otherwise G-EAIU, 'MJ, G-EBMD, 'OM and 'PK (see page 122). Brough was unique therefore as the only School offering seaplane and twin-engined training.

The aircraft were housed in one of the two large hangars built in 1917 for No. 2 Marine Acceptance Depot, which for obvious reasons is known to this day as the North Sea hangar. Pupils were accommodated in huts originally erected for personnel of the Depot and their off-duty entertainment was looked after by the Brough Aviation and Recreation Club formed by the Blackburn directors in April 1924.

Two of the Avros were disposed of to joyriding concerns in 1927 and the third in 1928, being replaced by two Blackburn Bluebird IIs, G-EBTA and 'TC, and the prototype Bluebird III G-EBWE.

When twin-engined Reserve training came to an end in 1928 all the gallant old Kangaroos were flown to Sherburn-in-Elmet to be broken up. At the same time the superannuated Darts were replaced by six Velos trainer sea-planes, which operated on wheels when the seaplane requirement also ended.

Reserve School and other aircraft in the North Sea hangar, Brough, during the Velos demonstrations of 28 October 1925. *Left to right:* Avro 548A G-EBIT, Kangaroo dual trainer G-EAIU, Avro 548A G-EBIV, Bluebird I prototype G-EBKD and the US Army Air Attaché's DH-4B.

28

Scene outside the North Sea hangar in September 1932, with Dart G-EBKH and Velos G-AAAW nearing the end of their careers and forming a background to the Baffin prototype B-5 running up for test flight. (*Flight Photo 12398.*)

The Khartoum–Kisumu Air Route

As soon as the Reserve School was in full operation and the North Sea Aerial and General Transport Co Ltd was on a fairly sound financial footing, Robert Blackburn's old air transport ambitions were re-awakened. With the expert assistance of Capt T. A. Gladstone, another North Sea director, who in the previous year had had a series of tactful interviews to ensure the co-operation of Governors of African States along the Nile, plans were laid for an experimental air route between Khartoum and Kisumu to test the feasibility of a service right through to the Cape.

A layout was then prepared by the Blackburn design staff for a suitable commercial float biplane designated C.A.3 (see page 515) powered by three Bristol Jupiter engines and able to carry eight passengers, mail and baggage at an all-up weight of 16,260 lb. To speed up the survey work, however, an order was placed with the de Havilland Aircraft Co Ltd for a D.H.50J four-seat seaplane similar to, but more powerful than, that used by Sir Alan Cobham for his African and Australian survey flights, the 420 hp Bristol Jupiter IV air-cooled radial driving a Fairey-Reed metal airscrew being stipulated, in preference to Cobham's 385 hp Armstrong Siddeley Jaguar III, in order to gain experience with this engine under tropical conditions in readiness for the projected Blackburn C.A.3.

Registered G-EBOP, the D.H.50J was taken by road from Stag Lane to Rochester, fitted with Short metal floats and christened *Pelican* by Lady Beatrice Ormsby-Gore on 15 November 1926. It then took off from the Medway to be shown off by de Havilland's test pilot Capt Hubert Broad

29

Launching the D.H.50J *Pelican* at Rochester on 15 November 1926.
(*Flight Photo 4169.*)

before Robert Blackburn, Oswald Short and guests, before shipment to the Sudan. Here disaster struck decisively and at once, for during take-off for the first test flight on 30 December, *Pelican* struck submerged wreckage and was seriously damaged. It was thereupon dismantled and, on a temporary wheel undercarriage, shipped as deck cargo to the nearest Blackburn repair shop, in this instance the Greek National Aircraft Factory at Athens.

To prevent the premature demise of the venture the Air Ministry loaned the North Sea company an RAF Fairey IIID seaplane with 450 hp Napier Lion engine and gave it temporary civil status as G-EBPZ. It was collected from Aboukir by Capt Gladstone and flown to Khartoum, arriving on 7 February 1927. He then left next day on a leisurely four-day survey flight to Kisumu via Jinja, arriving on 12 February, total flying time being seven hours. The return trip to Khartoum with 120 lb of mail was completed on 19 February, but heat and high altitude soon proved too much for the IIID. On 13 March, when leaving Kisumu on the second northbound flight, it failed to get properly airborne from Lake Victoria and on the fourth bounce the undercarriage collapsed. The pilot, Capt Boyle, and his mechanic, Mr Blacklock, were uninjured but the aircraft became a total loss during salvage operations.

In preparation for the return of *Pelican* from repair in Athens, an Imperial Airways flying-boat pilot, Capt F. J. Bailey, who had been flying on the Southampton–Guernsey route in Supermarine Sea Eagles, obtained leave of absence to join the North Sea Aerial and General Transport Co Ltd for six months from 1 September 1927. He ferried *Pelican* from Athens to Khartoum and left on the resumed service to Kisumu on 8 October, carrying Viscount Gage and a Belgian aviation expert M. Allard, but when landing from a test flight at Kisumu on 17 October, *Pelican* was completely wrecked and the whole project came to an end.

On 24 April 1928, the North Sea Aerial and General Transport Co Ltd merged its African airline interests with those of Alan Cobham Aviation Ltd, a company formed by Sir Alan Cobham to exploit the survey work he had done through Africa in his D.H.50J G-EBFO and around it with H. V. Worrall in the Short Singapore I G-EBUP.

Known as Cobham–Blackburn Air Lines Ltd, and with Sir Alan Cobham, Robert Blackburn, Col W. Wright and Capt T. A. Gladstone as first directors, the new company formulated a scheme for permanent services between Alexandria and the Cape via the Nile and African lakes with Blackburn Nile flying-boats. Soon afterwards, however, the British Government ruled that Imperial Airways would be the chosen instrument for operating such a route and so put an end to all Cobham–Blackburn air route aspirations in Africa.

The Humber Ferry

Air routes are never so profitable as when they cross water. This was proved in the 1930s by the success, for example, of the Portsmouth–Isle of Wight, Southend–Rochester, Weston–Cardiff and Wick–Kirkwall ferries. Then, as now, the Humber Estuary formed such an obstruction to north–south communications that it took $1\frac{1}{2}$ hours to travel from Hull to Grimsby by boat and train, and the need for a regular air service was quickly established after only a few taxi flights between the Hull Municipal Aerodrome at Hedon and Waltham Aerodrome, Grimsby. The machine used was National Flying Services' Desoutter I G-AANB in October 1932, but it was not until 1 July

The short-lived Fairey IIID seaplane G-EBPZ, loaned to the North Sea company by the Air Ministry in 1927, standing on the dockside at Kisumu.

31

of the following year that the North Sea Aerial and General Transport Co Ltd opened a thrice daily (except Sunday) return ferry service in conjunction with East Yorkshire Motor Services Ltd who conveyed passengers to and from the aerodrome.

Using Blackburn Segrave G-ABFR, the journey time was reduced to 15 min and over 500 passengers were carried during the summer. An hourly service was introduced on 4 September 1933 but there was little demand for it after the summer season and the last flight was made on 4 November. Another company operated the Airspeed Courier G-ACLF for a time in 1934, but it was not until Provincial Airways Ltd opened a Plymouth–Hull service on 4 March 1935, with de Havilland Dragons G-ACBW, 'DL and 'KD, and called at Grimsby on request that the service was restored. Even this facility was withdrawn in the following July, due to an inexplicable lack of public support.

Nos. 4 and 5 Elementary and Reserve Flying Training Schools

In the intervening years light aeroplanes had established themselves as more economical training machines than the converted military types of the past, and the North Sea company was quick to add a number of Blackburn Bluebird IVs to its fleet from 1930 onwards. They made it possible, for the first time, to offer *ab initio* training to British and foreign civilians, and the response was such that by 1937 no less than 13 different Bluebirds had been used at one time or another, classrooms had been provided for the ground subjects and arrangements made for practical engineering experience in the Blackburn factory.

From December 1932, however, the Bluebird IVs were gradually joined by Blackburn B-2s and by March 1933, 13 of these were in service with a total utilization exceeding 100 hr per week. Four others were added during 1934 but, with war clouds approaching, a great expansion took place in flying instruction and a number of civil flying schools were enlarged for training RAF pilots. Thus in 1935 the Brough Reserve School became No. 4 Elementary

The North Sea hangar in 1932 housing three Velos including G-EBWB (on the all-metal floats used for the South American tour) and three Bluebird IVs including G-AAUW centre and G-AATM right.

Eleven Blackburn B-2s of the Brough Reserve School outside the North Sea hangar in 1933 with Flt Lt A. G. Loton, chief flying instructor standing in front of G-ACER (*right*). (*Courtesy Peter W. Brooks.*)

and Reserve Flying Training School, and the North Sea Aerial and General Transport Co Ltd formed a subsidiary company known as Flying Training Ltd to operate No. 5 E and RFTS at Hanworth Aerodrome, Feltham, with Flt Lt N. H. Woodhead as chief flying instructor.

The new School opened on 1 June 1935 and was entirely Blackburn in organization and equipment, two-thirds of the share capital having been found by the North Sea company. Its initial equipment comprised 14 Blackburn B-2s, augmented by six others in February 1936.

Communications between Brough, Hanworth and the various sub-contractors and RAF stations were maintained by the Percival Gull G-ADOE, bought in August 1935 as a flying test bed for the new Blackburn Cirrus Major 1 engine and raced by C. S. Napier. It was assisted by a Stinson Reliant SR-9D, registered to Robert Blackburn in October 1937 as G-AFBI, but the name of the North Sea Aerial and General Transport Co Ltd, which had been a part of British civil aviation for so long, had by that time disappeared, having been absorbed with all the other Blackburn interests into Blackburn Aircraft Ltd in June 1936.

The flow of *ab initio* trainees increased at such a rate that in June 1938 15 B.A. Swallow II two-seat low-wing monoplanes, powered by 90 hp Blackburn Cirrus Minor 1 engines, were bought to supplement the Brough fleet. To cope with all this activity, the aerodrome was enlarged, new hangars erected on the north side, and a control tower, administrative building and mess was opened which is known to this day as The Flying Club even though instructional flying ceased many years ago. The Swallows were transferred to the London Air Park Flying Club at Hanworth for Civil Air Guard duties in February 1939, but after the outbreak of war all Flying Training's B-2s were evacuated to join their fellows at Brough.

By this time the School had been restyled No. 4 EFTS with Wg Cdr A. G. Loton as commanding officer and Sqn Ldr J. Stockbridge as his deputy. It boasted Hawker Hart, Fairey Battle and Avro Anson I advanced trainers in addition to the B-2s, but on 30 August 1939, a few days before the declaration of war, all flying ceased and the pupils were posted away. The Hawker Harts

33

were then ferried to RAF stations in Scotland, but the initial invasion scare was soon over and flying recommenced with the B-2s on 11 September. Before the end of the year the fleet was augmented by D.H. Tiger Moths and Miles Magisters, which for safety in the event of an air raid alert were evacuated to the satellite landing ground at Gilberdyke. At night they were dispersed round the airfield at Brough but after some 30 Tiger Moths were torn from their pickets and wrecked in a gale early in 1940, the light aeroplanes were put back into the hangar. The immensely strong B-2s safely rode out the storm, held by their ropes but in 1942 they were all given to ATC Squadrons as instructional airframes. Many Service types were then brought on charge and at its peak the School had 45 aircraft in use. After the war Brough became an all Tiger Moth RAFVR School under Sqn Ldr Howes, but this closed in 1950. Its hangars still housed the Chipmunks of the Hull University Air Squadron in 1968.

North Sea Air Transport Ltd

In a brave attempt to re-open the civil flying school after the war, Blackburns made airworthy the two surviving B-2s G-ACLD and G-AEBJ, the Swallow G-AFIH, and three ex RAF Tiger Moths which they civilianized as G-AHRL, 'RM and 'RN. Together with Austers G-AGOH and G-AHSN, they were all used by the short-lived Brough Flying Club (1946–1950) for teaching technicians to fly under a scheme sponsored by Blackburns. North Sea Air Transport Ltd, formed on 28 August 1944 as the postwar equivalent of the old North Sea Aerial and General Transport Co Ltd, began charter operations at Hanworth in July 1946 with Sqn Ldr B. S. Smallman as manager. The chief pilot, Capt H. P. Wilson, had been chief production test pilot at the parent company's factory at Sherburn-in-Elmet, where he had test flown over a thousand Blackburn-built Swordfish.

Through careful study of every aspect of its subsidiary's activities, the Blackburn company hoped to gain experience which would enable them to design and market the successful civil aircraft of the future, and initially the fleet consisted of a war surplus de Havilland Rapide, which they had converted at Brough as G-AHLU, and two of their former engine test beds, the Cirrus Minor powered Auster 5 hybrid G-AGOH and Miles Messenger 2B G-AGPX with Cirrus Major.

A Percival Proctor 1, G-AHAZ, added in the following month, was lost soon afterwards near Zürich while on hire to Olley Air Service Ltd; but business boomed and by November 1946 the Messenger alone had flown 490 hours and had made 12 return trips to Zürich. As a result two more Rapides, G-AIWG and 'WZ, were civilianized at Brough and painted in the company's newly adopted maroon and cream house colours. A Miles Aerovan 4, G-AISG, acquired in May 1947 for transporting outsize loads, flew furniture from France to Luton but, like the Proctor, was short-lived and met with a fatal crash on 14 June when leaving Croydon for Guernsey with 26 cases of pigeons.

34

The company had close ties with Universal Flying Services Ltd, based at Hanworth, from which in 1948 it acquired a converted Avro Anson 1, G-AIRX, for the lucrative Channel Islands traffic, and also the Miles Gemini 1A G-AKEI. When Hanworth closed in 1949, operations were transferred to Brough where Rapide G-AIWZ was destroyed in a fatal crash while landing after a flight from Newcastle. Most of the original aircraft were then replaced and a new fleet built up which consisted of three more Rapides, another Aerovan 4 G-AJOG, Percival Proctor 5s G-AHVG and G-AHWR as well as two fast American transports, the Lockheed 12A G-AGDT and Lockheed 14H G-AGBG.

Last of the test bed aircraft, acquired from RAF surplus stock in 1948, was the Miles Messenger 1 RH420 used for airtesting the Cirrus Bombardier 702 engine. Most of its life was spent in the Blackburn Class B marking G-2-1, but three years later it was at last painted up as Messenger 5 G-ALAC and flown by P. G. Lawrence in the South Coast Air Race of 22 September 1951, during which it was destroyed in a forced landing near Faversham, Kent.

After 1950 the scale of North Sea's operations was gradually reduced and several aircraft were sold abroad, the aged Lockheeds, expensive to run and difficult to maintain, being disposed of in Sweden. Proctor 5 G-AHWR came to grief in a field near Baginton on 18 June 1954 when it ran out of fuel while being flown in the National Air Races by Blackburn test pilot G. R. I. 'Sailor' Parker, leaving Rapide G-AHAG as the only survivor. This remained at Brough long after charter operations ceased, first as Blackburn's, and eventually as Hawker Siddeley's communications machine in partnership with a de Havilland Dove 1, G-ANMJ, acquired in October 1958. Early in 1967 this too was sold and went south to Gatwick for service with Cardinal Airways, being replaced by a late production Dove 8A registered G-ARBE.

The Greek National Aircraft Factory

Blackburn Managership

The Greek Ministry of Marine first recognized the need for aircraft manufacture and repair facilities as early as 1918 and some aircraft maintenance was attempted in the Naval Arsenal at Salonika. The results were hardly satisfactory and as a result Cdr J. Weston of the British Naval Mission in Greece submitted proposals for the construction of a properly equipped Greek National Aircraft Factory adjacent to the Naval Air Base at Old Phaleron, near Athens. His ideas were accepted and, towards the end of 1920, plant, machinery and tools arrived from the USA but the gas and oil engines to drive them were purchased in England.

Construction of the factory did not begin until 1923 because of political

Manhandling T 11, the first Greek-built Velos, out of the Old Phaleron factory ready for its first flight on 17 March 1926.

unrest, and progress was so slow that in 1924 the Ministry of Marine invited Robert Blackburn to visit Athens to discuss taking it over and building Blackburn and other British types in it under licence. As a result the Old Phaleron factory, although remaining the property of the Ministry of Marine, was run entirely by the Blackburn Aeroplane and Motor Co Ltd, the first contract being for five years commencing 1 July 1925, and during the first six months the company's personnel not only completed the buildings but installed the machinery and began the manufacture of a batch of 12 Blackburn Velos two-seat torpedo-bombers for the Greek Navy. A layout for a military flying-boat powered by two Rolls-Royce Condor engines to carry a crew of five, submitted to the Ministry of Marine on 26 April 1926, brought no response and was not proceeded with.

At first the scarcity of skilled local labour made the work extremely difficult and 1,000 men passed through the company's hands before the required 300 had been selected, but their efficiency improved after training, and by December 1930 only 12 of the original 30 British leading hands remained, the others having been replaced by Greeks.

The first product of the Greek factory, the Velos landplane T 11, made its first flight from rough ground behind the works piloted by Col the Master of Sempill on 17 March 1926, and the second, a seaplane T 12, was flown off Phaleron Bay by the same pilot on 31 March. There was no slipway and the latter aircraft had to be launched from the beach by an inexpert handling party beset by language difficulties. At the critical moment Blackburn's local manager, Maj F. C. Buck, shed his garments and led the remaining British staff into the water, and the proceedings then passed off without further

36

incident. After acceptance flights the Velos was handed over to the adjoining Naval Base but, with his assignment complete, the Master of Sempill returned home, leaving production test flying to Maj H. S. Travers.

The efficient manner in which the establishment of the National Aircraft Factory had been handled was a matter of deep satisfaction to the Greek Government, and in Athens on 10 March 1927—just a year after the completion of the first Greek-built Velos—the King of the Hellenes invested Robert Blackburn with the insignia of the Golden Cross of the Order of the Redeemer.

Production and Repair

During the five-year period of the contract the principal work executed was as follows:

New construction	Reconditioned
12 Blackburn Velos	10 D.H.9 landplanes
15 Avro 504N★ (Lynx)	2 D.H.9 seaplanes
9 Avro 504N★ (Mongoose)	1 D.H.50J seaplane
10 A.W. Atlas	1 Bristol Fighter Mk. IV
	10 Avro 504N
	2 Hanriot trainers
	13 Blackburn Velos
	3 A.W. Atlas
	1 D.H.60G Gipsy Moth
	1 Hawker Horsley

★ With float undercarriages for conversion to Avro 504O.

Col the Master of Sempill and a Greek naval officer standing on the port float of the Greek-built Velos T 12 in Phaleron Bay on 31 March 1926. (*Flight Photo 3936.*)

The factory also flourished by making wood and metal float undercarriages for Velos and Avro 504O aircraft as well as doing light engineering jobs and carrying out routine maintenance on Imperial Airways, Aero Espresso and Air Union commercial aircraft staging through Athens. In addition it repaired the North Sea Aerial and General Transport Co's D.H.50J seaplane G-EBOP *Pelican* which Capt T. A. Gladstone shipped from Khartoum to Athens for the purpose after it had struck submerged wreckage on the Nile in December 1926. Some years later the factory performed a similar service for J. H. Ford of the Asiatic Petroleum Co Ltd, who left Lympne on 23 March 1931 in his D.H.60G Gipsy Moth G-AADW to fly to Shanghai but on 29 March made a forced landing near Athens in a snowstorm and overturned.

Original Design

In a memorandum to the parent company late in 1926, Maj Buck indicated that the next logical step would be the construction of aircraft entirely designed in Greece. It was no surprise therefore when a small spruce and plywood open cockpit two-seat biplane, similar to a Sopwith Dove, appeared in the field behind the Old Phaleron factory. Known as the Chelidon (or Swallow) and powered by a 120 hp Salmson air-cooled radial, it first flew on 11 February 1927, only eight weeks after the commencement of drawings, all design and construction work having been done by Greeks under the supervision of Maj Buck and his colleague Mr Wylde.

It bore a superficial resemblance to drawings for a projected light aircraft for Greece produced by the Brough designers and dated 1 June 1926. These showed a two-seat biplane braced by sloping N-type interplane struts, possessed of good low-speed control and powered by a 240 hp Armstrong Siddeley Lynx radial. A floor-mounted camera was to be fitted for survey work, but a smaller variant depicted in another set of drawings, initialled by Maj Bumpus a month later on 1 July, showed a trainer version named the Helithon which had a 125 hp Armstrong Siddeley Mongoose radial. Neither was built and the Chelidon remained unique as the only light aeroplane wholly produced in Greece at that time. The surviving data on these types is as follows:

Survey biplane: Span 31 ft 0 in; length 24 ft 0 in; height 9 ft 3 in.
Helithon: Span 26 ft 10 in; length (landplane) 19 ft 0 in, length (seaplane) 21 ft 11 in; all-up weight 1,559 lb; maximum speed 103 mph; initial climb 900 ft/min; service ceiling 13,500 ft; endurance 3 hr.
Chelidon: Span 26 ft 3 in; maximum speed 90 mph.

The Second Managerial Period

In the middle of the fifth year the Greek Army and Naval Air Services were unified under the control of an Air Ministry into whose possession the factory passed. Blackburn's contract was thereupon extended, first for six months up to 31 December 1930 and then re-negotiated for a further period

The Bluebird IV, Segrave and Lincock III at Heston on 5 October 1931 prior to their departure for Brussels at the commencement of the European sales tour.

of seven years, to include all the engine repairs formerly done by the Army at Salonika and responsibility for modernizing the factory to deal with the manufacture and repair of all-metal airframes.

Additional aircraft types reconditioned during the period of the second contract were the Avro 621 Tutor, Fairey IIIF, Gloster Mars VI, Breguet XIX.A2, Breguet XIX.B2, Potez XXV, Morane Saulnier (130 hp or 230 hp Salmson) and Avia (Bristol Jupiter).

In an attempt to interest the Greek Government in purchasing its range of training, transport and light fighter aircraft, and with the possibility of building them at Old Phaleron well in mind, Blackburns conducted a European sales tour with the Bluebird IV G-ABPV, Segrave G-ABFP and Lincock III G-ABFK. They left Heston on 5 October 1931, with chief test pilot A. M. Blake and Robert Blackburn aboard the Segrave, H. J. Andrews in the Bluebird and T. Neville Stack flying the Lincock, all arriving in Athens on the 21st, where they were joined by Robert Blackburn whose business commitments had compelled him to go by train from Cologne. The enterprise achieved nothing, for the Bluebird was lost in a fatal accident while being flown by a Greek pilot at Tatoi Aerodrome on 24 October and, although the Lincock stayed on for demonstration for another fortnight in charge of H. J. Andrews, the Segrave was dismantled and shipped home.

By the end of the further contractual period Greek technicians were in complete control of the National Aircraft Factory and by 1938 the last of the original Blackburn personnel had returned home, including B. R. Rolfe who, after being chief test pilot at Old Phaleron since 1929, became assistant test pilot at Brough.

39

The Blackburn Modification and Repair Organizations

American Aircraft Modifications

A considerable number of American aircraft built to French, Dutch, Belgian and Balkan contracts, which remained undelivered because Europe had been overrun by the Germans, were acquired in 1940 by the British and Dominion Purchasing Commission and shipped to England. Having been designed without the backing of operational experience, it was necessary to convert them on arrival to standards acceptable to the RAF and the Royal Navy and to replace American ancillary equipment such as radio, batteries and the like by British equipment. Difficulties of this kind had been foreseen when the purchase was made, but in practice hundreds of other modifications were found essential before the aircraft could be cleared for operational use.

Thus in the summer of 1940 Blackburn Aircraft Ltd, with its specialist knowledge of FAA requirements, was appointed sister firm for Grumman aircraft and made responsible for all modifications to them. First to arrive, in 1940–41, was the Grumman Martlet single-seat carrier-borne fighter which ran from Mk I to Mk III, specimens of which were allotted to Blackburns who, in each instance, held an Arrival Conference at which representatives of various technical departments, after examining the aircraft, outlined the extent and variety of the work needed to satisfy British requirements.

Subsequent American deliveries were not by direct purchase but resulted from Lend–Lease agreements authorized on 11 March 1941. First to arrive at Blackburns were Martlets Mk IV and Mk V (renamed Wildcat in January 1944), and much later the Wildcat Mk VI. They were followed by the Avenger Mks I to III, deliveries of which commenced in January 1943; the Hellcat Mks I and II (with a night fighter variant of the latter); and the Corsair Mks I to IV, first of which arrived aboard *Illustrious* in the hands of No. 1830 Squadron in June 1943. Strengthening of machine-gun mountings on Brewster-built Corsairs, deliveries of which commenced a month later, was typical of the kind of modification called for. The company was also appointed sister firm for the Curtiss Helldiver, but only one machine was received at Brough and this was obsolete by the time it arrived.

As the modifications were often applicable only to certain marks it was necessary to have sample aircraft of each and on occasion the same modification had to be embodied in them all to prove its applicability, so that at one period 18 or 19 different aircraft were being worked on at Brough. By then the Skua and Roc, and later the Botha, had become obsolete so that room was available for an increasing number of US types.

When Admiralty requirements had been confirmed and the local technical committee had dealt with the routine promulgation of Modification Numbers and costs, the design office proceeded with drawings. The task facing the stress department was considerable, since lack of American stress analysis

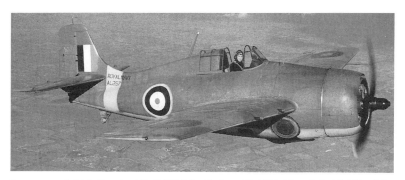

Grumman G-36A Martlet Mk I (Wright Cyclone R-1820-87 radial) AL257 of the type for which Blackburn Aircraft Ltd was the sister firm.
(*Imperial War Museum Photo.*)

data meant that it could not arrive at a true assessment of the effect of adding new items to the existing structure without recourse to a generous amount of commonsense. Gradually, however, the US drawings and technical data arrived but in most cases later than needed. Much of it was lost due to sinkings in the Atlantic so that eventually such data was always sent by air in the form of micro-films which had to be enlarged. When delays did occur there was no alternative but for draughtsmen to go down to the hangar to measure up the vital parts, an exercise which usually revealed that manufacturing standards among US subcontractors differed from those of the parent firm and affected interchangeability.

When a modification was at last satisfactorily fitted to the trials aeroplane and any necessary amendments had been made to the drawings, Blackburns began to manufacture modification sets at Brough but when, in June 1943, the need for sets escalated and the Fairey Barracuda production programme reached a peak, Messrs Boon and Porter Ltd of 163 Castelnau, Hammersmith (who had already done light engineering work for the Air Ministry), were appointed as a central firm responsible for manufacturing modification sets to Blackburn drawings. Thereafter the whole of this work was done at Hammersmith with the exception of a few high priority sets which were always in production at Leeds, Brough, Sherburn-in-Elmet or Dumbarton, or by closely linked specialist firms such as Slingsby Sailplanes Ltd at Kirbymoorside and Messrs Prince-Smith and Stells Ltd at Keighley. These firms made the rocket projectile modification sets for Wildcat and Hellcat aircraft.

The machines were shipped to England as deck cargo and re-assembled (often by Lockheeds at Speke and at Renfrew), but as few of the essential modifications could be embodied aboard a carrier much of the work of bringing them up to operational standard was done by the Blackburn repair factories at Sherburn-in-Elmet and Abbotsinch as well as at a number of their service depots overseas. It involved the installation of British gun sights, oxygen systems and IFF recognition equipment; clipping the aerial mast

41

of Avengers and removing Corsair wing tips to suit the limited headroom in British carriers; fitting British catapult spools and local structural strengthening to the Wildcat; exploratory work towards fitting all types with RATOG gear; wing strengthening modifications to carry rocket projectiles either on standard British rails or the US Mk. V zero-length launcher; fitting F.24 cameras; converting Hellcat Mk II and Corsair Mk IV aircraft at Abbotsinch for fighter-reconnaissance duties; completely reworking the Avenger internally to accommodate the navigator immediately behind the pilot; and a great deal of other work.

So that American aircraft destined for the Fleet Air Arm were not brought up to full US Navy operational standard only to be torn apart and converted to suit British requirements on arrival, a British Modification Centre was set up in 1943 at Roosevelt Field with Mr J. Hall of Blackburn Aircraft Ltd as chief engineer. Here all Hellcat and Corsair machines received a full quota of Blackburn-designed modifications as well as others evolved locally. This innovation not only saved time but enabled fully modified aircraft to be shipped direct from the USA to the Far East.

The size of this mammoth task can only be fully envisaged if it is realized that between the end of 1940 and the year 1945 Blackburns handled over 400 modifications and trial installations which were embodied in nearly 4,000 aircraft, 600 of which were completed under contract at its own factories. During that time the central firm, Messrs Boon and Porter Ltd, manufactured some 40,000 modification sets for four different types of aircraft.

The Blackburn Repair Organization

In addition to modification work, Blackburn Aircraft Ltd also undertook the repair of damaged aircraft. A separate section known as the Blackburn Repair Organization was set up under Mr H. Bentley which commenced repairing aircraft in the Brough works in May 1940 and also in the Sherburn Swordfish factory until January 1941 when it moved across to the old RAF hangars (floor area 54,000 sq ft) which had been altered to suit its purposes.

Unidentified Grumman Martlet I.

42

Chief engineer was Mr T. Bancroft and the local chief test pilot was H. P. Wilson, succeeded in 1943 by R. F. Stedman. Capt Norman Blackburn was in charge of Sherburn throughout the war and from 1944 was in full charge of all Blackburn factories in Yorkshire.

In 1941 additional hangars were constructed at Sherburn giving an additional 35,000 sq ft of floor space, and dispersal premises were requisitioned by the Ministry of Aircraft Production in Harehills Lane, Brown Lane and other districts of Leeds, adding another 30,000 sq ft to the repair facilities. This additional accommodation was urgently necessary for, besides repairing increasing numbers of complete aeroplanes, the Organization was being called on to repair quantities of spare mainplanes and other components and to undertake the breakdown and salvage of aircraft detailed for RAF and Naval Stores provisioning. In the same year repair work began at Abbotsinch, giving an additional 84,000 sq ft of hangar space in which to concentrate Botha repairs. In the following year, at the request of the Central Repair Organization, some breakdown and salvage work was sub-contracted to Messrs Ogston and Tennant, soap makers of Renfrew, who allocated 10,000 sq ft of floor space to the work.

During the period 1940–45 the various factories broke down for salvage between 400 and 500 aircraft and repaired hundreds of components for stores provisioning in addition to modifying complete airfames. By the time it shut down in 1945, the Blackburn Repair Organization had returned no less than 1,215 machines to serviceable condition, as detailed below:

Year	Aircraft totals	Details
1940	29	Major repairs to Blackburn types.
1941	111 ⎫	Major repairs to Blackburn types and Swordfish aircraft.
1942	157 ⎭	
1943	247	116 major repairs as above; 39 Swordfish converted to dual control; 92 Swordfish fitted with special electrical Mod. 397.
1944	451	141 major repairs as above; 91 Swordfish converted to dual control with electrical mods.; 130 Barracudas for fuselage strengthening and electrical mods.; 89 Avengers for electrical mods. and other work.
1945	220	25 major repairs as above; 115 Barracudas for electrical mods; 80 Avengers for electrical mods. and other work.
	1,215	

The Sherburn Repair Factory completed its 1,000th aircraft on 12 June 1945, the balance of 215 comprising 91 repaired on site, 84 at Abbotsinch and 40 at Brough or Sherburn in 1940. Peak monthly output occurred in February 1944 when 61 aircraft were completed, comprising three Rocs and four Skuas converted as instructional airframes; four Wildcats and one Brewster Bermuda repaired; as well as four Swordfish and 45 Barracudas modified.

43

Blackburn Designations and Markings

The Alphabetical Sequence

In common with most early British heavier-than-air experimenters, Robert Blackburn was far too preoccupied with designing and building, and in solving the basic problem of getting off the ground, to make detailed records of his individual aeroplanes or the continuous alterations to which they were subjected. In his modesty he put aside all thought of naming or numbering them until he had succeeded in building a machine capable of sustained flight, and it was not until the Olympia Aero Show of March 1911, therefore, when the rudders of his exhibit carried the wording Mercury Passenger Type, that a Blackburn machine first acquired a positive identity. Even so it was to be another year before the first actual designation appeared, on the Hucks tour aircraft which, in rebuilt form as a school machine, bore the inscription Blackburn Monoplane Type B on its rudders.

Exactly which aeroplane Robert Blackburn had in mind as his Type A is a matter for conjecture since there were many variations on the Mercury theme and, despite the fact that an alphabetical sequence was followed until the Type L was reached in 1914, designations for several well-known aircraft such as the Shuttleworth-restored 1912 Monoplane, went unrecorded.

For this reason only seven out of the possible twelve alphabetical identities are certain, as shown below:

Type B   1911   Military two-seater (50 hp Gnome)
Type D   1913   Single-seat monoplane (50 hp Gnome)
Type E   1912   All-metal military two-seater (70 hp Renault)
Type F   —   First Blackburn biplane—the 'hydro biplane'
Type G   1913   30 hp monoplane for Hart Engine Co.
Type I   1913   Two-seat monoplane for M. G. Christie (80 hp Gnome)
Type L   1914   Circuit of Britain seaplane (130 hp Canton-Unné)

The original Blackburn styling over the company's Improved Type I monoplane at Olympia, London, in March 1914. (*Courtesy C. H. Barnes.*)

44

The incomplete Swift prototype among potted palms on the Blackburn stand at Olympia, London, in July 1920.

During the alphabetical era Blackburn aeroplanes often bore the single word BLACKBURN in large unseriffed capitals on the sides of the fuselage or under the wings, but advertisements in the technical press always displayed the name in a uniform style with serifs. Eventually, at the Olympia Aero Show of March 1914, signwriting over the Blackburn stand employed a rather more elaborate styling which, from that time, was adopted as standard on all the company's catalogues and headings.

This was retained throughout the First World War and appeared again above the Swift at Olympia in July 1920. Times were changing, however, and the well-known Rockwell Italic trademark, introduced in 1919 and destined to be used for more than a quarter of a century, gradually replaced it. As a result of carefree punning with the founder's surname, black and red also became the accepted house colours and were used as edging on all brochures and publicity material. The familiar BA monogram divided vertically by a miniature airscrew within a circle of lettering, which had graced Blackburn aeroplanes ever since the T.B. seaplane and B.E.2cs of 1915, also gave way to Rockwell Italic.

The Mission Symbols

The award of contracts for the production of Sopwith Baby and Cuckoo aircraft during the 1914–18 war brought the company into close collaboration with the Sopwith Aviation Co. Ltd., who were using an ingenious type num-

45

The last Blackburn-built B.E.2c, only British military aircraft ever to carry a five-figure serial, bearing the company's original circular monogram on the fin.

Kangaroo G-EAIU carrying the Rockwell Italic styling in 1922.
(*Courtesy G. S. Leslie.*)

bering system in which fighters were lettered F followed by a mark number, bomber aircraft B and so on. Under this system their first torpedo-carrier, the Cuckoo, bore the designation T.1, almost exactly equivalent to the mission symbol used by United States military aircraft in later and more lethal wars.

The soundness of this principle was not lost on the Blackburn design office who used it to identify the firm's own projects and products from the R.T.1

Kangaroo (first Reconnaissance Torpedo type) of 1918 until the R.B.3A Perth of 1931. Within this period all Blackburn aeroplanes and major projects were grouped logically into classes according to the role they were to fulfil, as follows:

Class B.T.	Bomber-Torpedo	Class R.	Reconnaissance
C.A.	Commercial Aeroplane	R.B.	Reconnaissance Boat
C.Bo.	Civil Boat	R.T.	Reconnaissance-Torpedo
C.B.	Commercial Boat	S.	Survey
D.B.	Dive-Bomber	T.	Torpedo
F.	Fighter	T.C.	Troop Carrier
L.	Light Aeroplane	T.R.	Trainer
M.	Mailplane		

Detailed listing of aircraft and projects in each class is given in Appendix B.

Blackburn Works Orders

At the beginning of the century it was standard practice for large industrial concerns to manufacture their various products in batches and to authorize the work at factory level by means of Works Orders. Many aircraft firms began using this technique during the 1914–18 war, among them the Sopwith Aviation Co Ltd, and it is probable that the Blackburn Aeroplane and Motor Co Ltd followed suit while building Sopwith designs. There is, alas, no surviving documentation to prove this, and the earliest known example is Works Order 6368 under which the Swift prototype was built in 1920. After that date individual aircraft were identified within their own particular batch by means of sequence numbers, e.g. the civil Darts G-EBKF, 'KG and 'KH which were constructed under Works Order 8213 but identified individually as 8213/1, 8213/2 and 8213/3 respectively.

Deprived of that most useful common denominator the constructor's number, the author has found considerable but not insurmountable difficulty in preparing a complete list of Blackburn aircraft in the order in which they were constructed. The task was made difficult because Works Orders were issued for everything manufactured in the company's several factories and frequently covered items of a non-aeronautical nature such as car, coach and trolley-bus bodies. Some were for batches of A.G.S. parts or small aircraft components so that Works Orders relating to the construction of complete aeroplanes ran anything but consecutively.

Constructor's numbers of the more usual kind were used on Blackburn aircraft on two occasions only: in 1930–31 when Bluebird IVs built by Saunders-Roe Ltd carried Saro-Bluebird numbers SB.200-SB.254 in stencilling aft of the cockpit door, and in 1952–55 when the two Universal Freighter prototypes and the first two production Beverleys were allotted constructor's numbers 1000–1003 in order that application might be made for civil registration.

Flt Lt H. R. D. Waghorn with Bluebird IV G-AATN before the King's Cup race at Heston, July 1930. The Saro constructor's number, SB.218, is stencilled above the registration. (*Flight Photo 8803.*)

The B Series

In 1930 a special series of markings was introduced under which British aircraft manufacturers might fly their aircraft for experiment or test, for the purpose of qualifying for Certificate of Airworthiness, for its renewal or for the approval of modifications. Known as Class B registrations, they consisted of a single letter followed by a number and were roughly equivalent to the trade plates used for delivering or testing motor vehicles. They were allotted by the firms themselves, as and when required, and considerably reduced the expensive paperwork previously associated with test flying. The Blackburn Aeroplane and Motor Co Ltd was more fortunate than most for it was allocated its own initial letter B and from that time on the company commenced a numerical series of type designations which had its beginnings in the early issues of Blackburn Class B registrations. These were ten in number and all but the second (which was not painted on the aircraft) and eighth (which was not used) are illustrated in this book.

B-1   Segrave I prototype 1930, later registered G-ABFP.
B-2   Bluebird V prototype 1931, later known as the B-2 and registered G-ABUW.
B-3   Blackburn M.1/30A prototype 1931.
B-4   Tiger-engined Ripon V prototype 1932.
B-5   Pegasus-engined Ripon V prototype 1932.
B-6   Shark prototype 1933.
B-7   Private venture G.4/31 prototype 1933.
B-8   Reserved for two-seat light aeroplane but not used.
B-9   H.S.T.10 prototype 1935.
B-10 Bluebird IV used as Cirrus Minor I test bed 1936.

Thereafter the B Series continued purely as a convenient designation system and at the time of writing is still in use. The most recent to be built, the B-103 Buccaneer, has been followed by a number of freight and transport projects ending with the B-107A, a turboprop third-stage development of the B-101 Beverley.

A detailed listing of completed aircraft, design studies and layouts, from B-1 to B-107A is given in Appendix C.

Postwar Class B Markings

In 1945, when the Class B registration system was amended to include the national letter G and manufacturers were given an individual number which replaced the letter previously used, Blackburn Aircraft Ltd was issued with the numeral 2. It was first used at Brough to identify the Miles M.38 Messenger monoplane flown by the Company as G-2-1 for flying test bed duties during the development of the Cirrus Bombardier 702 engine in 1950–51. In this form it became the one and only Messenger 5, as described on pages 35 and 538.*

* See also the author's *British Civil Aircraft 1919–1972*, Vol. 3, pages 76–77.

Blackburn Class B registration G-2-1 applied to the Bombardier Messenger test bed in 1950.

Class B registration G-2-2 borne by the second Buccaneer S. Mk 50 for South Africa in 1965.

Blackburn Class B registrations then fell into disuse until the first South African Air Force Buccaneer S.Mk.50 also appeared as G-2-1 at Holme-on-Spalding Moor 14 years later, in January 1965. The 15 subsequent aircraft, 412–426, also flew under B conditions and were labelled in sequence right through to G-2-16.

SBAC Designations

Also in 1945 the Society of British Aircraft Constructors introduced a universal designation system during the lifetime of which Blackburn Aircraft Ltd re-indexed several of its designs but at the same time firmly retained its own type numbers. Under this system each manufacturer was given a letter with which to preface each series of nine designs with an additional sequence letter added. In this way Blackburn prototypes built during 1945–58 had SBAC designations which ran from Y.A.1 to Y.A.9 and then onward from Y.B.1, as follows:

Y.A.1	B-48 Firecrest prototype to Specification S.28/43 (1945).
Y.A.2	
Y.A.3	Design studies only.
Y.A.4	B-55 project for a Rolls-Royce Dart powered 24-seat commercial aircraft.
Y.A.5	B-54 anti-submarine two-seater to Specification G.R.17/45 with Napier Double Naiad.
Y.A.6	B-62 project for Firecrest with Armstrong Siddeley Python (1946).
Y.A.7	Y.A.5 two-seater with Rolls-Royce Griffon 56.
Y.A.8	Y.A.5 three-seater with Rolls-Royce Griffon 56 (1950).
Y.A.9	B-75 feeder-liner with two Blackburn Cirrus Majors or Bombardiers (1947).
Y.B.1	Y.A.8 with Armstrong Siddeley Double Mamba (1950).
Y.B.2	H.P.88 research aircraft using a Supermarine Attacker fuselage and Handley Page Victor scale model crescent wing (1951).
Y.B.3	B-103 (otherwise the N.A.39) low-level strike-fighter prototype (1955).

The technical details and operational histories of individual Blackburn aircraft which follow are presented in the order outlined in the previous chapter:

1909–17	Types with known alphabetical designations interspersed chronologically by undesignated types.
1918–31	The 'mission symbol' types in chronological order.
From 1931	Blackburn B designations in numerical order.

They should be read in conjunction with the following notes:

Mark numbers: Aircraft and engine mark numbers used throughout this book are faithful reproductions of those in use at the period under discussion. Before 1939 Roman numerals were already giving place to Arabic and were finally abandoned in 1945.

Abbreviations: These are confined to words and phrases which have first been used in full so that abbreviations are self evident or are well known in aviation terminology.

British civil registrations: It should be noted that the use of the letter Q was discontinued in 1927 and is not included in batches of aircraft built after that date.

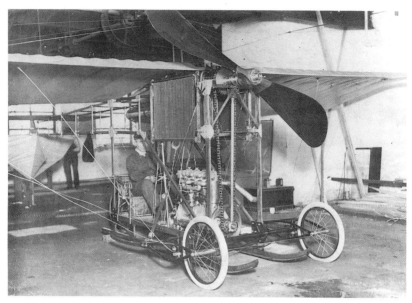

Robert Blackburn's First Monoplane in the workshop at Marske-by-the-Sea where it was housed between attempts to fly from the nearby sands, 1909–10.

The First Blackburn Monoplane

As might have been expected, Robert Blackburn's first aeroplane, being the product of a trained engineering mind, was no stick and string freak. Highly original in concept, it was a wire-and-kingpost braced high-wing monoplane built for strength rather than for economy in weight and in consequence was referred to in later years as the Heavy Type Monoplane to distinguish it from its successor. The parallel-chord square-cut mainplane was bolted across a wooden, wire-braced rectangular box structure which ran on three pneumatic-tyred, rubber-sprung wire wheels, the front being mounted on cantilevers whose trailing ends formed (as an additional safety measure) two long flat skids. A wicker chair from father's garden was pressed into service as a pilot's seat and was mounted on the floor of the box on runners as a means of C.G. adjustment. A 35 hp Green water-cooled engine (one of Gustavus Green's four-cylinder masterpieces and owing nothing to the firm of Thomas Green) was mounted on the floor ahead of the pilot and cooled by two side radiators under the wing. It drove a slow running 8 ft 6 in diameter airscrew of Blackburn's own make through a strong 2 to 1 roller chain and sprocket reduction gear. The overhead airscrew shaft ran in bearings at the front end of a long Warren girder boom which carried a fixed tailplane and, at the extreme end, a cruciform, all-moving, non-lifting, Santos Dumont type empennage mounted on a universal joint.

52

Not content to copy other experimenters, Blackburn dispensed with the feet for controlling direction, and fitted his patent 'triple steering column' consisting of a single car-type steering wheel which turned to operate the all-moving tail as a rudder, moved up and down when it functioned as an elevator and from side to side when warping the wings. He intended originally to fit his patented stability device in which a pendulum admitted air from an engine-driven compressor to one end or the other of a cylinder, according to which way the machine was banking, and an internal piston then operated the control surfaces so as to maintain straight and level flight. Although brilliantly anticipating the automatic pilot of the future, the device was not proceeded with and in any case would not have worked when the aeroplane was accelerating or decelerating.

The designs having been completed in Paris in 1908, the aircraft was built quite rapidly in the small workshop at Benson Street, Leeds, with the assistance of Harry Goodyear, and in April 1909, and in the face of much scepticism, Blackburn began his trials along the wide stretch of sand between Marske-by-the-Sea and Saltburn on the northeast Yorkshire coast. Painstaking taxying trials continued at intervals and the occasional absence of tyre marks proved that short hops were being made, but the 35 hp Green gave insufficient power for sustained flight and Blackburn dismissed these attempts as 'sand scratching'.

He had suspended such weighty items as engine, tanks and pilot, well below the mainplane in order to obtain a low C.G. position, but the disadvantages of such a pendulous arrangement were not immediately obvious and it was not until 24 May 1910 that he attempted a turn and paid the price. The aircraft sideslipped, dug in the port wing, skidded into a hole and threw the pilot from his seat.

One wing was a write-off, the airscrew broken and the undercarriage twisted and there was no alternative but to take the aeroplane back to Benson Street. There work began on an entirely new design and when the works moved to larger premises in Balm Road, Leeds, the fuselage of the First Monoplane went too. Illustrations in the company's 1911 catalogue show it being dismantled in stages at the end of 1910 during the overhaul of two

Front view of the First Blackburn Monoplane on the sands at Marske in 1909.

The fuselage of the Second Monoplane under construction in the Benson Street works, with the partly dismantled First Monoplane behind.

Blériot monoplanes for the Northern Automobile Co Ltd and the construction of Robert Blackburn's second monoplane. For no obvious reason it also received a two page descriptive write-up as the firm's new Military Type, increased in span and length and 'specially built for speed, with seating accommodation under the mainplanes and possessing thereby the chief advantage of the biplane—that of an unobstructed view'. The historic but undoubtedly defunct aircraft was then declared eminently suitable for warlike purposes!

Known as the '1909 Replica Group', enthusiastic Blackburn employees at the Brough works of Hawker Siddeley Aviation Ltd were preparing in 1966 to build a full-size replica for exhibition purposes.

SPECIFICATION AND DATA

Construction: By Robert Blackburn and Harry Goodyear at Benson Street, Leeds, Yorks.

Power Plant: One 35 hp Green

Dimensions: (First Monoplane)	Span 24 ft 0 in	Length 23 ft 0 in
	Wing chord 6 ft 5 in	Wing area 170 sq ft
(Military project)	Span 30 ft 0 in	Length 26 ft 0 in

Weights: All-up weight 800 lb

Performance: Estimated maximum speed 60 mph

Production: One aircraft only, completed September 1909, damaged beyond repair at Saltburn Sands 24 May 1910, dismantled at Balm Road, Leeds, about December 1910.

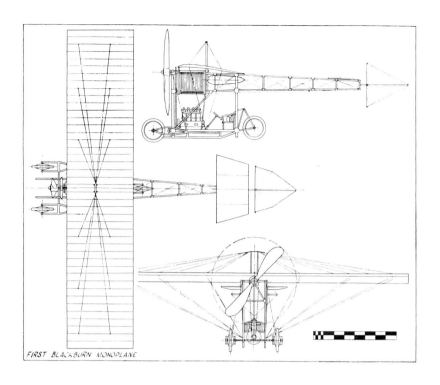

FIRST BLACKBURN MONOPLANE

The Second Monoplane in unfinished state at the Blackpool Flying Meeting,
August 1910, showing the original undercarriage and airscrew.

The Second Blackburn Monoplane

Although Robert Blackburn's second aeroplane bore a marked resemblance to
M. Levavasseur's Antoinette monoplane which he had seen in France, so
many detailed improvements were incorporated that the resemblance was
purely superficial. It was a single-seat, fabric-covered, wooden monoplane
with a square-ended, constant-chord mainplane wire-braced to a central
kingpost at a considerable dihedral angle, and the fuselage was of triangular
cross-section tapering rearwards from the pilot's seat.

The 'triple steering column' was used again but the little all-moving tail
was abandoned in favour of the Antoinette's long dorsal fin and its diminutive
triangular rudders above and below the elevator. Blackburn also fitted an
untried British engine of advanced design then being developed by R. J.
Isaacson, a skilled engineer employed by the Hunslet Engine Co of Leeds.
The Isaacson engine was a seven-cylinder air-cooled radial of 40 hp arranged
so that valves and other working parts were readily accessible for maintenance,
and its many novel features (for those days) included pushrod-operated overhead valves and a 2 to 1 reduction gear within the airscrew hub. Being a
stationary unit there were none of the gyroscopic problems with which the
rotary engine continually plagued designers and pilots alike.

The development of such an engine inevitably took a long time, so that although Blackburn and Goodyear took the monoplane to the Blackpool Flying Meeting of 28 July–20 August 1910, it could not participate because the engine was unfinished even though installed in the airframe. This was perhaps fortunate, for the undercarriage was so weak that the wing tips had to be supported with timber when in the hangar.

In its original form the undercarriage consisted merely of a downward extension of the wooden kingpost which terminated in a socket carrying a tubular-steel cross-member. Two ash skids, with pneumatic-tyred wire

The completed Second Monoplane with fuel and oil tanks in position, narrow-bladed airscrew, and the first undercarriage modification.

The Second Blackburn Monoplane at Filey in 1911 with wing tip skids and the second undercarriage modification.

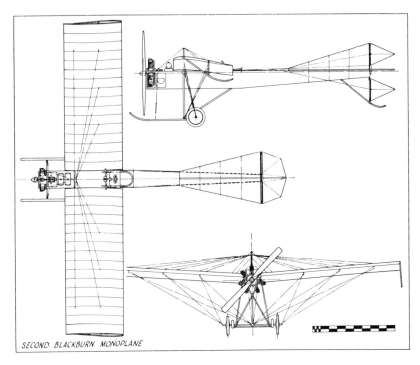

SECOND BLACKBURN MONOPLANE

wheels in forks at the rear ends, pivoted about this steel cross member, all landing shocks being taken by a powerful coil spring at the apex of a triangle of struts under the engine. However, after Blackpool, and while he was awaiting the completion of the engine, Blackburn added a stout pair of main undercarriage struts and refitted the wheels on an overlength axle to give a measure of sideways movement under the control of coiled springs. He then took the monoplane to a new stretch of sands on the Yorkshire coast at Filey, but the undercarriage was still unsatisfactory. The front struts with their central coiled spring were removed almost immediately and replaced by four skeins of bungee rubber connecting the ends of each skid via cables to the longerons of the fuselage.

Not long after reaching Filey, the machine attracted the attention of B. C. Hucks who thereupon joined forces with Blackburn to try out the machine and, on Tuesday, 8 March 1911, taxied it for a distance of three miles along the sands before making the initial take-off. He then headed for Filey Brigg at a height of 30 ft and at an estimated speed of 50 mph, but in attempting a turn, always a hazardous manoeuvre when there is negligible difference between maximum speed and stalling speed, he sideslipped into the ground.

After repairs the Second Monoplane flew well and saw a great deal of service as an instructional aircraft at Filey and established Robert Blackburn as one of the foremost British designers of the day.

SPECIFICATION AND DATA

Construction: By R. Blackburn and H. Goodyear at Benson Street, Leeds, Yorks.

Power Plant: One 40 hp Isaacson

Dimensions: Span 30 ft 0 in   Length 32 ft 0 in

Weights: All-up weight 1,000 lb

Performance: Maximum speed 60 mph

Production: One aircraft only, completed July 1910, first flown at Filey 8 March 1911.

The Mercury I monoplane (50 hp Isaacson) flying at Filey in 1911. The slipway below the machine led to Robert Blackburn's hangar on the right.

Blackburn Mercury

The Mercury, Robert Blackburn's next aeroplane, was a larger, two-seat development of his Second Monoplane powered by a new 50 hp version of the Isaacson radial. It was built with the assistance of Harry Goodyear, Mark Swann and George Watson in large premises which Blackburn acquired in Balm Road, Leeds. Whereas the earlier machine (with which the Mercury is still frequently confused) had a two-wheeled undercarriage, the Mercury had four wheels mounted in pairs on short, bungee-sprung axles astride two long ash skids attached to the fuselage by a substantial wire-braced, 12-strut, multiple A frame calculated to resist the efforts of the most inexpert pupil. Steel springs projecting sideways under the axle were intended to counteract the effects of landing with drift.

To make wire bracing unnecessary, the triangular-section lattice-work fuselage, also of English ash, was precision-built with vertical and diagonal struts butting accurately on the longerons. The forward part accommodated pilot and passenger in tandem and was planked with polished, veneered wood, but the tapering rear fuselage was fabric-covered.

Constant-chord, shoulder-mounted mainplanes were built up from closely spaced ribs supported on two I-section ash main spars and two subsidiary spars. To reduce the stresses associated with wing warping the mainplane was pivoted about the rear spar and wire-braced to a kingpost built into the fuselage in line with the front spar. The patent 'triple steering column' was used again and the tail surfaces were similar to those of the second Blackburn mono-

60

Robert Blackburn (*standing right*) and B. C. Hucks with the Mercury I in the cliff-top hangar, Filey 1911. (*Courtesy Royal Aeronautical Society*,)

plane, with the long dorsal fin, the 10 ft bird-like tailplane, and the one-piece semi-octagonal elevator moving between two small triangular rudders.

The first Mercury (which for convenience will be referred to hereinafter as the Mercury I) was exhibited at the Olympia Aero Show during the last two weeks of March 1911 and then went to Filey to join the Blackburn Second Monoplane at the newly established Blackburn Flying School, where a new airscrew with wider blades was fitted. On 17 May B. C. Hucks flew it to Scarborough and back in 19 min, averaging 50 mph and reaching a height of 1,200 ft, the highest flight made in North England up to that time. Next day he flew the handling and height tests for his Aviator's Certificate, but differences of opinion between the Aero Club observers about the validity of doing both tests in the course of one flight led Hucks to make a second take-off. Minutes later the airscrew sleeve overheated, seized up and broke, allowing the airscrew to fly off. Hucks received slight injuries when he sideslipped

B. C. Hucks fuelling the Mercury I before the Filey–Scarborough flight of 17 May 1911. The high-mounted tanks which identify this machine are clearly illustrated. (*Courtesy Royal Aeronautical Society*.)

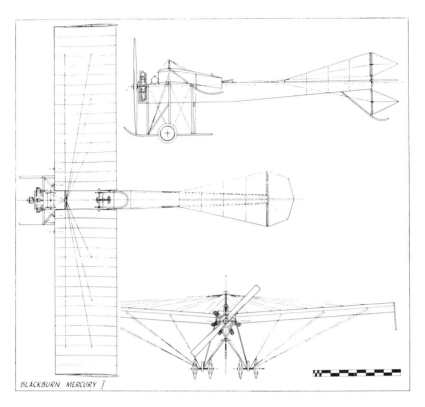

BLACKBURN MERCURY I

into the ground but nevertheless was granted Certificate No. 91, no mean
achievement for a pilot who was entirely self-taught.

In the repaired machine Hucks (by then the Filey School instructor) made
several remarkable flights, notably a cross-country to Scarborough and back
on 7 July and a 40 mile moonlight trip over the same route on 10 July.
Leaving Filey at 10.10 pm he circled Bridlington, reached Scarborough without difficulty, nursed a failing engine which picked up when he was about to
make a forced landing in a cornfield, and landed on the beach by the light of
bonfires 45 min after take-off.

Hubert Oxley who succeeded Hucks as the Filey School's instructor, flew
Mercury I for the first time on 3 September 1911, and to give new pupils
(one of whom was engine designer R. J. Isaacson) an opportunity of watching
his control movements, the front passenger seat was turned round to face aft.
The aircraft was also used for joyriding, as on 11 October when a local resident, Miss Cook, became the first lady passenger in Yorkshire.

Robert Blackburn was now calling himself 'The Blackburn Aeroplane Co'
and advertised the Mercury at £825 with 50 hp Isaacson; £925 with 50 hp
Gnome; £730 with 35 hp Green; and £1,275 with 100 hp Isaacson. None

was in fact ever fitted with the Green or the big Isaacson, the first of a production run of eight aircraft which appeared at intervals during the next couple of years being two single-seaters (referred to in this book as Mercury IIs), built for the Daily Mail £10,000 Circuit of Britain contest, powered by 50 hp Gnome rotaries. They had reduced span and shorter fuselages, the space normally occupied by the front seat was faired over with fabric, and fuel and oil tanks were lowered partially into the fuselage and covered by a curved metal fairing to reduce drag.

Both were entered for the contest by Stuart A. Hirst of the Yorkshire Aeroplane Club—racing No. 22 to be flown by F. Conway Jenkins and No. 27 by B. C. Hucks—and each made its maiden flight at Filey early in July 1911. During the first flight of No. 22 on 7 July, Hucks made a return flight to Scarborough, 15 miles in 15½ minutes, and reached 3,000 ft, but on the 14th, while attempting to win Hirst's £50 prize for a flight to Leeds in a Yorkshire-built aeroplane, he damaged it extensively in avoiding grazing cattle and carried away the undercarriage on a barbed-wire fence during a forced landing at East Heslerton Grange. By a prodigious effort it was repaired on site by Robert Blackburn's working party in time for it to be on the line at Brooklands on 22 July, but although Hucks reached Hendon successfully, he retired the next morning after a forced landing with engine trouble at Barton-in-the-Clay, near Luton. Conway Jenkins' machine turned over and was wrecked while taxying out at Brooklands, but there are conflicting reports on the cause, one blaming a strong cross-wind, another crossed warping controls.

Mark Swann and Harry Goodyear once again repaired No. 27 on site and Hucks flew it back to Hendon. It was then converted to two-seater, dismantled and sent by train from Paddington to Taunton where Hucks began a West Country tour in aid of charity, taking with him a portable hangar, Harry Goodyear as mechanic and C. E. Manton Day as manager. After two opening flights before 10,000 people at Taunton Fête on Bank Holiday Monday, 7 August, the aircraft was sent by train to Burnham-on-Sea, but, late on 17 August, because of a railway strike, Hucks flew the next 25 miles

F. Conway Jenkins in the first single-seat Mercury II at Filey in July 1911.

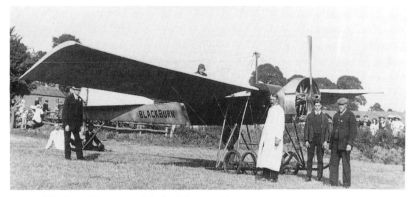

Hucks at Taunton with the Mercury II two-seater on 7 August 1911.
(*Courtesy Royal Aeronautical Society.*)

across to Minehead in 22 minutes, outflying the telegram which was to have announced his arrival. The next port of call was Locking Road aviation ground, Weston-super-Mare, where considerable publicity attended his 5.10 am take-off on 1 September for a nonstop flight to Cardiff, Whitchurch, Llandaff and back. Attired in a cork life-jacket, he reached 2,250 ft, dropped handbills over Cardiff and landed at Weston 40 minutes later, having made the first double crossing of the Bristol Channel by air. The Weston visit over, Hucks made another early start on 11 September, flew 16 miles to Cardiff in 16½ minutes and landed at Whitchurch polo ground at 6.01 am. Static exhibition for two days at the Westgate Road skating rink was a prelude to daily flying from Cardiff's Ely Racecourse and, while flying at 85 mph at a height of 700 ft on 23 September, Hucks made further history by receiving wireless telegraphy signals transmitted by H. Grindell Matthews.

The tour continued with a 6.16 am take-off for Newport, Mon., on 27 September and on to Cheltenham on 1 October where the aircraft was put on show at the Drill Hall, North Street. Flying took place from Whaddon Farm, Cemetery Road, from 4 October until his departure for Gloucester on 16 October where, two days later, he caused a sensation by flying higher than the cathedral tower, although an attempt to better his personal record of 3,500 ft failed. Eventually, on 21 October, a gale lifted the travel-stained aircraft and its hangar completely clear of the ground, but quick repairs enabled the last three flights of the tour to be completed the same afternoon.

In three months, weather had prevented flying on only two of the 30 advertised flying days and an estimated 1,000 miles had been covered in 90 flights, impressive figures for those days particularly when it is remembered that all take-offs and landings were from unprepared surfaces. The wings, originally white but now black with signatures, were replaced while the aircraft was at Cheltenham. Apart from this, the only other major replacement was the result of a forced landing at Cheltenham during which Hucks ploughed up yards of cabbages with his skids until eventually a wheel came off and rolled forward, breaking the airscrew.

From 7 to 10 January 1912 the aircraft flew at Holroyd's Farm, Moortown, Leeds, and was then sent to Shoreham, Sussex, by rail on loan to Lt W. Lawrence of the 7th Essex Regiment pending the delivery of a special steel-framed monoplane he had ordered from Blackburn for service in India. His immediate objective was a cross-Channel flight with society hostess Mrs Leeming as passenger. Taxying practices, begun on 25 January under the watchful eye of Hucks, led to first solos on 29 January and on 26 February to a half hour, 28-mile flight to Eastbourne where he landed down wind on the

The Blackburn Type B monoplane at Hendon in 1913. (*Flight Photo 018.*)

Laurence Spink at the controls of the Type B, Hendon 1913. Details of the Blackburn patent triple steering column are clearly visible. (*Courtesy H. F. Cowley.*)

65

Robert Blackburn beside the Type B, racing number 33, before the start of the Aero Show Trophy Race at Hendon on 22 February 1913. (*Courtesy Royal Aeronautical Society.*)

beach with engine trouble. F. B. Fowler of the Eastbourne Aviation Co gave the Gnome a complete overhaul and fitted a hand pump to overcome fuel starvation in the climb, but test flights on 30 March ended in a bad landing which put the machine on its back with sufficient damage to end Lawrence's cross-Channel aspirations. While under repair in Leeds, the opportunity was taken to modify it for school work and it emerged a month or so later as a single-seater with wing span increased to 36 ft, the wing roots cut away to improve the pilot's downward view, the undercarriage simplified, and the engine cowling extended rearward to form a scuttle over the instrument panel and afford some protection for the pilot. In this form it was historically important as the first Blackburn aircraft to exhibit a designation, each rudder bearing the inscription 'Blackburn Monoplane Type B'. One of the first pupils to fly it at the Filey School in April 1912 was M. G. Christie, DSc, for whom a special Blackburn aircraft was built in the following year.

With the possibility of military contracts looming ahead, it was considered expedient to bring the Blackburn monoplanes more closely to the notice of the War Office. The School therefore moved to Hendon in September that year under a new instructor, Harold Blackburn (no relation of Robert). There the 'brevet' machine, as it was called, was allotted racing No. 33 for the frequent weekend competitions and also bore the maker's name in large capitals on the fuselage. In this guise it was flown by Harold Blackburn on 28 September at the Hendon Naval and Military Aviation Day and on 22 February 1913 in the Aero Show Trophy Race in which he came third.

The soundness of the Mercury design, well-proven by the Hucks tour, prompted the construction of a third variant inscribed 'Mercury Passenger Type' with 60 hp Renault vee-8 air-cooled engine, now usually known as the Mercury III. This was a three-seater structurally similar to the earlier marks but with mainspars of wood-filled tubular-steel around which the cottonwood ribs were free to swivel and thus reduce twisting strains during wing

66

warping. Other refinements included a foot accelerator which could override the hand throttle, and aluminium panels covering the engine bay. Although ready for flying at Filey on 29 October 1911, bad weather prevented Hubert Oxley from making the first flight until 9 November when the machine took off in 30 yards with one passenger and fuel for four hours. It proved very manoeuvrable and had a top speed around 70 mph.

Oxley, who began a series of passenger flights over the sands in bright moonlight at 1 am on 27 November, was the only pilot to fly this machine. On 6 December, with Robert Weiss in the passenger seat, he passed low over Filey bent on his favourite trick of diving steeply over the edge of the 300 ft cliff and then suddenly flattening out to land. This occasion was the last, for on pulling out of a particularly steep dive at a speed estimated at 150 mph, the fabric stripped from the wings which immediately broke up, leaving the wingless fuselage to plummet into the sands with fatal results for both occupants.

At first this machine had a constant-chord mainplane, but at some point

The Mercury Passenger Type (the first Mercury III) with 80 hp Renault and the original parallel-chord mainplane.

Hubert Oxley and passenger in the ill-fated Mercury Passenger Type outside the Filey hangar after the tapered mainplane was fitted.

Jack Brereton climbing into the second Mercury III (50 hp Isaacson) at Filey in May 1912. The raised top rudder distinguished it from the Isaacson-powered Mercury I. (*Courtesy G. S. Leslie.*)

during its brief six-week existence it was fitted with new wings having a root chord of 9 ft and tapering to 7 ft at the tip. Despite statements to the contrary made in the Press at the time, this was the only Blackburn Mercury fitted with a tapered wing.

A second Mercury III, with 50 hp Isaacson and faired tanks as on Mercury II, was then built for Oxley's successor Jack Brereton who attempted the Filey–Leeds flight on 29 May 1912. This machine further differed from the Isaacson-powered Mercury I in having the top rudder raised above the fin, removable inspection panels behind the engine, and no wing tip skids. After a 6 am take-off, Brereton forced landed 22 miles away at Malton with engine trouble, and the flight ended in a second forced landing at Welham Park later in the day. The machine went back to Filey by rail and after this episode R. J. Isaacson modified the engine and fitted ball bearings to the connecting rods and crankshaft. It was flying again on 9 June and went to Hendon with the Type B in the following September.

The third Mercury III, built for naval flying pioneer Lt Spenser Grey, RN, had polished aluminium side panels as far aft as the cockpit and for this reason has been continually misrepresented as one of the all-steel monoplanes which Blackburn built in 1912. Redesign of the front fuselage, which began when the tanks on the Mercury IIs and the second Mercury III were lowered and covered, reached finality in Spenser Grey's machine. This had a curved decking over the tanks which continued the line of the circular cowling over the 50 hp Gnome back as far as the cockpit where it formed a 'scuttle-dash' to deflect some of the slipstream from the pilot. This modification was embodied in the Hucks tour machine when it was rebuilt as Type B in 1912. Grey's Mercury III was delivered by rail to Brooklands where Hucks made the first engine runs on 16 December 1911, and the owner flew it for the first time on 25 December. A few days later he made a cross-country flight to Lodmoor, near Weymouth, where he had had a hangar built and on 7 January 1912 crossed Weymouth Bay to Portland and circled over the Home Fleet. Unfortunately, after exhibition flights on 10 January, he returned to find his landing ground full of sightseers and the machine was damaged in the ensuing avoiding action. After repairs at Leeds the redoubtable Harry Goodyear took the machine to Eastchurch by train and re-erected it. Spenser Grey then made the first of many flights there on 21 February. The aircraft was eventually repurchased by Blackburns, fitted with the simplified Type B undercarriage, and put to work as a school machine at Hendon where it took part in the Naval and Military Aviation Day on 28 September 1912.

The fourth Mercury III, identified by a combination of cut-away wing roots and six-strut undercarriage, was built for the Blackburn School and flew at Filey in March 1912. Yet another is said to have had a 50 hp Anzani radial. For the summer season that year, a special single-seat machine with partially cowled 50 hp Gnome, similar to the Type B and with 'Blackburn' in bold lettering under each wing, was built to enable Jack Brereton to give demonstrations similar to those of B. C. Hucks the year before. Although it had the cut-away wing roots of Mercury III No. 4, its undercarriage differed from those of all other Mercury monoplanes. Basically of the simplified type fitted to the Type B, it had a tubular-steel spreader bar between the front struts and laminated skids with turned-down rear ends. It was first flown at Filey on 7 June 1912, and initial engagements were at Bridlington on 15 July and the Lincolnshire Agricultural Show, Skegness, two days later.

Despite the oft repeated assertion that nine Mercury IIIs were built, careful research has failed to identify more than six, so that in the absence of further information it can only be assumed that the total of nine included the Mercury I and the two Mercury IIs. The company's Flying School activities seem to have been maintained throughout by four aircraft. At Filey they appear to have been Blackburn's second monoplane, the Mercury I and Isaacson- and Gnome-powered Mercury IIIs, but at Hendon the veteran second monoplane and the old Mercury I were replaced by the Type B and the modified ex-Spenser Grey two-seater. They remained in service until the School closed in the spring of 1913 and were flown by a select band of pupil

The fuselage of Lt Spenser Grey's two-seat Mercury III (50 hp Gnome) outside the Balm Road works ready for despatch to Brooklands, December 1911. These views show clearly the third and final stage in Mercury fuselage evolution.

pilots, only three of whom actually gained Royal Aero Club Aviators' Certificates on the Blackburn types on which they had learned, viz:

No. 91	B. C. Hucks	Filey	30 May 1911
No. 409	H. A. Buss	Hendon	4 February 1913
No. 410	M. F. Glew	Hendon	4 February 1913

Jack Brereton flying the fourth Mercury III (50 hp Gnome, cut-away wing roots and six-strut undercarriage) at Filey in May 1912.

Mark Swann (*no hat*) and Jack Brereton (*right*) with the last of the Mercury monoplanes on the promenade at Bridlington on 15 July 1912. The machine is identified by the undercarriage modification. (*Courtesy G. S. Leslie.*)

SPECIFICATION AND DATA

Constructors: The Blackburn Aeroplane Co (the Aeroplane Dept of Robert Blackburn and Co, Engineers), Balm Road, Leeds, Yorks.

Power Plants: (Mercury I)   One 50 hp Isaacson
       (Mercury II)   One 50 hp Gnome
       (Mercury III)   One 60 hp Renault
                  One 50 hp Isaacson
                  One 50 hp Gnome
                  One 50 hp Anzani

Dimensions, Weights and Performances:

	Mercury I	Mercury II	Mercury III
Span	38 ft 4 in	32 ft 0 in*	32 ft 0 in
Length	33 ft 0 in	31 ft 0 in	31 ft 0 in
Height	6 ft 9 in	8 ft 6 in	8 ft 6 in
Wing area	288 sq ft	200 sq ft*	195 sq ft
All-up weight	1,000 lb†	700 lb	800 lb
Maximum speed	60 mph	70 mph	75 mph‡

   * Second aircraft later rebuilt with 36 ft span, 220 sq ft mainplane
   † With Isaacson engine   ‡ With Renault engine

Production:

(a) *Mercury I*
One aircraft only, 50 hp Isaacson, shown at Olympia March 1911 and used by the Blackburn Flying School, Filey, until 1912.

(b) *Mercury II*
Two aircraft only, both with 50 hp Gnome engines:

1. Racing No. 22, first flown at Filey in July 1911, wrecked at Brooklands 22 July 1911.
2. Racing No. 27, first flown at Filey 7 July 1911, converted to two-seater August 1911, crashed at Eastbourne 23 March 1912, rebuilt as a single-seat school machine for the Filey School April 1912, to the Hendon School September 1912 as racing No. 33, withdrawn from use when the school closed June 1913.

(c) *Mercury III*
Six aircraft as follows (in approximate production order):

1. 60 hp Renault	First flown 9 November 1911, crashed at Filey 6 December 1911.
2. 50 hp Isaacson	First flown May 1912, identified by raised top rudder, used by the Blackburn Flying School, Hendon, until June 1913.
3. 50 hp Gnome	First flown 25 December 1911, built for Lt Spenser Grey, RN, damaged at Weymouth 10 January 1912, first flown at Eastchurch after repair 21 February 1912, to the Blackburn Flying School, Hendon, by September 1912.
4. 50 hp Gnome	School machine, cut-away wing roots, first flown at Filey March 1912.
5. 50 hp Anzani	No details.
6. 50 hp Gnome	Exhibition machine first flown 7 June 1912.

71

Lt W. Lawrence's all-steel Blackburn Type E (60 hp Green) *L'Oiseau Gris*, No. 1 of the Indian Aviation Co Ltd, at Brooklands in May 1912. (*Flight Photo 0132.*)

Blackburn Type E

During 1911 the efforts of Robert Blackburn and other British pioneers produced a number of sturdy aeroplanes with good flying characteristics which challenged the supremacy of French machines to the point where the placing of military contracts for British-built aircraft could not long be delayed. As expected, the War Office issued its first military aircraft specification in November that year and called for a reconnaissance two-seater able to carry a useful load of 350 lb over and above essential equipment and to have an initial rate of climb of 200 ft/min, $4\frac{1}{2}$ hr endurance, 55 mph maximum speed and able to maintain 4,500 ft for 1 hr. It also had to be transportable in a crate from one operational area to another. Competing firms were given just nine months in which to design, build and test before the commencement of competitive trials on Salisbury Plain in August 1912.

To meet these requirements Robert Blackburn designed a two-seat 'military' aeroplane in metal which retained most of the principal features of his successful Mercury series. The mainplane was built up from two 18 swg tubular-steel spars, respectively 2 in and $1\frac{1}{2}$ in in diameter, with ribs of $\frac{1}{4}$ in cottonwood fretted out for lightness and edged with 1 in by $\frac{1}{4}$ in ash. A number of light ash strips ran transversely and the leading and trailing edges were reinforced with the same material. The tubular spars were filled at the root ends and securely bolted to steel plates through which passed the stout king-post carrying the wing warping and bracing wires.

For durability and to expedite repairs, the triangular fuselage had 32 detachable and interchangeable vertical struts and 58 cross-members, all of oval-section steel tubing, joined by specially riveted clips and covered with sheet aluminium. The tail unit was formed from fabric stretched over a steel-tube framework and ending in an ash trailing edge to which were hinged steel rods carrying the elevator and twin triangular rudders. Control wires ran inside the fuselage, and the much simplified, twin-skid, four-wheeled

72

undercarriage was of oval steel tubing and incorporated built-in anchorages for the flying wires.

The new monoplane was built in the Balm Road works alongside a single-seater (also with steel-tube fuselage) ordered by Lt W. Lawrence for use in India where he had seen Army service the year before. Both monoplanes consequently earned a place in aviation history as the first aircraft of British design and construction to have metal fuselages. Powered by a 60 hp Green four-cylinder inline water-cooled engine and closely resembling the Blackburn Type B, Lawrence's single-seater was taken to Filey for test in April 1912 and took off in 30 yards with fuel for four hours at approximately the same all-up weight as a standard wooden Mercury. Painted grey overall and bearing the inscription Indian Aviation Co Ltd on the lower rudder, the name *L'Oiseau Gris* on the engine cowling and with No. 1 painted on the radiator grill, it went to Brooklands for further trials in the following month. Although entered by the owner in the round-London Aerial Derby of 8 June 1912, the aircraft

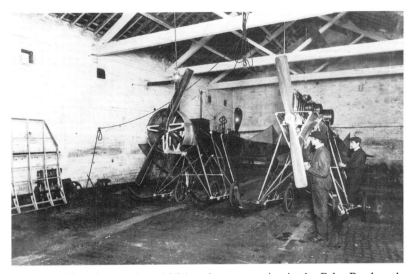

Lawrence's all-steel monoplane (*right*) under construction in the Balm Road works in April 1912, next to his damaged Mercury II which was awaiting conversion to Type B.

was scratched as 'not ready in time'. As this occurred some two months after the first flights at Filey, teething troubles are suggested which may have been the result of using an engine which required a heavy water cooling system and the reason for the end of Lawrence's interest in it.

Trouble of this sort was avoided in the military two-seater which appeared later in June 1912 fitted with a vee-8 air-cooled 70 hp Renault. It differed from the first in having a curved top decking, which extended as far aft as the forward tip of the dorsal fin, to accommodate the crew in tandem cockpits with the pilot and his triple control unit in the rear. Extra fuel, increasing the endurance to five hours, was carried in a cigar-shaped tank between the undercarriage struts and, following the precedent set by the Blackburn Type B trainer, the little triangular rudders bore the designation Type E.

The second or 'military' two-seat Blackburn all-steel Type E monoplane (70 hp Renault) on the playing fields of Cockburn High School, Leeds, at the end of 1912.

An early intention was for the Eastchurch pilots, Lt Spenser Grey, RN, and Capt R. Gordon, RMLI, to pilot these machines in the British Military Aeroplane Trials, but when the two-seater was taken to Knavesmire, York, for flight testing by Robert's brother Norman Blackburn and R. W. Kenworthy it proved too heavy to leave the ground and in fact never did so. It was taken back to the Balm Road works, and when the entry lists for the Trials were published in July 1912 Blackburn was not represented. The ultimate fate of the 'all-steel' monoplanes is uncertain but later on, in the winter of 1912, the two-seater appeared briefly on the playing fields of Cockburn High School off Dewsbury Road, Leeds, with Spenser Grey and Gordon in attendance.

A further development of the type was evidently contemplated since the company records refer to an undesignated two-seat military aircraft of 1912–13 with a specification which does not correspond to that of the Type E.

SPECIFICATION AND DATA

Manufacturers: The Blackburn Aeroplane Co, Balm Road, Leeds, Yorks.

Power Plants: (Single-seater)   One 60 hp Green
      (Type E Two-seater) One 70 hp Renault

Dimensions: (Type E) Span 38 ft 4 in Length 31 ft 2 in
                Wing area 290 sq ft
     (Project)   Span 40 ft 0 in   Length 32 ft 0 in
                Wing area 276 sq ft

Weights: (Type E) All-up weight 950 lb

Performance: (Type E) Maximum speed 80 mph (Project) 65 mph

Endurance: (Single-seater) 4 hr (Type E) 5 hr (Project) 5 hr

Production: Two dissimilar aircraft only:

1. Single-seater *No. 1 L'Oiseau Gris*, 60 hp Green, first flown at Filey April 1912, to Brooklands May 1912.
2. Two-seater military Type E, 70 hp Renault, completed June 1912, never flew.

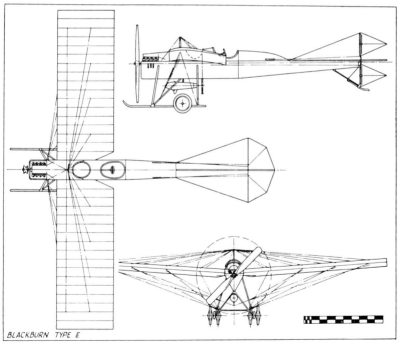

BLACKBURN TYPE E

The Single-Seat Monoplane after restoration by the Shuttleworth Trust, flying at the RAF Display, Farnborough, July 1950, piloted by Sq Ldr G. Banner. (*Flight Photo 26071S.*)

Blackburn Single-Seat Monoplane

On 19 October 1912 Mr Cyril E. Foggin qualified for Aviator's Certificate No. 349 on a Blériot monoplane of the Eastbourne Aviation Co and soon afterwards placed an order with Robert Blackburn for a private aeroplane. This was a single-seat monoplane built of selected English ash, fabric-covered and powered by a 50 hp Gnome rotary. It was smaller, more compact and streamlined than the Mercury but retained the triangular-section fuselage and wire-braced, square-cut warping wing which was rectangular in planform with I-section spars machined out of straight-grained ash over which were slipped silver spruce ribs with cottonwood flanges. The fabric was held in place by a beading of split cane along each rib. The mainplane was braced to the undercarriage by three flying wires and also to the top of a central pylon which also carried the pulleys for the upper warping cable.

External features which gave the new single-seater a modern appearance were the curved top-decking, the aluminium-plated front fuselage, the one-piece rudder with divided elevator, and the simplified, two-wheel, bungee-sprung undercarriage. For the first time in a Blackburn aeroplane the rudder was operated by a foot bar, and a small, universally mounted, wing-warping wheel was situated on top of the control column. From the pilot's point of view a most disconcerting feature was a crossbar, joining the root ends of the rear wing-spar, which clamped across his lap after he had taken his seat.

The machine was completed with commendable speed and first flew unpainted, in the hands of Harold Blackburn, at the end of 1912. Its rate of climb was a marked improvement on that of its predecessors, and the machine appeared for the first time in public at Lofthouse Park, Leeds, on Good Friday, 21 March 1913, when Blackburn began ten days of demonstration flying which included circuits of Wakefield. The owner, Cyril Foggin, flew it for the first time on Easter Monday, 24 March, and was airborne for 20 min. Exhaust fumes and hot oil, when thrown back into the cockpit do not make

* See note on page 80.

76

The Blackburn Single-Seat Monoplane, new and unpainted, out for its first engine run at Leeds late in 1912, with Harold Blackburn at the controls.

for safe and enjoyable flying, and after a few flights the rather abbreviated engine cowling was extended down to the line of the top longerons.

Further demonstration flying with Harold Blackburn at the controls then took place at Lofthouse Park (later known as the Yorkshire Aerodrome) at intervals until the end of May. Cross-country flights were also made to Stamford on 2 and 3 April, when he dropped 2,500 leaflets from 1,200 ft. With the aid of map and compass—one of the earliest attempts at accurate navigation—he flew to Harrogate on 29 April and landed on the Stray in front of the Queen's Hotel, having covered the 18 miles in as many minutes and reached a height of 4,000 ft en route. Finally, on 23, 24 and 25 July, he made daily newspaper flights between Leeds and York to deliver bundles of the *Yorkshire Post*.

The original hooked undercarriage skids were later replaced by the more usual and less lethal hockey stick variety, and a new mainplane with rounded

Cyril Foggin (*right*) and Harold Blackburn with the Single-Seat Monoplane at Lofthouse Park, Leeds, in March 1913. The original square-cut wing tips and hooked undercarriage skids are noteworthy.

77

M. F. Glew (cloth cap) sitting on the engine of the Single-Seat Monoplane after the crash at Wittering in 1914. (*Courtesy R. W. Kenworthy.*)

tips similar to that used on its two-seat derivative, the Type I, was also fitted. Foggin then sold the machine to Montague F. Glew, whom he had met at the Blackburn School, Hendon, earlier in the year. Glew, who on 4 February 1913 had qualified on a Blackburn Mercury for Aviator's Certificate No. 410, flew and eventually crashed the ex-Foggin machine on his father's farm at Wittering, Lincs., adjacent to the site of the present RAF aerodrome.

Reconstruction began by cutting 18 in off the fuselage longerons behind the engine bearer plate and this has been interpreted as a C.G. adjustment consistent with an attempt to install a heavier and more powerful engine, but such a scheme was never mentioned by M. F. Glew.

When war came later in 1914, the components were stored in a farm building, where they were discovered by the late R. O. Shuttleworth almost a quarter of a century later, in 1938. Several of the major airframe assemblies were lying under hay but all were collected together and conveyed to the Shuttleworth headquarters at Old Warden Aerodrome, Biggleswade, Beds. The dismantled Gnome engine and parts of a second were found in a barrel, but during the very considerable work of restoration (including the re-insertion of the missing 18-inch fuselage bay) it was decided to fit a 'new' engine. This was the 50 hp Gnome No. 683 which had formerly powered the single-seat Sopwith Type SL.T.B.P. biplane, Harry Hawker's 1914–18 war personal transport. This engine bore the date stamp 6.8.1916 and was sold to R. O. Shuttleworth by Mr R. C. Shelley of Billericay, Essex, who had owned the SL.T.B.P. for a time in 1926.

Work was held up by the outbreak of the 1939–45 war, and it is a tribute to the patience and skill of the Shuttleworth engineers, led by the indefatigable Sqn Ldr L. A. Jackson, that when the work was eventually completed the monoplane flew very well despite the low power output of the old Gnome engine. All the secondary structure of the mainplane, the fittings and wing tip bends are the originals, but new mainspars were made and fitted. The old engine cowlings, quite unserviceable, were replaced by replicas but, apart from this, a few small wooden members and the fabric, all the rest of the structure remains just as it was in 1913.

The first post-restoration flight was made by Air Commodore (then Grp Capt) A. H. Wheeler at Henlow on 17 September 1949 and by 1966 the Blackburn Single-Seat Monoplane had completed 10 hrs in the air. During two decades it has flown in public on many occasions, one of the first being the RAE At Home of 25 September 1949 when Air Commodore Wheeler made three very successful circuits of Farnborough. It performed well in the hands of Sqn Ldr Gordon Banner at the RAF Display, Farnborough, on 7–8 July 1950 and at the RAeS Garden Party, White Waltham, on 6 May 1951. More recently it posed alongside the latest Blackburn Buccaneer strike-fighter at Holme-on-Spalding Moor on 16 April 1962, to mark the 50th anniversary of military aviation, and at Booker among sundry replica aircraft of the period during the filming of 'Those Magnificent Men and their Flying Machines'. Built well over 50 years ago, it is the earliest British design in the Shuttleworth Collection and the oldest flyable British aircraft. For this reason it is regrettable that there is no record of its Blackburn type letter, the brass plate on its dashboard which reads Type B No. 725 being completely meaningless in any Blackburn context.

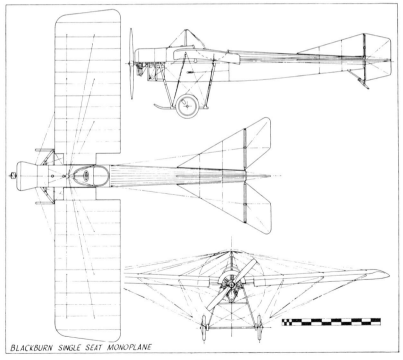

BLACKBURN SINGLE SEAT MONOPLANE

SPECIFICATION AND DATA

Manufacturers: The Blackburn Aeroplane Co, Balm Road, Leeds, Yorks.

Power Plant: One 50 hp Gnome

Dimensions: Span 32 ft 1 in   Length 26 ft 3 in
          Height 8 ft 9 in   Wing area 256 sq ft

Weights: Tare weight 550 lb.   All-up weight 980 lb

Performance: Maximum speed 60 mph   Endurance 2½–3 hr

Production: One aircraft only, first flown at Leeds March 1913; crashed at Wittering 1914; rebuilt by the Shuttleworth Trust 1938–47; preserved in airworthy condition at Old Warden, Beds.

The Single-Seat Monoplane outside the flying school hangar at Brough in 1950.

★   ★   ★

Since the publication of the original edition of this book doubts have been expressed about the identity of the Single-Seat Monoplane in the Shuttleworth Trust's collection. A. J. Jackson was in correspondence with several people about this aeroplane but the issue had not been resolved by the time of his death.

In order not to mislead readers some of the correspondence has been reproduced as Appendix G.

Editor

The first Blackburn Type I monoplane ready for one of its early flights, with M. G. Christie and Harold Blackburn aboard and showing the original engine cowling. (*Courtesy G. S. Leslie.*)

Blackburn Type I

M. G. Christie, DSc, who had done some flying at Filey and Hendon on earlier Blackburn types but had not qualified for an Aviator's Certificate, watched the performance of Cyril Foggin's new single-seat monoplane with interest, having known the owner as a fellow pupil at Hendon. It came as no surprise therefore when he ordered a two-seat version and engaged Harold Blackburn to give flying demonstrations and to act as his personal pilot. Similar in appearance to, and structurally identical with, the single-seater, the new Blackburn Type I two-seater had the span increased to 38 ft and was fitted with the more powerful 80 hp Gnome generously cowled in aluminium for about five-eighths of its circumference and driving a 9 ft Blackburn laminated walnut airscrew. The occupants sat in tandem in a large double cockpit, with the passenger in front over the C.G. so that the aircraft could be flown solo from the rear seat without ballast. Instrumentation included a large Hewlett and Blondeau inclinometer mounted externally on the starboard wing pylon strut, and the control column, conforming for the first time to contemporary practice, moved fore and aft for elevator control and had a large steering wheel for wing warping. A slightly redesigned undercarriage with forward instead of backward, sloping front struts imparted a rakish appearance to the whole machine.

The Type I was delivered at the Yorkshire Aerodrome, Leeds, on 14 August 1913, and it is said that on its first test flight Harold Blackburn climbed it to 7,000 ft in 10 min. His flying programme, which commenced at Harrogate about a week later, usually took the form of a week or so's demonstration and joyriding at each town, followed by cross-country flights with M. G. Christie, the owner, at weekends. Typical of these trips was one made on 24 August

Harold Blackburn and passenger in the Type I as it was in November 1913 with rudder inscription and modified engine cowling. The tail-up attitude was provided by two gentlemen whose likenesses were obliterated from the original print. (*Courtesy J. W. R. Taylor.*)

The Type I after the fuselage was covered-in to provide two separate cockpits. Oil stains of distinctive shape on the port side were a useful recognition feature of this machine in all configurations.

1913, from Bridlington to Leyburn (75 miles in 70 min) and then on via Ripon Racecourse to the Stray, Harrogate (40 miles in 23 min). Ripon was again visited on 10, 13 and 15 September—on the last occasion carrying Mrs Leigh, a local septuagenarian. Exhibition flying with steep turns took place at Doncaster and Wetherby on 20 and 21 September and a week or so later, on 2 October, Harold Blackburn secured the firm's first racing success by winning a challenge cup offered by the *Yorkshire Evening News*. In bad visibility and carrying Christie in the front seat, he groped his way to York, Doncaster, Sheffield, Barnsley, and back to Leeds in a 100-mile 'Wars of the Roses' air race against a Lancastrian entry in the shape of the Manchester-built Avro 504 prototype piloted by F. P. Raynham and carrying H. V. Roe as passenger.

After the 'Roses Race' the Type I monoplane was modified in two stages. To improve engine cooling and air supply to the carburettor, two large holes were cut in the nose cowling, and a hinged inspection panel was also provided, probably to facilitate engine priming. At the same time the inclinometer was

82

removed and refitted internally and the inscription 'The Blackburn Aeroplane Co, Leeds. Type I' appeared on the rudder in bold capitals. In December 1913 the aircraft reached its final configuration when the large single cockpit was covered in by a sheet-metal decking to form two separate open cockpits with padded edges.

A second Type I monoplane which followed was a single-seater with a small freight compartment replacing the front cockpit, and a single vertical king-post, encased in a wide-chord streamlined fairing, in place of the inverted V structure used for wing bracing on the previous machine. In this and two other respects it was a throw-back to the Blackburn Mercury since the cowling over the 80 hp Gnome was entirely open at the front, and it was controlled by means of the old 'triple steering column'.

Harold Blackburn flew it continually throughout the winter, and no better

The Type I and the prototype Avro 504 on tour in 1914. (*Courtesy C. H. Barnes.*)

Harold Blackburn unloading newspapers from the freight compartment of the single-seat 'single kingpost' Type I at Chesterfield on 4 April 1914.

testimony to its strength and airworthiness can be found than the readiness with which he braved first fog and then gales in flying from York to Moortown, Leeds, in two attempts on 8–9 January 1914. An ovation from 10,000 spectators in pouring rain is a measure of the enthusiasm he generated, and from 29 March to 4 April he took part with this machine in a 'Sheffield Aviation Week' organized by the *Sheffield Independent* and delivered copies of the early morning edition to Chesterfield on the last day. Passengers were also carried in Christie's Type I throughout the meeting. The 'single kingpost' machine was then exhibited at the Yorkshire Show but was damaged beyond repair in an accident at York later in 1914.

The success of these aircraft prompted the construction of a similar but somewhat improved two-seater which was the only monoplane of British design at the Aero Show which opened at Olympia on 16 March 1914. Then referred to as the Improved Type I, it differed significantly from its predecessors and can be distinguished from them quite easily in photographs. The 80 hp Gnome was more completely cowled and the engine bearers were modified to give a better nose shape in planform, while in side elevation the fuselage was noticeably deeper in the region of the undercarriage. The tailplane was cut back so that it did not extend forward of the fin, the tail skid consisted of two steel rods instead of one, and there were no wedge-shaped strengtheners where the front undercarriage struts were bolted to the skids. A small but useful identifying detail, not found on either of the other Type I machines, was a small brass engraved plate bolted to the nose cowling above the airscrew hub. Internally there were ash instead of cottonwood flanges to the wing ribs. The aircraft type and the manufacturer's name were inscribed on the rudder, though less boldly than on Christie's machine.

On 18 April 1914, Harold Blackburn took the Christie Type I to Saltburn, and during the first week in June was at South Shore, Blackpool. On 22 July he opened the first scheduled service in Great Britain by flying in it with the

The 'single kingpost' Type I, with virtually uncowled engine, being wheeled into the Yorkshire Show, Bradford, 22 July 1914.

Sydney Pickles with the Improved Type I at West Auckland on 11 July 1914. This view shows the twin tail skid and narrow-chord tailplane. (*Courtesy G. S. Leslie.*)

Lady Mayoress of Leeds on the first of the day's every-half-hour runs between Leeds and Bradford. He also tried out his old adversary the prototype Avro 504 biplane, and at the end of the month, when at Southport, took delivery of one of the first four production Avro 504s, but his plans for a flying circus ended at Harrogate in the following month when war was declared and both machines were commandeered by the Government. Guarded by Guy Wilton, one of Blackburn's pupils, they remained inert until a few days later saboteurs (local German waiters were suspected) soaked them in petrol and set fire to their canvas hangar. Somehow Wilton got both aircraft out safely but was badly burned for his trouble.

The first flight of the Improved Type I went unrecorded, but it is known to have been flown at the Knavesmire aviation ground, York, on 9 July 1914 in the hands of the Australian pilot Sydney Pickles, who left next day for West Auckland with a passenger, two suitcases and a two gallon tin of castor oil for the engine. Fog forced him to land in a small field at Darlington and the flight was completed next day. After demonstration flights sponsored by the *Yorkshire Post*, the name of which was painted under the mainplane, he returned to York on 13 July where one of his passengers was R. W. Kenworthy, destined to be Blackburn's chief test pilot before the 1914–18 war was over.

The Improved Type I outside the seaplane hangar at Scarborough on 26 September 1914, in the care of Blackburn engineers Copley and Swann and a detachment of soldiers after it had been commandeered. (*Courtesy G. S. Leslie.*)

D   85

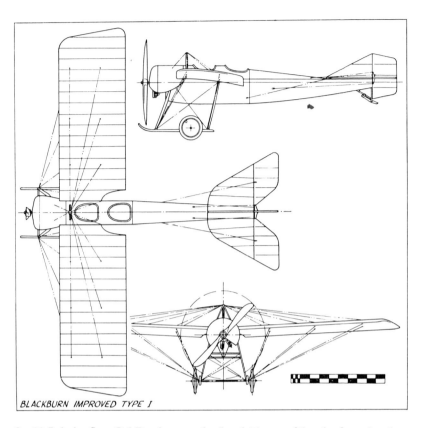

BLACKBURN IMPROVED TYPE I

On 22 July he flew Col Brotherton, the Lord Mayor of Leeds, from Leeds to Bradford on the day that Harold Blackburn inaugurated his half-hourly service by conveying the Lady Mayoress.

On Sunday, 26 July, Pickles flew the Improved Type I the 32 miles back to Knavesmire in 18 min at an average speed of 105 mph, and when war broke out this machine was also commandeered. It was taken to Scarborough in September and housed in the hangar built for the Blackburn Type L seaplane (q.v.). Obviously it was of little military value and in the following year was acquired by the Northern Aircraft Co, successors to the Lakes Flying Co of Windermere, for whom Blackburns rebuilt it as a floatplane trainer. They fitted an uncowled 100 hp Anzani radial, enlarged the cockpit openings, installed dual control, removed the wheels and axle and clamped the skids to the float spreader bars with U shackles. A small cylindrical float was fitted at the tail. Reconversion to landplane was only a matter of a few minutes so that in this form the aircraft was known as the Land/Sea monoplane. In actual fact the wheels were never re-fitted.

It was erected at Windermere by the Northern Aircraft Company and the first flight was made from the firm's slipway at Bowness by W. Rowland Ding on 26 October 1915. Despite the major engine change and the makeshift undercarriage, it needed no adjustments whatever although it was found expedient to remove the exhaust collector ring from the engine early in 1916. With Ding's name painted large on the underside of the mainplane, the aircraft was used for the initial training of a large number of RNAS pilots, and J. Lankester Parker, afterwards Short's famous test pilot, who also instructed on this aircraft, recorded an undated 2hr 39 min on it with pupils, as well as

W. Rowland Ding taking off from Lake Windermere in the 'Land/Sea monoplane', October 1915. The pupil in the front cockpit was Lt Stubbs, RN.

The 'Land/Sea monoplane', with exhaust collector ring removed, on Coniston Water on 18 March 1916, with H. P. Reid and J. Lankester Parker (*rear cockpit*) ready to go ashore. (*Courtesy C. H. Barnes.*)

a climb, two up, to 4,050 ft in 31 min. On Saturday, 18 March 1916, he flew it from Windermere to Coniston Water and, although the trip took only a few minutes, climbed to 2,900 ft. The machine was tied up at Waterhead Pier while the aviators lunched at a local hotel and on the return journey reached a height of 3,400 ft. It was the first seaplane to alight on Coniston where it attracted considerable attention, but a fortnight or so later on 1 April it capsized at Bowness and was written off.

Designs prepared in 1914 for a pure seaplane based on the Improved Type I were not proceeded with, probably because float drag and the 100 lb weight penalty would have made it underpowered with an 80 hp Gnome, the estimated maximum speed being a mere 60 mph.

SPECIFICATION AND DATA

Manufacturers: The Blackburn Aeroplane Co, Balm Road, Leeds, Yorks.

Power Plants: (Type I)   One 80 hp Gnome
            (Improved Type I)   One 80 hp Gnome
            (Land/Sea)   One 100 hp Anzani

Dimensions: Span 38 ft 0 in   Length 28 ft 6 in
             Length (seaplane) 29 ft 6 in   Wing area 252 sq ft

Weights: (Type I)   Tare weight   950 lb   All-up weight 1,500 lb
         (Land/Sea)   Tare weight 1,124 lb   All-up weight 1,733 lb

Performance: Maximum speed (Type I) 70 mph   (Land/Sea) 82 mph
               Initial climb 700 ft/min.   Endurance 4 hr

Production:

(a) *Type I*

Two aircraft only:

1. Two-seater for M. G. Christie, first flown August 1913.
2. Single-seater, with freight compartment, for Harold Blackburn first flown about December 1913, extensively damaged in accident at York about May 1914, stored.

(b) *Improved Type I*

One aircraft only:

Two-seater shown at Olympia, March 1914, commandeered September 1914, converted to Land/Sea Monoplane 1915.

(c) *Land/Sea Monoplane*

One aircraft only:

Conversion of the Improved Type I, first flown on floats at Bowness-on-Windermere 26 October 1915, capsized at Bowness and written off 1 April 1916.

The Type L seaplane in its original configuration outside the hangar on Scarborough beach, August 1914.

Blackburn Type L

Both in the United Kingdom and on the Continent, 1912 had been a year marred by fatalities caused by the structural failure in the air of monoplanes and as a result the British Government banned them from service with the RFC. A departmental committee was set up to enquire closely into such accidents and although its report, issued early in 1914, 'saw no reason to recommend the prohibition of the use of monoplanes', the ill-advised ban, though temporary, created prejudice in favour of biplanes that was to last for close on two decades.

Blackburn monoplanes, rugged and reliable, experienced none of these failures, but nevertheless Robert Blackburn considered it expedient to follow the popular trend and in 1913 designed a two-seat 'hydro biplane' on twin floats, to be powered by either an 80 hp Gnome or a 100 hp Anzani. It was to have had unequal span and cruise at 65 mph at an all-up weight of 1,250 lb, but when, in 1914, the *Daily Mail* announced a £10,000 prize for a Circuit of Britain seaplane race, the project was dropped and a larger, more powerful version built. Designated Type L, it was the company's first biplane and the first Blackburn aircraft since the First Monoplane to have a square instead of triangular-section fuselage. Four ash longerons converged rearwards until they were all bolted to the rudder post and, as before, internal bracing was by precision-fitted diagonal wooden struts instead of the wire bracing favoured by other manufacturers.

Although the component parts of the Type L were fabricated at Balm Road, the seaplane itself had the distinction of being the first of the many hundreds of aircraft assembled in the disused roller-skating rink known as Olympia in Roundhay Road, Leeds, which had been acquired as a new works in the spring of 1914, just prior to the firm's expansion into a limited company. The aircraft was powered by a 130 hp Canton-Unné nine-cylinder water-cooled radial, an engine of Swiss origin, named after its co-designers, and built under licence in Britain by the Dudbridge Iron Works Ltd at Stroud, Glos. Money was distinctly scarce at this time and Robert Blackburn was only able to proceed with the Type L through the kindness of Dudbridge's Mr Kimmins who provided an engine on exceptionally favourable terms. It gave full power at 1,250 rpm and was cooled by two radiators mounted vertically on each side of the front seat. An aluminium cowling over its upper part extented rearwards to form a curved decking which concealed the 32-gallon main fuel tank mounted on the top longerons between the cockpits. There was also a partitioned tank behind the engine holding five gallons of oil and an additional 16 gallons of fuel. The pilot sat in the rear cockpit, where the end of the main fuel tank sloped slightly forward to form an instrument panel carrying revolution counter, altimeter, compass and clock. Controls were conventional and similar to those of the Improved Type I, with a rudder bar for directional control and a large aileron wheel mounted at the top of a tubular control column.

Fabric-covered, wooden mainplanes constructed in the usual Blackburn manner were rigged unstaggered in two bays and the considerable top wing overhang was supported by sloping struts. Long-span ailerons were fitted only to the upper mainplanes, with the balancing cables running through pulleys mounted on its upper and lower surfaces. Tail surfaces were similar in outline to those of the earlier machine but rudder area was increased by a large horn balance under the rear end of the fuselage.

The Type L seaplane under construction in the disused skating rink which was to become the great Olympia Works.

90

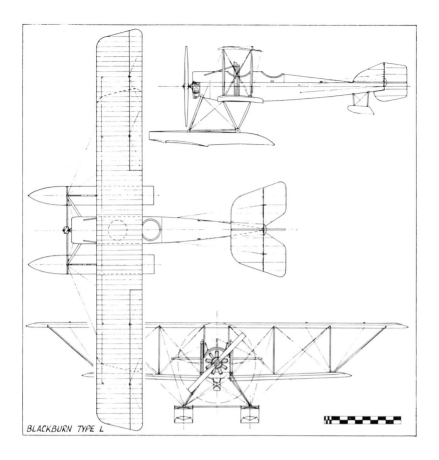

BLACKBURN TYPE L

The twin wooden floats were of unusual design with two steps, the first being only some two feet from the front end. Up to this point there was a pronounced vee bottom which gradually lessened until, aft of the second step, the bottom of the float became quite flat although concave in side elevation. Each float was clipped to tubular steel spreader bars and attached to the fuselage by six stout ash struts. Buoyancy at the tail was provided by a small float attached to four short steel tubes.

The Circuit of Britain seaplane race attracted nine entries from the Sopwith, Beardmore, Grahame-White, Eastbourne, White and Thompson, Avro and Blackburn companies, the Type L, which was to have been flown by Sydney Pickles, receiving racing number 8. Considering the power loading of over 19 lb/hp, its prospects appeared good, the top speed being over 80 mph, and the range of 445 miles was exceptional for those days. Competitors were scheduled to start from Calshot at 6 am on Monday, 10 August 1914, and to proceed via Ramsgate, Great Yarmouth, Scarborough, Aberdeen, Fort

The Type L afloat off Scarborough in 1915, with short-span ailerons, repositioned radiators and uncowled engine.

George, Oban and Kingstown (Dublin) to Falmouth but, as described in a previous work in this series,* entries were actually on their way to the starting point when war was declared against Germany. The race never took place and all the competing aircraft were commandeered by the Admiralty.

The Type L was taken to a section of beach north of Scarborough known as Scalby Mills where Blackburns had built a large wooden hangar. There it was used for offshore reconnaissance duties, thereby forging a link between the company and the Royal Navy that remains unbroken to the present day. The pilot was Sydney Pickles, who had flown the Improved Type I monoplane earlier in the year, and it seems that he experienced control and cooling problems, as it was found necessary to replace the long-span ailerons by short-span, wide-chord, inversely-tapered units which extended well behind the trailing edge of the upper mainplane; to remove the engine cowlings and move the radiators back to the rear centre section struts; and to fit a curved, wide-bladed airscrew. The aircraft was then armed with a machine gun, probably a Lewis, and spent some six weeks at Scarborough in the care of Blackburn mechanics, but its Service career was brief. Early in 1915 the company's test pilot, W. Rowland Ding, struck the top of the cliffs at Speeton in poor visibility while en route from Scarborough to RNAS Station, Killingholme. The undercarriage was wiped off and the rest of the airframe became a total loss in the ensuing crash.

Proposals made late in 1914 for an even larger naval development of the Type L, having staggered mainplanes and powered by a 200 hp Gnome, were shelved.

* See the author's *Avro Aircraft since 1908*, page 68.

SPECIFICATION AND DATA

Manufacturers: The Blackburn Aeroplane and Motor Co Ltd, Olympia Works, Roundhay Road, Leeds, Yorks.

Power Plants: (1913 project) One 80 hp Gnome
                           One 100 hp Anzani
       (Type L)   One 130 hp Canton-Unné
       (1914 project) One 200 hp Gnome

Dimensions, Weights and Performance:

	1913 project	Type L	1914 project
Span upper	44 ft 0 in	49 ft 6 in	62 ft 0 in
lower	36 ft 0 in	35 ft 0 in	47 ft 6 in
Length	33 ft 0 in	32 ft 6 in	—
Height	—	12 ft 6 in	—
Wing area	410 sq ft	481 sq ft	—
Tare weight	1,250 lb	1,717 lb	1,450 lb
All-up weight	—	2,475 lb	3,000 lb
Maximum speed	65 mph	81 mph	—
Climb to 5,000 ft	—	34 min	—
Ceiling	—	11,000 ft	—
Range	—	445 miles	—

Production: One aircraft only, Type L, impressed by the Admiralty August 1914, crashed at Speeton, Yorks., in 1915.

One of the Gnome-powered T.B. prototypes at the RNAS experimental establishment on the Isle of Grain in 1916.

Blackburn T.B.

In May 1914 the Blackburn company received an Admiralty order for a batch of the Farnborough-designed B.E.2c biplane trainers which, together with larger and later batches, were built in new and bigger premises, the Olympia Works. They also built the Sopwith Cuckoo torpedo-bomber in quantity but still found time to work on a number of their own original prototypes. The first of these, first Blackburn design to bear the now legendary 'BA' monogram of the new company, and its first true military aircraft, was built in 1915 to an Admiralty specification which called for a long-range Zeppelin interceptor capable of operating over the sea at night. Its warload of Ranken incendiary steel darts, carried in canisters of 24, was intended to penetrate the airship's envelope and ignite the gas inside.

Known as the T.B. or Twin Blackburn, the machine was a large biplane of unusual design having two wire-braced, fabric-covered, box girder fuselages, each with its own rotary engine, joined by a 10 ft centre section forward and a common tailplane at the rear. The fuselages were supported on the water by separate and unconnected bungee-sprung, stepped pontoons, and small tail floats were attached at the rear by short steel struts.

Fabric-covered wooden mainplanes, built up from I-section spruce spars and ribs of three-ply spruce braced internally with drift struts and tie rods, were rigged in three bays. The considerable overhang at each end of the upper mainplane was wire-braced to triangular steel pylons above the outboard interplane struts. Fins and rudders were B.E.2c components taken from the Blackburn company's own production and slightly modified in shape.

Long-range capability was to have been achieved by fitting the T.B. seaplane with a new type of 150 hp engine said to have an exceptionally low fuel consumption and a dry weight of only 380 lb. This was the ten-cylinder Smith radial, designed by John W. Smith, an American who brought his designs to England in January 1915 and somehow gained immediate Admiralty interest.

94

A prototype engine was bench-tested successfully and a production contract was awarded to Heenan and Froude Ltd of Worcester, but only a few were delivered. When flown experimentally later in 1915 in the A.D. Navyplane and Vickers F.B.5 pusher biplane, the Smith engine proved unsatisfactory, and so eight of the nine T.B. seaplanes ordered by the Admiralty were completed with 100 hp Gnome Monosoupape rotary engines and the ninth and last with 110 hp Clergets.

The first Gnome-powered machine, 1509, was rolled out at the Olympia works in August 1915 and, together with 1510 and the final Blackburn T.B., 1517 with Clergets, underwent type trials at RNAS Isle of Grain in 1916. In his memoirs, the flight test observer E. W. Stedman recalls how the pilot J. W. Seddon sat in one fuselage with all the flying and engine controls, while he sat several feet away in the other with no controls except the starting handle for the engine on his side. Starting on the water needed discipline, courage and agility, for a pool of excess petrol, which formed on the float when the Gnome was primed, promptly ignited when the engine fired. The observer's job was to lie on the lower centre section and put out the fire on the pilot's side

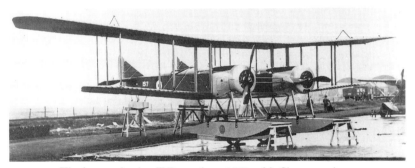

The last production T.B. seaplane, 1517, with Clerget engines.
(*Courtesy Royal Aeronautical Society.*)

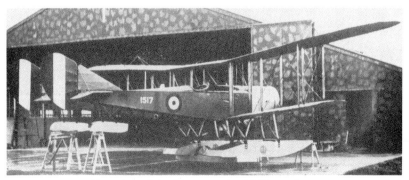

Rear view of the Clerget-engined T.B. seaplane.
(*Imperial War Museum Photo Q.67574.*)

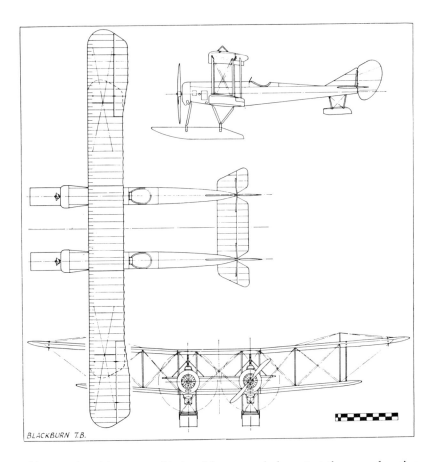

BLACKBURN T.B.

with an extinguisher, scramble into his own cockpit to start the second engine and then leap out again to extinguish the fire on his own float.

Once in the air, mainplane deflection was such that the aileron control cables became slack and all lateral control was lost. This defect was soon put right by the manufacturers but there remained a disconcerting amount of relative movement between the fuselages caused by flexibility in the wire-braced centre section. Furthermore, on only two-thirds of the designed power, performance was mediocre, and to achieve a worthwhile four-hour endurance the military load had to be limited to 70 lb of steel darts. Hand signalling, the only means of communication between the crew members, was hardly an ideal arrangement when in action against an enemy airship, thus, despite the fact that the three trials aircraft and four others were sent to RNAS Killingholme, they were little used and were eventually broken up. This fate also overtook the two remaining aircraft, 1511 and 1512, which were held in store at the RNAS Depot, Crystal Palace, London, until struck off charge.

SPECIFICATION AND DATA

Manufacturers: The Blackburn Aeroplane and Motor Co Ltd, Olympia Works, Roundhay Road, Leeds, Yorks.

Power Plants: Two 150 hp Smith
Two 100 hp Gnome Monosoupape
Two 110 hp Clerget 9b

Dimensions: Span (upper) 60 ft 6 in   (lower) 45 ft 0 in
Length 36 ft 6 in   Height 13 ft 6 in
Wing area 585 sq ft

Weights: (Gnomes) Tare weight 2,310 lb   All-up weight 3,500 lb

Performance: (Gnomes) Maximum speed at sea level 86 mph
Climb to 5,000 ft 12 min   Endurance 4 hr

Production: Nine aircraft 1509–1517, all Gnome-powered except 1517 with Clergets. 1509, 1510 and 1517 Isle of Grain trials aircraft 1916, broken up at RNAS Killingholme August 1917; 1511 and 1512 stored at RNAS Crystal Palace, s.o.c. June 1917, broken up July 1917; 1513–1516 to RNAS Killingholme, broken up August 1917.

97

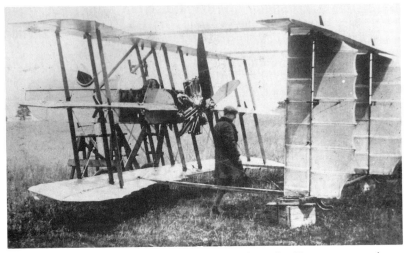

The Blackburn Triplane as first constructed with 110 hp Clerget rotary engine driving a four-bladed airscrew.

Blackburn Triplane

While the batch of T.B. seaplanes was going through the Blackburn works, the firm was also engaged in the construction under contract of two examples of another anti-Zeppelin fighter, the A.D. Scout (later known as the Sparrow), designed by Harris Booth of the Air Department of the Admiralty. This aircraft was a heavily-staggered, single-bay biplane of extremely unorthodox appearance, built to meet an Admiralty requirement for a fighter built from commercially obtainable materials and which could be armed with the Davis two-pounder quick-fire recoilless gun. This lay in the bottom of a short, single-seat nacelle, the top longerons of which were bolted directly to the main spars of the upper wing. With the 100 hp Gnome Monosoupape rotary driving a 9-ft pusher airscrew behind his back, the pilot had a superlative view in nearly every direction.

The aircraft's extraordinary appearance stemmed from the fact that the abnormally large mainplane gap was below instead of above the nacelle, and because the twin fins and rudders, no less than 11 ft apart, were mounted on two pairs of parallel outriggers and supported a vast tailplane of 21-ft span. A suitably bizarre undercarriage reversed the usual pattern, the three points of contact with terra firma being widely spaced skids under the fins and a pair of small wheels mounted close together centrally under the lower mainplane. In this respect it was similar to the Armstrong Whitworth F.K.12 triplane and the projected Bristol F.3A escort and anti-Zeppelin fighters, for it seems that Harris Booth believed in the 'pogo stick' type of landing gear as a means of simplifying cross-wind landings at night.

Four prototype aircraft only were ordered, 1452 and 1453 from Hewlett and Blondeau Ltd of Leagrave, Beds., and two others, 1536 and 1537, from Blackburns. They were all delivered to RNAS Chingford, but being considerably above their estimated all-up weight and difficult to handle in the air, were scrapped.

In 1916 Harris Booth left the Air Department of the Admiralty to join the Blackburn Aeroplane and Motor Co Ltd for whom he immediately designed what can only be regarded as a modified version of his A.D. Scout. To impart the high rate of roll needed by a slow machine taking evasive action round a target Zeppelin, the span was reduced from 33 ft 5 in to 24 ft but the lost wing area was regained by adopting a triplane configuration. It was then fitted with six inversely-tapered ailerons, those on the centre mainplane being

Two views of the first Blackburn-built A.D. Scout, 1536, at RNAS Chingford in 1915 with H. C. Watt in the cockpit. (*Courtesy National Aviation Museum, Ottawa.*)

The Blackburn Triplane with 100 hp Monosoupape and two-bladed airscrew.

cable-controlled from the cockpit and operating those above and below through link struts. The aircraft inherited the A.D. Scout's ugly nacelle and heavy stagger as well as the four parallel tail booms and outsize tailplane of no less than 18 ft 10 in span. The rudders were more enormous than ever so that altogether the Triplane was one of the most extraordinary looking aircraft ever built.

The two-wheel arrangement of the A.D. Scout was replaced by a bungee-sprung, V-type, cross-axle undercarriage of moderate track, but the bottom wing was so close to the ground that substantial wing tip skids were also necessary. In other respects the Triplane was structurally similar to its predecessor and had a wire-braced, fabric-covered wooden airframe which used metal fittings of commercial mild steel. Wing, tailplane and rudder trailing edges were formed from stout wire which gave under the tautening effect of the dope to form a scalloped shape between the ribs.

Only one prototype Triplane, N502, was built, and although contemporary photographs clearly show the gun port in the nose of the nacelle, it is doubtful if the Davis gun was ever fitted. The aircraft was erected in the Soldiers' Field at Roundhay Park, Leeds, where initial engine runs were made before despatch to Eastchurch at the end of 1916. The aircraft flew first with a 110 hp Clerget driving an 8ft-diameter four-bladed airscrew and later with a 100 hp Gnome and two-bladed airscrew. Admiralty acceptance took place at Eastchurch on 20 February 1917, but the Blackburn Triplane proved no more successful than the A.D. Scout and was struck off charge as unsatisfactory one month later on 19 March. Its end, like that of many another undeveloped pusher aircraft, was no doubt hastened by the invention of interruptor gear which enabled machine-guns to fire through the airscrew disc on tractor machines.

SPECIFICATION AND DATA

Manufacturers: The Blackburn Aeroplane and Motor Co Ltd, Olympia Works, Roundhay Road, Leeds, Yorks.

Power Plants: (A.D. Scout) One 100 hp Gnome Monosoupape
 (Triplane)   One 110 hp Clerget
 One 100 hp Gnome Monosoupape

Dimensions: (A.D. Scout) Span 33 ft 5 in   Length 22 ft 9 in
 Height 10 ft 3 in
 (Triplane)   Span 24 ft 0 in   Length 21 ft $5\frac{5}{16}$ in
 Height 8 ft 6 in   Wing area 221 sq ft

Weights: (Triplane, Gnome) Tare weight 1,011 lb   All-up weight 1,500 lb

Performance: No confirmed details

Production: (A.D. Scout) Four aircraft only, 1452 and 1453 by Hewlett and Blondeau
 Ltd; 1536 and 1537 by Blackburn, to Contract 38552/15
 (Triplane)   One aircraft only, N502, to Contract C.P. 120730/16

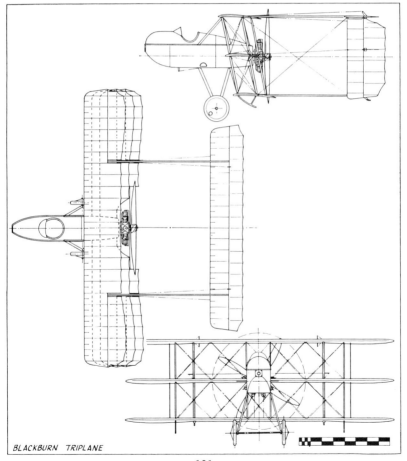

BLACKBURN TRIPLANE

Blackburn test pilot W. Rowland Ding in the cockpit of the White Falcon
monoplane at Roundhay Park, Leeds.

Blackburn White Falcon

Very few technical and historical details of the Blackburn White Falcon
monoplane have survived and little is known of it apart from the fact that it
was built for the personal use of the firm's test pilot W. Rowland Ding.

A photograph taken inside the Olympia works showing it under construction at the same time as the two A.D. Scout biplanes fixes the date as mid-
1915, and comparison with an adjoining Blackburn-built B.E.2c shows that
the machine used the B.E.2c undercarriage and tail skid. Otherwise it bore a
striking resemblance to the float-equipped Type I derivative which preceded
it and which Ding flew at Windermere. Like this machine, it was powered
by a 100 hp Anzani radial driving a 9-ft diameter four-bladed airscrew and
carried the pilot's monogram on the rudder. It used the same type of mainplane, one foot greater in span, and rigged and warped from the same type of
pylon. It also had the same curved decking over a 30-gallon fuel tank and the
same deep, roomy cockpits, but there the similarity ended because the fuselage, like those of most Blackburn aircraft subsequent to the Type I, was of
square instead of triangular section.

Unlike the wire-braced structure of the B.E.2c, the fuselage of the White
Falcon was typically Blackburn and took the form of a precision-built Warren
girder with wooden diagonal members secured by plywood 'biscuits'. The
top of the rudder continued upwards as a rearward projection of the line of
the fin, and all struts were this time of wide-chord streamlined section. The
engine exhaust collector ring was removed during the early part of the aircraft's career. It is doubtful if it ever flew with the B.E.2c main undercarriage;
this was replaced by a neat, wire-braced structure without skids, but the bungee-sprung tail skid and its supporting pyramid of steel tubes was plainly a
standard B.E.2c assembly. During the early stages of construction, the flying
controls were grouped in the front cockpit but seem to have been repositioned
in the rear before the machine flew.

102

There is no definite information as to why a one-off type of this kind should have been constructed during a major war but it is significant that in the few photographs of the machine which exist it is invariably shown outside the little wooden hangar at Soldiers' Field, Roundhay Park, or by the park's distinctive iron railings. With so many B.E.2c aircraft to be test flown at Soldiers' Field, it is probable that the White Falcon was intended as a communications aircraft in which Ding could liaise with RNAS stations to which

The Olympia Works, Leeds, in mid-1915 with the A.D. Scout airframes at the far end, B.E.2cs on the right and the incomplete Land/Sea monoplane (on wheels), facing left.

Close-up of the White Falcon from the starboard side showing cockpit and simplified undercarriage.

Blackburn-built B.E.2cs had been delivered and as a means of returning the firm's ferry pilots to base. Later in its career the machine had the exhaust collector ring replaced and was painted up in Service roundels with the name White Falcon on the engine cowlings, but it did not receive a military serial number.

SPECIFICATION AND DATA

Manufacturers: The Blackburn Aeroplane and Motor Co Ltd, Olympia Works, Roundhay Road, Leeds, Yorks.

Power Plant: One 100 hp Anzani

Dimensions: Span 39 ft 6 in   Length 26 ft 11¼ in
                Wing area 209 sq ft

Production: One aircraft only, built 1915.

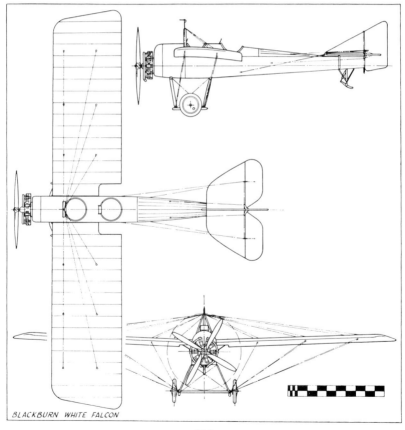

BLACKBURN WHITE FALCON

The White Falcon in military marks during the winter of 1916–17.

The first Blackburn G.P. seaplane, 1415, at the RNAS experimental
establishment, Isle of Grain, in 1916.

Blackburn G.P.

Lack of success with the twin-fuselage T.B. design prompted the Blackburn
company to set about the construction of a more conventional twin-engined
type. This was a three-seat, long-range, anti-submarine patrol bomber known
as the G.P. or General Purpose seaplane. It had mainplanes of modified
RAF 3 section, a long, slim fuselage of unusually small cross-section, inline
water-cooled engines housed in nacelles on the lower mainplane and a large
twin-ruddered biplane tail unit. Nevertheless, the G.P.'s long, wire-braced
upper mainplane extensions and wide-track, divided float undercarriage
proclaimed its T.B. ancestry, but this time the pontoons were bungee sprung
and divided internally into twelve watertight compartments. For ease of
storage the two-spar mainplanes folded backwards outboard of the engine
nacelles, reducing the overall width to 27 ft 10 in.

Blackburns built only two of the type and these differed considerably in
detail. The first, which appeared in July 1916 with the naval serial 1415, was
powered by two opposite-handed 150 hp Sunbeam Nubian engines driving
four-bladed airscrews and cooled by vertical radiator blocks clamped to struts
at the rear of each nacelle.

Three crew members sat in open cockpits, with the bomb-aimer/gunner in
the nose, the pilot just ahead of the centre section and the rear gunner aft of
the wings. A bomb sight was mounted externally on the starboard side of the
front cockpit and, in addition to the two Scarff-mounted Lewis guns, armament consisted of four 230-lb bombs carried on racks under the wings. As
there were no connecting struts between the main floats, alternative armament

106

was a torpedo carried centrally under the fuselage. Although there is no evidence that the G.P. seaplane was ever airborne with a torpedo in position, it was one of the first British aircraft with this capability, and one of the first designed to carry W/T apparatus as standard equipment.

On completion, the G.P. seaplane went to the Isle of Grain for trials which included mooring in a rough sea for several days, an ordeal realistically described at the time as a 'destructive test'.

Meanwhile, the site for Blackburn's new aerodrome and seaplane base had been chosen on the River Humber at Brough, where the first experimental hangar and slipway were completed by the time the second G.P. seaplane was ready for erection later in 1916. Numbered 1416, this was a developed version of the original, and was sometimes known as the S.P. or Special Purpose seaplane. It was powered by two opposite-handed 190 hp Rolls-Royce engines (later named Falcons) cooled in the same manner as the Sunbeams and likewise driving four-bladed airscrews. However, unlike the Sunbeam engines of the first aircraft, the Rolls-Royces had exhaust manifolds on the outside walls of the cylinder blocks, making it convenient to run exhaust pipes along the sides instead of over the tops of the nacelles. Oil tanks were suspended between the inboard nacelle struts ahead of the radiator blocks.

The new machine was structurally stronger than 1415 through the greater use of heavier-gauge metal fittings, and whereas the first had ailerons only on the upper mainplane, the second boasted four ailerons—two of increased length on the upper mainplane connected by link struts of faired tubular steel to short-span units on the lower wing. A wire trailing edge, first employed on the Triplane, was also used for all flying and control surfaces, so that unlike 1415 which had straight edges, those of 1416 were of the familiar scalloped pattern. It was, in fact, a retrograde step as wire trailing edges on seaplanes were a constant source of trouble because they rusted through and split the fabric.

In a lecture given before the Brough branch of the Royal Aeronautical Society in November 1958, G. E. Petty recalled the nightmare of conducting

Launching G.P. seaplane 1416 at the Isle of Grain in 1916.
(*Courtesy R. W. Kenworthy.*)

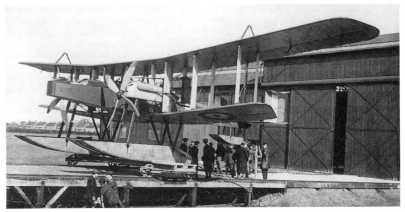

The second G.P. seaplane, 1416, at Brough in 1916 showing the raised nacelles and ailerons on all four wings.

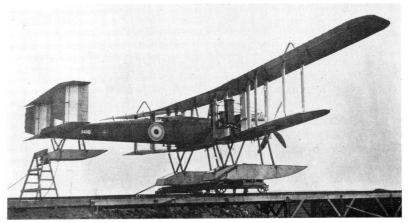

The second G.P. seaplane ready for launching and showing the scalloped trailing edges to all flying surfaces.

manufacturer's trials on the G.P. seaplane in midwinter with drift ice on the Humber. Launching was simple and the first flight successful, but the strong tide made recovery difficult, and the wading team led by Robert Blackburn's brother-in-law, R. R. Rhodes, were literally frozen stiff and had to be carried in on planks and thawed out in front of fires lighted in the hangar. Afterwards the machine was flown to the Great Yarmouth Air Station for Service trials but did not secure a production contract. Nevertheless a landplane version was built in small numbers as the Blackburn Kangaroo.

SPECIFICATION AND DATA

Manufacturers: The Blackburn Aeroplane and Motor Co Ltd, Olympia Works, Leeds, and Brough, East Yorks.

Power Plants: Two 150 hp Sunbeam Nubian
Two 190 hp Rolls-Royce

Dimensions: Span (upper) 74 ft 10¼ in   (lower) 52 ft 10½ in
Length 46 ft 0 in   Height 16 ft 10 in
Wing area 880 sq ft

Weights: (Sunbeam) All-up weight 8,100 lb
(Rolls-Royce) Tare weight 5,840 lb   All-up weight 8,600 lb

Performance: (Rolls-Royce) Maximum speed at sea level 97 mph
Climb to 5,000 ft 10 min
Ceiling 11,000 ft   Endurance 8 hr

Production: Two aircraft only.
1415 with Sunbeam engines, first flown at RNAS Isle of Grain July 1916.
1416 with Rolls-Royce engines, first flown at Brough late 1916 and delivered to the Great Yarmouth Air Station.

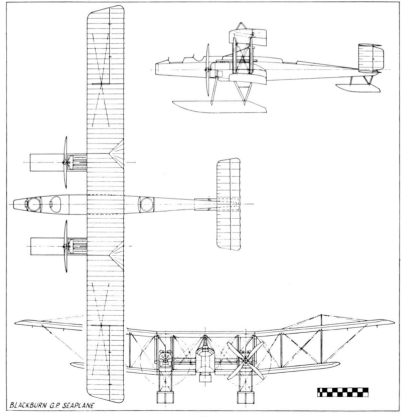

BLACKBURN G.P. SEAPLANE

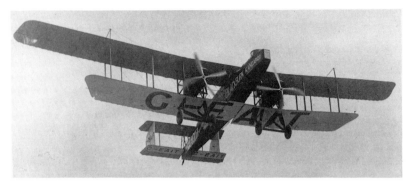

R. W. Kenworthy taking off in the North Sea Aerial Navigation Company's first civil Kangaroo, G-EAIT, at the ELTA Exhibition, Amsterdam, in August 1919. Note full registration under both sides of tailplane.

Blackburn R.T.1 Kangaroo

The landplane version of the G.P. seaplane referred to in the previous section was designated R.T.1 or Reconnaissance-Torpedo type 1 and constructed in the Blackburn Olympia Works under the type name Kangaroo. The Air Board's decision to operate over the sea with land machines instead of marine aircraft was not merely a tribute to the reliability of the Kangaroo's Rolls-Royce engines and to its exceptional range and bomb load when relieved of the heavy float undercarriage, but to a realization that the ability of patrols to take-off must no longer be dependent on sea conditions.

The fabric-covered, wooden airframe of the G.P. was retained, complete with the wing-folding mechanism, but all the main metal fittings were machined from forgings instead of being built up from sheet metal, and the top decking of the fuselage was almost entirely deleted, further emphasizing its already exceptionally slim lines. A number of other structural changes were made, including raising the engine nacelles into the mid-gap position by means of complicated strutting; replacing the side-mounted radiators by the frontal honeycomb type; increasing the rudder area by means of a rounded extension of the trailing edge; and fitting rectangular instead of triangular pylons to brace the massive 11-ft upper mainplane overhang. The four-wheeled land undercarriage was in two separate units, one under each engine nacelle, and consisted of two simple V struts with cross axle. These were quite rigid and devoid of shock absorbers, the only springing being the give in the 900 × 200 mm pneumatic tyres.

The divided undercarriage made the Kangaroo ideal for torpedo-carrying but despite the original intention and designation it was not used in this role, offensive armament consisting of four 230-lb bombs, or a single 520-lb bomb, suspended tail-down in a special internal compartment between the main spars of the lower mainplane. Four smaller bombs were carried externally

110

on racks bolted to the bottom longerons of the fuselage, all under the control of the front gunner whose cockpit was equipped with an RNAS Mk IIA low-altitude bomb sight. Defensive armament comprised two Lewis guns on Scarff rings, one in the nose and one aft of the wing, so that the normal crew was finalized at three—the front gunner/observer/bomb-aimer; the pilot, sitting 8 ft back from the nose; and the rear gunner/wireless operator. Night-flying and W/T equipment were fitted as standard, and dual purpose ailerons, rigged with a droop of $\frac{3}{4}$ in for normal use, could be lowered to act as landing flaps and were operated by a large wheel mounted on the control column. For reasons which defy deduction, the rear gunner's cockpit was provided with rudder and engine controls but had no control column or ignition switches. An early intention to raise the tail by means of a long, pylon-mounted tail skid giving adequate ground clearance for a prone gun position under the fuselage was not proceeded with, and all Kangaroos had short tail skids of welded steel.

Two 250 hp twelve-cylinder vee-type water-cooled Rolls-Royce Falcon II engines driving four-bladed wooden airscrews gave the machine a maximum speed of 98 mph at ground level, and the total fuel capacity of 215·5 gallons (97·5 in the front tank and 118 in the rear) gave an operational endurance of eight hours. Each nacelle carried its own 8-gallon oil tank and an M.L. exciter which made engine starting so easy that a Kangaroo could be airborne in under 20 min.

Martlesham

Clifford B. Prodger, an experienced American freelance test pilot, at that time under contract to Handley Page Ltd to test their big H.P. O/400 bombers, was engaged by the Blackburn company to flight test the prototype Kangaroo, B9970, and on 3 January 1918 it was delivered to the Aeroplane Experimental

The prototype Blackburn Kangaroo, B9970, with the unsprung undercarriage.

111

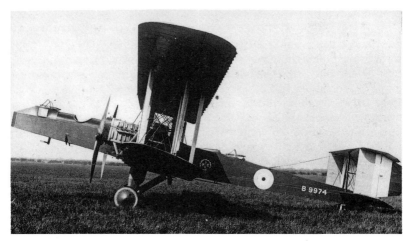

Production Kangaroo B9974 with shock-absorbing undercarriage and revised gunner's cockpit in the nose. (*Imperial War Museum Photo Q.63799.*)

Station, Martlesham Heath, where it was put through official trials which lasted some three weeks. Martlesham's evaluation included comparative trials between the Kangaroo and the Avro 529 one-off, long-range bomber prototype 3694*. These were staged on 19 January. It is difficult to see what conclusions could be drawn from such a comparison since the Avro 529, powered by two early 190 hp Rolls-Royce Falcon engines, was smaller and in a lower weight class. Later that day the undercarriage of the Kangaroo collapsed with the tests only partly completed, and as a result the device for lowering both ailerons to act as landing flaps was never tried. After the necessary repairs, all the remaining performance testing was completed by 26 January, and by 2 February the makers had been advised that the aircraft was ready for collection. A Blackburn working party began to dismantle and pack it on 9 March and it left for Brough by rail on 27 April.

The resulting Martlesham Report M.169 stated that the machine was pleasantly light on the controls at cruising speed but became markedly nose heavy in an engine-off glide, with excessive loads on the control column. Lateral control was very light but undergeared, and the twin rudders were difficult to operate because foot trolleys had been fitted in place of a rudder bar and the control wires passed through the rear cockpit where they were liable to be trodden on. Lack of torsional rigidity caused the rear fuselage to twist when the aircraft came out of a steep turn; the front gun was so far in front of the C.G. that it was off balance; lack of fuselage depth made it impossible for the gunner to get down low enough to work it, and his seat was extremely uncomfortable; and the aft gunner was prevented from firing in a backward direction by the biplane tail unit.

* See the author's *Avro Aircraft since 1908*, pages 92–94.

A requirement for up to 50 Kangaroos had been foreseen, but in the light of the defects enumerated by Martlesham and in response to a departmental enquiry, Lt Col J. G. Weir, Chief of the Technical Department, stated in a memorandum dated 4 February 1918 that . . . 'The 20 Kangaroos which are already well in hand at Blackburns will be similar to the machine in the attached report. It is understood that no more are to be ordered and no steps have been taken to modify the machine . . .' Despite this statement the 19 subsequent aircraft, all of which were test flown by Blackburn's chief test pilot R. W. Kenworthy, must have had strengthened rear fuselages and other modifications because no further twisting or other difficulties were ever experienced. The scheme for using the ailerons as flaps was abandoned and the aircraft were fitted with sprung undercarriages, each front leg incorporating rubber shock absorbers in a streamlined wooden fairing. At the same time, the front fuselage was built up to improve the lot of the front gunner, and his mounting was raised 9 in to give freedom of fire in all forward directions. B9970 was also modified to this standard and retained its 250 hp Rolls-Royce Falcon IIs. This mark of engine also powered the next four Kangaroos, but the remaining 15 aircraft had 270 hp Rolls-Royce Falcon IIIs.

The 20 Kangaroos, intended originally as G.P. seaplanes for the Admiralty, were at first allotted serial numbers N1720–N1739 in a series reserved almost entirely for marine aircraft but, following the usual practice in those days, they were renumbered on transfer to the RFC and completed as landplanes for anti-submarine work as B9970–B9989, but Blackburn's production rate was slowed by a shortage of cypress timber and absorption into the RAF had taken place before any were delivered.

B9976 of No. 246 Squadron bombed up and ready to leave Seaton Carew on anti-submarine patrol in 1918. (*Crown Copyright Reserved.*)

113

Although the Kangaroo was to have been used in the alternative role of night bomber, none were so employed and ten were delivered to No. 246 Squadron, RAF, at Seaton Carew near the mouth of the River Tees, for oversea reconnaissance duties during 1918. Their working-up period was brief and between 1 May 1918 and the Armistice of 11 November, they flew 600 hr over the North Sea on convoy protection, sighted twelve U-boats, attacked eleven, sank one and damaged a further four. Two of these attacks were made by B9972 on 8 and 13 June 1918, respectively, but the only confirmed sinking resulted from prompt action by Lt E. F. Waring and his gunner Lt H. J. Smith while on patrol in B9983. At 15.25 hrs on 28 August 1918, they discovered the *U.C.70* lying on the bottom in 14 fathoms close inshore near Runswick Bay where a near miss with the 520-lb bomb sufficiently damaged the submarine for it to be finished off with depth charges by HMS *Ouse*. B9983 did not survive the war, being destroyed in a serious crash at Seaton Carew.

From an Admiralty report on the 1918 anti-submarine campaign it would appear that only seven or eight were airworthy at Seaton Carew at any one time, although ten were on charge in October 1918. At that time B9984 was at the Anti-Submarine Inshore Patrol Observers' School, Aldbrough, and three more at No. 2 (N) Marine Acceptance Depot, Brough, were probably never used operationally. In January 1919, when the Anti-Submarine School at Aldbrough became No. 1 Marine Observers' School, B9984 was joined by B9986 and B9987. Very surprisingly the report then goes on to say that '. . . notwithstanding the fact that all the twin-engined machines were fitted with Rolls-Royce engines, the number of their patrols curtailed by engine trouble compares unfavourably with that of other types. . . .' This suggests that Kangaroo utilization was by no means as high as had been expected and contrasts sharply with the experiences of the company's pilot who flew them all and never had engine trouble of any kind on Kangaroos throughout 1918 and 1919.

Commercial Kangaroos

After the Armistice, all available Kangaroos and spares were put up for sale by the Disposals Board and early in 1919 R. W. Kenworthy and Harry Goodyear were sent off to Seaton Carew to pick out the best. They were subsequently ferried to Brough, Blackburns having purchased them *en bloc* in a transaction completed on 10 May 1919. There was some competition for the Kangaroos at Seaton Carew as Lt Valdemar Rendle was there looking for a machine with which to compete for the Australian Government's £10,000 prize. He eventually selected the prototype machine B9970 and flew it to Brough for modifications, while three others, B9981, B9982 and B9985, were acquired by the Grahame-White Aviation Co Ltd and flown to Hendon on 11 May 1919, to be used as joyriding aircraft. For this purpose they were stripped of gun mountings and other military equipment and fitted with plywood floors aft of the wings. Fabric on top of the rear fuselage was then

114

Kangaroo G-EADG of the Grahame-White Air Service being wheeled out at Hounslow, from where on 1 October 1919 it operated a mail flight to Newcastle. (*Courtesy B. A. Hewitt.*)

opened up to form two large cockpits accommodating seven passengers, an eighth being carried in the extreme nose. They retained their drab green camouflage and military serial numbers, and it was not until 8 June 1919 that they were allotted civil registrations G-EADE, 'DF and 'DG respectively. By that time B9982/'DF had already been wrecked when a wing struck the ground after the port engine cut when the machine was taking off from Hendon with a load of joyride passengers on Saturday, 31 May, during the official reception to H. G. Hawker and Cdr Mackenzie Grieve, pilots of the unlucky Atlantic Sopwith, and Cdr Read of the successful American trans-atlantic flying-boat NC-4. No one was hurt in this Kangaroo accident nor in a later one when the first of the three was damaged beyond repair in July of that year. The third Kangaroo survived to be repainted with 'Grahame-White Air Service' in white outline letters along the length of the fuselage and took part in Hendon's week-end racing, dropped parachutists, gave foreign missions their baptisms of the air and carried hundreds of joyriders during the two year currency of its C. of A. By 28 September 1919, when it was pressed into service to carry passengers and mail from the London terminal aerodrome at Hounslow Heath to Roundhay Park, during the rail strike, it had been painted up in full civil marks as G-EADG. From 1 October, it was commandeered by the Government to fly the mail to Newcastle via Leeds, and left Hounslow at 7.50 am with about 50 letters weighing a total of 3 lb 8 oz! Needless to say the service was promptly suspended when 'DG returned south next day.

On 23 April 1919, Blackburns formed an operating subsidiary known as the North Sea Aerial Navigation Co to run commercial services, and their first recorded movement took place on 10 May 1919, when Kenworthy flew a load of freight from Gosport to Leeds. The first leg to Hounslow took 40 min and the remainder of the journey to Roundhay Park 1 hr 45 min. This machine, almost certainly B9978, later civil-registered G-EAIT, was quickly fitted with a large glazed cabin seating seven passengers. Glass sides were also fitted to the gun pit in the nose to accommodate an eighth. With this machine Kenworthy inaugurated a short-lived West Hartlepool–Brough service with three passengers on 26 May. Two other North Sea Kangaroos B9972 and B9973, later G-EAKQ and 'IU respectively, were similarly modified but differed in detail. G-EAIU had the glazed nose compartment and a large open cockpit in the rear for freight carrying or joyriding in the manner of the Grahame-White machines, and while still in military marks gave pleasure flights at Roundhay Park, during the victory celebrations in the same month. G-EAKQ had the same type of cabin roof as 'IT, but the nose was reshaped to form two standard pilot's cockpits in tandem and almost certainly had dual controls.

The First Air Traffic Exhibition—ELTA—held at Amsterdam in August 1919, attracted exhibits from all the leading European aircraft manufacturers, and the stand of the Blackburn Aeroplane and Motor Co Ltd displayed large detailed models of the cabin-type commercial Kangaroo in both land and seaplane configurations. Some 20 years later, in March 1939, the model of the unbuilt seaplane project was presented by the company to the Hull Municipal Museum. On 8 August 1919, R. W. Kenworthy left Leeds for the Exhibition with five passengers in G-EAIT, cleared Customs at Hounslow and made Brussels as darkness fell. After inspection next morning by the King and Queen of the Belgians, the remaining distance to Amsterdam was covered in 1 hr 35 min. Tremendous Dutch enthusiasm kept the machine hard at joyriding for six weeks, except for a five-day delay caused by the destructive effect of the aerodrome's sandy surface on the airscrew coverings. G-EAIT also took second prize in a starting, climbing and short-landing competition. Joyriding profits were so satisfactory that the company thought it worthwhile to despatch a second Kangaroo, G-EAIU, which Capt S. J. Woolley flew out via Hounslow and Lympne on 28 August. Next day the exhibition organizers

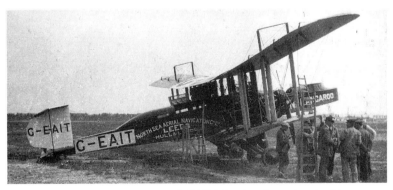

Ground view of Kangaroo G-EAIT showing the enclosed cabin.

presented him with a gold watch when 'IU came last in the Circuit of Holland Race for commercial aircraft!

With only a week to go before ELTA closed, Kenworthy and Woolley were joined by Maj Veale in G-EAKQ, and at the final count they had carried between them 1,400 fare-paying passengers and given many free rides without incident. All three Kangaroos then returned to Brough, and on the way home Kenworthy flew 'IT from Amsterdam to Lympne in 3 hr and from Hounslow to Brough in 2 hr, total fuel consumption working out at 25 gallons per hour.

On 30 September 1919, and coincident with the activities of the Grahame-White Kangaroo during the rail strike, the North Sea Aerial Navigation Co Ltd commenced a regular service between Leeds and Hounslow. They used the cabin machines G-EAIT and 'KQ, despatching the southbound machine from Leeds at 10 am and the northbound from Hounslow at noon. The fare was 15 guineas single or £30 return. Kenworthy flew the first southbound service with only one passenger (the company's secretary travelling free!) but on arrival at Hounslow he and the aircraft were commandeered by the Government to fly the strike-bound mail to Glasgow next morning at dawn. After some haggling with the GPO officer concerned, a price of £945 was agreed for the round trip, worked out on the basis of 13½ hr flying at £70 per hour. The mail load was similar to that carried to Newcastle by the Grahame-White Kangaroo, so on reaching Glasgow Kenworthy promptly sold the seven vacant seats at £20 per head for the return trip to Hounslow.

The North Sea Aerial Navigation Co Ltd also acquired a pair of Avro 504Ks, G-EAGV and 'GW, which were converted to three-seaters to be used for joyriding and a short-lived Harrogate–Brough (Hull)–Scarborough service. The Kangaroos were maintained at Brough and went on service at the old Leeds aerodrome at Roundhay Park, a comparatively small field which was eventually abandoned as unsuitable. Brough then became the terminal, the service was extended to Amsterdam and the company re-formed as the North Sea Aerial and General Transport Co Ltd.

The first 'service' was, in fact, a charter flight for Heatons (Leeds) Ltd to beat a dock strike in the Netherlands, flown by R. W. Kenworthy in G-EAKQ with Mr T. Bancroft as engineer. The Kangaroo left Brough at 12.30 pm on 5 March 1920 and landed at Lympne at 5 pm, arriving in Amsterdam at 10.30 am next day. The load, consisting of over 1,000 lb of ladies' raincoats and garments in West Riding cloth, was rushed through Dutch Customs and away by lorry, but strikers became hostile and Kenworthy had to take the machine over to Soesterberg Aerodrome for military protection before it could take off on the return flight on 13 March. The inbound load consisted of 1,200 lb of German aniline dyes for the Bradford Dyers' Association, each-way aircraft operating costs being approximately £150. The service ran weekly for a time and carried 2½ tons of freight a month initially, but the long detour to the Customs aerodromes in the south was a severe handicap

R. W. Kenworthy and T. Bancroft in Kangaroo G-EAKQ at Amsterdam on 6 March 1920 at the conclusion of the first commercial flight from England. Only the braking effect of the railway track prevented it terminating in the ditch. (*Courtesy R. W. Kenworthy.*)

and financially the scheme was a failure. Thus, after some 20,000 miles had been flown, 18,000 lb of goods and 1,200 passengers carried, this gallant pioneer attempt at airfreighting was abandoned.

Kangaroos G-EAIT and 'IU were retained by the company for training purposes, as related later, but 'KQ, at that time the only one fitted with two pilots' cockpits in tandem, was sold in July 1921 to the Peruvian Centro Militar or Army Flying Service. Along with twelve Avro 504Ks, it was based at Las Palmas air station, 9 miles from Lima, and was still there in 1923.

Long Distance Flights

One of the four aircraft competing for the prize of £10,000, offered by the Australian Government for the first flight from England to Australia by a British-built aircraft manned by an Australian crew, was Kangaroo G-EAOW, which at the beginning of the previous year had been the performance trials machine B9970. When the Blackburn company submitted its entry on 26 May 1919, the crew was to have been Lt Valdemar Rendle, Charles Kingsford Smith and Cyril Maddocks, but the FAI would not permit the last two to fly. Thus when the Kangaroo took off from Hounslow at 10.37 am on 21 November 1919—nine days after the departure of Ross and Keith Smith in the victorious Vickers Vimy G-EAOU—it was flown by Rendle with Lt D. R. Williams as co-pilot, explorer Capt (later Sir) Hubert Wilkins, MC, as navigator and commanding officer, and Lt G. H. Potts as engineer. Its

Falcon II engines were expertly tuned by Rolls-Royce, fitted with special carburettors and provided with enlarged radiators for tropical flying. A large auxiliary gravity tank was mounted on top of the upper centre section and a duplicated set of flying and engine controls was fitted in the front cockpit.

G-EAOW reached Romilly, 60 miles from Paris, the first day, but progress was slow because of bad weather and head winds, the itinerary being as follows:

21 November	Hounslow–Romilly	30 November	Pisa–Rome
28 November	Romilly–St Raphaël	3 December	Rome–Taranto
29 November	St Raphaël–Pisa	5 December	Taranto–Suda Bay

By the time it reached Suda Bay, in Crete, the magnetos had twice been tampered with and a further instance of suspected sabotage ended the flight three days later. When 80 miles out from Crete on 8 December, the pipe from the scavenge pump to the oil tank on the port engine (Rolls-Royce Falcon II No. 59) fractured, apparently as a result of fatigue caused by bending it backwards and forwards. Lt Rendle managed to fly back to Crete on one engine and made a difficult downwind landing, but the aircraft ran over a small ditch, punctured a tyre, slewed round, ran up an embankment and tipped slowly on its nose. No-one was hurt and the machine was undamaged, but cables to England for a spare engine were so distorted in transit that no engine was ever sent and the machine still lay at Suda Bay in July 1921.

When a second £10,000 prize was put up, this time by the *Daily Express* for a flight to India and back, the Blackburn Aeroplane and Motor Co Ltd

The England–Australia Kangaroo, G-EAOW, after the forced landing at Suda Bay, Crete, on 8 December 1919.

Kangaroo G-EAIU with wings folded at Croydon on the eve of the first King's
Cup Air Race on 8 September 1922. (*Courtesy H. C. Rayner, OBE.*)

were quick to enter Kangaroo B9977, civil-registered G-EAMJ and crewed
by R. W. Kenworthy as pilot and Capt Hubert Wilkins, MC, as navigator.
Operating expenses for the flight were guaranteed by the *Yorkshire Evening
News*, and the aircraft was fitted out as a three-seater with a cabin of the type
first devised for G-EAIT. This housed the overload fuel tanks, a compre-
hensive selection of spares and the compulsory commercial load, in this case
a ton of crated whisky donated by a Scottish distillery. Oversize tyres were
fitted to improve handling on sandy aerodrome surfaces, and Rolls-Royce
carefully tuned the Falcon III engines and fitted large tropical radiators of the
type used on G-EAOW. Only one other entry materialized, the Handley
Page O/400 G-EASO *Old Carthusian II* to be flown by Maj A. S. MacLaren,
but the flight never took place. On 11 May 1920, the Air Ministry postponed
the start indefinitely on receipt of a telegram from the AOC, RAF Middle
East, prohibiting flights east of Cairo because of strained relations with the
Arabs.

A Kangaroo was to have accompanied the British Aerial Antarctic Expedition later that year, but this scheme too was abandoned.

Racing and Training

Probably the most memorable day in the history of the Blackburn Kangaroo
was 8 September 1922, when the cabin machine G-EAMJ intended for the
India flight (modified to eight-seater) and the open-cockpit G-EAIU lined
up at Croydon for the start of the first-ever King's Cup Race. Powered by
Falcon IIIs specially tuned for the race by Rolls-Royce, they had both arrived
at Croydon from Brough on the previous Tuesday, 5 September. G-EAMJ
was entered by no less a person than the Rt Hon Winston S. Churchill, MP,
and flown by Lt Col Spenser Grey, DSO, who had owned a Blackburn Mercury III back in 1911. G-EAIU, entered by Sir Walter de Frece, was flown
by R. W. Kenworthy. Accompanied by Cdr Risk and some mechanics,
Spenser Grey got away 10 min ahead of Kenworthy, but both aircraft made

120

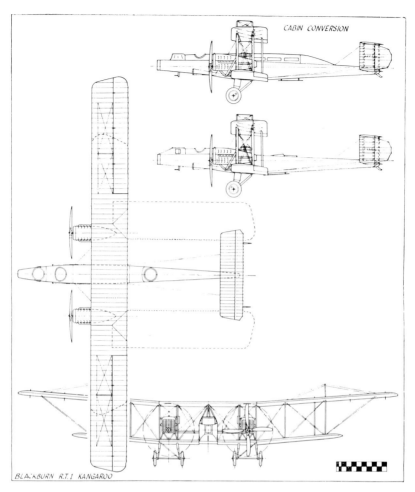

CABIN CONVERSION

BLACKBURN R.T.1 KANGAROO

slow progress and eventually Spenser Grey's compass failed and he was compelled to land at Jarrow-on-Tyne to enquire the way. The two Kangaroos night-stopped at Town Moor, Newcastle, and pressed on over the mountains to Renfrew next morning, but without a compass Spenser Grey had no alternative but to follow Kenworthy and, after refuelling, they turned south for Manchester where both retired. The race was won by F. L. Barnard flying the famous D.H.4A G-EAMU and a few days later the four specially-tuned Falcons were removed from the Kangaroos and advertised for sale at £485 each!

After its attempt to operate commercial services failed in 1920, the North Sea Aerial and General Transport Co Ltd was kept in being with joyriding and exhibition flying until 1924, when an RAF Reserve School was established

121

at Brough under its management. To provide refresher courses in twin-engined flying for serving RAF pilots and for Reservists, the surviving Kangaroos were fitted with dual control in tandem cockpits. In the training role they appeared in silver dope for the first time and, following the loss of the veteran G-EAIT in a crash at Brough on 5 May 1925 in which a pilot named Macdonald was killed, three more old Kangaroos were taken out of storage and modified to the standard of G-EAIT. They were fitted with Falcon II engines, for at that time all available stocks of Falcon IIIs were earmarked for Bristol Fighters. The names of the famous *Daily Mirror* cartoon characters Pip, Squeak and Wilfred, were painted across their flat noses and, with registrations G-EBOM, 'PK and 'MD respectively, they ended their days doing a useful, if unspectacular, training job and were a common sight in the Humber area until withdrawn from use in 1928. By March 1929 they had all been flown to Sherburn-in-Elmet and completely filled the hangars of the Yorkshire Aeroplane Club until taken out one at a time and broken up.

All that now remains is an airscrew which has been cleaned and polished by the present Yorkshire Flying Club and fitted with a clock to serve as a mural decoration in their clubhouse at Leeds/Bradford Airport, Yeadon. Until uncovered by a contractor's bulldozer in 1965, it had lain there under an immense pile of sand once used as ballast during test flights of Yeadon-built Avro Lancasters more than 20 years previously.

SPECIFICATION AND DATA

Manufacturers: The Blackburn Aeroplane and Motor Co Ltd, Olympia Works, Roundhay Road, Leeds, and Brough Aerodrome, East Yorks.

Power Plants: Two 250 hp Rolls-Royce Falcon II
Two 270 hp Rolls-Royce Falcon III

Dimensions: Span (upper)	74 ft 10¼ in	(lower) 53 ft 1 in
(folded)	46 ft 1 in	Wing area 868 sq ft
Length 44 ft 2 in		Height 16 ft 10 in

Loadings: Three crew	540 lb	Tare weight	5,284 lb
Two Lewis guns	33 lb	Military load	1,003 lb
Ammunition	127 lb	Fuel 215½ gallons	1,570 lb
Equipment	303 lb	Oil 16 gallons	160 lb
Military load	1,003 lb	All-up weight	8,017 lb

Performance:			
Speed at 6,500 ft	98 mph	Maximum height reached	10,600 ft
Speed at 10,000 ft	86 mph	Time to max. height	44 min 0 sec
Initial climb	480 ft/min	Climb at max. height	90 ft/min
Climb at 5,000 ft	305 ft/min	Absolute ceiling	13,000 ft
Climb at 10,000 ft	115 ft/min	Endurance	8 hr

* *Ref. A. & A.E.E. Report M/169 dated 25 January 1918—prototype Blackburn Kangaroo aircraft B9970 powered by Rolls-Royce Falcon II engines No. 9 (port) and No. 2 (starboard), each giving 250 hp at 2,000 rpm and driving 9 ft 10 in diameter S.D.440 airscrews.*

Comparative trials with Avro 529 prototype 3694 held at Martlesham 19 January 1918:

	Kangaroo	Avro 529
All-up weight	8,017 lb	6,309 lb
Maximum speed at 10,000 ft	86 mph	89 mph
Climb at 2,000 ft	430 ft/min	640 ft/min
Climb at 5,000 ft	305 ft/min	500 ft/min
Climb at 10,000 ft	115 ft/min	260 ft/min

Production:
Prototype B9970 and nineteen production aircraft B9971–B9989 (originally N1720–N1739) to Contract A.S.7469, monthly deliveries as under:

January 1918	B9970	July 1918	B9981–B9984
April 1918	B9971–B9972	August 1918	B9985–B9988
May 1918	B9973–B9976	September 1918	B9989
June 1918	B9977–B9980		

B9973 and B9977 were delivered to the RAF on 8 May and 18 June 1918 respectively; B9983 crashed at Seaton Carew while in service with No. 246 Squadron; one new and unidentified Kangaroo (vandals cut out the identity panels), crashed at Hornsea, East Yorks., while on delivery to Seaton Carew.

The dual-control Kangaroo trainer G-EBOM at Brough in 1926.

123

Civil Conversions:

	Cabin model	Dual trainer
Tare weight	5,300 lb	5,150 lb
All-up weight	8,100 lb	8,020 lb
Maximum speed	98 mph	98 mph
Climb to 1,000 ft	2 min	2 min
Range	410 miles	580 miles

(a) *For the Grahame-White Aviation Co Ltd (delivered from Seaton Carew to Hendon 11 May 1919)*

G-EADE   ex B9981, registered June 1919, C. of A. issued 21 June 1919, crashed at Hendon 29 June 1919.

G-EADF   ex B9982, registered 8 June 1919, no C. of A., crashed on take-off at Hendon 31 May 1919.

G-EADG   ex B9985, C. of A. issued 6 June 1919, registered 11 June 1919, C. of A. renewed 8 June 1920, withdrawn from use at C. of A. expiry 7 June 1921.

(b) *For the North Sea Aerial Navigation Co Ltd (style changed to the North Sea Aerial and General Transport Co Ltd in 1920)*

G-EAIT   ex B9978, cabin type registered 1 August 1919, C. of A. issued 11 August 1919, out of service from 11 August 1921 until C. of A. re-issued 2 March 1925 after conversion to dual trainer, crashed at Brough 5 May 1925.

G-EAIU   ex B9973, open type registered 1 August 1919, C. of A. issued 1 September 1919, out of service from 12 September 1923 until C. of A. re-issued 18 May 1924 after conversion to the prototype dual trainer *Bonzo*, withdrawn from use at C. of A. expiry 19 April 1929 and broken up at Sherburn-in-Elmet.

G-EAKQ   ex B9972, cabin type registered 18 August 1919, C. of A. issued 9 September 1919, renewed 5 September 1920, sold to the Peruvian Army Flying Service July 1921.

G-EAMJ   ex B9977, cabin type for India Flight registered 8 September 1919, no C. of A., King's Cup Race 1922, converted to dual trainer *Felix the Cat* in 1924, C. of A. issued 20 June 1924, withdrawn from use at C. of A. expiry 2 February 1929 and broken up at Sherburn-in-Elmet.

G-EAOW   ex B9970, registered to the Blackburn Aeroplane and Motor Co Ltd for Australia Flight 24 October 1919, C. of A. issued 17 November 1919, abandoned in Crete 8 December 1919.

G-EBMD   origin unknown, registered 13 August 1925 for conversion to dual trainer *Wilfred* to Works Order 8837, C. of A. issued 21 January 1926, withdrawn from use at C. of A. expiry 7 February 1929 and broken up at Sherburn-in-Elmet.

G-EBOM   origin unknown, registered 18 June 1926 for conversion to dual trainer *Pip* to Works Order 8839, C. of A. issued 13 July 1926, crashed at Brough due to engine failure 29 May 1928. Pilot F/O E. B. Fielden.

G-EBPK   origin unknown, registered 29 October 1926 for conversion to dual trainer *Squeak* to Works Order 8840, C. of A. issued 3 February 1927, withdrawn from use at C. of A. expiry 2 July 1929 and broken up at Sherburn-in-Elmet.

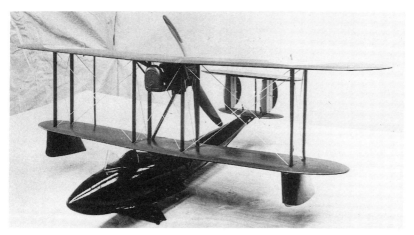

The wind-tunnel model of the Blackburn N.1B single-seat flying boat.

Blackburn N.1B

Designs to an Admiralty requirement for a single-seat fleet escort bomber to replace the Blackburn-built Sopwith Baby seaplane, made known in 1916 as category N.1B, were prepared by the Blackburn Aeroplane and Motor Co Ltd at Leeds, the Supermarine Aviation Works Ltd at Southampton, and the Westland Aircraft Works at Yeovil. Contracts were placed for eight prototypes, three by Blackburn, three by Supermarine and two by Westland. All were known as N.1B, but whereas the Westland machines N16 and N17 were twin-float seaplanes somewhat similar to the Sopwith Baby, the three Supermarines, N59, N60 and N61, were small pusher flying-boats.

The Blackburn N.1B design resembled Supermarine's concept of the requirement in that it too was a pusher flying-boat employing a hull of Linton Hope design. This was built to a system created by Lt Linton Hope, RN, and consisted of circular wooden formers spaced by stringers and planked diagonally with narrow mahogany strips one-eighth of an inch in thickness, in two laminations so that the layers crossed each other at 90 degrees. There the resemblance ended, for the Supermarine boat was constructed on strictly utilitarian lines and had a monoplane tail while the Blackburn N.1B was a sesquiplane of inspired design using a hull of refined and delicate aerodynamic form. Armament was to have been a single Lewis gun mounted on the nose in front of the pilot.

The hand of Harris Booth, who had joined Blackburns from the Air Department of the Admiralty in 1915, can be detected in the design of Blackburn's machine, not only through general similarity of layout to the early A.D.

125

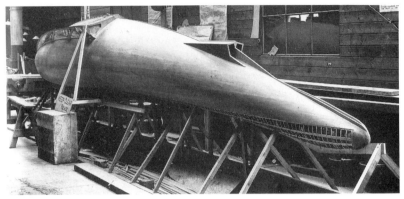

The hull of the Blackburn N.1B under construction in the Olympia Works, Leeds, in 1918.

Flying-Boats (of which the Supermarine N.1B was a descendant), but in minor design features such as the shape of the wing tip floats and the retention of a biplane tail using an inverted RAF14 aerofoil section on the upper tailplane to hold the tail down with engine on if nose heavy and automatically take up a correct gliding angle if the engine failed.

The mainplanes were built round rectangular box spars with two-ply spruce webs and spruce flanges. They were designed to fold to a mean width of 11 ft 2 in, and it is probable that it was intended to have jettisonable wheels for taking-off from the decks of naval vessels.

The two-step hull swept gracefully upwards at the rear, but even so the lower tailplane would have been awash when the aircraft was taxying. It is probable therefore, in the absence of precise details, that this was to have been a watertight plywood structure as on the A.D. Flying-Boats. The ends of all aerofoil surfaces were elliptical, directional control was by twin rudders, and ailerons were fitted to all four wings. Power was supplied by a 200 hp Hispano-Suiza engine, mounted high up under the top centre section, driving a two-bladed, fabric-covered, mahogany airscrew and cooled by a circular radiator mounted in front. Fuel was carried at the C.G. in a midships tank.

Supermarines and Westlands built and flew their prototypes during 1917–18, but successful deck operations by the Sopwith Pup and a promise of an even better performance by its successor the Camel, led to a cancellation of the N.1B contracts in November 1918. Non-availability of the engine slowed down the work of construction at Leeds and, when work ceased, Blackburns had completed only the hull of their first machine N56, and the other two, N57 and N58, existed merely as a number of sub-assemblies.

The completed hull of N56 was put into storage, but was taken out in 1923 and used in the construction of Blackburn's Schneider Trophy entry, the Pellet.

SPECIFICATION AND DATA

Manufacturers: The Blackburn Aeroplane and Motor Co Ltd, Olympia Works, Roundhay Road, Leeds, and Brough Aerodrome, East Yorks.

Power Plant: One 200 hp Hispano-Suiza

Dimensions: Span (upper) 34 ft 10 in   (lower) 29 ft 4 in
                      Length 28 ft 3½ in   Wing area 314 sq ft

Weights: Tare weight 1,721 lb   All-up weight 2,390 lb

*Performance: Maximum speed 114 mph   Climb to 5,000 ft 7 min
                      Ceiling 16,000 ft   Range 340 miles

Production: Hull of N56 only; N57 and N58 incomplete.

* Estimated.

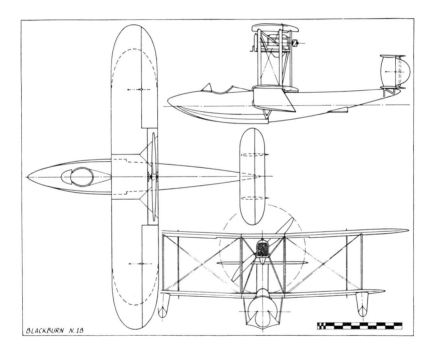

BLACKBURN N.1B

127

N113 with wheels fitted and showing the constant-depth fuselage, unbraced tail unit and small rudder. (*Courtesy Royal Aeronautical Society.*)

Blackburn Blackburd

Although Robert Blackburn had made a valuable contribution to the war effort by building large numbers of B.E.2c biplanes and had been awarded sizeable contracts for Sopwith Baby seaplanes and Sopwith Cuckoo single-seat torpedo-bombers, it was well known that his real interest lay in the construction of naval aeroplanes of Blackburn design. Opportunity was not long delayed, for, despite the excellence of the Cuckoo as an aeroplane, its 1,086 lb Mk IX torpedo was not capable of sinking a large warship. Thus, in the autumn of 1917, the Admiralty formulated a requirement for a generally similar single-seater capable of carrying the large Mk VIII torpedo weighing 1,423 lb and mounting a warhead 50 per cent more powerful than that of the Mk IX. Details were set out in Specification N.1B (Torpedo-Carrying Ship Aeroplane), but when the RNAS lost its separate identity in April 1918 the N.1B aeroplanes were restyled Type XXII in the new RAF system of numbering by functional category.

Contracts were placed in February 1918 for six Rolls-Royce Eagle VIII powered prototype aircraft, three from Short Bros Ltd which were given the name Short Shirl and numbered N110–N112, and three others N113–N115 from the Blackburn Aeroplane and Motor Co Ltd for which Robert Blackburn created the name Blackburd simply by changing the last letter of his surname. As stated in a previous chapter on the little Blackburn single-seat flying-boat, N.1B aircraft were all single-seat bombers, but as this category also included torpedo aircraft, the Shirl and the Blackburd came within it.

Competitive trials were to decide which of the two types was to be built in quantity, but so determined were Blackburns to secure a production contract and to establish themselves as specialists in naval aircraft, that they supplied these prototypes at £2,200 each, or approximately two-thirds of the actual cost.

Designed by Harris Booth and intended eventually for shipboard service on Britain's first aircraft carrier *Argus*, commissioned in September 1918, the Blackburd was a large, three-bay, unstaggered biplane with folding wings, conceived on the simplest possible lines for cheap and rapid production. For this reason the mainplanes were of constant chord and uniform section throughout so that if the Blackburd were ordered in quantity they could, like those of the D.H.6, be 'made by the mile and cut off by the yard'. They retained the wire trailing edges of the S.P. and Kangaroo machines and were built up from rectangular-section box spars and ribs of spruce three-ply, braced with steel tie rods. The same principle was applied to the design of the square-section fuselage which was built around four rectangular spruce box longerons. It maintained a constant depth from nose to tail and was thus little more than a flying box under which the torpedo was carried in steel crutches. Although the strength/weight ratio was unusually good, it is doubtful whether the fuselage could, in fact, have been produced quickly as the work of building up the struts and box longerons was considerable, particularly as the latter tapered towards the rear.

Lateral control was by four interconnected long-span ailerons which could all be lowered to act as flaps for shortening the take-off run, but the pilot

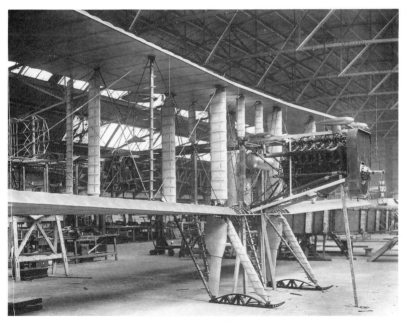

Blackburd N113 under construction in the Olympia Works, May 1918, showing the steel landing skids and built-up fairings.

only had positive control over them in a downward direction, the upward movement being effected by the dashpot-controlled tension of bungee rubber cord anchored to the rear spar of the wing.

A single 350 hp Rolls-Royce Eagle VIII water-cooled engine on a tubular-steel mounting drove a two-bladed left-hand tractor wooden airscrew and was equipped with doper and hand starter which made it possible to despatch the Blackburd within 15 min of an alert. Fuel was pumped from a 74-gallon tank in the second bay of the fuselage, and a 9-gallon oil tank was fitted crosswise some 2 ft behind the engine.

Tubular-steel interplane and undercarriage struts were streamlined with an exceptionally light, if complicated, fairing built up of fabric doped over three-ply formers linked by wires and secured to metal clips soldered to the main tube. Weight saving over the usual spruce fairings was estimated as 120 lb. The enormous undercarriage was built in the form of a pin-jointed parallelo-gram with stout diagonal main legs incorporating solid rubber shock absorbers, the shock legs projecting vertically below the inboard interplane struts and carrying short steel skids of Warren truss construction at their lower ends. The 900 $\times$ 200 mm pneumatic wheels and their transverse axle weighing 70 lb had to be jettisoned before the torpedo could be dropped, and on its return to the carrier the Blackburd was expected to make a deck landing on the skids. This was not so hazardous a procedure as it would appear, much preparatory work having been done with skid-equipped Sopwith Pups and 1½ Strutters at the Marine Experimental Aircraft Depot, Isle of Grain.

Ability to jettison the wheels was, of course, a distinct advantage if the pilot were faced with the necessity of making a forced landing at sea, the risk of nosing over being greatly reduced. Ditching characteristics on the third Blackburd prototype, N115, were further improved by increasing the chord of the front undercarriage struts so that they acted as mountings for multiple hydrofoils, an additional pair being fixed to the skids. Flotation gear in the form of inflatable air bags was carried in the fuselage.

The pilot's cockpit was situated 9 ft behind the centre section and approx-imately half-way between the trailing edge of the mainplane and the leading edge of the tailplane, a remote position from which forward view must have been negligible, and the fuselage was so wide that he had difficulty in looking over the side. Control was by a wooden rudder-bar and a stick-mounted aileron wheel which projected out of the cockpit in true pre-1914 manner. The pilot sat in a large wicker seat protected from the slipstream by a fairing of doped fabric surmounted by a small Triplex wind screen. No guns were carried and the aircraft was armed solely with the torpedo.

Delivery of the first Blackburd, N113, was scheduled for 6 May 1918 but, after the engine had been installed, the men were taken off it to rush out the first few Cuckoos but even so it was finished by the end of the month. R. W. Kenworthy, Blackburn's chief test pilot, then flew it on a series of trials in which the wheels and a dummy torpedo were dropped repeatedly into the

River Humber to be picked up by motor boat. The aircraft then returned to Brough to make its fearsome skid landing. The skids were modified a number of times but according to Kenworthy the landings went off fairly satisfactorily, the 'feel' to the pilot being similar to landing a seaplane. He flew it south to the Aeroplane Experimental Station at Martlesham Heath on 4 June 1918 for official performance trials, beating the first Short Shirl, N110 (delivered by John Lankester Parker), by several days.

In Report M.208 dated 21 June 1918, the Blackburd's combined aileron and flap system was criticized on the grounds that if the flaps were down for take-off the machine was without ailerons and therefore uncontrollable laterally. Their effectiveness was proven, however, when the fully-loaded Blackburd unstuck in less than one-third of the distance required without flaps.

Flight testing showed that the Blackburd was only stable laterally, and the Report went on to say that it was excessively nose heavy in climbing, gliding and level flight, both with and without torpedo, and that it was '. . . only possible to fly for any length of time by relieving the pilot of the continuous elevator load by means of "sandow" (bungee rubber) on the control stick'.

The second Blackburd, N114, with torpedo in position, wing tip floats, braced tail unit and modified rudder.

Front view of the second Blackburd, N114, to show the large rectangular radiator. Short-span ailerons, separate from the flaps, are distinguishable on the starboard side.

131

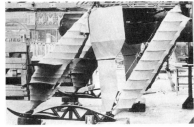

Left: The cockpit of Blackburd N113. (*Courtesy Royal Aeronautical Society.*) *Right:* The undercarriage of Blackburd N115 showing the steel landing skids, wheel-jettison control cable running parallel to the rear strut, and the experimental hydrovanes. (*Courtesy G. S. Leslie.*)

In gusts and bumps, rudder area was inadequate; and while landing, the rudder became ineffective as flying speed was lost, making it difficult to keep the aircraft into wind during slow landings, and impossible to taxy in winds of more than 8 mph. When the trials were almost complete, Blackburd N113 crashed, and some of the tests, including flapped take-off distance measurements with varying loads, were never completed. Comment was made, however, on the excellent way in which the tubular engine mounting, the fuel tank and all the joints in the wooden structure stood up to the impact.

The second Blackburd, N114, was doped silver overall, and although first flown without them, was delivered with small wing tip floats bolted to the underside of the lower mainplane below the outboard interplane struts. It also had a large rectangular tropical radiator of the type fitted later to the special long-distance Blackburn Kangaroos. As a result of recommendations made after the Martlesham trials with N113, the tail unit was redesigned, strengthened internally, fitted with improved rudder and elevator hinges and a larger rudder, having the trailing edge in the form of a smooth curve instead of in vertical scalloping. To prevent deflection of the tailplane under load (which by altering the incidence had probably affected fore and aft control on N113), twin bracing cables were anchored to both front and rear spars. Take-off flaps were retained but were controlled separately from the ailerons.

On completion in mid-August 1918, N114 was flown straight to the RAF station at East Fortune, Scotland, for torpedo trials, but it later returned to Brough for servicing before being flown to Martlesham Heath on 16 October for full performance testing. Performance measurements with and without torpedo were completed by 9 November, but a week later manoeuvrability trials were temporarily suspended to permit a detailed examination of the fuselage structure. The third Blackburd, N115, completed in November 1918, was sent from Brough to the Development Squadron at Gosport. N114 was also posted to the strength of this squadron but was dismantled and sent to Devonport to be held as spares for N115. The latter was certainly serviceable at Gosport on 10 May 1919, and it later operated experimentally from *Argus* in the Mediterranean.

R. W. Kenworthy recalled how a second cockpit was made over the C.G. of a Blackburd—it could only have been N115—and how he flew with Lady Mary Savile as passenger from Gosport to Hounslow en route for Brough but forced landed on the golf course at Hurst Park. This aeroplane was also to have been used by Miss Florence Parbery, the singer, for airborne Marconi wireless tests at the Hague, but she eventually made them at Croydon Airport in a Westland Limousine piloted by A. F. Muir on 12 January 1922.

As the Shirl's performance was marginally better than that of the Blackburd, an order was placed with Blackburns for 100 Shirls (see Appendix A), but this was cancelled soon afterwards in favour of additional Sopwith Cuckoos which were better able to take evasive action after launching their torpedoes. Nevertheless, despite the brevity of their careers, the three Blackburd prototypes served to renew and strengthen the Blackburn company's link with the Royal Navy, first forged with the Type L four years previously.

SPECIFICATION AND DATA

Manufacturers: The Blackburn Aeroplane and Motor Co Ltd, Olympia Works, Roundhay Road, Leeds, and Brough Aerodrome, East Yorks.

Power Plant: One 350 hp Rolls-Royce Eagle VIII

*Dimensions: Span (extended) 52 ft 5 in   (folded) 17 ft 1 in
             Length 34 ft 10 in   Height 12 ft 4½ in
             Wing area 684 sq ft

*Loadings:				
Pilot	180 lb	Tare weight	3,228 lb
Mk VIII torpedo	1,400 lb	Military load	1,851 lb
Torpedo gear	50 lb	Fuel 74 gallons	534 lb
Equipment	221 lb	Oil 9 gallons	87 lb
Military load	1,851 lb	All-up weight	5,700 lb

*Performance:

	Without torpedo	With torpedo
Speed at 6,500 ft	95 mph	90·5 mph
Speed at 10,000 ft	94·5 mph	84·5 mph
Speed at 16,500 ft	87 mph	—
Initial climb	845 ft/min	505 ft/min
Climb at 5,000 ft	685 ft/min	345 ft/min
Climb at 10,000 ft	480 ft/min	140 ft/min
Maximum height reached	17,000 ft	11,000 ft
Time to max. height	37 min 15 sec	41 min 45 sec
Climb at max. height	195 ft/min	100 ft/min
Absolute ceiling	21,500 ft	13,000 ft
Endurance	3 hr	3 hr

* *Ref. A. & A.E.E. Report M/208 dated 2 July 1918—prototype Blackburn Blackburd aircraft N113 powered by Rolls-Royce Eagle VIII engine No. 8 giving 352 hp at 1,800 rpm and driving a two-bladed, left-hand tractor airscrew type A.B.8580.*

133

Production:

Three prototype aircraft only as follows:

N113   Completed May 1918, flown to Martlesham 4 June 1918, crashed at Martlesham on or about 2 July 1918.

N114   Completed August 1918, to East Fortune, September 1918, flown to Martlesham 16 October 1918, dismantled and sent to Devonport as spares on or about 7 December 1918.

N115   Completed November 1918, to the Development Squadron, Gosport; temporary two-seater later.

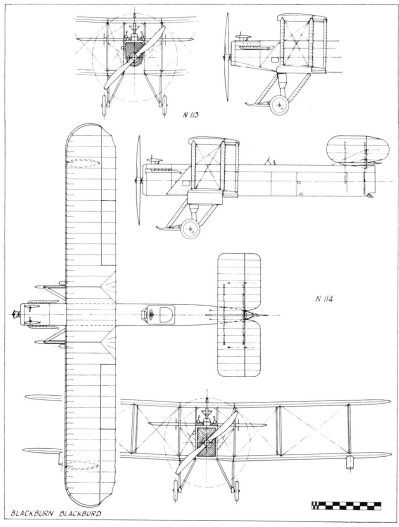

N 113

N 114

BLACKBURN BLACKBURD

134

The Blackburn Sidecar from the starboard side, showing the wind-driven fuel pump. The exhaust port, which served both cylinders, is ahead of the wing leading edge.

Blackburn Sidecar

Anticipating the birth of the light aeroplane movement by more than six years, Blackburns began work late in 1918 on designs for a small, wire-braced, mid-wing monoplane which would be regarded today as an ultra light. It was christened the Sidecar because the traditional tandem cockpit arrangement was abandoned in favour of side-by-side seating, a configuration which was to be a characteristic feature of Blackburn private and training aeroplanes for more than two decades. True to the tradition of the Blackburn Mercury monoplanes of old, the Sidecar had a triangular-section fuselage of fabric-covered wooden construction, each of the three sides being a lattice girder built up with diagonal spruce struts. Above the top longerons the main fuselage was surmounted by a light plywood superstructure which swept upwards from the tail to the shoulder height of the crew. At the top of this fairing the landing wires were attached to a specially strengthened cross-member which also served as an instrument panel, and above this were twin Triplex windscreens. Entry was by downward hinging doors of the type used on motorcycle sidecars, and provision was made for quick conversion to a cabin type if required.

The mainplane was built in two halves using spruce box spars with spruce and plywood ribs, spruce drift struts, and leading and trailing edges of flattened steel tube. The whole structure was wire-braced internally and externally. A cable running below, and well clear of, the leading edge of the mainplane gave the pilot positive downward control of the short-span ailerons against the action of bungee cords which provided the upward deflection as on the Blackburd. The rectangular, balanced rudder and the halves of the all-moving tailplane were built up on tubular-steel spars with spruce and plywood ribs and steel-tube edging. They appear to have been interchangeable.

135

The legs of the V-type undercarriage were attached at their upper ends to the wing root fittings, the forward leg on each side consisting of two steel tubes, spaced one behind the other and faired with wood veneer. Bungee-sprung half axles, hinging on the centreline of the deep front fuselage, were slung between the lower ends of these tubes. Wire wheels were streamlined with fabric discs and fitted with 450 × 60 Palmer cord tyres, the rear end of the fuselage being supported by a diminutive rubber-sprung tail skid.

The engine was the tiny, two-cylinder, horizontally-opposed, air-cooled A.B.C. Gnat, the power of which has been described variously as 30, 40 and 45 hp; in actual fact it gave 40 hp at the stipulated maximum cruising revolutions and drove a two-bladed wooden airscrew. Fuel from a 14-gallon tank underneath the seats reached the carburettor through a wind-driven pump on the starboard side of the cockpit assisted by a hand pump which supplied the necessary air pressure. Consumption was estimated at $3\frac{1}{2}$ gallons per hour, giving 27 miles per gallon at cruising speed and an endurance of four hours. Exhaust gases from both cylinders were ejected through a common orifice on the starboard side. With full tanks, crew of two and 55 lb of luggage, the all-up weight was 850 lb.

The Sidecar was built at the Olympia Works early in 1919 and made a brief public appearance at Harrods department store in London, at a small exhibition opened by Lady Drogheda on 7 April 1919. Priced at £450, it carried no markings other than 'Sidecar' in ornate signwriting in front of the windscreens and the circular 'B.A.' monogram on the sides of the fuselage. A Norman Thompson N.T.2B flying-boat and various interpretations of the 'latest thing' in natty flying clothing displayed by mannequins, completed the exhibition. Later the machine was shown in a similar manner by Heelas Ltd in their store in Broad Street, Reading.

Blackburn's Sidecar was thus in existence some two months before civil flying was officially permitted in the United Kingdom but did not come on the British civil register—as G-EALN—until 26 August 1919. The certificate

The Sidecar on exhibition at Harrods, Knightsbridge, in March 1919. The engine access door is open, and the aileron control cables can be seen running externally under the wing. (*Flight Photo 167.*)

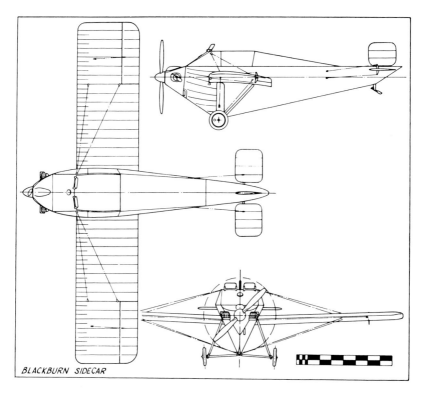

BLACKBURN SIDECAR

of registration was in the name of K. M. Smith, c/o Elder, Smith and Co, 3 St Helen's Place, London, EC3, with an alternative address at Stephen Terrace, Gilberton, South Australia. The Sidecar did not leave the country, however, and being sadly underpowered, never left the ground with the Gnat engine. Little is known of its subsequent history but, following an advertisement in the magazine *Flight* dated 23 June 1921, the Sidecar was acquired by Blackburn's London manager B. Haydon-White and re-engined with a 100 hp Anzani ten-cylinder, ungeared, air-cooled radial. Contemporary airworthiness records showed that it was no longer complete at 4 October 1921.

SPECIFICATION AND DATA

Manufacturer: The Blackburn Aeroplane and Motor Co Ltd, Olympia Works, Roundhay Road, Leeds, and Brough Aerodrome, East Yorks.

Power Plants: One 40 hp A.B.C. Gnat
One 100 hp Anzani

Dimensions: Span 27 ft 3 in   Length 20 ft 6 in
Height 6 ft 3 in   Wing area 123 sq ft

Weights: Tare weight 392 lb   All-up weight 850 lb

Performance: Maximum speed 83 mph   Landing speed 48 mph
              Range about 300 miles

Production: One aircraft only, Works Order unrecorded, completed February 1919, registered to K. M. Smith 26 August 1919 as G-EALN, last reported 4 October 1921.

            * Estimated performance with Gnat engine.

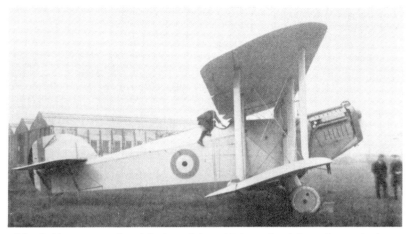

The Swift prototype, in original condition with long-chord fin and no mainplane sweepback, being prepared for first flight at Brough in 1920.

Blackburn T.1 Swift

At the end of 1919, after the Short Shirl and the Blackburn Blackburd had been found unsuitable, the Air Ministry re-issued its requirement for a carrier-based torpedo-carrying Sopwith Cuckoo replacement. In collaboration with D. Napier and Son Ltd, who provided the 450 hp Napier Lion, twelve-cylinder water-cooled engine, Blackburns at once went ahead with the construction of a private venture machine of advanced conception.

The prototype, called the Blackburn T.1 Swift, was built in five months to the designs of Maj F. A. Bumpus and by July 1920 was sufficiently complete to be exhibited at the Olympia Aero Show, albeit with dummy radiator and no controls. Even its underwater missile had to rest on the ground between the undercarriage legs because the aeroplane was at that time on the secret list and could only be shown without torpedo release gear or other specialized naval equipment.

The Swift was a large, single-seat, two-bay biplane of rugged appearance fitted with folding wings for economy in stowage space aboard an aircraft carrier. Thus the Blackburn company holds the distinction of being the first British firm to solve the problem of folding a staggered wing cellule. To achieve the immense strength needed in a machine which was to carry a heavy concentrated load and withstand the hard knocks of deck flying, Maj Bumpus built the aircraft round a central nucleus in which the centre fuselage, top centre section, lower wing roots and undercarriage attachments, were integrated into a single rigid structure built entirely of steel tubing for ease and economy of maintenance and repair. All the necessary fittings were machined

139

out of the solid, and to this primary structure was attached the tubular-steel rear fuselage, the two-spar T.64 section wooden wings and a detachable mounting which permitted time-expired engines to be replaced as complete power units in a matter of hours. Tubular-steel interplane struts had narrow chord fairings of fabric over wooden formers as on the Blackburd. Advanced features for those days were a fireproof bulkhead between the engine bay and a 66-gallon self-sealing fuel tank in the fuselage from which a Vickers pump distributed fuel via a three-way cock to the carburettors and to a 15-gallon gravity tank in the top centre section. The third branch led to an emergency hand pump.

Unlike that of the Blackburd, the fuselage had a curious humped appearance because the decking ahead of the pilot sloped sharply downwards to ensure maximum forward view over the engine when landing-on. It was not necessary to jettison the wheels before releasing the torpedo because the Swift boasted an early form of divided undercarriage, each half consisting of a triangulated structure supporting a long stub axle and incorporating a rubber-in-compression shock absorber leg. Nevertheless the wheels themselves were releaseable to minimize the risk of nosing over in a forced descent on the water, and flotation bags were installed in the fuselage. Slings were housed in the top centre section for hoisting the Swift aboard ship.

The Prototype Swift

After the Olympia Aero Show the prototype Swift was taken to Brough for completion, but when the firm's chief test pilot R. W. Kenworthy took off on the first flight, later in 1920, he quickly found he had no elevator control and that the machine climbed steeply even with the control column fully forward. It was only too clear that the C.G. was in the wrong place, but fortunately he carried no torpedo and there was only minimum fuel aboard, so that by closing the throttle, applying a little right rudder and lowering the star-

The Swift prototype, N139, at Martlesham Heath in January 1921, with the original fin and rudder. (*Imperial War Museum Photo MH. 5396.*)

140

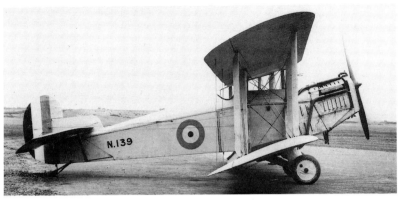

The Swift Mk I, N139, with the Martlesham-built vertical tail surfaces.
(*Imperial War Museum Photo MH. 3557.*)

board wing, he took up an attitude which enabled him to creep over the village of Brough and make a wide flat circuit by using the throttle as an elevator. Kenworthy then dropped the Swift back on to the aerodrome, bounced twice and came to rest entirely without damage some $7\frac{1}{2}$ minutes after take-off. The matter was corrected by giving the mainplanes a few degrees of sweepback.

A certificate of registration in the name of the manufacturer was filed on 22 September 1920 giving the Swift civil status as G-EAVN, but it is almost certain not to have appeared in civil colours since, by the end of October, it was nearly ready for handing over to the RAF, and a dummy Mk IX torpedo had been sent up from the Aeroplane Experimental Establishment, Martlesham Heath, for the manufacturer's pre-delivery trials. Designated Swift Mk I and bearing RAF serial N139, it flew from Brough to Martlesham on 23 December 1920 for radiator tests and full performance trials with Mk VIII and Mk IX torpedoes. At this stage it was still fitted with the original long-chord fin and rudder with oblique horn balance, but after initial handling trials in January 1921 the Blackburn company was asked to build a larger rudder. A weekly report on the aircraft state at Martlesham dated 3 February 1921 stated that N139 had, by that date, flown with the larger Blackburn rudder and also with another manufactured at Martlesham. Both proved unsatisfactory and were replaced with a horn balanced rudder, of entirely new outline, and a smaller fin, both built at Martlesham following consultations with the Swift's designer. Flight tests with the new tail assembly proved wholly satisfactory and by 20 April all trials were complete. A new engine was then installed, the cowling stiffened, some fabric restrung and arrester claws fitted to the stub axles, before the machine was despatched by air to the Development Squadron, Gosport, on 9 May.

First deck landings were then made on the carrier *Argus* by the Canadian pilot Gerald Boyce in the presence of assistant chief designer G. E. Petty.

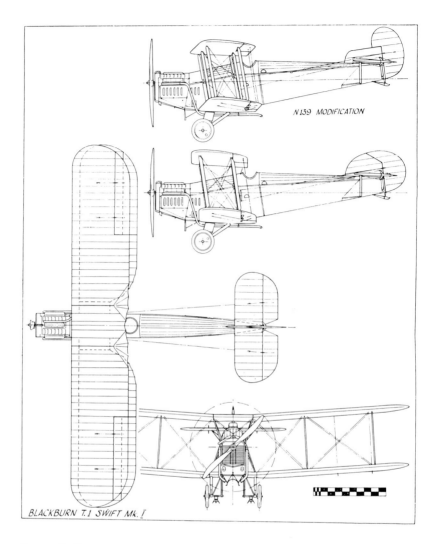

N139 MODIFICATION

BLACKBURN T.1 SWIFT MK. I

Export Swifts

Attracted by the Swift's ability to carry either an 18-inch naval torpedo of 1,500 lb weight or its equivalent in bombs on wing racks, several foreign governments placed sorely-needed orders. The export model, delivered to the United States, Japanese, Spanish and Brazilian navies, differed externally from the prototype mainly at nose and tail. The radiator was removed from the frontal position and bolted to the bottom engine bearers in a downward facing position, and new engine cowlings were devised to form a radiator compartment into which the pilot could admit cooling air by means of controllable shutters. A coolant header tank was fitted on top of the nose, and a silencer formed part of a new and modified exhaust system to improve the chances of surprise attack. All the tail surfaces were redesigned, slightly enlarged, and fitted with horn balances. The tailplane was provided with variable incidence gear and the interplane struts were streamlined with wide-chord fairings. The wheels could not be dropped.

Two aircraft, A-6056 and A-6057, built for the US Navy and known as the Swift F, were crated at Brough and transported to Hull Docks on a primitive wooden 'low loader' drawn by a team of four stout carthorses. They were consigned to the Manager, Naval Aircraft Factory, Navy Yard, Philadelphia, via the US Army Port Commander, Antwerp, and were among the five types of torpedo-bomber tested at the US Navy base at Anacostia between October 1922 and March 1923. These included three new American types and three examples of the 400 hp Liberty-powered Fokker FT-1 twin-float, low-wing monoplane. Convinced that three was the minimum crew for effective torpedo operations, the US Navy placed production orders for the Douglas DT-2 float biplane. The Swifts were therefore returned to Philadelphia on 19 March 1923 for storage until sent to San Diego for experimental use in the following January. As a result of a minor accident on 23 October 1924, A-6056 lay partially submerged in salt water for two hours but was salvaged to provide spares for A-6057, having flown 15 hr in US service. A-6057 remained airworthy until struck off charge at the Naval Reserve Unit, Sand Point, Washington, in March 1925.

A statement made in the Italian *Notiziarrio di Aeronautica* for September 1923 that the Swift Mk II had an increased span of 52 ft and operated at an all-up weight of 7,084 lb must surely be disregarded, because five subsequent aircraft, all built for export and designated Blackburn T.1A Swift Mk II, were completely identical to the US Navy version. All were test flown for the

A-6056, first of the two Swift F machines for the US Navy, photographed at San Diego on 20 April 1924. (*US Navy Photo.*)

143

M-NTBB, second of three Swift Mk IIs for the Spanish Navy, flying at Brough in 1923.

The second Japanese Navy Swift Mk II, serial 2, at Kasumigaura, Japan, in 1922. (*Courtesy AiReview, Tokyo.*)

manufacturers at Brough by R. W. Kenworthy who also flew acceptance trials on behalf of the foreign governments concerned.

Two Swift Mk IIs were among several aircraft types which accompanied the British Aviation Mission sent out to modernize and organize Imperial Japanese naval aviation in 1922. Numbered 1 and 2 they were based at Kasumigaura, a naval air station about 40 miles north of Tokyo, where, under

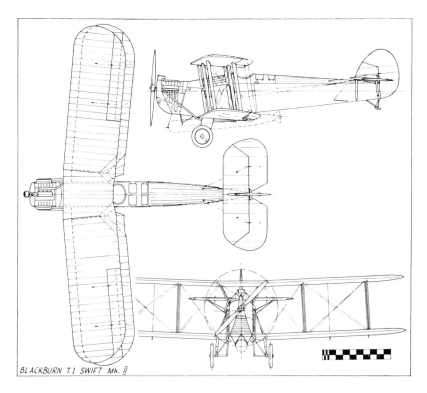

BLACKBURN T.1 SWIFT MK. II

the direction of the mission's senior pilot Lt Cdr H. G. Brackley, IJN, they were used to train Japanese pilots in torpedo-dropping and in simulated deck landings. Later they made actual landings on the IJN carrier *Hosho* at sea, but low-altitude flying over the Pacific in the prevailing atmospheric conditions made it necessary to reduce the compression ratio on the Lion engines to 5 to 1. In a letter to the Master of Sempill, leader of the mission, dated 10 July 1923, Brackley stated that the Swifts were no longer in use for torpedo work.

As was the custom in those days, the Spanish Government allotted pseudo-civil registrations to its three Swift Mk IIs which ran in sequence from M-NTBA, the first letter being at that time the Spanish nationality mark and the last the aircraft's individual identification. Thus, in order, the first four signified Spanish Naval Torpedo Bomber. Supermarine Scarabs ordered in the following year began at M-NSAA, i.e. Spanish Naval Ship's Amphibian. The second Swift, M-NTBB, flown by Kenworthy, was used at Brough on 27 August 1923 to demonstrate the torpedo-dropping technique to representatives of the Air Ministry, Admiralty and several foreign governments. Climbing to 2,000 ft, he dived steeply with engine off and discharged the missile into the Humber at a speed of 120 knots, afterwards climbing away at full throttle.

The Swifts retained their original markings throughout their Service careers and formed the Torpedo Section of the Campa Aviacione Navale at Prat de Llobregat, ten miles south of Barcelona. There M-NTBB made the first flight of a Swift in Spain on the evening of 30 November 1923, before making a demonstration flight over Barcelona next day.

The first Spanish pilot to convert on to Swifts was the unit's commanding officer, Capt F. T. de Andrade, whose British instructor J. R. King merely removed the first of the two access hatches on the port side behind the pilot, climbed inside and leaned over his pupil's shoulder. Dual instruction was given in the same manner by the other British instructors, H. A. Brown, George Moxon and Capt H. J. Andrews (CFI), which explains the many unconfirmed references to a two-seat Swift. Surprisingly enough, these large aircraft were aerobatic if flown light, and the flying instructors at Prat de Llobregat reported that the Swift had sufficient reserves of power to fly right over the top of a loop with no tendency to 'hang on top', and that only light stick forces were necessary. This was effectively demonstrated when M-NTBA gave an aerobatic display before King Alfonso at a Royal Review of the Forces at Barcelona in 1925.

The Projects

One of the last Swifts to be built, probably M-NTBC, was to have been shown at the International Aeronautical Exhibition at Gothenburg opened by the King of Sweden on 20 July 1923, but unfortunately it was held up at Hull by a dock strike. This was particularly regrettable as only a few weeks before, on 19 June, the Royal Swedish Navy had issued a specification for a similar machine and might well have ordered the Swift in modified form. Quick to meet the Swedish requirement, the Blackburn company prepared a design study for a Napier Lion powered three-seater which it called the T.O.1. Based on the Swift, it was armed with an 18-in torpedo, a fixed gun firing forward through the airscrew and another on a rotatable mounting aft. It envisaged an alternative wheel and float undercarriage and a top speed of 102 mph at the maximum all-up weight of 8,000 lb.

Although the standard Swift could be fitted with an alternative float undercarriage, there is no record of any being so equipped, and a project dated 14 April 1923 for the Blackburn T.1B Swift Mk III amphibian also never saw the light of day. Two versions of this were planned, one with a 400 hp Bristol Jupiter air-cooled radial engine and one with a 550 hp Packard vee-type water-cooled unit. The undercarriage comprised twin floats of rectangular cross-section and manually operated retractable wheels. Tankage was to have been increased from 66 to 95 gallons.

According to the Italian journal previously mentioned, the projected Lion-powered Swift Mk IV was to have been a three-seat fleet spotter, very similar to the Blackburn T.O.1 and chiefly differing from the basic design in having a deepened fuselage which filled the entire mainplane gap so as to provide an observer's glazed cabin amidships. The pilot was raised into a

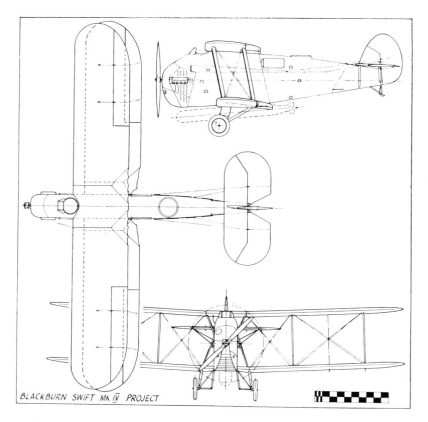

BLACKBURN SWIFT MK. IV PROJECT

position level with, and ahead of, the leading edge of the upper mainplane,
and the third crew member worked a gun on a rotatable mounting on top of
the rear fuselage. It was to be equipped with a standard divided undercarriage for alternative operation as a two-seat torpedo-bomber.

That these projects contemplated doubling or even trebling the crew on a
machine already carrying a heavy military load merely serves to highlight the
immense weight-lifting potential of the Swift, and the manufacturers were not
slow to realize its commercial possibilities. Stripped of warlike equipment
and with the fuselage widened, as well as deepened as on the Swift Mk IV
project, side-by-side seating was to be provided for two crew in an open cockpit ahead of the wings and with no less than eight passengers in two rows of
four in a small cabin. Known as the Blackburn 10 seater, it was to have had
Triplex sliding windows built into the sides of the cabin, with crew and passenger doors fore and aft respectively. A further proposal was for a Swift
M.1 Night Mailplane to carry a 500-lb mail load over the C.G. in a compartment of 30 cu ft capacity loaded from a strengthened platform on the top
surfaces of the lower centre section. Neither the Swift Mk IV, its ten-seat

147

commercial variant, nor the Swift M.1 Night Mailplane went beyond the drawing-board stage, but the scheme to deepen the fuselage bore fruit eventually in a later development of the Swift known as the Blackburn Blackburn fleet spotter.

SPECIFICATION AND DATA

Manufacturers: The Blackburn Aeroplane and Motor Co Ltd, Olympia Works, Roundhay Road, Leeds, and Brough Aerodrome, East Yorks.

Power Plants: (Swift Mk I, Swift F and Swift Mk II)
    One 450 hp Napier Lion IB
  (Swift Mk III project)
    One 400 hp Bristol Jupiter
    One 550 hp Packard
  (Swift Mk IV, Swift ten-seater and Swift M.1 projects)
    One 450 hp Napier Lion

Dimensions, Weights and Performance:

	Swift Mk I* and Mk II	Swift Mk III projects		Swift Mk IV project
		Bristol Jupiter	Packard	
Span	48 ft 6 in	48 ft 6 in	48 ft 6 in	48 ft 6 in
Span folded	17 ft 6 in	16 ft 10 in	16 ft 10 in	17 ft 6 in
Length	35 ft 6 in	36 ft 0 in	36 ft 0 in	36 ft 0 in
Height	12 ft 3 in	13 ft 3 in	13 ft 3 in	13 ft 3 in
Wing area	720 sq ft	720 sq ft	720 sq ft	720 sq ft
Tare weight	3,550 lb	—	5,296 lb	—
All-up weight	6,300 lb	—	7,100 lb	5,360 lb
Maximum speed	106 mph	104 mph	124 mph	112 mph
Initial climb	650 ft/min	600 ft/min	750 ft/min	960 ft/min
Service ceiling	15,000 ft	12,400 ft	13,800 ft	15,200 ft
Range	350 miles	300 miles	—	—

* *Ref. A. & A.E.E. Report M/281 dated July 1921—prototype Blackburn Swift aircraft N139 powered by one Napier Lion IB engine giving 450 hp at 2,000 rpm.*

Production:

(a) *Swift Mk I*

    One prototype aircraft only, to Works Order 6368, exhibited at Olympia, 9–20 July 1920; civil-registered as G-EAVN in the name of the Blackburn Aeroplane and Motor Co Ltd by C. of R. No. 600 dated 22 September 1920; to the AEE, Martlesham Heath, as N139 by air 23 December 1920; to the Development Squadron, Gosport, 9 May 1921; to Farnborough for test (Flg Off Hope) 2–9 June 1921.

(b) *Swift F*

    Two aircraft only for the US Navy.

    A-6056 received at Anacostia for competitive trials 29 June 1922; to the National Aircraft Factory, Philadelphia, for storage 19 March 1923; received at San Diego for experimental flying 3 January 1924; front end submerged, with damage to airscrew and fabric, 23 October 1924; reduced to spares and struck off charge 17 December 1924; total flying time 15 hr 01 min.

A-6057 received at Anacostia for competitive trials August 1922; to the National Aircraft Factory, Philadelphia, for storage 19 March 1923; received at San Diego for experimental flying 3 January 1924; to the Naval Reserve Unit, Sand Point, Washington; struck off charge 10 March 1925; engine to US Navy Laboratory for stripping and inspection.

(c) *Swift Mk II*

Five aircraft for export.

Two for the Imperial Japanese Navy, numbered 1 and 2, delivered in 1922 and based at Kasumigaura. Three for the Spanish Navy registered M-NTBA, M-NTBB and M-NTBC, delivered in 1923 and based at Prat de Llobregat until struck off charge in 1927.

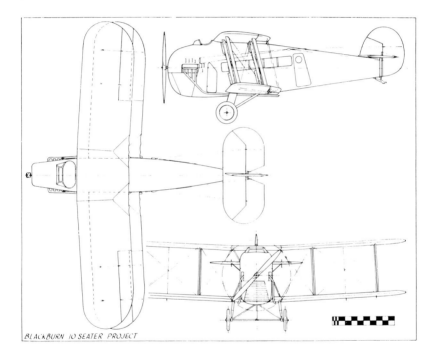

BLACKBURN 10 SEATER PROJECT

N9542, the seventh production Dart, with torpedo in position.

Blackburn T.2 Dart

Martlesham evaluation of the re-rigged Swift prototype N139 led, in 1921, to an Air Ministry contract for three trials aircraft, N140–N142, to Specification 3/20 (D. of R. Type 8) and to limited production for foreign governments. Export models retained the name Swift, but the British version for the Fleet Air Arm, with span reduced by 2 ft 11 in and fully equipped to Admiralty requirements, was renamed Dart. Externally distinguishable from the Swift because the shortened mainplanes brought the wing tips noticeably nearer to the outboard interplane struts, the Dart was powered by a later mark of Napier Lion. A standard fitment to the undercarriage stub axles was the early form of claw arrester gear which had been tried experimentally on the carrier *Argus* with the Swift prototype. It carried either the Mk VIII or Mk IX 18-in naval torpedo, but could be adapted quickly to carry an equivalent bomb load under the wings, the largest bomb being a 520 pounder. There was no other armament, for the Dart did not carry guns. A Vickers wind pump on the rear spar of the port bottom mainplane fed fuel from a 65-gallon tank in the fuselage to a $13\frac{1}{2}$-gallon gravity tank in the top centre section.

N140, first of the three Dart prototypes, was flown from Brough to Martlesham on 24 October 1921 for full performance testing but after delays caused by a leaky cooling system it was transferred to *Argus* for deck-landing trials and replaced at Martlesham by N141, flown down from Brough on 12 January 1922. Performance measurements with and without the Mk IX torpedo then proceeded and were complete by 15 February. The third prototype, N142, flown from Brough to Martlesham on 9 February, was fitted with a simple stick-type control column for comparative trials with N141 which had the standard fore and aft control column surmounted by an aileron wheel. The relative merits of the two systems had been assessed by 6 March, when it was stated that aileron loads were too great for the stick control, and after modifications to the tailplane fittings and variable-incidence gear, N141 and N142 were flown to Gosport and handed over to the Development Squadron on 9 March and 13 May 1922 respectively.

After competitive trials at Gosport with three Handley Page H.P.19 Hanley prototypes, N143–N145, to the same specification, the Dart was adopted as the Fleet Air Arm's standard single-seat carrier-borne torpedo-bomber and the Blackburn company was awarded an initial production contract for 26 aircraft. They were all built at the Olympia Works, and the airframe sections were taken by road to Brough for erection, test and delivery. Before he left Blackburns in 1925, R. W. Kenworthy test flew the three trials aircraft and the majority of early production Darts before they were collected by Service pilots and ferried via Northolt or the Stores Depots at Henlow and Spittlegate to Farnborough en route to Gosport. Deliveries began in March 1922, and many machines later returned to the RAE, Farnborough, for the fitting and testing of short-wave radio.

Although unusually large for single-seat aircraft, the Darts had those subtle handling qualities which made them 'pilots' aeroplanes'. With a wing loading of only 9 lb/sq ft and a stalling speed of 38 knots, they were easy to land on the deck of an aircraft carrier, particularly after 1928 when they were all fitted with Handley Page slots as they came up for reconditioning. Although not a high performance type, the Dart remained in service for ten years, a period in which its rugged dependability played an important part in enabling the Fleet Air Arm to develop and perfect its torpedo-dropping techniques.

The first production Dart, N9536, was shown statically along with one of the trials aircraft in the New Types Park at the Hendon RAF Display of

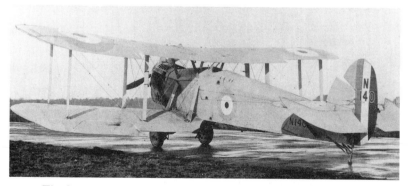

The first prototype Dart, N140, at Martlesham Heath, January 1922.
(*Courtesy Royal Aeronautical Society.*)

151

24 June 1922, and two others, N9542 and N9545, were sent to Martlesham for proving trials later in the year, afterwards being flown to Gosport on 25 November 1922 and 22 February 1923, respectively. In the following year the first Darts went into service with Nos. 460 and 461 (Fleet Torpedo) Flights based on the aircraft carriers *Eagle* and *Furious* serving with the Mediterranean and Home Fleets respectively. Three further batches of ten Darts laid down in 1923–24 were followed in August 1924 by a larger contract for 32 and during 1925–26 by three orders for replacement aircraft. In late production Darts, the Napier Lion IIB gave way to the newer 450 hp Lion V, and the last contract for ten machines, dated November 1926, stipulated interchangeable wheel and float undercarriages. When production ceased in 1928, the total number built for the Fleet Air Arm amounted to 117.

The Dart and the taxpayer rarely met, as, apart from those in use by 'D' (Torpedo Training) Flight at Gosport which taught naval pilots the technique of flattening out 15 ft above the water and aiming the whole aircraft at the target, the majority were normally at sea with the aircraft carriers. Nevertheless a single aircraft, N9549, coded 1, did appear at the Hendon RAF Display on 30 June 1923, and another disported itself (with dummy torpedo) at an air display organized for the Dominion Premiers at Croydon on 10 November the same year. A new aircraft, N9689, just off the production line, was exhibited at the Third International Aero Show, staged at the Palace of Industry in Prague, from 31 May to 9 June 1924, but at that year's Hendon RAF Display on 28 June, no less than five Darts appeared from *Furious*. Led by N9549, now coded 4, they 'torpedoed' the dummy enemy ship *Slevik* before thousands of spectators and brought the display to a spectacular conclusion amid splendid noises.

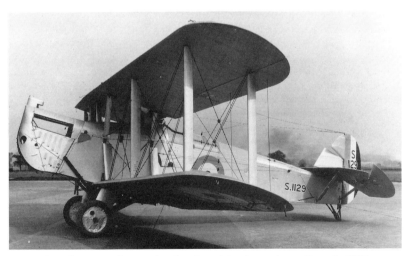

Dart S1129 newly completed and awaiting its engine at Brough, 1927.

152

Dart N9997 airborne near Leuchars, with smoke-producing apparatus in the torpedo crutch and long ejection pipe under the fuselage. (*Crown Copyright Reserved.*)

An event of more profound and lasting importance took place after dark on 1 July 1926, when Flt Lt Gerald Boyce touched down on *Furious* in N9804 to demonstrate the feasibility of night landings on a carrier at sea. In a few years night flying from carriers became a normal operation and, at Fleet Exercises held in 1931, the Darts of No. 463 Flight from *Courageous* were re-doped in night camouflage. This Flight and its companion, No. 464, each equipped with six Darts (Lion V), embarked on *Courageous* when it was commissioned on 21 February 1928 and, after a working-up period, during which the first deck landing was made by Sqn Ldr S. Watkins in a Dart, sailed in it for the Mediterranean on 2 June. Malta was reached on 10 June and next day both Flights were flown off to Hal Far Aerodrome, but in the first-ever take-off from the deck of *Courageous*, Lt Nicholson, RN, was killed when his Dart struck the superstructure and went over the side.

Crews reached a high pitch of efficiency, and in a Fleet and Air Exercise, held off the Isle of Wight on 9 September 1930, a combined force of 15 Darts of Nos. 461 and 462 Flights based at Lee-on-Solent scored eight hits on the battleships *Nelson* and *Rodney*. Attempts to shoot them down were invariably foredoomed to failure as, when pursued, they slowed right up and took evasive action at a speed well below that at which any fighter could stay in the air.

Nos. 463 and 464 Flights were combined in April 1933 to form No. 810 Squadron, which flew Darts for a few months before converting to the Black-burn Ripon Mk II, and on 22–23 September 1933 (during this transition period) it was armed with six Darts and six Ripons and took part in Coastal Defence Exercises off the Firth of Forth.

During its long career the Dart was seldom used experimentally, but tests with stannic chloride apparatus, similar to that developed by Maj Jack Savage for his skywriting S.E.5As, were commenced by Flt Lt E. F. Shales at the RAE, Farnborough, in N9822 on 8 July 1926, after which N9997, similarly equipped, operated with the Fleet Air Arm at Leuchars. Another was flown from Gosport to Donibristle on 1 January 1929 to be taken on charge by No. 36 (Bomber) Squadron as the RAF's only Dart. In experiments which began on 12 February, it laid truly voluminous smoke around ships under dummy attack by the squadron's Hawker Horsley torpedo-bombers. The only other significant development work with Darts was by the Instrument Flight of the RAE which fitted and flew anti-stall gear in N9719 from September to November 1927 and a later smoke-producing device in N9694 in September 1931. This was tested at Porton on 9 October before fitment to the Dart's successor, the Blackburn Ripon.

The Civil Darts

Following the award of an Air Ministry contract in 1924 to provide re-fresher courses and annual training for officers of the RAF Reserve, Blackburn's subsidiary, the North Sea Aerial and General Transport Co Ltd, opened a civilian flying school at Brough with Robert's brother, Capt Norman Blackburn, as manager. Initial equipment consisted of several Kangaroo dual

A Dart of No. 463 Flight with Handley Page slots and night camouflage during the Fleet Exercises in 1931. (*Crown Copyright Reserved.*)

154

The two-seat Dart seaplane G-EBKF flying past the hangars at Brough in 1925.

conversions, but during 1925 they were joined by three civil Darts, G-EBKF, 'KG and 'KH, converted from single-seaters to two-seat dual control advanced trainers while under construction on the Leeds production line. Under the wings were large white circles where the RAF roundels would have been and, in view of the fact that several Darts in the RAF batch commencing S1115 were never delivered, it is possible to draw a reasonable but unconfirmed conclusion. On completion the civil Darts were equipped with large-volume, boat-built, mahogany floats designed by the company's chief seaplane designer, Maj J. D. Rennie. They were of the long-heeled type to make a tail float unnecessary, and located between them was a pair of pilot-operated retractable beaching wheels, sprung-steel skids being provided at the rear of each float for taxying up the slipway.

In seaplane form the Dart lost none of its docility, the floats rode easily on the step, ran clean with no tendency to porpoise, and in suitable weather conditions the aircraft would unstick from the Humber 'hands off' in 20 sec. With these machines on the strength, Brough became the only British civil seaplane flying school, the chief instructor being Flt Lt N. H. Woodhead. All three operated on floats until Reserve seaplane training terminated in 1929. G-EBKG was then scrapped, and the other two were given wheeled undercarriages to continue as landplane Reserve trainers under chief instructor A. G. Loton and his assistant J. B. Stockbridge. G-EBKF was severely damaged and written off at Digby, Lincs., on 7 January 1932 without injury to the pilot Flg Off McCash, and the last aircraft, 'KH, was retired in 1933 and sold to Mr Reg Fowler who put it on show outside his garage in Doncaster Road, Hatfield, Yorks., for publicity purposes. He carefully preserved the log books and the original Certificate of Airworthiness, and 'KH soon became a well-known landmark in South Yorkshire, particularly after 1950 when it was renovated and repainted to make good the ravages of time. In later years it became a fabric-less skeleton and was broken up.

SPECIFICATION AND DATA

Manufacturers: The Blackburn Aeroplane and Motor Co Ltd, Olympia Works Roundhay Road, Leeds, and Brough Aerodrome, East Yorks.

Power Plants: One 450 hp Napier Lion IIB
One 465 hp Napier Lion V

★Dimensions: Span (extended) 45 ft 5¾ in   (folded) 17 ft 6 in
Length (landplane) 35 ft 4½ in   (seaplane) 40 ft 2½ in
Height (landplane) 12 ft 11 in   (seaplane) 17 ft 0 in
Wing area 654 sq ft

★Loadings:

Pilot	180 lb	Tare weight	3,599 lb
Mk VIII torpedo	1,500 lb	Military load	2,140 lb
Torpedo gear	115 lb	Fuel 78½ gallons	584 lb
Equipment	345 lb	Oil 6 gallons	60 lb
Military load	2,140 lb	All-up weight	6,383 lb†

† With Mk IX torpedo 5,973 lb

★Performance (prototype aircraft with torpedo):

Speed at 1,000 ft	107 mph	Time to max. height	44 min 18 sec
Speed at 5,000 ft	104 mph	Climb at max. height	80 ft/min
Speed at 11,000 ft	93·5 mph	Service ceiling	10,200 ft
Initial climb	575 ft/min	Endurance at 107 mph	2¼ hr
Maximum height reached	12,700 ft	Endurance at 95 mph	3 hr

★Take-off and landing distances, wind approximately 15 mph:
Without torpedo the aircraft took off in 132 yards; landing run 153 yards.

★ *Ref. A. & A.E.E. Report M/294 dated 21 February 1922—second prototype Blackburn Dart aircraft N141 powered by one Napier Lion IIB engine giving 465 hp at 2,100 rpm. Pilots: Flt Lt A. H. Orlebar and Flg Off Breakey.*

†*Performance* (production aircraft with dummy torpedo):

Speed at 3,000 ft	107 mph	Climb at 3,000 ft	485 ft/min
Speed at 7,000 ft	104·5 mph	Climb at 7,000 ft	327 ft/min
Speed at 10,000 ft	100 mph	Climb at 10,000 ft	207 ft/min
Initial climb	600 ft/min	Absolute ceiling	15,200 ft
		Service ceiling	12,700 ft

† *Ref. A. & A.E.E. Report M/303A dated 30 November 1922—seventh production Blackburn Dart aircraft N9542 powered by one 465 hp Napier Lion IIB engine and equipped with dummy Mk VIII torpedo.*

Production: (a) *Ship-planes for the Fleet Air Arm*

Requisitioned	Quan- tity	Serials	Requisitioned	Quan- tity	Serials
1921	3	N140–N142	August 1924	32	N9792–N9823
1922	26	N9536–N9561	January 1925	10	N9990–N9999
1923	10	N9620–N9629	1926	6	S1115–S1120
1923	10	N9687–N9696	November 1926	10	S1129–S1138★
May 1924	10	N9714–N9723			

★ With interchangeable wheel and float undercarriages.

Deliveries ex Brough:

(i) *Trials aircraft*

N140 to Martlesham 24 October 1921, to *Argus* 15 November 1921; N141 to Martlesham 12 January 1922, to Gosport 9 March 1922; N142 to Martlesham 9 February 1922, to Gosport 13 May 1922, still there August 1926; N9542 to Martlesham November 1922, to Gosport 25 November 1922; N9545 to Martlesham November 1922, to Gosport 22 February 1923.

(ii) *Production aircraft*

To Farnborough and Gosport: N9536 via Northolt (Flg Off Hempel) 23 March 1922; N9537 via Henlow (Flg Off Harrison) 24 March 1922; N9538 via Henlow (Flg Off Mason) 24 March 1922; N9543 via Spittlegate (Flg Off Harrison) 29 November 1922; N9544 via Spittlegate (Flg Off Mason) 29 November 1922; N9550 via Northolt (Flg Off Harrison) 22 January 1923; N9551 via Northolt (Flg Off Hempel) 22 January 1923; N9552 via Northolt (Flg Off Harrison) 22 February 1923; N9557 via Northolt (Flt Lt Giffard) 28 February 1923; N9723 via Northolt (Flg Off Harrison) 15 August 1924.

G-EBKF, the first Dart two-seat seaplane trainer, standing on its retractable beaching wheels.

157

Notes on individual aircraft:
N9723 coded 75 of No. 460 Flight; N9808 coded 63; N9811 sank in the Mediterranean 26 June 1929; N9817 coded 73 sank in the Mediterranean in 1931; S1115 broke its back at Gosport 8 May 1929; S1129 sank in the Solent while on frame deck practice 11 March 1929; one Gosport-based Dart crashed at Brook Down, Isle of Wight, 17 August 1926.

Yearly totals of Darts reconditioned at Brough:
1924   Three aircraft comprising N9551 redelivered Brough–Farnborough en route to Gosport 17 May 1924; N9688 and N9689 redelivered by the same route 31 October 1924.
1925   (18 aircraft); 1926 (8); 1927 (nil); 1928 (9); 1929 (9); 1930 (3).
1931   Six aircraft comprising N9540 and N9623 to Works Order 3420/1; N9823 to Works Order 3420/2; N9692 to Works Order 3420/3; the others being N9802 and S1134.
1932   One aircraft N9723 to Works Order 4701/1.

(b) *Civil two-seat seaplanes*
Three aircraft only, Works Orders 8312/1 to 8312/3, registered 20 October 1924 to the North Sea Aerial and General Transport Co Ltd, Brough.

G-EBKF, first flown at Brough 17 January 1925, C. of A. issued 21 April 1925, damaged beyond repair in accident near Digby, Lincs., 7 January 1932.
G-EBKG, C. of A. issued 13 June 1925, withdrawn from use at Brough 25 January 1928.
G-EBKH, C. of A. issued 26 October 1925, withdrawn from use at C. of A. expiry 9 May 1933, towed to Reg Fowler's Garage, Doncaster Road, Hatfield, Yorks., broken up by Hatfield Motor Wreckers *circa* 1952.

Service Use:
(a) *The Fleet Torpedo Flights*

Date	Flight	Base	Station
1923–31	No. 460	HMS *Eagle*	Mediterranean
1923–29	No. 461	HMS *Furious* or Gosport	Home
1924–29	No. 462	HMS *Furious* or Gosport	Home
1928–33	No. 463	HMS *Courageous*	Mediterranean
1928–33	No. 464	HMS *Courageous*	Mediterranean

Nos. 463 and 464 Flights were merged in April 1933 to form No. 810 Squadron which embarked on *Courageous* 8 May 1933 with 12 Darts, six of which were replaced by Blackburn Ripons by 18 September 1933.

(b) *Training*
'D' (Torpedo Training) Flight formed at Gosport in 1925, re-styled the Torpedo Training Flight in 1927.

(c) *Royal Air Force*
One aircraft only to No. 36 (Bomber) Squadron, Donibristle, 1 January 1929.

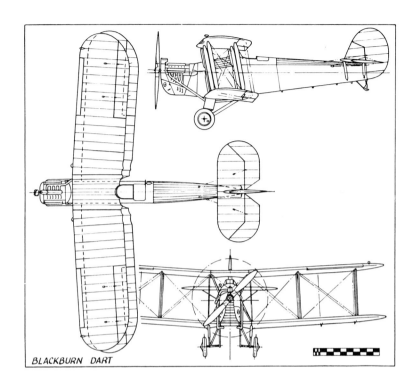

BLACKBURN DART

159

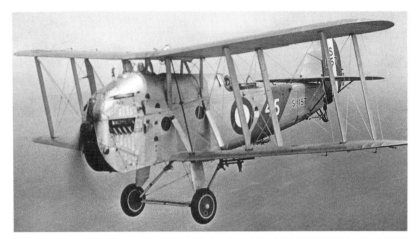

Blackburn Blackburn Mk II S1157 showing the raised centre section and simplified undercarriage.

Blackburn R.1 Blackburn

Named after the Lancashire town which bore the same name as its manufacturer, the Blackburn Blackburn was a deck-landing biplane intended, as the symbol R.1 indicated, for reconnaissance and gunnery fire control. It was designed to Specification 3/21 (D. of R. Type 7A) and therefore contemporary with the Avro 555 Bison* with which it shared many common features and which fulfilled the same naval requirement. In each case functional considerations took absolute priority over refinement of aerodynamic shape, so that both Bison and Blackburn were little short of grotesque in appearance and ungainly and slow in the air. Nevertheless they were very successful in their designed role and remained in service for almost a decade.

Designed by Maj F. A. Bumpus, the Blackburn was a two-bay biplane of fabric-covered wood and metal construction with folding wings, and powered by a 450 hp Napier Lion IIB twelve-cylinder water-cooled engine arranged as a detachable power unit and installed in a Dart-type louvred engine bay with controllable shutters. To simplify the Fleet Air Arm spares holding, the basic structure was almost identical with that of the Dart, being built up from lengths of tubular steel fitted into joint-clusters machined from the solid. As before, the centre fuselage unit formed the nucleus to which a number of sub-assemblies were bolted to form the complete aeroplane. Mainplanes, tail unit and all control surfaces except the rudder were interchangeable with those of the Dart, but aft of the tubular-steel centre unit the fuselage was of semi-

* See the author's *Avro Aircraft since 1908*, page 202.

160

monocoque construction and of greatly increased girth to provide cabin accommodation for the two crew members during long reconnaissance sorties. The wireless-operator/gunner sat in the forward end with his gear mounted above a folding table, while a rearward extension of the cabin roof shielded the navigator/observer from the slipstream when he moved into the open rear cockpit to use sextant, range finder or camera.

The pilot sat in an open cockpit in a cut-out in the leading edge of the top centre section, with the decking in front of him cut away to clear the control wheel, the gap being closed by a Triplex windscreen. The engine cowling then sloped away sharply to give him a good view of the carrier's deck when landing-on. Armament consisted of one Vickers gun (with 500 rounds) mounted externally on the port side of the pilot's cockpit and firing through the airscrew, and a rearwards and downwards firing Lewis gun (with three drums of ammunition) on a Scarff ring immediately aft of the rear cockpit. There were thus four crew positions but the machine was nevertheless a three-seater.

In the manner of the three Avro Bison prototypes, N153–N155, ordered to the same specification, the top centre section was bolted straight on to the cabin roof so that the fuselage filled the entire mainplane gap, a feature which sprang directly from design studies for the fat-fuselaged Swift IV and the Blackburn civil ten-seater. Main fuel was carried in a saddle tank under the centre section, over the C.G. and behind the pilot, but the total was brought up to 90 gallons by means of two streamlined tanks on top of the upper main-plane.

The first prototype Blackburn, N150, in its original form with extra struts
in the undercarriage.

161

As the Blackburn was not intended for torpedo carrying it did not use the Dart undercarriage, but was equipped with the conventional wheel-and-axle type strengthened centrally with additional struts for deck landing at a high rate of descent. Claws were fitted for engaging the fore and aft arrester wires used at that time.

Martlesham Trials

Three prototype Blackburns, N150–N152, built in the Olympia Works in 1922 alongside the first batch of Fleet Air Arm Darts, were test flown at Brough by R. W. Kenworthy, who gave Robert Blackburn his first flight ever as a passenger in one of them. Handling tests on N150 had been completed at the Aeroplane and Armament Experimental Establishment, Martlesham, by 12 August 1922, and the machine was flown to Gosport on 19 August for deck-landing trials on the carrier *Argus* which began on 23 August.

The second prototype, N151, flew from Brough to Martlesham on 5 September 1922 for performance tests, but fuel surging and the fitting of new undercarriage oleos delayed their completion until 20 January 1923. The return flight to Brough was made on 24 January. Martlesham's Report contained favourable comments on the efficiency of the undercarriage, criticism of the draughty and uncomfortable pilot's cockpit, and stated that N151 had flown successfully with a Dart rudder, recommending it as standard fitment in order to reduce the length of the aircraft slightly and save stowage space aboard a carrier.

Fuel-surging trouble was also experienced with the third prototype, N152, which forced landed with loss of oil pressure in a field at Lowestoft while on delivery from Brough to Martlesham on 30 September 1922. Attempts at take-off only succeeded when the half-full tanks were topped up to within 10 gallons of full. While at Lowestoft the machine fell prey to a local photographer whose picture of this unheard-of 'hush hush' machine found its way into *The Aeroplane* for 15 November 1922. With typical candour C. G. Frey described it as an 'apparatus with the aspect of a docile bull in a field', thus unwittingly coining the name 'Bull' later given unofficially to the side-by-side two-seat trainer variant. Surging tests were made at Martlesham on N151 and N152 and the trouble was cured by building up a tank pressure of 1 lb/sq in with a hand pump on take-off. Unfortunately N152 was completely destroyed in a hangar fire at Martlesham during the week ending 7 October 1922. N151 was employed as a trials aircraft and after reconditioning was re-delivered from Brough to Farnborough by Flg Off Harrison on 19 September 1924 but sometime later was destroyed in a crash.

In production aircraft large portholes were provided to lighten the gloom of the Blackburn's cavernous interior, and it is evident that brief consideration was given to using the type in the Torpedo-Spotter-Reconnaissance role since twelve Mk I aircraft N9579–N9590, built to the initial production contract awarded in 1922, were fitted with Dart-type divided undercarriages. Deliveries to Gosport began in April 1923, but the machines later went to Farnborough

The performance trials aircraft, N9581, at Stag Lane after the 1923 RAF Display with the rudder of the second prototype, N151. (*Courtesy P.T. Capon.*)

An early production Blackburn Mk I, N9586, showing the fuselage-mounted top wing, fuel tanks, large cabin portholes and original divided undercarriage. (*Courtesy P. L. Gray.*)

for the fitting and testing of short-wave radio, five of the first six production aircraft, N9579, '80, '82, '83 and '84, being flown back to Gosport in formation after this treatment on 4 June 1923. The absent third production machine, N9581, was ferried from Brough to Martlesham on 28 April for acceptance tests which continued until 23 June, and a week later, on 30 June, it formed Exhibit No. 5 in the New Types Park at the Hendon RAF Display. The rudder was damaged on this occasion and a replacement, donated by the second prototype, N151, was fitted at de Havilland's nearby aerodrome at Stag Lane a few days later. The same machine was demonstrated at the Imperial Conference Air Display at Croydon along with a Service Dart on 10 November that year. Eighteen more Mk Is were also built during 1923–24.

The Blackburn Mk II

Further production contracts for 29 aircraft to Specification 11/23 placed between January 1925 and December 1926 were for the Napier Lion V powered Blackburn R.1A Blackburn Mk II. As in the case of the Avro Bison Mk IA, the mainplane gap of the Blackburn was increased by 22½ in by raising the top centre section clear of the fuselage on short struts in order to overcome the elevator blanketing experienced with the Mk I aircraft. The structure was cleaned up inside and out, the wing fuel tanks eliminated and a much simplified cross-axle undercarriage substituted, modifications which led to an appreciable increase in performance and which were the subject of prolonged trials with the modified first prototype, N150. This was still at Martlesham in April 1925 but spent a month under test at Farnborough and returned to the makers at Brough on 21 May.

Two Flights of Blackburns went into service with the Fleet Air Arm. The Mk I, first issued to No. 422 Fleet Spotter Flight in 1923 for Mediterranean service with the carrier *Eagle*, also operated from Hal Far Aerodrome, Malta, but many eventually returned to Brough to be modified up to Mk II standard. Then, in 1926, Mk II aircraft replaced the Westland Walrus biplanes in No. 420 Fleet Spotter Flight at Gosport before embarking in the carrier *Furious* for service with the Home Fleet. These Flights were renumbered Nos. 450 and 449 Fleet Spotter Reconnaissance Flights, respectively, in 1929 and served with the carrier *Argus* on the China Station and HMS *Courageous* in

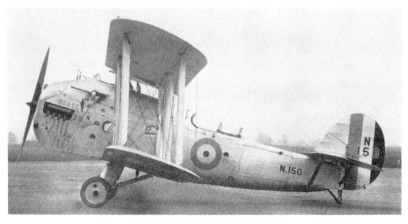

N150 after conversion into the Blackburn Mk II prototype.

164

Side view of the Blackburn Mk II dual trainer N9589 showing the cockpit entry ladder necessary on this variant.

the Mediterranean. In ordinary weather and with the carrier steaming into wind, take-off distance was often as little as 60 ft.

No. 449 Flight took part in exercises off the Isle of Wight on 9 September 1930 but all Blackburn Blackburns were replaced by Fairey IIIFs in 1931 and finally declared obsolete in March 1933.

The dual control conversion used in small numbers for deck-landing training at No. 1 Flying Training School, Leuchars, was known unofficially as the Blackburn 'Bull'. The first, N9589, built as a Mk I, retained the split undercarriage, the arrester claws and upper wing tanks, but had the raised centre section of the Mk II. Above the top longerons the front fuselage was widened to accommodate pupil and instructor side-by-side in an open cockpit in the manner of the projected two-crew Dart ten-seater. Drag was increased to such an extent that, according to contemporary accounts, the whole of Leuchars' 600 yard take-off run was needed to unstick, and the initial rate of climb was said to be about 100 ft/min. On 21 April 1926, it was flown all the way from Leuchars to Farnborough by Flg Off Bryer for the installation and testing of a camera gun. Records show that he flew it to Gosport on 20 May but forced landed at Basingstoke on the way back on 4 June.

One other 'Bull', N9989, built as a Mk II and issued to Leuchars in January 1927, was fitted with the simplified undercarriage and had the upper wing tanks of the Mk I.

Experimental work with the Blackburn included Fairey-Reed metal airscrew tests on N9982 and a modification of the second prototype, N151, to carry a 16-ft gunnery glider target. Installation and test took place at Farnborough in May 1925 and Service trials began at Gosport in the following July.

165

The Blackburn Mk I seaplane N9833 with strengthened floats for experimental deck landings.

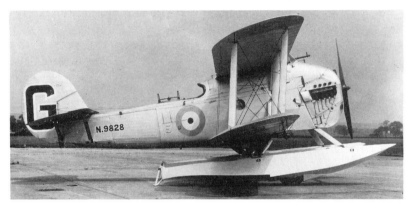

The Blackburn Mk I amphibian N9828 fitted with the rudder from Dart G-EBKH.

Twin-float conversions were also made at Brough to two Mk I aircraft. The first, N9833, had a four-bladed airscrew and was fitted with float set No. 15 from the Greek Navy Velos programme (q.v.), equipped with oleo rear struts and specially strengthened keels for landing on the deck of an aircraft carrier. These landings inevitably caused slight damage and strain, and when N9833 arrived at Felixstowe in May 1926 the floats were no longer fully watertight. Handling trials proved the Blackburn to be viceless in the air but unsuitable for use as a seaplane.

The second aircraft, N9828, was an amphibian equipped with the same type of floats but with landing wheels housed internally and projecting just forward of the step. Sprung tail skids supported the heel of each float when taxying on deck or on the slipway. The machine was evaluated at Felixstowe and later, as a reminder of Martlesham's original suggestion that the Dart rudder should be fitted, this machine flew with one borrowed from a civil Dart, G-EBKH, of the RAF Reserve School at Brough.

A projected flying-boat trainer using Blackburn Blackburn mainplanes and tail unit, capable of development as an operational type, was shelved.

SPECIFICATION AND DATA

Manufacturers: The Blackburn Aeroplane and Motor Co Ltd, Olympia Works, Roundhay Road, Leeds, and Brough Aerodrome, East Yorks.

Power Plants: (Mk I) One 450 hp Napier Lion IIB
(Mk II) One 465 hp Napier Lion V

Dimensions:

	*Blackburn Mk I		Blackburn Mk. II
	Landplane	Seaplane	
Span (extended)	45 ft 6½ in	45 ft 6½ in	45 ft 6½ in
Span (folded)	17 ft 6 in	17 ft 6 in	17 ft 6 in
Length	36 ft 2 in	38 ft 8 in	36 ft 2 in
Height	12 ft 6 in	15 ft 5½ in	14 ft 4½ in
Wing area	650 sq ft	650 sq ft	662 sq ft

Blackburn Mk I landplane

Loadings:				
Three crew	720 lb		Tare weight	3,929 lb
Equipment	573 lb		Military load	1,293 lb
	———		Fuel 90 gallons	680 lb
Military load	1,293 lb		Oil 4½ gallons	60 lb
			All-up weight	5,962 lb

Performance:

Speed at 3,000 ft	122 mph	Time to max. height	49 min
Speed at 10,000 ft	112·5 mph	Climb at max. height	80 ft/min
Initial climb	690 ft/min	Absolute ceiling	15,500 ft
Climb at 3,000 ft	566 ft/min	Service ceiling	12,950 ft
Climb at 10,000 ft	224 ft/min	Endurance at 122 mph	3¼ hr
Maximum height reached	13,450 ft	Endurance at 103·5 mph	4¼ hr

* *Ref. A. & A.E.E. Report M/312 dated October 1922—second prototype Blackburn Blackburn Mk I aircraft N151 powered by Napier Lion IIB engine No. 24484 driving a two-bladed wooden airscrew made by the Lang Propeller Co. Pilots: Flg Off Gray and Flg Off Potter.*

Blackburn Mk I seaplane

†*Loadings:*				
Pilot	180 lb		Tare weight	5,330 lb
Equipment	533 lb		Military load	713 lb
	———		Fuel 73 gallons	554 lb
Military load	713 lb		Oil 7 gallons	65 lb
			All-up weight	6,662 lb

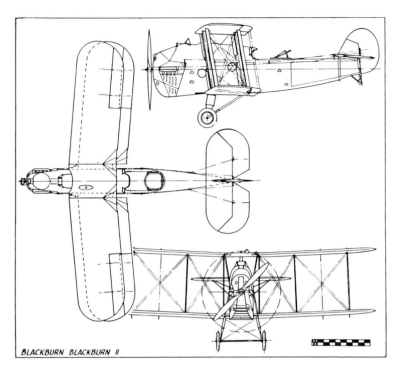

BLACKBURN BLACKBURN II

†*Performance:*

Speed at sea level	97·8 mph	Climb at 6,500 ft	118 ft/min
Speed at 3,000 ft	93·5 mph	Maximum height reached	7,125 ft
Speed at 6,500 ft	85·8 mph	Time to max. height	34 min 40 sec
Cruising speed	74 mph	Climb at max. height	92 ft/min
Initial climb	385 ft/min	Absolute ceiling	9,375 ft
Climb at 2,500 ft	282 ft/min	Service ceiling	6,942 ft

†Take-off and landing distances, wind approximately 12 mph:
    Aircraft took off in 35 sec. in a distance of 465 yards; landing run 117 yards.

    † *Ref. M.A.E.E. Report F/17 dated 29 May 1926—production Blackburn Blackburn Mk I N9833 powered by one Napier Lion II engine giving 465 hp at 2,000 rpm and mounted on two 24 ft 2 in boat-built deck-landing floats, track 12 ft 6¼ in. Pilot: Flg Off A. R. Wardle.*

Production:

(a) *Blackburn R.1 Blackburn Mk I*
    Three prototypes and 30 production aircraft:

Requisitioned	Quantity	Serials
1922	3	N150–N152
1922	12	N9579–N9590
1923	6	N9681–N9686
June 1924	12	N9824–N9835

Notes on individual aircraft:
N9581 delivered Brough–Martlesham 28 April 1923, RAF Display 30 June 1923, sank in the Solent 2 January 1929; N9587 delivered Brough–Farnborough–Gosport 2 July 1923; N9589 dual trainer ('Bull') conversion; N9686 converted to Mk II; N9826 to No. 420 Flight from December 1924 to December 1925, then to No. 1 FTS, Leuchars; N9828 amphibian, later converted to standard Mk II; N9829 converted to Mk II, to No. 449 Flight, HMS *Furious* 1929; N9833 deck-landing floatplane; one Gosport-based crashed at Lee-on-Solent 4 September 1925.

(b) *Blackburn R.1A Blackburn Mk II*
Prototype conversion and 29 production aircraft.

Requisitioned	Quantity	Serials
1924	1	N150
January 1925	12	N9978–N9989
October 1925	12	S1046–S1057
December 1926	5	S1154–S1158

Notes on individual aircraft:
N9989 dual trainer ('Bull') conversion; S1045 lost overboard from *Furious* in 1930; S1047 coded 46; S1052 to No. 449 Flight in 1929, coded 21; S1056 performance trials at Martlesham, delivered to Gosport 12 November 1926; S1157 coded 45.

Yearly totals of Blackburn Mks I and II reconditioned at Brough:
1925 (8 aircraft); 1926 (9); 1927 (3); 1928 (1); 1929 (4).

Service Use:
(a) *Fleet Spotter Flights*
No. 422 Flight served in the Mediterranean aboard *Eagle* and on the China Station on *Argus* 1923–28.
No. 420 Flight, initially based at Gosport, served with the Home Fleet aboard *Furious* 1926–28.

(b) *Fleet Spotter Reconnaissance Flights*
No. 449 Flight served with the Home Fleet on *Furious* and aboard *Courageous* in the Mediterranean 1929–31.
No. 450 Flight served on the China Station aboard *Argus* and in the Mediterranean with *Courageous* 1929–31.

The Pellet in its original form with wooden airscrew, ready for the first launching at Brough, September 1923.

Blackburn Pellet

When Great Britain became host country for the 1923 Schneider Trophy contest as a result of H. C. Biard's victory at Naples in the Supermarine Sea Lion II the previous year, Blackburns decided to build a challenger and in March 1923 announced that a small, fast, single-seat flying-boat was being made ready.

Choice of configuration came naturally since an eminently suitable hull already existed in the shape of the unfinished Blackburn N.1B flying-boat N56, which was still in excellent condition despite the fact that it had lain in storage at Brough ever since November 1918. Furthermore it had been built to the same specification as the Supermarine Baby flying-boat which had sired the Sea King II military amphibian and its highly successful racing conversion renamed Sea Lion II. Work began at once on the design and construction of suitable racing mainplanes and the aircraft emerged as the Blackburn Pellet, with a narrow-gap, single-bay, sesquiplane wing structure mounted directly on top of the circular-section hull and strut-braced to its sides. The wings were rigged with dihedral on the upper mainplane only and this also carried the large push-rod operated ailerons. Wooden wing tip floats (at this stage almost certainly those first built for the N.1B) were bolted to the lower mainplane directly beneath V-type interplane struts, and a system of N-struts amidships supported a 450 hp Napier Lion engine mounted on top of the upper centre section in a streamlined nacelle tailored for a smooth, close fit, the only projections being the stub exhausts and camshaft casings. The engine drove a large two-bladed wooden airscrew, which came uncomfortably close to the top of the hull and the back of the pilot's head, and was cooled by surface radiators fitting flush in the underside of the upper mainplane. The pilot's head was faired in by a streamlined headrest and a long, tapering windscreen which hinged forwards for access to the cockpit.

To ensure sufficient time for clearing up teething troubles and to enable him to become familiar with an untried prototype, R. W. Kenworthy stipulated that the Pellet should be available for practice flying by August 1923, a month before the race. Thus, on 23 July, it was allotted civil registration G-EBHF in readiness for the first flight, but in the event the company narrowly missed its target date and the Pellet was launched during the first days of September, when, immediately after leaving the Brough slipway it was caught by the tide, dipped the starboard wing tip float and slowly turned turtle, throwing Kenworthy into the water. Although only three weeks remained before the race Robert Blackburn was undaunted. He salvaged the machine and worked night and day with his dedicated band to strip the engine down to its smallest components, dry out the airframe, effect repairs and fit larger wing tip floats.

No time remained for another attempt to fly the Pellet at Brough, and the machine was sent by rail to Southampton and assembled at the works of the Fairey Aviation Co Ltd at Hamble. Bearing racing No. 6, it was launched from Fairey's slipway in the early dawn of 26 September 1923, the day before the race, and, although a great deal of water was shipped while taxying, it took off smartly enough. Once in the air, however, the Pellet proved excessively nose heavy and Kenworthy had to exert all his strength to prevent a dive. The situation was further complicated when the water in the engine cooling system boiled because of insufficient radiator area. A successful forced alighting was made on the sea south of the RAF seaplane base at

The Blackburn Pellet on the Hamble River after launching from Fairey's slipway on the morning of 26 September 1923. (*Topical Press.*)

171

The Pellet in Saunders' hangar at Cowes later on 26 September 1923, with work in progress on changing the airscrew and fitting the cylindrical Lamblin radiator between the centre section struts. (*Flight Photo.*)

Calshot, but the Pellet drifted for an hour before a motor-boat from S. E. Saunders Ltd hove in sight to tow it to Cowes, Isle of Wight. Here, mechanics under Mr Newman worked through the night to bypass the wing radiators and to fit a large Lamblin radiator under the nacelle among the centre section struts. At the same time a two-bladed metal airscrew was fitted in place of the wooden original which had almost certainly suffered spray damage the day before.

The Pellet was ready with the engine running by 11.48 am next morning, with only minutes to spare before last launching time for the navigability and watertightness tests. It left Saunders' slipway without incident but, as Kenworthy opened up the Lion engine and began his take-off run down the River Medina, he was baulked by a small rowing boat, and the aircraft began to porpoise, hitting the sea with a series of resounding smacks. It then became prematurely airborne in a semi-stalled condition, turned slowly to the right under the torque of the airscrew, touched with the starboard float, stuck in its nose, turned right over and dived below the surface.

Grave fears arose for Kenworthy's safety, for he had been trapped in an airlock inside the hull and it was not until 61 seconds later that he was able to wriggle clear of the cockpit and bob to the surface. He then climbed on top of the overturned machine and was picked up by the motor-launch *Vivid*. The wreck itself was brought ashore during the night by engineer Newman and taken back to Saunders' hangar.

172

SPECIFICATION AND DATA

Manufacturers: The Blackburn Aeroplane and Motor Co Ltd, Olympia Works, Roundhay Road, Leeds, and Brough Aerodrome, East Yorks.

Power Plant: One 450 hp Napier Lion

Dimensions: Span (upper) 34 ft 0 in   (lower) 29 ft 6 in
              Length 28 ft 7 in   Height 10 ft 8 in

Weights: All-up weight 2,800 lb

Estimated performance: Maximum speed 140 knots

Production: One aircraft only, Works Order number not recorded, allotted civil marking G-EBHF in the name of the Blackburn Aeroplane and Motor Co Ltd by Certificate of Registration No. 1008 dated 23 July 1923. First flown at Hamble 26 September 1923, sank in take-off accident at Cowes, IOW, 27 September 1923.

Sequence shots of the Pellet bouncing off the Solent on 27 September 1923, with only seconds to go before disaster. The small hub identifies the metal airscrew with which it had been fitted overnight.

173

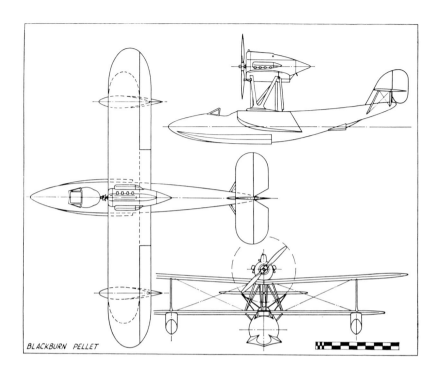

BLACKBURN PELLET

174

The second Leeds-built tandem-cockpit T.3 Velos for Greece, mounted on wooden float undercarriage No. 12, ready for demonstration at Brough on 28 October 1925. *(Flight Photo 3273.)*

Blackburn T.3 Velos

The Velos was a two-seat development of the Dart and, being the third in the firm's series of torpedo aircraft, was designated T.3. Powered by a 450 hp Napier Lion V, it was designed by Maj F. A. Bumpus in 1925 to meet a Greek Navy requirement for a coastal defence type having torpedo-dropping, reconnaissance, bombing and training capabilities. The Velos was essentially a seaplane which, if the need arose, could be fitted with a wheeled undercarriage and thus differed in concept from the Dart which was regarded as a deck-landing type easily convertible to seaplane.

The aircraft was structurally identical to the Dart but was wired for night flying and carried a considerable additional load of specialized equipment, including slings in the top centre section, electric intercom between pilot and gunner, 200-mile range W/T gear, and bomb racks.

The first and second of a batch of Velos machines—believed four—built in the Olympia Works for the Greek Navy and identified by wooden float undercarriages numbered 11 and 12, were flown at Brough on 28 October 1925 before a distinguished gathering which included the Italian Air Attaché, Gen Guidoni, who in 1912 had been the first pilot ever to drop a torpedo, when he released it from a float-equipped Farman biplane; Air Vice-Marshal Sir Vyell Vyvyan; the US Army Attaché, Maj Davidson, who flew up from Stag Lane in his American Army DH-4B*; Maj Shirley Kingsley of the

* See the author's *De Havilland Aircraft since 1915*, page 59.

River Plate Aviation Co; and officers of the British, Australian, Argentine and Spanish Navies. During a torpedo demonstration with the second aircraft, by Flt Lt N. H. Woodhead, DSC, accompanied in the rear seat by Capt T. A. Gladstone of Blackburn's subsidiary, the North Sea Aerial and General Transport Co Ltd, a precision drop was made close enough inshore to wet the spectators and demonstrate the need for the strengthened, splash-resistant bottom fitted to the Velos fuselage. Despite its size and loading, the aircraft was very manoeuvrable in the air, and Maj J. D. Rennie's work in designing the long, boat-built wooden floats and special airscrew was evident when the machine left the water fully loaded in about 20 sec. When alighting, the fine tapering stern of each float sank cleanly into the water and the machine ran smoothly without porpoising.

During the second half of 1925 the Blackburn company had taken over and completed the construction of the Greek National Aircraft Factory at Old Phaleron, obtained a five year contract to run it and, using local labour, began to manufacture further Velos aircraft. The two machines demonstrated at Brough were therefore built with identical cockpits and dual controls for shipment to Athens for training purposes prior to the delivery of the first all-Greek aircraft. The others were fully equipped for coastal defence work, with a Lewis gun on a flush-mounted Scarff ring behind the pilot. The second cockpit was also fitted with a full set of dual controls but was used only on bombing, reconnaissance or instructional sorties. When carrying a torpedo, the Velos was flown as a single-seater.

For bombing, part of the torpedo gear was replaced by a rack unit to carry four 230-lb bombs connected to selector levers permanently installed in the rear cockpit, and a sighting slot was provided close to the starboard side of the fuselage to give a good forward and downward view. When used for armed, long-range reconnaissance, the normal fuel (66-gallon main tank at the

The Velos used at Brough for trials with the prototype metal floats, showing also the original Scarff ring position. It became G-AAUM in 1931.

176

The first Greek-built T.3A Velos, T 11, taking off from Tatoi on 18 March 1926 for Greek Navy acceptance trials, piloted by Col the Master of Sempill.

C.G. and a 15-gallon gravity tank in the centre section) was supplemented by two cylindrical 45-gallon tanks under the lower mainplane to give an additional 1½ hours endurance at full power. Fuel was fed from these to the gravity tank by a duplicated system of hand- and wind-operated pumps.

It is evident that at least one operational Velos was not delivered but remained at Brough for trials with the duralumin floats which Blackburns offered as an optional alternative to overcome water soakage and shrinkage in hot climates. They followed closely the lines of their wooden counterparts but were fitted with large rectangular water rudders and fittings for a simple lever-type beaching trolley.

Further trials with this machine showed that the upper mainplane somewhat restricted the field of fire of the aft gun, and for this reason the Greek-built machines, designated T.3A, differed externally from their British equivalent in having the rear cockpit built up to raise the Scarff ring, and by having a slightly larger radiator to improve engine cooling in high-temperatures.

The maiden flight of T 11, the first Greek-built Velos landplane, took place on 17 March 1926, when Col the Master of Sempill flew it out of a small piece of rough ground behind the Old Phaleron factory to the military aerodrome at Tatoi, 15 km away on the other side of Athens, in readiness for acceptance trials, which he flew next day in the presence of Robert Blackburn and Gen Pangalos, the Greek Prime Minister. The second machine, T 12, was a seaplane on wooden floats first flown from the waters of Phaleron Bay by the same pilot on 31 March. The remainder were air tested by Maj H. G. Travers, DSC, who delivered five more, including T 15, to the adjoining naval base by January 1927. Production terminated at the twelfth aircraft, and up to the end of 1930 the factory had also reconditioned 13 Velos airframes including those built at Brough. Many were still in use in 1934.

177

The South American demonstrator at Brough, January 1927, showing the built-up rear cockpit, long-range tanks, modified metal floats and water rudders, and the Blackburn patent beaching trolley.

H. V. Worrall (*second from right*) in Brazil with the T.3A Velos demonstration aircraft in 1927. It became a civil trainer, G-EBWB, in 1928.

Early in 1927, H. V. Worrall, one of Blackburn's pilots, toured South America with a Leeds-built Velos fitted as a flying show-piece, with built-up rear gunner's cockpit, full torpedo gear, the long-range tank system, and the handsome streamlined production version of Maj Rennie's metal floats with smaller water rudders; but the tour was abortive and no orders were received from Brazil or any of the other South American governments who had had demonstrations. In 1928 it was converted into a tandem-cockpit seaplane trainer. Registered G-EBWB, it was the first of the type to be fitted with Handley Page slots, the first to have civil markings, and the first of six registered to the North Sea Aerial and General Transport Co Ltd for operation at the RAF Reserve School at Brough. It was followed in 1929 by four more, lettered G-AAAW to 'AZ, but, after Reserve seaplane training ended later in the year, they operated on wheeled undercarriages and were joined in 1930 by the sixth, registered G-AAUM. This was a conversion of the frustrated Greek machine, which had been used for the first metal-float trials, fitted with an old Napier Lion IIB normally found only in early production Darts, and re-certificated just three years after initial issue. When withdrawn from service at the end of 1932, all the Velos school machines were, with one exception, sold as scrap and their decaying hulks could be seen in several breakers' yards in Yorkshire right up to 1939.

The sole exception was G-AAAW which private owner Ian Parker acquired for £15 and flew home from Brough to Hooton in April 1933. A month later on 19 May he made the only known Velos flight to the south, landing at Heston for an overnight stop before proceeding to Brooklands next day to attend a display organized by the Guild of Air Pilots. The Velos is said to have consumed 63 gallons of petrol on the journey and afterwards to have flown to Northolt where it was eventually discovered in a closed hangar by Air Commodore A. H. Wheeler, trustee of the Shuttleworth Collection, who purchased it for a guinea after a previous offer of £1 had been refused!

Subsequently Wheeler, finding that 15 gallons of fuel remained in the tank, secured volunteers to help in starting the engine. One cylinder, anxious to prove that it was full of water, discharged it through the exhaust system and all over the man turning the starter. After two test flights Wheeler left for Old Warden on a flight that was not without hazard. In his words.

Compass-swinging the Velos trainer G-AAAX of the North Sea Aerial and General Transport Co Ltd, at Brough in 1930 by means of a power-driven tail trolley designed and made by Blackburns.

179

... 'The inside of the compass was covered in white froth like a Guinness, making it quite useless, and at 700 ft over Watford there was a colossal bang in the engine. Curiously enough it flew perfectly after this, having previously operated half as an internal combustion and half as a steam engine.' Regrettably, this largest and noisiest of all contemporary private aircraft was then broken up to provide aircraft grade timber for rebuilding Shuttleworth's Blériot and Deperdussin monoplanes. All that now remains is the Lion V engine No. 50108, refurbished and kept in exhibition condition by the vintage aero engine connoisseur, R. C. Shelley of Billericay, Essex.

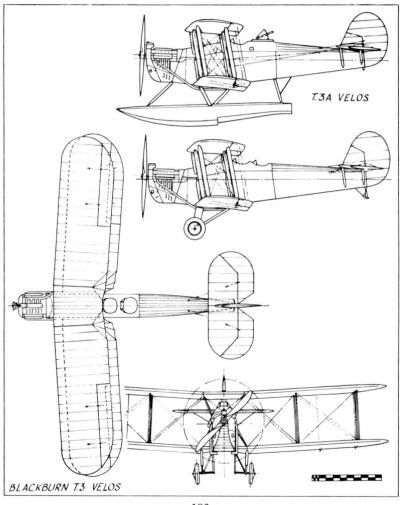

T.3A VELOS

BLACKBURN T.3 VELOS

180

SPECIFICATION AND DATA

Manufacturers: The Blackburn Aeroplane and Motor Co Ltd, Olympia Works, Roundhay Road, Leeds, and Brough Aerodrome, East Yorks.
  The Greek National Aircraft Factory, Old Phaleron, near Athens, Greece

Power Plants: One 450 hp Napier Lion IIB
  One 450 hp Napier Lion V

Dimensions: Span 48 ft 6 in   Length 35 ft 6 in
  Height 12 ft 3 in   Wing area 654 sq ft

Weights and Performance:
(a) *Torpedo versions*

	T.3 Velos		T.3A Velos	
	Landplane	Seaplane	Landplane	Seaplane
Tare weight	3,890 lb★	4,520 lb	3,765 lb	4,395 lb
All-up weight	6,200 lb★	6,830 lb	6,370 lb	7,000 lb
Maximum speed	107 mph	101 mph	107 mph	100 mph
Cruising speed	73 mph	70 mph	71 mph	75 mph
Initial climb	650 ft/min	480 ft/min	620 ft/min	460 ft/min
Absolute ceiling	16,600 ft	12,200 ft	16,000 ft	11,700 ft
Service ceiling	14,100 ft	9,700 ft	13,400 ft	9,200 ft
Endurance	4½ hr	3¾ hr	4½ hr	3½ hr

  ★ Civil trainer G-AAAX: Tare weight 3,945 lb   All-up weight 6,300 lb

(b) *T.3A Velos—other roles*

	Bomber		Reconnaissance	
	Landplane	Seaplane	Landplane	Seaplane
Tare weight	3,890 lb	4,520 lb	3,885 lb	4,715 lb
All-up weight	6,200 lb	6,830 lb	5,700 lb	6,330 lb
Maximum speed	107 mph	101 mph	108 mph	101 mph
Cruising speed	70 mph	73 mph	67 mph	71 mph
Initial climb	650 ft/min	480 ft/min	720 ft/min	536 ft/min
Absolute ceiling	16,600 ft	12,200 ft	18,500 ft	13,700 ft
Service ceiling	14,100 ft	9,700 ft	16,000 ft	11,100 ft
Endurance	4½ hr	3¾ hr	8½ hr	6½ hr

Production:
(a) *Built at Leeds for the Greek Navy*
  Total believed to be four comprising T.3 Velos seaplanes fitted initially with float sets Nos. 11–14 in 1925–26. One built to Works Order 9762/1, fitted with gun ring and used for prototype metal float trials was issued with a Certificate of Airworthiness on 28 January 1927 and converted into a civil trainer G-AAUM in 1931.

(b) *Built at the Greek National Aircraft Factory*
  Twelve T.3A Velos land and seaplanes commencing T 11 in March 1926.

G   181

Velos G-EBWB in the scrap-yard at York Road, Leeds, in 1934. (*E. J. Riding Photo.*)

(c) *Built at Leeds for the South American tour*

One aircraft only to Works Order 9593/1 built 1926 as prototype T.3A Velos with production metal floats. Converted to civil trainer G-EBWB in 1928.

(d) *For the North Sea Aerial and General Transport Co Ltd*

G-EBWB   Works Order 9593/1, built for South American tour 1926, C. of A. issued 28 March 1928. To scrap yard in York Road, Leeds, December 1933, still recognizable in 1939.

G-AAAW   Works Order 1440/1, C. of A. issued 23 April 1929, sold 28 April 1933 to I. R. Parker, Hooton. Broken up at Old Warden Aerodrome, Biggleswade, Beds., in 1935.

G-AAAX   Works Order 1440/2, C. of A. issued 9 May 1929. To scrap yard in York Road, Leeds, after C. of A. expiry 10 May 1933, still recognizable in 1939.

G-AAAY   Works Order 1440/3, C. of A. issued 22 May 1929. Scrapped at Bentley, Yorks., after C. of A. expiry 31 March 1933.

G-AAAZ   Works Order 1440/4, C. of A. issued 9 October 1929. Scrapped at C. of A. expiry 15 March 1932.

G-AAUM   Built 1926 to Greek order but used for metal float trials. Works Order 9762/1, C. of A. issued 28 January 1927. Converted to civil trainer 1930, C. of A. re-issued 2 January 1931. Scrapped after C. of A. expiry 22 January 1934.

P. W. S. Bulman demonstrating the first Cubaroo I biplane, N166, at Brough on 21 August 1924.

Blackburn T.4 Cubaroo

The Cubaroo was an extremely large biplane designed by Maj F. A. Bumpus, and built in the Olympia Works during 1923–24, to meet Air Ministry Specification 16/22 (D. of R. Type 9) for a long-distance coastal defence aircraft capable of carrying a 21-inch torpedo or equivalent bomb load. The Avro company also tendered to this specification with their Avro 557 Ava* (two 650 hp Rolls-Royce Condor III), but the Blackburn contender was designed round one of the six prototype 1,000 hp Napier Cub sixteen-cylinder water-cooled engines which the Ministry had ordered in 1919 at a cost of £10,000 each, one of which had already flown successfully in the Avro 549 Aldershot II* in 1922.

First intimation that such a project was in hand came in an article accompanying a set of drawings in the Italian *Notiziarro di Aeronautica* late in 1923; yet in this country the machine was very firmly on the secrets list. It remained shrouded in mystery until a privileged party representing the Press, the Air Ministry and the Governments of Spain, Japan, Greece and the United States, were invited to inspect it on the ground and see it in the air at Brough on 21 August 1924.

With a span of 88 ft, the Cubaroo was probably the largest aeroplane in the world in its day, yet its tubular-steel structure closely paralleled that of the Swift–Dart–Blackburn family. It was constructed round a central fuselage unit built integral with two tubular-steel girders which projected on each side to carry two separate undercarriages and form the front and rear spars of the bottom centre section. The two-bay mainplanes were of medium high-lift section having a constant chord of 11 ft 6 in and enough dihedral and sweepback on the outer panels to ensure adequate lateral stability. To cut down on the space needed to house so large a machine, the outer panels were hinged to the centre section and folded back along the sides of the fuselage, with a

* See the author's *Avro Aircraft since 1908*, pages 170 and 207.

Detail view of N166 showing the folding wing arrangement and the slender rear fuselage. (*Flight Photo 2737.*)

jury strut supporting the inboard ends of the top and bottom front spars. The undercarriages were each fitted with a pair of 4-ft diameter Palmer wheels and were spaced well apart with an unobstructed space between for the torpedo and its heating gear. The rear fuselage was supported on a bungee-sprung tail skid, braced to the bottom longerons by two slanting struts and to the top by two others lying parallel with and external to the fuselage sides. A biplane tail unit, chosen for its structural advantages, was equipped with two normal fins with balanced rudders, a large additional central rudder, horn-balanced elevators and variable-incidence tailplanes.

Pilot and navigator sat side by side in an open cockpit ahead of the leading edge of the upper mainplane and over the rear part of the engine where the fuselage tapered sharply away on each side to give a clear downward view, as on the dual trainer version of the Blackburn Blackburn. The Napier Cub engine, weighing more than a ton, was built in the form of an X, with four cylinders in each row, but was not symmetrical in front elevation. The upper banks were closer than the lower because they were inclined at $26\frac{1}{4}$ degrees to the vertical, whereas the lower banks lay $26\frac{1}{4}$ degrees below the horizontal. This feature enabled the designer to enclose the engine completely within the nose except for the lower cylinder blocks and part of the exhaust system. Despite its size and complexity, the Cub could be started from cold in under two minutes by means of a 5 hp gas starter installed in the engine bay. In front of the pilot's windscreen was a curved radiator conforming to the rounded shape of the nose and providing a convenient means of warming the cockpit in cold weather.

All the crew members were in direct communication with one another, and a hatch in the floor of the cockpit gave access to an enclosed cabin lit by circular portholes and equipped with a chart table and wireless telegraphy gear. The floor of the cabin incorporated a bomb-aimer's window and provided prone positions for two gunners firing through rotating trap doors in the fuselage adjacent to the lower wing root fittings. These guns had a clear field of fire under the tail, since aft of the cabin the fuselage was of triangular

184

section like the Blackburn monoplanes of old. A passage led aft from the cabin to a ladder giving access to an elevated gun ring on top of the rear fuselage with a wide field of fire over the tail unit.

In RAF colours and bearing serial N166 in the group reserved for experimental naval aircraft, the Cubaroo was first flown at Brough in the summer of 1924 by Flt Lt P. W. S. Bulman, MC, AFC, well known in later years as chief test pilot of Hawker Aircraft Ltd, but at that time a Service test pilot at the RAE, Farnborough. He had done a good deal of research-flying with the Cub-engined Avro Aldershot, and at the Brough demonstration of 21 August 1924 he took off towards the river in an 8 knot wind, and in the words of an onlooker '. . . the Cubaroo floated into the air in half the available distance'.

Fully equipped, the great machine carried nearly 2 tons of fuel and a 3½-ton useful load (including a 1½-ton torpedo) at a maximum loaded weight of nearly 9 tons, yet Bulman reported that its imaginative control surface design made it no more tiring to fly than a D.H.9A and its manoeuvrability was reminiscent of a Bristol Fighter. After a series of slow and fast runs and impressive climbing turns, he concluded the demonstration with a gentle wheel landing and came to rest in 100 yards.

Following the precedent of the little Pellet flying-boat the year before, the large two-bladed wooden airscrew was eventually changed for a Leitner-Watts three-bladed, all-metal, adjustable-pitch model made by Metal Propellers Ltd. The Cubaroo then went to Martlesham Heath for official performance trials.

A second Cubaroo, N167, first flown in 1925, was almost identical to the first, but the radiator was quite flat and stood up almost vertically above the airscrew shaft. Fitted from the outset with a three-bladed metal airscrew, it made a brief appearance at the Hendon RAF Display of 27 June 1925, where it dwarfed all other aircraft and formed exhibit No. 6 in the New Types Park.

Cubaroo I N166 at Martlesham Heath, with three-bladed metal airscrew and the torpedo in position. (*Imperial War Museum Photo MH. 5389.*)

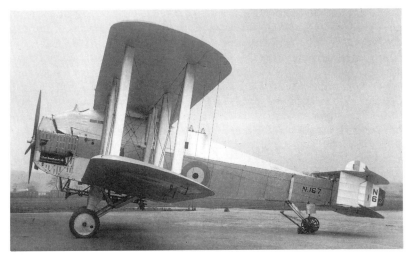

The second Cubaroo I, N167, at first roll-out in 1925 with Napier Cub engine, showing the angular shape imparted to the nose by the flat radiator.

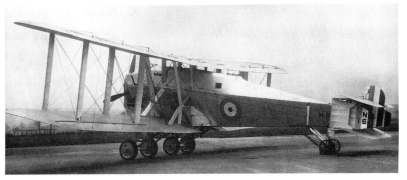

View of N167 showing the rotating gun position in the fuselage adjacent to the wing root. The two-wheel tail dolly was purely for ground handling.

In the fly-past it was nothing short of impressive, floated off the ground with its usual equanimity and thundered past the Royal Enclosure belching flames and smoke as unburned mixture ignited on the exhaust pipes as the pilot throttled back.

Later in 1925, the Air Ministry abandoned its large single-engined bomber policy in favour of twin-engined reliability. To counter this move Blackburns made detailed design studies for twin-engined versions of the Cubaroo powered by Rolls-Royce Condor engines. General arrangement drawings dated September 1927 show that three possibilities were considered, the

T.4A Cubaroo II with two 650 hp Rolls-Royce Condor IV direct-drive water-cooled engines, with frontal radiators, mounted in tubular-steel nacelles in the mid-gap position directly above the undercarriages; the T.4B Cubaroo III, similar but with geared Condor IIIs; and the T.4C Cubaroo IV with direct-drive Condor IVs in nacelles lowered on to the bottom wing.

None of these were built, and the two Cubaroo I prototypes ended their days as experimental hacks, N166 being delivered from Kenley to Farnborough for this purpose by Flt Lt Hilton on 2 February 1925. It was employed on engine, airscrew and wireless development work but, during a demonstration at Farnborough on 16 July that year, the port undercarriage collapsed, causing damage which evidently ended its career. N167 was still at Brough in June 1926 but in the following year was employed as a flying testbed for the 1,100 hp Beardmore Simoon Mk I eight-cylinder, inline inverted water-cooled engine.

SPECIFICATION AND DATA

Manufacturers: The Blackburn Aeroplane and Motor Co. Ltd, Olympia Works, Roundhay Road, Leeds, and Brough Aerodrome, East Yorks.

Power Plants: (T.4 Cubaroo I)
　　　　　One 1,000 hp Napier Cub
　　　　　One 1,100 hp Beardmore Simoon Mk I
　　　　　(T.4A Cubaroo II project dated 21 September 1927)
　　　　　Two 650 hp Rolls-Royce direct drive Condor IV
　　　　　(T.4B Cubaroo III project dated 16 September 1927)
　　　　　Two 650 hp Rolls-Royce geared Condor III
　　　　　(T.4C Cubaroo IV project dated 21 September 1927)
　　　　　Two 650 hp Rolls-Royce direct drive Condor IV

Dimensions: Span 88 ft 0 in　　Length 54 ft 0 in　　Height 19 ft 4 in

Weights and Performance:

	T.4 Cubaroo I Torpedo or bombs	T.4A, T.4B and T.4C projects	
		Torpedo only	Bombs only
Tare weight	9,632 lb	6,200 lb	8,146 lb
Military Load	—	5,290 lb	2,790 lb
All-up weight	19,020 lb	21,617 lb	21,487 lb
Maximum speed	115 mph	105 mph	105 mph
Absolute ceiling	11,800 ft	11,600 ft	11,600 ft
Maximum range	1,800 miles	740 miles	740 miles

Production: Two T.4 Cubaroo I aircraft only:
　　　　　N166　Completed July 1924 with Napier Cub engine, damaged beyond repair at Farnborough 16 July 1925.
　　　　　N167　Completed in 1925 with Napier Cub, later re-engined with experimental Beardmore Simoon Mk. I.

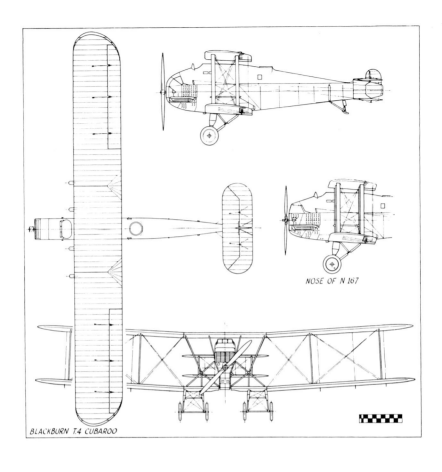

NOSE OF N 167

BLACKBURN T.4 CUBAROO

188

The Blackburn Bluebird I prototype with 1,100 cc Blackburne Thrush radial.
(*Flight Photo 3039.*)

Blackburn L.1 Bluebird I

In Robert Blackburn's view, side-by-side seating in light aircraft was not only more sociable than the usual tandem arrangement but was essential for effective flying instruction. This opinion, given practical effect in his 1919 Sidecar monoplane, was reaffirmed when he approved the same arrangement for the company's entry for the Air Ministry low-powered two-seater trials held at Lympne from 29 September to 4 October 1924. This was the Blackburn Bluebird I designed by A. C. Thornton and built under his personal supervision in the Olympia Works. With commendable foresight the Bluebird was designed from the outset as a robust instructional or touring machine rather than a competition freak and, although the rules limited engine capacity to 1,100 cc, it was stressed to take engines of much greater power.

In front elevation the Bluebird's fat and distinctive fuselage was square with rounded corners, and was made in two sections. The plywood-covered front portion was built round two rigid spruce plywood and steel box frames, but the rear fuselage was a fabric-covered, wire-braced structure consisting of four longerons with spruce struts, all joints being reinforced with three-ply and duralumin gusset plates. Although the seats were side by side in a single cockpit, the occupants' heads were separated by a strip of decking, necessitating deep individual entry doors on each side. Dual controls consisted of two parallel-acting rudder bars and a single control column placed centrally.

To satisfy the rules of the competition, the fabric-covered, single-bay wings were made to fold, and were built up on orthodox lines with two spruce spars and Warren girder ribs, internal drag-bracing being of duralumin tubing and 4 B.A. steel tie rods. They were rigged with slight stagger, 3 degrees of dihedral and 6 degrees of sweepback, and the interplane struts, also of duralumin tubing, were taper-pinned into metal sockets. Elevator and rudder control cables were routed vertically upwards behind the cockpit to emerge via a bank of pulleys and run externally rearwards along the fuselage. The undercarriage was of the simplest kind, with a transverse axle in an auxiliary aerofoil fairing supported by two rubber-in-compression legs projecting vertically from the root end fittings of the lower wing. There was no splay-out since the width of the fuselage imparted a wide enough track.

For the Lympne Trials the Bluebird was powered by a 1,100 cc Blackburne (with an 'e') Thrush three-cylinder, direct-drive radial engine giving about 37 hp and built by Burney and Blackburne Engines Ltd of Bookham, Surrey. It drove a metal airscrew and was mounted on a triangulated structure of steel tubes bolted to the fireproof bulkhead with the thrust line inclined slightly upwards. Fuel was gravity fed from a semi-cylindrical $4\frac{1}{2}$-gallon tank above the top centre section.

The qualities gaining highest marks in the competition—a maximum speed in excess of 60 mph combined with ability to fly slowly and maintain full controllability below 45 mph—were precisely those necessary in a deck-landing aircraft. The Blackburn company was, of course, very experienced in this field, and when the Bluebird emerged as a miniature Dart with the same T.64 wing section and folding capability, its chances in the competition were rated highly. Although pushed aside from time to time so as not to hold up Dart production at the Olympia Works, the Bluebird was finished on time and carried its competition No. 12, but engine teething troubles prevented A. G. Loton, CFI, of the Brough RAF Reserve School, from taking it to Lympne. As late as October 1924 the Thrush engine was still not giving

The Bluebird I re-engined with the Armstrong Siddeley Genet I engine in readiness for the Lympne Trials of September 1926.

190

full power but nevertheless the Bluebird performed well at Brough, where take-off and landing runs were a measured 150 ft. At this stage the competition fuel tank was replaced by one of aerofoil shape under the top centre section, the nationality mark G replaced No. 12 on the rudder, the machine was painted up with its full registration marks, G-EBKD, and an application made for a Certificate of Airworthiness. Performance trials for this were made at Brough by Flt Lt Gray, an RAE pilot, on 19 January 1926.

As predicted, even the best of the 1,100 cc Lympne machines were obviously unsatisfactory for touring or instruction, and this led the *Daily Mail* to sponsor a similar competition at Lympne on 10–17 September 1926 and to devise rules which encouraged sturdy airframes but imposed a weight limitation of 170 lb on the engines. Certification of the Bluebird prototype with Thrush engine was therefore abandoned, and the machine was promptly fitted with one of the first of the new Armstrong Siddeley Genet I five-cylinder radial engines driving a two-bladed wooden airscrew and giving a full 60 hp. The decking strip was removed from between the occupants, and the cockpits were staggered slightly in order to give the seat width called for in the competition. The pilot's seat on the port side was now somewhat behind that of the passenger, making it necessary to replace the shared control column by duplicated controls.

The Bluebird was first flown at Brough in this form by Flt Lt N. H. Woodhead on 4 June 1926 and the C. of A. was issued three months later. For the 1926 trials it was doped silver and blue and carried the competition No. 1, the pilot being Sqn Ldr W. H. Longton, DFC, AFC, who had the misfortune to bend an undercarriage fitting slightly in a landing test. The stewards of the meeting refused to allow even trivial replacements and the Bluebird had to be withdrawn.

Set on demonstrating the complete dependability of his mount and its superiority over the machines still left in the competition, Longton spent the whole of 14 and 15 September incessantly lapping the 12½-mile Lympne–Postling–Hastingleigh circuit. He deliberately flew low over the stewards' tent on every lap, covered 800 miles in the two days, and only landed for fuel and refreshments at three-hourly intervals. This splendid performance was rounded off on 18 September, the day after the end of the trials, when Longton and the Bluebird I scored a notable victory over 20 other entries in the 75-mile Grosvenor Trophy Race, averaging 84·95 mph over six laps of the 12½-mile course. At the end of the meeting it was flown back to Brough via Croydon and Manchester.

Air racing successes brought valuable publicity to a new type of aeroplane in those days, and the Bluebird's reputation was further enhanced by a win in the Yorkshire Aeroplane Club's 25-mile Open Handicap from Sherburn-in-Elmet to Selby, Tadcaster and return 2 October 1926. Two months later G-EBKD became one of the first of the new generation of light aeroplanes to cross the English Channel when an RAF officer used it for a honeymoon trip from Croydon to Le Bourget via Lympne and Beauvais on 1–2 December.

He returned on 12–13 December via Abbeville and Lympne after a trouble free trip in poor visibility, but recommended an increase in the wheel track for taxying over rough ground.

These performances persuaded Robert Blackburn in the following year to enter the machine for the Killjoy Trophy Race and the Holiday Final Handicap at the Easter Meeting held at Ensbury Park Racecourse, Bournemouth, during 15–18 April 1927. Two local hotels, the Westover and the Central, entered it in the Business Houses, and Hotels and Restaurants Association Handicaps, respectively. Thus on 6 April W. H. Longton flew from Netheravon to Sherburn-in-Elmet in an RAF D.H.9A and motored over to Brough with the Bluebird's designer, A. C. Thornton, for tuning and practice flights. The machine now had a Fairey-Reed metal airscrew, the auxiliary aerofoil was removed from the undercarriage, and the whole cockpit was faired over to leave only a small opening on the port side, with a streamlined fairing behind the pilot's head. A week later Longton flew it to Bournemouth where, on Good Friday, 15 April, it was riddled with shot from the ground as it passed over the village of West Parley during practice laps of the circuit. Fortunately Longton was unhurt and the following day won his heat

W. H. Longton taxying out for the Bournemouth Business Houses Handicap on 16 April 1927. Although arranged as a single-seater, the staggered seating is clearly visible. (*Flight Photo.*)

in the Business Houses Handicap at an average speed of 83·5 mph and was only just beaten in the final by A. B. Youell in the Avro 548 G-EBAJ.

The machine took part in the Hampshire Air Pageant at Hamble on 15 May and was again entered for four races at the Bournemouth Whitsun Meeting. It was allotted racing No. 2, and the large cylindrical fuel tank was replaced by one fitting closely to the underside of the top centre section. On 6 June 1927, however, last day of the meeting, it was in collision with the Westland Widgeon III flown by Westland's pilot L. P. Openshaw, both he and Longton being killed when the machines crashed and burned.

SPECIFICATION AND DATA

Power Plants: One 1,100 cc Blackburne Thrush
One 60 hp Armstrong Siddeley Genet I

Dimensions: Span (extended) 28 ft 3 in★ (folded) 9 ft 8 in
Length 21 ft 8 in Height 7 ft 11 in
Wing area 243 sq ft

★ 28 ft 0 in with Genet I engine.

Weights and Performance:

	Thrush	Genet I	Lympne trials 1926
Tare weight	495 lb	705 lb	721 lb
All-up weight	875 lb	1,150 lb	1,300 lb
Maximum speed	74 mph	85 mph	—
Cruising speed	60–65 mph	70 mph	—

Production: One prototype aircraft only with 1,100 cc Blackburne Thrush, allotted
civil markings G-EBKD in the name of Robert Blackburn by Certificate of
Registration No. 1118 dated 27 September 1924. Modified 1926 under Works
Order 9803/1 to take the 60 hp Armstrong Siddeley Genet I; Certificate of Airworthiness No. 1026 issued 4 September 1926; crashed and burned out following
collision with Westland Widgeon III G-EBPW at Bournemouth 6 June 1927.

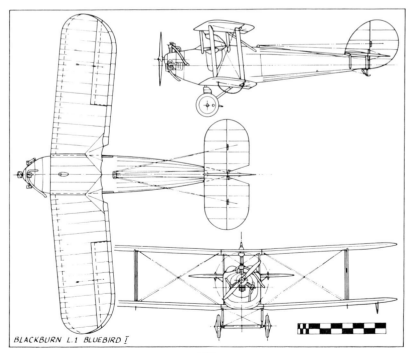

BLACKBURN L.1 BLUEBIRD I

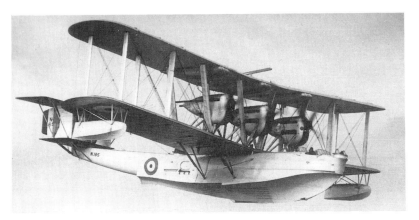

Flt Lt H. G. Sawyer flying low at Cromer in N185, the white-hulled Iris I, on 29 September 1926. The projection over the centre engine was a retractable radio mast.

Blackburn R.B.1 Iris

As a result of experience of outsize aircraft structures gained with the great Cubaroo biplane, Blackburns commenced work in 1924 on a very large long-range reconnaissance flying-boat. It was designed by Maj J. D. Rennie to Air Ministry Specification R.14/24, was equipped with three engines to minimize the risk of a forced descent at sea and could maintain height fully loaded on any two.

The hull was of plywood-covered wooden construction and of good stream-lined form with a sharp two-step, vee bottom which gave exceptionally clean running on the water. The biplane wing structure consisted of a massive three-bay centre section mounted directly on top of the hull and braced to its sides by duplicated steel struts. To it were attached two-bay outer wing panels identical in appearance to those of the Dart, all wing construction being of the composite type with wooden spars and ribs braced internally by tubular duralumin drag struts and steel tie rods. The upper centre plane was similar, but tubular-steel main spars were used in the lower. Ailerons were fitted to all four wings, and large wooden wing tip floats were supported on short steel rods below the outboard interplane struts.

An enormous biplane tail unit of similar construction to the mainplanes had a 30 ft span upper plane which carried the elevator and a 15 ft span lower plane which was purely a variable-incidence tail trimming device moving under the control of a lever in the cockpit. Directional control was by three aerodynamically-balanced rudders.

194

The flying-boat was powered by three 650 hp Rolls-Royce Condor III water-cooled engines mounted between the wings as self-contained power units, each with its own oil tank, starting gear and Dart-type radiator shutters. They drove 12 ft 5 in diameter wooden airscrews. Mounted under the top centre section above each engine was a 302-gallon fuel tank fitted with a direct-reading fuel contents gauge visible from the cockpit. Fuel was gravity fed to a junction box in the lower centre section from which pipes led up to the three engines, and six cocks (one in each pipe), operable from within the hull, enabled the crew to maintain lateral trim when fuel did not drain equally from the two outboard tanks.

Two pilots sat side by side, 12 ft ahead of the mainplanes, in an open cockpit with full dual control. A similar cockpit (without controls) was situated immediately behind, with in-flight access to the rear gun position and to a large cabin in the hull equipped with navigator's chart table, W/T gear, four sleeping bunks and a small galley. In addition to the two rotatable ·303 Lewis Mk III guns, the machine could be fitted with two others outside the hull alongside the after portholes, and bomb racks under the wing roots with selective salvo gear for dropping two 520-lb, four 230-lb bombs or eight 20-lb practice missiles. The usual crew was five but, stripped of armament, the boat could have carried 3 crew and 18 passengers, and a quotation for a commercial version of this kind was sent to a Mr Barker in New York in December 1926.

Many of the components were built in the Olympia Works, but the hull was constructed at Brough where final assembly took place two years after commencement of designs. Painted white and bearing RAF serial N185, the machine was named Iris by Mrs Robert Blackburn prior to launching and first flight on 19 June 1926. After acceptance tests by an RAF crew, it was moored in the Humber and left next day for the MAEE, Felixstowe, where Flt Lt H. G. Sawyer, AFC, flew full performance trials during July and August. Inevitably the indefatigable Sir Samuel Hoare, Secretary of State for Air, was impatient to fly in it and arrangements were made for this to be combined with a public debut at Cromer. Thus, on 29 September 1926, the Iris was flown up from Felixstowe by Flt Lt Sawyer but the sea was too rough for a boat to go alongside and the pilot merely flew up and down the seafront using various engine combinations.

Water soakage in a large wooden flying-boat often amounted to several hundred pounds and work was already in progress on an all-metal hull before the wooden Iris had flown. Also designed by Maj Rennie, this was of rigid duralumin construction built up from widely-spaced transverse frames and longitudinal stringers, the frames being attached to a central keelson, with the result that the planing bottom was built integral with the hull with two steps and a deep, well-flared fore foot to keep down spray and give a clean and rapid take-off. It differed in detail from the wooden original in having small circular portholes to illuminate the cabin and a widened, upswept rear end to provide a firing position aft of the tail unit.

Iris II

After performance trials at Felixstowe which included twin-engined flying and tests in March 1927 with a servo device on the centre rudder, the Iris I prototype returned to Brough for the superstructure to be fitted to the new metal hull. The opportunity was also taken to fit improved metal wing tip floats on simplified strutting and to instal three 675 hp Condor IIIA geared engines in low-drag nacelles with chin radiators. To make way for a tail gunner, the centre rudder was removed, converted into a servo unit and moved forward into the position formerly occupied by its fin. It was linked to two new unbalanced outer rudders, but in an emergency the servo mechanism could be de-clutched by the pilot. To make the Iris independent of shore bases, a small duralumin dinghy, capable of carrying five people and weighing about 80 lb, was carried in an inverted position on the lower centre section.

Still numbered N185 but now designated R.B.1A Iris II, the machine was re-launched at Brough on 2 August 1927 and, after acceptance tests by Flt Lt Sawyer and his crew next day, left once more for Felixstowe.

On 12 August 1927, only ten days after re-delivery to the RAF, the Iris II

Rear views of N185 before and after conversion to Iris II to show the deletion of the centre rudder and the change of rear hull design to provide a tail gunner's position.

left Felixstowe in company with the Short Singapore I (N179) and Saunders Valkyrie (N186) prototype reconnaissance flying-boats on a 3,000-mile tour of Scandinavian capitals. The threefold purpose of the flight was to show the the flag in the North, to evaluate the boats under Service conditions and to convey Sir Samuel Hoare to the Air Traffic Exhibition which opened at Copenhagen on 20 August. Seen off by Robert Blackburn and flown by Sqn Ldr C. L. Scott, DSC, with Flt Lt W. E. Dipple as second pilot, the Iris got off cleanly in under half a minute and reached Oslo the same evening. It flew Sir Samuel to Copenhagen on the 19th and returned him to Felixstowe on the 24th before rejoining the Flight at Gdynia, the full itinerary being:

August 12	Felixstowe–Oslo	August	31	Danzig–Helsinki
19	Oslo–Copenhagen	September	5	Helsinki–Stockholm
24	Copenhagen–Felixstowe		7	Stockholm–Copenhagen
26	Felixstowe–Gdynia		11	Copenhagen–Felixstowe
27	Gdynia–Danzig			

The Iris II covered 300 miles from Oslo to Copenhagen in a heavy gale, and its seaworthiness compelled great admiration when it alighted at its destination in rough seas and rode out the storm at anchor. It was almost lost in a gale at Felixstowe early in 1928 and on 10 August was forced down off Exmouth with engine trouble, but nevertheless plans went ahead to study its behaviour under tropical conditions while flying Sir Philip Sassoon, Under Secretary of State for Air, and Air Commodore Sir Arthur Longmore on a tour of RAF stations in the Mediterranean and the Middle East. For this purpose two wicker chairs were fitted in the cabin, with a folding table for meals in the air, a Clyde cooker with two primus stoves was installed aft, and the large double cockpit behind the pilots was permanently faired over to leave only a small navigator's hatch on the port side which could be covered with a sliding panel.

Again piloted by Sqn Ldr Scott, this time assisted by Flt Lt Martin, the machine left Felixstowe on 27 September, picked up its passengers at Plymouth and left for l'Étang de Berre, Marseilles, next day. Operating at an all-up weight of 27,400 lb the normal fuel load was 680 gallons, but on this flight the full 960 were carried and the Iris weighed 30,350 lb at take-off, still well inside the 33,000 lb maximum gross weight at which it had flown on test at Felixstowe; on most stages of this flight, however, it carried only 700 gallons which reduced the take-off weight to 28,850 lb.

N185 proceeded via Naples and Athens to Aboukir, and six days later left for Alexandretta and Baghdad. After off-loading 100 gallons of fuel, in high temperature and no wind, it got off at a second attempt at an all-up weight of 28,070 lb, but although Scott climbed to 5,500 ft, storms prevented him from getting through the mountains. He succeeded next day, refuelled at Habbani-yah, picked up his passengers (who had gone ahead in a Fairey IIIF) at Basra and landed at Jask on 12 September with engine trouble. The homeward trip began at Karachi on 24 October, but more serious trouble with the star-board engine caused a seven-day delay at Jask while a replacement was flown

197

The Iris II N185 taxying on the River Humber and showing the curved chin radiators.

from Bombay. A duststorm necessitated a precautionary alighting on the Shatt al Arab, off Abadan, on 1 November, choked filters led to an alighting on the Tigris at Zeidan next day, and Scott had to taxi the last ten miles to Hinaidi. The flight eventually terminated at Calshot on 13 October. The Iris returned to Felixstowe next day having covered 11,360 miles in 125 hr 5 min flying time at an average ground speed of 92 mph, the full itinerary being:

September 27	Felixstowe–Plymouth	November 2	Abadan–Basra
29	Plymouth–Marseilles	3	Basra–Zeidan‡
30	Marseilles–Naples	4	Hinaidi–Habbaniyah
October 1	Naples–Athens	5	Habbaniyah–Alexandretta
2	Athens–Aboukir	6	Alexandretta–Aboukir
8	Aboukir–Alexandretta	7	Aboukir–Benghazi
11	Alexandretta–Hinaidi	8	Benghazi–Malta
12	Hinaidi–Basra	10	Malta–Naples
13	Basra–Henjam	11	Naples–Marseilles
14	Henjam–Jask*	12	Marseilles–Hourtin
15	Jask–Karachi	13	Hourtin–Calshot
24	Karachi–Jask†	14	Calshot–Felixstowe
November 1	Jask–Abadan		

* Engine trouble.   † Engine replacement.   ‡ Precautionary landing.

A fortnight later, on 28 November, N185 flew briefly with three-bladed wooden airscrews and in March 1929 made test flights on various combinations of two engines, but, there being no centre rudder, directional control proved less effective than that of the Iris I. It was detached from Felixstowe to search for the lost submarine *H 47* off Plymouth in June but returned in the following month for tests with two-bladed airscrews outboard and an 11 ft diameter four-blader on the centre engine. Later still, it was flown at an all-up weight of 27,358 lb with the centre engine removed.

On 10 October 1929, Flt Lt C. H. Cahill and the North Sea Aerial and General Transport Co's seaplane instructor, N. H. Woodhead, flew it up from Felixstowe and alighted on the Humber off Hedon, 10 miles east of Hull, to attend the official opening of the adjacent Hull Municipal Aerodrome.

198

Iris III

Impressed by the soundness of the Iris II design, the Air Ministry decided to equip one squadron with a developed version, issued Specification R.31/27 to cover it and called for a full-scale mock-up. This led to a contract being signed on 4 February 1928 for three improved boats designated R.B.1B Iris III to equip No. 209 (Flying Boat) Squadron RAF, which re-formed on 15 January 1930 at Mount Batten (formerly Cattewater), Plymouth, to operate them. The Iris III was essentially similar to its predecessor, but the super-structure, although fabric-covered, was built entirely of duralumin, the main-planes were of slightly greater aspect ratio, and narrow-chord servo tabs were fitted to the trailing edges of both rudders. Power was provided by three Condor IIIB engines in aerodynamically cleaner nacelles with radiators mounted vertically at the rear. Wing tip floats were again redesigned, over-load fuel tanks were slung under the lower wing roots, the central corridor was carried right through to the bow compartment to enable the pilots to leave their seats in flight, and additional portholes were provided in the cabin. Behind the pilots there was a navigator's compartment with chart table and sliding roof hatch, and aft of that again, on a lower level, was the W/T station, sleeping quarters for the officers and men, engineer's seat, cooker and col-lapsible dinghy stowage. A raised platform gave access to the midships gun. The tail gun position, provision for which was made in the Iris II, was now brought fully into use so that armament consisted of three ·303 Lewis Mk III guns on Scarff mountings. Bomb load was similar to that of the Iris II.

The prototype Iris III, N238, was launched at Brough on 21 November 1929 and first flown by Sqn Ldr C. A. Rea, an experienced flying-boat pilot on the staff of Boulton and Paul Ltd, Norwich. He was accompanied by Maj J. D. Rennie and the second pilot was N. H. Woodhead. After half an hour's local flying, N238 was handed over to an RAF crew and flown to the

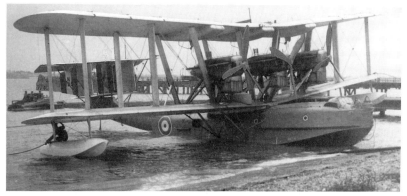

The Iris II beached for an engine change on 20 November 1928 at the conclusion of the Felixstowe trials with three-bladed wooden airscrews.
(*Crown Copyright Reserved.*)

MAEE, Felixstowe, where take-off, climb and two-engined performance were found to be markedly better than on the Iris II. By this time work on the two production boats was well advanced and the first, S1263 *Leda*, was test flown by Sqn Ldr Rea on the morning of 5 February 1930. Sqn Ldr J. H. O. Jones and Flt Lt L. B. Maxton of No. 209 Squadron then tried it out on the Humber and left at 10.20 hrs to fly right round the coast of Kent and down the Channel. They reached Mount Batten at 15.15 hrs at the end of a 500-mile non-stop flight. After crew training it left on 20 May for a navigation, photographic and public schools liaison exercise to the Isle of Man, Stranraer, Belfast, Tarbert, Bute, Tobermory, Skye and Stornoway, during which flights were given to the boys of King William College, IOM, and Campbell College, Belfast. S1263 returned to base on May 28 having flown 26 hr 15 min.

The prototype Iris III N238 was delivered from Felixstowe on 15 May but, being just off extended trials, needed considerable servicing and was not operational until 30 September. The third boat, S1264, arrived direct from Brough on 4 June and to it, therefore, fell the task, in August 1930, of air testing a new automatic pilot, later removed and fitted to the leader of three Short Rangoon flying-boats for their ferry flight to Basra.

During their period of service the Iris IIIs were the largest aircraft in the RAF and made a number of remarkable overseas flights. S1263 and S1264, flown respectively by Flt Lt Maxton and Sqn Ldr Jones, were detailed to leave Mount Batten for Reykjavik on 22 June 1930 to represent Great Britain at the Icelandic Parliament's millenary celebrations. They completed the first leg, to Stornoway non-stop, in $5\frac{1}{2}$ hr. Here S1263 was stranded with water-contaminated fuel but, carrying on alone on 24 June, S1264 made a re-fuelling stop at Thorshaven in the Faroes and reached Reykjavik in 11 hr flying time. The 630-mile return flight direct to Stornoway in $7\frac{1}{4}$ hr on 2 July was the first non-stop RAF flight between Iceland and Britain.

The prototype Iris III, N238, ready for launching at Brough in October 1929. This view shows the vertical radiators, redesigned ailerons and extra portholes.

S1263, the first production Iris III, flying along the Devon coast. The centrally-placed navigator's cockpit can be seen behind the pilots, and the redesigned lightweight radio mast lies retracted on the upper mainplane. (*Flight Photo 10029.*)

On 25 August Flt Lt Maxton with six crew flew S1264 non-stop to the Portuguese Navy seaplane base at Bom Succeso on the Tagus near Lisbon in 10 hr 50 min, making the first crossing of the Bay of Biscay by flying-boat. He continued to Gibraltar on 28 August and, leaving again on 1 September, returned to Mount Batten on 4 September. On 24 March 1931, Maxton and Jones left for l'Étang de Berre, Marseilles, in S1263 and S1264, to pick up Air Chief Marshal Sir John Salmond, Chief of Air Staff, and fly him to the Near East. They covered the 730 miles to Kalafrana, Malta, in $7\frac{3}{4}$ hr on 31 March and on 3 April made the first direct crossing of the Mediterranean from Malta to Sollum en route to Aboukir. Here S1263 was delayed by an engine change but, on 9 April, S1264 was flown to Lake Timsah on the Suez Canal before both boats returned via Crete, Athens, Naples and Marseilles. They flew overland to Hourtin via the Garonne valley on 14 April but gales and engine trouble in S1264 forced a diversion to St Nazaire. S1263 returned to base on 24 April, leaving S1264 to be warped through locks into St Nazaire's minor harbour where the centre and port engines were changed before it flew back to Mount Batten on 3 May.

The prototype Iris III crashed in Plymouth Sound on 4 February 1931 after too steep an approach during an instructional flight. It struck the water at 70 mph and broke up and sank, with the loss of nine lives, making it necessary to order a replacement. This was S1593 *Zephyrus* built in under 20 weeks and first flown at Brough on 25 June 1931. It was delivered to No. 209 Squadron on 6 July but differed significantly from the others, being battleship-grey instead of silver, and having bluff bows and an enlarged bow compartment ahead of the gun ring to take a 37 mm Coventry Ordnance Works quick-firing cannon. Flown by Sqn Ldr Jones, and accompanied by Flt Lt D. C.

201

Prance in S1263, its first operational flight was to East Loch Tarbert, in Argyll, on 16 September to survey 26 ports and anchorages in the Hebrides before returning to Mount Batten on 1 October.

Iris V

Progressive increases in fuel and equipment loads raised the all-up weight of the Iris from the 27,000 lb of the Mk I to over 30,000 lb for the fourth Mk III. As a result it now rode low in the water and both engine reliability and performance in the air were much reduced. To overcome these difficulties the company pointed out in July 1931 that the 675 hp Condor IIIBs of the Iris III could be replaced by 825 hp Rolls-Royce Buzzard IIMS moderately supercharged engines, with only minor alterations to the structure and without any appreciable weight penalty. Furthermore their ·552 reduction gears would make possible the use of large-diameter airscrews to take greater advantage of the take-off power, and streamlining could be improved by mounting new, low-drag nacelles of advanced design directly on the interplane struts.

A further improvement in power/weight ratio was considered possible by using aluminium instead of tinned-steel fuel tanks in conjunction with evaporatively-cooled Buzzards.

Late in 1931 the Air Ministry decided to act on the first of these suggestions and to modernize all three Iris IIIs, and the first, S1263, was flown from Mount Batten to Brough for the purpose on 18 November that year. Blackburn's estimate of one month for the conversion proved inaccurate, and it was not until 5 March 1932 that it flew with Buzzards as the first R.B.1D Iris V, with test pilot A. M. Blake at the controls. It proceeded at once to Felixstowe where flying qualities were adjudged outstanding, but the aircraft still sat low in the water and threw up considerable spray on take-off. It was redelivered to Mount Batten on 6 June and left on detachment to East Loch Tarbert on 16 June for Service trials with N240, the prototype Saro A.7.

Before finally entering service with No. 209 Squadron, S1263 spent July 1932 at Felixstowe where a Blackburn working party temporarily fitted an enclosed pilots' cabin of duralumin construction with sliding windows. At the normal loaded weight of 31,050 lb, maximum speed was increased by two knots but forward view was restricted and it was removed.

Meanwhile the Iris III S1264 had been damaged in collision with the fishing vessel *Erycina* in Plymouth Sound while taking off for Holyhead on 27 January 1932. It was left at its moorings, but there was undetected damage and it sank during the night, the subsequent salvage operations delaying until 4 March its shipment to Hull en route to Brough for repairs and Iris V conversion.

S1593 was flown to Brough for modification on 10 December 1932, and flew again as an Iris V in the hands of A. M. Blake on 31 March 1933 and was delivered to Mount Batten later the same day. Since it already had the 37-mm nose gun, it can properly be regarded as prototype of the Blackburn Perth

202

S1264 at Brough on 2 January 1933 after reconstruction and launching as an Iris V with the improved Buzzard installation. It was destroyed next day by a gale at Felixstowe.

that was to follow. Sometimes referred to as the R.B.3 or Iris VI, it flew with a number of experimental installations including Fairey-Reed metal airscrews, two-bladed outboard and four-bladed on the centre motor.

The second Iris V, S1264, re-launched at Brough, after rebuild, on 2 January 1933, left at once for Felixstowe but sank at its moorings in a gale next day and was written off. S1263, which survived it by only a few days, collided with a naval steam pinnace, with the loss of one life, while alighting in Plymouth Sound on 12 January. The Squadron was thus without aircraft, since S1593 did not return from Brough until 31 March. On 6 June it left for Malta by the 1930 Iris route, but take-off proved difficult even with normal fuel in conditions of high temperature and flat calm and it was eventually flown back, arriving at Mount Batten on 29 April 1934. On 12 June it was ferried to Brough for reconditioning and struck off squadron charge.

In response to an Air Ministry enquiry, designs had been submitted on 4 September 1933 for the completion of an experimental Iris with an entirely new superstructure to take four Junkers Jumo IVC.1 diesel engines. Two versions were envisaged, one with four engines in-line driving tractor airscrews, the other a twin-tandem arrangement. Parallel-chord centre sections were to be used with elliptically tapering outer wing panels, and it was expected to operate at a maximum permissible weight of 33,000 lb and cruise at 130 mph with sufficient fuel reserves to fly UK–Malta or non-stop across the Atlantic against normal headwinds.

This aircraft remained a project, but the surviving Iris V, S1593, on its return to Brough, was converted under Contract 354295/34 as a flying test bed for the 720 hp Napier Culverin Series I engine, the name given to the Jumo IVC built under licence at Acton by D. Napier and Son Ltd. The three Culverins were installed in close-fitting cowlings with controllable cooling gills and twin silenced exhausts which protruded from the pointed rear extremity of each nacelle. Long range no longer being of any consequence, the centre fuel tank was removed leaving two of 575-gallon capacity as on the new Blackburn Perths.

The first flight of S1593 with Culverins was made by A. M. Blake at Brough on 9 June 1937, and it was delivered to Felixstowe in the following September purely for engine trials and no aircraft performance measurements were made. It took from October 1937 to April 1938 to complete ground running, taxying and flight tests, first with two- and later with four-bladed airscrews. Tests were handicapped because the minimum engine speed of 800 rpm did not permit the flying-boat to taxi slowly enough to pick up moorings. In flight it was spectacular and on the climb white smoke persisted and became black and dense at 4,000 ft, leaving long trails as if three aircraft were skywriting in formation. Including the ferry flight from Brough, S1593 flew 15 hr 35 min with Culverins before its days ended kaleidoscopically when it became a test vehicle for anti-corrosive paints.

Iris IV

As early as December 1926 Maj Rennie had prepared a scheme for an Iris II powered by three 700 hp Armstrong Siddeley Leopard two-row air-cooled radials. He envisaged a saving of 2,100 lb structural weight coupled with improved performance, normal loaded weight being estimated at 25,520 lb. At an all-up weight of 29,000 lb with maximum overload fuel, still air range was expected to be as high as 1,250 miles.

No action was taken immediately, but, while work was in progress on the Iris III contract, Iris II N185 was sent back to the makers to be reworked and fitted with three of the latest 800 hp Leopard IIIs but with the centre engine reversed for investigations into the cooling of pusher radials and to compare the efficiency of tractor and pusher airscrews. Its first flight in this condition, as the R.B.1C Iris IV, was made on 6 May 1931 piloted by A. M. Blake, after which it went to Felixstowe where, in the following October, it took off on test in 60 sec at a record Iris all-up weight of 35,000 lb. After further work at

The final Iris V, S1593, at Brough in 1937 with Napier Culverin diesel engines.

Two views of N185 at Felixstowe in 1933, after conversion to Iris IV with
three Armstrong Siddeley Leopard III radial engines.

Brough it was redelivered to the MAEE in March 1932. From this conversion
can be traced the origins of a projected 14–28 passenger commercial development of the Iris considered in 1931, under the company designation C.B.1
(first commercial boat), which was to have had redesigned mainplanes of
RAF 28 section, greater range and speed and a maximum gross weight of
30,890 lb.

SPECIFICATION AND DATA

Manufacturers: The Blackburn Aeroplane and Motor Co Ltd, Olympia Works,
Roundhay Road, Leeds, and Brough Aerodrome, East Yorks.

Power Plants: (Iris I)   Three 650 hp Rolls-Royce Condor III
          (Iris II) Three 675 hp Rolls-Royce Condor IIIA
          (Iris III) Three 675 hp Rolls-Royce Condor IIIB
          (Iris IV) Three 800 hp Armstrong Siddeley Leopard III
          (Iris V)   Three 825 hp Rolls-Royce Buzzard IIMS
                    Three 720 hp Napier Culverin Series I

205

Dimensions: (Iris I, II and IV)

Span 95 ft 6 in	Length 66 ft 6⅛ in
Height 24 ft 6½ in	Wing area 2,461 sq ft

(Iris III and V)

Span 97 ft 0 in	Length 67 ft 4¾ in
Height 25 ft 6 in	Wing area 2,229 sq ft

Weights and Performance:
(a) *Iris I, Iris II and Iris IV*

	Iris I*	Iris II†	Iris IV
Tare weight	19,096 lb	18,930 lb	17,500 lb
Military load	2,802 lb	2,961 lb	6,720 lb
All-up weight	27,608 lb	27,358 lb	30,250 lb
Speed at sea level	115 mph	111 mph	130 mph
Cruising speed	86 mph	92 mph	100 mph
Initial climb	602 ft/min	450 ft/min	665 ft/min
Absolute ceiling	14,000 ft	13,100 ft	—
Service ceiling	11,850 ft	11,200 ft	10,350 ft
Range	560 miles	805 miles	505 miles

  * *Felixstowe Report F/21 dated September 1926.*   † *Felixstowe Report F/21F dated November 1928.*

(b) *Iris III and Iris V*

	Iris III*	Iris V†
Tare weight	19,048 lb	21,510 lb
Military load	2,719 lb	3,200 lb
All-up weight	29,489 lb	32,300 lb
Speed at sea level	118 mph	129 mph
Cruising speed	97 mph	103 mph
Initial climb	503 ft/min	660 ft/min
Absolute ceiling	12,800 ft	—
Service ceiling	10,600 ft	12,000 ft
Range	800 miles	985 miles

  * *Felixstowe Report F/54A dated 11 July 1930.*   † *Felixstowe Report F/93 dated May 1932.*

Production:
(i) *Contracts*

Ordered	Spec.	Contract	Qty.	Type	Serials
Jan. 1925	R.14/24		1	R.B.1 Iris I	N185
1927	R.14/24	740774/27	1	R.B.1A Iris II	N185
Feb. 1928	R.31/27	812143/27	3	R.B.1B Iris III	N238, S1263, S1264
1930		58821/30	1	R.B.1C Iris IV	N185
Feb. 1931	R.31/27	812143/27	1	R.B.1B Iris III	S1593
1932			3	R.B.1D Iris V	S1263, S1264, S1593

(ii) *Manufacture and delivery*
(*a*) Iris I

One aircraft only, N185, Condor III engines No. 360, 356 and 364, first flown 19 June 1926, to Felixstowe 20 June 1926.

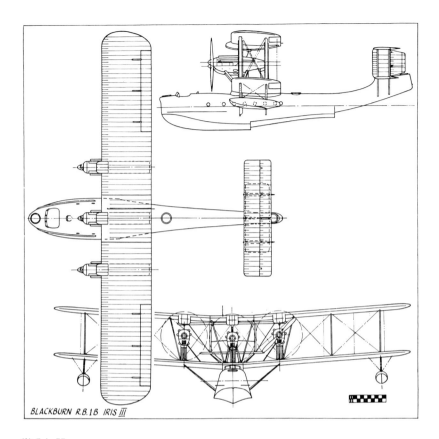

BLACKBURN R.B.1B IRIS III

(b) Iris II

One aircraft only, N185 converted from Iris I, first flown 2 August 1927; Condor IIIA engines No. 110, 368 and 16 fitted for return flight from the Middle East; overhauled at Brough October 1929 to Works Order 2458/1, converted to Iris IV in 1931.

(c) Iris III

Four aircraft only: (i) N238, Works Order 870/1, initially with Condor IIIB engines No. 438, 436 and 440, first flight and delivery to Felixstowe 21 November 1929, to Mount Batten 15 May 1930, crashed in Plymouth Sound 4 February 1931, reduced to produce. (ii) S1263 *Leda*, Works Order 870/2, first flight and delivery to Mount Batten 5 February 1930, to Brough for Iris V conversion 18 November 1931. (iii) S1264, unnamed, Works Order 870/3, first flight and delivery to Mount Batten 4 June 1930, sank in Plymouth Sound 27 January 1932, to Brough by sea for Iris V conversion 4 March 1932. (iv) S1593 *Zephyrus*, replacement aircraft to Works Order 3310/1, first flown 25 June 1931, to Mount Batten 6 July 1931, to Brough for Iris V conversion 10 December 1932.

(d) Iris IV

One aircraft only, N185 converted from Iris II, first flown 6 May 1931, to Felixstowe.

207

(*e*) Iris V

Three aircraft only: (i) S1263, first flight and delivery to Felixstowe 5 March 1932, to Mount Batten 6 June 1932, wrecked in Plymouth Sound 12 January 1933. (ii) S1264, first flight and delivery to Felixstowe 2 January 1933, sank at moorings off Felixstowe 3 January 1933. (iii) S1593, first flight and delivery to Mount Batten 31 March 1933, to Malta 6 June 1933, returned 29 April 1934, to Brough 12 June 1934, first flight with Culverins 9 June 1937, to Felixstowe September 1937, to anti-corrosive paint experiments April 1938.

The first Airedale prototype, N188, with the original transverse axle undercarriage.

Blackburn R.2 Airedale

Named after the Yorkshire town and designed by Maj F. A. Bumpus during 1923 to Air Ministry Specification 37/22, the Airedale was a three-seat, deck-landing reconnaissance land or sea monoplane intended as a replacement for the Fleet Air Arm's Blackburn R.1 Blackburn and Avro 555 Bison fleet spotter aircraft. A high-wing layout was chosen to give the crew the best possible downward view, and the machine was powered by one 385 hp Armstrong Siddeley Jaguar III radial but provision was made for installing any air-cooled radial of similar power.

The tail unit was almost identical to that of the Blackburn Blackburn and though the fuselage was slimmer there was no mistaking the family resemblance to the earlier machine. The pilot sat high up ahead of the mainplane for maximum field of view during deck-landing approaches, and there was the same enclosed cabin for navigator and wireless operator opening on to an observation cockpit in the rear, as before, protected from the slipstream by the familiar overhanging roof. Farther aft still was a gunner's cockpit.

The fuselage was of semi-monocoque construction and consisted of four spruce longerons supporting a number of ash and plywood formers covered with a three-ply skin. A pressed-steel engine mounting was anchored to the front ends of the longerons where they projected through the fireproof bulkhead and behind this lay the pilot's cockpit on a raised platform under which was located a prone bombing position. When released by a lever, the pilot's seat was free to rotate, enabling him to step down into the cabin to communicate with the crew. The cabin was provided with sliding Triplex windows, and at the rear end there was a folding seat and duplicated controls with which the navigator could fly the machine in an emergency or when the pilot left his seat. These controls took the form of an aileron wheel mounted centrally on a steel arch, moving fore and aft, which could be connected up to

209

The first Airedale, N188, after the front radius rods were fitted.
(*BAe.*)

the elevators when required. Entry to the cabin was made by ducking through the arch, and rudder pedals were permanently installed against the sides of the fuselage.

The thick-section, square-ended mainplane was of typical Blackburn composite construction with wooden spars and ribs braced internally by tubular-metal drag struts and steel tie rods. It was built in two hexagonal halves braced to the bottom fuselage longerons by tubular-steel N struts of streamlined section. Each half of the mainplane was hinged about an inclined axis so that it not only folded back but also rotated to lie flat against the fuselage with the trailing edge uppermost, a system which, though ingenious, proved very heavy. The tail unit was of similar construction with tubular-steel edging and incorporated a worm-driven variable-incidence gear operated by a trimming wheel in the cockpit.

The Airedale was fitted with the same simple wide-track undercarriage as late production Blackburn Blackburns and was equipped with arrester claws at each end of the transverse axle, landing shocks being taken by two telescopic rubber-in-compression struts braced by rear radius rods.

Armament consisted of a pilot's fixed ·5-in Vickers gun firing through the airscrew, a ·303 Lewis gun on a Scarff ring aft and a bomb load carried on racks under the fuselage.

The Jaguar engine was uncowled and drove a Leitner-Watts adjustable-pitch, hollow-bladed metal airscrew made by Metal Propellers Ltd of Croydon, and during development flying a domed fairing was fitted over the crankcase. Fuel was gravity fed from two 60-gallon tanks in the root ends of the mainplane through piping running down the centre wing bracing struts parallel to the aileron control cables.

Blackburns received a contract for the construction of two prototypes,

N188 and N189, built at Leeds in 1924 for competitive trials with the Hawker Hedgehog biplane N187, the first machine, N188, being glimpsed publicly for the first time during the Velos demonstration at Brough on 28 October 1925. It was the firm's first completely semi-monocoque fuselage and its first post-war monoplane, so that a prodigious amount of effort went into all stages of design, construction and testing, but the only major modification found necessary was the strengthening of the undercarriage. This was done by fitting front radius rods which met on the centre line of the fuselage and struts from the undercarriage attachment points to the middle of the axle as on the Blackburn Blackburn prototypes.

At the conclusion of the contractor's test flights, the Airedale was unfortunately crashed at Brough by a Service pilot when he took off cross wind in

The first and second stages in folding the wings of the Airedale N188.

211

The second Airedale prototype, N189, with auxiliary fins under the tailplane and Fairey-Reed airscrew.

Front view of N189 showing the strengthened undercarriage and the arrester claw attachment points.

an unfamiliar aircraft while attempting to ferry it to Martlesham Heath for official trials. He was unhurt but N188 was wrecked, and the remains lay in the Flying School hangar for a very long time before being broken up.

The second Airedale, N189, differed slightly from the first, being fitted from the outset with the multi-strut undercarriage and with auxiliary fins under the tailplane to improve directional stability. Its engine also had the crankcase fairing but this time drove a Fairey-Reed metal airscrew. The machine went to Martlesham for performance testing in June 1926 but did not represent a sufficient advance over those it was intended to replace. This, and the Air Ministry's long-standing aversion to monoplanes, killed the Airedale in that form and Maj Bumpus redesigned it as a biplane, and drawings dated 20

August 1926 show that this retained the name Airedale and carried the Blackburn type number R.3A. The fuselage, undercarriage and tail unit remained unchanged and the same structural methods were proposed for the mainplanes, but the extra drag and weight inherent in a biplane necessitated the greater power of a 425 hp Bristol Jupiter VI. The machine was rigged as a single-bay

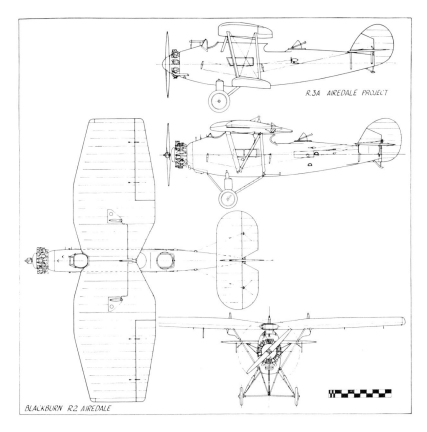

R.3A AIREDALE PROJECT

BLACKBURN R2 AIREDALE

sesquiplane with a short-span, narrow-chord bottom wing to give the crew a good downward view, and the whole wing structure was designed to fold back along the fuselage. The result was a handsome, businesslike aeroplane, but by this time the Air Ministry had cancelled the requirement and the Airedale biplane remained only a project.

Specification and data appear on page 214.

SPECIFICATION AND DATA

Manufacturers: The Blackburn Aeroplane and Motor Co Ltd, Olympia Works, Roundhay Road, Leeds, and Brough Aerodrome, East Yorks.

Power Plants: (R.2 monoplane) One 385 hp Armstrong Siddeley Jaguar III
(R.3A biplane)   One 425 hp Bristol Jupiter VI

Dimensions, Weights and Performance:

	R.2 monoplane	R.3A biplane†
Span	46 ft 0 in	46 ft 0 in
Length	36 ft 4 in★	36 ft 6 in
Height	14 ft 3 in★	12 ft 9 in
All-up weight	4,942 lb	5,030 lb
Maximum speed at sea level	120 mph	120 mph
Maximum speed at 5,000 ft	—	124 mph
Maximum speed at 10,000 ft	—	123 mph
Initial climb	—	672 ft/min
Service ceiling	—	18,800 ft
Endurance	—	4 hr

★ Seaplane 37 ft 0 in and 14 ft 6 in respectively.   † Estimated.

Production: Two prototype R.2 Airedale monoplanes only: N188 crashed at Brough in 1925; N189 tested at Martlesham.

A standard production Ripon II, S1270, with Fleet Air Arm coding.

Blackburn T.5 Ripon

The Ripon had its beginnings in Air Ministry Specification 21/23 for a torpedo or reconnaissance aircraft to replace the Dart in Fleet Air Arm service. In the reconnaissance role it was required to operate at great distances from base and to have an endurance in excess of 12 hr, so that a second seat was called for to accommodate a navigator/gunner. A further requirement was for interchangeable wheel and float undercarriages. Design work began in 1925 under the direction of Maj F. A. Bumpus who produced an aircraft with Napier Lion V engine which was plainly a cleaned-up version of the Velos, structurally similar but with single-bay wings and pronounced anhedral to the bottom centre section. The lower mainplane was of slightly greater span than the upper, and a new and unusual feature was a lower wing-root fairing in the form of three ribs radiating from the rear spar and fabric covered to form a fillet between the trailing edge and the fuselage. A large 155-gallon fuel tank was fitted in the centre fuselage, defensive armament consisted of one Lewis gun on a rotating mounting round the rear cockpit, and the alternative offensive loads were six 230-lb or three 520-lb bombs, or an 18-in torpedo.

Two prototypes were built and the first, N203, made its maiden flight at Brough in the hands of Flt Lt P. W. S. Bulman on 17 April 1926. The second, N204, fitted with a pair of 24 ft 9 in wooden floats designed by Maj J. D. Rennie, and strutted precisely as on the Velos, was first flown off the Humber by Flt Lt N. H. Woodhead on 12 August 1926 and went to the MAEE, Felixstowe, for trials in the following December.

Following Velos practice, the 4-gallon coolant header tank on N203 was mounted upright on the extreme nose, but on N204 it was fitted inside the top centre section. As usual, all three cylinder blocks of the Lion engine were exposed to the slipstream, but later the lines of N203 were improved consider-

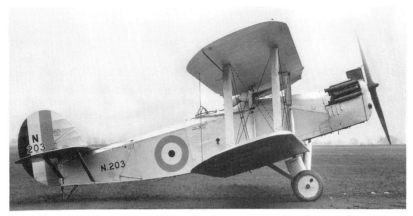

The first prototype Ripon I, N203, showing the exposed engine and the coolant header tank.

ably by raising the rear decking to tailplane level, banishing the coolant header tank to the top centre section as on N204, and eliminating the front fuselage 'kink' that had been a feature of Blackburn deck landing aircraft for so long. Increased sweepback on the mainplane coupled with close-fitting engine cowlings subtly changed the aircraft from Velos to true Ripon configuration, and in this form N203 emerged triumphant from competitive trials at Martlesham with the Avro 571 Buffalo G-EBNW and the Handley Page H.P.31 Harrow N205. In consequence, Blackburns were awarded a contract for an improved version, the T.5A Ripon II, first flown at Brough late in 1927.

Ripon II

This was scarcely recognizable as a derivative of the Ripon I, for the radiator and its time-honoured shuttering was entirely removed from the nose and the 570 hp Napier Lion XI was enclosed in well-tailored cowlings. This gave the nose a distinctly pointed appearance, further emphasized by the spinner of the large two-bladed wooden airscrew. Cooling was now by means of quadrant-shaped retractable radiators which, under the control of the pilot, emerged from each side of the fuselage just aft of the engine bay. A tall balanced rudder of greatly increased area was fitted, and the undercarriage was entirely redesigned, each half consisting of a bent axle attached to the bottom longerons to leave space below the fuselage for the torpedo. Telescopic oleo-pneumatic legs were taken to fittings on the outboard ends of the bottom centre section front spar.

Despite its highly refined external appearance, the main fuselage structure of the Mk II aircraft was basically the same as that of its ancestors, stressed for catapulting and comprising the usual three detachable units—steel engine mounting, steel tubular centre structure and tie rod braced wooden rear section. The sweptback, single-bay mainplanes were of composite construction, with spruce spars and ribs, metal compression struts and steel interplane struts in streamlined fairings. They were hinged to the rear spars of the top and bottom centre sections and folded back as on previous Blackburn shipborne aircraft. Ailerons were fitted to all four wings. Following standard Blackburn practice, the 145-gallon main fuel tank was located in the centre fuselage at the C.G. and fuel was then pumped into a 17-gallon service tank alongside the 4-gallon coolant tank in the top centre section. If the machine was required for reconnaissance duties, armament could be removed to permit an increase in endurance to 14 hr by means of a 120-gallon auxiliary fuel tank slung on the torpedo crutches, with a wind-driven fuel pump built into its nose to maintain a flow of fuel to the main system.

Originally the Fairey high-speed gun mounting was fitted externally about the rear cockpit as on the Ripon I, but early in 1928 the Ripon II rear fuselage was remodelled to lower the gun ring below the rim of the cockpit, with the Lewis gun locked into a slot in the rear decking when not in use. The cockpit

Two views of the second Ripon I, N204, at Felixstowe on 8 December 1926.

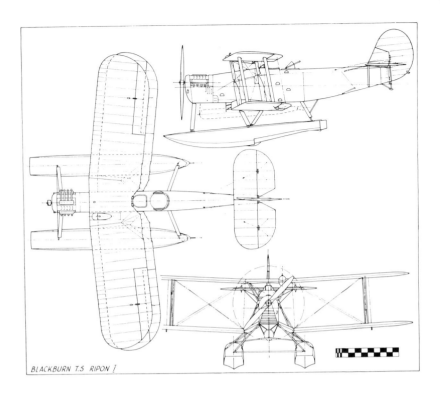

BLACKBURN T.5 RIPON I

was also extended rearwards to house the W/T gear under a sliding cover, an arrangement adopted as standard on the production machines which followed. In this form the machine received the RAF serial N231 for its début before the Press at Brough on 15 May 1928, when Blackburn test pilot A. M. Blake dropped a one-ton practice torpedo into the Humber before climbing away straight into a tight loop. Although not fitted with wing tip slots, the machine was rolled and yawed convincingly to demonstrate aileron effectiveness while sinking rapidly after the stall. A month later, on 30 June, the aircraft made its first appearance in public as exhibit No. 12 at the Hendon RAF Display, flown by a Farnborough pilot, but afterwards returning to Brough as a trial installations machine during the manufacture of the early production aircraft.

Contracts placed in 1928–29 were for 20 pre-production Ripon IIs, S1265–S1271 and S1357–S1369, which were of composite wood and metal construction and in every way similar to the prototype apart from large wing tip slots interconnected with the ailerons. The fourth aircraft, S1268, mounted on handsome semicircular-topped all-metal floats with water rudders, was evaluated at the MAEE, Felixstowe, in 1929 but, although the floatplane version was called for in the original specification and large numbers of floats were actually constructed, the Ripon, like the Dart before it, was seldom used

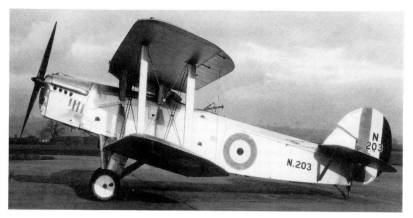

N203 in the transition stage between Velos derivative and true Ripon, with
improved fuselage lines, close-fitting cowlings and increased sweepback.

as a seaplane by the Fleet Air Arm and normally operated from aircraft carriers
as a landplane.

Following reports of mild tail flutter on Ripon IIs in service, S1268 was
flown experimentally in May 1930 with a smaller, lighter rudder reduced by
2·7 sq ft in area by clipping 1 ft from the tip. The cropped rudder was tested
on the seaplane in dives of up to 190 mph at an A.U.W. of 7,984 lb. and,
proving completely effective, was adopted for all later marks. Existing Ripons
were similarly modified including the prototype, N231, which, after nearly
four years at Brough, was delivered on 15 February 1932 to the Gosport
Torpedo Training Flight, in whose colours it appeared briefly at the Hendon
RAF Display on 25 June that year.

The eighth aircraft, S1357, was exhibited at the Olympia Aero Show on
16–27 July 1929, and the type first entered service on the carriers *Glorious*
and *Furious* in the following month, replacing some of the Darts of Nos.
460, 461 and 462 (Fleet Torpedo Bomber) Flights.

Ripon IIA

The main production version with 570 hp Napier Lion XIA and known as
the T.5B Ripon IIA, sizeable orders for which were placed in 1930 to Specification 2/29, was of slightly shorter span and had duralumin wing ribs and
the small rudder. Operating at a slightly increased all-up weight, the Ripon
IIA was fitted with catapulting spools and armed with one forward-firing
Vickers gun and one Lewis gun on a Fairey high-speed mounting in the rear.
The warload was one Mk VIII or Mk X torpedo, or alternatively one 1,100-lb
smoke canister or a bomb load of either six 250-lb or three 550-lb bombs under
the wings and fuselage. For precision bombing an aiming window was provided in the floor.

Orders placed in the first few months of 1930 totalled 40 Ripon IIAs (four

219

The prototype Ripon II in its original condition with the gun ring mounted on top of the rear fuselage.

The prototype Ripon II with RAF serial N231 and remodelled rear cockpit.
(*BAe.*)

of which had non-standard engines) and, to maintain a production rate of two aircraft per week, the manufacture of some components was sub-contracted to Boulton and Paul Ltd whose chief test pilot, Sqn Ldr C. A. Rea, flew the much-modified prototype N231 on further contractor's light- and full-load tests at the company's Mousehold Aerodrome, Norwich, on 29 August and 9 September 1933 respectively. These tests, which took place long after the termination of Ripon production, were probably in connection with component production for the Ripon's Bristol Pegasus engined successor, the Baffin.

Five Ripon IIAs of No. 460 Flight were transferred temporarily to the carrier *Eagle* for shipment, with a number of manufacturers' demonstration aircraft, to the British Empire Exhibition which opened at Buenos Aires on 14 March 1931. Operating from the deck of the carrier they demonstrated the FAA's impeccable formation flying at the El Palomar air display on 20 March, repeated it 100 miles away at the Argentine naval base at Punta Indio on 26 March and over their carrier off Mar del Plata on 3 April.

Ripon IIC

The Ripon IIA was followed in 1931–32 by 31 examples of a final version rigged with more sweepback than the earlier marks and incorporating built-up steel spars and duralumin ribs made from specially rolled and drawn sections to eliminate all wood from the mainplane structure as on the Iris III. Despite these major changes the aircraft was still designated T.5B and quite inexplicably known as the Ripon IIC, for no reference to a Ripon IIB occurs anywhere in manufacturer's or Air Ministry records and there is no vacant Blackburn designation to which it might have applied.

Two views of the Ripon II trials seaplane S1268 before and after the tip of the rudder was cropped by 1 ft.

221

The prototype Ripon II, N231, was modified to this standard in time for the air display for the Dominion Premiers at Croydon on 25 October 1930, but the prototype Ripon IIC proper, S1468, was a Mk IIA modified on the production line and completed in January 1931 with twin metal floats for handling trials at Felixtowe, made with a 1,420-lb torpedo in position. The aircraft earned considerable praise for its good flying and seaworthiness qualities before being sent to Martlesham Heath for performance tests with the land undercarriage. In July 1931 it was joined by S1571 which remained at the A. & A.E.E. through the next year, with occasional visits to Gosport.

In 1932 it was decided to modernize the earlier Ripons and when the carriers returned to the Solent and the Mk IIs and Mk IIAs came off service, they were sent back to the makers in batches for modification up to Mk IIC standard. One such batch, comprising all the Ripons of No. 460 Flight, newly disembarked from HMS *Glorious*, was ferried from Gosport to Brough on 10 November 1932.

Ripon IICs formed the initial equipment of Nos. 465 and 466 (Fleet Torpedo Bomber) Flights which were raised at Gosport on 20 and 31 March 1931, respectively, prior to embarking in HMS *Furious*. In common with all other Fleet aircraft, they carried individual codings in the form of huge white numerals on a blue diagonal fuselage stripe, but no listing of these is possible since any given aircraft carried several different codings during its Service life.

In 1933 the Flights were reformed as Nos. 810, 811 and 812 (Fleet Torpedo Bomber) Squadrons, No. 810 with six Ripons and six Darts on *Courageous*, No. 811 (formerly Nos. 465 and 466 Flights) with 12 Ripons on *Furious* and No. 812 on *Glorious*. During the Coastal Defence Exercises in the Firth of Forth on 22–23 September 1933, No. 810 Squadron formed part of the attacking force and No. 811 was temporarily detached to Donibristle to join the

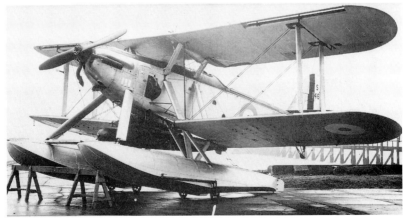

S1468, the Ripon IIC prototype, showing the exhaust manifold fitted to subsequent machines.

Ripon IIC conversion, S1567 of No. 462 Flight, *Furious*, fully cluttered with Fleet Air Arm impedimenta. (*Courtesy Capt W. B. Axford, RN.*)

defenders. From January 1934, however, the Ripon was gradually replaced by the Blackburn Baffin, the last in service being those of No. 811 Squadron.

The last four Ripon IIC aircraft to be built, K2884–K2887, were not used operationally but were ferried direct to Cardington for storage, the last by Sqn Ldr Gerald Boyce on 17 February 1933. At the end of the year they were flown back to Brough for conversion into Blackburn Baffins with Bristol Pegasus air-cooled radial engines, and many older specimens, often with several years of service behind them, and including every Ripon from S1473 onwards, were similarly converted.

Ripon IIF

The Blackburn company tried very hard to sell the Ripon overseas, and versions were offered with the 600 hp Hispano-Suiza Type 51-12Hb and 520 hp B.M.W. water-cooled engines. Their hopes were not realized but in response to an enquiry, details of a variant to suit the needs of the Spanish Navy and designated T.5C were the subject of a brochure sent to Madrid in May 1928. The Napier Lion IX, still on the secret list, gave place to a '570 hp Napier Lion', with the 530 hp Bristol Jupiter VIII air-cooled radial as the alternative. No orders resulted, but in August 1928 the Finnish Government purchased a single pattern aircraft, designated T.5D, with Jupiter engine and interchangeable wheel and float undercarriages and acquired a licence to build others in Finland.

The example aircraft, RI-121, had the high-aspect-ratio rudder of the early

Ripon IIC S1563 taking off from *Furious* with smoke-producing apparatus, June 1932. (*Courtesy Capt W. B. Axford, RN.*)

Ripon II but was known as the Ripon IIF, the F signifying Finland and the serial prefix RI indicating Ripon. After test flying at Brough on wheels and floats, it was delivered to the Finnish Air Force on 20 September 1929, and on receipt of the drawings from Blackburns, the Valton Lentokonetehdas, or National Aircraft Factory, commenced production of 25 Ripon IIFs at Tampere. Seven (RI-129 to RI-135) were completed with 480 hp Gnome-Rhône Jupiter VI 9AK radials by September 1931, a further eight (RI-136 to RI-143) with 535 hp Armstrong Siddeley Panther IIAs by November 1931, and a final batch of ten (RI-150 to RI-159) with the 580 hp Bristol Pegasus IIM.3 by the end of 1934. All had clipped rudders, those with the Pegasus being roughly equivalent to the Blackburn Baffin (q.v.). RI-129, RI-132 and RI-159 were used for trials with the 525 hp Wright Cyclone R-1750, 525 hp B.M.W. 132-A, 525 hp Pratt & Whitney Hornet B, 650 hp Armstrong Siddeley Tiger I and 600 hp Hispano-Suiza 12Nbr.

Finnish-built Ripons had plywood instead of fabric-covered rear fuselages and were armed with Vickers and Lewis guns, later replaced by the Finnish-made L-33 machine-gun. Torpedo tests made in 1935 were not successful and in 1936 diving speeds were limited to 155 mph and all diving with floats forbidden.

Six took part in the great air display at Suur-Merijoki in 1937, but Finnish Ripons were normally stationed at Santahamina, Turkinsaari and Sortavala, operating on wheels or Finnish-built floats and skis. When the Winter War broke out against the Russians in October 1939, 21 Ripon IIFs (including the Brough-built camouflaged RI-121 on skis and also six under repair) were in service with three reconnaissance squadrons—LLv 16, 36 and 39. Survivors of this brief conflict numbered 17 (including 11 under repair), almost all of which were lost in service with LLv 6 and 16 during the Continuation War. Flying mainly at night, they were engaged on U-boat patrols, leaflet dropping, casualty evacuation and supply delivery. RI-132 and RI-142 were cannibalized for spares in 1941, leaving RI-140 as the only Ripon IIF left to be struck off charge on 15 December 1944. In 1968 it was still in existence, albeit in poor condition, in a hangar at the disused military airfield at Vesivehmaa, 22 km north of Lahti, awaiting restoration for the Finnish Air Force historical collection.

Ripon III

The single Blackburn T.5E Ripon III prototype, S1272, ordered in May 1928, bore only a superficial resemblance to production machines. Not only

RI-121, the Jupiter VIII powered Ripon IIF built at Brough for the Finnish Government, 1928–29.

RI-129, first Finnish-built Ripon IIF, with Gnome-Rhône Jupiter VI 9AK and constructor's number R.29 No. 1 under the tailplane. (*Courtesy C. H. Barnes.*)

225

RI-132, first of the three Ripon IIF engine test beds, with 525 hp Wright Cyclone R-1750 installed.

RI-137, 535 hp Armstrong Siddeley Panther IIA, camouflaged and mounted on floats of Finnish design. (*Courtesy Eino Ritaranta.*)

was it of metal construction throughout, including the wing spars and ribs, the rear fuselage structure and the internals of the tail unit, but the fuselage lines were quite different. The decking ahead of the pilot was noticeably humped and the rounded wing tips and rudder were changed to a rectangular shape for ease of fabrication. The aircraft was first flown at Brough on 26 November 1929 and in January 1930 was put through the usual performance trials at the A. & A.E.E., Martlesham Heath, which revealed that the target was obscured by the top wing in a diving attack and by the nose when levelling off to drop the torpedo.

S1272 therefore returned to the manufacturers for the nose lines to be straightened and the upper mainplane raised by fitting longer interplane and centre-section struts. In Martlesham tests dated 31 May 1930, it was found that improved forward view had been obtained at the expense of performance which was reduced by extra drag and a 100-lb increase in structural weight. At a later date the machine was evaluated on floats at Felixtowe and later still returned to Brough to join the Ripon prototype, N231, as an experimental hack.

The experimental Ripon III, S1272, with prominent metal stringers in the rear fuselage, humped nose and rectangular wing tips and rudder, in January 1930.

The Ripon III in modified form with straightened nose lines and raised top wing, May 1930. (*Flight Photo.*)

227

SPECIFICATION AND DATA

Manufacturers: The Blackburn Aeroplane and Motor Co Ltd, Olympia Works, Roundhay Road, Leeds, and Brough Aerodrome, East Yorks. The National Aircraft Factory, Tampere, Finland.

Power Plants: (Ripon I)   One 467 hp Napier Lion V
(Ripon II)   One 570 hp Napier Lion XI
(Ripon IIA)   One 570 hp Napier Lion X, XI or XIA
(Ripon IIC)   One 570 hp Napier Lion XIA
(Ripon IIF)   One 530 hp Bristol Jupiter VIII
One 480 hp Gnome-Rhône Jupiter VI 9AK
One 535 hp Armstrong Siddeley Panther IIA
One 580 hp Bristol Pegasus IIM.3
One 525 hp Wright Cyclone R-1750
One 525 hp B.M.W. 132-A
One 525 hp Pratt & Whitney Hornet B
One 650 hp Armstrong Siddeley Tiger I
One 600 hp Hispano-Suiza 12Nbr
(Ripon III)   One 570 hp Napier Lion XIA

Dimensions:

	Ripon I	Ripon II	Ripon IIA, IIC and IIF	Ripon III
Span upper	44 ft 8½ in	44 ft 8½ in	44 ft 10 in	45 ft 2 in
Span lower	45 ft 6 in	45 ft 6½ in	45 ft 6½ in	45 ft 10½ in
Span folded	17 ft 8 in	18 ft 0⅝ in	17 ft 10 in	18 ft 4 in
Length landplane	36 ft 9 in	36 ft 9 in	36 ft 9 in	37 ft 1 in
Length seaplane	41 ft 3 in	—	39 ft 4 in	—
Height landplane	—	13 ft 4¼ in	12 ft 10 in	12 ft 8 in
Height seaplane	15 ft 6½ in	—	15 ft 0 in	—
Wing area	677 sq ft	720 sq ft	683 sq ft	711 sq ft

Weights and Performance:

	Ripon I		Ripon II	Ripon III
	Landplane	Seaplane (1)	Landplane	Landplane (2)
Tare weight	4,566 lb	5,027 lb	4,132 lb	4,676 lb*
Military load	2,502 lb	2,198 lb	3,150 lb	2,187 lb
All-up weight	7,068 lb	8,014 lb	7,282 lb	7,663 lb*
Speed at sea level	111 mph	101 mph	132 mph	118 mph
Speed at 5,000 ft	108 mph	94 mph	—	113 mph
Initial climb	602 ft/min	524 ft/min	800 ft/min	675 ft/min
Absolute ceiling	11,250 ft	7,500 ft	15,000 ft	12,000 ft
Service ceiling	9,700 ft	4,600 ft	13,000 ft	10,000 ft
Endurance	5 hr	5 hr	4 hr	4 hr

* With raised top wing 4,776 lb and 7,763 lb respectively.

(1) *Ref. M.A.E.E. Report F/22A dated January 1928.*
(2) *Ref. A. & A.E.E. Report M/553 dated March 1930.*

	Ripon IIA		Ripon IIF	
	Landplane	Seaplane	Landplane	Seaplane
Tare weight	4,255 lb	4,716 lb*	3,850 lb	4,311 lb
Military load	3,150 lb	3,150 lb*	3,150 lb	3,150 lb
All-up weight	7,405 lb	7,866 lb*	7,000 lb	7,461 lb
Speed at sea level	126 mph	120 mph	118 mph	112 mph
Speed at 5,000 ft	118 mph	122 mph	128 mph	118 mph
Initial climb	610 ft/min	575 ft/min	510 ft/min	360 ft/min
Service ceiling	10,000 ft	9,100 ft	8,700 ft	8,700 ft
Range (torpedo)	815 miles	315 miles	428 miles	488 miles
Range (reconn.)	1,060 miles	960 miles	1,127 miles	1,284 miles

* Ripon IIC seaplane 5,159 lb, 2,239 lb and 8,197 lb respectively.

Ref. M.A.E.E. Report F/71 dated 26 February 1931.

Production:
(a) *By the Blackburn Aeroplane and Motor Co Ltd at Brough*
 (i) Contracts

Ordered	Qty.	Type	Serials	Spec.	Contract
Sept. 1925	2	Mk I prototypes	N203–N204	21/23	
Nov. 1927	1	Mk II prototype	N231		
May 1928	7	Mk II production	S1265–S1271		833137/28
May 1928	1	Mk III prototype	S1272		833137/28
Aug. 1928	1	Mk IIF example	RI-121		Finnish
Jan. 1929	13	Mk II production	S1357–S1369	2/29	897808/29
Jan. 1930	9	Mk IIA production	S1424–S1432	2/29	957968/29
May 1930	9	,,	S1465–S1473	2/29	38676/30
May 1930	9	,,	S1553–S1561	2/29	38676/30
May 1930	6	,,	S1562–S1567	2/29	38676/30
May 1930	7	,,	S1568–S1574	2/29	38676/30
1931	22	Mk IIC production	S1649–S1669 and S1671	13/31	106668/31
1931	5	,,	S1670 and S1672–S1674	13/31	106668/31
1932	4	,,	K2884–K2887	13/31	170234/32

Total production: 96 aircraft.

Works Order	Serials	Engines	Delivery
	N203–N204	Lion V	N203 first flown 17 April 1926; N204 first flown 12 August 1926
	N231	Lion XI	First flown 1927; to Ripon IIC prototype 1929 under Works Order 2339; to Gosport 15 February 1932; to Boulton and Paul 1933
	S1265–S1271	Lion XI	S1265 first flown 8 January 1929; S1268 to Felixstowe on floats; S1270 to Martlesham March 1930
1420	S1272	Lion XIA	First flown 26 November 1929; to Martlesham January 1930
	RI-121	Pegasus VIII	Shipped to Finland in September 1929
1850	S1357–S1369	Lion XIA	Delivered January–February 1930: S1357–62 and S1364–65 to Northolt; S1363 and S1367–69 to Gosport
2690	S1424–S1432	Lion XIA	Delivered July–December 1930: S1424 to Martlesham July 1930; S1425–27 to Sealand; S1428–32 to Gosport September 1930
3130	S1465–S1473	Lion XIA	Delivered November 1930–January 1931: S1468 prototype Mk IIC to Felixstowe on floats, to Martlesham March 1930; remainder to Sealand
3320	S1553–S1554 S1555–S1558 S1559 S1560–S1561	Lion X Lion XIA Lion XI Lion XIA	All delivered to Gosport February–April 1931
3330	S1562 S1563–S1567	Lion X Lion XIA	All delivered to Gosport May 1931
3340	S1568–S1574	Lion XIA	Delivered June–July 1931: S1568–69 and S1572–74 to Gosport; S1570 to Sealand; S1571 to Martlesham
3810	S1649–S1669 and S1671	Lion XIA	Delivered October 1931–March 1932: S1655–56, S1661–62 and S1667 to Sealand; remainder to Gosport
4060	S1670 and S1672–S1674	Lion XIA	Delivered March–April 1932: S1670 to Martlesham; S1672–74 to Sealand
4570	K2884–K2887	Lion XIA	All to Cardington for storage: K2884 (6 January 1933), K2885 (25 January 1933), K2886 and K2887 (17 February 1933); to Brough for Baffin conversion —K2884 and K2885 (13 October 1933), K2886 and K2887 (11 January 1934)

(b) *By the National Aircraft Factory at Tampere, Finland*
Twenty-five aircraft built under licence 1931–34 together with float and ski under-carriages of local design.
   (i) RI-129 to RI-135 with 480 hp Gnome-Rhône Jupiter VI 9AK
   (ii) RI-136 to RI-143 with 535 hp Armstrong Siddeley Panther IIA
   (iii) RI-150 to RI-159 with 580 hp Bristol Pegasus IIM.3

(c) *Examples of Ripons converted at Brough to Ripon IIC*
S1270 redelivered to the F.A.A. 11 March 1932; S1557 converted in 1932 to Works Order 3971; S1366 to Works Order 4804/4, test flown by Flt Lt N. H. Woodhead 4 July 1933, delivered to Cardington by Flt Lt Rogers 28 July 1933; S1368 test flown by A. G. Loton 21 April 1933, delivered to Cardington 22 May 1933; S1369 test flown by J. Stocken, redelivered 7 July 1933 by Lt Price, RN; S1667 collected by Flt Lt Rogers 2 June 1933 but forced landed after 10 min at South Ferriby; S1553 collected by Flt Lt Rogers 15 June 1933 for catapult launching at the RAE, Farnborough, 6 July 1933.

(d) *The conversion of Ripon aircraft to Baffin standard* is listed in full on pages 360–362

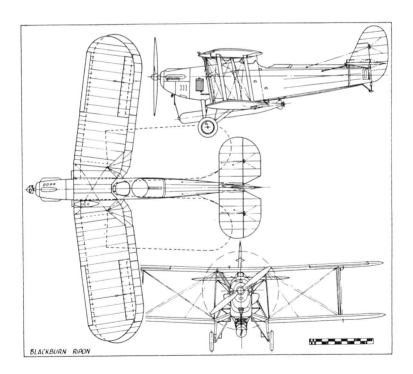

BLACKBURN RIPON

Service Use:

Date	Flight	Base	Station
August 1929	No. 460	HMS *Glorious*	Mediterranean Fleet
„	No. 461	„	„
„	No. 462	HMS *Furious*	Home Fleet
March 1931	No. 465	„	„
„	No. 466	„	„

Date	Squadron	Base	Station
1933	No. 810	HMS *Courageous*	Home Fleet
„	No. 811	HMS *Furious*	„
„	No. 812	HMS *Glorious*	Mediterranean Fleet

Notes on Individual Units:

No. 460 Flight (HMS *Glorious* codings): 60/S1360, 63/S1363, 74/S1270 (later S1358), 75/S1265, 81/S1437 (crashed on deck), 83/S1430, 86/S1429 (used as seaplane).

No. 462 Flight (HMS *Furious* codings): 4/S1565 (later S1574), 5/S1554 (later S1674), 6/S1554, 7/S1364 (later S1566), 8/S1567, 9/S1556. Ripon IIC aircraft in use June 1933: 10/S1559, 12/S1562, 13/S1564, 14/S1560, 15/S1563, 16/S1567.

The Torpedo Training Squadron, Gosport, used codes 1 to 6, e.g. 4/S1654.

Other codings: D4/S1573 (later on S1659), D5/S1651, D6/S1650, D9/S1654.

O1/S1531, O4/S1574, O5/S1657, O9/S1666.

The Blackburn Sprat taking off from Brough in 1926. (*Flight Photo 3949.*)

Blackburn T.R.1 Sprat

In 1925 the Air Ministry issued Specification 5/24 for a small two-seater, with interchangeable wheel and float undercarriages, which would be suitable for Royal Air Force advanced training, Fleet Air Arm deck-landing practice, and seaplane conversion courses. To ensure good deck-flying characteristics on low power, the Air Ministry took the unprecedented step of demanding no complicated gadgetry such as wing flaps, radio or provision for various forms of armament and allowed designers a free hand at producing machines with good take-off acceleration, low stalling speed and maximum low-speed controllability.

Three promising designs were selected from the many tendered, and in September 1925 orders were placed for three prototypes, the Blackburn T.R.1 Sprat, the Vickers Type 120 Vendace I and the Parnall Perch. They were allotted serial numbers N207, N208 and N217, respectively, in the series reserved for experimental marine aircraft and all were powered by 275 hp Rolls-Royce Falcon III water-cooled engines. In the case of the Blackburn entry, the designation T.R.1 signified the firm's first trainer aircraft, and provision was made for fitting the 240 hp Siddeley Puma or 300 hp A.D.C. Nimbus as alternative power plants.

The Sprat was designed by Maj Bumpus and in reality was a scaled-down version of the Velos two-seater, with similar fuselage lines, wing planform and tail unit shape. As before, the decking sloped steeply away to give maximum forward view, and the mainplanes, this time single-bay, used the same T.64 wing section and for shipboard use were designed to fold. The wide-track, divided undercarriage was a simplified version of the larger Velos original incorporating heavy-duty, rubber-in-compression main legs and deck arrester claws.

233

The machine was built in the same manner as its immediate forebears and was the essence of robustness, with engine mounting and wire-braced wooden rear fuselage bolted to a tubular-steel centre structure. As before, this consisted of a section of the fuselage from the fireproof bulkhead back to a point in line with the rear spar of the bottom mainplane, built integral with the bottom centre section. This in turn was braced at its extremities to the top longerons, the whole forming a rigid structure to take the undercarriage.

The Falcon III engine drove a four-bladed wooden airscrew and was arranged as a self-contained power unit complete with gas starter, radiator compartment (for either temperate or tropical radiators) and neat controllable shutters. By removing four bolts the whole unit was quickly detachable from the fireproof bulkhead and could be lowered to the hangar floor, where its mounting acted as an engine stand to facilitate maintenance. Main fuel was carried in a slim 56-gallon tank between the mainspars of the bottom centre section, with the rear of the tank faired into the underside of the fuselage by fabric over formers and stringers. A wind-driven pump on a port bracing strut pumped fuel to a streamlined gravity tank on the top centre section as on early versions of the Blackburn Blackburn.

For best possible view, both cockpits were aft of the trailing edge of the upper mainplane, and the dual controls were fitted with a device for disconnecting the pupil's set in an emergency. Following standard Blackburn practice, a hand wheel was fitted on top of each control column for operating the four ailerons. The instructor sat in the rear seat and both he and the pupil shared a common set of instruments mounted in line along the rear spar of the top centre section, a cumbersome arrangement of easily damaged, drag-producing piping and electrical leads.

By means of special adjustable trestles positioned at jacking points under nose and tail, the Sprat could be lifted clear of the ground so that the whole undercarriage could be removed and quickly replaced by twin floats designed

Front view of the Sprat showing the divided undercarriage, deck arrester claws, radiator shutters and splayed-out centre section struts. (*Flight Photo.*)

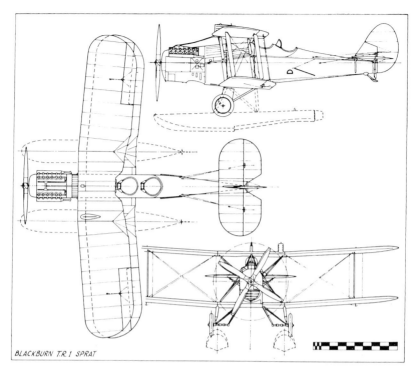

BLACKBURN T.R.1 SPRAT

by Maj J. D. Rennie. These were of the all-duralumin, vee-bottomed, rounded-deck type, identical to, but smaller than, those fitted to the demonstration Velos for the South American tour. They were well known for their incomparable behaviour on the water, having been built in the light of data obtained from an intensive programme of model testing in the tank at Brough, and if the Sprat were correctly trimmed it would leave the water quickly and cleanly with the pilot's hands completely off the controls.

It was first flown at Brough by Flt Lt P. W. S. Bulman on 24 April 1926 and then went to the A. & A.E.E., Martlesham Heath, and the M.A.E.E., Felixstowe, for competitive trials on wheels and floats with the Vendace I and Perch. The Vendace I was chosen finally as the most suitable machine but soon afterwards the requirement was cancelled as an economy measure and no production order was placed.

The Sprat was still at Felixstowe as late as 23 June but at the conclusion of the trials was refitted with the wheeled undercarriage in time to form exhibit No. 2 in the New Types Park at the Hendon RAF Display on 3 July 1926, alongside its successful rival the Vendace I. Later in the programme it gave a spirited flying display comparable to that of contemporary first-line aircraft and clearly would have made an ideal intermediate trainer for pilots who had learned on the RAF's standard Avro 504K.

235

Manufacturers: The Blackburn Aeroplane and Motor Co Ltd, Olympia Works, Roundhay Road, Leeds, and Brough Aerodrome, East Yorks.

Power Plant: One 275 hp Rolls-Royce Falcon III

Dimensions: Span 34 ft 9 in Length (land or seaplane) 29 ft 3 in
Height 11 ft 0 in Wing area 406·5 sq ft

Loadings:

(a) *Useful Load*

Two crew	360 lb
Instruments	55 lb
Very pistol	
and 12 cartridges	7 lb
	422 lb

(b) *All-up Weight*

	Landplane	Seaplane
Tare weight	2,318 lb	2,648 lb★
Useful load	422 lb	422 lb
56 gal petrol	425 lb	425 lb
4 gal oil	40 lb	40 lb
1½ gal water	15 lb	15 lb
	3,220 lb	3,550 lb★

★ 3,339 lb and 3,762 lb respectively at Felixstowe trials.

Performance:

	Landplane	Seaplane
Maximum speed at sea level	115 mph	112 mph
Maximum speed at 5,000 ft	112 mph	109 mph
Initial climb	1,100 ft/min	937 ft/min
Time to 5,000 ft	5½ min	6½ min
Time to 10,000 ft	13 min	16 min
Service ceiling	17,500 ft	15,700 ft

Production: One aircraft only, N207, first flown 24 April 1926; to Martlesham May 1926; to Felixstowe June 1926; to RAF Display, Hendon, 3 July 1926.

The Sprat on floats at Felixstowe on 23 June 1926.

236

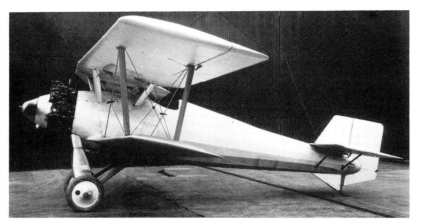

Side view of the unarmed Turcock showing the Jaguar two-row radial engine, two-bladed wooden airscrew and Hucks starter claw.

Blackburn F.1 Turcock

In 1926 the Blackburn company broke briefly away from its preoccupation with naval aircraft to build an interceptor fighter capable of production in six main variants according to the choice of engine. Designed by Maj Bumpus and his colleague B. A. Duncan to either F.9/26 or N.21/26, it was an extremely clean single-seat, unequal-span biplane and, being the first fighter since the introduction of the firm's designation system, was styled F.1. The design was an entirely private venture and aimed at the export market. The general arrangement drawings were dated 22 December 1926.

The range of engines consisted of the 585 hp Bristol Mercury and 446 hp Armstrong Siddeley Jaguar VI air-cooled radials and the 510 hp Rolls-Royce Falcon X (later renamed Kestrel) water-cooled vee-12 in naturally-aspirated and supercharged versions, and although the name Blackcock was assigned to the basic aircraft, it was the intention to allot separate names to variants as and when they were built.

Apart from the front fuselage and wing root fairings, which were duralumin-panelled, the machine was of light-weight, fabric-covered all-metal construction with a typically Blackburn fuselage consisting of detachable engine mounting, tubular steel centre structure and rear section. The wings were rigged as a single-bay with stagger, and the upper mainplane, which carried the ailerons, was of greater span and chord than the lower. Wing spars were built up from high-grade steel strips riveted together and the ribs were assembled from specially drawn duralumin sections, the whole braced internally by duralumin drag tubes and steel tie rods. External bracing was by steel interplane struts and streamlined wires.

The tail unit was braced to the bottom longerons by parallel struts and

237

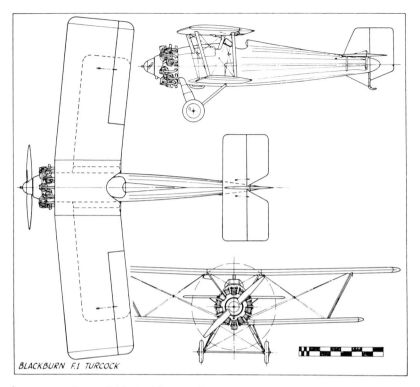

BLACKBURN F.1 TURCOCK

incorporated a variable-incidence tailplane operated by a trimming wheel in the cockpit. Additional fin area was provided below the fuselage by fairing in the tail skid and its support strut. A unique feature was a movable tail cone built integral with the rudder. The main undercarriage consisted of two long-travel oleo-pneumatic main legs supporting a through axle carrying the landing wheels, while shocks at the rear end were taken by rubber buffers in compression inside the sternpost tube.

Fuel was gravity fed from two 27-gallon tanks in the top mainplane and a 3-gallon oil tank was fitted in the centre structure behind the fireproof bulkhead. If the Falcon X water-cooled engine were requested it was proposed to fit retractable side radiators as on the Blackburn Ripon and to install a coolant header tank inside the top centre section.

The cockpit was situated immediately aft of the splayed-out centre section struts in such a position that the pilot could see vertically downwards behind the trailing edge of the bottom mainplane, and the top centre section was cut away to give him a good field of view forwards and upwards. The seat incorporated a parachute recess and was adjustable for height, with ample room on each side for the two ·303 Vickers guns and boxes for 1,000 rounds of ammunition. Controls were of the normal stick and rudder-bar type.

238

None of the Blackcock variants were ordered by the British Air Ministry. Only one example was built, an unarmed aircraft fitted with the Armstrong Siddeley Jaguar VI supercharged engine to a contract placed by the Turkish Government. It was constructed in the Leeds factory, assembled at Brough and first flown by A. G. Loton on 14 November 1927. In deference to the purchaser it received the name Turcock and, being a private order, was allotted the civil registration G-EBVP in January 1928 for test flying and ferrying to destination but on the 23rd of that month it was destroyed in an accident.

SPECIFICATION AND DATA

Manufacturers: The Blackburn Aeroplane and Motor Co Ltd, Olympia Works, Roundhay Road, Leeds, and Brough Aerodrome, East Yorks.

Power Plants: One 585 hp Bristol Mercury
One 446 hp Armstrong Siddeley Jaguar VI
One 510 hp Rolls-Royce Falcon X

Dimensions: Span (upper) 31 ft 0 in   Length 24 ft 4 in   Height 8 ft 11 in

Weights and Performances (supercharged engines):

	Mercury	Jaguar VI	Falcon X
Tare weight	2,172 lb	2,282 lb	2,447 lb
All-up weight	2,616 lb	2,726 lb	2,885 lb
Speed at 15,000 ft	202 mph	176 mph	197 mph
Initial climb	1,520 ft/min	1,300 ft/min	1,400 ft/min
Time to 10,000 ft	6 min	8 min	6½ min
Service ceiling	32,000 ft	27,500 ft	31,500 ft
Endurance	1·65 hr	1·75 hr	1·8 hr

Production: One Turcock only to Works Order 9725, first flown at Brough 14 November 1927, allotted civil markings G-EBVP in the name of the Blackburn Aeroplane and Motor Co Ltd by Certificate of Registration No. 1546 dated 6 January 1928, crashed at Martlesham Heath 23 January 1928.

Three-quarter rear view of the Turcock showing rigging details and the movable tail cone.

239

The Nautilus in original condition at Brough, May 1929, with large elevator and flat, vertical-sided radiator compartment.

Blackburn 2F.1 Nautilus

As indicated by the company designation, the Nautilus was Blackburn's first two-seat fighter and was designed by Maj Bumpus to meet Air Ministry Specification O.22/26 dated 8 June 1926 for a carrier-borne fleet spotter with limited interceptor capability. To design an aeroplane having fighter performance, full controllability at low speeds for carrier landings and strength enough for catapult discharge while encumbered with heavy wing-folding gear, and, in the extreme case, a float undercarriage, was in itself a very difficult assignment. The task was further complicated by the Air Ministry's vacillating power plant demands, for, although forms of tender were not issued until 11 November 1926, the 510 hp Rolls-Royce Falcon X called for in the original specification was discarded and the 520 hp Falcon XI requested on 2 December, and then as late as 17 October 1927 this was changed again to the 525 hp Rolls-Royce F.XIIMS. Thus it was not until January 1928 that the contractors' proposals were far enough advanced for the Air Ministry to place prototype contracts. Even then full-scale mock-ups were called for and it was well into 1929 before the four chosen firms had aircraft ready for competitive trials. These were the Short Gurnards N228 and N229, Blackburn Nautilus N234, Fairey Fleetwing N235, and the Naval Hart J9052 which ultimately won the production contract for Hawkers.

All were powered by the 525 hp Rolls-Royce F.XIIMS moderately-supercharged twelve-cylinder water-cooled engine, a much slimmer power unit than the famous broad-arrow, three-bank Napier Lion, which enabled the designers to produce fuselages of exceptionally good streamlined shape. The Nautilus in particular had a long and pointed nose terminating in the spinner of an 11-ft diameter two-bladed wooden airscrew and, unlike the others, was built with the fuselage in the mid-gap position. This left a space between the

240

bottom centre section and the cockpit floor for a neatly-faired radiator compartment with controllable shutters.

The airframe was constructed in three main sections in the standard Blackburn manner. The centre fuselage consisted of four tubular-steel longerons and a number of transverse frames, the foremost being the fireproof bulkhead and the remainder alternately open duralumin frames and steel tubular units cross-braced and carrying the fairing formers. From the nose to just aft of the rear cockpit the fuselage was covered by reinforced detachable duralumin panels but the rest was fabric covered.

Mainplanes were of all-metal construction, fabric covered and similar internally to those of the Turcock but were fitted with Frise-type ailerons on all four wings and were so balanced that they folded back along the fuselage without the use of jury struts. The machine was rigged as a two-bay biplane with splayed-out interplane struts as well as having considerable stagger and sweepback, features which combined with the slim lines of the fuselage to give it a distinctly rakish appearance. This was further accentuated by the absence of dihedral on the top wing. The bottom centre section was of much greater span than the top in order to carry the undercarriage and was braced externally to the bottom longerons by inverted W-struts.

A strut-braced tail unit carried the horn-balanced rudder and unbalanced elevator, and the worm-driven variable-incidence tailplane was controlled by a trimming wheel on the port side of the pilot's cockpit. An unusual feature was the provision of directional trim applied by a similar hand wheel on the starboard side which imparted sideways movement to the fin. The undercarriage was of the wide-track divided type with oleo-pneumatic main legs and disc wheels with brakes. To meet the specification two seaplane undercarriages were proposed, one with twin floats of 8 ft 8 in track and an alternative single-float arrangement to give the observer a better field of view vertically downwards.

The Nautilus with narrow-chord elevator and tapered radiator compartment with vee-shaped rear orifice.

The pilot's cockpit was situated below a cut-out in the trailing edge of the top centre section, with the observer/gunner's cockpit immediately behind so that the crew could communicate without using Gosport tubes. Armament consisted of a forward-firing ·303 Vickers gun in a trough in the port side of the engine cowling and a ·303 Lewis gun on a rotatable gun ring on the rear cockpit. The front gun was replaceable by a G.3 camera gun for training purposes. Radio equipment was carried in the rear cockpit, through the starboard side of which protruded a retractable wind-driven generator.

Fuel was carried in two 39-gallon tanks in the inner bays of the top main-plane and there was provision for a 20-gallon auxilliary tank in the centre fuselage behind the fireproof bulkhead.

The Nautilus was first flown at Brough in May 1929 by T. Neville Stack, but apparently there were control and cooling problems, for an elevator of smaller chord was built and fitted and the sides of the radiator compartment, formerly vertical, were repositioned to toe inwards towards the bottom, with louvres inserted at frequent intervals; in this form trial flights were begun by A. M. Blake on 21 August 1929. These modifications prevented the Nautilus from appearing at the Olympia Aero Show in July as advertised.

By 1 November 1929 the competitive trials at Martlesham Heath were over, and the Fairey Fleetwing N235, Hawker Naval Hart J9052, and the Nautilus were flown to Gosport to be formed into No. 405 Flight, Fleet Air Arm. They were embarked in the aircraft carrier *Furious* in the Solent on 1 January 1930, the Nautilus being flown-on by Flt Lt Ward. At a later date the gun ring was removed to enable the rear cockpit to be remodelled to take a passenger seat, with standard three-piece windscreen, to enable the Nautilus to be used for ship-to-shore communication duties, for which purpose it received a blue

The Nautilus at Martlesham on 1 November 1929, ready for delivery to Gosport and showing the heavy-duty inboard front interplane struts.

fin and the large white numeral 18 on a diagonal blue fuselage band, uniform with those of the carrier's Blackburn Ripons. To make room for it the roundel was moved aft, reduced in size and the N prefix positioned above the numerals.

It appeared several times in this form at Gosport, Brooklands and elsewhere in 1931, but was later sent back to Martlesham. From this establishment the Nautilus did a considerable amount of cross-country communications flying throughout 1932, mainly to Kenley, Farnborough, Upavon and Gosport. The well-known light aeroplane exponent and RAE test pilot, Flg Off H. H. Leech, flew it from Martlesham to Farnborough on 25 November 1932, and the last recorded movement was on 25 January 1933 when Sqn Ldr Martingale flew it from Martlesham to Farnborough and back.

The Nautilus at Brooklands in 1931 while in service with No. 405 Flight, FAA, as a communications aircraft with rear passenger cockpit. (*Aeroplane Photo AE/100/521.*)

SPECIFICATION AND DATA

Manufacturers: The Blackburn Aeroplane and Motor Co Ltd, Olympia Works, Roundhay Road, Leeds, and Brough Aerodrome, East Yorks.

Power Plant: One 525 hp Rolls-Royce F.XIIMS

Dimensions: Span 37 ft 0 in   Span (folded) 14 ft 3 in
     Length (landplane) 31 ft 8 in   (seaplane) 33 ft 2 in
     Height 10 ft 10 in   Wing area 458 sq ft

Loadings:			
Two crew	360 lb	Tare weight	3,223 lb
78 gal petrol	580 lb	Military load	1,527 lb
$7\frac{1}{2}$ gal oil	75 lb		
Equipment	512 lb	All-up weight	4,750 lb
Military load	1,527 lb		

Performance: Maximum speed at 5,000 ft 154 mph
Initial climb 1,260 ft/min   Absolute ceiling 20,000 ft
Service ceiling 18,800 ft   Range 375 miles

Production: One aircraft only, N234, to Contract 792248/27 dated 21 January 1928, Works Order 761. To No. 405 Flight, Fleet Air Arm 1 January 1930; to the A. and A.E.E., Martlesham 1932.

* Landplane.

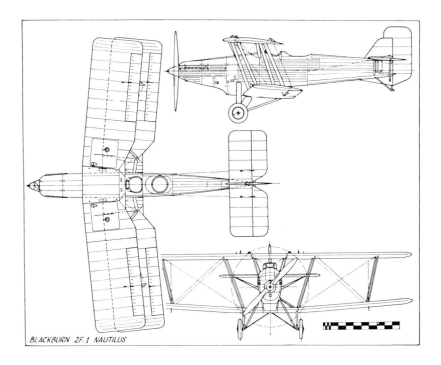

BLACKBURN 2F.1 NAUTILUS

The Beagle, as first built, with closely-cowled Bristol Jupiter VIIIF and large rudder horn balance.

Blackburn B.T.1 Beagle

The Beagle was designed by G. E. Petty, AFRAeS, initially to Air Ministry Specification 24/25 for a high-altitude bomber which could be used in a secondary role as a coastal defence torpedoplane with the military load considerably increased at the expense of performance. In March 1926, however, before the drawings were finalized, the design was modified to meet Specification 23/25, dated 18 January 1926, for a single-engined day bomber with long-range reconnaissance as well as torpedo-dropping capability. At this stage the 495 hp Bristol Orion (a supercharged development of the famous Jupiter) was suggested, but unsuccessful bench tests with this engine led eventually to the installation, in the finished aircraft, of the well-tried 460 hp Bristol Jupiter VIIIF air-cooled radial. A tender to the Air Ministry on 17 June 1926 led to a contract signed in December 1926 for one prototype, and drawings dated 16 September 1927 show the Beagle in final form as a large single-bay biplane with a strong family resemblance to the Ripon IIF.

It was built by the standard Blackburn method with the famous steel-tube centre fuselage with its machined-from-the-solid fittings, but this time terminating at the front end in an engine bearer plate for the radial engine although provision was made for alternative mountings for the Napier Lion XI or Rolls-Royce F.XII water-cooled engines. The rear fuselage reverted to wooden construction and was built from four spruce longerons spaced by cross struts and braced by steel tie rods, but the last fuselage bay, housing the tailplane incidence mechanism, was of tubular steel.

The Beagle fitted with underslung long-range tank and modified rudder.

Single-bay, equal-span, equal-dihedral, staggered mainplanes were rigged with slight sweepback, fitted with four Frise ailerons and also wing tip slots. They were of the usual Blackburn composite construction, with spruce spars and ribs braced internally by tubular-duralumin compression struts and steel tie rods, supported and braced externally by faired tubular-steel interplane struts and streamlined wires. A departure from normal practice was the attachment of the rear flying wires to the front, instead of the rear, bottom root end fittings. The mainplanes did not fold, but the outer panels were easily detachable from the top and bottom centre section for storage.

The two cockpits were arranged close together as on the Blackburn Nautilus and were similarly equipped, but extra facilities in the Beagle comprised pilot's controls for arming and releasing the torpedo and a prone bombing position beneath his seat which was reached from the gunner's cockpit. This position was equipped with bomb fusing and release controls as well as a bomb sight operated through a sliding door in the bottom of the fuselage. There was also a small dashboard with airspeed indicator and altimeter for use with an auxiliary rudder control handle which enabled the bomb-aimer to make small, last-minute directional corrections on to target. This control could be over-ridden by the pilot in emergency. A normal stick and rudder bar operated the control surfaces through a torsion-rod, push–pull layshaft system to a point between the cockpits and thence by cable.

Each half of the divided undercarriage consisted of an oleo-pneumatic main leg braced by a V of axle tubing hinged at the bottom centre-section root fittings so that each half could deflect sideways as the undercarriage took the landing load. Between the undercarriage legs was a dual purpose crutch used in the Beagle's long-range reconnaissance role to carry a 185-gallon, cigar-

246

shaped, auxiliary fuel tank with a wind-driven pump in the nose. This device was first used on the Blackburn Ripon. At other times the crutch was used to carry an 18-in naval torpedo in the usual way.

Main fuel from two 62-gallon tanks in the inner bays of the upper mainplane was gravity fed to the engine via a three-way cock operated by the pilot, and a 16-gallon oil tank (normally containing $10\frac{1}{2}$ gallons) was fitted just behind the fireproof bulkhead.

Armament consisted of a pilot's forward-firing Vickers gun mounted externally on the port side and a Lewis gun on a ring mounting round the rear cockpit.

The Beagle was first flown at Brough by Flt Lt P. W. S. Bulman on 18 February 1928 in its original form with the leading edge of the rudder horn balance conforming to the lines of the fin, but the balance area evidently proved

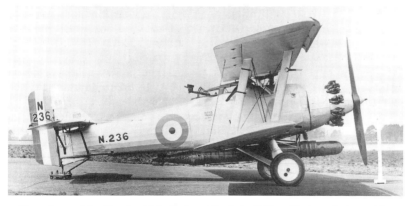

Two views of the Beagle at Martlesham Heath in 1931, with torpedo in position and powered by the Bristol Jupiter XF in more pointed nose cowlings.

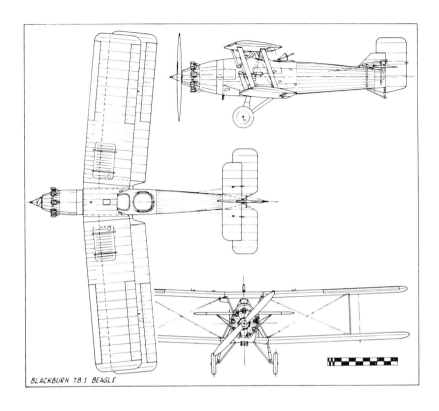

BLACKBURN T.B.1 BEAGLE

excessive, for its leading edge was subsequently clipped to give it a stepped appearance similar to the Nautilus. The machine was then retained at Brough for contractor's trials until July 1929 before being flown to the A. & A.E.E., Martlesham Heath, for performance and competitive testing with the Gloster Goring, Handley Page Hare, Westland Witch and Hawker Harrier. None of these met performance requirements, and the Beagle went back to Brough for a number of recommended improvements, not the least of which was the installation of the geared and supercharged 590 hp Bristol Jupiter XF radial in redesigned cowlings which improved the cooling by leaving more of each cylinder exposed. A proposal to fit a standard exhaust collector ring in the extreme nose was dropped and the Beagle was redelivered to Martlesham with stub exhausts on 19 March 1931. After tests it was sent to the Development Squadron at Gosport, made a brief visit to the RAE, Farnborough, on 2 November piloted by Flg Off Pearce and was afterwards returned to the manufacturers for overhaul. It was test flown at Brough on 6 June 1932 and last heard of when it landed at de Havilland's aerodrome at Stag Lane, Edgware, on 3 October that year.

248

SPECIFICATION AND DATA

Manufacturers: The Blackburn Aeroplane and Motor Co Ltd, Olympia Works, Roundhay Road, Leeds, and Brough Aerodrome, East Yorks.

Power Plants: One 460 hp Bristol Jupiter VIIIF
One 590 hp Bristol Jupiter XF

Dimensions: Span 45 ft 6 in   Length 33 ft 1 in
Height 11 ft 9 in   Wing area 570 sq ft

Loadings (Bristol Jupiter VIIIF):

(a) *Bomber*		(b) *Torpedo*	
Two crew	360 lb	Two crew	360 lb
124 gal petrol	942 lb	124 gal petrol	942 lb
10½ gal oil	105 lb	10½ gal oil	105 lb
Armament	1,218 lb	Armament	2,598 lb
Military load	2,625 lb	Military load	4,005 lb

Weights and Performance:

	Bomber		Torpedo
	Jupiter VIIIF	Jupiter XF	Jupiter VIIIF
Tare weight	3,495 lb	3,685 lb	3,495 lb
Military load	2,625 lb	2,435 lb	4,005 lb
All-up weight	6,120 lb	6,120 lb	7,500 lb★
Speed at 5,000 ft	140 mph	137 mph	133 mph
Cruising speed	115 mph	115 mph	—
Climb at 5,000 ft	740 ft/min	740 ft/min	380 ft/min
Climb at 10,000 ft	430 ft/min	—	145 ft/min
Absolute ceiling	18,000 ft	—	14,000 ft
Service ceiling	16,000 ft	16,000 ft	11,200 ft
Endurance	3½ hr†	3½ hr	3½ hr

★ Maximum permissible gross weight 7,750 lb.   † With maximum fuel 8½ hr.

Production: One prototype only, N236, ordered December 1926 to Contract 693541/26, first flown 18 February 1928, to Martlesham July 1929. Reworked with Bristol Jupiter XF to Contract 960797/29, Works Order 2689, to Martlesham 19 March 1931, to Gosport, flown again at Brough 2 June 1932.

249

Flg Off Stewart Birt taking off from Hendon in the Suffolk Aero Club's Bluebird II G-EBSZ at the start of the King's Cup Air Race on 20 July 1928. (*Flight Photo 5195.*)

Blackburn L.1A and L.1B
Bluebird II and III

Such keen interest was shown in the side-by-side seating and general sturdiness of the Bluebird prototype that Blackburns decided on limited production of an improved version to be known as Bluebird II and incorporating a number of detail modifications to suit the requirements of flying clubs and private owners.

It was fitted with the later and more powerful 80 hp Genet II five-cylinder radial on a new sheet duralumin box-mounting, lowered to bring the thrust line down to tailplane level and to improve the symmetry of the nose. It also permitted 4 hours' fuel to be carried in a 19-gallon tank in the front fuselage without forfeiting the advantages of gravity feed. The wing structure was strengthened by the use of deeper spruce spars, the mainplane gap was increased from 4 ft 9 in to 5 ft 4 in for easier entry to the cockpit, and wider doors were fitted. The top centre section was cut away to improve the backward and upward view, and a single bench-type seat was fitted right across the cockpit, with separate pneumatic cushions for the occupants. Engine controls were re-sited in a central quadrant and each control column was removable so that the machine could be flown from either seat when not used for instruction.

As on the prototype, the mainplanes folded back for stowage in minimum space, but the tailplane was made adjustable for incidence on the ground and a wider track undercarriage was fitted to improve crosswind taxying.

Thirteen Bluebird IIs were built during 1927–28, three of which, G-EBRE, 'SZ and 'UH, formed the initial equipment of the Suffolk and Eastern

250

Counties Aero Club (later known as the Suffolk Aero Club) at Hadleigh, near Ipswich. Three others, G-EBRF, 'RG and 'SV, were acquired by the Yorkshire Aeroplane Club at Sherburn-in-Elmet. Two of them were early in the news when Col the Master of Sempill returned to Hucknall in 'RF with loss of oil pressure soon after the start of the King's Cup Air Race on 30 July 1927; and Blackburn's pilot J. B. Stockbridge flew 'SV to Hendon on 8 October, picked up the Director of Civil Aviation, Sir Sefton Brancker, and flew him to the opening of the Bristol and Wessex Aeroplane Club at Filton. Members of both clubs were very enthusiastic about the new Bluebirds and on 21 March 1928 the Suffolk Aero Club's chief flying instructor, G. E. Lowdell, flew the first production machine 'RE to Croydon for inspection by King Amanullah of Afghanistan. Unfortunately the Yorkshire Club had already lost 'RG in a fatal crash at Sherburn, necessitating replacement by the tenth production machine G-EBTB in the following May.

Blackburns retained G-EBSW and 'TA as demonstration aircraft and despatched the latter to Croydon in November 1927 in charge of Flt Lt H. V. Worrall and Charles Blackburn, the company's commercial manager, for a three-day demonstration prior to an extensive tour of British flying clubs. After H. V. Worrall was recalled to take the Bluebird IIs G-EBSX and 'SY to Brazil (where he had recently demonstrated a Velos), the tour was completed by A. M. Blake with calls at Lympne, Hamble, Stag Lane, Sherburn-in-Elmet, Middlesborough, Renfrew, Cramlington (Newcastle), Woodford, Hooton (Liverpool), Filton, Castle Bromwich, Whitley, Mousehold, Wittering (CFS), Hucknall, and so back to Brough.

The Bluebird II G-EBSW with single-step floats.

251

The Bluebird II Seaplane

The machine was also offered as a seaplane, the other demonstrator, G-EBSW, being mounted on twin, single-step, anodically treated duralumin floats and its wooden airscrew replaced by a metal Fairey-Reed to avoid water damage. Col the Master of Sempill commenced a long association with this aircraft when he flew it from Brough, down the East Coast and up the Thames to the Welsh Harp, Hendon, in 4¾ hours on 14 July 1928, with an alighting on Barnes Reservoir to refuel from cans carried in the machine. On 1 August he alighted on the Thames at Westminster alongside the Imperial Airways Short Calcutta G-EBVG, which was anchored there for Parliamentary inspection, and left the Bluebird at moorings until 5 August before taking-off for Yarmouth on the first stage of a 3,000-mile holiday trip round the British coast.

Sempill reached Hartlepool the first day and then proceeded via the Farne Islands to the Firth of Forth, alighting next evening on Gladhouse Reservoir, 800 ft up in the hills north of Peebles. He then flew to Aberdeen and on, by way of Wick and Thurso, to Cape Wrath which he rounded en route to Strome Ferry and Oban before crossing to Belfast. The Bluebird seaplane was then flown the full length of the Irish coast to Wexford and on 18 August crossed 50 miles of open sea to Cornwall, flying overland from Newquay to a night alighting at Falmouth. Next day it was refuelled in Chichester Harbour before rounding the Foreland and flying up the Thames to make another night alighting, on the Welsh Harp aided by the lights of the Wembley by-pass and a few flickering matches at the water's edge.

On 5 October Sempill took off again and flew G-EBSW overland to Felixstowe for fuel and thence 100 miles across the North Sea to Amsterdam en route to the Berlin Aero Show. He alighted on the Wansee, close to the centre of the city, where, with only occasional engine runs and successfully riding out two violent winter storms, the Bluebird remained at moorings until 4 December. Sempill then flew back in appalling weather, being forced down on the Elbe by fog and held up at Amsterdam by gales. He alighted on the Zuider Zee to refuel at a Dutch waterside garage and made the North Sea crossing to Felixstowe nonstop in 4 hr on 8 December. On being flown back to the Welsh Harp, the Bluebird seaplane's ordeal came to a climax when it became frozen in. The ice had to be broken up with croquet mallets and part of the roadside fence taken down so that the machine could be towed on a trolley to Hendon to be stored for the rest of the winter. While there it was fitted with a 19-gallon centre section fuel tank.

Its final sortie on floats took place on 17 April 1929 when Sempill alighted on the Thames between Blackfriars and Waterloo Bridges to attend, at the Savoy Hotel, the inaugural luncheon of National Flying Services Ltd, who were to place an order for 25 metal Bluebird IVs later in the year. The aircraft was then fitted with wheels, and the famous float undercarriage was reconditioned at Brough for exhibition on the stand of Auto Auctions Ltd at the Olympia Aero Show during 16–27 July, 1929.

Although King's Cup honours eluded the wooden Bluebird II—Flg Off L. S. Birt retired at Hucknall in G-EBSZ in the 1928 event on 20 July—it gave faithful service in its intended role and, as the ageing Reserve School Darts were pensioned off at Brough, the North Sea Aerial and General Transport Co Ltd made increasing use of G-EBTA and 'TC for *ab initio* training. The enterprising Suffolk Aero Club, which flew 600 hours on Bluebirds in 1928 and whose CFI, G. E. Lowdell, put up such memorable aerobatic displays, formed a branch at Conington near Cambridge and from 19 November 1928 carried fare-paying passengers on the so-called Ipswich–Cambridge Airway at 30 shillings single, or 50 shillings return in the course of their Monday and Thursday positioning flights. There was also a flight to Grantham on Tuesdays to connect with the *Flying Scotsman*.

The prototype Bluebird III, G-EBWE *Friend Ship*, with its original Genet engine.

Bluebird III

Late in 1927 an improved model, the Bluebird III, was already being envisaged and the final Bluebird II, G-EBWE, was completed to this standard on the production line. External differences were twofold; the fabric-over-stringers rear decking was replaced by curved plywood incorporating a built-in locker behind the starboard seat, and to reduce fire risk the fuel was banished to a 19-gallon tank in the top centre section as on Sempill's seaplane.

G-EBWE was certificated as the prototype Bluebird III with Genet II engine in March 1928, and named *Friend Ship* for a tour of towns and villages to promote airmindedness among young people, but by the following May it had been fitted with a 90 hp A.D.C. Cirrus III as a trial-installation vehicle in readiness for the adoption of this and similar engines for the all-metal Bluebird IV which was to follow. 'WE was then acquired by Capt T. A. Gladstone, manager of the North Sea Aerial and General Transport Co Ltd's African airline interests, but it later reverted to that company before it was sold

253

to K. V. Wright, an inspector with the Fairey Aviation Co Ltd, and then transferred to Farnborough in May 1929. Aviation suffered a great loss when Wright was killed in it with Fairey's chief test pilot, Capt C. R. McMullin, on 8 September 1931 when the airscrew failed on take-off from Nivelles at the end of a visit to inspect Fairey Firefly fighters newly delivered to the Belgian Air Force.

Six Genet Bluebird IIIs were built in addition to the prototype, and the first, G-AABB, was shown with wheel undercarriage and a specimen float at the Berlin Aero Show of 7–28 October 1928, to which Sempill had flown in the Bluebird II seaplane G-EBSW. The second, 'BC, was exhibited for ten days in the motor showrooms of Francis E. Cox at 101 Water Lane, Leeds, in November 1928 before sale in Spain. The third, 'BD (originally destined for Armstrong Siddeley Motors Ltd), was delivered to the Yorkshire Aeroplane Club on 2 April 1929 to replace G-EBTB which had been written off in an accident.

The remaining three, G-AABE, 'BF and 'BG, were built for the Suffolk Aero Club, but the final machine and its float undercarriage were never

G-EBWE, with the inline A.D.C. Cirrus III engine, before and after painting.

254

The first production Bluebird II, in the Suffolk Aero Club's later colour scheme after modification to 'Bluebird Mk 2½' with the centre section fuel tank of the Bluebird III. (*Flight Photo 7789.*)

completed due to lack of support for a proposed seaplane section at Brightlingsea, Essex. Nevertheless, vigorous landplane activity continued at Marshall's, Cambridge (which replaced Conington in April 1929) and at Hadleigh, with the two Bluebird IIIs and two modernized Bluebird IIs with new centre-section fuel tanks.

In 1929 the Yorkshire Aeroplane Club flew 1,125 hr 25 min with its three Bluebirds but from 1930 followed the example of the Suffolk Aero Club and began to phase them out in favour of more up-to-date equipment. Thus G-EBRF and 'SV went south to L. J. C. Mitchell at Chard, Somerset, and F. R. G. Spikins at Hanworth respectively, and G-EBSZ passed via C. N. Prentice at Blue Barns Aerodrome, Colchester, into the hands of R. D. Gerrans at Broxbourne. In February 1933 G-AABE arrived at the old Rochford Aerodrome to become the Southend Flying Club's first light aeroplane, and 'BF went via private-owner H. R. Law to Miss Sicele O'Brien who was killed when it spun in when taking off from Hatfield after a refuelling stop on its delivery flight from Brough to Hanworth on 18 June 1931. The last survivor of this small but select band was the veteran G-EBRF which ended its career as the set piece in a fire-fighting display at Gravesend Airport in 1937.

In New Zealand

After its return from the Berlin Aero Show, the first production Bluebird III G-AABB was shipped to New Zealand, arriving in Auckland in February 1929 consigned to H. T. Merritt. Together with a D. H. Moth it formed the equipment of Southern Cross Airways Ltd, a short-lived concern based at Ihumatao (now known as Mangere). When that company ceased operations 'BB was acquired by James Tidd and Roy Kemp of Hamilton, but the latter collided with a fence on his first flight, and the aircraft was shipped to Hobsonville for repair. New Zealand registration ZK-AAQ was then allotted and the machine traded to S. J. Blackmore who went solo on it after only

Bluebird III G-AABB in Southern Cross Airways markings at Ihumatao Aerodrome, Auckland, New Zealand, in April 1929, prior to repainting as ZK-AAQ. (*Courtesy K. Meehan.*)

2 hr 20 min dual instruction. The new owner then fitted floats and flew the Bluebird to Hokianga Harbour, North Auckland, where, after some local flying, it was sold to A. and C. Brazier of the Waikato Aero Club and refitted with the wheeled undercarriage. It was used for instruction until it stalled off a turn and crashed in a swamp near Te Rapa Aerodrome, Hamilton, on 2 April 1933, with fatal results for its 19-year-old pilot.

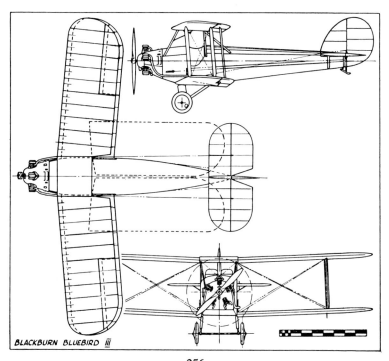

BLACKBURN BLUEBIRD III

SPECIFICATION AND DATA

Manufacturers: The Blackburn Aeroplane and Motor Co Ltd, Olympia Works, Roundhay Road, Leeds, and Brough Aerodrome, East Yorks.

Power Plants: One 80 hp Armstrong Siddeley Genet II
One 90 hp A.D.C. Cirrus III

Dimensions, Weights and Performance:

	Genet II		Cirrus III	
	Landplane	Seaplane	Landplane	Seaplane
Span	28 ft 0 in	28 ft 0 in	28 ft 0 in	28 ft 0 in
Span folded	9 ft 8 in	9 ft 8 in	9 ft 8 in	9 ft 8 in
Length	22 ft 6 in	—	22 ft 6 in	—
Height	8 ft 4 in	10 ft 3 in	8 ft 4 in	10 ft 3 in
Wing area	237·5 sq ft	237·5 sq ft	237·5 sq ft	237·5 sq ft
Tare weight	915 lb	—	1,050 lb	—
All-up weight	1,400 lb★	1,503 lb	1,500 lb	1,576 lb
Speed at sea level	88 mph	84 mph	90 mph	86 mph
Speed at 5,000 ft	86 mph	82 mph	89·5 mph	85 mph
Cruising speed	75 mph	70 mph	75 mph	70 mph
Initial climb	400 ft/min	330 ft/min	660 ft/min	540 ft/min
Absolute ceiling	11,300 ft	9,300 ft	—	—
Service ceiling	9,000 ft	7,500 ft	13,400 ft	11,000 ft
Range	300 miles	280 miles	217 miles	207 miles

★ 1,465 lb when modernized with centre-section tank.

Production:

(a) *Blackburn L.1A Bluebird II*
    Thirteen aircraft, Works Orders 9803/2 to 9803/14 as follows:

G-EBRE, C. of A. 25 August 1927, Suffolk and Eastern Counties Aero Club, damaged beyond repair at Hadleigh 6 January 1930.

G-EBRF, C. of A. 27 July 1927, Yorkshire Aeroplane Club; to L. J. C. Mitchell, Chard June 1930; B. Paddon, Heston August 1932; to R. H. Henderson, Hanworth February 1935; to Hon. A. B. Mildmay, Gravesend July 1936, burned at Gravesend 3 August 1937.

G-EBRG, C. of A. 13 September 1927, Yorkshire Aeroplane Club, crashed at Sherburn-in-Elmet 5 February 1928.

G-EBSV, C. of A. 18 September 1927, Yorkshire Aeroplane Club; to F. R. G. Spikins, Hanworth December 1930, dismantled in his Twickenham garage 1932.

G-EBSW, C. of A. 19 September 1927, seaplane for the Blackburn Aeroplane and Motor Co Ltd; to landplane for Flt Lt G. E. Lywood June 1930; to Norman Edgar, Whitchurch, Bristol, July 1933, withdrawn from use December 1933.

G-EBSX and G-EBSY, Cs. of A. 31 October and 8 October 1927 respectively, the Blackburn Aeroplane and Motor Co Ltd, shipped to Brazil 17 October 1927, registrations cancelled 11 November 1927.

257

G-EBSZ, C. of A. 20 September 1927, the Blackburn Aeroplane and Motor Co Ltd; to the Suffolk Aero Club 3 March 1928; to C. N. Prentice, Blue Barns March 1931; to R. D. Gerrans, Broxbourne January 1932, dismantled 1936.

G-EBTA, C. of A. 13 October 1927, the Blackburn Aeroplane and Motor Co Ltd; to the North Sea Aerial and General Transport Co Ltd, Brough April 1928, crashed December 1930.

G-EBTB, C. of A. 27 March 1928, the Blackburn Aeroplane and Motor Co Ltd; to the Yorkshire Aeroplane Club, Sherburn May 1928, crashed March 1929.

G-EBTC, C. of A. 8 July 1928, the North Sea Aerial and General Transport Co Ltd, Brough; to the Blackburn Aeroplane and Motor Co Ltd July 1928; to the North Sea Aerial and General Transport Co Ltd October 1928, crashed March 1930.

G-EBUH, C. of A. 17 May 1928, the Blackburn Aeroplane and Motor Co Ltd; to the Suffolk and Eastern Counties Aero Club, withdrawn from use 1932.

G-EBUI, C. of A. 5 October 1928, the Blackburn Aeroplane and Motor Co Ltd, crashed March 1929.

(b) *Blackburn L.1B Bluebird III*

One prototype and six production aircraft, Works Orders 1450/1 to 1450/6 as follows:

G-EBWE, laid down as a Bluebird II to Works Order 9803/15 but completed as the prototype Bluebird III with Genet II engine to Works Order 629/1, C. of A. 17 March 1928, Blackburn Aeroplane and Motor Co Ltd *Friend Ship*; re-engined with Cirrus III April 1928; to T. A. Gladstone, Brough October 1928; to the North Sea Aerial and General Transport Co Ltd, Brough May 1929; to K. V. Wright, Farnborough May 1930, crashed at Nivelles, Belgium, 8 September 1931.

G-AABB, C. of A. 4 December 1928, H. T. Merritt, Auckland, NZ; to J. Tidd and R. Kemp, Hamilton; to S. J. Blackmore, Hamilton as ZK-AAQ; to seaplane; to landplane for A. and C. Brazier, trading as the Waikato Aero Club, crashed at Te Rapa, Hamilton, 2 April 1933.

G-AABC, C. of A. 8 November 1928, sold in Spain to Señor Fernando Pedioza August 1929.

G-AABD, C. of A. 27 March 1929, Armstrong Siddeley Motors Ltd; to the Yorkshire Aeroplane Club April 1929; to T. Martin November 1930; to C. E. Dooks, Bridlington March 1931, dismantled 1931.

G-AABE, C. of A. 27 March 1929, the Blackburn Aeroplane and Motor Co Ltd; to the Suffolk and Eastern Counties Aero Club March 1929; to Southend-on-Sea Flying Services Ltd February 1933; to Aircraft and Autos Ltd, Croydon September 1935; to G. H. Charlton, Chilworth March 1936 crashed near Lichfield 22 March 1936.

G-AABF, C. of A. 31 May 1929, Suffolk and Eastern Counties Aero Club; to H. R. Law May 1930; to Mrs G. Gallien and Miss S. O'Brien, Hanworth June 1931, crashed at Hatfield 18 June 1931.

G-AABG, laid down as a seaplane for the Suffolk and Eastern Counties Aero Club, order cancelled and aircraft not completed.

Sqn Ldr Jack Noakes in the helmeted Lincock I preparing to leave Hendon in the King's Cup Air Race of 20 July 1928. (*Courtesy P. T. Capon.*)

Blackburn F.2 Lincock

To give Blackburn's design staff an opportunity of creating a high-performance aeroplane unencumbered by excessive armament, bomb racks, external stores, wireless, night-flying gear and other heavy, drag-producing impedimenta called for in Government contracts, the company decided in 1928 to resurrect the light fighter concept and build a small, private-venture single-seater. It was an attractive little biplane designed by Maj F. A. Bumpus, with G. E. Petty as his chief assistant, and was powered by a 240 hp Armstrong Siddeley Lynx IVc seven-cylinder air-cooled radial driving a two-bladed wooden airscrew. Although designated F.2, it inevitably acquired the name Lincock, a corruption of Lynx-cock, and with a performance approximating to that of a heavily laden standard fighter, but on only half the power, was intended for small nations whose economies could not support high-powered machines.

High performance was obtained by designing an exceptionally low-drag airframe, carefully balancing the controls and concentrating the main loads, including the 35-gallon fuel tank, near the C.G.

The first machine was an unarmed aerodynamic prototype of all-wood construction with a near-perfect plywood monocoque fuselage located between the mainplanes in the mid-gap position by steel N struts below, and short centre-section struts above. Mainplanes and tail unit were built up from spruce spars and ribs in the usual way and fabric covered. High rate of roll was ensured by fitting four ailerons, the tailplane was adjustable for incidence in flight, and the tail cone was built integral with the rudder as on the Turcock. Civil-registered G-EBVO, it was first seen in public on 15 May 1928, when Sqn Ldr Jack Noakes ferried it back to Brough to attend the·Press pre-view of the Ripon II prototype after performance trials at Martlesham Heath and

259

gave the first of the aerobatic shows for which it later became famous in the hands of G. E. Lowdell and A. M. Blake.

Robert Blackburn then entered it for the two-day, round-Britain King's Cup Air Race which began at Hendon on 20 July that year. Again flown by Noakes, it was 9th at Renfrew at the end of the first day and crossed the finishing line at Brooklands in 10th place at an average speed of 145·32 mph (often misquoted as 115·32 mph). For this event the engine was streamlined with metal cylinder helmets but they caused overheating and were removed after the race.

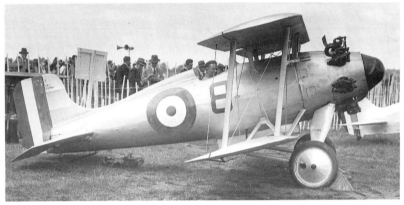

The Lincock I masquerading as a military aircraft in the New Types Park at the Hendon RAF Display, 28 June 1930. (*Flight Photo.*)

At the Lympne and Cambridge Easter Meetings 1929, at the Norfolk and Norwich Aero Club meeting at Mousehold on 19–20 May, and at Heston during the Olympia Aero Show in July, Lowdell's upward rolls, never before seen on such a low-powered machine, were the sensation of the year. At this time the Lincock was plain silver with black lettering outlined in white, but for the 1930 season it was repainted in a garish colour scheme of alternate black and yellow fuselage bands. After A. M. Blake's polished performances at the Stoke-on-Trent Air Pageant on 6 May, at the opening of Bristol Airport, Whitchurch, on 30 May, and at the Whitsun meeting of the Berks, Bucks and Oxon Aero Club at Woodley on 9 June, it was hurriedly resprayed silver. With crudely-painted RAF roundels, it became Exhibit No. 8 in the New Types Park at the Hendon RAF Display on 28 June, replacing an all-metal Lincock III which had been damaged a week before.

After the display it was painted blue overall and, as described later, was taken to Chicago by Flt Lt R. L. R. Atcherley. Its aerobatic displays were resumed in the following year, one of the last being at the Stanley Park Air Display, Blackpool, on 8 July 1931. It was back at Brough by 31 July and there withdrawn from use and dismantled when the C. of A. expired in the following month.

Lincock II

The Lincock at once attracted the attention of the Canadian Government and as a result Wg Cdr E. W. Stedman, Director of Technical Services, and RCAF liaison officer Sqn Ldr A. L. Cuffe, arrived at Brough by air on 13 August 1928 to inspect it. Possible delivery dates for six machines, less engines, were requested in the following October, and on 2 November the RCAF asked for a demonstration in Canada, at the same time suggesting an alternative model in metal. Blackburns agreed to send the Lincock I, G-EBVO, but shortly afterwards the RCAF said that it would insist on a metal aircraft for Canadian conditions and were advised on 17 January 1929 that a metal Lincock could be built and delivered in Canada by the end of July that year.

No more wooden Lincocks were constructed and translation into metal began at once, the second aircraft having a steel and duralumin fuselage, and mainplanes with drawn-steel spars and stamped-out duralumin ribs of the type used on the metal Bluebird IV. Fuselage construction reverted to the time-honoured Blackburn system of bolting the engine mounting and rear fuselage to a rigidly built steel centre fuselage, the whole being fabric covered apart from removable duralumin panels forwards from the cockpit. It was slightly longer than the original and, as a result of wind tunnel experiments and flight trials with a temporary structure fitted to the Lincock I, a slim ventral fairing was fitted inside the steel N struts to smooth the airflow between the under-fuselage and the bottom centre section.

A tall, oleo-pneumatic, split-type undercarriage replaced the rubber-in-compression type with transverse axle used on the Lincock I, and the machine was fitted with a more powerful geared Lynx driving a Fairey-Reed metal airscrew. It was not finished in time to go to Canada by the appointed date,

The Lincock II at Brough in October 1928.

261

The Lincock II in civil marks at Rockcliffe RCAF base, Canada, in 1930.
(*Courtesy National Aviation Museum of Canada.*)

being exhibited instead at the Olympia Aero Show of 16–27 July 1929 under the designation F.2A and type name Lincock II. It was still incomplete and was fitted with oversize wheels apparently from a Ripon, the airscrew was temporary, and there was no pitot head.

After the Show the Lincock II returned to Brough to be fitted with standard wire wheels and a metal airscrew with undersized spinner for C. of A. flight trials by test pilot A. M. Blake. It was registered G-AALH as a civil aeroplane and according to surviving records was packed for shipment by 3 January 1930, consigned to de Havilland Aircraft of Canada Ltd, Toronto (who had been appointed Blackburn agents), by the SS *Manchester Producer* due to leave on 8 February. It was, in fact, despatched on the SS *Manchester Division* on 13 February, arriving at St John, New Brunswick, about 23 February and at Toronto a week later.

Its arrival on 28 February 1930 coincided with the issue of its Certificate of Airworthiness, and it was first flown at Downsview by G. S. O'Brian on or before 21 March and all re-erection test flying was complete by 30 April. Fitted with a wooden airscrew, it was demonstrated to the RCAF at Camp Borden and on 20 May A. T. Cowley flew it at Montreal. Further RCAF demonstrations took place at Ottawa and Rockcliffe, and on 19 June Wg Cdr E. W. Stedman, Director of Technical Services, noted the favourable comments of pilots who had flown it and there was talk of establishing a factory to build it in Canada. This possibility came a step nearer on 7 July 1930 when Flt Lt F. B. Beamish, OC of 'F' Flight at Camp Borden, submitted an extremely favourable report on a 10-hour evaluation test which underlined the ease with which the Lincock was maintained, flown and manoeuvred. It was easy to land, and he considered it ideal for advanced training and aerobatics.

262

In the end it was not adopted for the same reason that the RAF did not purchase it, viz. it was not a first line fighter and there was no necessity for a transition machine between the standard trainers and fighters of the day. In August 1930 E. Leigh Capreol ferried it from Toronto to Montreal so that Flt Lt Beamish could use it for aerobatic displays at the Light Aeroplane Club's air pageant on 6–7 September, after which the machine went back to the de Havilland plant and was still there on 31 December awaiting shipment to England.

Meanwhile Flt Lt R. L. R. (later Air Marshal Sir Richard) Atcherley had been invited to give crazy-flying exhibitions at the International Air Meeting at Chicago from 23 August to 1 September 1930. The most suitable mount then available was unquestionably G-EBVO, the wooden Lincock I, which Robert Blackburn sold him for a nominal 10 shillings because serving RAF officers, though permitted to perform publicly in their own private aeroplanes, were not allowed to do so in manufacturers' demonstration aircraft. He sailed in the *Leviathan* with the dismantled Lincock on 10 August and was joined at Cherbourg by the other European performers—Marcel Doret (France), Dewoitine D.27; Pietro Colombo (Italy), Breda 18; and Fritz Lohse (Germany), Junkers Junior.

Throughout the Meeting the superbly matched Atcherley/Lincock combination brought the great Chicago crowd to its feet with a breath-taking aerobatic sequence which included an inverted falling leaf and did much to enhance the prestige of British aircraft design and standards of piloting. A remarkable and little publicized fact was that, for a brief period, both prototype Lincocks were in North America at the same time.

The Lincock I, at Chicago in August 1930, with the fairing in the gap between the fuselage and bottom wing. (*USAF Photo A-15399.*)

Lincock III

As a result of oriental interest in the Lincock II, Blackburns built five others, two each for the Governments of Japan and China and one as their own European demonstrator. Designated F.2D, they were powered by the new 270 hp Lynx Major with exhaust collector rings and two-bladed wooden airscrews and were known as Lincock IIIs.

The first of these flew for the first time at Brough on 6 June 1930, and it was scheduled to appear in the New Types Park at the Hendon RAF Display on 28 June but was prevented from doing so by slight damage incurred the week before, its place being taken therefore by the Lincock I.

Lincock IIIs differed from the unarmed Lincock I and II in carrying two Vickers guns in troughs along each side of the front fuselage, with their mechanisms inside the cockpit within easy reach of the pilot for clearing stoppages. To keep the all up weight down to 2,000 lb, the split undercarriage gave place to a lighter type with transverse axle and oleo-pneumatic main legs, while in the rear the helical tail spring was removed from inside the stern post and fitted externally.

The Japanese Lincock IIIs were despatched in September 1930; the final pair, for China, were shipped from the Royal Victoria Docks, Woolwich, in the SS *Glengarry* in December 1930 consigned to the agents, Arnhold and Co, Sassoon House, Shanghai, and they are said to have been used against the Japanese in 1932. A version for Spain with Lynx Major or Lynx IVC, designated F.2E, was not built.

The Lincock III demonstrator was registered to the manufacturers as G-ABFK in October 1930 and a year later on 4 October 1931 left Brough for Customs clearance at Heston, piloted by T. Neville Stack, and was accompanied by the Blackburn Bluebird IV G-ABPV, flown by H. J. Andrews (formerly of the Spanish Navy Swift squadron), and the Blackburn Segrave G-ABFP flown by A. M. Blake and carrying Robert Blackburn as passenger. They made a 5,700-mile sales tour of France, Belgium, Germany, Czechoslovakia, Austria, Hungary, Yugoslavia and Greece, terminating at Tatoi Aerodrome, Athens, where the aircraft was flown by several Greek pilots, but after the fatal crash of the Bluebird on 24 October the party returned home, leaving the Lincock behind in charge of H. J. Andrews.

Despite the considerable interest aroused in many of the countries visited, no further orders were received for the Lincock, but the Italian Regia Aeronautica saw it as a potential fighter trainer and the Piaggio company acquired a licence for its construction in Italy. The result was the Piaggio P.11, a tandem two-seater which was a cross between the Lincock I and III combining a wooden monocoque fuselage with the Lincock III under-fairing and tail surfaces. Piaggio designed a strengthened undercarriage and fitted the Lynx Major engine built under licence in Italy by Alfa Romeo. Only one P.11 was built, first flown in 1932.

The Brough flight shed in October 1930 showing the Lincock I in blue colour-scheme with experimental fairing under the fuselage, the demonstration Lincock III, G-ABFK, and the two Chinese Lincock IIIs under construction.

Running-up the Lincock III European demonstrator G-ABFK at Brough in October 1930. (*Flight Photo 9475.*)

Japanese pilots running-up the first two production Lincock IIIs in Japan 1931.

265

The two-seat Lincock trainer built under licence in Italy as the Piaggio P. 11.
(*Courtesy John Stroud.*)

The Lincock II with Cobham's Circus, showing the Lincock III undercarriage,
non-standard gun ports and radio aerial installation.

Air Displays

Writing about a visit to the Blackburn works on 25 February 1932, the
late F. D. Bradbrooke noted that the Lincock II G-AALH was in the Flight
Shed being fitted with the light-weight, transverse-axle undercarriage and a
270 hp Armstrong Siddeley Lynx Major engine. With these modifications it
was similar externally to the Lincock III G-ABFK, and early in 1933 Sir
Alan Cobham acquired both aircraft for the 'radio controlled' aerobatic act
in his National Aviation Day Displays.

266

To heighten its resemblance to 'FK, G-AALH was fitted with grooved side cowlings of odd shape which would certainly never have housed guns. It was doped yellow overall and joined No. 1 Display in charge of Geoffrey Tyson, and after a test flight at Brough by A. G. Loton on 31 May 1933, G-ABFK joined No. 2 Display. They performed at countless towns and villages until the following October, wintered at the Display's base at Ford Aerodrome, Sussex, and resumed their respective tours in a mauve colour scheme in the following April.

Two months later, however, G-ABFK was flown to Brooklands and handed over to the College of Aeronautical Engineering as an instructional airframe. In 1936, as an exercise in aircraft engineering, the students re-engined it with an Alfa Romeo radial engine which, being of lighter weight, necessitated the insertion of an additional bay into the front fuselage.

Lincock III G-ABFK in the workshops of the College of Aeronautical Engineering, Brooklands, in 1936 with extended front fuselage and Alfa Romeo radial.

SPECIFICATION AND DATA

Manufacturers: The Blackburn Aeroplane and Motor Co Ltd, Olympia Works, Roundhay Road, Leeds, and Brough Aerodrome, East Yorks.
Societa Anonima Piaggio, Finalmarina, Italy.

Power Plants: (Lincock I)   One 240 hp Armstrong Siddeley Lynx IVC
          (Lincock II)   One 255 hp Armstrong Siddeley Lynx IV (geared)
          (Lincock III)   One 270 hp Armstrong Siddeley Lynx Major
          (Piaggio P. 11) One 270 hp Alfa Romeo Lynx Major

Dimensions, Weights and Performance:

	Lincock I	Lincock II	Lincock III
Span	22 ft 6 in	22 ft 6 in	22 ft 6 in
Length	18 ft 1½ in	19 ft 6 in	19 ft 6 in
Height	7 ft 4½ in	7 ft 10 in	7 ft 4 in
Wing area	170 sq ft	170 sq ft	170 sq ft
Tare weight	—	1,244 lb	1,326 lb
Disposable load	438 lb	674 lb	756 lb
All-up weight	2,000 lb	2,000 lb	2,082 lb
Speed at sea level	146 mph	155 mph	164 mph
Speed at 10,000 ft	—	142 mph	159 mph
Speed at 15,000 ft	—	136 mph	153 mph
Cruising speed	—	128 mph	141 mph
Initial climb	1,220 ft/min	1,450 ft/min	1,660 ft/min
Climb at 10,000 ft	1,060 ft/min	—	1,000 ft/min
Climb at 15,000 ft	—	380 ft/min	640 ft/min
Service ceiling	24,000 ft	20,000 ft	23,000 ft
Range	—	390 miles	380 miles

Production:

(a) *Lincock I*

One aircraft only to Works Order 9906, civil registered G-EBVO in the name of the manufacturers by C. of R. No. 1545 dated 6 January 1928, C. of A. No. 1508 issued 14 July 1928, dismantled at Brough after C. of A. expiry 2 August 1931.

(b) *Lincock II*

One aircraft only to Works Order 2050/1, civil registered G-AALH in the name of the manufacturers by C. of R. No. 2129 dated 22 August 1929, shipped to Canada 13 February 1930, C. of A. No. 2424 issued 28 February 1930, shipped back to Brough 1931, re-registered to Sir Alan Cobham 9 May 1933, C. of A. renewed 1 June 1933, to National Aviation Day Displays Ltd 27 November 1933, dismantled after C. of A. expiry 27 March 1935.

(c) *Lincock III*

Five aircraft as under:

Two unregistered for Japan (i) to Works Order 2741/1, first flown 6 June 1930, C. of A. No. 2681 issued 5 August 1930; (ii) to Works Order 2920/1, C. of A. No. 2725 issued 10 September 1930.

One European demonstrator to Works Order 2920/2, civil-registered in the name of the manufacturers as G-ABFK by C. of R. No. 2842 dated 27 September 1930, C. of A. No. 2784 issued 11 October 1930, re-registered to Sir Alan Cobham 9 May 1933, C. of A. renewed 3 June 1933, to instructional airframe at Brooklands at C. of A. expiry 2 June 1934, still there without engine June 1936.

Two unregistered for China to Works Orders 2920/3 and 2920/4, first flown 31 October 1930 and 10 November 1930 respectively, Cs. of A. Nos. 2818 and 2819 issued 18 November 1930 in the name of Arnhold and Co., Shanghai, shipped from Woolwich December 1930.

(d) *Piaggio P11*

One prototype only, first flown 1932.

268

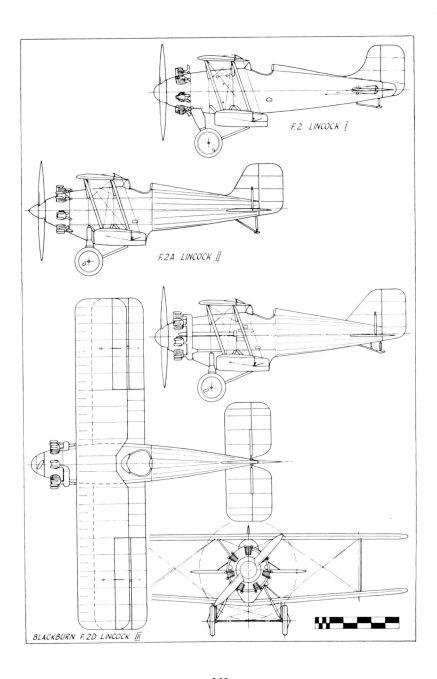

F.2 LINCOCK I

F.2A LINCOCK II

BLACKBURN F.2D LINCOCK III

269

The Sydney N241 ready for first flight in the all-silver colour scheme at Brough on 18 July 1930. (*Courtesy J. W. R. Taylor.*)

Blackburn R.B.2 Sydney and C.B.2 Nile

As the company designation implied, the Sydney was Blackburn's second maritime reconnaissance flying-boat. Considerable operational experience with the Iris II left no doubt that its all-metal hull was very good indeed, not only on account of its behaviour in the air and on the water, but also from the point of view of accommodation. Maj J. D. Rennie, the company's chief seaplane designer, therefore made it the basis of his proposals to Air Ministry Specification R.5/27, and the Sydney was conceived virtually as a monoplane version of the Iris. The design was approved by Grp Capt J. A. Chamier on behalf of the Directorate of Technical Development on 23 June 1927, and a contract was placed on 23 February 1928 for one boat with three 510 hp Rolls-Royce Falcon X engines. To keep pace with the rapid development of this power plant, however, the Air Ministry requested 525 hp Rolls-Royce F.XIIAs on 22 June that year and the F.XIIMS (with which it was eventually completed) on 23 January, 1929.

Designs for Britain's first large monoplane flying-boat were completed by mounting the wing on a duralumin-covered tubular-steel pylon amidships so that the thrust line of the three engines was in the same position relative to the tailplane as on the biplane boat. Pilot comfort was improved by fitting a cabin top incorporating sliding roof and side windows, and the biplane tail gave place to a monoplane unit.

The value of such a flying-boat for civil purposes was obvious and Black-

270

burns decided to build two, one to carry five crew and Iris-type armament for the Air Ministry and the other furnished to the airline standards of the day. Designated C.B.2 (i.e. Blackburn's second commercial boat), it was intended to carry three crew, 14 passengers, baggage and mail, on the Alexandria to Cape Town route of Cobham–Blackburn Air Lines Ltd, formed for the purpose on 24 April 1928 by a fusion of interests between the North Sea Aerial and General Transport Co Ltd, operators of the pioneer Khartoum–Kisumu route with the de Havilland D.H. 50J seaplane *Pelican*, and Alan Cobham Aviation Ltd which had surveyed air routes in and around Africa.

This new civil flying-boat was given the appropriate type name Nile, but whereas the Sydney followed Iris tradition and used three water-cooled engines, the fine serviceability record of the *Pelican's* Bristol Jupiter air-cooled radial under tropical conditions led to the choice of three 515 hp Jupiter IX geared engines for the Nile.

The two flying-boats took shape side by side at Brough during 1928–29, and the hull of the Nile, with large square passenger windows replacing the circular portholes of the military Sydney, was completed and furnished in time for transportation to London to form the *pièce de résistance* at the Olympia Aero Show of 16–27 July 1929. There was a compartment in the extreme nose for storing marine tackle or picking up moorings and behind this lay the pilots' cabin with dual controls. These compartments were still incomplete, but the main cabin was furnished with leather armchairs arranged in groups of four in facing pairs. Two additional seats faced one another in the starboard rear corner, and an instrument panel with altimeter, airspeed indicator and clock was fitted to the front bulkhead for the interest of passengers. Aft of the cabin was a toilet, a steward's pantry and a companion ladder leading down from the entry hatch above. Baggage and mail were stowed in the extreme tail.

After the Aero Show the hull was taken back to Brough and re-inserted into the production line between the Sydney and the Iris IIIs, S1263 and

A model of the Bristol Jupiter engined Nile civil transport.

271

The hull of the Nile on the Blackburn stand at Olympia in July 1929.

The Sydney (*top*), Nile, and Iris III S1264 under construction at Brough on 20 October 1929. (*Central Press Photo.*)

S1264, where it was very much in evidence bearing the name *Nile*, legacy of the Show, on the occasion of the launching of the prototype Iris III, N238, on 21 October 1929. By February 1930 it was almost complete and Canadian Airways were also showing interest in a production version designated C.B.2F. Prices quoted were £21,500 each for the first five boats and £19,000 each for subsequent aircraft for delivery 9–12 months from receipt of order. Not long afterwards, however, the British Government ruled that Imperial Airways should be responsible for all Empire air communications, using existing equipment. This ended Cobham–Blackburn's African trunk route aspirations, all work on the Nile ceased forthwith, and Canada never saw a Blackburn flying-boat.

The discarded hull lay neglected in the works for over five years until placed in a test rig of steel girders in 1935. It was then subjected to increasing loads during an investigation into the strength of stressed-skin structures which led first to progressive buckling and eventually to final destruction.

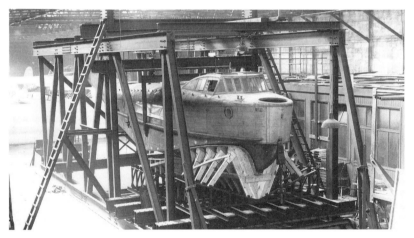

The hull of the Nile commercial flying-boat in the rig ready to be tested to destruction, August 1935.

The Sydney

Work was then concentrated on the Sydney, whose hull, like that of the unhappy Nile, was roomier than that of the Iris because its sides were perpendicular above the waterline instead of sloping inwards to the top decking. The tailplane and semi-cantilever mainplane were fabric covered but their internals were all-metal, constructed of duralumin box spars and girder-type ribs. The mainplane was 2 ft $4\frac{1}{2}$ in deep at its thickest point and consisted of a parallel-chord centre wing of RAF 30 section, embodying the dihedral and metal-clad on its upper surface to form a walkway round the engines. It was

273

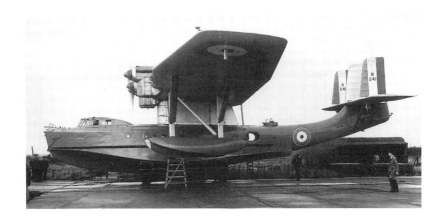

The Sydney before and after launching in battleship-grey on 28 November 1930. (*Flight Photos 9491 and 9494.*)

braced to the chines of the hull by parallel struts of faired steel tubing which intersected the stabilizing float-support struts at a point immediately below the outboard engines. The outer wing panels tapered in plan and thickness and carried the Frise-type ailerons.

Engine nacelles were similar to those of the Iris II but with built-in radiator shutters operated by the flight engineer from his station in the hull, and fuel was pumped to the engine from a 560-gallon main tank inside the wing pylon via a distributor control. Oil coolers lay flush in the sides of the pylon and a gas starter system was installed.

There were no fins, and the three rudders were unbraced externally, the centre rudder acting purely as a trimmer and the outer pair carrying trailing edge servo tabs which could be engaged or disengaged as required. Similarly, the two inner sections of the four-part elevator acted solely as trimmers.

274

From a research point of view, the most important feature of the hull design was the venting of the front step in an attempt to assist take-off by breaking the surface tension between the planing bottom and the water at high speeds. This was a simple device without working parts, air from two scoops on the sides of the hull just above the waterline being ejected from twenty-two $\frac{11}{16}$ in diameter holes in the vertical wall of the step.

Armament was similar to that of the Iris, with ·303-in Lewis guns in the bows, amidships and behind the tail unit, as well as bomb racks under the wings for two 550-lb (or 520-lb) or four 250-lb (or 230-lb) bombs as well as four 20-lb practice missiles. The main difference was that torpedoes were, for the first time, to be carried by a flying-boat, crutches and release gear for two 1,850-lb Mk VIII or Mk X Whitehead torpedoes being installed.

Sprayed all-silver and carrying RAF serial N241, the Sydney was rolled out on its beaching trolley for first engine runs in June 1930. It was launched and made a first flight, flying light, of nine minutes duration in the hands of Sqn Ldr C. A. Rea on 18 July, take-off time being 26 seconds. The second and third flights, with loads, were made on 28 July and 13 August respectively. After this the Sydney went back into the works for detailed inspection and emerged in the following October resprayed in the same battleship grey as the Iris II.

When test flown by Sqn Ldr Rea on 15 October, the centre engine seized, delaying the completion of tests at Brough until 28 November, but after a timed climb to 4,000 ft next day the Sydney was collected on 30 November by a Felixstowe ferry crew with Flt Lt Weblin as pilot. He took off at 1.40 pm and proceeded south in worsening visibility until fog in the Wash forced him to return to Brough where an alighting was made at 3.10 pm. The Sydney was then moored out overnight and taken up the slipway next afternoon, so that delivery to the M.A.E.E., Felixstowe, did not take place until 9 December.

On arrival it was allocated to 'A' Flight for performance testing, and a series of modifications to the tail unit, to the mainplane, its external bracing and its points of attachment to the hull. Chief of these was to remove the diagonal bracing strut above each float and replace it by a pinjointed horizontal strut with wire cross-bracing below and a diagonal strut above, as shown in the illustration on page 276. Horizontal struts were also fitted to the tail unit between the rudder posts.

In flight the large central pylon was found to cause partial blanketing of the elevator control, particularly in the glide below 100 mph, so that the Sydney had to be flown on to the water with a 'trickle' of engine; this was corrected by increasing the elevator chord by 20 per cent.

Tests to determine the effect of the vented step were made in Harwich Harbour and on the open sea at gross weights of 21,500 lb and 25,000 lb, but the improvement in take-off time was negligible, even with the scoop raised into the slipstream of the centre engine. Full performance tests were frustrated by recurring unserviceability and the aircraft was struck off charge in

1934, plans to produce a higher-powered version designated R.B.2A with Rolls-Royce Kestrel MS engines being shelved.

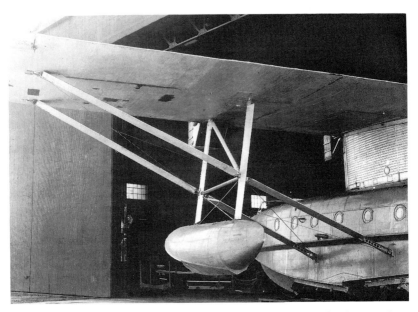

Close-up of the Sydney's modified wing struts. The air scoop for the vented step is visible below the third and fourth portholes.

SPECIFICATION AND DATA

Manufacturers: The Blackburn Aeroplane and Motor Co Ltd, Olympia Works, Roundhay Road, Leeds, and Brough Aerodrome, East Yorks.

Power Plants: (Sydney)   Three 525 hp Rolls-Royce F.XIIMS
(Nile)   Three 515 hp Bristol Jupiter IX

Dimensions and Performance:

	Sydney*	Nile
Span	100 ft 0 in	100 ft 0 in
Length	65 ft 7 in	65 ft 7 in
Height	20 ft 4 in	19 ft 2½ in
Wing area	1,500 sq ft	1,500 sq ft
Speed at sea level	117 mph	121 mph
Speed at 5,000 ft	123 mph	—
Cruising speed	100 mph	100 mph
Initial climb	390 ft/min	700 ft/min
Service ceiling	16,500 ft	14,000 ft
Maximum endurance	7·5 hr	8 hr

* *Ref. M.A.E.E. Report F/127 dated July 1934.*

Loadings:

Sydney		Nile	
Tare weight	17,065 lb	Tare weight	11,785 lb
Military load	1,442 lb	Disposable load	8,915 lb
590 gal petrol	4,543 lb		
30 gal oil	300 lb	All-up weight	20,700 lb
All-up weight	23,350 lb		

Production:

(Sydney) One aircraft only, N241, to Contract 781162/27 dated 23 February 1928, Works Order 369, first flown 18 July 1930, to Felixstowe 9 December 1930, s.o.c. 1934.

(Nile) One aircraft only, unregistered, hull completed July 1929, work ceased February 1930, tested to destruction at Brough in the period 31 August 1935 to 14 October 1935.

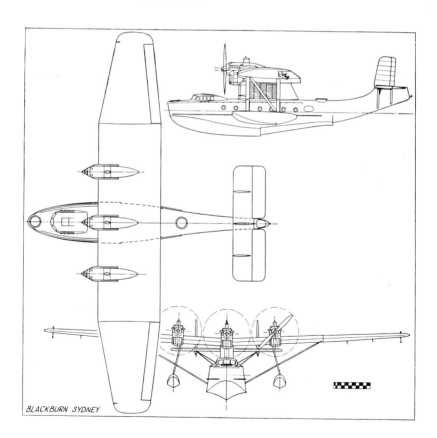

BLACKBURN SYDNEY

The prototype Bluebird IV, G-AABV, Gipsy I engine, used by Sqn Ldr L. H. Slatter for the England–South Africa flight in 1929. (*Aeroplane Photo.*)

Blackburn L.1C Bluebird IV

In 1928 G. E. Petty completely redesigned the Bluebird as an all-metal aeroplane after a series of wind tunnel experiments to improve the fuselage lines. Flight experience with the Cirrus-engined Bluebird III had already underlined the advantage of the slimmer, streamlined nose resulting from the use of an inline engine instead of the time-honoured radial, and the 90 hp A.D.C. Cirrus III or 100 hp D.H. Gipsy I engines were chosen initially as alternative standard power plants. At the same time the rounded rudder was replaced by a rectangular horn balanced unit without fin, Frise-type ailerons were fitted to the bottom mainplane only, and for better taxying over rough ground or long grass, the cross-axle undercarriage was abandoned in favour of the divided type.

The internal structure was translated into metal with considerable ingenuity and simplified as much as possible for quick and easy manufacture. The fuselage consisted of four sub-assemblies—engine mounting, cockpit section, rear fuselage and stern bay—only one gauge of steel tubing being used throughout. The rectangular-section basic structure consisted of four longerons of equal length rounded out by fabric over U-section duralumin stringers sprung on to supporting stubs in order to be quickly removable for inspection of the main structure.

The mainplanes were built up from hollow **I**-section spars of rolled steel strip and the ribs were stamped out of flat duralumin plate. They folded with the aid of jury struts and were rigged with slight dihedral and sweepback. The tail unit had duralumin ribs and steel-tube spars, the tailplane being adjustable for incidence in flight by means of a lever in a notched quadrant in the cockpit. Telescopic main undercarriage legs incorporated oil-damped spiral steel springs, and a twin-float undercarriage was available on demand.

The bench-type seat of the Bluebird III was replaced by two aluminium bucket seats with parachute recesses and the starboard seat could be removed altogether. A neat instrument panel was fitted centrally, with a glove compartment on each side and the tail incidence lever just below. Normal stick-type control columns were fitted and push–pull rods were used wherever possible, cables being employed only on straight runs without pulleys or fairleads. A large luggage compartment was provided under the decking aft of the cockpit with a door on the port side.

Fuel was gravity fed from a 22-gallon centre-section tank which was unique in being built integral with the front spar. It was easily removable when the wings were folded and could be replaced by a 30-gallon tank if desired.

Late in 1928, during early stages of construction, the prototype all-metal Bluebird IV attracted the interest of Sqn Ldr L. H. Slatter (senior officer of the RAF High Speed Flight which won the 1927 Schneider Trophy and later Air Marshal Sir Leonard Slatter, KBE, CB, DSO, DFC) who approached the Blackburn directors for permission to fly home in it on leave to South Africa. Even though his intended date of departure left insufficient time for complete flight trials, Blackburn's confidence in their new product was such that they sold it him a month before completion.

Gipsy I powered, registered G-AABV and bearing the revived circular B/A monogram on the rudder, it first flew at Brough on 23 February 1929.

The second pre-production Bluebird IV on Blackburn floats at Cowes in 1929.
(*Courtesy Beken and Sons, Cowes.*)

Only a few minor modifications were needed and with manufacturers' trials still incomplete Slatter flew the Bluebird IV from Brough to Stag Lane for engine tuning on 3 March and left Croydon on the first stage of the journey on 8 March. The cockpit heating system was used to advantage during a very cold trip from Lyons to Marseilles on 9 March, and Sicily was reached via Pisa, Rome and Catania on 13 March. Next day the Bluebird crossed the 90 miles of open sea to Tunis where a fuel tank leak was welded in preparation for a five-hour, 400-mile non-stop flight to Tripoli on 17 March. At Aboukir, reached on 22 March, it received an overhaul and a new fuel tank and left for Cairo on 29 March. In tropical heat Slatter covered 1,195 miles in $13\frac{3}{4}$ hr flying time between Luxor and Khartoum on 30–31 March, arriving at Nairobi on 5 April, Broken Hill on 10 April and Durban on 15 April. During the flight he made 47 landings on all sorts of unprepared fields without trouble.

Series Production

Only two more Bluebird IVs were Blackburn-built at this time, N-40 with a Gipsy I in totally enclosed cowlings for operation in Norway and flown at Cowes on Blackburn floats, and a demonstrator, G-AACC, fitted with a 90 hp A.D.C. Cirrus III which made its first public appearance at Croydon piloted by G. E. Lowdell in April 1929. In the following month pressure of work on the newly-awarded Baffin contract and other military commitments compelled Blackburns to sub-contract main Bluebird IV production to Saunders-Roe Ltd of Cowes, Isle of Wight, mainplane construction being entrusted to Boulton and Paul Ltd at their Riverside Works, Norwich. At the same time arrangements were made for Auto Auctions Ltd to handle all Bluebird marketing in the United Kingdom. G-AACC was on show when their new Burlington Gardens car showrooms were opened on 18 June 1929, and the first completed Cirrus III Saro Bluebird IV, G-AAIR, was kept at Heston for customer demonstration.

On its return (by sea) from Cape Town, Slatter's prototype Bluebird IV G-AABV reverted to the manufacturers to be shown on Auto Auctions' stand at the Olympia Aero Show during 16–27 July 1929 along with their own G-AAIR. A complete skeleton airframe also stood on Blackburn's stand.

Between the end of 1929 and May 1931, at least 55 Bluebird IVs were built, the majority at Cowes under the direction of H. E. Broadsmith*, an old Avro employee who had gone to Saunders-Roe Ltd with Sir Alliott Verdon Roe and Mr John Lord and who had built Avro 504Ks and aircraft of his own design in Australia. Detail changes were made to the structure in order to simplify and speed construction, notably in riveting the fuselage stringers direct to the formers, components such as fuselage box girders being made in the company's Maresfield Works at Cowes and ferried across the Medina to their Solent Works where complete Bluebirds were erected at the rate of four per week.

* See author's *Avro Aircraft since 1908*, page 116.

There were great hopes of Bluebird sales in the United States, where the Blackburn Corporation of America Inc was formed at Detroit by A. R. Martine, who had inspected the Bluebird III at the Berlin Aero Show in 1928, to manufacture the Bluebird and other Blackburn types. The company also held sales rights for the whole of North and South America, excluding Brazil, and ordered six Cirrus III engined seaplanes from Saunders-Roe, only one of which was ever delivered.

Air Racing

During the 1929 Olympia Aero Show an order for 25 Cirrus III Bluebird IVs was placed by Hanworth-based National Flying Services Ltd which had just commenced flying instruction and charter work there and in the provinces. The first six, G-AAOA to 'OF, resplendent in NFS orange and black, were delivered in formation from Cowes to Hanworth on 14 January 1930. G-AAOG to 'OJ arrived in the following month, but NFS did not survive long enough to take delivery of 'OK to 'OZ and these marks were never used. This enabled private owners to take delivery much earlier than anticipated, so that the round-Britain King's Cup Air Race on 5 July 1930, in which the following 14 were entered by celebrated pilots, will long be remembered as a highlight in the career of the Bluebird IV.

No. 21	G-AACC	Hermes I	T. Rose	109·8 mph
No. 22	G-AABV	Gipsy I	Norman Blackburn	retired at Brough
No. 27	G-AATO	Gipsy I	Flt Lt G. G. H. du Boulay	93·2 mph
No. 28	G-AAVG	Hermes I	Sqn Ldr L. H. Slatter	retired at Barton
No. 29	G-AAIR	Gipsy I	The Master of Sempill	retired at Brough
No. 30	G-AAOI	Hermes I	J. W. Gillan	95·2 mph
No. 31	G-AAUV	Gipsy I	Loel Guinness	non-starter
No. 32	G-AATN	Gipsy I	Flt Lt H. R. D. Waghorn	99·5 mph
No. 47	G-AAUW	Gipsy I	Flt Lt H. V. Rowley	91·3 mph
No. 64	G-AATS	Gipsy I	H. J. Andrews	non-starter
No. 89	G-AAUU	Gipsy I	Sqn Ldr A. H. Orlebar	95·8 mph
No. 90	G-AASV	Gipsy I	C. L. Pashley	non-starter
No. 93	G-AAVF	Gipsy II	Sqn Ldr J. W. Woodhouse	99·6 mph
No. 96	G-AAOB	Cirrus III	Lord Malcolm Douglas Hamilton	non-starter

The various racing modifications included not only more powerful engines but also streamlining such as on G-AACC which was a single-seater with passenger seat faired over, and G-AAVF which had pointed nose cowlings and miniature windscreens. Best performances were by Schneider Trophy pilot Flt Lt H. R. D. Waghorn in G-AATN who came third, and Tommy Rose in the much modified 'CC who recorded the high average speed of 109·8 mph despite cowling trouble at the start.

The Bluebird IV's first taste of success came in the following year when G-AACC, re-engined with a new 115 hp Hermes II and piloted by Flg Off E. C. T. Edwards, won the round-England King's Cup Air Race on 25 July

281

The first Saro-built Bluebird IV, G-AAOA, Cirrus III engine, arriving over Hanworth at the end of its delivery flight from Cowes on 14 January 1930. (*Flight Photo 8153.*)

1931 at the incredible average speed of 117·8 mph. A month later, on 22 August, Sqn Ldr J. W. Woodhouse won the Grosvenor Trophy Race at Cramlington, Newcastle, in G-AAUU with the owner Harold Peake as passenger, at an average speed of 102·5 mph round the 53·5-mile course.

Instructional Flying

A number of clubs and schools made good use of the Bluebird's side-by-side feature to speed and improve instructional methods, the first so used being G-AASU of the Airwork School of Flying at Heston during the first six months of 1930. In the North, G-AAVH was delivered to Coal Aston on 11 August of that year for motor magnate George Kenning and displayed in his showrooms at Vicar Lane, Chesterfield in the following October. He then presented it to the Sheffield Aero Club and added G-AACC and G-ABPN to the club fleet in 1931.

The York County Aviation Club, established at Sherburn-in-Elmet with the former NFS-owned G-AAOI in May 1932, took over G-AACC as a replacement in May 1934 and added G-AATP; while over at the Hull Municipal Aerodrome, Hedon, H. R. Field's machines G-AAOF, 'OI and 'VG were used by the Hull Aero Club. G-AAOF outlived the others and was joined eventually by the prototype aircraft G-AABV, then owned by T. E. Richardson.

By far the largest user was, of course, the North Sea Aerial and General Transport Co Ltd which, between February 1930 and April 1937, used no less than 13 Bluebird IVs for Reserve School training at one time or another. In order of acquisition they were G-AATM, 'TS, 'UF, 'UG, 'UT, 'UW,

'TO, G-ABEU, 'VZ, 'ZX, G-AAVF, G-ABPN and G-AAUX, but the last two were invariably at Waltham Aerodrome, Lincs., on loan to the Grimsby Aero Club. Equipped temporarily as twin-float seaplanes, two, G-AAUG, flown off the Humber by Flt Lt N. H. Woodhead on 30 June 1930, and 'TS, flown by A. M. Blake on 1 October, were followed by a third, G-AAUT, first flown on 17 December. This last was then ferried to Felixstowe for performance testing, presumably in preparation for the certification of the Bluebird IV seaplane used by Miss Delphine Reynolds for the survey flight along the West African coast described later in this chapter. Unfortunately, G-AAUT sank after alighting at sea off Felixstowe on 12 January 1931.

Overseas Sales

Among the Bluebird IVs sold overseas was an early Gipsy I production aircraft, G-AAJC, shipped to Bulawayo to the order of Cobham–Blackburn Air Lines. It was assembled by the Rhodesia Aviation Co at Wynberg in February 1930 and flown by Capt B. Roxburgh Smith on pleasure flights over the Victoria Falls until taken over by Rhodesia and Nyasaland Airways Ltd in June 1932. Eventually it migrated to South Africa with a subsequent owner, the Hon J. Grimston.

Two others, VH-UNS and 'OC, were delivered to the Larkin Aircraft Supply Co Ltd at Essendon Aerodrome, Melbourne, early in 1930. The first had a Gipsy I engine and the other was the only Bluebird IV known to have been fitted with an Armstrong Siddeley Genet Major I radial engine. They were used by the Lasco School of Flying, but after the loss of 'OC a few months later, 'NS was sold. Piloted by Ludwig Nudl and R. W. McKenzie, it had the distinction of making the first purely commercial flight round Australia—a sales tour which started and finished at Essendon and lasted from 24 October to 6 December 1931.

During 1931–32 three new Bluebird IV aircraft were also sold in India, VT-ACP imported by Coromandel Automobiles of Madras and VT-ADD and 'DK by the Indo-American Automobile Co of Bombay. Two secondhand examples, G-AATN and 'VI, were acquired by private owner A. S. Gallimore of Karachi and the Delhi Flying Club as VT-ACR and 'DI respectively.

Long-distance Flights

The most famous of all Bluebird IVs was undoubtedly the Gipsy II engined G-ABDS *Bluebird* in which the Hon Mrs Victor Bruce made the first solo light aeroplane flight round the world. Total fuel capacity was increased to 90 gallons by means of an overload tank occupying the port half of the cockpit and decked over so that the machine flew as a single-seater. It was fitted with long-range W/T equipment which automatically transmitted a clockwork-driven Morse signal every 15 min on 35·1 m, and carried a Dictaphone for recording the pilot's impressions of the flight.

With only 40 hr solo flying in her log book, Mrs Victor Bruce left Heston on 25 September 1930 and eventually reached Karachi on 27 October after a forced landing in the mountains near Istanbul and another in the Kohimborak Hills 20 miles north of Jask on the Gulf of Oman, where the machine was damaged. Thereafter G-ABDS flew eastwards with truly impressive reliability and reached Tokyo on 24 November after a magnificent 600-mile crossing of the Yellow Sea to Seoul, Korea, on 18 November. The Bluebird was then shipped to Seattle, and flown to Vancouver on 18 December. A flight south to San Francisco heralded her departure for New York on 13 January 1931, but she was again delayed a fortnight later when 'DS overturned in thick mud at the Glenn Martin Co's aerodrome at Baltimore. After local repair the aircraft reached New York on 5 February for shipment to Le Havre, via Plymouth, on the liner *Ile de France*. Mrs Victor Bruce then flew to Le Bourget before returning via Lympne to a triumphal reception at Croydon on 20 February, followed next day by a welcoming party at Heston attended by nearly every existing Bluebird, including Robert Blackburn's private G-ABEU. G-ABDS was then shown to the public in the booking hall of Charing Cross Underground Station throughout the first week of March.

The world flight itinerary was as follows:

25 September 1930	Munich	6 November 1930	Hanoi
26	Vienna	9	Hong Kong
27	Belgrade	12	Amoy
28	Istanbul	14	Shanghai
30	Eski-Shehr★	18	Seoul
2 October	Konia	24	Tokyo†‡
3	Baghdad	17 December	Seattle
4	Bushire	18	Vancouver
5	Kohimborak★	23	San Francisco
7	Jask†	13 January 1931	Los Angeles
27	Karachi	27	Baltimore†
28	Jodhpur	5 February	New York‡
29	Calcutta	15	Plymouth
30	Rangoon	16	Le Havre
31	Bangkok	17	Le Bourget
1 November	Lakhom★	20	Croydon

★ Forced landing.   † Repairs.   ‡ Left by sea.

After the Bluebird IV had been in production at Cowes for some 15 months, Saunders-Roe needed factory space for the construction of their new Cutty Sark/Windhover/Cloud series of amphibians, and with sales falling off, the last 20 or so Bluebird airframes were completed at Brough as and when required. Drawings dated 2 January 1932 show that Blackburns' well-known Bluebird pilot H. J. Andrews designed an engine mounting and cowlings which enabled several of these to be fitted with the new 120 hp de Havilland Gipsy III inverted engine, including two for the Curtiss-Reid Aircraft Co in Canada, G-ABMI *Bluebird II* for the Hon. Mrs Victor Bruce to replace her worn-out 'DS, and G-ABGF ordered by Miss Delphine Reynolds for a survey flight down the West African coast.

Miss Delphine Reynolds' Bluebird, G-ABGF, with W. G. Pudney as pilot, left Hanworth on 1 March 1931 and flew by way of Paris, Bordeaux, Toulouse, Perpignan, Tangier and Casablanca, and reached Bathurst, Gambia, on 16 March. A Blackburn float undercarriage awaited its arrival and, with this fitted, a number of local survey flights were made, including one of 3 hr 15 min up the Gambia River to McCarthy Island where the Bluebird was rammed at its moorings by a boat. Temporary repairs to the port elevator, tailplane and aileron enabled it to return to Bathurst for new components to be fitted, and on 2 April Pudney flew a one-day experimental air mail service for the French Government and carried 80 lb of mail 100 miles north to Dakar in 1 hr 30 min.

The next port of call, Freetown, Sierra Leone, was base for the main survey flying, but after 2½ months the machine became a total loss because acid in the water of the mangrove swamps corroded the metal airframe beyond repair even though the cadmium-plated floats and undercarriage struts were not affected.

Two flights to Australia were also undertaken in Bluebird IVs. After a test flight from Croydon to Rotterdam on 16 March 1931, H. F. 'Jim' Broadbent left Hanworth in his Gipsy II powered G-ABJA *City of Sydney* on 29 March in an attempt to lower the record, reaching Nuremberg the same evening, and Budapest, Sofia and Istanbul on successive days. On 2 April he left for Aleppo but was forced down in a swampy valley near Ismidt, but although the machine was undamaged it was in too inaccessible a spot for quick salvage and the flight was abandoned. G-ABJA was eventually recovered, shipped home, overhauled and sold to Irish Air Lines Ltd, a joyriding company based

Miss Delphine Reynolds' West African survey seaplane G-ABGF with metal airscrew and Gipsy III engine in short-chord cowlings.

285

at Waterford. During 1932 it accompanied two Avro 504Ks on a barn-storming tour of 30 Irish towns, rivalling the Cirrus III engined G-AAIR which was touring England with Cobham's Circus that year.

A more leisurely and successful trip to Australia in three weeks and three days was accomplished by Lt Cdr G. A. Hall, RAN, who left Croydon in the former Hull Aero Club machine G-AAVG on 8 August 1932. Apart from the specially-installed 115 hp Hermes II, it was similar to the Hon Mrs Victor Bruce's machine with extra tankage in place of the port seat. He arrived at Kuala Lumpur on 24 August, Singapore on 26 August, reached Wynd-ham from Koepang on 1 September and landed at Melbourne on 18 September. This machine afterwards flew under Australian registry for several years.

The last long-distance Bluebird flight started on 8 October 1934 when R. W. H. Knight left Heston with his wife in G-AAIR to fly 3,648 miles to his place of employment at Agades, Nigeria. Flying via Lympne, Paris, Marseilles, Barcelona, Oran, Algiers, Laghouat, In Salah, Arak and Agades, Kano was reached on 24 October in $54\frac{1}{2}$ hr flying time. Regrettably, the owner was killed when G-AAIR crashed at Agades in the following April.

Final Production

In July 1931 several of the earlier production machines remained unsold, one example being the 38th aircraft which was eventually completed as G-ABOT and fitted with a Gipsy III in July 1931. After several private owner-ships it passed into the hands of S. G. Cummings at Brooklands who flew it in the Isle of Man Tynwald Air Race on 29 May 1939 but forced landed in the sea off Kirkmichael. After salvage a few days later it was given to the local ATC squadron.

The 41st and 42nd aircraft both had involved careers. The former, first ordered by an Indian prince in 1930 as G-ABEX, remained at Brough until registered G-ABVZ for the Reserve School in April 1932. Two of its German pupils, Karl Winkler and Kurt Breugmann, then bought it, took part in the Weekend Aerien tour of British flying clubs during 1–4 September 1932, and then flew it home to Germany. The other was to have been G-ABEY but served with the Brough Reserve School as G-ABZX until withdrawn at the end of 1935 and converted into a flying testbed for the Blackburn Cirrus Minor engine, becoming G-ADXG in theory but actually flying under B conditions as B-10 with the words Cirrus Minor in large signwriting on the cowlings.

The penultimate Bluebird IV was the Gipsy II engined company demon-strator G-ABPV which H. J. Andrews flew from Brough to Heston on 8 October 1931 for Customs clearance at the beginning of a 5,700-mile European sales tour in company with the Lincock III G-ABFK and the Blackburn Segrave G-ABFP. Unfortunately, a Greek military instructor, Sub-Lt Sakelariou, when flying 'PV prior to going solo in the Lincock, spun out of cloud with insufficient recovery height and was killed at Tatoi Aerodrome, Athens, on 24 October.

The last Bluebird IV in existence was G-AATE, sent by owner P. H. Ford from Heston to the former Hamsey Green Aerodrome, Warlingham, Surrey, for overhaul in October 1938 and broken up there in 1947 after nine years of progressive decay.

SPECIFICATION AND DATA

Manufacturers: The Blackburn Aeroplane and Motor Co Ltd, Olympia Works, Roundhay Road, Leeds, and Brough Aerodrome, East Yorks.
Saunders-Roe Ltd, East Cowes, Isle of Wight.

Power Plants: One 90 hp A.D.C. Cirrus III
One 100 hp de Havilland Gipsy I
One 105 hp Cirrus Hermes I
One 115 hp Cirrus Hermes II
One 120 hp de Havilland Gipsy II
One 120 hp de Havilland Gipsy III
One 135 hp Armstrong Siddeley Genet Major I

Dimensions: Span 30 ft 0 in   (folded) 9 ft 10 in
Length 23 ft 2 in   Wing area 270 sq ft

Loading: Pre-production landplane

	Gipsy I
Pilot and passenger	320 lb
Luggage	40 lb
Fuel 22 gallons	144 lb
Oil 2 gallons	20 lb
Equipment	12 lb
Disposable load	536 lb

Weights and Performance:
(a) Blackburn-built pre-production aircraft

	Landplane		Seaplane	
	Cirrus III	Gipsy I	Cirrus III	Gipsy I
Tare weight	960 lb	960 lb	1,030 lb	1,030 lb
Disposable load	536 lb	536 lb	536 lb	536 lb
Normal loaded wt	1,496 lb	1,496 lb	1,566 lb	1,566 lb
Maximum speed	107 mph	109 mph	101 mph	103 mph
Cruising speed	82 mph	84 mph	80 mph	82 mph
Initial climb	780 ft/min	810 ft/min	650 ft/min	670 ft/min
Service ceiling	15,000 ft	15,600 ft	12,800 ft	13,300 ft
Range	330 miles	340 miles	310 miles	320 miles

287

(b) Saro-built production landplanes

	Cirrus III	Gipsy I	Hermes I	Genet Major I
Tare weight	1,042 lb	1,040 lb	1,067 lb	1,012 lb
Disposable load	553 lb	553 lb	553 lb	563 lb
Normal loaded wt	1,595 lb	1,593 lb	1,620 lb	1,575 lb
Max. aerobatic wt	1,500 lb	1,500 lb	1,500 lb	1,500 lb
Max. permissible wt	1,643 lb	1,750 lb	1,750 lb	1,750 lb
Maximum speed	100 mph	103 mph	112 mph	112 mph
Cruising speed	85 mph	86 mph	94 mph	94 mph
Initial climb	700 ft/min	720 ft/min	730 ft/min	730 ft/min
Range	480 miles	470 miles	320 miles	320 miles

(c) Saro-built production seaplanes

	Cirrus III	Gipsy I
Tare weight	1,118 lb	1,116 lb
Disposable load	525 lb	525 lb
Normal loaded wt	1,643 lb	1,641 lb
Max. aerobatic wt	1,500 lb	1,500 lb
Max. permissible wt	1,750 lb	1,750 lb
Maximum speed	95 mph	98 mph
Cruising speed	84 mph	85 mph
Initial climb	600 ft/min	650 ft/min

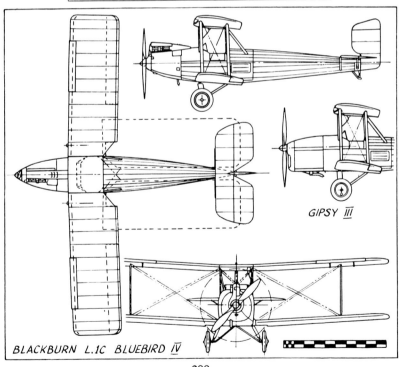

GIPSY III

BLACKBURN L.1C BLUEBIRD IV

288

Production:
(a) *By the Blackburn Aeroplane and Motor Co Ltd at Brough*
  Three pre-production aircraft as under:

G-AABV   Works Order 1430/1, Gipsy I, registered to Blackburns 14 September 1928; to Sqn Ldr L. H. Slatter January 1929, first flown 23 February 1929, restricted C. of A. 28 February 1929; to Blackburns September 1929, fitted Hermes II, full C. of A. 6 February 1930; to Dr C. S. Glass, Stoke-on-Trent February 1931; to T. E. Richardson, Hedon November 1933, crashed at Hedon 6 March 1934.

G-AACB   Works Order 1730/1, Gipsy I, registered to Blackburns 11 October 1928, no C. of A., registered in Norway October 1929 as floatplane N-40, believed to the order of a Mr Harr in north Norway, registration not taken up.

G-AACC   Works Order 1730/2, Cirrus III, registered to Blackburns 11 October 1928, restricted C. of A. 28 June 1929, full C. of A. 25 June 1930; to Auto Auctions Ltd, Heston February 1931; to R. McAlpine May 1931; to G. Kenning, Coal Aston October 1931; to York County Aviation Club, Sherburn May 1934; to R. J. Pattison, Yeadon July 1935; to F. Evans, Sherburn October 1936; to R. A. G. Kent and P. H. Forth, Hooton July 1937; dismantled 1938, destroyed in hangar fire at Hooton 11 July 1940.

(b) *By Saunders-Roe Ltd, East Cowes*
  Fifty-five production aircraft, constructor's numbers SB.(Saro Bluebird) 200 to SB.254 as under:

SB.200   G-AAOA, Cirrus III, registered to National Flying Services Ltd, 10 October 1929, C. of A. 7 January 1930, delivered Cowes–Hanworth 14 January 1930, crashed at Feltham 6 April 1930.

SB.201   unregistered, shipped to the Blackburn Corporation of America, Detroit, October 1929.

SB.202   G-AAIR, Cirrus III, registered to Blackburns 18 June 1929 (duplicate registered in error as G-AAJD 18 June 1929, cancelled January 1930); C. of A. 20 January 1930; to Auto Auctions Ltd, Heston 26 January 1930; fitted Gipsy I; to the Master of Sempill May 1931; to Flg Off J. W. Gillan June 1931; to Lord Douglas Hamilton December 1931; to C. Berens, High Post February 1933; to R. W. H. Knight, Christchurch 26 July 1934, crashed at Agades, Nigeria, 17 April 1935.

SB.203   G-AAJE, Cirrus III, registered to Blackburns 18 June 1929; re-registered to National Flying Services Ltd 10 October 1929 as G-AAOB, C. of A. 7 January 1930, delivered Cowes–Hanworth 14 January 1930, dismantled at Hanworth December 1930.

SB.204   G-AAOC, Cirrus III, registered to National Flying Services Ltd 10 October 1929, C. of A. 7 January 1930, delivered Cowes–Hanworth 14 January 1930; fitted Hermes I; to A. V. M. Longmore March 1931; to Mrs Elizabeth Scott, Madrid November 1933; registered in Spain 21 December 1933 to A. Fernandez Matamoro as EC-UUU.

SB.205   G-AAOD, Cirrus III, registered to National Flying Services Ltd 10 October 1929, C. of A. 10 January 1930, dismantled at Hanworth December 1930.

SB.206   G-AAOE, Cirrus III, registered to National Flying Services Ltd 10 October 1929, C. of A. 11 January 1930, to R. E. H. Allen, Hanworth September 1931; fitted Hermes II, sold abroad December 1934.

SB.207 G-AAJC, Gipsy I, registered to Blackburns 18 June 1929; to Cobham–Blackburn Air Lines, Bulawayo December 1929, C. of A. 8 January 1930; to RANA June 1932 as VP-YAI; to Dr Gane March 1935; to Hon J. Grimston, Cape Town August 1935.

SB.208 G-AASU, Gipsy I, registered to Airwork Ltd, Heston 9 December 1929, C. of A. 10 January 1930, crashed at Hendon 7 June 1930.

SB.209 G-AAOF, Cirrus III, registered to National Flying Services Ltd 9 December 1929, C. of A. 14 January 1930; to H. R. Fields, Hedon August 1931; fitted Gipsy I for loan to Grimsby Aero Club; to Reykjavik Flying Club 1937 as TF-LOA, first flight in Iceland 1 June 1937, last flew 15 August 1939.

SB.210 G-AATE, registered to J. Ellis, Sherburn 31 December 1929, C. of A. 18 January 1930; to Ellis (Leeds) Ltd August 1931; to J. M. Ferrier and G. H. Daniels, Gloucester April 1937; to P. H. Ford, Heston October 1938; to Hamsey Green, Surrey, for overhaul November 1938; to S. Bicham, Orkney May 1945 (not delivered); to C. & L. Aircraft Ltd, Hamsey Green January 1947, reduced to produce December 1947.

SB.211 G-AASV, Gipsy I, registered to E. L. Gandar Dower, Dyce 14 December 1929, C. of A. 4 April 1930, registration cancelled at census December 1937.

SB.212 Gipsy I, C. of A. 24 January 1930, registered in Australia to the Larkin Aircraft Supply Co Ltd as VH-UNS, crashed at Essendon, Melbourne, 30 January 1937.

SB.213 G-AAOG, Cirrus III, registered to National Flying Services Ltd 9 December 1929, C. of A. 24 January 1930, registration cancelled at census December 1930.

SB.214 G-AAOH, Cirrus III, registered to National Flying Services Ltd 9 December 1929, C. of A. 10 February 1930; to S. Hargreaves, Hanworth January 1931, crashed at Bushey Park, Middlesex, 27 January 1931.

SB.215 G-AATS, Gipsy I, registered to H. J. Andrews 30 January 1930, C. of A. 5 February 1930; to Maj H. P. L. Higman, Hooton 12 June 1933, crashed December 1936.

SB.216 Genet Major I, C. of A. 31 March 1930, registered in Australia to the Larkin Aircraft Supply Co Ltd May 1930 as VH-UOC, crashed at Essendon, Melbourne, 20 November 1930.

SB.217 G-AATM, Gipsy I, registered to North Sea Aerial and General Transport Co Ltd, Brough 4 February 1930, C. of A. 13 February 1930, crashed at Coal Aston 27 August 1932.

SB.218 G-AATN, Gipsy I, registered to Auto Auctions Ltd, Heston 25 February 1930, C. of A. 27 February 1930; to Sir Robert McAlpine April 1930; Indian registration VT-ACR allotted 31 March 1931; taken up 13 September 1932 by A. S. Gallimore, Karachi; crashed at Lingeh May 1933 on India-England flight, engine salvaged.

SB.219 G-AATO, Gipsy I, registered to Auto Auctions Ltd, Heston 4 February 1930, C. of A. 27 February 1930; to Norman Holden, Selsey June 1930; to Blackburns 6 January 1932, fatal crash Broomfield, near Brough, 4 August 1932.

SB.220 G-AATP, Gipsy I, C. of A. 24 February 1930, registered to Auto Auctions Ltd, Heston 25 February 1930; to P. Dujardin, Sherburn April 1930; to York County Aviation Club, Sherburn 24 May 1934; crashed and burned at East Heslerton 24 June 1934.

SB.221 G-AAOI, Cirrus III, registered to National Flying Services Ltd 4 February 1930, C. of A. 10 March 1930; fitted Hermes II; to J. W. Gillan April 1931; to H. R. Fields, Hedon May 1932; to York County Aviation Club, Sherburn 13 May 1932, crashed at Sherburn 20 January 1934.

SB.222 G-AAOJ, Cirrus III, registered to National Flying Services Ltd 4 February 1930, C. of A. 14 March 1930; to Miss Winifred S. Slack, Renfrew May 1931, fitted Gipsy I, dismantled at Gatwick March 1937.

Registrations G-AAOK to 'OZ, reserved by National Flying Services Ltd for Bluebird IVs, were not taken up due to the winding-up of the firm.

SB.223 G-AAUF, Gipsy I, C. of A. 25 March 1930, registered to Auto Auctions Ltd 31 March 1930; to North Sea Aerial and General Transport Co Ltd, Brough 11 April 1930, damaged beyond repair at Brough 16 July 1932.

SB.224 G-AAUG, Gipsy I, registered to Auto Auctions Ltd, Heston 4 February 1930, C. of A. 28 March 1930; first flown as seaplane 25 June 1930; to North Sea Aerial and General Transport Co Ltd, Brough August 1932; to R. Giddings, High Post, Salisbury, July 1937; crashed at High Post 20 March 1938 and sold as scrap.

SB.225 G-AAUT, Gipsy I, registered to North Sea Aerial and General Transport Co Ltd 8 May 1930, C. of A. 16 May 1930, first flown as seaplane 17 December 1930, sank off Felixstowe 12 January 1931.

SB.226 G-AAUU, Gipsy I, registered to Harald Peake MP 4 April 1930, C. of A. 4 April 1930; to Henlys Ltd, Heston May 1934, sold abroad June 1935.

SB.227 G-AAUV, Gipsy I, registered to Hon Loel Guinness 5 May 1930, C. of A. 5 May 1930; to D. Ripley, Heston February 1931; to Brooklands Aviation Ltd November 1931, registration cancelled at census December 1932.

SB.228 G-AAUW, Gipsy I, registered to Auto Auctions Ltd, Heston 20 May 1930, C. of A. 21 May 1930; to Blackburns 4 June 1930; to Maj A. Holt 11 June 1930; to North Sea Aerial and General Transport Co Ltd, Brough February 1931, registration cancelled at census December 1932.

SB.229 G-AAUX, Gipsy I, registered to Auto Auctions Ltd, Heston 26 May 1930, C. of A. 27 May 1930; to the North Sea Aerial and General Transport Co Ltd April 1935; to Blackburns December 1936 (on loan to the Grimsby Aero Club), crashed at Waltham, Grimsby, 29 April 1937.

SB.230 G-AAUY, Gipsy I, registered to Auto Auctions Ltd Heston 18 June 1930, C. of A. 19 June 1930, sold abroad July 1930.

SB.231 G-AAVF, Gipsy I, registered to Auto Auctions Ltd, Heston 24 June 1930, C. of A. 26 June 1930; to Capt the Earl of Amherst, Heston September 1930; to F. A. I. Muntz, Heston December 1931; to North Sea Aerial and General Transport Co Ltd, Brough November 1932, crashed September 1936.

SB.232 G-AAVG, Gipsy I, registered to Auto Auctions Ltd 24 June 1930, C. of A. 25 June 1930; to H. R. Fields, Hedon May 1931; to Lt Cdr G. A. Hall, RAN, July 1932, fitted Hermes II, re-registered in Australia July 1933 as VH-UQZ, registration cancelled March 1936.

SB.233 G-AAVH, Gipsy I, registered to Kennings Ltd 5 August 1930, C. of A. 5 August 1930, delivered to Coal Aston 11 August 1930, loaned to the Sheffield Aero Club; to S. Laurence, Alfreton April 1931, registration cancelled at census December 1934.

291

SB.234   G-AAVI, Gipsy I, registered to A. F. Horsman 29 August 1930; re-registered in India to the Delhi Flying Club 13 April 1932 as VT-ADI, withdrawn from use 5 August 1941.

SB.235   G-AAVJ, registration not taken up ⎱ Believed crated for shipment to Japan.
SB.236   G-AAVK, registration not taken up ⎰

SB.237   G-ABOT, Gipsy III, registered to Blackburns 30 July 1931, C. of A. 14 November 1931; to Norman Holden, Selsey November 1931; to J. B. Taylor, Heston September 1935; to S. G. Cummings, Brooklands October 1938, sank off Kirkmichael, Isle of Man, 29 May 1939, to local ATC 3 June 1939.

SB.238   G-ABEV, registration not taken up; registered to Kennings Ltd September 1931 as G-ABPN, C. of A. 20 November 1931; to Blackburns September 1933 (on loan to the Grimsby Aero Club), crashed at Waltham, Grimsby, 16 October 1935.

SB.239   G-ABEW, registration not taken up, C. of A. 3 May 1932 in the name of the Indo-American Automobile Co, Bombay, re-registered in India 23 June 1932 as VT-ADK.

SB.240   G-ABEX, Gipsy II, reserved for Prince Ghansbyam Singh, C. of A. 20 September 1930, registration not taken up; registered to Blackburns 19 April 1932 as G-ABVZ, C. of A. 22 April 1932; to K. Winkler December 1932 as D-2536.

SB.241   G-ABEY, registration not taken up; registered to North Sea Aerial and General Transport Co Ltd, Brough 29 September 1932 as G-ABZX, registration cancelled November 1935 in favour of new marks G-ADXG issued 15 November 1935, fitted Cirrus Minor I, to Class B marking January 1936 as B-10.

SB. 242 to SB.244   no details.

H. F. Broadbent's Australia-flight Bluebird IV G-ABJA *City of Sydney*, Gipsy II engine, at Brough in February 1931.

B-10, the Bluebird IV flying test bed for the Cirrus Minor I engine.

The Hon Mrs Victor Bruce's G-ABMI, last Bluebird IV to be built, was fitted with a wooden airscrew and a Gipsy III engine in long-chord cowlings with improved exit for the cooling air. (*Flight Photo 10102.*)

SB.245 G-ABDS, Gipsy II, registered to Hon Mrs Victor Bruce 26 July 1930 C. of A. 23 September 1930, named *Bluebird*, world flight machine withdrawn from use December 1931.

SB.246 G-ABEU, Gipsy I, registered to Robert Blackburn 10 September 1930, C. of A. 8 October 1930; to North Sea Aerial and General Transport Co Ltd January 1932; registered to H. Lauri, Belp, Switzerland, 4 July 1932 as CH-345, later HB-ULU; to E. Moret, Belp 1934, crashed at Gütterlitz, Germany, 6 October 1936.

SB.247 Gipsy I, British C. of A. issued 22 December 1930 in the name of Coromandel Automobiles, Madras; registered in India 2 February 1931 as VT-ACP, withdrawn from use February 1933.

SB.248 Gipsy III, C. of A. issued 18 April 1931 in the name of the Curtiss-Reid Aircraft Co, packed for shipment to Canada to Works Order 3347 as CF-AUP; to L. Bisson, Hull, Quebec September 1933; to Rev. J. M. Couture, Long Lac, Ontario, August 1934; withdrawn from use October 1936.

SB.249 G-ABJA, Gipsy II, registered to H. F. Broadbent 25 February 1931, C. of A. 19 March 1931, named *City of Sydney*; to G. N. Wilson, Heston January 1932; to Irish Air Lines, Waterford, December 1932 as EI-AAO.

SB.250 C. of A. issued 2 December 1931 in the name of the Indo-American Automobile Co, Bombay, registered in India 28 January 1932 as VT-ADD; to the Kathiawan Flying Club 26 September 1932, withdrawn from use 4 April 1939.

SB.251 CF-ALN, Gipsy III, packed for shipment to Canada to Works Order 3347, registered to the Curtiss-Reid Aircraft Co, Cartierville, Montreal, 9 March 1931, C. of A. 9 March 1931; to Curtiss-Reid Flying Service June 1932, withdrawn from use June 1933.

SB.252 G-ABGF, Gipsy III, registered to Miss Delphine Reynolds 7 November 1930, C. of A. 17 February 1931, to seaplane March 1931, totally unserviceable in Sierra Leone through acid corrosion May 1931.

SB.253 G-ABPV, Gipsy II, registered to Blackburns 14 September 1931, C. of A. 1 October 1931, crashed at Tatoi, Athens, 24 October 1931.

SB.254 G-ABMI, Gipsy III, registered to Hon Mrs Victor Bruce 11 May 1931, C. of A. 1 July 1931, named *Bluebird II*, crashed February 1933.

Running-up the Hispano-Suiza engine of the Blackburn T.7B in the presence
of Mitsubishi representatives, Brough, December 1929.

Blackburn T.7B (or 3MR4)

Early in 1927 the Imperial Japanese Navy decided to replace its Mitsubishi
B1M1 Type 13 carrier attack bombers and issued a specification to the Aichi,
Kawanishi, Mitsubishi and Nakajima companies for a new carrier-borne
torpedo-bomber with long-range reconnaissance capability. Mitsubishi, to
improve its chances of securing a lucrative contract on which depended not
only its reputation as the leading Japanese naval aircraft manufacturer but,
at that time, its very existence, took the unusual step of by-passing its own
design staff and requested basic layouts from Herbert Smith, a former
Sopwith designer who had been responsible for some of Mitsubishi's earliest
designs when in Japan in 1921, and from the Handley Page and Blackburn
companies.

One prototype of the winning design was to be built in England, under the
Mitsubishi designation 3MR4—which according to the Japanese system then
in use indicated primary duty (torpedo), manufacturer (Mitsubishi), secondary
duty (reconnaissance) and model number (fourth torpedo-bomber)—and
production aircraft in Japan. The stipulated engine was the 600 hp vee 12
water-cooled Hispano-Suiza Type 51-12Lb for which Mitsubishi had just
acquired licence rights.

Following receipt of the Japanese enquiry, Maj Bumpus issued a memorandum dated 17 March 1927 outlining his company's first 3MR4 proposals.
At this stage an enlarged 49-ft span Hispano-Suiza powered two-seat Ripon
with an all-up weight of 7,500 lb and a maximum speed of 139 mph was envisaged under the Blackburn designation T.6. After further study however the
design emerged as the T.7, a truly massive aeroplane of typical Blackburn

The Blackburn T.7B (or 3MR4) taxying out at Brough, December 1929, with torpedo in position.

appearance, much larger than the Ripon and incorporating the high aspect ratio, narrow-gap mainplanes and other characteristics of the Beagle.

Particulars of a variant described as the Blackburn T.7A, sent to Madrid following a Spanish enquiry for a Velos replacement, led to discussions which lasted well into 1931 but produced no orders. The main 3MR4 design, eventually finalized in detail by G. E. Petty as the Blackburn T.7B powered by a 625 hp Hispano-Suiza Type 51-12Lbr and equipped with three instead of two seats, was submitted to Mitsubishi's London office, together with the licence agreement, on 23 May 1928. No doubt influenced by Blackburns' pre-eminence in the field of naval aircraft construction and remembering the efficiency of the Swifts and Blackburn-built Cuckoos with which they had been initiated into torpedo-dropping techniques seven years earlier, the Japanese Government selected the Mitsubishi-sponsored Blackburn design as winner of the competition. The expected prototype order was placed at once, and when construction began Mitsubishi are known to have referred to it occasionally as the Ka-3.

It was a two-bay staggered biplane with Frise ailerons on all four wings and equipped with Handley Page leading edge slots, but the lower mainplane was some 13 inches greater in span than the upper and the outer interplane struts were not parallel to the inner. The fabric-covered all-metal wing structure followed standard Blackburn practice, using high-grade steel box spars built up from specially rolled and drawn sections in conjunction with duralumin ribs, the outer panels being hinged to the centre section rear spars. They folded with the aid of a jury strut, but the lower centre section, being of greater span than the upper, imparted some 45 degrees of tilt to them when folded.

The fuselage was of the usual Blackburn three-piece weldless steel-tube construction faired by aluminium panels to a point aft of the cockpits for ease of servicing and re-arming. The fabric-covered rear section was filled with flotation bags except for the stern bay, which housed the ballast weights used for C.G. adjustment when changing from three to two-crew operation.

296

Although larger, the divided oleo-sprung undercarriage and rectangular tail unit were similar in design and construction to those of the Beagle, and the tailplane was adjustable in the air by means of the usual handwheel on the starboard side of the cockpit. The tail skid was oleo-pneumatically sprung from the sternpost, and attachment points for a float undercarriage were an integral part of the fuselage structure although floats were, in fact, never fitted.

The closely-cowled Hispano-Suiza engine drove a two-bladed wooden airscrew and was mounted on duralumin bearers supported on a steel-tube structure, but for simplicity the old Swift/Dart/Velos cooling system was revived using a radiator compartment under the engine but with vertical instead of horizontal shutters. Total fuel capacity was 202 gallons housed in two 37-gallon gravity tanks in the top centre section, a 44-gallon tank between the pilot and the fireproof bulkhead, and a fourth of 84-gallon capacity below the pilot's floor. For long-range operation an 85-gallon streamlined overload tank with nose-mounted, wind-driven fuel pump, could be carried in the torpedo crutches. A 9-gallon oil tank was fitted under the decking ahead of the pilot and the coolant header tank was in the centre section as on the Ripon.

For reconnaissance duties the crew consisted of pilot, wireless operator/bomb-aimer and observer/gunner sitting in three separate cockpits and placed close together for ease of intercommunication, either verbally or by handwritten notes. An aperture in the floor of the centre cockpit served the dual purpose of course-setting bomb sight mounting and optional fourth gun position, the Lewis being carried on rails in the floor and stowed under it when not in use. For torpedo-carrying the crew was reduced to two and the fuel to 100 gallons.

Standard armament consisted of a fixed Vickers gun along the port side of the front fuselage, synchronized to fire through the airscrew, and twin Lewis guns on a double rotating mounting over the observer's cockpit. On the

The 3MR4 prototype in Japan with Japanese Navy markings and two 250-lb bombs between the undercarriage legs.

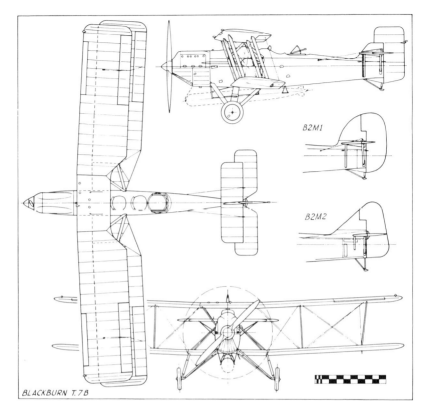

B2M1

B2M2

BLACKBURN T.7B

limited 100-gallon fuel load the 3MR4 could carry a pilot-released 2,000-lb torpedo or alternatively full fuel and two 250-lb bombs side by side between the undercarriage legs, the associated high-altitude bomb sight, fusing and release controls being fitted in the rear cockpit.

The prototype Blackburn T.7B, or 3MR4, was completed at the end of November 1929 and first flown at Brough without markings by A. M. Blake on 28 December that year. Test flights were made with and without torpedo but no time was lost, for records show that it was packed for shipment to Japan on 3 January 1930 and was accompanied on the voyage by G. E. Petty and a Blackburn working party. On arrival it was painted up with the Japanese red disc insignia and closely examined by Mitsubishi engineers who immediately began tooling up the factory and making ready for production. Their examination was, if anything, rather too searching, for the handle of the starting magneto was placed in the cockpit in such a position that it could not rotate (and therefore the engine could not start), unless the main oil cock was turned on; failing to see the wisdom of this arrangement, the Japanese re-positioned the handle without reference to the designer, with the inevitable result that one of their pilots took off without turning on the main oil supply and the aircraft crashed upside down in a paddy field when the engine seized.

Licence-built machines with the 650 hp Mitsubishi-Hispano Type 7 which appeared in 1932 bore the short naval designation B2M1 indicating, in order, carrier attack-bomber, the second design adopted for service by the Imperial Japanese Navy, Mitsubishi and the mark number. Its popular name, the Type 89 Model 1, stemmed from a Japanese system introduced in 1919 of basing type numbers on the last two digits of the Japanese year, in this case 2589 (or 1929 by Western calendars).

Unlike those of Blackburns' prototype, the fin and rudder were a rounded shape and the elevator horn balances were reduced in size. The nose was made slimmer by deleting the shuttered chin compartment and fitting a retractable radiator, and the tailplanes of late production machines had rounded ends and unbalanced elevators.

A variant armed with two instead of four guns and able to carry 1,764 lb of bombs over short distances appeared in 1934 as the B2M2 or Type 89 Model 2, with further modifications including reduced span, a triangular fin and rudder and an even slimmer nose. Even allowing for 50 per cent greater tankage, both variants came out much overweight compared with the Blackburn T.7B.

Although total production of the B2M1 and B2M2 amounted to 205 aircraft, it is said not to have been a worthwhile undertaking for Mitsubishi, who found the new constructional techniques very costly, compared with the machine's wooden predecessor, and the manufacturing licence for the Handley Page slots expensive. In addition, the unreliability of Japanese-built engines is believed to have led to a number of fatal accidents. Both variants served in the carriers *Ryujo*, *Akagi* and *Kaga* from 1933 until the Sino-Japanese war of 1937 and were operational on the Japanese mainland with the Tateyama Air Corps and as carrier trainers with the Omura Air Corps.

A Mitsubishi-built B2M1, identified by the rounded vertical tail surfaces, numbered 397 and bearing the identifying mark of the Omura Air Corps on the fin. (*Courtesy AiReview, Tokyo.*)

SPECIFICATION AND DATA

Manufacturers: The Blackburn Aeroplane and Motor Co Ltd, Brough Aerodrome, East Yorks.
Mitsubishi Shoji Kaisha, Nagoya Aircraft works, Oe-Machi, Minami-ku, Nagoya.

Power Plants: (Blackburn T.7B)   One 625 hp Hispano-Suiza Type 51-12Lbr
                (Mitsubishi 3MR4)   One 650 hp Mitsubishi-Hispano Type 7

Dimensions:

	Blackburn T.7B	Mitsubishi 3MR4	
		B2M1	B2M2
Span upper	48 ft 2 in	48 ft 9 in	48 ft 0 in
Span lower	49ft 3½ in	49 ft 11 in	49 ft 1 in
Length	33 ft 3 in	33 ft 7 in	33 ft 5 in
Height	12 ft 5 in	10 ft 4 in	11 ft 8 in
Wing area	592 sq ft	592 sq ft	527 sq ft

Loadings (Blackburn T.7B):

(a) Torpedo-bomber

Two crew	320 lb	Tare weight	3,896 lb
Armament	2,368 lb	Military load	3,070 lb
Equipment	382 lb	Fuel and oil	1,000 lb
Military load	3,070 lb	All-up weight	7,966 lb

(b) Reconnaissance-bomber

Three crew	480 lb	Tare weight	3,916 lb
Armament	957 lb	Military load	1,758 lb
Equipment	321 lb	Fuel and oil	1,826 lb
Military load	1,758 lb	All-up weight	7,500 lb

Weights and Performance:

	Blackburn T.7B		Mitsubishi 3MR4	
	Torpedo	Recon-naissance	B2M1	B2M2
Tare weight	3,896 lb	3,916 lb	4,982 lb	4,805 lb
Military load	3,070 lb	1,758 lb	2,854 lb	3,130 lb
All-up weight	7,966 lb	7,500 lb	7,936 lb	7,936 lb
Speed at sea level	132 mph	135 mph	132 mph	140 mph
Speed at 6,000 ft	124 mph	128 mph	—	—
Cruising speed	112 mph	115 mph	112 mph	119 mph
Initial climb	680 ft/min	810 ft/min	600 ft/min	900 ft/min
Service ceiling	11,500 ft	14,300 ft	—	—
Range	390 miles	800 miles	1,100 miles	1,090 miles

Production:
(a) *By the Blackburn Aeroplane and Motor Co Ltd*
 One T.7B, or 3MR4, for Mitsubishi Shoji Kaisha to Works Order 1930/1, final inspection 29 November 1929, first flown 28 December 1929, packed for shipment 3 January 1930, crashed in Japan.

(b) *By Mitsubishi Shoji Kaisha*
 Total licence production 205 aircraft in two variants, B2M1 and B2M2, 1933–35. Typical serial numbers: 301 (aircraft carrier *Kaga* 1937); 303 (aircraft carrier *Akagi* 1937); 312 (aircraft carrier *Ryujo* 1937); 349 (Tateyama Air Corps 1935); 379 (Omura Air Corps 1935). Each serial was preceded by a Japanese character indicating the unit to which it belonged.

301

The Blackburn biplane and monoplane together at Brough in October 1932.
(*Flight Photo 12384.*)

Blackburn C.A.15C Monoplane and Biplane

In the years following the 1914–18 war the name Blackburn became synony-
mous with naval aircraft and, apart from building a number of Bluebird light
aeroplanes and the unhappy Nile flying-boat, the company was thought to
take little interest in the design of civil aircraft. This was very far from being
the case for throughout those years many transport layouts were prepared
under the aegis of Maj F. A. Bumpus, with from one to four engines either as
private design studies or to meet the requirements of the North Sea Aerial and
General Transport Co Ltd, Imperial Airways Ltd and others.

As might be expected of a firm specializing in marine aircraft, the majority
of landplane layouts had their seaplane equivalents, but in July 1929 the design
department went a stage further and produced a scheme designated C.A.15A
(see page 516) for an 11-passenger monoplane with three 240 hp Armstrong
Siddeley Lynx IV radials which not only envisaged alternative wheel and float
undercarriages but could also be built in biplane form if the operator preferred
it. This ceaseless design activity was never publicized and the only hints to
appear in the technical press were a brief announcement in 1925 concerning
the proposed C.A.3 for the North Sea company's Khartoum–Kisumu route
and an artist's impression in a 1929 Blackburn advertisement. This depicted
a three-engined cabin monoplane bearing the appropriate but spurious
registration G-ROBT and having the centre engine nacelle conspicuously
mounted on struts above the wing. It was, of course, intended to represent
the C.A.15A in land monoplane form, and later in 1929, when the company
produced drawings of a slightly smaller nine-passenger variant designated
C.A.15B (see page 516), it attracted the attention of the Air Ministry who saw
it as a means of solving the age-old problem of whether a monoplane or
biplane was the more efficient.

Blackburns were therefore asked to prepare detailed designs for a pair of
transport aeroplanes of this type for comparative trials, identical in every

302

respect except wing arrangement, having similar payloads and range, the same engines, and all major components matched as far as possible for weight. They were to carry two crew, 10 passengers, baggage and mail, and have two 400 hp Armstrong Siddeley Jaguar IVC two-row radial engines in place of the three Lynx.

The revised design, known as C.A.15C, was covered by Specification 6/29 and, following the signing of the contract early in 1931, construction began at Brough alongside the Mk V conversion of the Iris S1263. In the drawing office they were known as 'The Duncan Sisters' (contemporary vaudeville stars), a reference to B. A. Duncan, designer responsible for the detailed layout.

With the exception of the fabric covering of mainplanes and tail units, they were built entirely of metal because at that time it was the Air Ministry intention to hand them over after the trials to Imperial Airways for experimental operation out of high-altitude tropical aerodromes on the Cairo–Cape Town route. Throttle controls for the Jaguars were of the Arens flexible type instead of the usual control rod and bell crank variety. The engines, driving large two-bladed wooden airscrews, were mounted between the wings of the biplane, with extension exhaust pipes leading from the collector rings

Two views of the Blackburn ten-seat civil biplane G-ABKW.

303

Rear view of the Blackburn ten-seat civil monoplane G-ABKV.

to below the bottom wing, and projected from the leading edge of the mono-plane with the exhaust led away over the top. Each engine was provided with its own $5\frac{1}{2}$-gallon oil tank, reached through a door in the bottom of the nacelle which could not be closed if the handle of the oil cock was inadver-tently left in the 'off' position.

Tail units and non-folding mainplanes were of standard Blackburn type with steel spars and duralumin ribs, the biplane rigged with two bays and the monoplane strut braced. Frise-type ailerons were fitted to both aircraft, and uniformity of design extended even to such details as wing and undercarriage attachment points. This forced the designers to inflict unnecessarily complex strutting on the monoplane in order to use a divided undercarriage identical with that of the biplane. They were equipped with Blackburn oleo-pneumatic main legs, disc wheels, differential hydraulic brakes and oleo-sprung castoring tail wheels.

Fuel tanks of 304 gallons total capacity were fitted inside the wing roots of the monoplane but the biplane had two of 70 gallons in the upper wing roots and a 30-gallon reserve tank in the top centre section, giving it the advantage of gravity feed. The monoplane fuel system was consequently heavier because pumps were incorporated, and its wing, being of greater chord and span, came out a great deal heavier than those of the biplane. When the greater area of the monoplane wing was taken into account, however, struc-ture weights per square foot were not greatly different.

The main cabin of 540 cu ft capacity was fitted with large push-out rec-tangular windows which acted as emergency exits, and was sound-proofed with a thick Kapok lining. It was divided into two compartments, the rear containing three comfortable upholstered seats on each side of a central gang-way and the front two per side. Each passenger was provided with a univer-sally-mounted ventilation louvre and in cold weather was warmed by air fed in from heater muffs round the exhaust pipes. A door in the front cabin bulk-head led to an enclosed pilots' cockpit in the nose via a luggage compartment of 127 cu ft capacity loaded through a door in the starboard side. The cockpit had a celluloid roof and vertical glass windscreen panels, two of which opened to give better visibility in rain and two others to act as emergency exits.

Although registered as civil aeroplanes G-ABKV and 'KW as early as April

1931, neither aircraft was completed until the following year, the first being the biplane G-ABKW, first flown by A. M. Blake on 10 June 1932 and flown by him to Farnborough on 20 June. Familiarization flights were made next day by RAE pilots who then flew it to Hendon for its first public appearances as exhibit No. 14 in the New Types Park at the Hendon RAF Display on 25 June and at the SBAC Show there two days later. It then returned to Brough for contractor's test flying and to be prepared for C. of A. trials which took place at Martlesham Heath in October 1932, but from the outset the aircraft was plagued by trouble with the brakes. These were not of Blackburn manufacture and, despite continual adjustment, made taxying extremely difficult and on one occasion seized on landing and tipped the aircraft on its nose. Tail wheel shimmy, then hardly known but destined to be a headache for many designers during the 1939–45 war, also caused vibratory troubles in the rear fuselage structure.

The aircraft proved tiring to fly, needing wheel rather than stick control, and would not maintain height on one engine with a reasonable load, and cabin ventilation was inadequate in warm weather. Nevertheless the aeroplane was recommended for issue of C. of A., but only at a maximum permissible weight of 11,750 lb, and the application was not proceeded with. The machine consequently returned to Brough for servicing at the end of November but returned to Martlesham on 27 January 1933 for full performance testing which continued in competition with the monoplane throughout the summer.

The monoplane G-ABKV was not finished until four months after the biplane and did not fly at Brough until 4 October 1932 but was the first to complete manufacturer's tests and the first to leave for Martlesham. It was a clean aeroplane with a flat glide and could be landed in a comparatively small space by gentle sideslipping. Post-trials overhaul at Brough culminated in a test flight by A. M. Blake on 14 June 1933 in preparation for the machine's public debut at Hendon where, by coincidence, it too became exhibit No. 14 among the New Types during the RAF Display on 24 June and the SBAC follow-up, just as the biplane had done the previous year.

The monoplane G-ABKV in RAF markings as K4241.

305

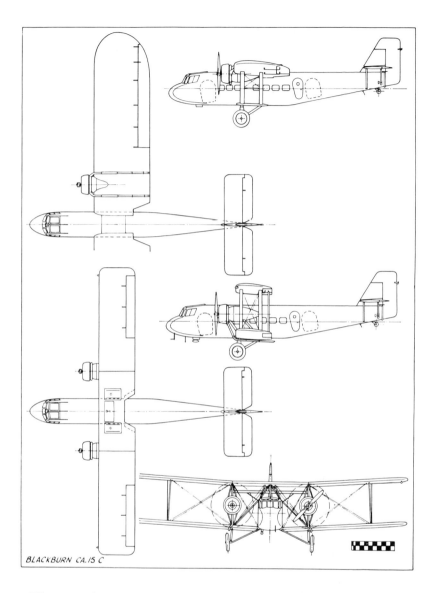

BLACKBURN CA.15 C

The monoplane then returned to Martlesham for the all-important comparative trials with the biplane, but despite the fact that a great deal of time, effort and money had been spent on their construction and flying, it was very difficult to say which was the better. At the same all-up weight the biplane was slower, but the structural weight of the monoplane was greater so that its payload was less.

Neither aeroplane was ever used in its designed role by Imperial Airways in Africa because a fleet of much larger Short Calcutta flying-boats and D.H.66 Hercules landplanes were already operating, and a batch of more modern four-engined A.W.XVs was on order. The biplane was consequently scrapped, but on 13 January 1934 the monoplane G-ABKV was flown from Martlesham to Farnborough and handed over to the RAE for automatic-pilot trials by Flt Lt Ubee which lasted throughout February. In the following July the aircraft was transferred from the Instrument to the Wireless and Electrical Flight and taken on RAF charge as K4241 for various W/T experiments, flown by Flt Lt Buckle and others. Three years later, on 11 February 1937, it went to No. 2 Aircraft Storage Unit, Cardington, for use as a taxi aircraft by its ferry pilots but in the following December was transferred to the Directorate of Technical Development at Martlesham Heath, having flown 232 hr 10 min. It was then used for what were described picturesquely as 'firing trials' and almost immediately put up for sale as scrap.

SPECIFICATION AND DATA

Manufacturers: The Blackburn Aeroplane and Motor Co Ltd, Brough Aerodrome, East Yorks.

Power Plants: (Monoplane)   Two 400 hp Armstrong Siddeley Jaguar IVC
           (Biplane)   Two 400 hp Armstrong Siddeley Jaguar IVC

Dimensions and Performance:

	Monoplane (1)	Biplane (2)
Span	86 ft 0 in	64 ft 0 in
Length	55 ft 3 in	55 ft 0 in
Height	16 ft 9 in	16 ft 0 in
Wing area	1,068 sq ft	1,037 sq ft
Maximum speed	128 mph	118 mph
Cruising speed	110 mph	110 mph
Initial climb	665 ft/min	535 ft/min
Absolute ceiling	16,000 ft	11,000 ft
Service ceiling	13,500 ft	9,000 ft
Range	350 miles	350 miles

Loadings: (a) *Monoplane* (1)

Tare weight	8,818 lb
Disposable load	1,569 lb
304 gal petrol	2,325 lb
11 gal oil	100 lb
Equipment	262 lb
All-up weight	13,074 lb

(b) *Biplane* (2)

Tare weight	7,931 lb
Disposable load	2,596 lb
170 gal petrol	1,284 lb
11 gal oil	100 lb
Equipment	239 lb
All-up weight	12,150 lb

(1) *Ref. A. & A.E.E. Report M.611A dated August 1933.*
(2) *Ref. A. & A.E.E. Report M.611 dated August 1933.*

Comparative Weights Envisaged at the Design Stage:

	Monoplane		Biplane	
	Weight	Percentage of total wt	Weight	Percentage of total wt.
Wing structure	2,621 lb	20·85	2,154 lb	17·73
Fuselage	2,001 lb	15·92	2,037 lb	16·77
Tail unit	262 lb	2·09	244 lb	2·01
Undercarriage	557 lb	4·43	557 lb	4·59
Power Plants	2,314 lb	18·32	2,314 lb	19·05
Fuel	1,339 lb	10·66	1,392 lb	11·46
Fuel system	160 lb	1·26	121 lb	1·00
Payload	2,340 lb	18·62	2,340 lb	19·27
Equipment	986 lb	7·85	986 lb	8·12
All-up weight	12,580 lb*	100·00	12,145 lb	100·00

* Maximum permissible weight 13,038 lb.

Production:

(a) *Monoplane*

One aircraft only to Specification 6/29 ordered 1931 to Contract 2669/30, Works Order 2780/1. Fitted with Armstrong Siddeley Jaguar IVC serial A.S.2170 port, A.S.438 starboard. Civil registered G-ABKV in the name of the Air Council by C. of R. No. 3105 dated 1 April 1931, first flown 4 October 1932, registration cancelled March 1934. On charge July 1934 at RAE, Farnborough as K4241, to No. 2 ASU, Cardington 11 February 1937; to DTD, Martlesham 2 December 1937, s.o.c. 30 April 1938.

(b) *Biplane*

One aircraft only to Specification 6/29 ordered 1931 to Contract 2669/30, Works Order 2781/1. Fitted with Armstrong Siddeley Jaguar IVC serial A.S.2153 port, A.S.572 starboard. Civil registered G-ABKW in the name of the Air Council by C. of R. No. 3106 dated 1 April 1931, first flown 10 June 1932; to Martlesham October 1932, registration cancelled January 1934.

The Blackburn F.7/30 with wheel spats and tail skid.

Blackburn F.3 (or F.7/30)

The unparalleled success of the water-cooled Rolls-Royce Kestrel engine in contemporary first line aircraft led to Air Ministry Specification F.7/30 issued to the aircraft industry late in 1931 for a single-seat day and night interceptor fighter powered by its evaporatively-cooled development, the Kestrel IV, which had nearly completed flight development and was about to go into production as the Goshawk. The stipulations were severe—a maximum speed in excess of 250 mph and superiority over existing fighters in range, manoeuvrability, rate of climb and service ceiling while carrying four synchronized Vickers guns and ammunition, full two-way radio and night-flying equipment. For night operations a low wing loading and a good field of view free of exhaust glare were also essential requirements.

From among the several tenders to the specification, the Air Ministry selected the Supermarine Type 224, Westland P.V.4 and Blackburn F.3 as the most promising, ordered one prototype of each and allotted serials K2890, K2891 and K2892 respectively. Competitive trials were scheduled to take place at the A. and A.E.E., Martlesham, during 1934, and the Bristol and Hawker companies, although not selected for prototype construction, also built their Type 123 and P.V.3 designs as private ventures.

If anything, the contractors interpreted the specification too literally and built some highly unusual aeroplanes, none of which, including Blackburn's design by G. E. Petty, was ordered into production.

This was the smallest biplane that could be built round the 660 hp Rolls-Royce Goshawk III and, drawing on the firm's experience with flying-boat hulls, Petty used a duralumin-covered stressed-skin fuselage with integral fin.

L   309

Front view of the Blackburn F.7/30 with spats removed.

The rest of the structure was of standard Blackburn fabric-covered steel and duralumin construction with horn balanced rudder. The upper mainplane was greater in span and chord than the lower and carried the ailerons which, like the elevators, were unbalanced.

The strange appearance of the completed aeroplane stemmed from the fact that the fuselage was raised from its usual position between the mainplanes until the entire wing cellule was below the pilot's field of vision. This was nigh on perfect in all forward and upward directions because the nose, with its cleanly-cowled Goshawk engine and flame-damped exhaust system, sloped sharply away ahead of the cockpit. A special honeycomb steam condenser replaced the usual coolant radiator and was sited in a streamlined tunnel which filled the gap between the fuselage and the bottom mainplane as on the Blackburn Nautilus. A Hucks starter dog was fitted to the large two-bladed wooden airscrew through which all four guns fired by means of interrupter gear, two being sited in the upper wing roots firing through troughs above the exhaust stacks, and the other two fired through ports on each side of the condenser fairing.

The exceptionally wide-track undercarriage consisted of two disc wheels running in steel cantilever crutches incorporating oleo and coil spring shock absorbers and bolted directly to the front spar of the lower mainplane. Landing loads were then transmitted to the main structure by parallel sloping struts on each side. The wheels were almost totally enclosed in large spun-duralumin spats and a typical Blackburn braced skid supported the tail.

Preliminary taxying was done at Brough by A. M. Blake on 20 July 1934 and ground handling tests proper began on 17 August, but the aircraft was plagued by cooling problems just as the other Goshawk-powered prototypes had been. A further complication was the difficulty of taxying an aircraft with a short fuselage and high C.G. Removal of the spats and the replacement of the skid by a castoring tail wheel made little difference and an inspection on 5 September revealed cracks and dents in the metal fuselage skin as a result of continued taxying.

The Blackburn F.7/30 was thus not ready for delivery by the agreed date and the Air Ministry withdrew its support for the project. This unique aeroplane consequently never flew despite the vast amount of skill and effort that had gone into creating it and in July 1936 was transferred to the Electrical and Wireless School at Halton as an instructional airframe.

SPECIFICATION AND DATA

Manufacturers: The Blackburn Aeroplane and Motor Co Ltd, Brough Aerodrome, East Yorks.

Power Plant: One 660 hp Rolls-Royce Goshawk III

Dimensions: Span 36 ft 10¾ in   Length 27 ft 0 in
Height 10 ft 0 in

Weights: Tare weight 2,500 lb

Estimated performance: Maximum speed 190 mph

Production: One aircraft only, K2892, first taxied 17 August 1934, not taken on RAF charge until 14 July 1936, struck off charge on the same day on transfer to the Directorate of Technical Development as 874M for use as an instructional airframe at the Electrical and Wireless School, Halton.

The F.7/30 in final form with tail wheel but with fabric-covered surfaces still in red dope.

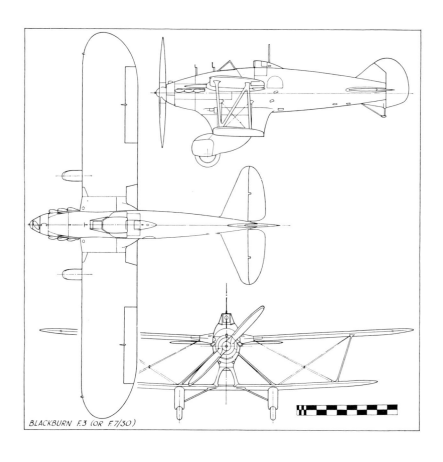

BLACKBURN F.3 (OR F.7/30)

312

The first Perth, K3580, ready for launching at Brough on 9 October 1933, with the 37-mm C.O.W. gun in the bows and eight Blackburn B-2s of the Reserve School in the background. (*Flight Photo.*)

Blackburn R.B.3A Perth

Sometimes known as the Iris VI, the third production Blackburn R.B.3 Iris V, S1593, with 37-mm Coventry Ordnance Works quick-firing cannon in the bows, can properly be regarded as prototype of the R.B.3A Perth, the ultimate Iris development and largest biplane flying-boat ever used by the Royal Air Force. Four Perths built at Brough 1933–34 to replace the Iris Vs of No. 209 Squadron, Mount Batten, only differed externally from S1593 in having enclosed pilots' cockpits of the type tried briefly and experimentally on an earlier Iris V, S1263, at Felixstowe in July 1932.

Designed by J. D. Rennie to Air Ministry Specification 20/32, the Perth was a long-range, all-metal coastal patrol flying-boat with fabric-covered, two-bay mainplanes and 30 ft span biplane tail unit, powered by the same mark of Rolls-Royce Buzzard engines driving 14 ft diameter two-bladed wooden airscrews. Extra buoyancy to prevent the new and heavier boat from sitting as low in the water as the Iris V was obtained by increasing the beam of the hull from 11 ft 0½ in to 12 ft 6 in. An important technical development was the use of Alclad for planking the hull, a new corrosion-resistant material consisting of a duralumin sheet coated on each side with layers of pure aluminium.

Mainplanes were rigged with slight dihedral and sweepback and were built almost entirely of duralumin, using box spars, and ribs with flanged outer edges and round section tubular girder work. Walkways, reached by a tubular-metal ladder carried in the hull, were built into the upper surface of the lower mainplane for engine starting and into the top mainplane and tailplane to enable engineers to reach, inspect or repair the control surfaces.

As on the Iris, the top tailplane and elevator were greater in span than the lower, the latter being used solely as a trimmer. All three rudders were fitted

313

with servo control which could be declutched by a small hand-lever in the cockpit.

The crew of five, consisting of captain, second pilot/navigator, bow gunner, wireless operator/midships gunner and engineer/rear gunner, were provided with Iris-type accommodation in the more spacious hull. The bow compartment not only mounted the 37-mm anti-shipping cannon, capable of firing $1\frac{1}{2}$-lb shells at 100 rounds per minute, but was also equipped with a bomb sight and the fusing and release controls for four 500-lb or eight 250-lb bombs carried on racks under the wing roots. It was also fitted with a compass, mooring and towing tackle, an anchor winch, two chain lockers and a parachute stowage. When the cannon was not in use, a ·303 Lewis gun on a rotating mounting slid forward over the bow compartment on rails to augment the tail and midship guns and make defensive armament identical with that of its predecessor, the Iris.

The pilots' cockpit, reached from the bow compartment through a door in the central gangway, was equipped with side-by-side seats, dual handwheel control columns and engine controls, those on the starboard side being detachable. The cabin top was built of Alclad, with safety glass panels in front and sides and two sliding panels in the roof through which the crew could stand up to supervise mooring operations.

Aft of the cockpit, and separated from it by a sliding door in the bulkhead, was the navigator's compartment equipped with chart table and chart racks and leading to two wardrooms with sleeping bunks for officers and men. The wardrooms were separated by an engineer's station with an instrument panel carrying oil pressure, oil and water temperature, and electrical fuel contents gauges. Three hand-levers projecting downward from a shaft in the roof were for operating the radiator shutters. A bomb-loading winch was fitted

K3580 entering the water for its first flight at Brough on 11 October 1933.
(*Topical Press Photo.*)

The second Perth, K3581, over the Cornish coast in 1934.
(*Flight Photo 13793.*)

in the men's quarters and an inflatable dinghy and oars were lashed to frames on the starboard side. In the after part, underneath the midships gun position, there was a wireless compartment on the port side, with the galley opposite. Toilet facilities were provided in the tail section adjacent to the walkway to the tail gunner's cockpit.

Each of the three Rolls-Royce Buzzard IIMS engines was installed as a self-contained power unit in a built-up duralumin nacelle of improved aerodynamic form, the centre one mounted on struts above the hull and the outboard pair directly on the sloping interplane struts. Radiators with controllable shutters were mounted at the rear of each nacelle, which also housed a complete oil system, hand-turning gear and a compressed-air starter. For starting, engines were first primed by means of the hand-turning gear and then started from the midships gunner's cockpit where the two air bottles, starting magneto and various cocks were situated.

Fuel was gravity fed from three 575-gallon aerofoil-section, tinned-steel tanks bolted to the underside of the upper mainplane, one above each engine, giving a maximum still-air range of 1,500 miles, equivalent to a complete circuit of the North Sea. A distributor outside the hull enabled any tank to feed any combination of engines and also served as the refuelling point, the important feature of the fuel system being that fire risks were reduced by excluding all piping and cocks from inside the hull.

315

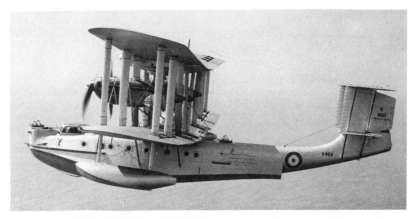

The fourth Perth, K4011, with C.O.W. gun removed and the sliding Lewis gun mounting fully forward over the bow compartment.

Service Use

First fog and then gales interfered with the official launching ceremony of the first Perth, K3580, at Brough on Monday 9 October 1933, but the Blackburn and Rolls-Royce companies' distinguished guests were able to watch the naming ceremony (all four aircraft of the type carried the name *Perth* on the bows) and to see the 37-mm gun fired across the Humber. K3580 eventually flew on 11 October and was ferried to Felixstowe on 10 November, remaining there for performance testing and post-test overhaul for some six months.

The first Perth to enter squadron service was thus K3581 which Blackburns readied for launching on 12 December 1933. Persistent fog prevented it from entering the water until the early morning of 5 January 1934, when A. M. Blake test flew it prior to handing over to Sqn Ldr J. H. O. Jones and the No. 209 Squadron crew that ferried it nonstop to Mount Batten. They routed the long way round via the East Coast and the English Channel and took 4 hr 55 min for the flight. The aircraft was then used for intensive crew training until the arrival of the third Perth, K3582, a month later.

The delivery flight of this boat was the occasion of a full-load trial and it left Brough with maximum fuel, taking off without difficulty at an all-up weight of 36,900 lb. Its first patrol was to the Scillies on 23 April 1934, and between 25 May and 1 June it made an extended cruise to Stornoway piloted by Wg Cdr G. Livock and P/O Jenkins during which HRH Duke of Gloucester was escorted on a sea crossing to Belfast.

The squadron was eventually brought up to strength when K3580 was delivered from Felixstowe on 31 May. The boats remained all-silver, but for identification purposes the hulls of K3581 and '82, respectively, were painted with one and two vertical black lines front and rear. They left Mount Batten

316

with these markings for a North Atlantic air route survey and training cruise on 12 September flown respectively by Wg Cdr G. Livock and Flt Lt Bainbridge. After a refuelling stop at Oban and a day's delay by bad weather, they reached the Faroes on September 14, but two days later the Air Ministry ordered their return because of dangerous ice conditions in Arctic waters.

The Perth's only appearance in the flying-boat event at the Hendon RAF Display was on 30 June 1934 when Flg Offs Gurney and L. F. Brown positioned K3581 at Felixstowe before flying past at Hendon in formation with a Short Singapore II, Supermarine Scapa, Short R.24/31, Saro London and three Saro Clouds.

The Perths normally patrolled over the Irish Sea and used an advance base at Stranraer, but were grounded on 8 October 1934 by HQ Coastal Area until their tail units had been checked. Flying was resumed on 6 November but ceased again on 27 November when the boats were brought ashore for further inspection. Following a conference with the manufacturers at Mount Batten on 6 December, the tail units were removed from all three Perths and sent back to Brough in the following March for modification. Devoid of aircraft, the squadron was hurriedly re-equipped with three prototype boats which had appeared at Hendon the previous year—the London, the Scapa and the Short R.24/31—all of which understudied the Perths at the next Hendon RAF Display on 29 June 1935. The Perths themselves returned to service during July and August 1935 but soon afterwards,

Perth K4011, on the 50-ton crane at Felixstowe, with experimental four-bladed airscrews and the nose gun mounting entirely removed. (*Flight Photo 12793S.*)

317

on 14 September, K3580 was lost off Stornoway when a wing tip float was torn off during an attempted take-off in heavy seas during naval exercises, the crew being rescued.

The fourth and final Perth, K4011, first flown on 16 April 1934 and subsequently on 18 and 19 April before delivery to Felixstowe on 20 April, had only two gravity fuel tanks instead of the usual three. It was nominally on Coastal Area's charge and bore No. 209 Squadron's 'Venture Far' crest but spent its entire Service life with 'A' Flight at the MAEE, Felixstowe, to which it was formally transferred for experimental use in May 1936. The armament and gun mountings were then removed and it was fitted with four-bladed wooden airscrews specially manufactured with alternate 80 degree and 100 degree angles between the blades. Eventually it made a heavy landing and was towed into harbour in a sinking condition.

SPECIFICATION AND DATA

Manufacturers: The Blackburn Aeroplane and Motor Co Ltd, Brough Aerodrome, East Yorks.

Power Plants: Three 825 hp Rolls-Royce Buzzard IIMS moderately supercharged engines with 0·552 : 1 airscrew reduction gear.

Dimensions: Span 97 ft 0 in   Length 70 ft 0 in
            Height 26 ft 5½ in   Wing area 2,511 sq ft

Loadings:

(a) *Normal*		(b) *Overload*	
Tare weight	20,927 lb	Tare weight	20,927 lb
Five crew	1,000 lb	Five crew	1,000 lb
Military load	2,230 lb	Military load	1,975 lb
1,000 gal fuel	7,700 lb	1,725 gal fuel	13,300 lb
54 gal oil	523 lb	70 gal oil	678 lb
12 gal water	120 lb	12 gal water	120 lb
All-up weight	32,500 lb	All-up weight	38,000 lb

Performance:	
Maximum speed at sea level	132 mph
Maximum speed at 5,000 ft	126 mph
Economical cruising speed	109 mph
Initial climb	800 ft/min
Time to 10,000 ft	22 min
Service ceiling	11,500 ft
Normal range at cruising speed	898 miles
Maximum range at cruising speed	1,500 miles

Production:

(*a*) Three aircraft to Contract 199604/32:

(i) K3580, Works Order 4970/1, launched 11 October 1933, taken on charge by the Directorate of Technical Development 20 October 1933, delivered to Felixstowe 10 November 1933, transferred to Coastal Area on 27 February 1934, delivered to

No. 209 Squadron 31 May 1934, lost off Stornoway 14 September 1935, struck off charge 17 October 1935. (ii) K3581, Works Order 4970/2, taken on charge by Coastal Area on 8 December 1933, first flown and delivered to No. 209 Squadron 5 January 1934, transferred to the Directorate of Technical Development 4 May 1936, struck off charge 1936. (iii) K3582, Works Order 5220/1, taken on charge by Coastal Area on 15 January 1934, delivered to No. 209 Squadron 5 February 1934, struck off charge 24 January 1936.

(b) One aircraft to Contract 265687/33:

K4011, Works Order 5240/1, taken on charge by Coastal Area on 21 March 1934, first flown 16 April 1934, delivered to Felixstowe 20 April 1934, transferred to the Directorate of Technical Development at Felixstowe 4 May 1936, struck off charge 2 February 1938.

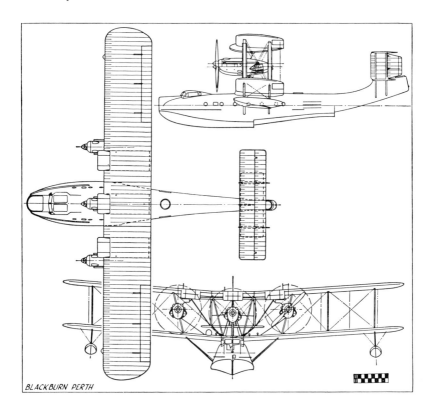

BLACKBURN PERTH

The first Blackburn Segrave I at Heston in March 1931 in its original form with cantilever tail skid, Saro-built wire-braced tail unit and slanting rudder horn balance. (*Flight Photo 9932.*)

Blackburn B-1 Segrave

As the name indicates, the layout for this high-performance light twin was the work of the late Sir Henry Segrave, ex-RFC fighter pilot, member of the British Aviation Mission to Washington in 1918, leading Sunbeam racing driver and holder of the world's land speed record in the Napier Lion engined car *Golden Arrow*, who, in 1929, became technical advisor to the Aircraft Investment Corporation Ltd. This was a powerful financial group with an interest in Saunders-Roe Ltd of Cowes, Isle of Wight, and close links with Brough through Blackburn Consolidated Ltd formed in the same year. His first, and only, task on their behalf was to design what he considered to be the ideal touring aeroplane possessed of an impressive cruising speed, yet able to land slowly and climb on one engine with full load. None knew better than he the improvement in performance and economies in power to be obtained by careful streamlining and thus, in a biplane age with several of Britain's classic biplane types yet unbuilt, his proposals for this twin-engined four-seater with cantilever mainplane were little short of revolutionary.

Its oval-section streamlined fuselage with totally enclosed cabin and 120 hp de Havilland Gipsy III engines faired into the leading edge of the wing, put it years ahead of its time and even today only the narrow-track fixed under-carriage and the crudity of its cabin glazing would hint at its true age.

Construction of the prototype was entrusted to Saunders-Roe Ltd who produced an all-white, plywood-covered wooden prototype, G-AAXP, which made its first flight at Cowes on 28 May 1930. Although popularly known as the Segrave Meteor I, its correct name, derived from mixed parentage and shown on the Certificate of Registration, was Saro Segrave Meteor I, the Saro type number being A.22.

320

The aircraft went to Martlesham Heath for performance testing in the following month and on its return was entered for the King's Cup Air Race of 5 July by Maj A. P. Holt of the Aircraft Investment Corporation Ltd. The crew comprised Flt Lts Atcherley (later Air Marshal Sir Richard) and Stainforth of the 1929 RAF High Speed Flight, but unfortunately a defect in the fuel system caused intermittent cutting of the starboard engine and 'XP limped back to Hanworth soon after the start. As a result of Martlesham test recommendations, the Meteor I then returned to Cowes for modifications which included increase in wing incidence and tailplane and rudder areas. It was also re-doped in an all-red colour scheme before reappearing at Croydon and Heston for demonstrations by the Corporation's pilot Flt Lt J. G. D. Armour on 26 and 27 September respectively.

It was the highlight of the opening of the Surrey Aero Club at Gatwick on 4 October and then paid a second visit to Martlesham for the effectiveness of the modifications to be assessed. Flt Lt Armour then flew it from Heston to St Inglevert on 23 October on the first stage of a flight to Rome for a special demonstration before the Italian Air Minister, Signore Balbo. Its performance drew enthusiastic comments from all the Italian Air Force officers who flew it and a contract was signed for its production under licence for the Italian Government by Piaggio at Finalmarina as the Piaggio P.12 trainer. Although a report dated November 1930 stated that an initial batch of six had been laid down, only two were completed and flown.

Flt Lt Armour brought the Meteor back to Heston after a nonstop flight from Paris on 14 November 1930 and eventually acquired it for his own use, but in June 1932 it was taken over by the Aircraft Investment Corporation's director G. E. de Lengerke, for whom it was overhauled at Brough and test flown for C. of A. renewal by A. M. Blake on 17 June. Entered by the owner and flown by Armour, it averaged 131 mph after leaving Brooklands at the start of the King's Cup race on 8 July but retired on the second day with a broken fuel pipe. After a few business trips abroad via Heston it returned to Brough in September to be dismantled.

The Saro-built Segrave Meteor I G-AAXP at Brough in 1931.

Blackburn C.A.18 Segrave I

A less remarkable type could hardly have survived the events which retarded its development during 1930. Its first and greatest setback was the tragic death of Sir Henry Segrave in an accident to the Saro-built speedboat *Miss England II* (two 1,900 hp Rolls-Royce R aero engines) during an attempt on the world's water speed record on Lake Windermere on 13 June 1930, only a fortnight after the prototype flew. Furthermore, Saunders-Roe Ltd, needing factory space for building their new Cutty Sark amphibian and its derivatives as well as London flying-boats for the RAF, were already handing back Bluebird IV production to Blackburns, so that, even before the prototype had been completed, all existing Meteor sub-assemblies and manufactured components had been sent to Brough. Simultaneously the Aircraft Investment Corporation announced that the production version would be built in metal by the Blackburn Aeroplane and Motor Co Ltd and known as the Meteor II.

Thus during the autumn of 1930 the Blackburn design staff translated the fuselage into a semi-monocoque metal structure supported internally by duralumin frames attached to four longerons, the skin being stiffened in shear by diagonal tubular struts in addition to the horizontal stringers. No welding or wire-bracing was used, and the skin was of Alclad reinforced with longitudinal swagings riveted to the frames.

The pilot's windscreens were of non-splinterable glass, and access to the cabin was through the hinged roof and side panels, the latter incorporating sliding windows. In the cabin area the structure was reinforced by steel frames and a central tubular pillar to protect the occupants if the machine turned over.

The mainplane was built in one piece with two deep box spars, which tapered towards the tips, spruce and plywood ribs, and a plywood covering glued and bradded to the main structure. Narrow-chord ailerons were inset at each wing tip and, although structurally identical with Saunders-Roe's prototype, the wing was mounted farther aft (no doubt because the C.G. of the metal fuselage was further aft than the wooden one), so that its leading edge was level with the second, instead of the first side window. The rudder was horn balanced and the tailplane adjustable.

Two 120 hp Gipsy III inverted engines were mounted on the main spar, each with its own 27-gallon fuel tank and $1\frac{1}{2}$-gallon oil tank, a fuel distributor cock in the cockpit enabling one tank to feed both engines if necessary. The fixed, divided undercarriage was similar to that of the prototype and consisted of rubber-in-compression telescopic struts attached to the main spar midway between the centreline of the fuselage and the wing engine and braced by two steel-tube Vs. Palmer wheels and brakes and a simplified cantilever tail skid were fitted.

Now regarded as a Blackburn aircraft, it was added to the firm's civil aircraft designation system as the C.A.18 and the Saro-inspired type name Meteor II was abandoned in favour of Blackburn Segrave I.

322

Segrave I G-ABFP at Brough in July 1931 with temporary Class B marking B-1, spatted undercarriage and Blackburn-built tail unit.

Two metal-fuselage Segrave Is, laid down for the Aircraft Investment Corporation Ltd in October 1930 and registered in the name of J. G. D. Armour, were fitted with Saro-built plywood-covered wooden mainplanes, and the first, G-ABFP, flown for the first time at Brough on 9 February 1931, also had Saro-built wire-braced tail surfaces and an inclined rudder horn balance similar to the Meteor I. Painted red overall to match this machine, which had been at Brough ever since its return from Italy, G-ABFP went immediately to Martlesham for tests which were pushed through very rapidly so that the machine could be delivered to Gordon Selfridge Jnr at Heston in time for an Easter tour of Spain. Carrying baggage and spares for the five accompanying light aircraft and with R. H. McIntosh as co-pilot, the Segrave left Heston on 31 March but got no further than Perpignan.

On its return the machine went back to Brough to be fitted with an improved cantilever tail unit entirely designed and built by Blackburns and incorporating standard Blackburn variable-incidence gear and externally sprung tail skid. The most noticeable differences lay in the shape of the rudder horn balance, which now formed a right angle, and in the close-fitting metal wheel spats, later discarded. Coincidentally the British aircraft industry was at this time allotted Class B markings for use on new or experimental aircraft under test, a system in which the Blackburn company was allotted letter B, to be followed by a number of their own choice. The Segrave I G-ABFP accordingly acquired Class B marking B-1 for manufacturers' trials in July 1931, but, by the time it went to Martlesham for handling trials in the following September with the new tail unit, B-1 had been adopted as the first of a new and simplified Blackburn type numbering system which remains in use to the present day.

The Segrave I's stalling speed of 69 mph was considered high for an aircraft of its class but it handled very nicely in the air and was able to maintain level flight with either engine switched off. Rudder and aileron controls were rather heavy and the fitting of rudder bias gear was suggested for asymmetrical flying.

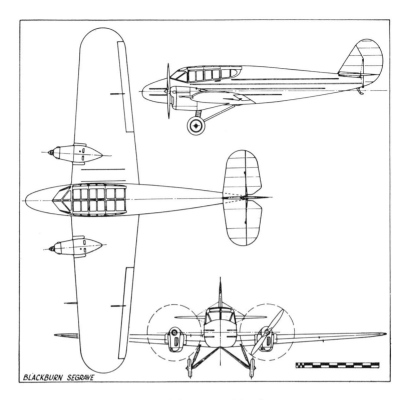

BLACKBURN SEGRAVE

No real order having resulted from the visit of the Saro Segrave Meteor I G-AAXP to Italy in the previous year, Robert Blackburn organized a European sales tour and left Heston as passenger in Segrave G-ABFP on 5 October 1931 piloted by A. M. Blake, and accompanied by the Lincock III G-ABFK and the Bluebird IV G-ABPV. The aircraft were demonstrated in Brussels on 5 and 6 October, Prague on 12 and 13 October, Vienna on 15 October, Budapest on 16 October and Belgrade on 19 October. They then flew to Tatoi Aerodrome, Athens, via Uskub and Salonika, arriving on 21 October, Robert Blackburn having travelled from Cologne by train in order to keep other business engagements.

The Segrave was flown by a number of Greek military pilots but, after the loss of the Bluebird IV G-ABPV in a fatal crash at Tatoi, it was dismantled, crated and shipped home. Again no foreign orders materialized, almost certainly because it was so far in advance of its time, and on its return G-ABFP was sold to BANCO, the British Air Navigation Co Ltd, formed at Heston in February 1932 by I. C. MacGilcrist with A. J. 'Bill' Styran as chief pilot, to operate fast air-taxi services with modern twin-engined equipment. The Segrave was fitted with navigation lights and Marconi A.D.22 radio and thereafter figured frequently in the cross-Channel movements lists, but its com-

324

mercial career was short, for a few months later it passed into the hands of J. G. D. Armour who flew it in the Brooklands–Cramlington (Newcastle) Race of 6 August 1932 and averaged 126·5 mph.

Early in 1933 it was acquired by Mrs Burnside of Redhill and flown out to Nairobi, Kenya, eventually arriving back at Croydon on 7 October after a leisurely return flight piloted by a South African Air Force officer named Mossett. Aircraft Exchange and Mart Ltd then added it to their fleet of miscellaneous training aircraft for the benefit of pilots requiring twin-engined experience. This scheme was short-lived, and the aircraft was sent to Brough for the trial installation of two of the new 120 hp Blackburn Cirrus Hermes IVA four-cylinder inverted air-cooled engines with which it was first flown on 17 January 1934. Records show that W. A. Burnside flew it at Brough with these engines on 21 February, with Blackburn's single-spar wing designer F. Duncanson as passenger, but when the C. of A. expired a few weeks later the aircraft was withdrawn from use.

The second Segrave I, G-ABFR, was first flown at Brough on 26 April 1932 and demonstrated at the SBAC Show at Hendon on 27 June that year before transfer to the North Sea Aerial and General Transport Co Ltd. A. M. Blake flew it at Brough after C. of A. renewal on 8 June 1933, and on 1 July it commenced a thrice-daily (except Sunday) return ferry service between the Hull municipal aerodrome at Hedon and Waltham Aerodrome, Grimsby. Some 500 passengers had been carried by 4 September when an hourly service was introduced, a frequency maintained until the service was permanently withdrawn on 4 November. G-ABFR then languished at Brough until purchased in October 1935 by F. R. Evans, former owner of a Bluebird IV, who evidently found it too large for his requirements, for in May 1936 he sold it to British Air Transport Ltd who used it for taxi work and twin-engined commercial licence training at the Redhill Flying Club up to the end of 1937, the rates being £5 15s. 0d. per hour dual and £5 solo. It is evident that BAT also acquired at least the mainplane of the original wooden Meteor as a spare, for this was still hanging in a small shed at Redhill in 1947.

Blackburn C.A.20 Segrave II

Construction of a third Segrave I, G-ABZJ, ordered in the name of J. G. D. Armour in September 1932 was halted before the end of the year, but shortly afterwards when F. Duncanson, who had patented a novel form of single-spar construction, joined the firm Blackburns decided to complete it for full-scale research into the rigidity of a single-spar mainplane of his design. This was built round a tapering, circular section, thin-walled duralumin tubular spar supported by baffles internally and stiffened by corrugations on top and bottom. With the duralumin ribs and fabric covering attached, a mainplane of great simplicity with a good strength/weight ratio resulted.

The tubular spar formed not only a rigid base for the attachment of engine mountings and undercarriage but was used to house the fuel which reduced

325

The sharply-tapered Duncanson wing is well shown in this view of the Segrave II G-ACMI flying near Brough. Wool tufts on the tail were for investigations into airflow behaviour at the rudder hinge.

the bending moment when distributed along the spar. Furthermore, the entire 39-gallon fuel load was carried exactly in line with the C.G. thus reducing torsional stresses and trimming loads. Frise-type ailerons were fitted and all balance weights and controls were entirely inside the wing, the leading edge of which was reinforced by sheet metal over closely spaced nose ribs.

Even though it was necessary to use an adaptor for attaching the new main-plane to the two-spar pick-up points on the fuselage, a direct saving in weight of 260 lb (or 42 per cent) was made over the wooden wing. Tare weight was reduced by 275 lb (a 12¼ per cent decrease), payload went up by the same amount (an increase of 52 per cent) and the elimination of fuel tanks saved a further 55 lb. Collectively these economies permitted the use of 130 hp Gipsy Major engines and the provision of a fifth seat in the cabin without exceeding the original all-up weight of 3,300 lb.

With its tapering wing, voluminous root fairings, tail wheel, Gipsy Major engines and revised exhaust system, it was markedly different from the original and received the amended designation C.A.20 Segrave II and a new registra-

The Segrave II showing the internal construction of the Duncanson single-spar wing.

326

tion, G-ACMI, painted in black on bare metal. Although completed in October 1933, the first flight at Brough by A. M. Blake and J. B. Stockbridge did not take place until 2 February 1934, and further manufacturers' trials were completed by N. H. Woodhead on 7 February. It was delivered to the RAE, Farnborough, by J. B. Stockbridge on 15 February, with F. Duncanson as passenger, but later returned to Brough for 50 hr of test flying to prove the wing construction. In the course of this it visited Sherburn-in-Elmet on 10 May 1934.

A second and identical single-spar wing, exhibited at the Hendon SBAC Show on 2 July 1934 was never fitted to an aeroplane.

Projected Variants

Although no other Segraves were built a number of variants were projected, the earliest being the C.A.18/1 Segrave Ambulance and a cleaned up version known as the C.A.18A Segrave High Performance Tourer, both with 120 hp Gipsy IIIs. Proposals to fit the single-spar Segrave II with two Cirrus Hermes IVAs under the designation C.A.20A did not materialize, but data gained from tests with its Duncanson wing was used in designing the larger Black-burn C.A.21A or B-9 transport, better known as the H.S.T.10, with retract-able undercarriage and two Napier Rapier engines.

The origins of this aircraft can be traced to discussions held at Brough on 30 June 1933 between Capt Snook, a Mr Lamb, and Blackburn engineers G. C. F. Ely and F. Duncanson, concerning an eight-passenger Segrave III with two 260 hp Armstrong Siddeley Lynx Major radials to suit Australian requirements. A less ambitious version of this project, also known as Segrave III, was produced in the following month to meet a specification submitted by ex-RCAF officer L. E. Cook for a convertible land, sea and ski-plane for airline service in the far north of Canada. With a span of 53 ft 0 in, both versions would have been rather larger than the original Segrave, and the Canadian machine would have carried 12 including crew; but neither aircraft was built.

These projects led in turn to a layout numbered C.A.19/1 in which the H.S.T.10 was now clearly taking shape, the main difference being the use of two 340 hp Armstrong Siddeley Serval radials in place of the Napier Rapiers. Full surviving data for these and allied projects is listed in Appendix B.

SPECIFICATION AND DATA

Manufacturers: (Saro Segrave Meteor I)
       Saunders-Roe Ltd, East Cowes, Isle of Wight.
      (Blackburn Segrave)
       The Blackburn Aeroplane and Motor Co Ltd, Brough Aerodrome, East Yorks.
      (Piaggio P. 12)
       Societa Anonima Piaggio, Finalmarina, Italy.

Power Plants: (Saro Segrave Meteor I)
            Two 120 hp de Havilland Gipsy III
            (Blackburn C.A.18 Segrave I)
            Two 120 hp de Havilland Gipsy III
            Two 120 hp Cirrus Hermes IVA
            (Blackburn C.A. 20 Segrave II)
            Two 130 hp de Havilland Gipsy Major

Dimensions, Weights and Performance:

	Saro Segrave Meteor I	Blackburn Segrave	
		C.A.18 Segrave I*	C.A.20 Segrave II
Span	39 ft 6 in	39 ft 6 in	41 ft 6 in
Length	27 ft 6 in	28 ft 6 in	28 ft 0 in
Height	7 ft 9 in.	7 ft 9 in	8 ft 8 in
Wing area	230 sq ft	230 sq ft	246 sq ft
Tare weight	1,948 lb	2,246 lb	1,971 lb
Disposable load	1,000 lb	1,054 lb	1,329 lb
All-up weight	2,948 lb	3,300 lb	3,300 lb
Maximum speed	132 mph	138 mph	142 mph
Cruising speed	110 mph	112 mph	120 mph
Initial climb	900 ft/min	800 ft/min	875 ft/min
Absolute ceiling	17,000 ft	17,000 ft	17,000 ft
Service ceiling	14,000 ft	14,000 ft	14,000 ft
Range (42 gallons)	340 miles	340 miles	300 miles†
Range (52 gallons)	450 miles	450 miles	—

* Ref. A. & A.E.E. Report M/566A dated 25 September 1931.
†39 gallons

Loadings: (a) *Segrave I*

Tare weight	2,240 lb
Disposable load	690 lb
52 gal petrol	340 lb
3 gal oil	30 lb
All-up weight	3,300 lb

(b) *Segrave II*

Tare weight	1,971 lb
Disposable load	1,029 lb
39 gal petrol	270 lb
3 gal oil	30 lb
All-up weight	3,300 lb

Production:

(a) *By Saunders-Roe Ltd, East Cowes*

One prototype only as under:

G-AAXP   c/n 1, registered to the Aircraft Investment Corporation Ltd 1 May 1930, first flown at Cowes 28 May 1930, C. of A. issued 27 June 1930; to J. G. D. Armour October 1931; to G. E. de Lengerke 8 June 1932, C. of A. renewal at Brough and air test by A. M. Blake 21 June 1932, withdrawn from use September 1932, mainplane at Redhill in 1947.

(b) *By the Blackburn Aeroplane and Motor Co Ltd, Brough*
Three production aircraft only as under:

G-ABFP Works Order 3169/1, registered to J. G. D. Armour 14 October 1930, first flown 9 February 1931, C. of A. issued 18 March 1931; to Gordon Selfridge Jnr, Heston March 1931; to Blackburns August 1931; to BANCO, Heston February 1932; to J. G. D. Armour June 1932; to Mrs F. S. Burnside, Redhill March 1933; to Aircraft Exchange and Mart Ltd, Hanworth October 1933; withdrawn from use at Brough at C. of A. expiry 10 March 1934.

G-ABFR Works Order 3169/2, registered to J. G. D. Armour 14 October 1930, first flown 26 April 1932, C. of A. issued 26 May 1932; to North Sea Aerial and General Transport Co Ltd, Brough June 1932; to F. R. Evans, Brough October 1935; to British Air Transport Ltd, Redhill May 1936, withdrawn from use at Redhill at C. of A. expiry 14 February 1938.

G-ABZJ Works Order 3854/1, registered to J. G. D. Armour 17 September 1932, registration cancelled at census December 1932; aircraft completed to same Works Order and registered to Blackburns 22 November 1933 as G-ACMI with Duncanson wing, first flown 2 February 1934, dismantled October 1935.

(c) *By Piaggio*
Two P.12 aircraft only, completed 1933, MM203 and MM204.

329

The Gipsy III powered Blackburn B-2 G-ACEM, first of the second batch.

Blackburn B-2

The Blackburn B-2 was a side-by-side two-seat trainer developed from the Gipsy III version of the Bluebird IV, using the same type of fabric-covered steel and duralumin single-bay mainplanes mated to an entirely new all-metal semi-monocoque fuselage built on the same principle as that of the Blackburn Segrave. This was deliberately made immensely strong to withstand the hard knocks of instructional flying and consisted of a structure of hollow frames reinforced by light stringers and strengthened by diagonal steel tubes. The stressed covering of Alclad was stiffened by three longitudinal swagings along each side and there was no welding or wire-bracing anywhere in the fuselage.

Fuel was gravity fed from a 22-gallon aerofoil-section tank carried above the fuselage on six struts, two vertical in front and four in the form of inverted Vs at the rear which permitted easy access to the cockpit by eliminating wire-bracing from the side panels. The outer wing panels folded round the rear spar hinges and were fitted with Handley Page slots on the upper mainplane and Frise-type ailerons on the lower. The tail unit was of similar construction to the mainplanes and the elevator trimmer was in the form of adjustable spring loading applied by a lever in the cockpit.

The front telescopic legs of the wide-track, divided undercarriage incorporated steel springs with oil dampers, and the engine was supported on a tubular-steel mounting bolted directly to the fireproof bulkhead, cooling air being ejected through fluting built into the fuselage plating aft of the engine bay. A 2½-gallon oil tank was mounted below the bearers and oil was circulated by an engine-driven pump.

Main external differences between the B-2 and the Bluebird IV were a tailplane and elevator of increased span, splayed-out interplane struts, slightly staggered mainplanes, a rounded horn balanced rudder (with fin) cut away to accommodate the tail skid spring, and main undercarriage legs which were raked forward.

All who flew the B-2 were unanimous that Blackburns had produced one of those outstandingly fine aeroplanes which appear all too rarely. There was little difficulty in taxying in a strong wind and take-off was easy without any tendency to swing. Controls were effective right down to the stall, making the aircraft a delight to fly, and on the approach at 65 mph it was very manoeuvrable and could be sideslipped with ease to the simplest possible landing.

In common with most early production B-2s, the prototype, G-ABUW, owned initially by Robert Blackburn as a replacement for his Bluebird IV G-ABEU, was powered by a 120 hp de Havilland Gipsy III inverted air-cooled engine. First flown at Brough on 10 December 1931, it made its public debut at the Hendon SBAC Show on 27 June 1932, and on 8 July was on the starting line at Brooklands for the two-day round-England King's Cup Air Race. Flown by Flg Off J. W. Gillan, it finished 18th, with the first production B-2, G-ABWI, piloted by Flg Off P. G. Sayer close behind, their average speeds being 113·75 and 115 mph respectively. G-ABWI, which differed from 'UW in having a Fairey-Reed metal airscrew, was then flown in the Brooklands–Cramlington Race on 6 August by Flt Lt N. H. Woodhead who averaged 112·5 mph and came 12th.

At this time the Portuguese Government was inviting manufacturers of training aircraft to submit examples for competitive trials, so in September 1932 the prototype B-2 was crated, taken 150 miles by road to the London Docks and shipped as deck cargo on the SS *Fayal*. It was accompanied by the demonstration pilot Flt Lt W. E. P. Johnson and consigned to the Engineering Company of Portugal, Lisbon. On arrival, 'UW was off-loaded on to a picturesque Tagus barge which, since it was impossible to take the machine, either boxed or towed with the wings off, through the narrow streets to the Government Flying School at Cintra 25 km distant, took it to the Naval Seaplane Base farther down river.

Within 40 min of leaving the crate, the B-2 had been erected, fuelled and flown off the Base football pitch on its way to Cintra. After 900 miles on a heaving deck, this performance drew very favourable comment from the Portuguese before the trials had even started and before Johnson had put the machine through its paces at Cintra, Amadora and Alverca, where he had to compete with Christopher Clarkson in a de Havilland Tiger Moth, an American Fleet trainer and a Caproni biplane of Moth-like aspect. The Portuguese did not like side-by-side seating and, after Johnson and Clarkson had impressed the populace with the superiority of the British product by flying an inverted formation right down the main street of Lisbon, the contract was awarded to the Tiger Moth.

After a five-week stay G-ABUW landed back on the football pitch to be

331

shipped home, where in March 1933 and following Air Ministry approval of the type for RAF Reserve training, it joined 'WI and 11 others at the Brough Reserve School of the North Sea Aerial and General Transport Co Ltd. This fleet comprised G-ACAH and G-ACBH to 'BK (five aircraft which formed the balance of the first production batch of six) and the complete second batch of six registered G-ACEM to 'ES.

Although the B-2 was developed primarily for military training, the Blackburn company had, at this time, every hope that Bluebird IV operators, clubs and schools would also re-equip with it. Brough CFI Flt Lt A. G. Loton flew G-ACBK to the opening of the Lincolnshire Aero Club at Waltham Aerodrome, Grimsby, on 10 June 1933 and put on a publicity display of aerobatics before handing over to T. Neville Stack who flew it into second place in the 30-mile Grimsby News Race, averaging 93 mph. With G-ACEM, the same machine formed an exhibit at the Hendon SBAC Show on 26 June. No orders came, but in the following year a new sales drive was mounted when Blackburn test pilot Sqn Ldr J. L. N. Bennett-Baggs left Brough on 20 April 1934 in the newest Hermes IVA engined machine G-ACLD for the Geneva Aero Show which opened a week later.

The works of the Cirrus Hermes Engineering Co Ltd, manufacturers of a series of engines similar to the de Havilland Gipsy range, having recently been transferred from Croydon to Brough, Blackburns had not been slow in fitting

The second production machine, G-ACAH, equipped for advanced training with camera gun, ring and bead sight, Cirrus Hermes IVA engine and Haw adjustable-pitch metal airscrew. (*Aeroplane Photo.*)

this company's 120 hp inverted air-cooled four-cylinder unit into the B-2. First to have it was the second production machine, G-ACAH, which the company fitted out as an advanced trainer with a Haw adjustable-pitch hollow-bladed metal airscrew, blind-flying hood, ring and bead sight, camera gun and P.7 vertical camera. In this form it gave an aerobatic display at the Hendon SBAC Show on 2 July 1934 but was then stripped of all specialist equipment and fitted with a fixed-pitch Fairey-Reed metal airscrew for the King's Cup Race on 14 July. Flown round four short courses centred on Hatfield by Flt Lt H. M. David, it averaged 114·18 mph and came fourth.

In a final bid to put it on an equal footing with the popular tandem cockpit types through the medium of a racing success, Capt Norman Blackburn entered 'AH for the Yorkshire Trophy Race at Sherburn-in-Elmet; but it fared no better, flown by C. S. Napier it again came fourth, this time at an average speed of 112·75 mph.

The Elementary and Reserve Flying Training Schools

At the 1934 SBAC Show G-ACAH had been supported by three other B-2s bearing the AEM monogram of Aircraft Exchange and Mart Ltd of Hanworth, sole B-2 concessionaires, on their rudders. During solo aerobatics by 'AH they flew round in formation to draw attention to the choice of three engine installations and were registered G-ACLC (Gipsy III), G-ACPZ (Gipsy Major) and G-ACRA (Hermes IVA), leased from Blackburns to form part of a miscellaneous fleet available for hire at Hanworth.

Their real importance lay in the fact that they introduced the B-2 to Hanworth (also known as London Air Park) at a time when great expansion was taking place in flying instruction, new schools were being founded and existing ones enlarged. When they reverted to the manufacturers in 1935, 'LC, 'PZ and 'RA formed the nucleus round which the North Sea Aerial and General Transport Co established No. 5 Elementary and Reserve Flying Training School run by a specially-formed Hanworth-based Blackburn subsidiary known as Flying Training Ltd, with Flt Lt N. H. Woodhead as CFI. At the same time, the parent school at Brough became No. 4 ERFTS, but in 1936, when all Blackburn interests were merged, its aircraft were re-registered to the new and all-embracing Blackburn Aircraft Ltd.

Additional equipment at Hanworth, all of which carried fleet numbers, included the Gipsy III powered G-ACZH, sixth and last of the third production batch, and all 10 of the Hermes IVA powered fourth batch registered G-ADFN to 'FV, 'LF and 'LG. At the end of 1936, however, when it was decided to standardize the Hermes IVA in the Hanworth fleet, 'ZH was replaced by G-ACEO, one of three with this engine which, up to that time, had been in use at Brough.

Rapid increases in trainee intake resulted in a batch of 10 B-2s G-ADZM, 'ZN and G-AEBE to 'BL, being issued alternately to Brough and Hanworth, and to a final batch of three, originally destined for civil status as 'BM to 'BO, which the Air Ministry purchased during construction in 1937 and issued

333

to No. 4 ERFTS with RAF serials. The total number of B-2s built thus reached 42 but none had been sold privately or overseas and Blackburn's entire output was for RAF and Reserve training.

Of the rugged strength of the B-2 there was no doubt, even if there was only a germ of truth in the story that G-ACEP came off best in a collision with a steam locomotive when it forced landed on the line at Brough on 14 August 1933. But casualties there were. Those recorded in the production list at the end of this section brought about the occasional transfer between the two Schools and included two highly spectacular landing accidents at Hanworth. The first took place on 28 May 1937 when G-ACEO was seriously damaged during an attempt to demolish the Stinson Reliant G-AEJI. The other was on 31 January 1938 when a Hawker Hart landed on top of G-AEBI, killing the pilot.

The Blackburn B-2 fleets at Brough and Hanworth continued the endless training process until just after the outbreak of war in October 1939 when all the Hanworth aircraft were evacuated to Brough. They were then merged with those of the Brough School which, from 15 October, was restyled No. 4 Elementary Flying Training School, the entire fleet being hastily re-doped with training-yellow fuselage and earth and dark green wings. Two aircraft, G-ACEO and G-ADZN, which came up for overhaul and C. of A. renewal in November 1939 were re-engined with early examples of the new 135 hp Blackburn Cirrus Major 1, the flight testing of which had been undertaken in Blackburn's communications Percival Gull G-ADOE which C. S. Napier was to have flown with this engine in the abortive 1939 King's Cup Air Race.

The B-2 fleet continued in operation until taken on RAF charge in February 1942 for issue to ATC Squadrons as instructional airframes, but not before

L6891, first of three for the RAF and photographed at Brough on 30 April 1937, was originally to have been G-AEBM.

An early Gipsy III powered Blackburn B-2, G-ACBJ, flying near Brough in 1940, in RAF training colours but with civil registration.

four more had been lost in crashes, two in an air collision over the River Humber on 24 June 1940. Several ATC instructional B-2s briefly survived the war and it is evident that in many, if not all, cases the maintenance serials were never actually painted on the aircraft. Over 20 years later several relics of these aircraft were still about, including the front half of G-ADFV at Caterham School, Surrey, and the remains of the fuselage of G-ACBH at Dixon's Yard, Ramsden Heath, Essex.

The only two to fly again were G-ACLD and G-AEBJ which Blackburn Aircraft Ltd retained and cherished at Brough throughout the war. G-AEBJ was fitted with a Gipsy Major 1 engine in 1944 and given a new C. of A. for communications duties, and 'LD reappeared in bare metal with a Gipsy III in 1946. At the next C. of A. renewal on 6 August 1947, 'LD was fitted with a 150 hp Blackburn Cirrus Major 3 engine but competed unsuccessfully for the Southend and Folkestone Trophies on 9 and 30 August, piloted by G. F. Bullen. Together with its sister machine 'BJ, it was then used for instruction by the Blackburn-sponsored Brough Flying Club, for which purpose it was repainted dark blue. It also proved a popular vintage exhibit at Royal Aeronautical Society garden parties and other air meetings, came 3rd in the Grosvenor Trophy Race at Elmdon on 30 July 1949 piloted by P. G. Lawrence, but crashed classically by stalling off a turn at low altitude during a display at York on 16 June 1951.

Used for the same purpose and piloted by Mr B. J. Watson and others, G-AEBJ attended the International Air Display at Burnaston, Derby, on 21 June 1947 and the RAeS garden party at Hatfield on 14 June 1953. In the following year it took part in the SSAFA* Display at Yeadon on 6 June, the veterans' fly-past at the King's Cup Air Race, Baginton, on 19 June and the Fairoaks Air Display on 28 June. It was used for making recordings of old-

* Soldiers', Sailors' and Airmen's Families Association.

335

aircraft noises for the BBC at Brough on 16 January 1957 and year by year was a familiar sight at most air meetings. It also landed and took off from the sands at Filey on 12 July 1960 to commemorate the 50th anniversary of the opening of the old Filey Flying School. On 15 June 1960 it was flown in formation with the company's Rapide G-AHAG for the air-to-air photograph which heads this section and was still in immaculate airworthy condition in the school hangar at Brough in 1988.

SPECIFICATION AND DATA

Manufacturers: The Blackburn Aeroplane and Motor Co Ltd, Brough Aerodrome, East Yorks.

Power Plants: One 120 hp de Havilland Gipsy III
One 120 hp Cirrus Hermes IVA
One 130 hp de Havilland Gipsy Major 1
One 135 hp Blackburn Cirrus Major 1
One 150 hp Blackburn Cirrus Major 3

Dimensions: Span 30 ft 2 in   Length 24 ft 3 in
Height 9 ft 0 in   Width folded 10 ft 9 in
Wing area 246 sq ft

Weights: Tare weight 1,175 lb
All-up weight (Normal) 1,850 lb   (Aerobatic) 1,770 lb

*Loading (aerobatic):

Tare weight	1,169 lb
Two crew	340 lb
22 gal petrol	170 lb
2 gal oil	18 lb
Equipment	73 lb
All-up weight	1,770 lb

* *Ref. A. & A.E.E. Report M/613 dated November 1932 on the first production aircraft G-ABWI fitted with Gipsy III engine No. 3406.*

Performance: Maximum speed 112 mph   Cruising speed 95 mph
Initial climb 600 ft/min   Range 320 miles

Production:

(a) *Prototype*

One aircraft only to Works Order 3580/1:

G-ABUW   Gipsy III, registered to the Blackburn Aeroplane and Motor Co Ltd, Brough 7 March 1932; first flown by A. M. Blake 13 April 1932; to Robert Blackburn April 1932; C. of A. issued 23 June 1932; to the North Sea Aerial and General Transport Co Ltd, Brough March 1933; to Blackburn Aircraft Ltd, Brough December 1936; to No. 4 EFTS 15 October 1939; impressed 17 February 1942, believed as 2887M, and handed over to the ATC at Blackburn's Olympia Works, Leeds.

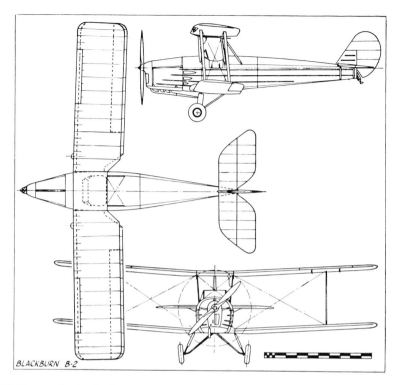

BLACKBURN B-2

(b) *First production batch*
Six aircraft to Works Orders 4700/1 to 4700/6 inclusive:

G-ABWI   Gipsy III, registered to the Blackburn Aeroplane and Motor Co Ltd,
          Brough 9 May 1932; C. of A. issued 30 June 1932; to the North Sea Aerial
          and General Transport Co Ltd, Brough March 1933; fatal crash at
          Ellerton, Selby, Yorks. 9 October 1936.

G-ACAH   Hermes IVA, registered to the Blackburn Aeroplane and Motor Co Ltd,
          Brough 1 November 1932; C. of A. issued 15 March 1933; to the North
          Sea Aerial and General Transport Co Ltd, Brough March 1933; to
          Blackburn Aircraft Ltd, Brough December 1936; to No. 4 EFTS
          15 October 1939; impressed 17 February 1942 as 2907M and handed over
          to No. 1187 ATC Sqn, Hemel Hempstead, as an instructional airframe.

G-ACBH   Gipsy III, registered to the North Sea Aerial and General Transport Co
          Ltd, Brough 1 December 1932; first flown 10 March 1933, C. of A. issued
          22 March 1933; to Blackburn Aircraft Ltd, Brough December 1936; to
          No. 4 EFTS, Brough 15 October 1939; written off in accident 4 miles
          west of Brough 16 March 1940; impressed 17 February 1942 as 2895M
          but only the fuselage had survived and this remained G-ACBH when
          handed over to No. 692 ATC Sqn, Brentwood Institute, Essex, as an
          instructional airframe; transferred to Dixon's Yard, Ramsden Heath,
          Essex, *circa* 1945. Fuselage with Cole Auto Supplies 1986.

337

G-ACBI   Gipsy III, registered to the North Sea Aerial and General Transport Co Ltd, Brough 1 December 1932; first flown 10 March 1933, C. of A. issued 22 March 1933; to Blackburn Aircraft Ltd, Brough December 1936; fatal crash at Brough Haven, East Yorks. 30 July 1937.

G-ACBJ   Gipsy III, registered to the North Sea Aerial and General Transport Co Ltd, Brough 1 December 1932; first flown 14 March 1933, C. of A. issued 22 March 1933; to Blackburn Aircraft Ltd, Brough December 1936; to No. 4 EFTS, Brough 15 October 1939; impressed 17 February 1942 as 2900M and handed over to No. 1069 ATC Sqn, Wimborne Minster, Dorset, as an instructional airframe.

G-ACBK   Gipsy III, registered to the North Sea Aerial and General Transport Co Ltd, Brough 1 December 1932; first flown 17 March 1933, C. of A. issued 22 March 1933; to Blackburn Aircraft Ltd, Brough December 1936; to No. 4 EFTS, Brough 15 October 1939; impressed 17 February 1942 as 2906M and handed over to No. 218 ATC Sqn, Rotherham, Yorks., as an instructional airframe; in use until all fabric covered surfaces were burned 5 November 1947.

(c) *Second production batch*

Six aircraft to Works Orders 5093/1 to 5093/6 inclusive, all registered to the North Sea Aerial and General Transport Co Ltd, Brough 28 February 1933:

G-ACEM   Gipsy III, first flown 29 March 1933, C. of A. issued 3 April 1933; to Blackburn Aircraft Ltd, Brough December 1936; repaired after accident at Brough Haven, East Yorks., 13 July 1937; to No. 4 EFTS, Brough 15 October 1939; impressed 17 February 1942 as 2890M and handed over to No. 438 ATC Sqn, Thanet, Kent, as an instructional airframe; to Manston 18 July 1946; to No. 1 Metal Produce and Recovery Depot, Cowley, Oxon., for reduction to scrap 21 February 1947.

G-ACEN   Gipsy III, first flown 31 March 1933, C. of A. issued 3 April 1933; to Blackburn Aircraft Ltd, Brough December 1936; to No. 4 EFTS, Brough 15 October 1939; fatal crash as Osgodby, Selby, Yorks, 26 December 1940.

G-ACEO   Hermes IVA, first flown by Flt Lt Bailey 2 April 1933, C. of A. issued 5 April 1933; to Flying Training Ltd, Hanworth December 1936; to No. 4 EFTS, Brough 15 October 1939; fitted with 135 hp Cirrus Major 1 at C. of A. overhaul 30 November 1939; impressed 17 February 1942 as 2899M and handed over to No. 1028 ATC Sqn, Eden Valley, Cumberland, as an instructional airframe.

G-ACEP   Gipsy III, first flown by Flt Lt Bailey 6 April 1933, C. of A. issued 10 April 1933; to Blackburn Aircraft Ltd, Brough December 1936; to No. 4 EFTS, Brough 15 October 1939; registration cancelled February 1943.

G-ACER   Gipsy III, first flown by Mr Downer 7 April 1933, C. of A. issued 12 April 1933; seriously damaged by fire in crash at Brough 8 May 1936; rebuilt for Blackburn Aircraft Ltd, Brough December 1936; to No. 4 EFTS, Brough 15 October 1939; crashed at Brough 11 September 1940.

G-ACES   Hermes IVA, first flown 1 May 1933, C. of A. issued 11 May 1933; to Blackburn Aircraft Ltd, Brough December 1936; to No. 4 EFTS, Brough 15 October 1939; impressed 17 February 1942 as 2904M and handed over to No. 1283 ATC Sqn, Gelligaer, Wales.

(d) *Third production batch*

Six aircraft to Works Orders 5290/1 to 5290/6 inclusive, the first five registered to the Blackburn Aeroplane and Motor Co Ltd on various dates and the last, G-ACZH, registered to Flying Training Ltd, Hanworth 31 October 1934

G-ACLC   Gipsy III, registered 24 October 1933, first flown 5 December 1933, C. of A. issued 2 February 1934; to the North Sea Aerial and General Transport Co Ltd, Brough April 1934; to Flying Training Ltd, Hanworth February 1936; to Blackburn Aircraft Ltd, Brough December 1936; to No. 4 EFTS, Brough 15 October 1939; destroyed in air collision with Blackburn B-2 G-ADFS over the River Humber 24 June 1940.

G-ACLD   Hermes IVA, registered 24 October 1933, first flown 10 April 1934, C. of A. issued 12 April 1934; to North Sea Aerial and General Transport Co Ltd, Brough November 1934; to Blackburn Aircraft Ltd, Brough December 1936; to No. 4 EFTS, Brough 15 October 1939; impressed 17 February 1942 as 2885M and allotted to No. 304 ATC Sqn but was retained by Blackburns; C. of A. renewal 2 July 1946 with Gipsy III; further renewal 6 August 1947 with Cirrus Major III; crashed at Rawcliffe, York 16 June 1951; wreck cannibalized at Brough as spares for G-AEBJ.

G-ACPZ   Gipsy Major, registered 17 April 1934, first flown 10 May 1934, C. of A. issued to Aircraft Exchange and Mart Ltd, Hanworth 18 May 1934; to Flying Training Ltd, Hanworth May 1935 (Fleet No. 4); to No. 4 EFTS, Brough 15 October 1939; impressed 17 February 1942 as 2902M and handed over to No. 1098 ATC Sqn at RNAS, Gosport, Hants., as an instructional airframe.

G-ACRA   Hermes IVA, registered 17 April 1934, first flown 12 May 1934, C. of A. issued 24 May 1934; to Flying Training Ltd, Hanworth May 1935; to No. 4 EFTS, Brough 15 October 1939; impressed 17 February 1942 as 2905M and allotted to No. 1345 ATC Sqn, Malden and Coombe, Surrey, but remained G-ACRA and was scrapped at Witney, Oxon., in 1946.

G-ACLD, outside the flying-school hangar at Brough in May 1951, with 150 hp Cirrus Major III engine and dark blue fuselage.

339

G-ACUE	Gipsy III, registered 11 June 1934, first flown 28 June 1934, C. of A. issued 28 June 1934; to North Sea Aerial and General Transport Co Ltd, Brough October 1934; struck high tension cables and crashed at Little Weighton, East Yorks., 12 November 1935.
G-ACZH	Gipsy III, first flown by Mr Downer 8 January 1934; C. of A. issued 12 January 1934; registered to Flying Training Ltd, Hanworth 31 October 1934; to Blackburn Aircraft Ltd, Brough December 1936; to No. 4 EFTS, Brough 15 October 1939; impressed 17 February 1942 as 2886M and handed over to No. 1375 ATC Sqn, Napier Road School, East Ham, London, as an instructional airframe; still there in 1945.

(e) *Fourth production batch*

Ten Hermes IVA powered aircraft to Works Orders 5920/1 to 5920/10 inclusive, all registered to Flying Training Ltd, Hanworth; the first eight on 13 April 1935 and the last two on 10 July 1935:

G-ADFN	Fleet No. 6, C. of A. issued 30 May 1935; to No. 4 EFTS, Brough 15 October 1939; impressed 17 February 1942 as 2897M and handed over to No. 734 ATC Sqn at the Cambridgeshire Technical School, Durham, as an instructional airframe.
G-ADFO	Fleet No. 7, C. of A. issued 3 June 1935; to No. 4 EFTS, Brough 15 October 1939; written off in a forced landing at Newport, Yorks., 3 September 1940.
G-ADFP	Fleet No. 8, C. of A. issued 5 June 1935; to No. 4 EFTS, Brough 15 October 1939; impressed 17 February 1942 as 2892M and handed over to No. 463 ATC Sqn at Pontefract Secondary Modern Boys' School as an instructional airframe.
G-ADFR	Fleet No. 9, C. of A. issued 7 June 1935; to No. 4 EFTS, Brough 15 October 1939; impressed 17 February 1942 as 2894M and handed over to No. 628 ATC Sqn at Pinner Grammar School, Middlesex, as an instructional airframe; struck off charge as scrap 26 September 1946.
G-ADFS	Fleet No. 10, C. of A. issued 9 June 1935; to No. 4 EFTS, Brough 15 October 1939; fell into the River Humber following an air collision with Blackburn B-2 G-ACLC 24 June 1940.
G-ADFT	Fleet No. 11, C. of A. issued 17 June 1935; to No. 4 EFTS, Brough 15 October 1939; impressed 17 February 1942 as 2908M and handed over to No. 1176 ATC Sqn, Bexhill, Sussex, as an instructional airframe.
G-ADFU	Fleet No. 12, C. of A. issued 20 June 1935; to No. 4 EFTS, Brough 15 October 1939; impressed 17 February 1942 as 2903M and flown to Castle Bromwich to be handed over to No. 1415 ATC Sqn at King Edward's School, Birmingham; dismantled and stripped 1944; struck off charge as scrap and removed by the RAF 28 May 1947.
G-ADFV	Fleet No. 18, C. of A. issued 25 June 1935; to No. 4 EFTS, Brough 15 October 1939; impressed 17 February 1942 as 2893M and handed over to No. 574 ATC Sqn at Caterham School, Surrey, as an instructional airframe; still complete in 1946; dismembered in 1950, front fuselage preserved in HQ building, remainder of airframe buried nearby; reconstruction attempted in 1967.

340

G-ADLF   Fleet No. 14, C. of A. issued 16 July 1935, to No. 4 EFTS, Brough
          15 October 1939; impressed 17 February 1942 as 2891M and handed over
          to No. 449 ATC Sqn at Port Talbot, Wales, as an instructional airframe;
          to No. 63 MU, Carluke 25 June 1944 as scrap.
G-ADLG   Fleet No. 2, C. of A. issued 28 November 1935; to No. 4 EFTS, Brough
          15 October 1939; impressed 17 February 1942 as 2888M and handed over
          to No. 358 ATC Sqn, Welling, Kent, as an instructional airframe.

(f) *Fifth production batch*
   Ten Hermes IVA powered aircraft to Works Orders 6300/1 to 6300/10 inclusive,
registered alternately to the North Sea Aerial and General Transport Co Ltd, Brough,
and Flying Training Ltd, Hanworth:

G-ADZM   To North Sea 12 December 1935, C. of A. issued 12 February 1936; to
          Blackburn Aircraft Ltd, Brough December 1936; to No. 4 EFTS, Brough
          15 October 1939; impressed 17 February 1942 as 2896M and handed
          over to No. 702 ATC Sqn, Vaughan Road School, West Harrow, Middle-
          sex, as an instructional airframe.
G-ADZN   To Flying Training 12 December 1935 (Fleet No. 15), C. of A. issued
          27 February 1936; to No. 4 EFTS, Brough 15 October 1939; fitted with
          Cirrus Major 1 at C. of A. renewal 13 November 1939; impressed
          17 February 1942 as 2889M and handed over to No. 387 ATC Sqn at
          Airedale, Yorks., as an instructional airframe.
G-AEBE   To North Sea 3 February 1936, C. of A. issued 6 March 1936; to Black-
          burn Aircraft Ltd, Brough December 1936; to No. 4 EFTS, Brough
          15 October 1939; impressed 17 February 1942 as 2898M and handed over
          to No. 1233 ATC Sqn at Chipping Sodbury, Glos., as an instructional
          airframe.
G-AEBF   To Flying Training 3 February 1936 (Fleet No. 16), C. of A. issued
          20 March 1936; crashed at Sunbury, Middlesex, 9 September 1937.

G-ADLG, last of the Hermes IVA powered fourth batch, at Hanworth in 1936
with Flying Training's fleet No. 2 on the rudder.

G-AEBG   To North Sea 4 February 1936, C. of A. issued 16 April 1936; to Black-
          burn Aircraft Ltd, Brough December 1936; impressed 17 February 1942
          as 2938M and handed over to No. 1223 ATC Sqn at Caerphilly, Wales,
          as an instructional airframe.

G-AEBH   To Flying Training 4 February 1936, C. of A. issued 6 May 1936;
          crashed at Kingsbury, Middlesex, 17 August 1936.

G-AEBI   To North Sea 4 February 1936, C. of A. issued 29 May 1936; to Flying
          Training Ltd, Hanworth September 1936; destroyed in ground collision
          with Hawker Hart at Hanworth 31 January 1938.

G-AEBJ   To Flying Training 4 February 1936 (Fleet No. 17), C. of A. issued
          5 June 1936; to No. 4 EFTS, Brough 15 October 1939; retained by
          Blackburn Aircraft Ltd; C. of A. renewals 14 July 1942 and 9 May 1944;
          fitted Gipsy Major 1; still airworthy in 1988.

G-AEBK   To North Sea 4 February 1936, C. of A. issued 20 July 1936; to Flying
          Training Ltd, Hanworth September 1936; to No. 4 EFTS, Brough
          15 October 1939; impressed 17 February 1942 as 2901M and handed over
          to No. 1155 ATC Sqn at Cheshunt Grammar School, Herts., as an
          instructional airframe.

G-AEBL   To Flying Training 5 February 1936, C. of A. issued 29 April 1936; to
          No. 4 EFTS, Brough 15 October 1939; impressed 17 February 1942 as
          2973M and handed over to No. 1086 ATC Sqn at Hawick, Roxburgh-
          shire, as an instructional airframe.

(g) *Sixth production batch*

Three aircraft to Works Orders 6795/1 to 6795/3 inclusive, to the RAF by production line purchase June 1937, Air Ministry authority 618141/37:

G-AEBM   To North Sea 5 February 1936, C. of A. application No. 5987 not pro-
          ceeded with; to Blackburn Aircraft Ltd January 1937; sold to the Air
          Ministry June 1937; on charge at No. 4 ERFTS, Brough 15 June 1937 as
          L6891; to No. 4 EFTS, Brough 15 October 1939; struck off charge
          18 September 1941 and transferred to No. 2 School of Technical Train-
          ing, Cosford as instructional airframe 3158M.

G-AEBN   To Flying Training 5 February 1936, C. of A. application No. 5988 not
          proceeded with; to Blackburn Aircraft Ltd January 1937; sold to the Air
          Ministry June 1937; on charge at No. 4 ERFTS, Brough 15 June 1937 as
          L6892; to No. 4 EFTS, Brough 15 October 1939; struck off charge
          18 September 1941 and transferred to No. 2 S. of T.T., Cosford as
          instructional airframe 3159M.

G-AEBO   To North Sea 5 February 1936, C. of A. application No. 5989 not pro-
          ceeded with; to Blackburn Aircraft Ltd January 1937; sold to the Air
          Ministry June 1937; on charge at No. 4 ERFTS, Brough 24 June 1937 as
          L6893; to No. 4 EFTS, Brough 15 October 1939; struck off charge
          4 October 1941 and transferred to No. 9 S. of T.T., Morecambe as
          instructional airframe 3877M; reduced to scrap at No. 1 Metal Produce
          and Recovery Depot, Cowley, Oxon., April 1947.

S1640, the fabric-covered Blackburn M.1/30, showing the short-span ailerons and wide-chord lower mainplane.

Blackburn B-3

In 1931 the Blackburn Aeroplane and Motor Co Ltd was awarded an Air Ministry contract for the construction of a large single-bay, folding-wing, deck-landing torpedo-bomber to Specification M.1/30 for competitive trials with the Vickers Type 207 and Handley Page H.P.46. Following the usual practice in such circumstances, their serials, allotted in sequence, were S1640, S1641 and S1642 respectively.

The Blackburn design was based on a project dated 12 September 1928 for a 50-ft span biplane with Rolls-Royce F.XII engine to Specification M.5/28 and was reminiscent of the metal Ripon III after it had been rebuilt with increased gap. It had unequal-span wings, raked interplane and centre section struts and increased sweepback, but the tailplane was similar to that of the Ripon, with rectangular horn-balanced rudder and elevators, variable-incidence tailplane and oleo-pneumatic tail strut housed inside the sternpost. Chief point of difference, however, was in the tailplane position, now raised some way above the top decking of the fuselage. Pilot and observer/gunner were accommodated in tandem cockpits, with a prone bombing position for the observer underneath the pilot's floor, the fuselage itself being of time-honoured Blackburn three-piece, fabric-covered, steel tubular construction with integral bottom centre section. The mainplanes, also fabric covered, were hinged at the rear spar root attachments and had main spars built up from stainless steel strip. Ribs were also of stainless steel and the internal bracing included tubular-duralumin drag struts and steel tie rods.

343

Power was supplied by an 825 hp Rolls-Royce Buzzard IIIMS twelve-cylinder, water-cooled, moderately supercharged engine carried on two built-up girder-type duralumin bearers, completely cowled in and fitted with short, low-drag exhaust manifold. Air bottles for the RAE Mk III engine starting gear were mounted on the floor on the starboard side of the rear cockpit. The nose, which terminated in the conical spinner of a 15-ft diameter two-bladed wooden airscrew, was exceptionally clean aerodynamically because the radiator had been divided and banished to two aluminium compartments with vertical blade-type shutters under each lower wing root. To accommodate a torpedo, the undercarriage was of the divided type with a track of 12 ft, each half consisting of V struts from the bottom fuselage longerons which converged on a Y axle forging attached to the Blackburn oleo-pneumatic main leg.

Pilot's controls consisted of normal control column and Blackburn patent adjustable rudder bar, with tailplane incidence control wheel on the port side of the cockpit.

Numbered S1640 and known throughout its career as the Blackburn M.1/30, the aircraft was rolled out at Brough for first engine runs on 18 February 1932 and first flown by test pilot A. M. Blake on 8 March. On 31 August that year, RAE test pilot Flt Lt G. H. Stainforth commuted from Farnborough to Brough in the Hawker Fury K1926, to fly the machine for 1 hr 10 min, after which manufacturer's trials continued at some length until S1640 finally left for performance testing at the A. & A.E.E., Martlesham, on 29 January 1933 where it is said to have been lost in an accident.

The metal-fuselaged M.1/30A as first flown in Class B markings as B-3, showing part of the gear for lowering the ailerons as flaps.

344

The M.1/30A

As a result of experience gained in constructing the M.1/30, Blackburns went ahead with the construction of a private venture which they called the M.1/30A and which differed from the original in three important respects. The span and chord of the lower mainplane was reduced, cutting total wing area by nearly 70 sq ft; the fuselage was of all-metal semi-monocoque construction with transverse ring frames at 2 ft pitch connected by intercostal stringers; and the four Frise-type ailerons were equipped with operating gear of new and unique design which enabled them all to be depressed by means of a handwheel in the cockpit to act as camber-changing flaps.

The decking behind the observer was made removable to accommodate a separate gunner whose weapon, when not in use, lay retracted in a groove in the fuselage as on the Blackburn Ripon. The entire fuselage was Alclad-covered and divided internally into watertight compartments which gave far greater reserve bouyancy than the old-fashioned flotation bags. The most radical change, however, was to be found in the centre fuselage, which was built of stainless steel and sealed by riveted and soldered joints to form a fuel compartment which occupied the whole space below the decking between the pilot's cockpit and the front watertight compartment. Separate tanks suspended within the fuselage structure were thus dispensed with, and the stainless steel container was divided by bulkheads to provide a 135-gallon main tank, a 100-gallon rear tank and above them a 22-gallon gravity tank into which fuel was pumped en route to the engine. Each tank section was fitted with a large manhole through which maintenance staff could insert head and shoulders for inspection or repair of the interior, and the whole installation was considered more accessible and efficient than three independently-installed fuel tanks.

The M.1/30A also differed from the first aircraft in having long perforated extension exhaust pipes from each cylinder block; automatic wing tip slots; and 1095-mm × 250-mm heavy-duty Palmer tyres and pneumatically-operated brakes, the reinforced rubber air bottle for which was located inside the forward watertight compartment. Armament consisted of a fixed, forward-firing Vickers Mk II machine-gun in a tunnel on the port side of the front fuselage and a ·303 Mk III Lewis gun on a high speed rotatable mounting over the third cockpit. Racks were provided under the mainplanes for four 550-, 520- or 500-lb bombs, eight 250-lb bombs, or eight 20-lb bombs; the alternative load being one 1,900-lb Mk VIII, Mk X or 18-in K Type torpedo in crutches between the undercarriage legs. Internally the aircraft was equipped with marine distress signals, collapsible dinghy, a camera gun in the starboard lower centre section, T.R.4 wireless equipment and crew parachutes. When operating with torpedo, fuel was restricted to 188 gallons.

The aircraft was first flown at Brough by A. M. Blake on 24 February 1933 and, being a private venture, carried the Blackburn Class B civil test marking

B-3, and was delivered to Martlesham in this condition by the same pilot on 2 March. Evidently some unserviceability was encountered, for records show that it returned to the makers almost at once and that A. M. Blake redelivered it to the A. & A.E.E. for performance testing on 14 March. Trials which took place in the following month quickly established that this was an aeroplane of quite outstanding technical merit but its performance did not reach the requirements of the original M.1/30 Specification. The vulnerability of the fuel-filled front fuselage to damage or enemy action came in for justifiable criticism, yet nevertheless the Air Ministry was much impressed by the aircraft's sealed watertight fuselage, drew up a contract for its purchase and took it on charge at Martlesham as K3591 in May 1933. It was then shown to the public alongside the Vickers M.1/30 design in the New Types Park at the Hendon RAF Display on 24 June and to the industry at the SBAC Show two days later.

Rear view of the M.1/30A after being taken on RAF charge as K3591, showing the full-span ailerons which also acted as flaps.

On 2 August 1933 the aircraft went back to Blackburns for modifications to the control surface mass balance, which necessitated a flight test programme by A. M. Blake which continued until its re-allottment to the A. & A.E.E. on 23 October. Flg Off Woodhall collected it on 31 October, but its stay at Martlesham was short because the Air Ministry was now vitally interested in testing the buoyancy of the sealed fuselage, for this was to be a feature of Blackburn's forthcoming Ripon/Baffin replacement, the B-6 or Shark.

Thus on 25 January 1934 the M.1/30A was transferred to the Marine Aircraft Experimental Establishment, Felixstowe, for ditching trials, at the conclusion of which the airframe was salvaged, struck off charge in the following April and returned to the manufacturers at Brough for detailed examination of the effects of salt water corrosion. The satisfactory outcome of these tests is evident from the large contract for Sharks awarded later that year.

SPECIFICATION AND DATA

Manufacturers: The Blackburn Aeroplane and Motor Co Ltd, Brough Aerodrome, East Yorks.

Power Plants: (M.1/30) One 825 hp Rolls-Royce Buzzard IIIMS
(M.1/30A) One 825 hp Rolls-Royce Buzzard IIIMS

Dimensions, Weights and Performance:

	M.1/30	M.1/30A*
Span upper	49 ft 4½ in	49 ft 6 in
Span lower	44 ft 9 in	42 ft 0 in
Span folded	18 ft 4 in	18 ft 7 in
Length	39 ft 0½ in	39 ft 10 in
Height	14 ft 3½ in	14 ft 7 in
Wing area	719·5 sq ft	651 sq ft
Tare weight	—	5,853 lb
All-up weight	—	10,393 lb
Speed at sea level	—	142 mph
Speed at 10,000 ft	—	130 mph
Initial climb	—	770 ft/min
Time to 12,000 ft	—	35 min 45 sec
Absolute ceiling	—	13,800 ft
Service ceiling	—	12,000 ft
Range	—	750 miles

Loading: M.1/30A★

Tare weight	5,853 lb
Military load	2,735 lb
257 gal petrol	1,448 lb
9 gal oil	72 lb
Equipment	285 lb
All-up weight	10,393 lb

★ *Ref. A. & A.E.E. Report M/621A dated April 1934.*

Production:

(a) *M.1/30*

One aircraft only, S1640, to Works Order 3380/1 under Air Ministry Contract 55826/30, initial engine runs at Brough 18 February 1932, first flown by A. M. Blake 8 March 1932, delivered to Martlesham 29 January 1933.

(b) *M.1/30A*

One private venture aircraft only, B-3, to Works Order 3900/1, Rolls-Royce Buzzard IIIMS engine No. 39, first flown by A. M. Blake 24 February 1933; to Martlesham 2 March 1933; taken on charge 18 May 1933 as K3591 by the Directorate of Technical Development, Martlesham, under Contract 244326/33; returned to Brough for modification 2 August 1933; to Martlesham 31 October 1933; on charge by the D.T.D., Felixstowe 25 January 1934 for ditching trials; airframe transferred to Blackburns for examination 30 April 1934; sold as scrap in 1935 under Disposal Contract 404341/35.

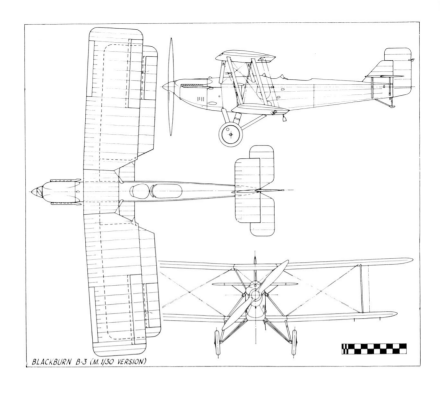

BLACKBURN B-3 (M.1/30 VERSION)

348

The first pre-production Baffin with Bristol Pegasus I.MS radial engine, on a test flight near Brough on 29 August 1933. (*Flight Photo 10051.*)

Blackburn B-5 Baffin

Advantages such as increased payload and simplified maintenance to be gained by replacing the Blackburn Ripon's water-cooled engine, its heavy radiators and water system, by a modern air-cooled radial had been recognized way back in 1928, when a scheme for a Ripon II with Bristol Jupiter VIII had been drawn up for the Spanish Government under the Blackburn torpedo-bomber designation T.5C. Reference to an earlier section dealing with the Ripon will show that, although none were sold in Spain, the Finnish Government bought a T.5D version named Ripon IIF, also with Jupiter VIII, and eventually built it under licence. They also installed other radial engines, one version having the Armstrong Siddeley Panther and therefore equivalent to Blackburn's projected T.5F with Armstrong Siddeley Jaguar Major, an earlier name for the same engine.

The Blackburn design department continued to explore in detail all possible results of using the many low-weight radial engines then becoming available, and in the process completed schemes for a T.5G Ripon IV long-range bomber without torpedo gear and a T.5H Ripon V to carry a standard torpedo. In each case choice of engine lay between the 650 hp Armstrong Siddeley Tiger I and the 545 hp Bristol Pegasus, and estimated performances were so promising that early in 1932 detailed designs were prepared for fitting these engines into standard Fleet Air Arm Ripon IIA and IIC aircraft under the designation T.5J Ripon V.

Being identical with the marks of Ripon in question, the airframe needs no

349

Blackburn's chief test pilot Flt Lt A. M. Blake flying B-4, the first prototype Ripon V, Armstrong Siddeley Tiger engine, at Brough on 12 June 1933. (*Flight Photo 13104.*)

description here, but a new type of engine mounting was fitted consisting of a circular engine bearer plate carried on steel struts projecting well forward from the fireproof bulkhead to keep the C.G. within limits. Fuel and oil systems, armament and all operational equipment were identical with those of the Ripon IIA and IIC.

Two prototype aircraft were completed at Brough in September 1932 for comparative trials, one with the Tiger two-row radial and the other with a single-row Pegasus which A. M. Blake first flew on 30 September. Being private-venture aircraft they respectively carried the manufacturer's Class B markings B-4 and B-5 which then became their type numbers under the newly established Blackburn system. B-5 flew initially in red undercoat with un-cowled engine but was sprayed silver with black markings before despatch to the A. & A.E.E., Martlesham, for evaluation alongside B-4 in February 1933. After its return to Brough B-5 was flown briefly with Blackburn patent bomb rails and a narrow-chord Townend ring.

As a result of these trials the Air Ministry selected the Pegasus version to replace the ageing Fleet Air Arm Ripons, wrote Specification 4/33 round it and standardized the Pegasus I.M3 giving 565 hp at 2,000 rpm at 5,000 ft but without the Townend ring. They then placed an initial order for two pre-production aircraft, K3589 and K3590, which were completed with consider-able rapidity, for by April 1933 K3589 was at Martlesham for acceptance tests and made its public debut as the 'Pegasus-Ripon' at the Hendon RAF Display on 24 June before inspection at close quarters by the industry at the SBAC Show two days later.

The second pre-production aircraft, K3590, remained at Brough as a trial installations aircraft, and in September 1933, when the Air Ministry approved the type name Baffin, K3589 was transferred to Gosport for deck-landing trials aboard the aircraft carrier *Courageous* before joining the strength of the

RAE, Farnborough, where Flt Lt Horniman was launched in it from the catapult on 2 February 1934.

By this time a batch of 14 aircraft, K3546 to K3559, originally laid down as Ripon IICs in 1932, had been completed as Baffins, and the first, K3546, made its first flight in the hands of A. M. Blake on 10 November 1933. This too went to Martlesham for tests but in January 1934 was flown to the RAF Packing Depot at Sealand to be crated with the rest of the batch and shipped to Malta. On arrival they were erected at the Kalafrana Depot and flown at Hal Far Aerodrome two miles away. Many were used for torpedo and deck-landing training in the Mediterranean, but others were merely test flown and then stored at the Depot to await onward shipment to the Middle East.

B-5 in finished state at Martlesham Heath, February 1933.

B-5 with Townend ring fitted after its return to Brough.

351

The Flight Shed at Brough on 30 November 1933 with the two dismantled Ripon V prototypes (*foreground*) and, in the background, the first pre-production Baffin K3589 with folded wings. (*Flight Photo 13757.*)

A widely-held theory that B-4 became K3546 and that B-5 was later K3589 is incorrect since the part numbers of their major components do not agree, and a photograph is included here which shows K3589 in the presence of the dismantled airframes of B-4 and B-5.

The Baffin was officially adopted as the standard Fleet Air Arm torpedo-bomber in succession to the Ripon on 7 March 1934 but issues to No. 812 Squadron aboard *Glorious* had begun in the previous January. The type was not widely used, and the only other Baffin squadrons were No. 810 which re-equipped aboard *Courageous* in August 1934 and No. 811 on *Furious* in May 1935.

To replace the six Blackburn Darts and six Ripons of No. 810 Squadron, a contract was placed with Blackburns for 10 more Baffins, K4071–K4080, which were produced with commendable speed and which, with two exceptions, were all ferried by air from Brough to Gosport during June–July 1934. These were by no means the only Baffins going through the works, for as Ripon aircraft were replaced by the newer type or came up for major overhaul, they were returned to the manufacturers for the engine change which would convert them into Baffins. Conversion also involved entire dismantling and complete rebuilding with reconditioned components, so that when the aircraft was finished, only the old RAF serial number revealed the fact that it was not brand-new. The programme of re-engining and refurbishing occupied the works for some two years, during which time it turned out a total of reconditioned machines which is often quoted as 62 but which cannot have been less than 68. These included the final batch of four Ripon IICs, K2884-K2887, which had not been issued to Service units but remained in store at Cardington until two were flown back to Brough for conversion in October 1933 and the remaining two in September 1934.

It appears that the first Ripon converted to Baffin standard was the Mk IIC S1665, since this was the aircraft submitted to Martlesham for handling trials with dummy Mk VIII torpedo in June 1934, but, with the new Blackburn Shark actually in being, the Baffin was already regarded as an interim type and only three more completely new aircraft were ordered to supplement the conversion programme. Designated T.8A, these were to Air Ministry Specification 17/34 which covered the replacement of the Bristol Pegasus I.M3 engine by the 580 hp Pegasus II.M3 which had replaced it in production. These machines had a slightly better climb at sea level, but, at the expense of inferior overall performance, higher fuel consumption and a weight penalty of 100 lb. All three were delivered to Sealand in June 1935 and shipped to No. 812 Squadron in Malta.

Despite original hopes, the Baffin's performance was only marginally better than that of the Ripon, even with the Pegasus II.M3, so that its Service life was only some three years. During this period six Baffins of No. 810 Squadron had the honour of leading the formation of Fleet Air Arm aircraft in the fly-past at the Jubilee Naval Revue off Spithead on 15 July 1935, and the type was also employed in some numbers by 'A' Flight, Gosport, for deck-landing and torpedo training. One Gosport aircraft which found notoriety in the Solent was S1562 which dropped a practice torpedo on 22 June 1936 and then flew round the French transatlantic liner *Normandie*, struck one of its derricks and crashed on the foredeck; with no suitable lifting gear available, there was no alternative but to take the wreck to Le Havre, whence it was retrieved by an RAF working party.

The three front-line Baffin squadrons re-equipped in 1936, Nos. 811 and 812 with Fairey Swordfish and No. 810 (its 12 Baffins at that time including nine converted Ripons) with the new all-metal Blackburn Shark. The last to fly in RAF service were those of No. 812 Squadron, the majority of whose

The first production Baffin, K3546.

353

Three Gosport-based Baffins in echelon formation. The nearest, S1562, is that which crashed on the liner *Normandie* on 22 June 1936. (*Imperial War Museum Photo MH.27.*)

Baffins were destroyed on the ground at Hal Far when their hangar was demolished by the tornado which swept Malta in December 1936. The type was then declared obsolete, all remaining Baffins in Malta being packed for shipment to England and struck off charge on 1 September 1937.

In New Zealand

In his 1937 report on the Royal New Zealand Air Force, Wg Cdr the Hon R. A. Cochrane recommended that Territorial Squadrons should be raised in the main cities to provide local coastal defence and, for reasons of economy, should be equipped with obsolescent aircraft. As a result, in August that year, the New Zealand Government purchased 12 Baffins from the British Air Ministry at a price said to have been as low as £200 each, and raised a Territorial Squadron in Wellington to operate them.

Simultaneously with the arrival at Auckland in November 1937 of the first four aircraft, S1364, S1430, S1573 and S1672 in Fleet Air Arm markings and codes, aboard the SS *Napier Star*, the Air Ministry offered New Zealand a further large batch. Seventeen of these were selected for delivery in 1938, bringing the total purchased to 29 and including K4777, one of the three T.8A Pegasus II.M3 machines.

The first four Baffins, still in crates, were taken by lighter to Hobsonville for assembly, and the first, S1573, made its first flight in the southern hemisphere piloted by Flt Lt A. G. Lester on 1 February 1938. After acceptance tests at Wigram, it was delivered to the Wellington General Reconnaissance Squadron's base at Rongotai where a special Baffin hangar had been erected.

354

Twelve Baffins allocated to the Wellington Squadron were S1266, S1426, S1430, S1527, S1556, S1558, S1573, S1649, S1654, S1655 and S1674, six of which, still in RAF serials, took part in a bombing demonstration on an off-shore target at the RNZAF Display at Rongotai on 4 June 1938. The Baffins also exercised at sea with HMS *Achilles* on 17 October 1938, but normally the 12 aircraft operated as two Flights of six, five aircraft of each Flight being stored at Ohakea and used only at annual training camps, the sixth being based at Rongotai for evening and weekend flying.

In November 1938 the 29 Baffins were allotted the RNZAF serial block NZ150–NZ178 and, although S1266 had already been repainted as NZ150 when it unwittingly severed the 110,000 volt grid system serving Wellington on 5 November, it was almost another year before many were re-serialled.

The second Territorial Squadron, formed at Christchurch in April 1938, was based at Wigram and received its first three Baffins, S1561, S1657 and K4078, in the following September and two others in November. At the same time, the third and final squadron was raised in Auckland and based at Hobsonville with six aircraft which included NZ155 and NZ157.

In September 1939 all three squadrons became fully operational, and the Wellington Squadron was moved to Woodbourne where it operated with NZ150, NZ151, NZ153–NZ157, NZ164, NZ167, NZ171, NZ173–NZ176 and NZ178. However, the first operation of the war was not flown until 16 November, when Baffins NZ162, NZ163, NZ165 and NZ167 of the Christ-

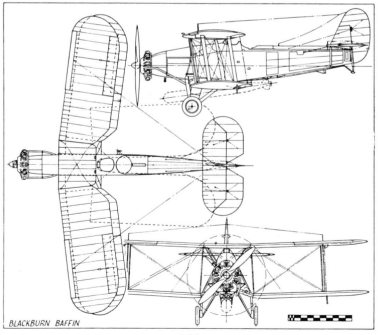

BLACKBURN BAFFIN

355

church Squadron, commanded by Sqn Ldr G. N. Roberts, were on patrol from 4 am to 9 am to locate and plot all shipping within a 50-mile radius of the Akaroa Light.

In March 1940 all three squadrons were combined to form the New Zealand General Reconnaissance Squadron based at Whenuapai, but early in 1941 it was renamed No. 1 G. R. Squadron and half the Baffins were then posted to Harewood to form the nucleus of the newly-formed No. 3 G. R. Squadron. This was responsible for patrolling the approaches to Lyttleton, Dunedin and the Foveaux Straits, in the course of which one Baffin penetrated as far as latitude 48 degrees 1 minute South.

SPECIFICATION AND DATA

Manufacturers: The Blackburn Aeroplane and Motor Co Ltd, Brough Aerodrome, East Yorks.

Power Plants: (Ripon V) One 650 hp Armstrong Siddeley Tiger I
  One 545 hp Bristol Pegasus I.MS
  (Baffin) One 565 hp Bristol Pegasus I.M3
  One 580 hp Bristol Pegasus II.M3

Dimensions: Span (upper) 44 ft 10 in   (lower) 45 ft 6½ in
  (folded) 17 ft 10 in
  Length 38 ft 3¾ in   Height 12 ft 10 in
  Wing area 683 sq ft

Loadings:
(a) *Ripon V*

	Tiger I		Pegasus	
	Landplane	Seaplane★	Landplane	Seaplane★
Tare weight	3,200 lb	3,638 lb	3,184 lb	3,622 lb
Two crew	360 lb	360 lb	360 lb	360 lb
Military load	3,070 lb	3,070 lb	3,070 lb	3,070 lb
120 gal petrol	925 lb	925 lb	925 lb	925 lb
7½ gal oil	71 lb	71 lb	71 lb	71 lb
All-up weight	7,626 lb	8,064 lb	7,610 lb	8,048 lb

★ Estimated—not flown as seaplanes.

(b) *Baffin*

T.8 with Pegasus I.M3		T.8A with Pegasus II.M3	
Tare weight	3,184 lb	Tare weight	3,284 lb
Two crew	360 lb	Two crew	360 lb
Military load	3,070 lb	Military load	3,070 lb
120 gal petrol	925 lb	120 gal petrol	925 lb
7½ gal oil	71 lb	7½ gal oil	71 lb
All-up weight	7,610 lb	All-up weight	7,710 lb

Performance:
(a) *Ripon V*

	Tiger I		Pegasus	
	Landplane	Seaplane*	Landplane	Seaplane*
Speed at sea level	134 mph	126 mph	127 mph	120 mph
Speed at 5,000 ft	148 mph	138 mph	136 mph	127 mph
Speed at 10,000 ft	143 mph	130 mph	128 mph	116 mph
Initial climb	650 ft/min	510 ft/min	520 ft/min	410 ft/min
Climb at 4,000 ft	850 ft/min	650 ft/min	510 ft/min	390 ft/min
Service ceiling	16,600 ft	13,600 ft	13,000 ft	10,400 ft
Endurance	4½ hr	4 hr	4½ hr	4 hr

* Estimated—not flown as seaplanes.

(b) *Baffin*

	Pegasus I.M3	Pegasus II.M3
Speed at sea level	125 mph	115 mph
Speed at 6,500 ft	136 mph	125 mph
Speed at 10,000 ft	128 mph	120 mph
Initial climb	480 ft/min	510 ft/min
Climb at 5,000 ft	600 ft/min	400 ft/min
Service ceiling	15,000 ft	13,000 ft
Endurance at 5,000 ft	4½ hr	3½ hr

Production:
(a) *T.5ʒ Ripon V prototypes*
Two private-venture aircraft only:

B-4 Tiger engine, first flown by A. M. Blake in 1932 and subsequently on 12 June, 17 July, 26 July and 12 August 1933, dismantled at Brough November 1933.

B-5 Pegasus engine, first flown 30 September 1932, to Martlesham 28 February 1933, dismantled at Brough November 1933.

(b) *T.8 Baffin pre-production to Specification 4/33*
Two aircraft only to Works Orders 5568/1 and 5568/2 under Contract 285466/33:

K3589 On charge by Directorate of Technical Development, Martlesham 6 April 1933; to Coastal Area 15 September 1933; to A Flight, Gosport 6 October 1933; Farnborough 31 January 1934; catapult launch 2 February 1934; to Gosport; struck off charge and sold as scrap 12 January 1937.

K3590 On charge by DTD 6 April 1933, retained by Blackburns; to Malta via Packing Depot, Sealand 18 May 1934; to Aboukir 14 November 1935; s.o.c. 30 January 1937.

(c) *T.8 Baffins to Specification 4/33*
Four aircraft completed as Ripon IIC, held on charge at No. 2 Aircraft Storage Unit, Cardington, Beds., from 5 December 1932 until returned to Brough for conversion:

K2884 Returned to Blackburns 13 October 1933; on charge as Baffin at PD, Sealand 15 January 1934; to Malta 30 June 1934; to Aboukir 14 November 1935; s.o.c. 30 January 1937.

357

K2885 Returned to Blackburns 13 October 1933; on charge as Baffin at PD, Sealand 15 January 1934; to Malta 30 June 1934; to Aboukir 14 November 1935; to Mediterranean Command, Malta 2 September 1936; s.o.c. 30 January 1937.

K2886 Returned to Blackburns 12 September 1934; on charge as Baffin by A Flight, Gosport 11 January 1935, coded 3; s.o.c. 12 January 1937 and sold as scrap.

K2887 Returned to Blackburns 12 September 1934; on charge as Baffin by A Flight, Gosport 11 January 1935; s.o.c. 12 January 1937 and sold as scrap.

(d) *T.8 Baffin further production to Specification 4/33*

Fourteen aircraft laid down as Ripon IIC but held up pending completion of Baffin prototype trials and then completed as Baffins to Works Orders 5120/1 to 5120/14 inclusive under the original Contract 217288/32:

K3546 First flown 10 November 1933; on charge by DTD, Martlesham 20 November 1933; to PD, Sealand 16 January 1934; to Malta 30 January 1934; s.o.c. 26 September 1935.

K3547 On charge at PD, Sealand 22 November 1933; to Malta 30 January 1934; s.o.c. 17 August 1934.

K3548 On charge at PD, Sealand 22 November 1933; to Malta 30 January 1934, coded 71; s.o.c. 12 March 1934.

K3549 On charge at PD, Sealand 22 November 1933; to Malta 30 January 1934; to Aboukir 14 November 1935; s.o.c. 24 August 1936.

K3550 On charge at PD, Sealand 22 November 1933; to Malta 30 January 1934 coded 64; to Mediterranean Command, Malta 2 September 1936; s.o.c. 1 September 1937.

K3551 On charge at PD, Sealand 22 November 1933; to Malta 30 January 1934; s.o.c. 9 February 1935.

K3552 On charge at PD, Sealand 5 January 1934; to Malta 30 January 1934; to Aboukir 14 November 1935; to Mediterranean Command, Malta 2 September 1936; s.o.c. 1 September 1937.

K3553 On charge at PD, Sealand 5 January 1934; to Malta 30 January 1934, coded 61; to Aboukir 14 November 1935; s.o.c. 8 March 1936.

K3554 On charge at PD, Sealand 5 January 1934; to Malta 30 January 1934; to Aboukir 14 November 1935; to Mediterranean Command, Malta 2 September 1936; s.o.c. 1 September 1937.

K3555 On charge at PD, Sealand 5 January 1934; to Malta 30 January 1934; to Aboukir 14 November 1935; s.o.c. August 1936.

K3556 Flown Brough–PD, Sealand 29 December 1933; on charge 5 January 1934; to Malta 30 January 1934, coded 60; to Aboukir 14 November 1935; to Mediterranean Command 2 September 1936; s.o.c. 1 September 1936.

K3557 Flown Brough–PD, Sealand 4 January 1934; on charge 5 January 1934; to Malta 30 January 1934; to Aboukir 14 November 1935; s.o.c. 1 September 1937.

K3558 Flown Brough–PD, Sealand 4 January 1934; on charge 5 January 1934; to Malta 30 January 1934; to No. 810 Sqn; to No. 1 Aircraft Storage Unit; sold to the RNZAF 6 December 1937, shipped per SS *Fordsdale*; became NZ175 with the Wellington G.R. Sqn; to instructional airframe INST.16 at Wigram 8 December 1939.

K3559 On charge 5 January 1934; flown Brough–PD, Sealand 8 January 1934; to Malta 30 January 1934; to Aboukir 14 November 1935; to Mediterranean Command 1 September 1936; to No. 812 Sqn; s.o.c. 30 January 1937.

(e) *T.8 Baffin further production to Specification 4/33*
Ten aircraft to Works Orders 5500/1 to 5500/10 inclusive under Contract 277109/33:

K4071 On charge by No. 810 Sqn 28 May 1934; to Coastal Area 12 June 1934; delivered Brough–Gosport 25 June 1934; to Mediterranean Command 24 September 1935; to Aboukir 14 November 1935; to No. 810 Sqn 31 March 1936, coded 01; sold to the RNZAF 6 December 1937 as NZ176; to Wellington G.R. Sqn, coded L; reduced to produce at Rongotai 1941.

K4072 On charge by No. 810 Sqn 28 May 1934; handed over at Brough 11 June 1934; flown to PD, Sealand 16 June 1934; to Fleet Air Arm 16 July 1934; to Mediterranean Command 24 September 1935; to Aboukir 14 November 1935; to No. 810 Sqn 31 March 1936; s.o.c. 12 January 1937.

K4073 On charge by No. 810 Sqn 28 May 1934; handed over at Brough 12 June 1934; flown to PD, Sealand 16 June 1934; to Fleet Air Arm 16 July 1934; to Mediterranean Command 24 September 1935; to Aboukir 14 November 1935; to No. 810 Sqn 31 March 1936; s.o.c. 12 January 1937.

K4074 On charge by No. 810 Sqn 28 May 1934; flown Brough–Gosport 14 June 1934; to Fleet Air Arm 16 July 1934; to Mediterranean Command; to Aboukir 14 November 1935; to No. 810 Sqn 31 March 1936; to No. 811 Sqn 17 September 1935; s.o.c. 5 January 1937.

K4075 On charge by No. 810 Sqn 12 June 1934; handed over at Brough 15 June 1934; flown to Gosport 19 June 1934; to Coastal Area and s.o.c. 11 October 1934.

K4076 On charge by No. 810 Sqn 12 June 1934; handed over at Brough 19 June 1934; flown to Gosport 25 June 1934; to Coastal Area; to DTD 14 December 1934; to Fleet Air Arm 30 January 1935; to Mediterranean Command 24 September 1935; to Aboukir 14 November 1935; to No. 810 Sqn 31 March 1936; s.o.c. and sold as scrap 12 January 1937.

K4077 On charge by No. 810 Sqn 14 June 1934; handed over at Brough 2 July 1934; flown to Gosport 12 July 1934; to Mediterranean Command 24 September 1935; to Aboukir 7 October 1935; s.o.c. 24 August 1936.

K4078 On charge by No. 810 Sqn 14 June 1934; handed over at Brough 2 July 1934; flown to Gosport 12 July 1934; to Mediterranean Command 24 September 1935; to Aboukir 7 October 1935; to No. 810 Sqn 31 March 1936; to Gosport 17 November 1936; to No. 1 ASU; sold to the RNZAF 6 December 1937 as NZ177; to the Christchurch G.R. Sqn, Wigram September 1939; to New Zealand G.R. Sqn, Whenuapai March 1940; reduced to produce at Rongotai 1941.

K4079 On charge by No. 810 Sqn 14 June 1934; handed over at Brough 5 July 1934; flown to Gosport 12 July 1934; to Mediterranean Command 24 September 1935; to Aboukir 7 October 1935; to No. 810 Sqn 31 March 1936; to Gosport 17 November 1936; to No. 1 ASU; s.o.c.

K4080 On charge by No. 810 Sqn 14 June 1934; flown Brough–Gosport 5 July 1934; s.o.c. 29 September 1934.

(f) *T.8A Baffins to Specification 17/34*
Three aircraft only to Works Orders 5830/1 to 5830/3 inclusive under Contract 324868/34:

K4776 Handed over at Brough 7 June 1935; flown to PD, Sealand for No. 812 Sqn 13 June 1935.

K4777 Handed over at Brough 7 June 1935; flown to PD, Sealand for No. 812 Sqn 15 June 1935; sold to the RNZAF 6 December 1937 as NZ178; to Wellington G.R. Sqn, coded 8; to New Zealand G.R. Sqn, Whenuapai March 1940; reduced to produce at Rongotai 1941.

K4778 Handed over at Brough 21 June 1935; flown to PD, Sealand for No. 812 Sqn.

(g) *Conversion of Ripon IIA to Baffin*
As detailed Service histories of individual aircraft in the S series no longer exist, this section is unavoidably incomplete.

Thirty-eight aircraft as follows:

S1266 To No. 811 Sqn, coded 614; sold to the RNZAF; shipped per SS *Waiwera*, became NZ150 with the Wellington G.R. Sqn; to the New Zealand G.R. Sqn, Whenuapai March 1940; crashed into the sea off Onerahi 25 June 1940; to Rongotai as instructional airframe INST.29.

S1269 In service at Gosport in 1936, coded 1.

S1358 Sold to the RNZAF as NZ164; to the Wellington G.R. Sqn; to the New Zealand G.R. Sqn, Whenuapai March 1940; reduced to produce at Rongotai 1941.

S1359 In service at Gosport 1936, coded 4.

S1364 To No. 811 Sqn, coded 604.

S1366 Based at Gosport in 1935.

S1368 First flown as Baffin 13 April 1933; sold to the RNZAF as NZ166; to instructional airframe INST.5 at Rongotai.

S1425 Sold to the RNZAF; shipped per SS *Fordsdale*; became NZ167 with the Wellington G.R. Sqn, coded F; to the New Zealand G.R. Sqn March 1940; reduced to produce at Rongotai 1941.

S1426 Sold to the RNZAF; shipped per SS *Waiwera*; became NZ151 with the Wellington G.R. Sqn; reduced to produce at Rongotai 1941.

S1427 Coded 81 in Fleet Air Arm service.

S1428 No details.

S1430 Coded 83 in Fleet Air Arm service; sold to the RNZAF; shipped per SS *Napier Star*; became NZ152; crashed into the sea, Pigeon Bay, Banks Peninsula 10 May 1939.

S1431 Sold to the RNZAF; became NZ168; to instructional airframe INST.6 at Rongotai.

S1432, S1470, S1473 No details.

S1553 Sold to the RNZAF; shipped per SS *Fordsdale*; became NZ169 with the Wellington G.R. Sqn; to the New Zealand G.R. Sqn, Whenuapai March 1940; reduced to produce at Rongotai 1941.

S1554 To No. 811 Sqn, coded 603; sold to the RNZAF as NZ170; to Wigram June 1939; to the New Zealand G.R. Sqn, Whenuapai March 1940; reduced to produce at Rongotai 1941.

S1555, S1556, S1557 No details.

S1558 Sold to the RNZAF; shipped per SS *Waiwera*; became NZ153 with the Wellington G.R. Sqn; crashed into the sea off Island Bay, Wellington, 14 December 1939; to instructional airframe INST.22 at Rongotai.

S1559, S1560 No details.

S1561 Sold to the RNZAF; shipped per SS *Hertford*; to the Christchurch G.R. Sqn, Wigram June 1939 as NZ161; crashed at Harewood 11 July 1941.

The erecting shop at Brough in 1934 with Ripon IIA and IIC aircraft undergoing complete reconditioning and Baffin conversion. S1432, S1672, S1662 and S1554 two of which went to New Zealand, are on the stocks.

S1562   In service at Gosport 1935, coded 8; crashed on the deck of SS *Normandie* in the Solent 22 June 1936.

S1563   Sold to the RNZAF; became NZ162 with the New Zealand G.R. Sqn, Whenuapai June 1940; reduced to produce at Rongotai 1941.

S1564   In service at Gosport 1934, coded O6.

S1565, S1566, S1567, S1568   No details.

S1569   Re-delivery after Baffin conversion 7 July 1934; to No. 812 Sqn in 1936.

S1570   To No. 811 Sqn, coded 609; sold to the RNZAF; shipped per SS *Waiwera*; became NZ154 with the Wellington G.R. Sqn, coded N; to the New Zealand G.R. Sqn, Whenuapai March 1940; reduced to produce at Rongotai 1941.

S1571   Sold to the RNZAF; became NZ171 with the Wellington G.R. Sqn, coded S; reduced to produce at Rongotai 1941.

S1572   No details.

S1573   To No. 810 Sqn, coded 524; sold to the RNZAF; shipped per SS *Napier Star*; became NZ155 with the Wellington G.R. Sqn; to the New Zealand G.R. Sqn, Whenuapai March 1940; reduced to produce at Rongotai 1941.

S1574   No details.

(h) *Conversion of Ripon IIC to Baffin*

Twenty-six aircraft as follows:

S1649   Sold to the RNZAF; shipped per SS *Waiwera*; became NZ172; to instructional airframe INST.7 at Rongotai.

S1650   Delivered Brough–Gosport after Baffin conversion 3 July 1934; sold to the RNZAF; shipped per SS *Fordsdale*; became NZ173 with the Wellington G.R. Sqn; to the New Zealand G.R. Sqn, Whenuapai March 1940; reduced to produce at Rongotai 1941.

S1651, S1652   No details.

S1653   To No. 810 Sqn, coded 528; sold to the RNZAF; became NZ174 with the Wellington G.R. Sqn; to the New Zealand G.R. Sqn, Whenuapai March 1940; reduced to produce at Rongotai 1941.

S1654   In service at Gosport 1934, coded 6; sold to the RNZAF; shipped per SS *Hertford*; became NZ156 with the Wellington G.R. Sqn; to instructional airframe INST.19 at Rongotai 4 February 1940.

S1655   Sold to the RNZAF; shipped per SS *Waiwera*; became NZ157 with the Wellington G.R. Sqn; to the New Zealand G.R. Sqn, Whenuapai March 1940; reduced to produce at Rongotai 1941.

S1656   To No. 811 Sqn, coded 612.

S1657   To No. 811 Sqn; sold to the RNZAF; shipped per SS *Waiwera*; to the Christchurch G.R. Sqn, Wigram September 1939 as NZ158; to the New Zealand G.R. Sqn, Whenuapai March 1940; reduced to produce at Rongotai 1941.

S1658 to S1664 inclusive   No details.

S1665, first Ripon to be re-engined with the Pegasus radial, which returned to service as a Baffin in June 1934.

S1665   In service at Gosport 1934, coded O2; to No. 810 Sqn.

S1666, S1667, S1668   No details.

S1669   In service at Gosport 1934, coded O9.

S1670   In service at Gosport 1934; sold to the RNZAF; shipped per SS *Hertford*; to Wigram June 1939 as NZ163; to the New Zealand G.R. Sqn, Whenuapai March 1940; reduced to produce at Rongotai 1941.

S1671   No details.

S1672   In service at Gosport 1936, coded 2; sold to the RNZAF; shipped per SS *Napier Star*; became NZ159; to instructional airframe INST.4 at Rongotai.

S1673   No details.

S1674   In service at Gosport 1934, coded 5; sold to the RNZAF as NZ160; shipped per SS *Waiwera*; reduced to produce at Rongotai 1941.

Service Use:

(a) *Fleet Air Arm*

   No. 810 Sqn in *Courageous*; No. 811 Sqn in *Furious*; No. 812 Sqn in *Glorious*; A Flight, Gosport; C Flight, Malta.

(b) *Royal New Zealand Air Force*
Wellington G.R. Sqn, Rongotai; Christchurch G.R. Sqn, Wigram; Auckland G.R. Sqn, Hobsonville; New Zealand G.R. Sqn, Whenuapai; No. 1 G.R. Sqn, Whenuapai; No. 3 G.R. Sqn, Harewood.

(c) *Conversion table for New Zealand Baffins*

NZ150	S1266	NZ156	S1654	NZ162	S1563	NZ168	S1431	NZ174	S1653
NZ151	S1426	NZ157	S1655	NZ163	S1670	NZ169	S1553	NZ175	K3558
NZ152	S1430	NZ158	S1657	NZ164	S1358	NZ170	S1554	NZ176	K4071
NZ153	S1558	NZ159	S1672	NZ165	S1364	NZ171	S1571	NZ177	K4078
NZ154	S1570	NZ160	S1674	NZ166	S1368	NZ172	S1649	NZ178	K4777
NZ155	S1573	NZ161	S1561	NZ167	S1425	NZ173	S1650		

The prototype Blackburn B-6 with short-chord engine cowling during deck-landing trials on *Courageous* 1934. (*Charles E. Brown Photo.*)

Blackburn B-6 Shark

Originally known as the Blackburn T.S.R., or torpedo-spotter-reconnaissance machine, the B-6 was a private-venture prototype built to Air Ministry Specification S.15/33 which also generated the Gloster T.S.R.38, S1705, and the Fairey T.S.R., K4190, forerunner of the famous Swordfish. The Blackburn machine was a large, unequal-span, folding-wing biplane designed for carrier operation, which bore the designation T.9 in the company's torpedo-bomber series. It was based on the earlier Blackburn M.1/30A from which it inherited the buoyant Alclad-skinned fuselage that had performed so well in ditching trials, but for carrier take-off carried only the Mk VIII or Mk X torpedo, not the heavier K type.

The new machine differed from all previous Blackburn naval biplanes, because streamlined wires were largely dispensed with; mainplane bracing consisted of a system of slanting struts forming a rigid Warren girder strong enough to support a full bomb load when the aircraft was stowed below decks with the wings folded. Mainplanes built on these lines were inevitably heavy and difficult to fold manually, particularly on a heaving flight deck, so Blackburns designed a hydraulic wing-locking device which was manufactured for them by the Lockheed Hydraulic Brake Co Ltd of Leamington Spa. This enabled ground crew to withdraw or re-engage top and bottom wing root bolts simultaneously by a few strokes of a small pump handle on the lower centre section. Further to assist deck handling and taxying, the machine was fitted with pneumatic wheel-brakes and a tracking tail wheel.

Using operational experience and data gained with the two Baffin prototypes, the B-6 was designed to take either the Armstrong Siddeley Tiger fourteen-cylinder two-row radial or the Bristol Pegasus nine-cylinder single-row unit, the prototype in this case being powered by an uncowled 700 hp Tiger IV driving a truly enormous two-bladed wooden airscrew. Bearing the Class B marking B-6, also adopted as its Blackburn type number, the unpainted prototype was first flown at Brough by A. M. Blake on 24 August 1933, just six months after the first flight of the M.1/30A.

Open cockpits, warmed from an exhaust pipe muff, accommodated pilot, observer/wireless operator and gunner, the customary prone bombing position being located below the pilot's floor. Bomb fusing controls were situated within reach of both pilot and observer, and the bombing hatch was fitted with a course-setting bomb sight on a hinged mounting, but was closed by a water-tight door when not in use. A special padded headrest was fitted to the front cockpit against which the pilot could brace himself during catapult take-off.

Armament comprised a Vickers air-cooled ·303 forward-firing gun in a tunnel in the forward decking and a Vickers-Berthier quick-firing gas-operated gun (or K-gun) on a ring mounting aft. Ten ammunition pans, each containing 60 rounds, were stowed in the gunner's cockpit. With a crew of two and a 1,500-lb torpedo or equivalent bomb load, range as a landplane was 625 miles, but in the reconnaissance role maximum range could be increased to 1,130 miles using a 150-gallon cylindrical long-range tank in the torpedo crutches. For lifting such a load from the deck of a carrier without the aid of catapult launching, and for landing again slowly, camber-changing flaps were essential. The B-6 was therefore equipped with the mechanism, first used on the M.1/30A, which by means of a small crank handle on the control column, lowered all four Frise-type ailerons.

Fuselage construction was similar to, but stouter than, that of the M.1/30A

The prototype B-6 with uncowled engine during early test flights, August 1933.

The prototype B-6 on floats after conversion to Shark I standard.

strengthened for catapult launching and cable arrest and divided into water-tight compartments in case of a forced descent at sea. Stainless steel tubular spars for the mainplanes were made by Boulton and Paul Ltd of Norwich, the upper set having tubular booms and plate webs and the lower a figure-eight section. Following normal Blackburn practice, ribs were of light alloy and all the components of the tail unit were of similar construction. All flying surfaces, except the Alclad-plated fin, were fabric covered, and a very practical innovation was the introduction of detachable wing tips, easily replaceable in case of damage.

In view of criticism levelled at the M.1/30A, the main fuel tanks did not form part of the fuselage structure; instead, two detachable welded duralumin tanks were carried in separate watertight compartments in front of the pilot, with a reserve tank under the top decking of the front fuselage. Total capacity was $172\frac{1}{2}$ gallons.

After manufacturer's trials at Brough, in the course of which the engine was totally enclosed in a long-chord cowling, the B-6 was delivered to the A. & A.E.E. by A. M. Blake on 26 November 1933. Early in 1934, at the conclusion of the Martlesham performance tests, it was flown to Gosport for deck-landing trials aboard *Courageous*, the success of which led to it being taken on charge by the Directorate of Technical Development as K4295 and to the placing of a contract for 16 production aircraft for the Fleet Air Arm in the following August. These were given the type name Shark I in October 1934 and embodied a number of modifications, chief of which was an engine cowling long enough to enclose the exhaust collector ring.

Flown by Flt Lt D. F. Anderson, K4295 made public appearances as exhibit No. 11 at Hendon for the RAF Display on 30 June 1934 and the SBAC Show on 2 July, before returning to Brough for overhaul. Being on DTD charge it was redelivered to Martlesham by Schneider Trophy pilot Flt Lt Boothman on 10 September, but the Shark I was already in limited production and one of the main stipulations of Specification S.15/33, viz. conversion to and performance testing as a seaplane, had still to be met. K4295 was therefore flown back to the makers on 22 November by Flt Lt Woodhall to be brought fully up to Shark I standard in readiness for trials on the Humber with a twin-float undercarriage. This was strutted to the same fuselage and wing root attachment points as the wheel chassis, lugs for the two additional struts being provided in the forward part of the fuselage. The floats, of Blackburn design, were built of Alclad, incorporated shock absorbers at their points of attachment and, to dispense with fenders, had solid rubber nose blocks. They were also unusual in not being handed, i.e. any given float would fit on the port or starboard side as required. Water rudders were pneumatically operated by jacks connected to the aircraft's normal differential braking system and were essential for safe slipway approach. As they were ineffective if the air pressure fell below 100 lb/sq in, it was necessary for pilots to check it before landing. First floatplane trials took place at Brough in April 1935, after which K4295 was ferried to Felixstowe by Flt Lt Bradbury for sea performance tests which proved very successful, and many favourable comments were passed on the Shark's behaviour in rough water.

The way was now clear for large-scale production and, as a result of further contracts over the next three years, Blackburns built a total of 238 Sharks for the Fleet Air Arm, or approximately two-thirds the total output of Darts, Blackburns, Ripons and Baffins during the previous decade or so.

None of these earlier Blackburn types saw service with the Fleet Air Arm as seaplanes except the Ripon, for which float sets were built to Air Ministry order and seldom used. The Shark, on the other hand, last of the famous Blackburn torpedo biplanes, was used by the Fleet Air Arm not only for deck landing but also as a seaplane, either by being hoisted overside from carriers

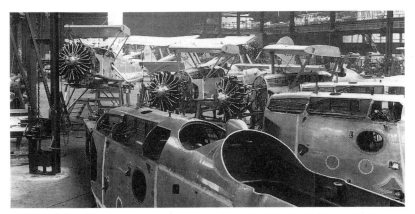

Shark I aircraft in the assembly shop at Brough with the Baffin production line in the background. (*Flight Photo 11083S.*)

367

The second production Shark I, K4350, in the colours of No. 820 Squadron, December 1934.

or being catapulted from battle cruisers. Its strength and buoyancy became legendary, and there is an instance on record of a Shark which lived to fly again after forced landing in the sea 20 miles off Gosport and being towed the whole distance inverted and with a torpedo in position.

In Squadron Service

Most of the initial batch of Shark I aircraft, K4349–K4364, was earmarked for No. 820 Sqn. to whom they were delivered at Gosport early in 1935, officially entering service in May that year to replace the squadron's Fairey Seals aboard HMS *Courageous*. K4349, first flown at Brough by A. M. Blake on 3 December 1934, was used for development work and, although delivered to Martlesham by Flt Lt Menzies on 31 December, spent most of its life at Brough. K4354 and K4364 were retained by the DTD for a similar purpose at Gosport, while a fourth machine of this batch, K4360, was delivered by air to the RAE, Farnborough, on 7 March 1935.

The only machine of this batch with any significant career was the last, K4364, which Blackburns retained at Brough for trials with the 760 hp Armstrong Siddeley Tiger VI radial engine. The aim of the flight test programme was to fly 100 hr in seven days with relays of pilots who included chief test pilot A. M. Blake, Reserve School instructors H. Bailey and C. A. Ball as well as Flt Lt G. M. Morris who was loaned by the RAF. The first take-off was at 3.45 am on Monday, 8 July 1935, and the 100 hr were completed at 8.15 am on Tuesday, 16 July, only $1\frac{3}{4}$ hr outside the seven days. The machine flew from 4 am to 10 pm daily to avoid night flying but was grounded on the Friday for maintenance. It did not reach No. 820 Squadron until September 1936, after which it served with the School of Naval Co-operation at Gosport in 1937 and with the RAE, Farnborough, where it was converted into a catapulting dummy and written off in the course of pilotless launching in 1938.

The T.9 Shark I became obsolete in May 1938, having been replaced by the T.9A Shark II, offered with either the 760 hp Armstrong Siddeley Tiger VI or the 840 hp Bristol Pegasus IX. There was also a number of airframe modifications, and the original B-6, K4295, again acted as prototype. Two of the pre-production batch of three, K4880–K4882, ordered for Service trials to Specification S.13/35 in June 1935, were Tiger-powered, but the third, K4882, was the first Shark fitted with the Pegasus IX. Main fuel was increased from 158 to 171 gallons in two main tanks of 108 and 43 gallons capacity with a further 20-gallon reserve gravity tank in the decking.

Main Shark II production began with a batch of 53, K5607–K5659, ordered in September 1935, the first machine going in the usual way to Martlesham and in 1936 to Felixstowe for acceptance tests, using the same float under-carriage that had been fitted to Shark I, K4295, a year earlier. The second, K5608, was delivered to No. 11 (Fighter) Group at Northolt on 11 February 1936 to replace its Fairey Seal communications aircraft, while others were flown to Gosport to replace the Seals of No. 821 Sqn which operated mixed landplane/seaplane Flights aboard *Courageous*. A number went to B and C Training Flights at Lee-on-Solent or were fitted with floats for catapult service with No. 444 Flight aboard the battle cruiser *Repulse* and the battle-ship *Warspite* on which special hangars had been built. Two at least found their way to Seletar, Singapore, and served with No. 4 Anti-Aircraft Co-opera-tion Unit, formed on 4 January 1939.

These were followed by 70 more, K8450–K8519, ordered in January 1936 to replace the Shark Is of No. 820 Sqn and to re-equip No. 822. Others served

The third pre-production Shark II, K4882, with Bristol Pegasus III engine (identified by the very short chord cowling) after conversion to Shark III prototype with sliding cockpit canopy, June 1936.

Shark II aircraft K8474, K8470, K8467 and K8454 of No. 820 Squadron in formation with Baffin S1653 of No. 810 Squadron over *Courageous* off Aboukir in 1937.

with A Flight of the Torpedo Training Squadron, Gosport, or on floats with A Flight of the Seaplane Training Squadron, Calshot.

Production for the Fleet Air Arm terminated with the final and largest contract, placed in January 1937 to Specification 19/36, for 95 aircraft designated Shark III. These were K8891–K8935 and L2337–L2386 delivered between 8 April 1937 and the end of the year, six of which went to No. 810 Sqn aboard *Courageous*. Another was demonstrated by Blackburn test pilot Flt Lt H. Bailey at the Hatfield SBAC Show on 28 June. They differed from the earlier marks in having a glazed, sliding canopy over the cockpits and Rotol three-bladed laminated wood airscrews. The Shark III had its origins in the Pegasus-engined pre-production Shark II, K4882, first delivered to Martlesham with open cockpits in February 1936 but which later went back to Brough to be fitted experimentally with the glazed canopy. Trials were resumed after its return to the A. & A.E.E. on 15 June 1936 and the aircraft made its first public appearance in the hands of Blackburn test pilot A. M. Blake at the Hatfield SBAC Show on 29 June that year.

Components of late production machines were sent to Blackburn's newly-opened Dumbarton works for assembly, the completed airframes afterwards going by road or by lighter on the Clyde for air testing at Abbotsinch, where the first such machine flew on 20 June 1938 piloted by Flg Off B. R. Rolfe.

Four Shark IIIs were used as trial installations machines at the RAE, Farnborough, K8460 and L2343 during July and August 1937 for tests on a modified oil system, and L2349 for an unspecified purpose in September. K8464, first delivered to Lee-on-Solent in October 1936, returned to Brough in December for the installation of an automatic pilot which was adjusted and subjected to flying checks at the RAE in 1937–38. In August 1938, L2343 was transferred to Gosport for further tests by the Admiralty, and one late

370

production Shark III, L2379, was delivered direct to Armstrong Siddeley Motors Ltd at Ansty, Coventry, for Tiger engine development and is believed to have served as test bed for the 880 hp Tiger IX used in the Armstrong Whitworth Whitley. Almost the last recorded use of the Shark for experimental purposes was on 6 November 1939, when a machine of No. 2 AACU was detached from Gosport to the RAE to tow an illuminated drogue (known as the Farnborough Illuminated Night Target) on night firing practices. Finally, in 1941 the RAE used a Shark III for JATO experiments which paved the way for carrying fighter aircraft on merchant ships.

Second Line Service

The Shark's frontline service was brief, for in 1938 Nos. 820, 821 and 822 Sqns re-equipped with the Fairey Swordfish, and the Shark was relegated to other duties such as target-towing, for which purpose more than 20 Shark II and III machines were returned to Brough or Dumbarton for conversion between November 1937 and April 1939. Earlier aircraft were brought up to Shark III standard and all were equipped with the D type winch with wind-driven re-winding gear on the port side of the rear cockpit controlling a drum carrying several hundred feet of wire cable for towing sleeve targets. Attachment brackets were also bolted to the top centre section for carrying the standard 16 ft glider target.

Thus equipped, and from 1939 fully camouflaged, the aircraft were issued to Target Towing Units at Abbotsinch, Gosport, Crail and Arbroath, and also to No. 2 AACU, Gosport, which sent K8909 on detachment to No. 269 Sqn at Bircham Newton on 4 October 1939 to provide air-to-air target practice for gun turret operators in its Avro Anson 1 aircraft. C Flight of No. 2 AACU operated at Roborough, Plymouth, with L2351, L2366 and L2375 until it moved to St Eval in April 1940, and two months later, during the Dunkirk

A late production Shark III trainer without arrester hook, ready for delivery from Brough, September 1937.

371

evacuation, the Unit's unarmed Gosport-based Sharks towed lighted flares from the North Foreland across the Channel to the mouth of the Schelde and back to illuminate German E-boats in the vicinity. Unfortunately, bad weather put a stop to this activity after only a few days. A small number was also detached to Detling, Kent, from 11 June to 3 July 1941.

At least 17 Shark target-tugs were shipped to No. 4 AACU, Seletar, via the Packing Unit at Sealand. These were K5621, '26, '46; K8505; K8904–'08; K8911, '12, '23, '26, '27, '33; L2343, '45, four of which were detached to Batu Pahat on January 3 1942 to attack Japanese army columns.

The Shark III was also widely used for training naval observers and telegraphists and was in service for this purpose until 1942 with Nos. 753 and 754 Air Observers' Schools, Lee-on-Solent; Nos. 755, 756 and 757 Air Gunnery Schools, Worthy Down; No. 758 Air Gunnery School, Eastleigh; and the Admiralty Air Observer Training Station at Piarco Airport, Trinidad, where, appropriately, they were used jointly with Fairey Albacores for training flights over the shark-infested Caribbean Sea! The way the Sharks stood up to heavy wear and tear in those arduous days was testimony to the strength and solidity of their construction and to the design of the magnificent Tiger engine which kept running even when losing oil or shedding spark plugs.

The Portuguese Shark IIA

At Lisbon in March 1935 Blackburns competed successfully against a number of firms from the USA, Germany, Czechoslovakia and Italy for a Portuguese Government contract worth £50,000 for the supply of six torpedo-bomber-reconnaissance seaplanes. Despite a vigorous sales and demonstration campaign by the Germans and Italians who took actual sample aircraft to Lisbon, final choice fell on the Blackburn Shark, and the contract, negotiated by Blackburn director and test pilot Sqn Ldr J. L. N. Bennett-Baggs, was signed on April 10.

The Portuguese machines were designated Shark IIA and equipped to carry four 112-lb, two 230-lb or one 550-lb bomb under each wing, but only three had torpedo-release gear. The other three were fitted with ungainly long-range tanks bolted directly to the underside of the fuselage, but all had metric instruments and Marconi A.D.37/38 wireless equipment. In most other respects they were identical with Fleet Air Arm machines, but, to make use of available Portuguese fuel supplies, they were powered by the 700 hp Armstrong Siddeley Tiger VIC, a version of the 760 hp Tiger VI with the compression ratio lowered from 6·2 to 5·35 for running on 77 instead of the customary 87 octane fuel.

The aircraft were numbered 73–78, coded 1–6, and appeared in a dove-coloured anodized finish similar to the British Sharks, but carried insignia supplied by Portugal consisting of black and white wing tip crosses and a red, blue and gold crest on a red and green rudder. The contract required each aircraft to have a full British Certificate of Airworthiness and laid down precise delivery dates, with penalties for late delivery. Nos. 73–75 were called for on 11, 18 and 25 January with Nos. 76–78 to follow on 1, 8 and 15 February 1936 respectively, but in the event slight delays occurred and the first aircraft did not fly until February. All six were still at Brough on 3 March when they

No. 74, second Shark IIA for the Portuguese Navy, on the slipway at Brough, 3 March 1936.

No. 75, third Portuguese Shark IIA, with 160-gallon long-range tank.
(*Flight Photo 15251.*)

were lined up for inspection by the Press in the presence of the Portuguese Air Attaché and three officers of the Portuguese Naval Air Mission, Lt Cdr José Aires Trigo de Sousa, Lt Cdr Antonio Guerreiro Telo Pacheco and Lt José de Saria é Silva. After the demonstration, during which Nos. 73 and 74 were flown off the glassy waters of the Humber for lively flying and gun firing demonstrations by Flt Lt A. M. Blake and Sqn Ldr Bennett-Baggs respectively, the Sharks were pushed into the Flight Shed to be dismantled for shipment. On arrival they were erected at the Portuguese Navy base at Bom Succeso on the River Tagus near Lisbon where they remained in service on coastal defence duties for several years.

Notes issued for the benefit of pilots flying the Shark IIA seaplane emphasized that it had no vices or unusual characteristics and that it was exceptionally easy to fly. For take-off the throttle was opened and the control column held forward until a slight porpoising signalled the moment for raising it on to the step. It then accelerated until it left the water at about 65 mph. It was not necessary to lower the ailerons as flaps unless the all-up weight exceeded 7,500 lb, when their use shortened the take-off and landing runs quite considerably. The recommended climbing and gliding speed for weights up to 8,000 lb was 92 mph, but gliding speed was increased to 98 mph when operating near the maximum permissible weight of 9,150 lb. Alighting presented no difficulty, the Shark merely being flown on to the water with the water rudders central.

Somewhat surprisingly, the large belly tank was found to improve the airflow over the Shark's fuselage and to put up the cruising speed of the three long-range machines by some 4 mph. This contributed in a small way to the fine non-stop flight made by Lt Trinidad of the Portuguese Navy from the Bom Succeso base to the RAF seaplane station at Calshot on 22 October 1936. With two other crew and a diplomatic courier packed into the rear cockpit, he conveyed an urgent Portuguese Government despatch to an international conference in London. The Shark flew back to Lisbon on 28 October.

Canadian Sharks

For sheer rugged strength and simplicity of maintenance the Blackburn Shark had no equal and consequently attracted the attention of the RCAF, which needed torpedo-bombers reliable enough for operating in areas remote from organized workshop facilities and capable of withstanding Canadian winters. Seven Mk II aircraft numbered 501–507 were therefore ordered from Blackburns and the first four were shipped in September 1936. After erection and test at No. 1 Depot, RCAF, Ottawa, during October–November, they went into service with No. 6 (Torpedo Bomber) Squadron at Trenton, Ontario, in January 1937, the remaining three being erected at Trenton for the same squadron in the following May.

In 1929, as part of a plan for expanding Canada's aircraft industry the United States firm of Boeing had, at Canadian invitation, established a subsidiary known as Boeing Aircraft of Canada Ltd with a factory at Sea

504, fourth Blackburn-built Tiger-engined Shark III for the RCAF, at Trenton in 1937 in the markings of No. 6 (T.B.) Squadron. (*Courtesy J. F. McNulty.*)

514, the short-lived first production Shark III (Pegasus engine) built by Boeing Aircraft of Canada Ltd at Vancouver in 1939. (*Courtesy J. F. McNulty.*)

Island Airport, Vancouver, among the first products of which were a further 17 Sharks built under licence. They were Mk III aircraft entirely fabricated by Boeing except for the Boulton and Paul stainless steel wing spars supplied by Blackburns but, unlike the British equivalent, were powered by the 840 hp Bristol Pegasus IX and therefore externally similar to the Pegasus III engined third pre-production Shark II, K4882, after it had been fitted with the sliding cockpit canopy.

Boeing-built Shark IIIs were numbered 514–524 and 545–550, but to assist in their production, two Pegasus-engined sample aircraft 525 and 526 were first supplied by Blackburns. A. M. Blake flew 525 at Brough with wheeled

The Pegasus IX engined RCAF Shark III 525, with incorrect rudder serial, on the compass-swinging base at Brough in November 1938.

525 fully painted and equipped with float undercarriage prior to delivery to Canada, December 1938.

undercarriage for the first time on 2 November 1938, at which stage, although correctly serialled under the wings, it was incorrectly numbered 508 on the rudder, probably because one too many rudders had been produced for the previous batch. This aircraft was at Martlesham for gunnery trials during 9–14 December 1938 and was adjudged a good gun platform with accessible weapons and a comfortable pilot's cockpit. Early in 1939 both aircraft arrived in Canada where, on 22 March, 525 was taken on charge by the RCAF Technical Detachment at Boeing's Vancouver plant. 526 was delivered to the Test and Development Flight, Ottawa, where trials lasted three months. In the following June this machine was taken on the strength of No. 10 (Bomber) Squadron on the east coast, but by this time it was realized that the Shark would be ineffective in modern war, so that when 526 came up for overhaul it was sent to Boeing at Vancouver and relegated to west coast duty with Western Air Command, to which all Boeing's deliveries were subsequently made.

No. 6 (T.B.) Squadron was also posted west to Sea Island Airport, Vancouver, and transferred to the bomber-reconnaissance role as No. 6 (B.R.) Squadron to escort shipping in and out of Vancouver Harbour and to patrol the Strait of Georgia. Two Sharks were also detached to Ucluelet, B.C., for sea patrol duty. Late-production Boeing machines joined the Supermarine Stranraer flying-boats of No. 4 (B.R.) Squadron at Prince Rupert on similar duties.

Inevitably the RCAF lost a number of Sharks in accidents, but the type gave thousands of hours of reliable, if unspectacular, service in arduous and hazardous conditions before they were withdrawn, with five exceptions, from use in August 1944. The five in question—502, 522, 546, 549 and 550—were reprieved and transferred to the Pacific coast for use on RN escort carriers for deck and lift drills.

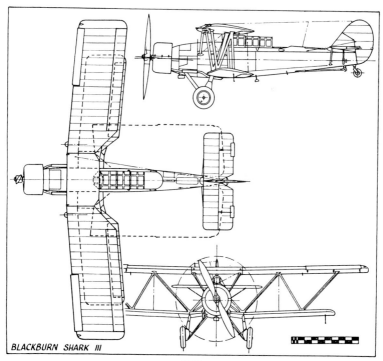

BLACKBURN SHARK III

SPECIFICATION AND DATA

Manufacturers: The Blackburn Aeroplane and Motor Co Ltd (restyled Blackburn Aircraft Ltd, April 1936), Brough Aerodrome, East Yorks. and Dumbarton, Dunbartonshire.

Boeing Aircraft of Canada Ltd, Sea Island Airport, Vancouver, British Columbia, Canada.

Power Plants: (B-6)   One 700 hp Armstrong Siddeley Tiger IV
(Shark I)   One 700 hp Armstrong Siddeley Tiger IV
(Shark II)   One 760 hp Armstrong Siddeley Tiger VI
One 800 hp Bristol Pegasus III
(Shark IIA) One 700 hp Armstrong Siddeley Tiger VIC
(Shark III) One 800 hp Bristol Pegasus III
One 840 hp Bristol Pegasus IX
One 760 hp Armstrong Siddeley Tiger VI

Dimensions: Span (upper) 46 ft 0 in   (lower) 36 ft 0 in
(folded) 15 ft 0 in
Length (landplane) 35 ft 3 in   (seaplane) 38 ft 5 in
Height (landplane) 12 ft 1 in   (seaplane) 14 ft 3 in
Wing area 489 sq ft

Weights and Performance: (a) *B-6 prototype*

	Torpedo		Reconnaissance	
	Landplane	Seaplane	Landplane	Seaplane
Tare weight	3,808 lb	4,287 lb	3,808 lb	4,287 lb
Military load	2,550 lb	2,550 lb	1,260 lb	1,260 lb
All-up weight	7,358 lb	7,837 lb	6,068 lb	6,547 lb
Speed at 5,000 ft	153 mph	144 mph	160 mph	151 mph
Speed at sea level	138 mph	130 mph	146 mph	138 mph
Initial climb	810 ft/min	640 ft/min	1,210 ft/min	990 ft/min
Service ceiling	18,500 ft	15,900 ft	23,200 ft	20,500 ft
Range	533 miles	476 miles	512 miles	463 miles

(b) *Shark I*

	Torpedo		Reconnaissance	
	Landplane	Seaplane	Landplane	Seaplane
Tare weight	4,039 lb	4,599 lb	4,039 lb	4,599 lb
Military load	2,712 lb	2,712 lb	1,595 lb	1,595 lb
All-up weight	8,050 lb	8,610 lb	7,040 lb	7,600 lb
Speed at sea level	150 mph	142 mph	157 mph	148 mph
Cruising speed	126 mph	118 mph	—	—
Initial climb	895 ft/min	680 ft/min	1,230 ft/min	1,000 ft/min
Service ceiling	16,400 ft	13,500 ft	20,400 ft	17,200 ft
Range	625 miles	548 miles	792 miles★	690 miles

★ Maximum range 1,130 miles with 150 gallon overload tank.

(c) *Shark II (760 hp Armstrong Siddeley Tiger VI)*

	Torpedo		Reconnaissance	
	Landplane	Seaplane	Landplane	Seaplane
Tare weight	4,039 lb	4,599 lb	4,039 lb	5,049 lb
Military load	2,712 lb	2,712 lb	1,595 lb	2,476 lb
All-up weight	8,050 lb	8,610 lb	7,040 lb	8,750 lb
Speed at sea level	150 mph	141 mph	157 mph	129 mph
Cruising speed	118 mph	118 mph	—	—
Initial climb	895 ft/min	700 ft/min	1,230 ft/min	770 ft/min
Service ceiling	16,000 ft	12,900 ft	20,400 ft	11,430 ft
Range	625 miles	548 miles	792 miles*	690 miles*

* Maximum range with 150-gallon overload tank 1,130 miles (landplane) and
990 miles (seaplane).

(d) *Shark II (800 hp Bristol Pegasus III)*

	Torpedo		Reconnaissance	
	Landplane	Seaplane	Landplane	Seaplane
Tare weight	3,939 lb	4,499 lb	3,939 lb	4,499 lb
Military load	2,712 lb	2,712 lb	1,595 lb	1,595 lb
All-up weight	8,050 lb	8,610 lb	6,940 lb	7,500 lb
Speed at sea level	140 mph	139 mph	157 mph	148 mph
Initial climb	990 ft/min	775 ft/min	1,340 ft/min	1,090 ft/min
Service ceiling	14,600 ft	11,600 ft	19,000 ft	15,800 ft
Range	717 miles	626 miles	829 miles*	731 miles*

* Maximum range with 150-gallon overload tank 1,260 miles (landplane) and 1,100
miles (seaplane).

(e) *Shark IIA and Shark III*

	Shark IIA seaplane		Shark III landplane
	Torpedo	Reconnaissance	Trainer
Tare weight	4,893 lb	4,893 lb	4,153 lb
Military load	2,735 lb	1,595 lb	3,130 lb
All-up weight	8,747 lb	7,894 lb	7,323 lb
Speed at 5,500 ft	133 mph	138 mph	162 mph
Speed at 10,000 ft	127 mph	134 mph	148 mph
Initial climb	580 ft/min	800 ft/min	1,350 ft/min
Service ceiling	11,700 ft	15,000 ft	20,400 ft
Range	430 miles	580 miles*	680 miles

* Maximum range 1,148 miles with 160-gallon overload tank.

379

Production:

(a) *B-6 prototype to Specification S.15/33*

One private venture aircraft only, B-6 to Works Order 5060/1:

Taxying trials at Brough 22 August 1933, first flown 24 August 1933, to Martlesham 26 November 1933, on charge 16 April 1934 by D.T.D. as K4295, brought up to Shark I standard by 20 March 1935 and converted to seaplane, Brough–Felixstowe by air 5 June 1935, struck off charge 21 January 1937, to instructional airframe as 931M.

(b) *T.9 Shark I to Specification S.12/34*

Sixteen aircraft, K4349–K4364, to Works Orders 5670/1 to 5670/16 inclusive, ordered August 1934 under Contract 334315/34. All flown to Gosport and handed over to No. 820 Sqn on the given date unless otherwise stated:

K4349 first flown by A. M. Blake 3 December 1934, delivered to Martlesham by Flt Lt Menzies 31 December 1934; K4350 first flown by A. M. Blake 11 December 1934, delivered by Flt Lt Edwards 15 December 1934, coded 738, later 674; K4351 first flown 19 December 1934, delivered by Flg Off Robinson 29 December 1934, coded 648, sank off Eastney 7 February 1939; K4352 first flown 31 December 1934, delivered 11 January 1935, coded 740, later 649; K4353 first flown by A. M. Blake 4 January 1935, delivered by Flg Off Hope 15 January 1935; K4354 first flown by A. M. Blake 17 January 1935, delivered by Lt Skene, RN, 23 January 1935, retained by D.T.D.; K4355 first flown by A. M. Blake 21 January 1935, delivered by Flg Off Doran 26 January 1935; K4356 first flown by A. G. Loton 23 January 1935, delivered 4 February 1935; K4357 delivered 8 February 1935; K4358 delivered 12 February 1935; K4359 delivered 23 February 1935.

K4360 delivered Brough–Farnborough for D.T.D. 7 March 1935; K4361 delivered 11 July 1935; K4362 delivered 30 June 1935, coded 645; K4363 delivered 1 August 1935; K4364 on charge at Blackburns 13 July 1935, to Gosport 21 September 1935, to D.T.D. 4 November 1935, to Coastal Area 22 January 1936, to No. 820 Sqn 3 September 1936, to School of Naval Co-operation Gosport 13 April 1937, to No. 4 Aircraft Storage Unit Ternhill 15 October 1937, to RAE Farnborough 25 June 1935, to catapult dummy 25 July 1938, written off 31 July 1938.

Many of the above were later modified to Shark II under Contract 708369/37.

(c) *T.9A Shark II pre-production to Specification 13/35*

Three aircraft only, K4880–K4882, to Works Orders 6020/1 to 6020/3 inclusive ordered June 1935 under Contract 334315/34:

K4880, Tiger VI, first flown by A. M. Blake 16 November 1935, to RAE Farnborough 21 January 1936, on charge by D.T.D.; K4881, Tiger VI, delivered 6 April 1936 and retained by Blackburns, 20 hr test flying by 15 January 1937; K4882, Pegasus III, to Martlesham 13 February 1936, returned to Blackburns 1 October 1936 for conversion to Shark III prototype and 20 hr test flying, to Martlesham June 1936.

(d) *T.9A Shark II production to Specification 13/35*

Fifty-three aircraft, K5607–K5659, to Works Orders 6120/1 to 6120/53 inclusive ordered September 1935 under Contract 400135/35:

K5607 to Martlesham 9 January 1936, to Felixstowe as seaplane; K5608 to No. 11 (F) Group at Northolt 11 February 1936; K5609–K5620 to Fleet Air Arm Pool Gosport for No. 821 Sqn in batches between 11 February 1936 and 26 March 1936 (K5619 coded 682, K5620 coded 683).

K5621 to FAA Pool Gosport 28 March 1936, to No. 821 Sqn 19 January 1937 coded 683 (later 690 as seaplane), to Lee-on-Solent 22 March 1937, to Gosport 21 May 1937, to No. 3 ASU Cardington 24 August 1937, to Blackburns Dumbarton 11 February 1938, to No. 36 Maintenance Unit Sealand 27 January 1939, to Far East 22 March 1939, written off at No. 4 AACU, Seletar; K5622 to Gosport 30 March 1936; K5623–K5624 retained at works, to No. 444 Flight Lee-on-Solent 15 March 1936 for HMS *Repulse*; K5625–K5626 retained at works, to No. 444 Flight Mount Batten 2 May 1936; K5627–K5629 to Gosport for No. 821 Sqn 18, 23 and 24 April 1936 respectively.

K5630–K5636 to C Flight Lee-on-Solent in batches on 4, 11 and 19 May 1936 respectively (K5634 to Weston-super-Mare September 1939); K5637–K5640 to B Flight Lee-on-Solent between 18 May 1936 and 22 May 1936.

K5641 to Gosport for No. 821 Sqn 27 May 1936; K5642–K5645 to B Flight Lee-on-Solent 4, 5, 7 and 15 June 1936 respectively; K5646 to B Flight Lee-on-Solent 15 June 1936, to No. 24 MU Ternhill 28 March 1938, to Blackburns Dumbarton 2 June 1939, to No. 36 MU Sealand 12 October 1939, to the Far East 3 November 1939, stored at Seletar; K5647 to B Flight Lee-on-Solent 15 June 1936, to No. 24 MU Ternhill 28 March 1938; K5648 to the Packing Depot Sealand 18 June 1936, engine removed, shipped to No. 820 Sqn at Aboukir, to No. 36 MU Sealand 7 October 1938, to Blackburns Dumbarton 2 March 1939, to Weston-super-Mare May 1940; K5649 to Packing Depot Sealand 18 June 1936, engine removed, to No. 820 Sqn at Aboukir 9 July 1936, to Mediterranean Command 11 August 1936, to No. 36 MU Sealand 10 October 1938, to Blackburns Dumbarton 2 March 1939.

K5650 to the Packing Depot Sealand, 23 June 1936; K5651–K5659 to No. 2 ASU Cardington between 23 June 1936 and 31 August 1936 (K5651 to No. 2 AACU 1939, crashed near Birmingham 5 February 1940; K5657 coded 902).

(e) *T.9A Shark IIA production for the Portuguese Navy*
Six aircraft, 73–78, to Works Orders 6180/1 to 6180/6 inclusive, to contract placed by the Directorate of Naval Aviation, Portuguese Government, on 10 April 1935:
No. 73, Certificate of Airworthiness No. 5347 issued 22 February 1936; Nos. 74–78, Cs. of A. Nos. 5451–5455 issued 20 April 1936.

(f) *T.9A Shark II further production to Specification 13/35*
Seventy aircraft, K8450–K8519, to Works Orders 6790/1 to 6790/70 inclusive, ordered January 1936 under Contract 467000/35. In each case the first date is that of the delivery flight from Brough.
K8450–K8452 to A Flight Calshot 4, 9 and 9 September 1936 respectively; K8453–K8455 to C Flight Gosport 10, 14 and 15 September 1936 thence to No. 820 Sqn coded 653, 658 and 659 respectively; K8456–K8458 to D Flight Lee-on-Solent 21, 24 and 24 September 1936 respectively; K8459 to D Flight Lee-on-Solent 25 September 1936, to No. 4 ASU Ternhill 15 December 1937, to Blackburns Dumbarton 2 June 1939; to Target Towing Unit Abbotsinch 19 March 1940, to RNAS Crail 2 December 1940.
K8460 to D Flight Lee-on-Solent 25 September 1936, to RAE Farnborough 24 July 1937, to Blackburns Dumbarton 1 July 1938, to RNAS Worthy Down 20 February 1941; K8461 to D Flight Lee-on-Solent 28 September 1936, to Blackburns Dumbarton 19 May 1939, to No. 8 MU Little Rissington 28 August 1939, to TTU Abbotsinch

17 April 1940, to RNAS Crail 5 December 1940, to catapulting dummy; K8462 to D Flight Lee-on-Solent 1 September 1936, to No. 4 ASU Ternhill 14 October 1937, to Blackburns Dumbarton 31 May 1939, to No. 8 MU Little Rissington 17 October 1939, to TTU Abbotsinch 27 March 1940, to RNAS Crail 5 December 1940; K8463 to D Flight Lee-on-Solent 7 October 1936; K8464 to D Flight Lee-on-Solent 8 October 1936, to Blackburns Brough 17 December 1936, to RAE Farnborough 8 October 1937, to No. 24 MU Ternhill 16 June 1938, to Blackburns Dumbarton 16 May 1939, to No. 8 MU Little Rissington 28 August 1939, to TTU Abbotsinch 27 March 1940, to RNAS Crail 9 November 1940; K8465 to D Flight Lee-on-Solent 8 October 1936; K8466 delivered to Gosport for No. 820 Sqn coded 659; K8467–K8470 to Gosport for No. 820 Sqn, coded 647, 654, 651 and 650 respectively.

K8471–K8472 to Gosport for No. 820 Sqn 28 October 1936 and 30 October 1936, coded 652 and 649 respectively; K8473 to Gosport for No. 820 Sqn 30 October 1936; K8474 to Gosport for No. 820 Sqn 4 November 1936, coded 648, to instructional airframe as 1127M; K8475–K8477 to Gosport for No. 820 Sqn 11 November 1936; K8478 to C Flight Gosport 11 November 1936; K8479–K8485 to A Flight Gosport in batches 13 November 1936, 20 November 1936, 30 November 1936 and 4 December 1936, coded A to G respectively; K8486 to Gosport for No. 822 Sqn 4 December 1936, coded 531; K8487–K8490 to Gosport for No. 820 Sqn 15 December 1936.

K8491 to Gosport for No. 820 Sqn 21 December 1936; K8492–K8494 delivered 16, 12 and 19 December 1936 but retained by Blackburns; K8495–K8496 to Gosport for No. 820 Sqn 30 December 1936; K8497–K8499 to Gosport for No. 822 Sqn 5 January 1937 (K8498 coded 523).

K8500 to FAA Pool Lee-on-Solent 14 January 1937; K8501 to No. 822 Sqn Gosport 27 January 1937; K8502 to No. 820 Sqn Gosport 27 January 1937; K8503–K8504 to No. 822 Sqn Gosport 27 January 1937; K8505 to No. 822 Sqn Gosport 27 January 1937, to No. 36 MU Sealand 24 August 1937, to Blackburns Dumbarton 10 February 1938, to Packing Depot Sealand 27 January 1939, to No. 4 AACU Seletar 22 March 1939; K8506 to Packing Depot Sealand 2 February 1937, to Malta for *Courageous*; K8507 to No. 822 Sqn Gosport 3 February 1937; K8508 to A Flight Lee-on-Solent 3 February 1937; K8509–K8510 to Packing Depot Sealand 4 February 1937, to Malta for *Repulse*.

K8511–K8515 to A Flight Lee-on-Solent between 11 February 1937 and 3 March 1937; K8516–K8517 to No. 3 ASU Cardington 27 February 1937; K8518–K8519 to FAA Pool Gosport 15 March 1937 (K8518 coded W4F).

(g) *T.9A Shark II for the Royal Canadian Air Force*

Seven aircraft, 501–507, with Tiger VI engines to Works Orders 6596/1 to 6596/7 inclusive, ordered 1936 under Contract 455279/35 to form the equipment of No. 6 (T.B.) Squadron, Trenton, Ontario; re-formed as No. 6 (B.R.) Squadron at Vancouver September 1939.

501 completed 6 October 1936, on RCAF charge 17 November 1936, s.o.c. 23 September 1943; 502 on charge 26 October 1936, to the British Admiralty Trinidad 5 June 1944; 503 on charge 15 October, coded XE-B, s.o.c. 3 August 1944; 504 on charge 17 November 1936, coded XE-C, s.o.c. 3 August 1944; 505 on charge 3 May 1937, s.o.c. 9 March 1939; 506 on charge 27 April 1937, beyond repair at Vancouver 18 June 1942; 507 on charge 3 May 1937, beyond repair at Vancouver 10 September 1939.

(h) *T.9B Shark III to Specification 19/36*

Ninety-five aircraft, K8891–K8935 and L2337–L2386, to Works Orders 7050/1 to 7050/95 inclusive, ordered January 1937 under Contract 510994/36. In each case the first date is that of the delivery flight:

K8891–K8893 to No. 821 Sqn Gosport 8 April 1937, 15 March 1937, 15 March 1937 respectively; K8894 to No. 820 Sqn Gosport 15 March 1937; K8895–K8897 to No. 822 Sqn Gosport 24 March 1937, 24 March 1937 and 8 April 1937 respectively; K8898–K8903 to No. 810 Sqn Gosport in two batches 8 and 19 April 1937 (K8898 to No. 2 AACU in 1939, crashed in sea off Hurst Castle 20 November 1939); K8904–K8909 to No. 2 ASU Cardington between 21 April 1937 and 5 May 1937 for shipment to Malaya (K8909 to No. 2 AACU in 1939) to No. 269 Sqn, Bircham Newton 4 October 1939.

K8910 to No. 822 Sqn Gosport 21 May 1937, to No. 820 Sqn Gosport 23 June 1937, to No. 3 ASU Cardington 9 August 1937, to Blackburns Brough 17 November 1937, to No. 2 AACU Gosport 1939, to TTU Gosport 5 January 1940, to TTU Gosport 19 March 1940, to RNAS Crail 11 December 1940; K8911–K8912 to No. 2 ASU Cardington 5 May 1937 for shipment to Malaya; K8913–K8920 to No. 2 ASU Cardington in two batches on 20 May 1937 and 31 May 1937 for *Warspite* (K8913 coded W4).

K8921–K8922 to FAA Pool Gosport 4 and 3 June 1937; K8923 to FAA Pool Gosport 3 June 1937, to No. 821 Sqn 22 July 1937, to No. 3 ASU Cardington August 1937, to Blackburns Dumbarton 13 January 1938, to No. 36 MU Sealand 31 October 1938, to No. 4 AACU Seletar 4 January 1939; K8924–K8925 to FAA Pool Gosport 17 and 15 June 1937; K8926 to FAA Pool Gosport 15 June 1937, to No. 821 Sqn 22 July 1937, to No. 3 ASU Cardington 24 August 1937 to Blackburns Brough 13 January 1938, to No. 36 MU Sealand 21 October 1938, to No. 4 AACU Seletar 4 January 1939; K8927 to FAA Pool Gosport 17 June 1937, to No. 3 ASU Cardington 27 August 1937, to Blackburns Brough 18 January 1938, to No. 36 MU Sealand 26 October 1938, to No. 4 AACU Seletar 4 January 1939; K8928 to FAA Pool Gosport 23 June 1937; K8929 to FAA Pool Gosport 22 June 1937, to No. 3 ASU Cardington 19 August 1937, to Blackburns Brough 18 November 1937, to No. 2 AACU Gosport 1938, to No. 17 Group Station Flight Gosport 11 July 1938, to C Flight No. 2 AACU Roborough 15 April 1942, to instructional airframe as 3490M.

K8930 to FAA Pool Gosport 22 June 1937; K8931 to FAA Pool Gosport 28 June 1937, to No. 821 Sqn 22 July 1937, to No. 3 ASU Cardington 24 August 1937, to Blackburns Brough 25 November 1937, to No. 17 Group Station Flight Gosport 24 August 1938, to No. 2 AACU Gosport 30 November 1939, to TTU Gosport 17 February 1940, to TTU Abbotsinch 8 April 1940, to RNAS Crail 2 December 1940; K8932 to FAA Pool Gosport 5 July 1937; K8933 to FAA Pool Gosport 5 July 1937, to No. 3 ASU Cardington 19 August 1937, to Blackburns Dumbarton 18 January 1938, to D Flight No. 17 Group Ford 8 September 1938, to No. 36 MU Sealand 14 November 1938, to No. 4 AACU Seletar 4 January 1939; K8934 to FAA Pool Gosport 5 July 1937, to No. 2 AACU 1939, crashed in sea off Hill Head Gosport 5 February 1940; K8935 to FAA Pool Gosport 8 July 1937.

L2337–L2342 to FAA Pool Gosport in two batches 14 July 1937 and 20 July 1937; L2343 to FAA Pool Gosport 21 July 1937, to RAE Farnborough 24 August 1937, to Blackburns Dumbarton 5 January 1938, to No. 820 Sqn Gosport 25 July 1938, to No. 17 Group Station Flight Gosport 29 August 1938, to Lee-on-Solent 9 February 1939, to No. 2 AACU Gosport 2 August 1940, to Blackburns Dumbarton 9 December 1940; L2344 to No. 36 MU Sealand 22 July 1937, to No. 3 ASU Cardington 29 July 1937, to

Blackburns Dumbarton 30 November 1938, to No. 4 AACU Seletar 4 January 1939; L2345 to No. 3 ASU Cardington 22 July 1937, to Blackburns Dumbarton 9 February 1938, to No. 36 MU Sealand 27 January 1939, shipped to No. 4 AACU Seletar 22 March 1939; L2346–L2348 to School of Naval Co-operation Lee-on-Solent 30 August 1937; L2349 to RAE Farnborough 20 September 1937, to FAA Pool Gosport July 1938.

L2350 to School of Naval Co-operation Lee-on-Solent 10 September 1938; L2351 to FAA Pool Lee-on-Solent 10 September 1937, to C Flight Lee-on-Solent 18 September 1937, to Blackburns Brough 3 January 1939, to No. 2 AACU Gosport 8 May 1939, to Mount Batten Station Flight 12 January 1940, to No. 2 AACU Gosport 19 April 1941, to Blackburns Brough 22 May 1941, to RNAS Worthy Down 4 March 1942; L2352–L2358 to FAA Pool Lee-on-Solent between 10 September 1937 and 23 October 1937; L2359 to C Flight, later 1760 Flight, Lee-on-Solent 24 September 1937, to Blackburns Brough 3 January 1939, to No. 2 AACU Gosport 11 May 1939, beyond repair at Blackburns Brough 22 December 1940.

L2360–L2365 to D Flight Lee-on-Solent between 11 October 1937 and 26 October 1937; L2366 to D Flight Lee-on-Solent 26 October 1937, to C Flight Ford 14 May 1938, to Blackburns Dumbarton 25 January 1939, to No. 2 AACU Gosport 16 May 1939, to Mount Batten Co-operation Flight 1 November 1939, to C Flight No. 2 AACU Roborough 30 November 1939, to St Eval 27 April 1940, to Blackburns Dumbarton 22 May 1941, to RNAS Worthy Down 27 April 1942; L2367–L2372 to D Flight Lee-on-Solent in two batches 11 November 1937 and 20 November 1937; L2373–L2374 to C Flight Lee-on-Solent 15 December 1937 and 20 November 1937 respectively; L2375 to C Flight Lee-on-Solent 20 November 1937, to Blackburns Dumbarton 25 January 1939, to No. 2 AACU Gosport 8 May 1939, to C Flight No. 2 AACU Roborough 25 November 1939, to St Eval 27 April 1940; L2376–L2378 to C Flight No. 17 Group Lee-on-Solent 20 November 1937, 20 November 1937 and 15 December 1937 respectively (L2376 to Gosport July 1938); L2379 on charge by D.T.D., to Armstrong Siddeley Motors Ltd Ansty 4 December 1937.

L2380 to C Flight Lee-on-Solent 15 December 1937; L2381 retained by Blackburns Brough 20 December 1937; L2382 to C Flight Lee-on-Solent 16 December 1937; L2383–L2386 on charge by Blackburns Brough 18, 22, 23 and 30 December 1937 respectively (L2386 to Gosport July 1938).

(i) *T.9B Shark III for the Royal Canadian Air Force*
Two aircraft, 525 and 526, with Pegasus IX engines to Works Orders 8780/1 and 8780/2, ordered April 1937 under Contract 667787/37:
525, first flown at Brough 2 November 1938, on charge by the RCAF Technical Detachment Vancouver 22 March 1939, beyond repair at Vancouver 18 July 1940, s.o.c. 4 October 1940; 526 on charge by the Test and Development Flight Ottawa 14 March 1939, to No. 10 (B) Sqn June 1939, beyond repair at Vancouver 3 September 1942, s.o.c. 4 December 1942.

(j) *T.9B Shark III by Boeing Aircraft of Canada Ltd*
Seventeen aircraft, 514–524 and 545–550, c/n 501–517, built at Sea Island Airport, Vancouver, BC under Blackburn licence granted April 1937.
514, c/n 501, delivered and on charge 2 August 1939, beyond repair 5 September 1939, s.o.c. 16 February 1940; 515, c/n 502, delivered 18 August 1939, on charge 22 August 1939 by No. 6 (B.R.) Sqn, Vancouver, s.o.c. 16 February 1940; 516, c/n 503, on charge 16 September 1939, delivered 18 September 1939, beyond repair at Vancouver 17 October 1939, s.o.c. 16 February 1940; 517 on charge 17 October 1939,

delivered 18 October 1939, beyond repair at Alliford Bay, BC 27 July 1940, s.o.c. 14 November 1940; 518, c/n 506, delivered and on charge 24 October 1939, beyond repair 4 January 1942, s.o.c. 4 February 1942; 519, c/n 507, delivered and on charge 22 November 1939 to No. 6 (B.R.) Sqn Vancouver, s.o.c. 13 July 1944.

520, c/n 505, delivered 5 December 1939, on charge 14 December 1939, beyond repair 2 March 1943, s.o.c. 25 May 1943; 521, c/n 504, on charge 5 December 1939 by No. 6 (B.R.) Sqn Vancouver, delivered 14 December 1939, s.o.c. 13 July 1944; 522 delivered and on charge by No. 6 (B.R.) Sqn, Vancouver 22 December 1939, to the British Admiralty Trinidad 5 June 1944; 523 on charge by No. 6 (B.R.) Sqn Vancouver 8 January 1940, delivered 9 January 1940, s.o.c. 13 July 1944; 524 delivered and on charge 24 January 1940, dived into the sea off Digby Island, BC, 20 June 1942, s.o.c. 13 July 1942.

545 delivered and on charge by No. 6 (B.R.) Sqn Vancouver 14 February 1940; 546 delivered and on charge 20 February 1940; 547 delivered and on charge 5 March 1940, beyond repair at Prince Rupert 27 January 1943; 548 (seaplane) delivered and on charge by No. 4 (B.R.) Sqn 19 March 1940, coded FY-F, destroyed by accidental depth charge explosion at Prince Rupert 21 September 1943; 549–550 delivered and on charge by Western Air Command 19 March 1940 and 4 April 1940 respectively.

(k) Conversion to Shark III Target Tugs

Deliveries to Brough for modification: K8909 and K8910 (17 November 1937), K8929 (18 November 1937), K8931 (25 November 1937), L2343 (5 January 1938), K8923 and K8926 (13 January 1938), K8927 and K8933 (18 January 1938), L2351 and L2359 (3 January 1939).

Deliveries to Dumbarton for modification: L2345 (9 February 1938), K8505 (10 February 1938), L2344 (30 November 1938), L2366 and L2375 (25 January 1939), K5648 and K5651 (2 March 1939), K8464 (16 May 1939), K8461 (19 May 1939), K8462 (31 May 1939, K8459 (2 June 1939).

Service use:

No. 269 Sqn, Bircham Newton; No. 810 Sqn, *Courageous*; No. 820 Sqn, *Courageous*; No. 821 Sqn, *Courageous*; No. 822 Sqn, *Furious*; No. 444 Flight, later renamed No. 705 (Catapult) Flight, *Repulse* and *Warspite*.

Nos. 753 and 754 Air Observers' Schools, Lee-on-Solent; Nos. 755, 756 and 757 Air Gunnery Schools, Worthy Down; No. 758 Air Gunnery School, Eastleigh; School of Naval Co-operation, Gosport; Air Observers' School, Trinidad.

A, B, C and D Flights, Lee-on-Solent; A, B and C Torpedo Flights, Gosport; A Flight, Seaplane Training Squadron, Calshot; TTU, Gosport; TTU, Abbotsinch; RNAS Crail; RNAS Arbroath; No. 2 AACU, Gosport; No. 4 AACU, Seletar; No. 11 (Fighter) Group Station Flight, Northolt; No. 17 Group Station Flight, Lee-on-Solent; Mount Batten Station Flight.

Side view of the Blackburn B-7 at Brough, January 1935. (*Flight Photo 11371S.*)

Blackburn B-7

In July 1931 the Air Ministry issued Specification G.4/31 for a two/three-seat general purpose type to replace the Westland Wapiti and Fairey Gordon, equipped to perform a multiplicity of duties which included Army Co-operation, day and night light bombing, dive-bombing and reconnaissance. Tenders were attracted from nearly all the major aircraft firms, but prototype contracts were awarded only to the Vickers 253, Parnall G.4/31 and Handley Page H.P.47, to which RAF serials K2771, K2772 and K2773 were allotted respectively. Competitive trials were scheduled to take place at Martlesham Heath and, since the winning aircraft could expect to be the RAF maid-of-all-work for many years to come, lucrative production contracts were in prospect which would keep an aircraft factory fully employed.

With this in mind, five other companies financed, built and submitted entries, so that when the three sponsored prototypes arrived at the Aircraft and Armament Experimental Establishment they faced competition from the Bristol 120, Westland P.V.7, Hawker P.V.4, Fairey G.4/31 and Armstrong Whitworth A.W.19 private venture machines. All were powered by various marks of the Bristol Pegasus radial engine except the A.W.19 which had the 810 hp Armstrong Siddeley Tiger VI.

In a period of stringent economy it was essential that maximum use be made of every piece of military equipment, and in October 1931 the Air Ministry added coastal defence and torpedo-dropping to the already long list of G.4/31 requirements. This brought the aeroplane within the Blackburn Aeroplane and Motor Co's specialist field, and design work was at once put in hand. Thus in 1933 a private venture prototype, the B-7 was built on the production line which, at that time, was assembling the first batch of Shark I aircraft for the Fleet Air Arm. The two types were almost identical struc-

386

turally, many components were interchangeable, both had the 700 hp Armstrong Siddeley Tiger IV, the watertight Alclad buoyant fuselage, the Warren girder wing-bracing and the aileron flap gear. Not being intended for shipboard operation, however, the wings of the B-7 did not fold, and although the span remained the same as that of the Shark at 46 ft 0 in, greater wing area for carrying really heavy loads was obtained by increasing the chord.

The B-7 was tropicalized, carried desert equipment and had the internal accommodation changed to make way for extensive military gear to suit the various specialist roles. Armament was essentially similar to that of the naval Shark and included underwing bomb racks, torpedo gear, a fixed forward-firing gun and a rear gun on a rotating mounting. It was also wired for night flying and carried navigation lights and magnesium flares.

Bearing Class B marking B-7, the new machine was first flown at Brough by A. M. Blake on 28 November 1934 and, following a lengthy after-flight inspection, the same pilot commenced manufacturer's trials on 5 January 1935.

It was flown to Martlesham on 28 May, but four years had passed since the issue of the Specification and the dive-bombing and other requirements had long since been dropped. Thus, by the time the competitive trials had been completed in October 1935, official interest in the Specification had ceased and none of the nine contestants was ordered into production. The B-7 was therefore flown back to Brough, dismantled and scrapped.

The B-7 soon after arrival at Martlesham, 28 May 1935.

SPECIFICATION AND DATA

Manufacturers: The Blackburn Aeroplane and Motor Co Ltd, Brough Aerodrome, East Yorks.

Power Plant: One 700 hp Armstrong Siddeley Tiger IV

Dimensions: Span 46 ft 0 in   Length 35 ft 4⅝ in
Height 12 ft 9 in

387

Weights and Performance:

	Bomber	General Purpose	Torpedo
All-up weight	7,027 lb	7,762 lb	8,338 lb
Speed at 6,000 ft	150 mph	149 mph	145 mph
Cruising speed	100 mph	100 mph	100 mph
Initial climb	1,200 ft/min	1,150 ft/min	980 ft/min
Service ceiling	20,000 ft	18,000 ft	10,500 ft
Range	540 miles	540 miles	475 miles

Production:

One prototype only, B-7, to Works Order 5590/1, first flown 28 November 1934, to Martlesham 28 May 1935, dismantled and scrapped at Brough 1936.

Side view of the Blackburn H.S.T.10 with Class B marking B-9, Brough 1936.

Blackburn B-9 (or H.S.T.10)

The origins of this 12-seat twin-engined low-wing cantilever transport mono-plane, outlined on page 327, can be traced to schemes considered in 1933 for an eight-passenger Blackburn Segrave III for Australia. This, with a similar proposal for Canada, led to a layout numbered C.A.19/1 (or *H.S.T.8) with two 340 hp Armstrong Siddeley Serval radials which, in turn, sired a family of 10-seat aircraft which were equally suitable for survey work. Offered with five different engine combinations and known as C.A.21, these projects led directly to the C.A.21A (or H.S.T.10), a larger and more sophisticated develop-ment with retractable undercarriage. It also featured hydraulically-operated trailing edge flaps and was powered by two 365 hp Napier Rapier moderately supercharged H-type inline air-cooled engines, themselves of entirely new design and driving two-bladed wooden airscrews.

In response to an Air Ministry enquiry dated 10 May 1934, a scheme for a military version known as the C.A.21B was prepared for the Directorate of Technical Development but was not proceeded with. Nevertheless, construc-tion of a purely civil private-venture prototype was commenced at Brough to drawings dated 27 August 1934, and by January 1935 the fuselage and Duncan-son tubular main spar were taking shape in the jigs. Although larger, the latter was essentially similar to the prototype spar used on the experimental Segrave II, being built of duralumin around internal rings and reinforced externally by corrugations. It was constructed in three sections with the central portion sealed to act as the main fuel tank and carrying at its outer ends the tubular-steel mounting for the Napier Rapier engines.

The mainplane was built in one piece and fitted into a recess in the under-side of the fuselage, the wing ribs of light-gauge duralumin tubing being

* High Speed Transport.

389

The H.S.T.10 under construction at Brough 1935, with the F.7/30 in the background. (*Aeroplane Photo 8687.*)

attached to the spar by angle plates riveted through both the spar wall and the flanges of the internal rings. The whole wing was fabric covered and the ailerons were aerodynamically as well as mass balanced.

The fuselage was a semi-monocoque structure consisting of stout transverse frames and longitudinal stringers covered with flush-riveted Alclad sheeting. Tailplane was also metal clad but the fin, elevator and rudder were fabric-covered duralumin frames.

As the whole concept of the design centred round high cruising speed, very careful consideration was given to fuselage shape and to streamlining. The H.S.T.10 was therefore unusual in side elevation because the pilots' compartment was wholly contained within its unbroken lines to avoid disturbing the airflow by breaking the contour with a conventional stepped windscreen. Two pilots were accommodated side by side in the nose, with dual controls comprising parallel-action rudder pedals to each seat and a central spectacle-grip control column with swing-over head. Emergency escape was via a transparent sliding roof and communication with the ground crew while starting engines was facilitated by sliding side windows.

The main cabin, 18 ft long, 4 ft 4 in wide, and 5 ft 6 in average height, was separated from the pilots' flight deck by a partition with communicating door, and was furnished to seat 12 passengers in pairs, one on each side of a central gangway, each with his own window. Individual heating and ventilation controls were fitted, a toilet was provided aft of the cabin door, and behind that, in the tail, was a luggage compartment of 37 cu ft capacity.

Retractable undercarriages were not yet in general use, and the H.S.T.10 is historically important as the first Blackburn design to include so revolutionary a feature. It was built in two separate units incorporating Blackburn oleo-pneumatic main struts which were hydraulically-retracted backwards and upwards into the engine nacelles. The medium-pressure wheels were fitted with differential brakes, the tail wheel was also retractable, and an undercarriage position indicator with audible warning device was fitted in the cockpit.

At an estimated cruising speed of 175 mph, range with 12 passengers was 320 miles, rising to 1,000 miles if only six passengers were carried. By removing the seats, the H.S.T.10 could be used for carrying freight or mail, for ambulance work or for aerial survey and photography.

Delays in the supply of materials and the firm's increasing military commitments during 1935 slowed up work on the H.S.T.10 very considerably. No sooner had the demand for Baffins eased and work was again in progress on the civil machine, when large orders were received for Sharks and the transport was again pushed into a corner. The tragic death of wing designer F. Duncanson in a road accident caused further delays but, with the prospect of even larger contracts for the new Blackburn Skua naval dive-bomber in the offing, a real effort was made to complete the H.S.T.10. It reached structural completion, functional testing and final inspection, so that by 4 July 1936 it was standing on its own wheels in the Flight Shed, complete but unpainted and at last on the point of flight test.

Although a very handsome aeroplane, it was completed too late and, instead of being a couple of years ahead of its time, which would have been the case had construction proceeded unhindered, was now merely one of a growing breed of twin-engined low-wing monoplanes with retractable undercarriages. On 7 July 1936 it appeared on the apron at Brough, with Class B marking B-9, ready for taxying trials but never flew because the RAF expansion scheme was at that time getting well into its stride and Blackburns were forced, reluctantly, to shelve the whole project in order to put maximum effort into the Shark/Skua programme. The H.S.T.10 was therefore banished to its corner of the Flight Shed where it remained until donated to the Loughborough College of Technology (Aeronautical and Automobile Engineering Dept) early in 1939 as an instructional airframe. Finally, in 1946, it was dismantled and reduced to produce, but the rudder is still preserved at the College as a souvenir of a unique prototype aircraft.

View of the H.S.T.10 showing the outsize wing root fillets and tapering wing.

391

So ended the H.S.T.10 and also three allied projects, the first of which, for an armed coastal reconnaissance/bomber transport with two Rapier VI, was dated 8 January 1935 and known as the H.S.B.T.10. Derived from this were the long-range H.S.T.20 bomber for the RAF with two 630 hp Napier Dagger I H-type engines and a general purpose version with two 500 hp Bristol Aquila radials designated H.S.N.T.10. Fuller details of these projects are given in Appendix B.

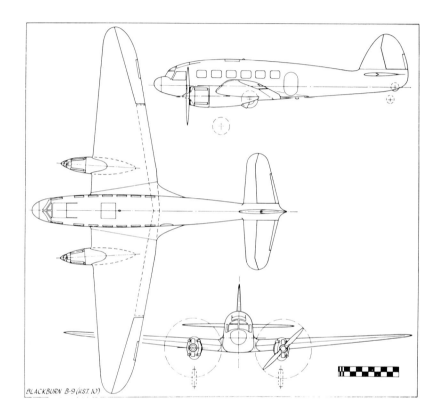

BLACKBURN B·9 (H.S.T.10)

SPECIFICATION AND DATA

Manufacturers: The Blackburn Aeroplane and Motor Co Ltd, Brough Aerodrome, East Yorks.

Power Plants: Two 365 hp Napier Rapier VI

Dimensions: Span 57 ft 4 in   Length 42 ft 0 in
Height 12 ft 0 in   Wing area 442 sq ft

Weights: Tare weight 5,490 lb   All up weight 8,850 lb

Estimated performance: Maximum speed at 5,500 ft   204 mph
                    Cruising speed   175 mph
                    Initial climb   1,000 ft/min
                    Service ceiling   23,800 ft
                    Ceiling on one engine   5,000 ft
                    Maximum range   1,000 miles

Production:

One prototype aircraft only, B-9, Works Order not recorded, commenced 1934, ready for taxying trials 7 July 1936, never flown and no civil registration allotted. Donated to the Loughborough College of Technology 1939, reduced to produce 1946.

The Blackburn B-20 on its beaching trolley outside the Dumbarton works, March 1940, with pontoon lowered and wing tip floats retracted

Blackburn B-20

At the Annual General Meeting of the newly-formed Blackburn Aircraft Ltd, held at Brough on 4 July 1936, Robert Blackburn announced that the company was about to receive a contract for a new type of flying-boat. At the time this was highly secret and details were not released for almost another nine years, for it was the culmination of a long period of research by Maj J. D. Rennie into the flying-boat designer's oldest problems, those of keeping the airscrews clear of the water without excessive hull depth and of obtaining large angles of wing incidence on take-off without the penalty of an awkward nose-down, drag-producing cruising attitude.

He solved both these problems by constructing the main portion of the hull separately from the planing bottom and mounting it high above it on a system of folding struts. This not only gave plenty of airscrew clearance but the struts were so proportioned that the aircraft sat on the water with the wing at the correct take-off incidence. Immediately the boat was airborne, four powerful hydraulic jacks retracted the planing bottom snugly into a recess in the hull and thereafter the boat cruised in the minimum-drag attitude. The principles of this invention were the subject of Patent No. 433925 which also included retraction of the wing tip floats into the engine nacelles.

This ingenious device was incorporated in the Blackburn B-20 design submitted to Specification R.1/36 for a medium-sized reconnaissance flying-boat with Bristol Hercules radial engines and, although the Saunders-Roe A.36 Lerwick gained the production contract, Air Ministry interest was such that a prototype of the B-20 was ordered to explore the practicability of the retractable planing bottom.

The B-20 was an all-metal high-wing cantilever monoplane with the engines mounted in nacelles protruding from the leading edge of the mainplane, and a hull of stressed skin construction built of Alclad plating flush-riveted to the usual transverse frames and longitudinal stringers. Construction of the separate planing bottom, or pontoon, was similar, but whereas flush riveting of the hull was achieved by dimpling, the plating used for the pontoon was thick enough to take countersunk rivets.

The pontoon was sub-divided into five watertight sections with four fuel tanks of 976 gallons total capacity carried in the midships compartment and accessible through large detachable manholes in the decking. Wing tip floats had four watertight compartments and were carried on hinged struts of box girder section built of Alclad with stainless steel fittings. When retracted, the supporting struts lay flush with the underside of the mainplane, the floats forming oversized wing tips similar in appearance to the tip tanks which were to appear later on other aircraft.

The all-metal tapering mainplane was built in one piece and attached to specially-strengthened frames in the hull, and was unusual in having three main spars and a covering of flush-riveted Alclad sheeting. Hydraulically operated metal-covered camber-changing flaps ran on curved rails inboard of the fabric-covered Frise-type ailerons.

Access to the interior of the aircraft was by a folding ladder from the deck of the pontoon through a hatch in the floor of the bomb-aimer's compartment, which was situated in the extreme nose behind an optically-flat glass panel. Behind the bomb-aimer was a spacious flight deck with first and second pilots side by side, and navigator, observer and engineer behind and on a lower level. In the interior of the hull was an officer's wardroom with two bunks, sleeping quarters for four crew, a compartment for loose equipment and with engineer's bench and tool kit, and behind this the galley and a toilet. All marine equipment not stowed in the hull, such as anchor, anchor winch, boat hook, mooring pennant and drogue, were stowed either on the pontoon itself or on the underside of the main hull to be instantly on hand during mooring operations.

Since the B-20 was an experimental aircraft, no defensive armament was

Rear view of the B-20 showing dummy tail turret.

395

carried, but in production machines it was proposed to fit two ·303 machine guns in the nose, with provision for two more in a power-driven turret amidships and four others in a tail turret. Four bomb cells, each to carry a 500-lb bomb, were built into the centre section of the mainplane, two inboard of each engine nacelle with bomb doors retracting into the thickness of the wing.

Construction took place in Blackburn's new Clydeside factory at Dumbarton, but the B-20 took some three years to complete and its camouflaged shape, serialled V8914, did not leave the slipway to find a place in the anchorage among the licence-built Short Sunderlands until early in 1940. It is possible that the structure weight came out higher than at first intended, for the boat was completed with two 1,720 hp Rolls-Royce Vulture X liquid-cooled engines driving three-bladed de Havilland Hydromatic variable-pitch airscrews. The importance attached to the project at that time can be deduced from the fact that these engines were supplied by the Air Ministry even though they were a somewhat specialized production and in short supply. First flights with the company's chief test pilot, Flt Lt H. Bailey, at the controls took place in late March or early April that year, the performance of the planing bottom on the water and of the retracting mechanism in the air being particularly successful. Unfortunately, these flights had shown aileron control to be unsatisfactory and during high-speed trials over the Clyde on 7 April 1940 the machine crashed in the sea off Gourock Head due to aileron flutter. Three crew escaped by parachute but Flt Lt Bailey was killed.

Close-up of the pontoon retraction gear and crew entrance with folding ladder.

The B-20 moored in the Clyde, April 1940, showing the wing tip floats in the lowered position.

Enough had been learned to prove the soundness of Maj Rennie's invention, but war requirements compelled Blackburns to apply themselves to the production of Sunderlands and other types so development was delayed and, although design work was undertaken for the B-44 retractable float fighter, advances in other fields had already made the idea obsolete.

SPECIFICATION AND DATA

Manufacturers: Blackburn Aircraft Ltd, Dumbarton, Dunbartonshire.

Power Plants: Two 1,720 hp Rolls-Royce Vulture X

Dimensions:		
Span with floats retracted		82 ft 2 in
Span with floats extended		76 ft 0 in
Length		69 ft 7½ in
Height with planing bottom lowered		25 ft 2 in
Hull depth with planing bottom retracted		11 ft 8 in
Wing area		1,066 sq ft

Weights: All-up weight   35,000 lb

Estimated performance:	
Maximum speed at 5,750 ft	288 mph
Maximum speed at 15,000 ft	306 mph
Cruising speed	200 mph
Endurance at economical cruise	8 hr
Range	1,500 miles

Production: One prototype aircraft only, ordered 1936 for retractable planing bottom development under Contract 498571/36 and built in the Dumbarton works to Works Order CL/39/128. On charge by the Marine Aircraft Experimental Establishment, Helensburgh March 1940 as V8914. First flown about March 1940, crashed in the River Clyde off Gourock Head, 7 April 1940.

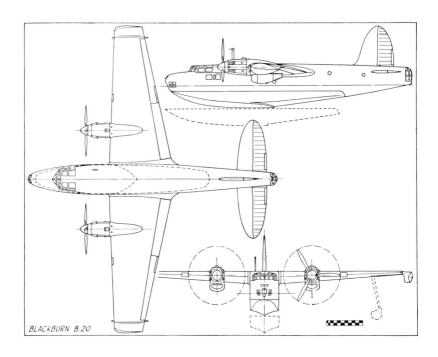

BLACKBURN B.20

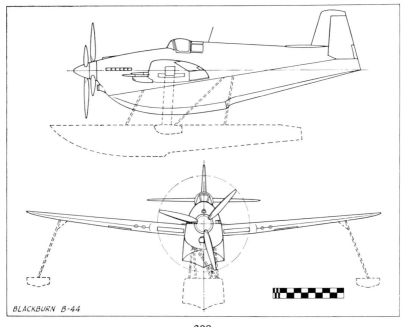

BLACKBURN B-44

398

Skua IIs of No. 803 Squadron pass HMS *Nelson* during exercises in the English Channel in 1939.

Blackburn B-24 Skua

The Skua two-seat fighter/dive-bomber earned a secure niche in aviation history because it was the first deck-landing machine produced in Britain to the modern all-metal cantilever monoplane formula with flaps, retractable undercarriage and variable-pitch airscrew, and the first British dive-bomber to equip Fleet Air Arm squadrons. Designed by G. E. Petty to Air Ministry Specification O.27/34, it was selected in preference to similar layouts submitted by Avro, Boulton Paul, Hawker and Vickers, the type number B-24 being allotted in the current Blackburn series; being the firm's first dive-bomber, it was also known in the drawing office under the time-honoured 'mission symbol' system as the D.B.1.

Painted in an unusual colour scheme, with grey fuselage and white mainplane, K5178, first of two prototypes ordered in April 1935, flew for the first time at Brough on 9 February 1937 piloted by A. M. Blake. It was powered by an 840 hp Bristol Mercury IX air-cooled radial engine, and featured the Shark-style flush-riveted Alclad fuselage incorporating two main watertight compartments, one under the pilot's floor and the other in the rear fuselage behind the gunner's cockpit, providing buoyancy in the event of a forced descent at sea. The crew compartment was also watertight up as far as the edge of the cockpits. The aircraft was stressed for catapult launching and arrested landing, the hook being fitted with a hydraulic damping device.

The mainplane, also of Alclad construction and covering, was built as three units with the two-spar, heavy-duty centre section bolted under the fuselage to form the bottom of the front watertight compartment. The outer wing panels tapered in plan and thickness, terminated in detachable upswept tips and were sealed between the main spars forward of the ailerons to form

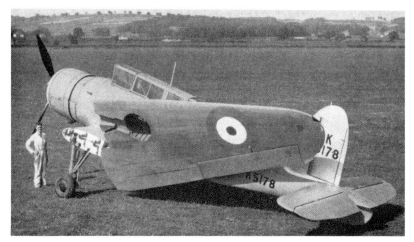

The first prototype Skua I, K5178, at Brough in 1937 showing the wheel wells, dive-brakes, unusual tail unit and method of wing folding. (*Flight Photo.*)

additional watertight compartments. Recesses in the under surface of the wing at the rear of the main spar between aileron and wing root, housed modified Zap flaps, the upper edges of which slid back as the flaps were lowered, their function being to shorten the take-off run, steepen the glide and limit the speed during steep bombing dives. They proved very effective and no difficulty was found in holding the aeroplane on target in a dive at 300 mph. Ailerons were fabric-covered and balanced by the use of inset hinges with mass balance assistance.

To combine wing folding and a retractable undercarriage required considerable ingenuity, but the problem was solved neatly by a development of the method first used in 1925 on the Blackburn Airedale monoplane. Folding was performed from ground level and the wings moved back about an inclined hinge housed entirely within the wing, twisting as they went so that in the folded position they rested parallel to the fuselage, leading edge uppermost. Latch pins were then inserted or withdrawn through linkage operated from a small hand lever and gear box in the wing root.

The undercarriage retracted outwards and upwards under the action of an engine-driven hydraulic pump into circular wheel wells which, with troughs for the various struts, were built into the undersurface of the outer wing panels. Each half undercarriage consisted of a Vickers oleo-pneumatic strut with stub-axle, medium-pressure wheel, pneumatic brake unit and light alloy fairing which completely closed the wheel well when in the up position. The last proved an unnecessary refinement and was not fitted to subsequent machines. The tail wheel unit consisted of a Dowty self-centring shock-absorber strut with castoring fork and electrically conductive tyre.

Tailplane and fin were both metal-clad cantilever structures bolted directly to the rear fuselage frames and carrying a fabric-covered elevator and horn balanced rudder on inset hinges. Controllable trim tabs were fitted and, to prevent blanketing and ensure rapid spin recovery, part of the tail-plane area and the whole of the elevator lay behind the trailing edge of the rudder.

The crew was accommodated under a glazed cockpit enclosure supported internally by two specially-strengthened fuselage frames which formed a crash pylon if the aircraft turned over on the ground. The pilot was provided with a sliding hood and was comfortably seated over the leading edge of the wing with a commanding view in most forward directions. Controls were conventional, the stick having a knuckle joint so that sideways movement gave aileron control, the rudder bar was adjustable, and large elevator and rudder trim wheels were located on the port side of the cockpit.

The gunner was seated aft of the wings under a tilting canopy which deflected the slipstream when the Lewis Mk IIIE machine gun was fired. When not in use this lay in a stowage in the rear decking, the tilting canopy then being shut to permit access to the wireless compartment behind the pilot. In addition to the Lewis gun on its Fairey Battle-type pillar mounting, the Skua was armed with four Browning Mk II guns in the leading edge of the main-plane, firing forward outside the airscrew disc. For dive-bombing a single 500-lb semi-armour-piercing bomb was carried on a retractable ejector arm in a recess in the underside of the fuselage. Additionally, eight 30-lb practice bombs could be carried on racks below the mainplane.

Main fuel, carried in two tanks between the crew members and in a reserve tank inside the front watertight compartment, reached the engine via an engine-driven pump and a selector cock which permitted fuel to be drawn from any combination of tanks. Oil was carried in a 12-gallon tank under the decking in front of the pilot's instrument panel.

Production

The prototype, K5178, was first flown at Brough by Flt Lt A. M. Blake on 9 February 1937, and it appeared in public in battleship grey as exhibit No. 8 in the New Types Park at the Hendon RAF Display on 26 June, and was demonstrated by the same pilot at the SBAC Show at Hatfield two days later. The type name Skua I was bestowed on it by an Air Ministry letter dated 17 August.

The machine then went to the A. & A.E.E., Martlesham, for handling trials which occupied 11 hr 15 min flying time between 20 October and 8 November. It left the ground with 20 or 30 degrees of flap at just under 70 mph, the wheels came up in 35 seconds and the aircraft then climbed away at 120 mph with the de Havilland two-position airscrew in coarse pitch. It was adjudged easy and pleasant to fly, landing was straightforward and its adequate brakes made taxying simple.

The aircraft remained at Martlesham for gunnery trials until early in 1939 when it was transferred to Gosport for ditching experiments, having flown 127 hr. Its place at Martlesham was taken by the second prototype, K5179,

Two views of the first prototype Skua I taken in February 1938. (*Flight Photos.*)

which first flew at Brough on 4 May 1938. This machine was also Mercury-powered but, in common with all subsequent Skuas, had the nose lengthened by 2 ft 4¾ in. It was first employed for comparative handling tests with wing tip slots locked and unlocked but, in view of the aeroplane's mild stalling characteristics, slots were not fitted to production aircraft. K5179 went to Farnborough on 24 August 1938 to be checked by the RAE after appearing briefly in public at the Ipswich Aero Club's annual display on 9 July.

The need for a naval dive-bomber was so urgent that the Blackburn machine was ordered in quantity straight off the drawing board, a contract for 190 aircraft to Specification 25/36 having been placed in July 1936, more than six months before the first flight of the prototype. To speed delivery, mainplanes were built in the old Olympia Works in Leeds and some fuselages were sub-contracted to General Aircraft Ltd at Hanworth. Unlike the prototypes, however, both of which had the Mercury IX poppet-valve engine, production aircraft (known as D.B.1A or Skua II) were powered by a Bristol Perseus XII sleeve-valve radial rated at 890 hp at 2,750 rpm at 7,000 ft, driving a de

Havilland D.H.5/8 three-bladed, two-position airscrew, all Mercury engines being earmarked for the expanding Bristol Blenheim programme.

L2867, the first production Skua II, first flew at Brough piloted by Flt Lt H. J. Wilson on 28 August 1938 and, to speed the clearance of the type for squadron issue, this and the second machine, L2868, were despatched to Martlesham in the following month so that performance testing with L2867 and armament trials with L2868 could proceed simultaneously. Unfortunately, the next three machines off the line met with accidents and were quickly relegated to instructional airframes, L2869 at Worthy Down in November 1938, L2870 on 16 December in the course of contractor's full-load trials on *Courageous* in the Firth of Forth, and L2871 on 6 January 1939 in a forced landing near Martlesham due to fuel starvation. L2870 was replaced by L2899 from No. 803 Squadron and the last, which was assisting L2867 on the A. & A.E.E. test programme, by L2888.

Considering the radical nature of the design, it was a compliment to the Blackburn company that few modifications were called for either by the Air Ministry or by the Bristol Aeroplane Co Ltd, manufacturers of the engine, to whom L2885 was despatched for engine proving in January 1939. The only changes of any significance were the strengthening of the up-turned wing tips (which had been introduced on the second prototype and all subsequent aircraft) and the substitution of a modified tail oleo (first fitted to L2883 delivered to Worthy Down on 10 January 1939) to overcome tail wheel juddering. L2883 was also the first Skua II to leave Brough with the arrester hook fitted, the second being L2903 delivered to Brize Norton on 2 February. Reference to page 404 will show that the majority of the 190 production aircraft were delivered during the year 1939, the peak month being July when 26 left the factory. In prewar days output on this scale was only possible by

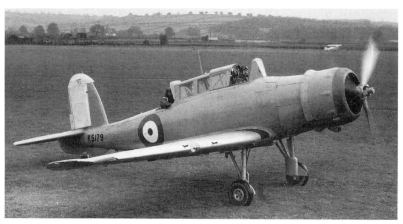

Test pilot Flt Lt H. Bailey in the long-nosed second prototype, K5179, with turned-up wing tips at Brough in May 1938.

Skua II L3007 in experimental red striped paint scheme.
(*Courtesy Bristol Aeroplane Co Ltd.*)

team work of the highest order and by untiring effort on the part of the three
Skua test pilots, Flt Lt H. J. Wilson, Flt Lt H. Bailey and Flg Off B. R. Rolfe.

Delivery record:				
	October 1938	3	June	17
	November	3	July	26
	December	6	August	14
	January 1939	9	September	11
	February	15	October	16
	March	15	November	5
	April	23	December	3
	May	23	March 1940	1
			Total	190

All this immense effort was largely nullified because the programme ran
more than a year behind schedule, for when the Skua requirement was formulated in September 1934, production aircraft were expected to enter service
in 1937. In the event deliveries did not commence until four years one month
later, in October 1938, so the Admiralty, faced with a deficit in fighter aircraft,
were compelled to order the Fairey Fulmar straight off the drawing board.

Squadron Service

First deliveries to the Fleet Air Arm were ferried to Worthy Down for
Nos. 800 and 803 Squadrons late in 1938 to supersede Hawker Nimrods and
Ospreys aboard the Navy's newest carrier *Ark Royal*. A temporary complication was the unserviceability of Brough aerodrome in December when, for a
short time, production Skuas were airtested at, and distributed from, Leconfield. At least up to L3006 (which Blackburns retained for target towing
trials in 1939), the aircraft were delivered in an all-silver colour scheme, but
the next, L3007, was experimentally painted with red bands on fuselage and
upper wing surfaces for ease of spotting if ditched. Later they were camouflaged and given red, white and blue striped fins, but one of the few public
occasions on which they appeared in silver was the opening of Derby Munici-

pal Aerodrome, Burnaston, on 19 June 1939 when a flight from Worthy Down gave a memorable demonstration of deck-landing techniques.

No. 801 Squadron also re-equipped with Skuas aboard the carrier *Furious*, and when war broke out a few months later 33 Skuas were on operational strength, including eight at Eastleigh with No. 806 Squadron but, though regarded as an effective dive-bomber, the type had already been outclassed as a fighter. Nevertheless, the Skua enjoyed a few brief months of glory and, before being ousted by faster and more lethal equipment, took part in several notable actions and made history as the first British type in the 1939–45 war to shoot down an enemy aircraft. This was a Dornier Do 18 flying-boat which fell to the guns of Lt B. S. McEwen and Petty Officer B. M. Seymour, crew of one of nine Skuas of No. 803 Squadron flown off by *Ark Royal* on 25 September 1939 while escorting the battleships *Nelson* and *Rodney* on patrol off Heligoland. In March 1944, the pilot, with the rank of Lt Cdr, visited Brough as guest of Robert Blackburn to give the company's employees a first-hand account of the action.

Ark Royal then took the two Skua squadrons to Freetown, Sierra Leone, base for convoy protection patrols over the South Atlantic, before returning to disembark them at Hatston, near Kirkwall in the Orkneys, in January 1940.

The Skua's greatest success was the classic dive-bombing attack which sank the German cruiser *Königsberg* alongside Skoltegrund Mole in Bergen Harbour at the very limits of range at dawn on 10 April 1940. The attack was mounted by seven Skuas of No. 800 Squadron, led by Capt R. T. Partridge, RM, in company with nine from No. 803 Squadron, led by Lt W. P. Lucy, RN, which made the 330-mile night crossing from Hatston. By a superlative feat of navigation, all but one returned safely to base, but eleven days later both squadrons re-embarked in *Ark Royal* to cover the Narvik operations, in the course of which practically all the Skuas were lost. Many failed to find the carrier and ditched at sea, others were shot down, two were interned in

Anonymous Skua II from *Ark Royal* on a frozen lake in Norway, April 1940.
(*Courtesy Leslie Hunt.*)

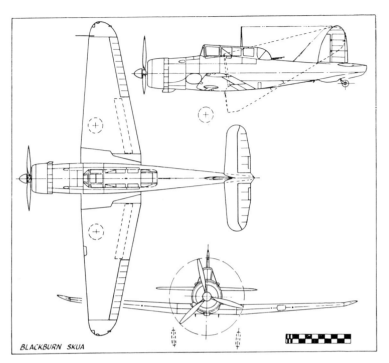

BLACKBURN SKUA

Sweden and others were abandoned on Norwegian soil where the remains of one which crash landed at Ålesund in April 1940 (fuselage number B3/LL/432 dated 7 June 1939 and probably from the sequence L2970–L2980) were still to be seen in 1968. One Skua navigated for the 18 Gloster Gladiators of No. 263 Squadron from the carrier *Glorious* to Lake Lesjaskog.

No. 801 Squadron was temporarily shore-based at Detling, Kent, during the Dunkirk evacuation in June 1940 and operated over the beaches as a fighter unit of Coastal Command. Losses among the *Ark Royal* squadrons were made good with new Skuas and crews for operations in the Mediterranean which, according to some sources, included a dive-bombing attack on the French battleship *Richelieu* in Oran Harbour in September 1940. Two Skuas were also embarked in the carrier *Argus* in November that year to repeat the role of lead ship played earlier in the year off Norway. This time they were to shepherd 12 Hawker Hurricanes to Malta, but movements of the Italian fleet in the Mediterranean compelled them to fly off at extreme range with the result that only one Skua and four Hurricanes reached Luqa.

In acknowledgement of the Skua's effective, if short-lived, part in the war at sea, L2950 was exhibited in Hull alongside a captured Bf 109 from 30 November to 12 December 1940.

Skuas remained operational until No. 800 Squadron came home from the Mediterranean aboard the carrier *Furious* in March 1941 to re-equip with

Fairey Fulmar Is at Lee-on-Solent. No. 806 also surrendered its eight Skuas and six Blackburn Rocs for Fulmars, Nos. 803 and 801 following in May and August 1941 to be re-equipped with Sea Hurricanes.

Thereafter the Skua was relegated to advanced training or target towing, in fact its future as a tug for air gunnery targets had been foreseen as early as August 1939 when drogue-towing tests had been conducted at Martlesham with the first production Skua, L2867. Seven aircraft, L2987–L2993, were shipped to No. 3 Anti-Aircraft Co-operation Unit, Malta, for this duty in October 1939, and L3006 was retained by Blackburns for the trial installation and testing of an improved target-towing gear and for test flying the production version. Many later Skuas were actually built as target tugs with windmill-driven cable drums, emerging wasp-like from the factory in the well-known black and yellow distinguishing stripes.

Target towing was also undertaken by No. 2 AACU whose first tug conversion, L2978, went into service on 12 February 1940. At this time the unit was operating A Flight at Gosport with four Sharks and eight Skuas, C Flight at Roborough, Plymouth, with six Sharks and D Flight at Eastchurch with two Sharks and four Skuas. D Flight co-operated with Chatham-based units of the fleet but was transferred to Donibristle on 18 May 1940 to work with *Nelson* and other capital ships in the Firth of Forth, the first Donibristle tug being L2982. In the south, A Flight's Skuas and Sharks illuminated the sea with towed flares during night anti-E boat patrols off Dunkirk in June 1940.

SPECIFICATION AND DATA

Manufacturers: Blackburn Aircraft Ltd, Brough Aerodrome, East Yorks.

Power Plants: (Skua I) One 840 hp Bristol Mercury IX
(Skua II) One 890 hp Bristol Perseus XII

Dimensions: Span 46 ft 2 in   Width folded 15 ft 6 in
Length (K5178) 33 ft 2¼ in (others) 35 ft 7 in
Height 12 ft 6 in   Wing area 319 sq ft

Weights and Performance:

	Skua I Prototype	Skua II		
		Dive bomber	Fighter	Target tug
Tare weight	5,722 lb	5,496 lb	5,496 lb	5,496 lb
Military load	1,069 lb	1,488 lb	977 lb	1,381 lb
All-up weight	7,807 lb	8,228 lb	8,124 lb	7,840 lb
Speed at 6,500 ft	—	225 mph	225 mph	229 mph
Speed at sea level	—	—	204 mph	205 mph
Maximum cruise	—	—	187 mph	189 mph
Economic cruise	—	—	114 mph	145 mph
Initial climb	—	—	1,580 ft/min	1,790 ft/min
Service ceiling	—	19,100 ft	20,200 ft	22,800 ft
Maximum range	—	—	435 miles	350 miles

Production:
(a) *D.B.1 Skua I prototypes to Specification O.27/34*
Two aircraft, K5178 and K5179, with Mercury IX engines to Works Orders 6290/1 and 6290/2, ordered April 1935 under Contract 400778/35:

K5178   First flown 9 February 1937, to A. & A.E.E. Martlesham 17 June 1937; to Blackburns Brough 29 June 1937, to RAE Farnborough 7 July 1937; to Blackburns Brough 30 July 1937; to A. & A.E.E. Martlesham 9 October 1937; to Blackburns Brough 8 November 1937; to RAE Farnborough 18 December 1937; to Blackburns Leconfield 20 January 1938; to A. & A.E.E. Martlesham 9 March 1938; to Gosport 30 January 1939; ditched February 1939.

K5179   First flown 4 May 1939, retained at Brough under Contract 769429/38; to RAE Farnborough 13 August 1938; to A. & A.E.E. Martlesham 26 September 1938; to RNAS Evanton 18 October 1938.

(b) *D.B.1A Skua II production to Specification 25/36*
One hundred and ninety aircraft with Bristol Perseus XII engines ordered July 1936 under Contract 534298/36:

(i) Sixty-nine aircraft, L2867–L2935, to Works Orders 7371/1 to 7371/69 inclusive. The first date given is that for the delivery flight from Brough. L2873–L2935 (except L2884, L2888 and L2892) were transferred to the Admiralty 24 May 1939.

L2867 to A. & A.E.E. Martlesham 14 September 1938, to Fleet Air Arm 15 February 1940; L2868 to A. & A.E.E. Martlesham 22 September 1938; L2869 to FAA Pool Lee-on-Solent 14 October 1938, to No. 800 Sqn, to No. 4 Wing Henlow 16 December 1938 as instructional airframe 1200M; L2870 to Leuchars 2 November 1938 for full load trials on *Courageous*, allotment to No. 4 Wing Henlow as instructional airframe 1201M cancelled 16 December 1938, to Worthy Down 11 January 1939, broken up 7 June 1940; L2871 to A. & A.E.E. Martlesham 14 November 1938, forced landing 6 January 1939, to RAF Locking 27 March 1939 as instructional airframe 1294M, flew 19 hr 55 min; L2872 to Blackburns Brough 17 November 1938 for trial installations, to RAE Farnborough 5 April 1939, to Blackburns 1 March 1940, still there December 1941; L2873 to No. 803 Sqn Worthy Down 2 January 1939; L2874 to No. 803 Sqn Worthy Down 30 December 1938, coded A7C; L2875 to Central Flying School Upavon 2 December 1938, to No. 803 Sqn Worthy Down, to No. 800 Sqn; L2876–L2887 to No. 803 Sqn Worthy Down between 6 December 1938 and 24 January 1939 (L2881 coded A7L, L2884 lost at sea 6 April 1939 having flown 25 hr 40 min, L2885 detached to Bristols Filton, L2887 coded A7F), all to No. 800 Sqn; L2888 to A. & A.E.E. Martlesham 7 February 1939, to No. 2 AACU Gosport 8 January 1940, to FAA Gosport 15 June 1940; L2889 to No. 803 Sqn Worthy Down 6 February 1939, coded A7G; L2890 to No. 803 Sqn Worthy Down 6 February 1939, coded A7H, s.o.c. at Blackburns Sherburn-in-Elmet 5 January 1942.

L2891 to No. 6 MU Brize Norton 16 February 1939, to A Flt No. 2 AACU June 1939, crashed in Fareham Creek 30 November 1939; L2892 to No. 800 Sqn 7 February 1939, s.o.c. 1 June 1939; L2893–L2896 to No. 6 MU Brize Norton 7 February 1939 except L2894 10 May 1939 due to taxying accident; L2897 to No. 6 MU Brize Norton 16 February 1939; L2898–L2899 to No. 803 Sqn Worthy Down.

L2900–L2905 to No. 6 MU Brize Norton between 16 February 1939 and 1 March 1939; L2906 to No. 10 MU Hullavington 7 March 1939; L2907–L2919 to No. 19 MU St Athan between 7 March 1939 and 13 April 1939; L2920 to No. 5 MU Kemble 13 April 1939; L2921 to No. 19 MU St Athan 13 April 1939; L2922 to No. 5 MU Kemble 13 April 1939; L2923–L2928 to No. 801 Sqn Donibristle 6 April 1939, (L2928 coded S); L2929 to No. 5 MU Kemble 28 April 1939; L2930–L2932 to No. 803 Sqn Worthy Down 15 April 1939; L2933–L2935 to No. 800 Sqn 18 April 1939 (L2934 coded N, L2935 replacement for L2892).

(ii) Twenty-one aircraft, L2936–L2956, to Works Orders 7375/1 to 7375/21 inclusive, with delivery dates from Brough. All transferred to the Admiralty 24 May 1939.

L2936–L2941 to No. 8 MU Little Rissington between 25 April 1939 and 27 April, 1939; L2942–L2956 to No. 10 MU Hullavington between 2 May 1939 and 22 May 1939.

(iii) Fifty aircraft, L2957–L3006, to Works Orders 7840/1 to 7840/50 inclusive, with delivery dates from Brough. All transferred to the Admiralty 7 October 1939.

L2957–L2966 to No. 27 MU Shawbury between 25 May 1939 and 1 June 1939, thence to No. 4 MU Prestwick, L2961 later to No. 801 Sqn; L2967–L2971 to No. 10 MU Hullavington between 9 June 1939 and 21 June 1939; L2972 to No. 36 MU Sealand 17 June 1939 for trial packing and despatch to No. 3 AACU Malta, project abandoned, s.o.c. 4 December 1939; L2973 to A Flt No. 2 AACU Gosport 19 June 1939, to Station Flight Gosport 13 June 1940, to Fleet Air Arm MU Yeovilton 20 March 1941; L2974 to A Flt No. 2 AACU Gosport 26 June 1939, to Station Flight Gosport 12 June 1940, packed at No. 76 MU Wroughton 13 February 1942, to Liverpool Docks 7 March 1942; L2975 as L2974, to Birkenhead Docks 15 January 1942; L2976 to A Flt No. 2 AACU Gosport 26 June 1939, damaged beyond repair 12 July 1939 having flown 13 hr 10 min; L2977 to A Flt No. 2 AACU Gosport 26 June 1939, crash landing 17 October 1939, to No. 4 MU Prestwick 23 November 1939, to No. 27 MU Shawbury 29 July 1941; L2978 to A Flt No. 2 AACU Gosport 26 June 1939, to FAA Gosport 15 June 1940; L2979 to A Flt No. 2 AACU Gosport 27 June 1939, to FAA Gosport 21 June 1940, to Blackburns Dumbarton 30 November 1941.

L2980 to D Flt No. 2 AACU Eastchurch, s.o.c. 16 January 1940; L2981–L2982 to D Flt No. 2 AACU Eastchurch 5 July 1939, to Donibristle 18 April 1940, to FAA Gosport 10 July 1940; L2983 to D Flt No. 2 AACU Eastchurch 6 June 1939, to No. 4 MU Prestwick 15 October 1940, to Blackburns Dumbarton 11 November 1941; L2984 to D Flt No. 2 AACU Eastchurch 6 June 1939, to Donibristle 18 April 1940, to Blackburns Dumbarton 15 October 1940; L2985–L2986 to D Flt No. 2 AACU Eastchurch 6 June 1939, to FAA Gosport 15 June 1940; L2987–L2993 to No. 5 MU Kemble between 7 July 1939 and 13 July 1939, to No. 3 AACU Malta 7 October 1939; L2994–L2998 to No. 9 MU Cosford 19 and 20 July 1939; L2999–L3005 to No. 20 MU Aston Down between 21 July 1939 and 31 July 1939 (L3004 to FAA Yeovilton 21 February 1941); L3006 retained by Blackburns Brough 29 July 1939 for towed target gear trials, to RAE Farnborough 19 October 1939, to No. 49 MU Lasham, to Blackburns Brough 1 July 1940, to No. 10 MU Hullavington 25 September 1940.

(iv) Fifty aircraft, L3007–L3056, to Works Orders 7842/1 to 7842/50 inclusive, with delivery dates from Brough. Mainly completed as target tugs and all transferred to the Admiralty 7 October 1939.

L3007–L3011 to No. 20 MU Aston Down between 8 August 1939 and 21 August 1939; L3012–L3020 to No. 9 MU Cosford between 21 August 1939 and 31 August 1939 (L3020 scrapped at Brown Lane, Leeds); L3021–L3028 to No. 6 MU Brize Norton between 5 September 1939 and 20 September 1939; L3029–L3035 to No. 19 MU St Athan between 17 September 1939 and 6 October 1939 (L3029 to Weston-super-Mare 9.40); L3036–L3044 to No. 5 MU Kemble between 18 October 1939 and 23 October 1939; L3045–L3056 to No. 9 MU Cosford between 27 October 1939 and 10 March 1940.

Service Use:

No. 800 Sqn, HMS *Ark Royal;* No. 801 Sqn, HMS *Furious,* Donibristle and Hatston; No. 803 Sqn, HMS *Ark Royal;* No. 806 Sqn, Eastleigh; No. 759 FAA Fighter School, Yeovilton; No. 760 FAA Fighter Pool Sqn, Eastleigh; No. 772 Ferry Return Unit, Bermuda; No. 792 ATTU, St Merryn; No. 2 AACU, Gosport, Eastchurch and Donibristle; No. 3 AACU, Malta.

Rocs from RNAS Donibristle in formation in November 1939. Rotation of the turret has lowered the rear fairings on the outboard machines L3118/O and L3114/E, the latter with modified cabin roof. (*Aeroplane Photo 11469/10.*)

Blackburn B-25 Roc

The Roc was a two-seat fleet fighter developed from, and structurally similar to, the Blackburn Skua. It was powered by the same mark of Bristol Perseus sleeve-valve radial but differed from the earlier machine in several important respects. The fuselage was widened amidships to accommodate a Boulton Paul Type A Mk II power-driven gun turret, the mainplane was rigged with 2 degrees of dihedral outboard of the centre section to avoid the need for upturned wing tips, attachment points for a float undercarriage were incorporated as standard, and provision was made for installing a close-fitting 70-gallon overload fuel tank under the centre section.

Designed by G. E. Petty to Air Ministry Specification O.30/35, it was the naval equivalent of the RAF's Boulton Paul Defiant and the first turret fighter to enter Fleet Air Arm service. The pilot sat up front under a sliding canopy, as in the Skua, with his observer behind in a minute wireless cabin from which there was ready access to the gun turret. This carried four ·303-in Browning guns mounted in pairs, rotation of the turret through a full 360 degrees and elevation of the guns to a maximum of 85 degrees above the horizon being effected by the movement of a single control column. Hydraulic power was provided by an electrically-driven pump, and the guns were also fired electrically by a button on the control column, with automatic interruption of the circuit if the tail unit or airscrew came into the line of fire. The turret fitted

411

The prototype Blackburn Roc L3057.

snugly between the roof of the W/T cabin and a continuation fairing which ran rearwards to the tail. A device at the bottom of the turret lowered this fairing into the fuselage when the guns were pointing in an aft direction. Marine equipment and a collapsible dinghy were carried in the rear fuselage, and additional armament consisted of a 250-lb bomb and four practice bombs under each mainplane.

A contract for 136 aircraft was placed with Blackburns on 28 April 1937, but preoccupation with the Skua programme and with preparations for large-scale manufacture of the twin-engined Botha, resulted in Roc production to Specification O.15/37 being sub-contracted to the Wolverhampton factory of Boulton Paul Aircraft Ltd, to whom sub-assemblies such as complete tail units were supplied by General Aircraft Ltd, Hanworth.

There were no special prototypes, and the first Roc, L3057, made its first flight in the hands of Blackburn test pilot Flt Lt H. J. Wilson on 23 December 1938. Testing of subsequent production aircraft was the responsibility of Boulton Paul's chief test pilot Flt Lt Feather, later assisted by R. Lindsay-Neale who joined him in February 1940.

L3057 went first to Brough for contractor's trials and in March 1939 to the A. & A.E.E., Martlesham, together with the next two aircraft, L3058 and L3059, so that handling and armament trials might proceed simultaneously. The latter were conducted between March and May 1939 using L3058 equipped with the prototype Mk II turret, rotation of which had little effect on the aircraft's flying characteristics. Although not an outstanding aerobatic aeroplane, the Roc could, like the Skua, be held steady in a steep dive without difficulty by means of the dive brakes. Performance was undoubtedly impaired by the weight and drag of the turret, and it is probable that comparative tests with L3057 and L3059 at Martlesham with the 12 ft diameter de Havilland Type 5/8 airscrew prescribed for the Roc and the 11 ft 6 in diameter Type 5/10 used on the Skua were first steps towards seeking an improvement.

When Martlesham closed on 19 September 1939, L3058 was flown to

Boscombe Down, Hants., new home of the A. & A.E.E., in a further search for better performance using a specially-built airscrew. This consisted of a standard Skua hub with blades from the type of airscrew normally fitted to Armstrong Siddeley Tiger engines in Whitleys, but this device proved ineffective.

Roc Floatplanes

Unlike the Skua fighter/dive-bomber which was purely a landplane for shore or carrier operation, the Roc was intended from the outset to meet Specification 26/36 for a twin-float seaplane fighter. Trials machines L3057 and L3059 were therefore sent to the Blackburn factory at Dumbarton in October 1939 to be fitted with the first two seaplane conversion sets. These were built to Specification 20/37 and consisted of Alclad covers for the wheel wells and Blackburn Shark interchangeable Alclad floats mounted on close-set N struts amidships and single front struts with spreader bar. As on the Shark, water rudders were operated pneumatically from the aircraft's normal braking system and the tail wheels were removed and replaced by mooring rings. At this stage the original all-silver colour scheme gave way to camouflaged upper surfaces with duck egg blue on the lower half of the fuselage and under the starboard mainplane, the underside of the port wing being black.

Transfer of the A. & A.E.E. to Boscombe Down coincided with a similar move by the M.A.E.E. from Felixstowe to Helensburgh, only 10 miles or so down the Clyde from the Dumbarton factory. Tests there with L3059 during November 1939 showed marked directional instability and it crashed just after

The ill-fated Roc seaplane L3059 at Helensburgh in November 1939, showing the wing-folding mechanism.

413

take-off on 3 December. Tests on the other machine, L3057, were therefore initiated in April 1940 to see if stability could be improved by means of additional fin area below the tailplane. Without the lower fin, turns at low altitude were hazardous, but after modification the aircraft was much more stable, although care was still needed if inward sideslip was to be avoided in low turns. Behaviour was normal in all other respects, both in the air and on the water, and in June 1940 take-off runs made from Loch Lomond and from the Clyde to compare the unstick times from fresh and salt water, showed little difference between the two.

A third Roc, L3060, also mounted on floats, was short-lived and ended its days as scrap at No. 49 MU, Horsham, in March 1940. Even L3057 itself, first of all the Rocs, faired little better and was relegated to the role of instructional airframe at No. 6 School of Technical Training, Hednesford, at the end of the year. A fourth seaplane conversion kit, despatched to the Hawker factory at Kingston-on-Thames, arrived on 26 April 1940 for experimental fitment to a Hurricane for the Norwegian campaign. Flight trials scheduled for June 1940 were cancelled when British forces were withdrawn from Norway.

The Roc's potential as a target tug was investigated at Helensburgh between March and September 1942 with seaplane L3174 fitted with Type B Mk IIA wind-driven winch in place of the turret and a metal container under the fuselage to carry two 3-ft diameter sleeve targets or three of the 5 ft 5 in flag type. It proved a useful tug capable of streaming its target on 6,000 ft of cable and flying at 10,000 ft, and a number of Rocs were used in this form as landplanes at Air Gunnery Schools.

Service use

Preparations for the Roc's entry into squadron service began in the usual way in April 1939 when the fifth production machine, L3061, was delivered

The second Roc seaplane, L3057, with enlarged under-fin.

414

A Roc fitted with the optional 70-gallon long-range tank.

to the Central Flying School, Upavon, for familiarization flying. This machine and four others, L3065–L3068, then went to Worthy Down for similar use by No. 800 Squadron, and three more, L3062–L3064, were issued to No. 803 Squadron, while at the same time L3141 was evaluated by No. 778 Service Trials Unit at Lee-on-Solent. But No. 800 was destined not to receive Rocs, the first of the type put into service being four landplanes which joined the eight Skuas of No. 806 Squadron at Eastleigh in February 1940. Six others joined the six Skuas of No. 801 Squadron at Hatston, Orkney, in June 1940, but the whole idea of four guns brought to bear in broadside attacks on enemy aircraft proved a failure. Thus the Roc's front-line service lasted only a few months and all production ceased in August 1940. Although intended for carrier operation, Rocs flew only from shore stations and never made a deck landing. No. 806 Squadron's Skuas and Rocs were replaced by Fairey Fulmar Is in July 1940 and No. 801 was re-armed with Hawker Sea Hurricanes in August 1941.

The majority of Rocs were delivered direct from Wolverhampton to RAF Maintenance Units for distribution to second-line FAA squadrons, the chief user being No. 2 Anti-Aircraft Co-operation Unit at Gosport where at least 16 Rocs joined the unit's Skuas in June 1940, replacing Sharks. On 16 August L3131 and L3162 were damaged beyond repair at dispersal as a result of dive-bombing attacks by German Junkers Ju 87s after which four Rocs were pressed into use as machine-gun posts placed strategically round the aerodrome with turrets permanently manned. The type was used also in sea searches for the survivors of sinking ships and aircraft in the Channel, and several were detached to Coastal Command at Detling, Kent, for similar duties in the Straits of Dover between 11 June and 3 July 1941.

Two aircraft, L3120 and L3161, were allotted to No. 22 (Army Co-Operation) Group and L3123 went to No. 102 MU, Abu Sueir. In 1940 many were added to fleets of miscellaneous aircraft operated by No. 759 Fighter School, Yeovilton; No. 760 Fighter Pool, Eastleigh; No. 769 Squadron, Donibristle; No. 792 Target Towing Unit, St Merryn; and Nos 772 and 773 Fighter Reconnaissance Units at Machrihanish and in Bermuda respectively.

L3087 is known to have survived until 21 July 1943 when it flew a Speke–Hooton–Woodvale round trip, and L3183 was at HMS *Phoenix*, RAF Fayid, in November 1942, but the last two Rocs in service appear to have been L3082 and L3072 which served with Nos. 1622 and 1623 Flights at Gosport and Roborough respectively until withdrawn from use through lack of spares in August 1943. Wearing black and yellow towing stripes, the wingless hulk of L3084 still stood in the long grass at Eastleigh in 1946 having been used for test running Perseus XII engines driving a four-bladed fan with wire-braced annular protecting ring in place of the airscrew.

SPECIFICATION AND DATA

Designers: Blackburn Aircraft Ltd, Brough Aerodrome, East Yorks.

Manufacturers: Boulton Paul Aircraft Ltd, Wolverhampton Aerodrome, Staffs.

Power Plant: One 890 hp Bristol Perseus XII

Dimensions: Span 46 ft 0 in   (folded) 15 ft 6 in
            Length 35 ft 7 in (seaplane) 39 ft 4 in
            Height 12 ft 1 in Wing area 310 sq ft

Weights and Performance:

	Landplane	Seaplane	
		Fighter	Target Tug
Tare weight	6,124 lb	—	—
Military load	870 lb	790 lb	—
All-up weight	7,950 lb	8,670 lb	8,670 lb
Speed at 10,000 ft	223 mph	193 mph	108 mph*
Speed at sea level	194 mph	170 mph	110 mph*
Cruising speed	135 mph	135 mph	—
Initial climb	1,500 ft/min	1,130 ft/min	—
Service ceiling	18,000 ft	14,600 ft	—
Endurance	6 hr	4½ hr	2 hr
Maximum range	810 miles	810 miles	—

* With target streamed.

416

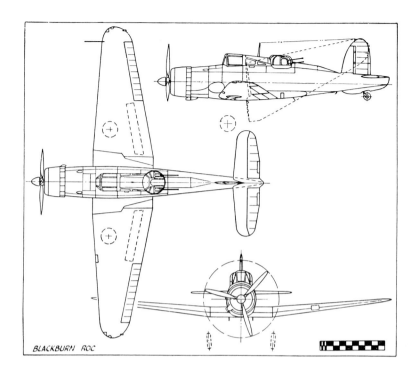

BLACKBURN ROC

Production:

One hundred and thirty-six aircraft, L3057–L3192, ordered 28 April 1937 under Contract 632260/37. All delivered from Wolverhampton on the first date given.

L3057 first flown 23 December 1938, to Blackburns Brough 7 February 1939, to Martlesham March 1939, to Helensburgh October 1939, to No. 6 S. of T.T. Hednesford 31 December 1940; L3058 to Martlesham 1 March 1939, to Boscombe Down September 1939; L3059 to Martlesham 13 March 1939, to Helensburgh October 1939, crashed 3 December 1939.

L3060 to Blackburns 20 March 1939 for seaplane conversion, to No. 49 MU Horsham 2 March 1940; L3061 to CFS Upavon 4 April 1939, to No. 800 Sqn Worthy Down 24 May 1939; L3062 to No. 803 Sqn Worthy Down 4 May 1939, to No. 2 AACU Gosport 1 November 1940; L3063–L3064 to No. 803 Sqn 19 and 22 May 1939 respectively; L3065–L3068 to No. 800 Sqn Worthy Down between 19 June 1939 and 10 July 1939; L3069 to Martlesham 26 June 1939, accident 25 September 1940, scrapped at site by Blackburns 3 October 1940.

L3070 to No. 10 MU Hullavington 29 June 1939, to No. 769 Sqn Donibristle, s.o.c. 7 November 1944; L3071 to No. 10 MU Hullavington 4 July 1939, to No. 2 AACU Gosport, struck gang mower landing Gosport 30 July 1941; L3072 to No. 10 MU Hullavington 7 July 1939, to No. 2 AACU Gosport, to No. 1623 Flt Roborough, s.o.c. 14 February 1943; L3073 to No. 6 MU Brize Norton 7 July 1939, to No. 759 Fighter School Yeovilton; L3074 to No. 6 MU Brize Norton 10 July 1939; L3075 to No. 6 MU Brize Norton 14 July 1939, to No. 2 AACU Gosport, forced landed on

417

Portsmouth Aerodrome 28 May 1941; L3076 to No. 5 MU Kemble 26 July 1939; L3077 to No. 5 MU Kemble 22 August 1939, to RNAS Donibristle 21 March 1941.

L3078–L3081 to No. 5 MU Kemble between 29 July 1939 and 3 August 1939, to No. 769 Sqn Donibristle; L3082 to No. 20 MU Aston Down 4 July 1939, to No. 2 AACU Gosport 1 November 1940, undercarriage collapse at Gosport 3 January 1941. to A Flt No. 2 AACU Gosport 27 July 1941, to No. 1622 Flt Gosport, s.o.c. 14 February 1943; L3083 to No. 27 MU Shawbury 5 August 1939; L3084 to No. 27 MU Shawbury 31 August 1939, converted to target tug; L3085 to No. 2 AACU Gosport 16 August 1940, crashed at Gosport after striking balloon cable 8 April 1941, scrapped at site by Blackburns 12 April 1941; L3086–L3088 to No. 19 MU St Athan between 24 and 31 August 1939; L3089 to Blackburns Brough 4 September 1939 for installation of ciné camera target marking gear, to Boscombe Down June 1940.

L3090–L3092 to No. 9 MU Cosford between 5 and 11 September 1939, to RNAS Worthy Down; L3093 to No. 9 MU Cosford 23 July 1940, to RNAS Worthy Down; L3094–L3097 to No. 24 MU Ternhill between 18 and 22 September 1939, to FAA October 1939; L3098–L3100 to No. 8 MU Little Rissington 25 September 1939.

L3101–L3104 to No. 20 MU Aston Down between 8 and 18 October 1939, to FAA October 1939; L3105 to No. 20 MU Aston Down 18 October 1939, later coded L6R; L3106–L3107 to No. 20 MU Aston Down 18 October 1939 as reserve aircraft; L3108–L3109 to No. 20 MU Aston Down 23 October 1940, to No. 2 AACU Gosport 1 November 1940.

L3110–L3111 to No. 5 MU Kemble 24 October 1939 as reserve aircraft; L3114 to No. 24 MU Ternhill 7 November 1939, to RNAS Donibristle coded E; L3115 to No. 24 MU Ternhill 7 November 1939; L3116–L3117 to RNAS Donibristle 9 November 1939; L3118 to RNAS Donibristle 9 November 1939, coded O; L3119 to No. 5 MU Kemble 13 November 1939, to Lee-on-Solent 10 March 1941.

L3120 to No. 5 MU Kemble 13 November 1939, to No. 22 A.C. Group, s.o.c. 12 November 1940; L3121 to No. 5 MU Kemble 1 December 1939; L3122 to No. 5 MU Kemble 1 December 1939, accident 29 August 1940, to Blackburns Brough 17 September 1940, to No. 11 S. of T.T. Hereford as instructional airframe 30 January 1941; L3123 to No. 10 MU Hullavington 29 November 1939, to No. 102 MU Abu Sueir 27 March 1941; L3124–L3125 to No. 10 MU Hullavington 29 November 1939;

Roc L3089 with catalytic engine heater and special light-weight cupola for ciné camera operator, June 1940.

418

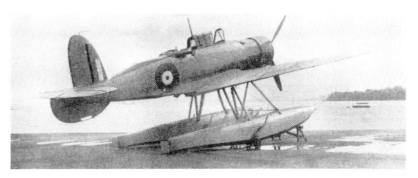

Roc seaplane L3174 with turret replaced by the wind-driven target towing winch.

L3126 to No. 12 MU Kirkbride 14 December 1939, to No. 2 AACU Gosport 1940, crashed in the sea off Gosport 1 August 1941; L3127 to No. 12 MU Kirkbride 14 December 1939, to No. 2 AACU Gosport 1940, belly landing Lee-on-Solent 7 November 1940; L3128 to No. 12 MU Kirkbride 14 December 1939, to Blackburns Brough 17 September 1940; L3129 to No. 12 MU Kirkbride 14 December 1939, to No. 2 AACU Gosport, accident 23 July 1940, to RNAS Donibristle 13 April 1941, to No. 2 AACU Gosport.

L3130 to No. 12 MU Kirkbride 15 January 1940; L3131 to No. 12 MU Kirkbride 14 December 1939, to No. 2 AACU Gosport, damaged by enemy action 16 August 1940, to No. 50 MU Oxford 17 September 1940, to Blackburns Brough 20 September 1940, to Donibristle Station Flt 26 February 1941; L3132 to No. 6 MU Brize Norton 16 December 1939, to No. 1 OTU Silloth 31 August 1940, to Donibristle Station Flt 7 December 1940, scrapped at Blackburns 24 July 1941; L3133–L3136 to No. 6 MU Brize Norton between 16 December 1939 and 16 January 1940; L3137–L3140 to No. 5 MU Kemble between 30 December 1939 and 16 January 1940.

L3141 to No. 5 MU Kemble 16 December 1939, to No. 778 Service Trials Unit Lee-on-Solent; L3142 to No. 10 MU Hullavington 19 January 1940; L3143 to No. 10 MU Hullavington 1 March 1940, to No. 2 AACU Gosport 21 March 1940, crashed at Gosport 11 October 1940; L3144–L3145 to No. 10 MU Hullavington 1 and 5 March 1940 respectively; L3146 to No. 10 MU Hullavington 5 March 1940, to No. 2 AACU Gosport 16 July 1940; L3147–L3148 to No. 12 MU Kirkbride 1 March 1940; L3149 to No. 12 MU Kirkbride 1 March 1940, to No. 2 AACU Gosport, damaged landing at Thorney Island 3 April 1941.

L3150–L3153 to No. 6 MU Brize Norton 24 February 1940; L3154 to No. 5 MU Kemble 1 March 1940; L3155 to No. 5 MU Kemble, to RNAS Donibristle coded I; L3156–L3157 to No. 52 MU Cardiff 1 and 9 March 1940 respectively; L3158–L3160 to No. 10 MU Hullavington between 9 and 21 March 1940.

L3161 to No. 10 MU Hullavington 21 March 1940, to No. 22 A.C. Group; L3162 to No. 12 MU Kirkbride 28 March 1940, to No. 2 AACU Gosport 13 June 1940, damaged by enemy action 16 August 1940, to No. 50 MU Oxford 16 September 1940; L3163–L3165 to No. 12 MU Kirkbride 5 and 6 April 1940 respectively; L3166–L3168 to No. 6 MU Brize Norton 10, 13 and 15 April 1940 respectively; L3169–L3170 to No. 23 MU Aldergrove 23 April 1940.

L3171 to No. 8 MU Little Rissington 3 June 1940; L3172 to No. 2 AACU Gosport 7 May 1940, crashed at Binfield Rd. Portsmouth 24 October 1940; L3173 to No. 2

AACU Gosport 7 May 1940; L3174 to No. 8 MU Little Rissington 9 May 1940, to Helensburgh for seaplane target tug trials March 1942; L3175 to No. 8 MU Little Rissington 9 May 1940, to No. 2 AACU Gosport 9 May 1941, struck hangar at Gosport 2 July 1941, scrapped at site by Blackburns Brough 6 August 1941; L3176–L3178 to No. 8 MU Little Rissington 23 May 1940 and 3 June 1940; L3179 to No. 8 MU Little Rissington 3 June 1940, to No. 2 AACU Gosport, crashed on take-off 29 May 1941.

L3180–L3187 to No. 8 MU Little Rissington between 3 and 19 June 1940; L3188–L3189 to No. 6 MU Brize Norton 24 June 1940 and 22 July 1940; L3190 to No. 6 MU Brize Norton 10 August 1940, to D Flt No. 2 AACU Donibristle; L3191 to No. 6 MU Brize Norton 13 August 1940; L3192 to No. 6 MU Brize Norton 19 August 1940, to D Flt No. 2 AACU Donibristle.

A late production Roc, L3186, in camouflage and training-yellow in May 1940.

Service use:
No. 801 Squadron, Hatston; No. 806 Squadron, Eastleigh; A Flt No. 2 AACU Gosport; D Flt No. 2 AACU, Donibristle; No. 759 Fighter School, Yeovilton; No. 760 Fighter Pool, Eastleigh; No. 769 Squadron, Donibristle; No. 772 FRU, Machrihanish; No. 773 FRU, Bermuda; No. 778 Service Trials Unit, Lee-on-Solent; No. 792 Airborne Target Towing Unit, St Merryn; No. 1622 Flight, Gosport; No. 1623 Flight, Roborough.

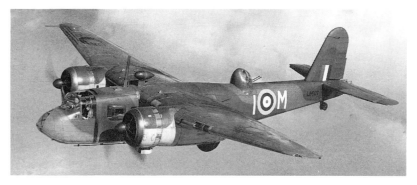

Botha I L6507 of No. 3 S. of G.R., Squires Gate, bearing the coding of its No. 1 training squadron. Delivered direct from Dumbarton on 24 January 1941, it was eventually scrapped in July 1943. (*Flight Photo 18136S.*)

Blackburn B-26 Botha I

M.15/35 was an extremely exacting Specification issued by the Air Ministry in September 1935 for a three-seat, land-based, twin-engined reconnaissance bomber with internal stowage for a torpedo. It was intended for the re-equipment of Coastal Command, and attracted proposals by Blackburn Aircraft Ltd and the Bristol Aeroplane Co Ltd which were accepted early in 1936, both designs employing 850 hp Bristol Perseus sleeve-valve radial engines. At a late stage, however, the Air Ministry decided that a crew of four was essential, and both companies produced modified designs, with enlarged fuselages, around which an amended Specification 10/36 was written to enable them to be ordered in quantity straight from the drawing board. They were named after General Botha and the Duke of Beaufort, respectively, but there has long been speculation about the pronunciation of the name allotted to the Blackburn machine. Correctly the 'o' is long as in 'oat', for in Afrikaans the word is pronounced 'Boater'; whereas 'Boather', introducing the 'th' sound as in 'myth', is the accepted English form.

In enlarged four-seat configuration, it was evident that with Perseus engines both types would be slower and have an all-round performance inferior to that envisaged in 1935. The Bristol Beaufort consequently entered Coastal Command service with two 1,130 hp Bristol Taurus radials, but supplies of this engine were limited and none was available for the Botha programme. The Blackburn company consequently submitted proposals for a variant designated B-27 Botha II using two large Bristol Hercules radials, but this suggestion was turned down. Following the placing of contracts for 442 Botha I aircraft in December 1936, tooling began for simultaneous production at Brough and Dumbarton, backed up by large-

421

scale component manufacture at the Olympia Works in Leeds. Unfortunately, the end product of this large organization remained underpowered throughout its Service life.

In order to give crews the best possible downward view on convoy duty or when on the look-out for enemy shipping, the Botha was arranged as a high-wing cantilever monoplane and was one of the first Service aircraft to have adequate space in the pilot's cabin, with well-planned instrument and control layout. The engines and nacelles cut off all sideways and rearward visibility, but in all forward directions the pilot had an exceptional field of view. Wireless operator and navigator were accommodated in a midships cabin reached through an entrance door with built-in step-ladder on the starboard side. It opened into a narrow gangway along which the navigator could reach both the pilot and the prone bombing position in the nose. The fourth crew member manned an egg-shaped power-driven gun turret situated behind the wing and reached from the rear of the cabin.

The front fuselage was essentially similar to that of the Skua and covered with flush-riveted Alclad plating, but the rear part was a metal skinned tubular metal structure. Rudder, elevator and ailerons were fabric covered. The parallel-chord centre section housed the main fuel tanks, two of which contained 146 gallons each at normal load and the third 132½ gallons, but for

Two views of the first Blackburn Botha, L6104, showing the inset elevator.

special operations this could be increased from a total of 435¾ gallons (including the 11¼-gallon distributor tank) to 565¾ gallons. The centre section also carried the hydraulically-operated trailing edge split flaps, the engine nacelles and the sharply tapered outer wing panels. These were set at a large dihedral angle and carried balanced ailerons.

Fin and tailplane were unbraced cantilevers of stressed-skin metal construction with the elevator projecting aft of the rudder as on the Skua and Roc. The undercarriage consisted of two oleo-pneumatic legs which retracted backwards into the nacelles until spring-loaded doors closed round the wheels. Hydraulic brakes were operated by a hand lever on the control column.

In production form, the Botha I was powered by 880 hp Bristol Perseus Xs enclosed in wide-chord cowlings with controllable cooling gills and driving de Havilland Type 5/11 Hydromatic three-bladed, constant-speed airscrews. Armament consisted of one pilot's forward-firing ·303-in Vickers gun and two Lewis guns in the rear turret. Alternative war loads were one Mk XII or Mk XIV torpedo (or one 2,000-lb bomb); four 250-lb bombs (or two 500-lb); or one 500-lb bomb (or two 250-lb) carried in a special cell inside the fuselage with hydraulically-operated bomb doors which were removed if the torpedo or 2,000-lb bomb were carried. Additional bomb racks could be attached to the mainplane outboard of the nacelles. The Botha's operational equipment also included full marine gear and collapsible dinghy with inflation bottle.

The first production Botha, L6104, which also served in lieu of a separate prototype, first flew at Brough on 28 December 1938 in the hands of the company's chief test pilot Flt Lt H. Bailey and was sent to the A. & A.E.E., Martlesham, on 25 March 1939 for performance and handling trials. These revealed inadequate elevator control which was cured on the second trials aircraft, L6105, first flown on 7 June 1939, by slightly increasing the tailplane area and fitting a large horn balanced elevator in place of the small inset type used previously. L6104 therefore returned to Brough in May 1939 as a trial installations vehicle for modifications. It was re-delivered to the A. & A.E.E. at Boscombe Down on 30 November and eventually despatched to St Athan as an instructional airframe in July 1940, joining L6105 which had arrived in the previous May after armament trials at Martlesham and Boscombe Down. The third aircraft, L6106, was delivered to the Central Flying School, Upavon, for instructor familiarization on 3 September 1939.

Although underpowered, it was still hoped at this stage that the Botha might be used for torpedo work, and two aircraft, L6107 and L6110, were delivered to the Torpedo Development Unit, Gosport, on 23 September and 2 December 1939 respectively. They were joined by the first two Dumbarton-built machines, L6347 (coded M) and L6348, on 26 October and 20 November, but the former remained only a few days before being flown to Boscombe Down for its handling characteristics to be compared with standard Brough-built products, in this case L6105 and L6109, from which it was found not noticeably different.

L6347 was replaced at Gosport by L6111 on 1 December for mine-laying experiments which terminated when the machine crashed into the sea off Spit Fort on 24 February 1940. Torpedo trials began with L6110 but, when enemy activity increased in the area, it was disposed of to No. 3 School of Technical Training, Blackpool, for instructional purposes.

L6109 later went to No. 770 Squadron, RNAS, Crail, for marine equipment proving, but L6108 was wrecked when it flew into a house while overshooting at Filton in bad weather on 22 December 1939 while in service with No. 2 Ferry Flight.

First delivery to the RAF was made on 12 December when the third Dumbarton-built Botha L6349 was flown from Abbotsinch to No. 5 MU, Kemble, there joined on the 27th by Brough-built L6112. Both were sent immediately to the TDU, Gosport, where they were coded O and L respectively, and such was the efficiency of the Blackburn production planning that Brough and Dumbarton reached peak production together six months later, in June 1940, when a total of 58 Bothas left the factories. Unfortunately this achievement was marred by a number of fatal accidents during factory

Dumbarton-built Botha I L6463, with horn-balanced elevator, in use at Filton as a Perseus engine test bed in 1941. (*Bristol Photo.*)

and RAF Maintenance Unit test flights, the first on 5 March 1940 when L6129, which had been retained at Brough to supplement L6104 on the modification programme, plunged to earth on the opposite side of the Humber at Flixborough, Lincs., with the loss of veteran test pilot B. R. Rolfe and his flight test observer. L6377 and L6390 shared the same fate at Abbotsinch on 26 May and 12 June, while another, L6205, was lost at Brough on 8 July.

If the reason for these accidents was ever established, it was certainly never disclosed, with the result that many harsh things have been said of the Botha for more than a quarter of a century. It must be remembered, however, that in wartime the loss of a handful of machines from a very large production run was of little consequence when viewed against the background of the tens of thousands of hours of punishing operational and instructional flying completed during the period 1940 to 1944. In an all-out war effort of this magnitude even the losses at the Schools cannot be considered excessive.

The ill-fated L6129 was replaced by L6133, and a third, L6143, was also retained at Brough to be prepared for tropical trials at Aden, but in fact this machine was despatched instead to No. 47 MU, Sealand, on 27 July 1940 for packing and shipment to Khartoum. By this time the Bristol company was providing some of the extra power the Botha I so badly needed with deliveries of a developed engine giving 930 hp and known as the Perseus XA, the first aircraft so powered being L6155. As it would have been pointless to conduct tropical trials with the lower-powered Botha, L6232 was substituted and consigned to Takoradi via Sealand en route to Khartoum but, as related later in this section, when the Botha was relegated to training, the Khartoum project was dropped and the machine in question was issued to No. 2 Bombing and Gunnery School, Millom.

Performance testing of the Perseus XA powered Botha was undertaken with Dumbarton-built L6212, ferried from Kirkbride to Boscombe Down for the purpose on 16 August 1940. This machine was also the first to have non-retractable bulge-type navigator's windows on each side of the fuselage. Other modifications introduced during production included a jettisonable main entrance door, first fitted to L6235, new-type flap jacks introduced on the first Dumbarton Perseus XA machine L6378 and improved undercarriage retraction and up-lock mechanism, commencing at L6421. Experiments conducted at Boscombe Down in October 1941 with 12-ft diameter airscrews borrowed from a Handley Page Hampden on L6188, and, at night in December 1942, with Bristol Hercules type flame dampers on L6325, were not successful.

Service use

First issues began on 3 June 1940 when four Bothas, L6107, L6123, L6124 and L6126 were delivered from No. 22 MU to No. 1 Operational Training Unit, Silloth, via Brough, in readiness for the introduction of the Botha into squadron service, and within a few months this unit had received 25 machines. First trainees came from No. 608 (North Riding) Squadron, then operating at Thornaby with Coastal Command, to which a first allocation of three Bothas, L6164-L6166, was delivered on 28 June to replace Avro Ansons on North Sea shipping patrols. With seven others (L6170-L6174, L6188 and L6388) received on 5 July, they were the first Blackburn aircraft to equip a land-based RAF squadron since the Kangaroos of No. 246 Squadron in 1918.

Wg Cdr Shaw, P/O Washington and P/O Tucker flew the first patrols on 10 August 1940 in L6173, L6170 and L6190 respectively, and during the next three months there were only 12 days on which the squadron's Bothas were grounded by bad weather. Airborne times were often as much as 4–5 hours but, although there are recorded instances of the squadron's Ansons being attacked by enemy aircraft, the Bothas were given no opportunity of gaining battle honours.

All told, a total of 30 Bothas was delivered to Thornaby, only one of which was lost—L6165 posted missing on 31 August. Alphabetical code letters allotted to 17 aircraft and listed on page 432, are used to present a complete survey of all Botha operational sorties, but, despite the impressive number of hours flown, the fall of France and the invasion of the Low Countries and Scandinavia ended the requirement for machines such as the Botha, and Ansons were gradually re-introduced. Last Botha sorties were flown on 6 November 1940 in L6209 (Sgt Burton) and L6198 (P/O Keates) after which the aircraft were dispersed to MUs and relegated to training. Blackburn's contracts were at once cut back, and production terminated at the 200th Dumbarton machine, L6546, in June 1941 and at the 380th Brough-built aircraft, W5169, in May 1942. Total Botha production was thus 580, with 676 cancellations.

The re-equipment of No. 502 (County of Ulster) Squadron, begun in August 1940 with the delivery of L6228, L6229 and L6231, was likewise cancelled and the aircraft handed over to No. 1 OTU, Silloth. During the rest of the war the only other Botha aircraft issued to squadrons were L6128 used for communications by No. 24 Squadron, Hendon, from May 1941 to October 1942; L6156 by No. 301 (Polish) Squadron August 1941 to May 1942; and L6114 by No. 304 (Polish) Squadron, Chedburgh, briefly in June 1943.

First of the second-line units to fly Bothas was No. 3 School of General Reconnaissance at Squires Gate, Blackpool, which trained Coastal and Bomber Command aircrews, work for which the machine was well suited since it had many of the characteristics of more advanced Service aeroplanes. From the arrival of the first machine in November 1940 until the type was withdrawn from Service three years later, No. 3 S. of G.R. had over 100 Bothas on charge. They were camouflaged and had training yellow undersides. The scale of the School's activities is now difficult to visualise, but the density of its Botha traffic would certainly cause a major control problem today, some 2,803 Botha hours being flown in April 1942 alone. Of the several fatal accidents, the worst occurred on 27 August 1941 when Boulton Paul Defiant N1745 collided with L6509 while making firing passes near Blackpool Tower, the wreckage crashing through the roof of the Central Station.

During 1941–43 hundreds of Botha aircraft were distributed to bombing, gunnery, navigation, radio and flying schools in Northern Ireland, Scotland, the Isle of Man, and Central and Northern England, as listed at the end of this section. Their withdrawal from squadron service limited their usefulness at flying training schools; 12 allotted to No. 3 (Pilot) Advanced Flying Unit, South Cerney, and 14 to No. 6 (P) AFU, Little Rissington, were never used but remained picketed in dispersal fields until taken away again by Air Transport Auxiliary pilots.

Staff pilots flew the Bothas at training schools, a typical example being No. 2 Bombing and Gunnery School, Millom, which opened with L6112, L6118 and L6262 flown in from No. 22 MU, Silloth, on 25 January 1941, this unit eventually having nearly 80 machines. No. 3 Air Observers' Navigation School, Bobbington, was less fortunate; initially its machines had to be kept

A late production Brough-built Botha I, W5065, with non-retractable navigator's window aft of the pilot. It served with No. 3 S. of G.R., Squires Gate, from April 1942 to July 1943.

at Cosford (including the first, L6466, collected from No. 33 MU, Lyneham, by Sqn Ldr R. B. Pakenham on 4 April 1941) due to unserviceability of the aerodrome and, later, maintenance difficulties with its 25 Bothas led to their replacement by Avro Ansons after only three months.

In common with nearly all other schools, No. 2 B. and G.S. lost a number of Bothas through the abrasive action of sand which caused engine failure in the air or, at best, excessive oil consumption. Continual replacement of these engines by reconditioned units, sent by rail from Filton or the BOAC engine shops at Pontypridd, made it difficult to maintain training schedules, and working parties were sent from the MUs in mid-1941 to fit all the Perseus engines with filter units. This reduced the failures at No. 2 B. and G.S., for example, from 21 in June 1941 to negligible numbers by the end of the year.

No. 3 Radio School, which boasted two Bellman hangars at Prestwick and received its first two Bothas L6178 and L6276 on 25 March 1941, introduced Air to Surface Vessel radar training in May 1942 using large numbers of ASV-equipped Bothas, first of which were L6158 and L6168. This unit re-formed as No. 11 Radio School on 1 December 1942 and ferried all its Bothas to a new base at Hooton Park Aerodrome, Wirral, Cheshire. The scale of its operations rivalled even those of No. 3 S. of G.R. at Squires Gate a little further north, 15 Bothas airborne together exciting little comment. The highest recorded number in the area at one time was 24, engaged on direction-finding flights on 26 March 1943. Unlike the Squires Gate machines, which were lettered 1-A, 1-B, etc., those of No. 11 R.S. were coded numerically from 1 to about 52.

Towards the end of 1942 a number of time-expired airframes were made available to Schools of Technical Training where they were used as instructional airframes or, with outer wing panels removed, for teaching engine starting and running procedures. The majority of Bothas, however, flew incessantly until declared obsolete in August 1943 and were then broken up on site or flown back to Blackburn Aircraft at Abbotsinch to be reduced to

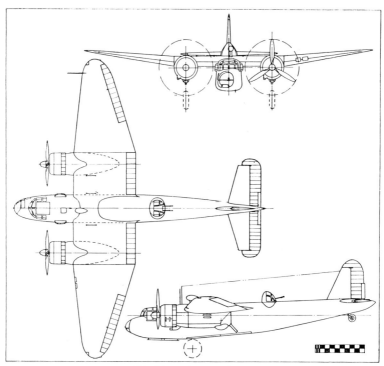

Blackburn B-26 Botha I.

produce at Paisley, or to Sherburn-in-Elmet where they met a similar fate. No. 11 R.S. was exceptional in keeping its Bothas until they were replaced by Avro Ansons in April 1944, and their last machine W5073 was not ferried to Sherburn until 23 September that year, having flown 916 hr 30 min.

Despite the variety of uses to which the ubiquitous Botha was put, it remained unchanged externally except in the case of a few aircraft issued to the Target Towing Unit at Abbotsinch. These had winch gear in place of the rear turret in the manner of the Roc and were designated Botha T.T.Mk I.

SPECIFICATION AND DATA

Manufacturers: Blackburn Aircraft Ltd., Olympia Works, Roundhay Road, Leeds; Brough Aerodrome, East Yorks.; Dumbarton, Dunbartonshire, and Abbotsinch Aerodrome, Renfrewshire.

Power Plants: (B-26 Botha I) Two 880 hp Bristol Perseus X
Two 930 hp Bristol Perseus XA
(B–27 Botha II project)
Two 1,400 hp Bristol Hercules III

Dimensions: Span 59 ft 0 in   Length 51 ft 0½ in
Height 14 ft 7½ in Wing area 518 sq ft

428

Weights and Performance:

	Perseux X	Perseus XA
Tare weight	11,830 lb	12,036 lb
All-up weight	17,628 lb	18,450 lb
Speed at sea level	—	209 mph
Speed at 15,000 ft	253 mph	220 mph
Initial climb	820 ft/min	985 ft/min
Climb at 15,000 ft	740 ft/min	355 ft/min
Absolute ceiling	24,900 ft	19,700 ft
Service ceiling	23,600 ft	18,400 ft
Range	—	1,270 miles

Production: (a) *380 Botha I aircraft at Brough to Specification G.10/36*
(i) Two hundred and forty-two aircraft built under Contract 563935/36:

Works Orders	RAF serials	Total
7860/1 to 7860/25	L6104–L6128	25
7862/1 to 7862/25	L6129–L6153	25
7864/1 to 7864/50	L6154–L6203	50
7866/1 to 7866/50	L6204–L6253	50
7868/1 to 7868/50	L6254–L6303	50
7870/1 to 7870/42	L6304–L6345	42
		Total 242

(ii) One hundred and thirty-eight aircraft built under Contract 69254/40:

Works Orders	RAF serials	Total
3240/1 to 3240/138	W5017–W5056	40
	W5065–W5114	50
	W5118–W5157	40
	W5162–W5169	8
		Total 138

(b) *200 Botha I aircraft at Dumbarton to Specification G.10/36 under Contract 583994/36*

Works Orders	RAF serials	Total
Dumbarton 13	L6347–L6371	25
„ 15	L6372–L6396	25
„ 17	L6397–L6421	25
„ 19	L6422–L6446	25
„ 21	L6447–L6471	25
„ 23	L6472–L6496	25
„ 25	L6497–L6521	25
„ 27	L6522–L6546	25
		Total 200

(c) *Cancelled orders*

RAF serials			Total
L6547–L6590			44
W5170–W5211,	W5216–W5235,	W5239–W5288,	
W5296–W5315			132
W7247–W7296,	W7300–W7339,	W7343–W7362,	
W7368–W7379,	W7382–W7409		150
W9396–W9415,	W9434–W9463,	W9469–W9545,	
W9558–W9597,	W9646–W9665,	W9702–W9741,	
W9748–W9772,	W9821–W9855,	W9880–W9899,	
W9936–W9975,	X1000–X1029		350
		Total	676

Delivery: (a) *ex Brough*

Month	Number completed	Latest delivery	A. & A.E.E., Boscombe Down	CFS, Upavon	TDU, Gosport	No. 5 MU, Kemble	No. 12 MU, Kirkbride	No. 19 MU, St Athan	No. 22 MU, Silloth	No. 23 MU, Aldergrove	No. 24 MU, Ternhill	No. 33 MU, Lyneham	No. 48 MU, Hawarden	Blackburns, Brough	RAE, Farnborough	No. 3 S. of G.R., Squires Gate	No. 2 B. & G.S., Millom	No. 4 AGS, Morpeth	No. 3(P) AFU, Sth. Cerney
October 1939	4	L6108	1	1	2														
November	2	L6109	2																
December	6	L6115			2	2	1	1											
January 1940	4	L6119					1		3										
February	3	L6122					3												
March	10	L6135		1			3		4							2			
April	19	L6152					10		9										
May	16	L6168					2		8		4					2			
June	32	L6185					9	14	4	1						3	1		
July	22	L6231					4	8	4	3						3			
August	31	L6252					11	7		2						10	1		
September	20	L6273					1		8	1		6				4			
October	12	L6287						3		5		4							
November	15	L6300					3	3		6		2	1						
December	15	L6314	1				2			6			6						
January 1941	9	L6323											9						
February	11	L6335											8	3					
March	16	W5020					4		5	3			4						
April	10	W5031					5	1					4						
May	9	W5039					5	4											
June	6	W5046						4										2	
July	nil																		
August	18	W5072					8	2					8						
September	9	W5081						2					7						
October	8	W5090											8						
November	10	W5099					2						8						
December	9	W5108							2				7						
January 1942	11	W5123						8				3							
February	10	W5132						8				2							
March	9	W5141					7		2										
April	12	W5153					3											9	
May	12	W5169					2	1	3	3								1	2
Total	380		4	2	4	2	84	63	57	30	4	17	71*	3	1	24	2	10	2

* W5047 and W5103 destroyed on test flights at Hawarden 23 November 1941 and 15 December 1941 respectively.

430

(b) *ex Dumbarton/Abbotsinch*

Month	Number completed	Latest delivery	TDU Gosport	No. 5 MU, Kemble	No. 12 MU, Kirkbride	No. 19 MU, St. Athan	No. 22 MU, Silloth	No. 23 MU, Aldergrove	No. 33 MU, Lyneham	No. 48 MU, Hawarden	Blackburns, Abbotsinch	No. 3 S. of G.R., Squires Gate	No. 2 B. & G.S., Millom
October 1939	1	L6347	1										
November	1	L6348	1										
December	2	L6351		2									
January 1940	1	L6350			1								
February	4	L6359			3	1							
March	7	L6372			4	3							
April	3	L6364			1	2							
May	4	L6377			1	2					1		
June	26	L6390			7	6	3	2	4	3	1		
July	23	L6419					4	10		9			
August	23	L6442					5	6		12			
September	13	L6457					6	2		5			
October	19	L6473					4		9	6			
November	10	L6483			3		3		4				
December	8	L6495			5		2		1				
January 1941	13	L6507			1		2	5				5	
February	17	L6522				2	3	3				9	
March	8	L6531			3		1		2				2
April	9	L6538			9								
May	3	L6541					3						
June	5	L6546					5						
Total	200		2	2	38	16	41	28	20	35	2	14	2

Front view of the Perseus test bed Botha, L6463, at Filton 1941.

431

Service use:

(*a*) Chronology showing user units in the order in which they were equipped and the period Bothas were on charge:

No. 608 (North Riding) Squadron, Thornaby	May 1940–December 1940
No. 1 Operational Training Unit, Silloth	June 1940–May 1941
No. 2 Electrical and Wireless School, Yatesbury	October 1940–September 1941
No. 3 School of General Reconnaissance	November 1940–December 1942
No. 2 Bombing and Gunnery School, Millom	January 1941–February 1942
No. 3 Radio School, Prestwick	March 1941–December 1942
No. 8 Bombing and Gunnery School, Evanton	April 1941–February 1942
No. 3 Air Observers' Navigation School	April 1941–July 1941
No. 4 Air Observers' School, West Freugh	May 1941–April 1942
No. 2 Air Observers' School, Millom	July 1941–February 1942
No. 1 Radio School, Cranwell	July 1941–February 1942
No. 4 Air Observers' Navigation School	August 1941–July 1942
No. 10 Air Observers' School, Dumfries	October 1941–July 1942
No. 8 Air Gunnery School, Evanton	February 1942–August 1943
No. 4 Air Gunnery School, Morpeth	April 1942–July 1943
No. 3 (Pilot) Advanced Flying Unit, S. Cerney	April 1942–July 1942
Target Towing Unit, Abbotsinch	April 1942–September 1942
No. 6 (Pilot) Advanced Flying Unit	June 1942–July 1942
No. 3 Air Gunnery School, C. Kennedy/Mona	July 1942–May 1943
No. 1 (Observer) Advanced Flying Unit, Wigtown	July 1942–July 1943
No. 3 Radio Direction Finding School	September 1942–August 1943
No. 11 Radio School, Hooton Park	December 1942–September 1944

Schools of Technical Training:

No. 1	Halton	from	November 1942
No. 2	Cosford		October 1942
No. 3	Blackpool		October 1942
No. 4	St Athan		May 1940
No. 5	Locking		October 1942
No. 6	Hednesford		September 1942
No. 7	Innsworth		December 1942
No. 9	Morecambe		March 1941
No. 10	Kirkham		April 1941

(*b*) Unit allocations in order of the foregoing table:

The aircraft listed were not all on charge at the same time and comparison of one unit's machines with another's will reveal a considerable interchange. They were usually ferried via one or more of the RAF Maintenance Units listed on page 430, where many not mentioned in this section remained in storage throughout the war.

No. 608 (North Riding) Squadron, Thornaby

Aircraft in use May–December 1940: L6128, L6155(P), L6164, L6165, L6166, L6170(F), L6171(A), L6172(E), L6173(D), L6174(B), L6188, L6189(K), L6190(L), L6191(M), L6192, L6193, L6194(V), L6195(R), L6198(G), L6208(N), L6209(O), L6213(Y), L6215(Q), L6237, L6238, L6239(Z), L6380, L6381, L6382, L6388.

Code letters not quoted above were used by the squadron's Avro Ansons.

Casualty: L6165 posted missing 31 August 1940.

Diary of North Sea Botha patrols by code letter, in order of take-off:

10. Aug. 1940	D F L	25. Sept. 1940	Q N E B
11.	K L	26.	P L N G V Q E
12.	K F N L	27.	Z Y K N
13.	N O	28.	V P Q B Y L
14.	M E O F	29.	P K Z B
15.	E L K N O	30.	Z V Y
16.	P M N E	1. Oct. 1940	Z O M P Y L
17.	O D M O P	2.	M R N
18.	E P N L	3.	Q M E
19.	D	4.	nil
20.	P	5.	P O L Z G
21.	L	6.	P Q N
22.	nil	7.	G M Q
23.	N P F D K F	8.	E M N Z P R O G
24.	M P E		Y
25.	D E K M P	9.	nil
26.	M L	10.	L Q E M
27.	K L	11.	R Q G B Z K N
28.	N D Z	12.	O G N
29.	D L N	13.	M E R N
30.	N P K	14.	nil
31.	E L F N D	15.	O B G Z E Q R M
1. Sept. 1940	N F E D L		K L
2.	P N F E F Y	16.	O Y K
3.	L P F E N	17.	nil
4.	M K E P	18.	nil
5.	K O E D A O L	19.	Z Y
6.	Y D A L P K	20.	nil
7.	M D	21.	nil
8.	nil	22.	nil
9.	M O D Y K	23.	G M
10.	F K Y P	24.	Y M O Q B N E
11.	D V F K Y	25.	P L M O G
12.	K D	26.	E K Y G
13.	P Z V Q	27.	Z G Y B E
14.	R O V Z R	28.	V K N L R
15.	N K G V Z N R F	29.	R Y Z
16.	G Z E	30.	L
17.	F	31.	Z V N
18.	E F N R V Q	1. Nov. 1940	Y V G Z
19.	R V G R Y E	2.	nil
20.	Z Y O L E	3.	Q V
21.	P G M L O	4.	nil
22.	M	5.	B Z G
23.	K	6.	O G
24.	L N Y Q M G		

No. 1 Operational Training Unit, Silloth

Aircraft in use June 1940–May 1941: L6107, L6123, L6124, L6126, L6156–L6163, L6174, L6182, L6183, L6192, L6202–L6204, L6214, L6215, L6228, L6229, L6231, L6355, L6399.

Casualties: L6126 forced landed in the sea 10 miles west of Workington 7 January 1941; L6160 crashed 3 miles from Silloth while night flying 24 August 1940.

No. 2 Electrical and Wireless School, Yatesbury

Aircraft in use October 1940–September 1941: L6172, L6175, L6191, L6195, L6270, L6277, L6279, L6281, L6398, L6456, L6467, L6469, L6477, L6478, L6480.

No. 3 School of General Reconnaissance, Squires Gate

Aircraft in use November 1940–December 1942: L6141, L6143, L6156, L6174, L6179, L6184(5-E), L6185, L6192, L6201, L6210, L6211, L6214, L6216, L6248, L6249, L6250(1-F), L6255, L6261, L6263, L6265, L6266, L6273, L6295, L6297(5-B), L6298–L6304, L6305(5-D), L6306(5-A), L6307–L6311, L6375, L6385(1-L), L6399, L6423, L6445, L6461(5-B), L6463, L6470–L6472, L6476, L6486, L6495, L6496, L6497(4-H), L6498–L6502, L6503(3-K), L6504, L6505(4-P), L6506, L6507(1-M), L6508–L6514, W5065, W5068, W5077(2-N), W5080, W5092(4-L) W5097(4-G), W5106, W5108, W5135, W5136, W5141, W5142, W5144

Coding was by internal squadron numbers followed by an individual letter, examples of these being shown above.

Examples of Botha hours flown in 1942: March, 1,471 hr 20 min; April, 2,808 hr 5 min; May, 2,451 hr 30 min; June, 1,461 hr 55 min; July, 1,359 hr 35 min; August, 1,874 hr 30 min; September, 2,331 hr 55 min; October, 1,307 hr 30 min; November, 635 hr; December, 432 hr.

Casualties: L6141 crashed in the sea 6 May 1942; L6210 forced landed on the foreshore, Blackpool, 24 April 1942; L6249 crashed in the River Mersey 7 February 1942; L6265 in the sea off Puffin Island, North Wales, 6 May 1941 (flew 52 hr 45 min); L6314 crashed near Port Erin, Isle of Man, 12 March 1942; L6315 total wreck 31 August 1941 (flew 91 hr); L6326 crashed in the sea off Ronaldsway, Isle of Man, 2 May 1941 (flew 245 hr 45 min); L6330 total wreck 2 May 1942; L6509 air collision with Defiant N1745 over Blackpool 27 August 1941 (flew 156 hr); L6512 total wreck 16 May 1942; W5141 struck at dispersal by Botha L6192 landing 27 October 1942.

L6508 and W5142 struck off charge 17 February 1943 and 20 July 1942 having flown 291 hr 50 min and 128 hr respectively.

No. 2 Bombing and Gunnery School, Millom

Aircraft in use January 1941–February 1942: L6118, L6135, L6139, L6169, L6181, L6185, L6186, L6220–L6222, L6224–L6227, L6231, L6232, L6236–L6239, L6246, L6247, L6251, L6254, L6262, L6271, L6277, L6278, L6283–L6285, L6288, L6290, L6296, L6299, L6351, L6354, L6361, L6378, L6379, L6383, L6384, L6386, L6392, L6393, L6395, L6402, L6413, L6416, L6422, L6424, L6425, L6427, L6430, L6431, L6440, L6441, L6443, L6444, L6446, L6447, L6456, L6460, L6462, L6469, L6474, L6475, L6487–L6490, L6525, W5038, W5039, W5045, W5053.

Casualties: L6262 total wreck 8 March 1941; L6277 crashed on take-off, Millom 25 September 1941; L6283 crashed at Barrow-in-Furness 14 April 1941 (flew 33 hr 40 min); L6354 landed in the sea 2 miles S.W. of Millom 15 August 1941; L6416 crashed near Castle Moss, Appleby, 22 August 1941; L6425 forced landing at Breadquarry, Ravenglass, 16 October 1941; L6431 struck by Fairey Battle L5785 landing Millom 15 April 1941; L6446 crashed near Stranraer 27 June 1941 (flew 56 hr 15 min); W5053 crashed near Millom 28 November 1941.

L6440 struck off charge 11 June 1941, having flown 80 hr 30 min.

No. 3 Radio School, Prestwick

Aircraft in use March 1941–December 1942: L6158, L6167, L6168, L6172, L6178, L6179, L6182, L6200, L6201, L6207, L6211, L6216, L6218, L6219, L6237, L6241, L6266, L6274, L6276, L6288, L6290, L6292, L6351, L6418, L6421, L6428, L6439, L6442, L6453, L6467, L6468, L6472, L6474, L6477, L6481–L6483, L6488, W5072–W5074, W5101, W5113, W5114, W5122, W5125, W5126, W5129, W5130, W5132.

Casualties: L6178 landed in the sea 14 October 1941 (flew 224 hr 30 min); L6201 landed in the sea 2 October 1942; L6207 crashed at Heathfield Aerodrome after air collision with Botha L6219, 21 April 1942; L6211 crashed on beach at Turnberry 23 February 1942; L6274 engulfed by tide on beach, Heads of Ayr, 26 October 1941; L6276 dived into the sea, Saligo Bay, 5 June 1942; L6351 belly landing at Turnberry 25 October 1942; L6418 landed in the sea near Girvan 19 June 1942; L6442 landed in the sea in bad weather 18 October 1942.

No. 8 Bombing and Gunnery School, Evanton
Aircraft in use April 1941–February 1942: L6147, L6153, L6164, L6166, L6171, L6189, L6191, L6213, L6215, L6229, L6230, L6233, L6252, L6253, L6264, L6267, L6268, L6272, L6289, L6291, L6388, L6389, L6391, L6400, L6401, L6404–L6411, L6434–L6438, L6448–L6451, L6461, L6491–L6494, L6515, L6516, L6522, L6527, L6541, W5017–W5019, W5026–W5028.
Casualties: L6268 burned out 25 June 1941 (flew 23 hr 40 min); L6404 crashed in the sea 18 July 1941; L6407 crashed in the sea 10 November 1941; L6435 burned out 4 October 1941; L6438 crashed in the sea 30 September 1941; L6449 total wreck 3 July 1941 (flew 11 hr 30 min); L6451 crashed in the sea 30 November 1940 (flew 126 hr 10 min); L6541 total wreck 25 May 1941; W5027 total wreck 25 May 1941 (flew 5 hr 5 min).

No. 3 Air Observer's Navigation School, Bobbington
Aircraft in use April 1941–July 1941: L6107, L6132, L6133, L6138, L6152, L6154, L6155, L6158, L6159, L6162, L6163, L6167, L6168, L6182, L6187, L6193, L6202, L6204, L6206, L6223, L6260, L6334–L6336, L6339, L6340, L6342, L6343, L6359, L6382, L6439, L6442, L6452, L6455, L6464–L6466, L6534, L6535, L6539, L6540, W5023, W5025, W5031–W5037, W5040–W5042.
Casualties: L6155 landing Bobbington struck motor vehicle 29 June 1941; W5031 crashed and burned near Enville 30 June 1941 (flew 55 hr 30 min).

No. 4 Air Observers' School, West Freugh
Aircraft in use May 1941–April 1942: L6107, L6117, L6125, L6131, L6134, L6136, L6143–L6145, L6156, L6157, L6170, L6172, L6173, L6175–L6177, L6180, L6183, L6184, L6191, L6193, L6195, L6197–L6199, L6217, L6242, L6243, L6245, L6253, L6256, L6258, L6259, L6270, L6275, L6281, L6286, L6293, L6294, L6299, L6332, L6333, L6337, L6338, L6341–L6343, L6345, L6353–L6355, L6373, L6394, L6396–L6398, L6402, L6412, L6414, L6417, L6419, L6420, L6422, L6429, L6432, L6433, L6478, L6484, L6517–L6521, L6523, L6524, L6528–L6530, L6532, L6533, L6536–L6538, W5020, W5022, W5024, W5029, W5030, W5048–W5050, W5055–W5067 W5076, W5090, W5091, W5136.
Aircraft were coded numerically, e.g. L6394(37).
Casualties: L6478 destroyed in accident 1 December 1941.

No. 2 Air Observers' School, Millom
Aircraft in use July 1941–February 1942: L6151, L6169, L6227, L6231, L6240, L6246, L6251, L6254, L6271, L6277–L6279, L6286, L6296, L6383, L6384, L6386, L6387, L6392, L6402, L6403, L6413, L6416, L6422, L6441, L6447, L6453, L6456, L6458, L6469, L6473, L6474, L6480, L6487, L6490, W5053, W5054, W5081, W5089.
Casualties: L6416 destroyed in accident 29 August 1941.

No. 1 Radio School, Cranwell
Aircraft in use singly July 1941–March 1943: L6218, L6219, L6428.

435

No. 4 Air Observers' Navigation School, West Freugh

Aircraft from No. 4 Air Observers' School in use August 1941–July 1942: L6259, L6337, L6355, L6412, L6478, W5049.

No. 10 Air Observers' School, Dumfries

Aircraft in use October 1941–July 1942: L6132, L6133, L6138, L6147, L6148, L6153, L6154, L6166, L6185, L6213, L6229, L6230, L6233, L6251–L6253, L6264, L6267, L6272, L6289, L6291, L6359, L6380, L6382, L6400, L6405, L6406, L6409, L6437–L6439, L6448, L6465, L6466, L6491, L6492, L6494, L6515, L6516, L6534, L6539, L6540, W5023, W5025, W5026, W5028, W5032–W5037, W5040–W5042, W5082, W5087.

Casualties: L6213 posted missing 17 January 1942; L6264 posted missing 1 December 1941 (flew 134 hr 45 min); L6289 forced landing on Dishforth Aerodrome 28 July 1942; L6539 crashed near Newton Stewart 2 March 1942; W5042 landed in the sea off Port May Bay 30 July 1942.

No. 8 Air Gunnery School, Evanton

Aircraft in use February 1942–August 1943: L6118, L6123, L6128, L6131, L6132, L6135, L6136, L6139, L6151, L6156, L6170, L6175, L6181, L6183, L6186, L6197, L6222, L6226, L6237, L6238, L6242, L6253, L6271, L6281, L6284, L6285, L6290, L6291, L6307, L6333. L6337, L6345, L6351, L6359, L6378, L6380, L6382, L6384, L6388, L6389, L6393, L6394, L6406, L6408, L6409, L6415, L6422, L6424, L6443, L6444, L6447, L6453, L6456, L6458, L6464, L6474, L6475, L6480, L6521, L6522, L6526, L6529–L6531, L6534–L6536, W5020, W5045, W5048, W5050, W5054, W5055, W5069, W5070, W5077, W5081, W5084, W5085, W5109–W5111, W5130.

Casualties: L6408 crashed in the sea 5 March 1943; L6444 destroyed in accident 9 August 1943; W5081 crashed on Dalcross Aerodrome and burned out 21 May 1942.

No. 4 Air Gunnery School, Morpeth

Aircraft in use April 1942–July 1943: L6115(26), L6116, L6122(28), L6140, L6153, L6161, L6194, L6239(21), L6247, L6281, L6296(55), L6339, L6372, L6374, L6379(27), L6381, L6409, L6441, L6450(17), L6494, L6506(44), L6510, L6513, L6516, L6525, L6531, L6537, L6542, L6544(43), L6546, W5034, W5039, W5043(9), W5044, W5052(18), W5066(2), W5089, W5093, W5096(41), W5107(42), W5112(35), W5119(39), W5120, W5121, W5123(34), W5124(37), W5131, W5133(20), W5134, W5137(14), W5138–W5140, W5145–W5149, W5150(6), W5151(7), W5152(8), W5153, W5154(10), W5155, W5156, W5164, W5165, W5166(58), W5167(29), W5168(30).

Aircraft were coded numerically, examples being shown above.

Casualties: L6247 crash landed at Morpeth 26 June 1942; L6339 used wrong runway, destroyed with Botha W5139 in collision at the intersection 16 November 1942 (flew 76 hr 35 min); L6441 crashed in grounds of Gateshead Mental Hospital 9 June 1943 (flew 323 hr 20 min); L6531 crashed on hillside, Rothbury, Northumberland, 10 May 1943; W5121 crashed at Bedlington 19 August 1942; W5134 (first for Unit) crashed near Ouston 11 April 1942 during delivery from 33 MU; W5137 air collision with Botha W5154, both wrecked 29 March 1943 (flew 136 hr); W5146 blown over on take-off at Morpeth 24 May 1942; W5153 crashed on take-off at Morpeth 17 June 1942; W5155 crashed in the sea 18 August 1942 after air collision with Lysander T1506; W5156 crashed on Morpeth Aerodrome 22 June 1943 (flew 153 hr 10 min); W5164 struck lorry on take-off, Morpeth, 8 March 1943 (flew 114 hr 35 min).

W5140 and W5154 scrapped 30 March 1943 having flown 49 hr 15 min and 138 hr 55 min respectively; L6494 and W5044 scrapped 27 July 1943 having flown 315 hr 40 min and 100 hr 10 min respectively.

Examples of Botha hours flown 1942–43: June 1942, 407 hr 10 min; July, 841 hr 35 min; August, 609 hr; September, 610 hr; October, 702 hr; November, 585 hr; December, 341 hr; January 1943 297 hr; February, 553 hr; March, 527 hr 45 min; April, 635 hr.

No. 3 (Pilot) Advanced Flying Unit, South Cerney
Aircraft in use April 1942–July 1942: L6143, L6180, L6198, L6217, L6245, L6256, L6259, L6429, L6484, L6532, W5157, W5162.

Target Towing Unit, Abbotsinch
Aircraft in use April 1942–September 1942: W5094, W5098–W5101, W5104, W5105, W5143.

No. 6 (Pilot) Advanced Flying Unit, Little Rissington
Aircraft on dispersal June 1942–July 1942: L6184, L6340, L6374, L6436, L6455, L6494, L6513, L6516, L6546, W5044, W5131, W5164–W5166.

No. 3 Air Gunnery School
Aircraft in use at Castle Kennedy, Northern Ireland, July 1942–December 1942. The unit then moved to Mona, Isle of Man, and used Bothas until May 1943: L6117, L6123, L6145, L6156, L6157, L6170, L6180, L6183, L6197, L6207, L6217, L6242, L6245, L6258, L6259, L6281, L6338, L6342, L6345, L6373, L6397, L6412, L6414, L6415, L6419, L6420, L6429, L6433, L6443, L6517, L6523, L6529, L6536–L6538, W5020–W5022, W5024, W5029, W5030, W5048, W5049, W5056, W5066, W5067, W5076, W5090, W5098, W5107.

Casualties: L6342 burned out 3½ miles from Castle Kennedy 26 August 1942 after air collision with Fairey Battle (flew 213 hr 40 min); L6373 collided with Avro Anson LT528 landing at Mona 14 May 1943 (flew 233 hr); L6414 destroyed in forced landing, Castle Kennedy, 27 October 1942; L6419 destroyed in forced landing, Mona 17 May 1943; W5024 crashed on Mona Aerodrome 28 February 1943; W5029 crashed near Mona 15 February 1943.

No. 1 (Observer) Advanced Flying Unit, Wigtown
Aircraft in use July 1942–July 1943: L6143, L6148, L6176, L6230, L6233, L6252, L6256, L6322, L6409, L6465, L6484, L6505, L6516, L6546, W5030, W5035, W5157, W5162.
Casualties: L6233 lost at sea 21 August 1942.

No. 3 Radio Direction Finding School
Aircraft in use September 1942–August 1943: L6162, L6187, L6221, L6238, L6351, L6447, L6476, W5071, W5114, W5162.
L6187 struck off charge 16 August 1944 having flown 793 hr 10 min.

No. 11 Radio School, Hooton Park
Aircraft listed below and a large number of those listed under No. 3 Radio School, in use December 1942–September 1944: L6142, L6158, L6171, L6188, L6202, L6219, L6220, L6237, L6238, L6241, L6243, L6288, L6292, L6300, L6313, L6331, L6361, L6393, L6395, L6421, L6459, L6463, L6524, L6540, W5046, W5072–W5074, W5113, W5118, W5127, W5129, W5130, W5132.

Examples of codes used: L6219(6–16), L6393(6–15), L6421(6–08), W5169(6–06).

Casualties: L6188 crashed in the sea 3 March 1944; L6202(6–20) crashed 7 miles S.E. of Bethesda 28 August 1943; L6220 destroyed in belly landing at Hooton 28 April 1944; L6237 crashed on Flint Bank, River Dee, 8 January 1943; L6459 destroyed in accident 6 March 1944; L6463 broken up after bad landing 29 March 1944.

W5163 scrapped in 1943 having flown 1,073 hr 25 min; L6171, L6331, L6421 and W5169 scrapped 16 August 1944 having flown 546 hr, 570 hr 40 min, 977 hr 35 min and 582 hr 10 min respectively; W5073 scrapped at Sherburn-in-Elmet 26 September 1944 having flown 916 hr 30 min.

W5132 struck off charge 15 September 1943 as instructional airframe 4148M.

No. 1 School of Technical Training, Halton
Aircraft in use from November 1942: L6532(3394M).

No. 2 School of Technical Training, Cosford
Aircraft in use from October 1942: L6232, L6240(3376M), L6322(3739M), L6364(3660M), L6428(3800M), L6472(3801M).

No. 3 School of Technical Training, Blackpool
Aircraft in use from October 1942: L6110, L6254(3375M).

No. 4 School of Technical Training, St Athan
Aircraft in use from May 1940: L6104(2217M), L6105, L6106, L6159(3364M), L6168(3794M), L6200(3799M), L6241(3796M), L6260(3363M), L6368(3078M), L6474(3797M), L6476(3798M), L6477(3796M), L6483(3795M).

No. 5 School of Technical Training, Locking
Aircraft in use from October 1942: L6198(3378M), L6204(3367M).

No. 6 School of Technical Training, Hednesford
Aircraft in use from September 1942: L6133(3379M), L6267(3380M).

No. 7 School of Technical Training, Innsworth
Aircraft in use from December 1942: L6152(3365M), L6205(3366M).

No. 9 School of Technical Training, Morecambe
Aircraft in use March 1941–December 1941: L6106.

No. 10 School of Technical Training, Kirkham
Aircraft temporarily on charge 31 December 1941–8 January 1942:L6368(3078M). The 'M' serial was not painted on while at Kirkham.

Firebrand T.F. Mk 5 EK691, coded 123/J, making an approach to *Eagle* in 1953, showing the horn-balanced elevator peculiar to this mark. (*Flight Photo.*)

Blackburn B-37 Firebrand

The Blackburn B-37 had its beginnings in N.8/39, first of two specifications circulated by the Air Ministry in March 1939 setting out requirements for two-seat short-range fleet fighters to replace the Gloster Gladiator, Blackburn Skua and Fairey Fulmar. The main difference between N.8/39 and the alternative N.9/39 specification was in the matter of gun installation, the former calling for four fixed 20-mm cannon and the latter a power-driven gun turret. In the light of operational experience with the Blackburn Roc, N.9/39 was re-written in the following year to exclude the turret, becoming N.5/40 met by the two-seat Fairey Firefly which was ordered in quantity. N.8/39, on the other hand, was reduced to a single-seater and re-issued as N.11/40, Blackburns being awarded a contract for three prototype aircraft in the face of competition from the Hawker P.1009 project, a folding-wing version of the famous Typhoon. Production orders followed, but the machine was subjected to such a long drawn out succession of changes in operational role, power plant and structure, that its development went on continuously at Brough throughout the 1939–45 war and it did not reach squadron service until 1945.

The Advisory Design Conference, under the leadership of Blackburn's chief designer G. E. Petty, took place in a golf clubhouse near the parent factory at Brough on 25 July 1940, after which events moved swiftly for, within two months, a full-scale mock-up had been completed, and only 18

439

DD804, the unarmed first prototype Blackburn B-37 Firebrand F. Mk I, at Brough 1942.

months later, on 27 February 1942, the first of three prototypes, DD804, made a first flight of ten minutes duration. It was a large single-seat, all-metal low-wing monoplane of elegant aspect designed round the new 2,305 hp Napier Sabre III liquid-cooled twenty-four cylinder H-type engine. Closely cowled and driving a de Havilland three-bladed variable-pitch airscrew with large conical spinner, this engine imparted unusually slim lines to the fuselage, the coolant radiators being housed in forward extensions of the centre section root ends.

Structurally, the B-37 combined Botha-type outer wing panels, rigged with a dihedral of 5 degrees, with a massive two-spar centre section built round a heavy-duty centreline frame. The undercarriage, consisting of two telescopic oleo-pneumatic legs with cantilever axles and fairings, retracted inwards hydraulically in a matter of 3–4 seconds into wheel wells with self-closing doors. The wells also housed major components of the aircraft's Lockheed hydraulic system where they were readily accessible for maintenance purposes.

Forged steel fork-end fittings located at the outer ends of the centre section main spars carried latch pins which on withdrawal permitted the wings to fold. Withdrawal or re-insertion was effected by a Skua-type crank and screwjack mechanism in the wheel well, the wings being folded manually to lie parallel to the fuselage, leading edge uppermost.

A combination of hydraulically-operated Fowler and subsidiary flaps, developed in the wind tunnel at Brough, to give increased lift for take-off and low approach speed for deck landings, occupied the whole trailing edge from the wing root to the inner ends of the Frise-type ailerons. The centre portion of each outer wing panel formed a heated, felt-lagged gun bay housing the two cannon with 200 rounds of ammunition for each.

The fuselage was built in two parts. In front it was a circular section tubular-steel structure covered with detachable metal panels housing main and auxiliary self-sealing fuel tanks of 239 gallons total capacity, but to the rear of the pilot's cockpit it was of oval-section, stressed-skin, semi-mono-coque construction. Fin and rudder were positioned well forward of the elevator to prevent blanketing, as on the Skua, and the extended tail cone formed a convenient housing for the hydraulic gear which retracted the castoring tail wheel, extended the arrester hook and damped the sudden load of an arrested landing.

Contractor's trials at Brough showed the need for tailplane and elevator modifications, and these were completed before the aircraft left for full performance testing by the A. & A.E.E., Boscombe Down, which took approximately a month from 23 June to 28 July 1942. Increases in flap and rudder area were recommended to reduce float and improve directional control at low carrier-landing speeds, and criticism was levelled at distortion of the forward view by the curved side-panels of the windscreen.

The B-37 was allocated type name Firebrand I on 11 July 1941 but, whereas the first machine had been purely an unarmed aerodynamic proto-type, the second, serialled DD810 and first flown on 15 July 1942, was armed with two 20-mm British Hispano cannon in each wing and if desired could also be fitted with racks for two 500-lb bombs. It was delivered to the Royal Navy on 11 October for deck-landing trials, which took place on *Illustrious* in the Clyde Estuary in February 1943. The third prototype, DD815, was delivered to Boscombe Down in May 1943 for armament trials, which included air firing tests over Poole Bay in the following September. By May 1944 it had flown approximately 60 hr.

On 25 May 1943, the first machine, DD804, was delivered to the Luton experimental establishment of D. Napier and Son Ltd, manufacturers of the Sabre engine, for a complete re-design of the engine installation as a removable power plant with the engine slung from forged light-alloy bearers. After only five such power plants had been manufactured, however, the Ministry of Aircraft Production saw fit to allocate all Sabre production to the

DD810, the four-cannon second prototype Firebrand F. Mk I, with de Havilland three-bladed variable-pitch airscrew.

Hawker Typhoon. Coupled with the entry into service of the fully-developed Supermarine Seafire fleet interceptor, this decision spelled the end of the Firebrand as a pure fighter, but the MAP, deciding to take full advantage of its enormous load-carrying capability, asked Blackburns to re-work the design as a fast, hard-hitting, carrier-borne, torpedo-carrying strike aircraft.

The second prototype, DD810, which had suffered damage in a forced landing with a seized engine after an oil pipe fractured in flight, was accordingly rebuilt with the centre section strengthened along the centreline and increased in width by 1 ft 3½ in to make room for a 1,850-lb, 18-in torpedo slung between the wheel well doors. In this form it was re-serialled NV636 and first flew as the prototype Firebrand T.F. Mk II at Brough on 31 March 1943. Reconstruction had little effect on performance, and the machine flew with torpedo for the first time on 2 April. Thus, having flown the Blackbird back in 1918, Blackburns that day gained distinction as builders of one of the world's first biplanes and the first monoplane, single-seat torpedo aircraft.

The first nine production aircraft, DK363-DK371, completed without torpedo modifications as Firebrand F. Mk Is, were all used for experimental purposes. The first was flown to Napiers at Luton on 29 July 1943 to be fitted with another of the interchangeable power plants; DK364 was retained by the manufacturers at Brough for trial modifications until flown to the RAE, Farnborough, on 29 February 1944; DK370 went to RNAS, Lee-on-Solent, for evaluation by the Royal Navy and the remaining five to the A. & A.E.E., Boscombe Down, where DK367 was used for air firing trials with rocket projectiles on rails under the mainplane. DK369 also went briefly to Lee-on-Solent in November 1944 before a final flight to Blackburn's establishment at Sherburn-in-Elmet to be broken up.

DK363, first production Firebrand F. Mk I, at Luton 1943, with Sabre III interchangeable power plant identified by the repositioned air intake under the nose.
(*Napier Photo.*)

The third prototype after reconstruction as the first Firebrand Mk II NV636. The torpedo was fitted with the M.A.T. Mk IV directional stabilising tail assembly.

Restrictions on the supply of Sabre engines limited production of the torpedo-carrying Firebrand T.F. Mk II to 12 aircraft, DK374-DK385, two of which, DK374 and DK379, were evaluated by the Torpedo Development Unit, Gosport, which conducted dropping trials in the Solent. DK375 went to RNAS, Leuchars, for familiarization flying, DK377 to Boscombe Down, and the remainder to RNAS, Lee-on-Solent, between 20 September and 30 October 1944. Here they were taken on charge by No. 708 Squadron, a shore-based trials unit, which fitted some of them with rails for eight rocket projectiles and flew combat practice sorties against Seafires.

Projects based on the Sabre-engined Firebrand were the Blackburn B-41 single-seat fighter for the RAF; the B-42 with high-lift wing; and the B-43 twin-float seaplane fighter. None of these was built.

Firebrand T.F. Mk III

The strike fighter requirement crystallized as Specification S.8/43 issued on 3 October 1943 and to which subsequent Firebrands were completed with 2,400 hp Bristol Centaurus VII two-row, eighteen-cylinder sleeve-valve radial engines driving 13 ft 6 in diameter four-bladed Rotol airscrews. This installation taxed the ingenuity of the design staff, since the fuselage had been built as slim as possible to take advantage of the lines of the Sabre and the large radial could not be allowed to obstruct the pilot's view during deck landings. They succeeded handsomely but, as it involved a major redesign, this variant was given the new type number B-45 and redesignated Firebrand T.F. Mk III. It also had spring-loaded tabs on all control surfaces as well as increased rudder chord, and the leading edge extensions to the centre section, formerly used for housing radiators, now contained the carburettor air intakes (with Blackburn-designed filters) in the port side and the oil cooler to starboard.

443

Torpedo-carrying Blackburn B-45 Firebrand T.F. Mk II DK383 of No. 708
Squadron flying near the South Coast in 1945.

The prototype T.F. Mk IIIs, DK372 and DK373, were conversions of airframes originally laid down as the 10th and 11th production Firebrand F. Mk Is, and the first, which flew at Brough on 21 December 1943, enjoyed a considerable career as a test aircraft which began at Boscombe Down in March 1944. It flew with a metal streamlined headrest and perspex sliding hood but was later fitted with a clear-view, tear-drop canopy before going to Rotol Ltd at Staverton for airscrew development work in March 1945. Trouble was again experienced with directional stability and DK373 was fitted experimentally with an offset fin to counteract take-off swing. It too went to Boscombe Down but was transferred to the RAE, Farnborough, on 2 June 1945 for a short period of radio altimeter testing before being flown to Sherburn-in-Elmet on 2 August to be scrapped.

Twenty-seven production aircraft, commencing with DK386, first flown in November 1944 by Sqn Ldr J. R. Tobin, a test pilot on loan from the RAF, were completed by the following May, bringing total Firebrand production (excluding the original prototypes) to 50. Many were retained at the works, but DK389 was flown to Farnborough on 1 February 1945 for arrester gear trials, both at the RAE and at Henstridge; DK387 also flew to Farnborough on 3 May for arrester gear, RATOG and torpedo-buffeting tests; the Boscombe Down trials machines were DK396 and DK400; and the last eight, DK405-DK412, were delivered to the Royal Navy at RNAS, Anthorn. The Bristol Centaurus VII engine was fitted to early examples but, commencing with DK396, it was replaced by the improved Centaurus IX with vibration dampers in the engine mounting.

Firebrand T.F. Mk 4, 5 and 5A

Problems encountered with the Mk III aircraft were rectified in the B-46 Firebrand T.F. Mk 4 main production variant by fitting a horn balanced

444

rudder of increased area, to give full measure of control during slow carrier-landings, and an unusually large fin, offset 3 degrees to port, to compensate for the natural tendency to swing on take-off. The aircraft's capability was extended to include dive-bombing with the military load increased by two 2,000-lb bombs on racks, one under each wing, diving speed being limited to 350 mph by means of retractable spoilers, 4 ft 6 in in length, developed in the wind tunnel at Brough and housed in recesses in the upper and lower wing surfaces. An alternative load of sixteen 60-lb rocket projectiles could be carried or, for long-range work, two 45-gallon drop tanks. Long range with bombs was also possible if a 100-gallon overload tank was carried in the torpedo crutches. Provision was also made for catapult and RATOG take-off. Drawings were prepared for fitting the Firebrand T.F. Mk 4 with a later mark of Sabre engine in an annular radiator but this scheme was not pursued.

The torpedo crutch was pin-jointed at the front end so that the missile could be winched up parallel to the ground, i.e. in the nose-down attitude relative to the fuselage, but on take-off, retraction of the undercarriage automatically tilted it into the minimum drag position parallel to the line of flight.

Firebrand T.F. Mk 4 production totalled 102 aircraft, the first of which, EK601, was airborne for the first time on 17 May 1945. On leaving the factory they were ferried to RNAS Arbroath, Anthorn, Stretton and Donibristle, exceptions being EK605 and EK630 retained at the works for trial installations, EK622 which crashed on test, EK608 used by Rotol Ltd at Staverton, EK629 by Bristols for engine development at Filton, EK631, EK633 and EK657 by the Aircraft Torpedo Development Unit, Gosport, and EK 633 by RAF Hullavington.

A single example was present at the ATA Farewell Display at White Waltham on 29 September 1945, and at Heston on 2 October a superb display of manoeuvrability at both ends of the speed range was given by EK602 (Lt Cdr Ivers) with torpedo and by EK665 without. On 1 September that year No. 813 Squadron was re-formed at RNAS Ford with 15 Firebrand T.F.

DK372, prototype Blackburn B-45 Firebrand T.F. Mk III with Centaurus engine, Rotol four-bladed variable-pitch airscrew and opaque rear headrest.

P. G. Lawrence flying the Blackburn B-46 Firebrand T.F. Mk 4 EK660, showing the tear-drop canopy and enlarged fin and rudder introduced on this mark.

Mk 4s, becoming the first Fleet Air Arm squadron to fly single-seat torpedo aircraft since the withdrawal from service of the Blackburn Dart 22 years earlier. After several months working-up, the squadron's aircraft, coded FD (signifying Ford) with individual letters, first appeared in public on 8 June 1946 in the Victory fly-past over London and at the subsequent air display at Eastleigh, using EK613 (FD-1H), EK672 (FD-1C) and EK633 (F). During this period EK746 was exhibited statically in Green Park, London, and at the British Aircraft Display, Farnborough, on 28 June.

Contracts for the last 50 aircraft were cancelled and production terminated at the end of 1947 with the 220th machine, final variants being the B-46 Firebrand T.F. Mks 5 and 5A. The Mk 5 embodied detailed improvements such as horn balanced elevators and long-span aileron tabs, and an early example, EK742, gave a memorable display of low-level aerobatics with torpedo at the Radlett SBAC Show of 12–13 September 1946. The pilot was P. G. Lawrence, MBE, who had conducted deck-landing trials with the T.F. Mk 4 while serving with the Firebrand Tactical Trials Unit at Lee-on-Solent in 1944 prior to leaving the Royal Navy to join Blackburns as test pilot. He demonstrated the next machine, EK743, with drop tanks at the 1947 SBAC Show, by which time No. 813 Squadron, which had received Mk 5 aircraft in April 1947, was displaying them to good advantage at Naval Air Displays up and down the country. At the end of 1947 No. 813's Firebrands were embarked on *Illustrious* and later served in *Implacable*.

The Firebrand's short but noteworthy racing career opened at Lympne on 31 August 1947 when Blackburn test pilot Grp Capt C. J. P. Flood flew a Mk 5, EK850, into second place in the High Speed Handicap Race at an average speed of 310·69 mph.

Small formations of Firebrand T.F. Mk 5s from No. 1 Carrier Air Group, and coded C (signifying home base Culdrose), took part in an attack on Ford as part of the Home Fleet Exercises in April 1948, and No. 813, operating from Arbroath, was engaged in Exercise Dawn a month later, afterwards operating at Culdrose before returning to *Implacable*.

To increase the rate of roll at high speeds, Blackburns introduced a final variant, the T.F.5A, fitted with hydraulically-boosted aileron controls, and the first of these, EK769, was demonstrated at the garden party of the Brough branch of the Royal Aeronautical Society by P. G. Lawrence on 21 August 1948. As part of the same display six Firebrand T.F. Mk 5s of No. 813 Squadron, temporarily based at Anthorn, were batted down to short carrier-landings on the airfield. Power-assisted elevators were fitted to one aircraft to allow Lawrence to conduct spinning trials, and a Mk 5A, EK844, was a static exhibit at the Farnborough SBAC Show in the following September. P. G. Lawrence also won the Air League Challenge Cup in a race at Elmdon on 30 June 1949 at an average speed of 302 mph in EK621, a conversion from Mk 5. In the repeat event at Sherburn-in-Elmet on 22 July 1950 he flew EK644, a one-off conversion with Centaurus 57 engine (using water-methanol injection for take-off) and the wing root air intakes faired over and replaced by a smaller unit on top of the cowlings.

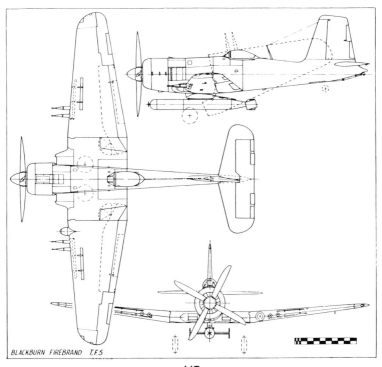

BLACKBURN FIREBRAND T.F.5

In the absence of catapulting facilities, short take-offs with heavy loads were made with rocket assistance, a little-known procedure which Firebrands from No. 1 Carrier Air Group, Culham, demonstrated in spectacular manner at the Lee-on-Solent Naval Air Display on 26 August 1950. In the following December No. 827 Squadron also re-armed, receiving 12 Firebrand Mks 5 and 5A. After a five-month working up period at Ford they were flown to Malta and in October 1951 embarked in *Illustrious* for the return journey to the United Kingdom. Then followed a cruise in *Eagle* in 1952 during which they took part in Exercise Castanets in the North Sea, bearing the carrier's code letter J. In 1953 Nos. 813 and 827 Squadrons were re-equipped with propeller-turbine powered Westland Wyverns, and the Firebrands were then used for fire-fighting practice at shore bases, as catapult dummies, or were disposed of as scrap at naval maintenance units, many being reduced to produce at a scrap yard at Milnathort, Kinross-shire.

SPECIFICATION AND DATA

Manufacturers: Blackburn and General Aircraft Ltd, Olympia Works, Roundhay Road, Leeds, and Brough Aerodrome, East Yorks.

Power Plants: (B–37 Firebrand F. Mk I and T. F. Mk II)
  One 2,305 hp Napier Sabre III
  (B–45 Firebrand T.F. Mk III)
  One 2,400 hp Bristol Centaurus VII
  One 2,520 hp Bristol Centaurus IX
  (B–46 Firebrand T.F. Mk 4, 5 and 5A)
  One 2,520 hp Bristol Centaurus IX
  One 2,520 hp Bristol Centaurus 57

Dimensions, Weights and Performance:

	Firebrand F. Mk I	Firebrand T.F. Mk II	Firebrand T.F. Mk III
Span	50 ft 0 in	51 ft 3½ in	51 ft 3½ in
Span folded	13 ft 6 in	13 ft 6 in	13 ft 6 in
Length	38 ft 2 in	38 ft 2 in	37 ft 7 in
Height	13 ft 4 in	13 ft 4 in	12 ft 10 in
Wing area	369 sq ft	383 sq ft	383 sq ft
Tare weight	11,100 lb	—	11,375 lb
All-up weight	13,643 lb	15,049 lb	15,753 lb
Maximum speed*	353 mph	355 mph	319 mph
Cruising speed	294 mph	274 mph	272 mph
Initial climb†	2,250 ft/min	2,300 ft/min	2,480 ft/min
Service ceiling	32,500 ft	—	29,400 ft
Range	805 miles	770 miles	530 miles

   ★ Without torpedo.   † With torpedo.

	Firebrand T.F. Mk 4	Firebrand T.F. Mk 5	Firebrand T.F. Mk 5A
Span	51 ft 3½ in	51 ft 3½ in	51 ft 3½ in
Span folded	16 ft 10 in	16 ft 10 in	16 ft 10 in
Length	38 ft 9 in	38 ft 9 in	38 ft 9 in
Height	13 ft 3 in	13 ft 3 in	13 ft 3 in
Wing area	383 sq ft	383 sq ft	383 sq ft
Tare weight	11,689 lb	11,835 lb	11,835 lb
All-up weight	15,671 lb	17,500 lb	16,700 lb
Maximum speed*	342 mph	340 mph	335 mph
Maximum speed†	320 mph	320 mph	—
Cruising speed	256 mph	256 mph	—
Initial climb*	2,440 ft/min	—	2,500 ft/min
Service ceiling	34,000 ft	28,500 ft	31,000 ft
Range	745 miles	740 miles	745 miles

* Without torpedo. † With torpedo.

Production: (a) *Prototypes to Specification N.11/40*
Three aircraft only with Napier Sabre III engines:

DD804 First flown 27 February 1942, delivered to D. Napier and Son Ltd, Luton, 20 May 1943.

DD810 First flown 15 July 1942, delivered to the Royal Navy 11 October 1942 for deck landing trials.

DD815 Delivered to the A. & A.E.E., Boscombe Down, 15 September 1942, converted to Firebrand T.F. Mk II prototype NV636, first flown as such 31 March 1943, s.o.c. 26 June 1945 and broken up at Sherburn-in-Elmet.

(b) *Blackburn B-37 Firebrand F. Mk. I*
Nine aircraft only, DK363–DK371, Napier Sabre III engines, Works Orders 3380/1 to 3380/9:

DK363 to Luton 29 July 1943; DK364 retained at Brough 28 April 1943 under Contract 2406, to RAE Farnborough 1944; DK365 and DK366 to Boscombe Down 29 July 1943 and 12 July 1943 respectively; DK367 to Boscombe Down 31 July 1943 for armament trials, undercarriage collapse 7 November 1943; DK368 retained at Brough; DK 369 loaned by Blackburns to the A. & A.E.E., Boscombe Down 22 March 1944, to RNAS Lee-on-Solent 9 November 1944, to Blackburns Sherburn-in-Elmet 1 December 1944, s.o.c. 22 August 1945; DK370 to RNAS Lee-on-Solent 18 September 1944; DK371 to Boscombe Down 12 September 1944.

(c) *Blackburn B-37 Firebrand T.F. Mk II*
Twelve aircraft only, DK374–DK385, Napier Sabre III engines, Works Orders 3380/10 to 3380/21:

DK374 to TDU Gosport 2 February 1944; DK375 to RNAS Leuchars 20 June 1944; DK376 retained by Blackburns; DK377 to Boscombe Down 6 September 1944, 13 hr 10 min flying by 16 September 1944; DK378 to RNAS Lee-on-Solent 16 September 1944; DK379 to TDU Gosport 9 September 1944; DK380–DK385 to No. 708 Sqn Lee-on-Solent, delivery dates 20 September 1944, 21 September 1944, 3 October 1944, 7 October 1944, 3 October 1944 and 3 October 1944 respectively, DK383 coded OC.

(d) *Blackburn B-45 Firebrand T.F. Mk III*
Two prototypes, DK372 and DK373, followed by 27 production aircraft, DK386–DK412, Bristol Centaurus engines, Works Orders 3380/22 to 3380/50:
DK372 first flown 21 December 1943, to Rotol Ltd Staverton 12 March 1945; DK373 on Royal Navy charge 8 May 1944, to Boscombe Down 28 December 1944, to RAE Farnborough 2 June 1944, to Sherburn-in-Elmet 2 August 1945; DK386 retained by Blackburns 27 November 1944 under Contract 3962; DK387 and DK389 to RAE Farnborough 3 May 1945 and 1 February 1945 respectively (the latter returning to Brough 23 April 1945); DK388 and DK390–DK395 completed April 1945 and retained by Blackburns, DK392–DK394 to Boscombe Down September 1945; DK396 to Boscombe Down 7 April 1945; DK398–DK403 retained by Blackburns (DK400 to Boscombe Down, to Farnborough 11 July 1945); DK404 to Rotol Ltd Staverton 16 June 1945; DK405–DK412 to RNAS Anthorn between 17 May 1945 and 29 June 1945.

(e) *Blackburn B-46 Firebrand T.F. Mk. 4*
Contract for 102 aircraft, EK601–EK638, EK653–EK694, EK719–EK740, Bristol Centaurus engines, Works Orders 3380/51 to 3380/152:
EK601 first flown 17 May 1945, to RNAS Arbroath 30 May 1945; EK602 to RNAS Arbroath 17 June 1945, to Boscombe Down September 1945; EK605 retained at Brough 29 July 1945, later to Boscombe Down; EK608 to Rotol Ltd Staverton 23 June 1945; EK614 retained at Brough 4 July 1945, converted to T.F. Mk 5A; EK622 crashed on test flight; EK628 converted to T.F. Mk 5A; EK629 to Bristols Filton 10 August 1945; EK630 at Boscombe Down 21 March 1946–January 1948; EK631, EK633, EK657 and EK725 to ATDU Gosport 10 August 1945, 20 August 1945, 5 September 1945 and 1 January 1946 respectively; EK636 to RAF Hullavington 31 August 1945, on Admiralty charge 15 November 1945; EK653 to No. 47 MU Sealand 30 August 1945 for trial packing; EK660 to catapult dummy; EK680 to RAE Farnborough; EK694 to RNAS Donibristle 11 December 1945; EK722 to Boscombe Down 1948–49; EK723 converted to T.F. Mk 5A, to RAE Farnborough 3 January 1946, at Boscombe Down November 1947–January 1948 for power-assisted aileron tests; EK726 converted to T.F. Mk 5; EK728 converted to T.F. Mk 5, scrapped at Bramcote 1956; EK730, EK733 and EK735 converted to T.F. Mk 5; EK740 to RAE Farnborough.
Deliveries to RNAS Anthorn between 4 June 1945 and 30 January 1947: EK603, EK604, EK606, EK607, EK609–EK613, EK628, EK632, EK634, EK635, EK637, EK638, EK654–EK656, EK658–EK664, EK666, EK719–EK722, EK727, EK729, EK731, EK734, EK737, EK738.
Deliveries to RNAS Stretton between 6 July 1945 and 24 July 1945: EK615–EK621, EK623–EK627. (EK619 later to RAE Farnborough.)

(f) *Blackburn B-46 Firebrand T.F. Mks 5 and 5A*
Contract for 70 aircraft, EK741–EK748, EK764–EK799, EK827–EK850, Bristol Centaurus engines, Works Orders 3380/153 to 3380/220. Also approximately 40 conversions of Mk 4 aircraft to Mk 5. First deliveries 31 January 1946. Contract completed 24 February 1947.

EK742 at Boscombe Down November 1947–January 1948 for cooling and handling trials; EK769 prototype Mk 5A; EK770 coded 180 exhibited at the Fifty Years of Flying Exhibition, Hendon, July 1951; EK844 burned at fire-fighting demonstration, Bramcote June 1953; EK848 to Boscombe Down January 1948 for radio and gunnery trials; EK850 rolled out at Brough 31 March 1947.
Fifty aircraft EK851–EK867, EK885–EK913, EK934–EK937 cancelled.

Service Use:
No. 708 Squadron, Lee-on-Solent 1944–45; No. 813 Squadron, Ford, *Illustrious* and *Implacable* 1947–53; No. 827 Squadron, Ford, Malta and *Eagle* 1950–53; No. 1 Carrier Air Group, Culdrose and Culham.

No. 708 Squadron
1944–45 DK383 (OC).

No. 813 Squadron
1945–47 EK613(M later FD-1H), EK624(FD-1P), EK628(FD-1N), EK633(F), EK672(FD-1C), EK719(FD-1K), EK729(FD-1A).
1948–53 EK609(100), EK614(103), EK627, EK628(102/A), EK636, EK655, EK662(121/A), EK665(121), EK678(122/A), EK680(102 later 102/A), EK694(100/A), EK721(123/A), EK723(121/C), EK727(102/A), EK731(103/A), EK734(110/A), EK736(101/A), EK737(124), EK738, EK748(123/C), EK755, EK764(124/C), EK766(121/FD), EK771(121/C), EK773(112/A), EK777(120/A), EK781(101 later 103/C), EK784(103/C), EK790(102/C), EK791(112/C later 112/A), EK793(113 later 110), EK831(113/C), EK832(110/A), EK845(111/C), EK846, EK847(122/C), EK849(101/C), EK850(110/C).

No. 827 Squadron
1950–53 EK691(123/J), EK693(125/J), EK795(123/J).
Code letters: A—*Illustrious/Implacable*; C—Culdrose; FD—Ford; J—*Eagle*.
Scrapped at Milnathort 1965: EK617, EK621, EK625, EK628, EK637, EK661, EK729, EK744, EK747, EK780.

P. G. Lawrence flying RT651, the first prototype B-48, near Brough in July 1947.

Blackburn B-48

In October 1943 the Blackburn design staff under G. E. Petty began work on a new all-metal single-seat, deck-landing strike aircraft which was covered by Specification S.28/43, issued on 26 February 1944, calling for a 'Firebrand T. F. with redesigned wing and improved pilot's view'. Known as the B-48 in the Blackburn series and also designated Y.A.1 under the SBAC system, it was a development of, and potential successor to, the Firebrand Mk 5, a fact reflected in the unofficial name Firecrest used for a time by the manufacturers.

Although the basic structure of the B-48 was similar to that of the Firebrand, it was powered by a 2,475 hp Bristol Centaurus 59—similar to the Centaurus 57 but equipped with a Coffman cartridge starter. Considerable attention was paid to giving the pilot an unobstructed view over the nose, achieved by raising the cockpit and moving it forward so that most of the fuel tankage was behind instead of in front. Chief engineering interest, however, centred round the mainplane, an entirely new design of the inverted gull type, with relatively thin laminar-flow section, which folded hydraulically in two places for economy in carrier stowage space. The downward sweep of the anhedral centre section also enabled the designers to use a short undercarriage built to withstand a vertical velocity of 12 ft/sec, the undercarriage, tail wheel and arrester hook all being retracted hydraulically.

Four Fowler high-lift flaps, with auxiliary flaps on the outer pair, imparted STOL characteristics for carrier work, and take-off is said to have been of the order of 430 ft in a 25-knot wind. As on the Firebrand, hydraulically-retracting dive brakes were fitted above and below the wing and electrically-operated trim tabs were used on all control surfaces.

Two prototypes were ordered but did not fly until after the end of the war, the first, RT651, being wheeled out at Brough in the snows of February 1947.

452

It was then taken by road to Leconfield where it flew for the first time on 1 April, making two low passes over Brough before landing again at Leconfield, to fold its wings while taxying in. When preliminary tests had shown that its short, slow landings were all that the designers intended, the machine was flown to Brough where its first take-off from the rather small factory airfield was made on 9 April.

Cooling of the closely-cowled Centaurus 59 radial engine was controlled electrically by gills and boosted by a multi-blade fan immediately behind the five-bladed Rotol constant-speed airscrew. The forward extension of the centre section, legacy of the liquid-cooled Firebrand I, was not retained on the B-48, the oil cooler being housed externally to starboard of the torpedo and the supercharger air intakes in the leading edge of each wing root.

Total fuel capacity was 236 gallons, 92 in each wing and 52 in the fuselage in two tanks, fore and aft of the pilot. For long-range work or ferrying, 45-gallon drop tanks could be carried under each wing as well as a 100-gallon tank in the torpedo crutches.

No armament was actually installed in RT651 but, in addition to the torpedo, there were pick-up points under the wing for two externally-mounted ·5-in machine guns replacing the normal armament of two 500-lb bombs or an equivalent load of rocket projectiles.

Test and development flying of the B-48 was in the hands of Blackburn's chief test pilot P. G. Lawrence, assisted by Grp Capt Flood and G. F. Bullen, its first public appearance being at the Naval Air Command Display at RNAS, Lee-on-Solent, on 26 June 1947 when Flood convincingly demonstrated its handling qualities at high and low speeds and folded the double knuckle-jointed wing as he taxied in. It gave a similar performance with torpedo at the Radlett SBAC Show of 9–11 September 1947 and afterwards returned to Brough for further test flying.

The intended second prototype, RT656, was not completed, but a modification of the design, serialled VF172, was built for research with the power-

RT651 in the snow at Brough, February 1947, showing the double wing fold.

453

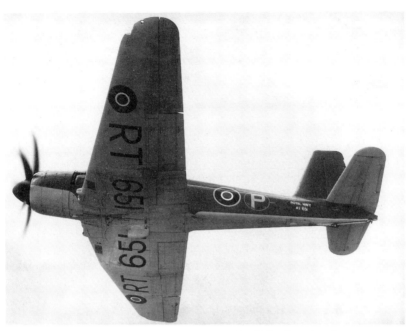

Underneath view of the B-48 showing its distinctive wing shape.
(*Flight Photo 20543S.*)

The second B-48, VF172, at Brough in June 1948.

boosted ailerons then being introduced on the Firebrand T.F.5A production line. For this reason the dihedral on the outer wing panels was reduced from the 9 degrees used on RT651 to only 3 degrees. This machine first appeared in public at the garden party of the Brough branch of the Royal Aeronautical Society held on 21 August 1948, when P. G. Lawrence demonstrated its high rate of roll and slow flying capabilities with flaps extended. The same pilot then flew it at the Farnborough SBAC Show of 7–12 September that year before it was sent to Boscombe Down for handling tests of the powered controls. Later it returned to Brough to rejoin the first prototype for further manufacturer's test flying.

The B-48 appeared at a time when piston engines were ceasing to be used as a means of propulsion for military aircraft and no production contracts were awarded, but projects first considered in July 1946, which envisaged its development with Armstrong Siddeley Python, Rolls-Royce Clyde or Bristol Proteus turbine engines driving six-bladed contra-rotating airscrews, led directly to the B-54, or Y.A.5, two-seat strike aircraft and its derivatives.

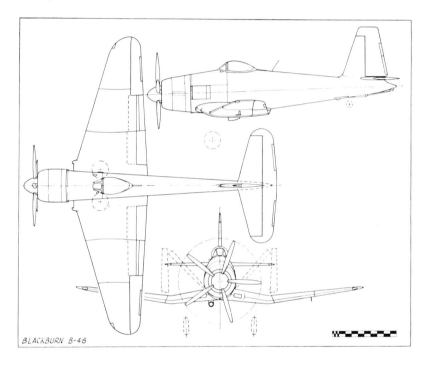

BLACKBURN B-48

SPECIFICATION AND DATA

Manufacturers: Blackburn and General Aircraft Ltd, Olympia Works, Leeds and Brough Aerodrome, East Yorks.

Power Plant: One 2,475 hp Bristol Centaurus 59

Dimensions: Span 44 ft 11½ in   (folded) 18 ft 0 in
            Length 39 ft 3½ in   Height 14 ft 6 in
            Wing area 361½ sq ft

Weights: Tare weight 10,513 lb   Military load 2,500 lb
        All-up weight 15,280 lb

Performance: Maximum speed at 19,000 ft   380 mph
Initial climb 2,500 ft/min
Absolute ceiling 33,500 ft   Service ceiling 31,600 ft
Range 900 miles at 213 mph at 15,000 ft
Best combat range with torpedo
750 miles at 272 mph at 10,000 ft

Production:
  Three prototype aircraft only:

RT651   First flown at Leconfield 1 April 1947, retained by the manufacturers for test purposes.
RT656   Aircraft not completed.
VF172   Built to Works Order 4400/1 and retained at Brough under Contract G/ACFT/2311/CB96.

WB797, the Double Mamba powered three-seat Blackburn B-88 or Y.B.1,
with the radome in the lowered position.

Blackburn B-54 (Y.A.5) and Derivatives

A change of naval policy in 1945, brought about by the recognition that in
modern war the submarine was a greater menace to shipping than the surface
vessel, ended the requirement for torpedo-carrying machines (among them
the Blackburn B-48) and led to the issue of Specification G.R.17/45 for a
specialized, carrier-borne, anti-submarine aircraft. In addition to carrying
weapons for the destruction of the enemy, this was to be equipped with search
and tracking radar able to detect the raider's snorkel in sea conditions which
would make detection by surface vessels impossible.

Blackburn's first ideas in this direction appeared in model form at the 1948
Farnborough SBAC Show as a B-48 variant with chin radome and either the
Armstrong Siddeley Python or Napier Double Naiad propeller-turbine
driving large-diameter contra-rotating airscrews. However, final design, by
G. E. Petty, which initially carried the SBAC designation Y.A.5, owed little
to the B-48. It used the same form of robust, easily maintained, all-metal
semi-monocoque construction, but had a deep and capacious fuselage, a
tricycle undercarriage designed to absorb high sinking speeds, an· inverted
gull wing with high-lift flaps for effective control at low speeds, and a dihedral
tailplane. The nosewheel retracted into the underside of the generously-
proportioned nose and behind it, running from the fireproof bulkhead aft to
a retractable radome under the tail, was an immense bomb trunk capable of
holding a large and flexible load of attack weapons.

Alternative wing stores were 60-lb rocket projectiles, depth charges or auxiliary fuel tanks, and there were also pick-up points for a large ferrying tank
in the weapons trunk.

The crew of two sat high up under individual sliding canopies with the best possible view in all directions, and deck handling was simplified and expedited by powered wing-folding, powered extension and retraction of the arrester hook, and automatic ejection of the arrester wire as the hook was retracted. Retractable spools and attachment points for four rockets enabled catapulting or RATOG to be used for take-off with heavy loads from carriers in adverse wind conditions or from restricted deck space.

It was the original intention to fit a Napier Double Naiad propeller-turbine, for which jet efflux ports were built into the fuselage sides amidships, but when development of this power plant was discontinued, the first of three prototypes ordered, WB781, was completed with a 2,000 hp Rolls-Royce Griffon 56 vee-12 piston engine and 13-ft diameter six-bladed contra-rotating airscrew so that test flying could proceed on schedule.

With the Griffon engine the machine was re-designated Y.A.7 and flew for the first time at Brough on 20 September 1949 piloted by P. G. Lawrence. It then went to the A. & A.E.E., Boscombe Down, for handling trials prior to delivery to a Naval Trials Unit for carrier proving flights. Its first deck landings, some of which were made by P. G. Lawrence, took place on the carrier *Illustrious* on 8 February 1950.

While the design work was still in its early stages the naval specification was modified to include an additional crew member, resulting in the second aircraft, WB788, which first flew on 3 May 1950, being equipped with a third seat to carry two observers face to face under a common canopy behind the pilot. It also had increased sweepback on the mainplane leading edge, revised

WB781, first Blackburn B-54, or Y.A.5, with the original fin and rudder. In this view the weapon trunk doors are open, radome lowered and arrester hook down.

The Griffon-engined first prototype in Y.A.7 condition.

outer wing panels, taller fin and narrow-chord mass balanced rudder, cut off at the bottom and replaced by an extension to the rear fuselage. This aircraft, which made its first landings on *Illustrious* on 19 June 1950, was also Griffon-powered but in view of the modifications carried the SBAC designation Y.A.8. The same vertical tail surface modifications were also incorporated in the first machine, WB781.

With piston engines these two aircraft became, in fact, aerodynamic test vehicles for the three-seat turbine-powered third prototype, WB797, with which it was hoped to secure the G.R.17/45 production contract. Known as the Y.B.1, or alternatively the Blackburn B-88, this machine was powered by an Armstrong Siddeley Double Mamba driving a six-bladed contra-rotating airscrew. It was first flown at Brough by P. G. Lawrence on 19 July 1950 and remains historically important as Blackburn's first propeller-turbine aircraft. The Double Mamba was chosen because it consisted of two gas-turbine units side by side and coupled together to drive the contra-rotating airscrew, thus enabling the firm's designers to produce a twin-engined aircraft in single-engined configuration. The port unit drove the front airscrew and each half of the engine could be shut down independently of the other so that after take-off on maximum power, fuel could be husbanded and the range extended by cruising on one engine with an airscrew feathered.

The Y.B.1 made its first public appearance at the Naval Air Display at Lee-on-Solent on 26 August 1950, and at the last minute it replaced the Y.A.8 at the Farnborough SBAC Show of 6–10 September because the earlier machine could not be spared from its Ministry of Supply test programme. P. G. Lawrence consequently took full opportunity of demonstrating the

The Y.B.1 after the folding wing tips were fitted.

high rate of roll imparted by the Y.B.1's power-boosted ailerons and completed his display with one engine and airscrew stopped.

When the Y.B.1 returned to Brough, extended wing tips were fitted to increase the aspect ratio and reduce induced drag in the single-engined cruise condition. To keep the folded height within limits, the wing tips were also arranged to fold down at the same time as the main wing panels folded up. Unfortunately for Blackburns, however, competitive trials with the Fairey 17 and Short S.B.3, which included deck landings aboard *Illustrious* on 30 October, led to the placing of production contracts for the Fairey aircraft (later named Gannet) on 14 March 1951. Its adoption meant that for the first time in nearly four decades, Blackburns had no work on hand for the Navy.

Throughout their short careers, the three Blackburn prototype aircraft were painted dark sea-grey on the upper surfaces with duck egg green undersides, and in the 14 months preceding the trials, the Griffon-engined pair, assisted for a short time by the Y.B.1, made more than 1,000 landings and exceeded 300 hr of test flying.

After the award of the Gannet contract, the Y.B.1 WB797 was handed over to Armstrong Siddeley Motors Ltd and spent the rest of its useful life at their test establishment at Bitteswell as a test bed for the Double Mamba engine. In the same year, 1951, both Griffon-engined prototypes were transferred to the RAE, Farnborough, where, in September 1954, the Y.A.8 was in evidence with a number of modifications, but by September 1956 it had degenerated into an engineless hulk in the scrap yard on the northwest side of the aerodrome where it was joined in the following year by the Y.A.7.

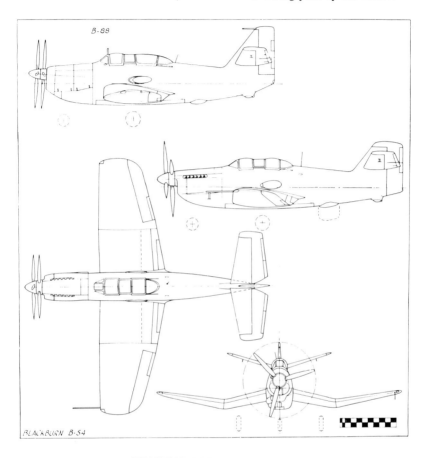

SPECIFICATION AND DATA

Manufacturers: Blackburn and General Aircraft Ltd, Brough Aerodrome, East Yorks.

Power Plants:		
(B-54/Y.A.7)	One 2,000 hp Rolls-Royce Griffon 56	
(B-54/Y.A.8)	One 2,000 hp Rolls-Royce Griffon 56	
(B-88/Y.B.1)	One 2,950 ehp Armstrong Siddeley Double Mamba	

Dimensions: Span 44 ft 2 in   (folded) 19 ft 6 in
Length (B-54) 42 ft 5 in   (B-88) 42 ft 8 in
Height (B-54) 17 ft 3 in   (B-88) 16 ft 9 in

Weights: All-up weight (B-54) 13,729 lb   (B-88) 13,091 lb

461

Performance: Maximum speed (B-54) 251 mph   (B-88) 320 mph

Production:

Three prototype aircraft only:

WB781   Blackburn B-54, Griffon 56, first flown 20 September 1949 as Y.A.7, scrapped at Farnborough 1957.

WB788   Blackburn B-54, Griffon 56, first flown 3 May 1950 as Y.A.8, scrapped at Farnborough 1956.

WB797   Blackburn B-88, Double Mamba, first flown 19 July 1950 as Y.B.1; to Armstrong Siddeley Motors Ltd in 1951; scrapped at Bitteswell July 1955.

XL149, a Beverley C. Mk 1 of No. 84 Squadron, Middle East Air Force, in camouflage, 1966. (*Crown Copyright Reserved.*)

Blackburn B-101 Beverley

First thoughts on the Beverley can be traced to the later stages of the 1939–45 war when F. F. Crocombe, chief designer of General Aircraft Ltd, Feltham, Middlesex, and his assistant C. W. Prower, were considering the possibility of large aeroplanes, designed specifically for carrying bulky loads and having immediate military potential as well as a future civil role. A military freighter of this kind had to be capable of the strategic transport of men and supplies from one theatre of operations to another and also of tactical use for delivering them right into the forward areas.

An attempt at solving the tactical transport problem formed the subject of a design study made by the company in 1945 using the specialist knowledge of outsize aircraft structures gained during construction of their Hamilcar tank-carrying glider. The proposal at this time was for a twin-finned, four-engined, fixed undercarriage, pod and boom aircraft with a detachable cargo compartment which bore a striking resemblance to the Hamilcar fuselage and was intended to be dropped from a height of 10 ft and to land on its own tracked undercarriage while the aircraft was flying over the dropping zone at about 90 mph. With four Rolls-Royce Merlin 90s it was expected to carry a payload of 20,000 lb at an all-up weight of 75,000 lb.

Of the several two- and four-engined studies which subsequently sprang from the first, one had a fixed freight compartment and four Bristol Hercules 100s for carrying a 20,000 lb load over medium distances and another was a much larger version, clearly recognizable as the embryo Beverley, with four Bristol Centaurus engines and a short-range payload of 38,000 lb at an all-up weight of 126,000 lb.

463

Thus, when Air Ministry requirements for a medium-range tactical transport were eventually finalized and Specification C.3/46 was issued calling for an aircraft with a still-air range of 500 miles while carrying a payload of 25,000 lb, General Aircraft Ltd were well prepared. Further demands were a service ceiling of 18,000 ft and suitability for trooping, parachuting, casualty evacuation, glider towing and the dropping of heavy loads by parachute. To meet the ceiling requirements, Bristols agreed to develop a new version of the Hercules, with two-speed supercharger, which would give 1,950 hp. Take-off and landing capability from small and restricted grass fields, all-important in military as well as civil context, was to be achieved by using large slotted flaps and reversible-pitch airscrews, modern devices which reduced the estimated full-load take-off distance to clear 50 ft to only 970 yd and cut the landing distance to a mere 225 yd.

Universal Freighter Mk 1 prototype

On receipt of a prototype order from the Air Ministry, construction began at Feltham of one complete aircraft, designated G.A.L.60, as well as a large number of components for a second, the name Universal Freighter being chosen as a reminder that it was aimed at both the civil and the military market. In keeping with the company's original design philosophy, it was constructed on the simplest possible lines with fixed nosewheel undercarriage, no pneumatics and no pressurization, features which brought immense savings in cost and weight and made for ease of maintenance when operating in remote areas away from specialist servicing facilities.

A high-wing layout was adopted to facilitate rapid cargo loading and give maximum head-room in the freight hold, the enormous 162-ft span mainplane being of RAF34 section built in four main parts and covered with riveted Alclad plating. The two-spar centre section, consisting of two separate halves bolted to the fuselage, carried the four Hercules engines installed as self-contained power plants driving 14-ft diameter four-bladed Rotol con-

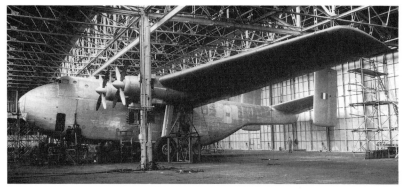

The G.A.L. 60 Universal Freighter Mk 1 in tail-down attitude during erection at Brough in March 1950.

464

The Universal Freighter Mk 1, WF320, on its way from Brough to Farnborough for the SBAC Show, September 1950. (*Charles E. Brown Photo.*)

stant-speed, feathering and reversible-pitch airscrews. As a result of model tests in the Fairey Aviation Co's wind tunnel, the nacelles were mounted low on the wing for minimum drag and optimum cooling, all the engines and their complete accessory bays being interchangeable as well as accessible in flight from the crawl-way in the leading edge of the wing.

The centre section also carried large-area NACA slotted trailing edge flaps, electrically controlled and synchronized down to a maximum flap angle of 60 degrees. Main fuel was carried in four 500-gallon Marston Excelsior flexible containers between the main spars outboard of the outer engines, and there was also room for a third on each side and for bag tanks in the outer wing panels which also carried the long-span set-back-hinge type ailerons. Wing deflection in flight coupled with the use of a high-wing layout reduced the need for dihedral to 54·5 min.

All-metal, two-spar, 42-ft span cantilever tail surfaces were set at a dihedral angle of 7 degrees 45 minutes to lift them clear of the slipstream of the inboard engines and carried twin, end-mounted rectangular fins and rudders. To reduce pilot fatigue in so large an aircraft, all controls were power-boosted, using the Fairey hydraulic control system with manual override, and the flight deck, reached by a ladder from the forward hold, accommodated two pilots side by side in the nose which shelved rapidly away to give the best possible downward view. The navigator and radio operator sat on back-to-back bench-type seats in the rear, with the navigator facing forward.

The Universal Freighter's most outstanding feature was the all-metal fuselage with its deep, rectangular-section, parallel-sided main cargo hold terminating in an outsize tail boom. A forward hold, 15 ft long and with 6 ft 8 in head-room, was situated in the extreme nose, and the rear of the fuselage formed a compartment with a slightly sloping floor and head-room of 5 ft 6 in, divided by structural bulkheads. Between lay the gargantuan, cathedral-like main hold, 36 ft long, 10 ft wide and 15 ft 6 in high, except forward under

465

the flight deck where the head-room was reduced to 10 ft. The floor, stressed to take a distributed load of 325 lb/sq ft, was constructed of light-alloy corrugations covered by flat sheeting, vehicles and bulky objects being secured to 5½-ton shackles let into the floor at 20-in intervals and by 1-ton rings in the side frames every 18 in.

Entry to the aircraft was by a crew door forward on the port side, a passenger door in the rear or through the rear freight-loading doors, the hinge lines of which were set at 30 degrees to the horizontal. A fore and aft ramp, lowered hydraulically by hand in 2½ min, gave easy access for heavy freight and vehicles. Typical loads were:

(a) Nine jeeps in two tiers, total weight 20,200 lb.
(b) Rearward-facing seats for 81 troops on two decks.
(c) 48 casualty stretchers in the main hold with six medical attendants in the rear fuselage.
(d) 38 paratroops back to back down the centre and 24 supply containers slung under the fuselage.
(e) One Angledozer, fully fuelled, weight 26,970 lb.
(f) One 3·7-in Army anti-aircraft gun, weight 20,560 lb.
(g) One Army vehicle with 10-cwt trailer and 75-mm gun on para-dropping pallets.
(h) One Bulldozer and accessories, weight 15,700 lb.
(i) Two Army vehicles, total weight 25,200 lb.

Lockheed semi-cantilever main wheel shock-absorber struts with vertical velocity absorption of 12 ft/sec for the short landing case, were attached to the wing main spar through a spherical joint and braced to the fuselage by built-up, aerofoil-section triangular sponsons. Very large low-pressure Dunlop single main wheels, 6·62 ft in diameter and inflated to 50 lb/sq in, gave a wheel load similar to that of a Dakota, and the double nosewheel assembly, with Lockheed hydraulic steering, reduced the ground turning circle to 33 ft.

When General Aircraft Ltd merged with Blackburn Aircraft Ltd on 1 January 1949 to form Blackburn and General Aircraft Ltd, it was agreed that

WF320 in 1952 with bogie undercarriage, showing the original loading doors and ramp.

466

all work in hand at Feltham, including the Universal Freighter, should be completed there, but when the great machine was ready in the following October, it was decided that the adjoining Hanworth Aerodrome was unsuitable for its first flight. It was consequently dis-assembled and transported in unpainted state by road to Brough where re-erection presented some difficulty, for even in the cavernous interior of the North Sea hangar, head-room was insufficient for the Universal's huge fins without chocking up the nosewheel.

Now known as the Blackburn and General Aircraft Universal Freighter Mk 1, the aircraft made a trouble-free first flight at Brough in RAF markings as WF320 on 20 June 1950, just four years after the start of the design, piloted by the company's chief test pilot Harold 'Tim' Wood with D. G. Brade as co-pilot. As the Bristol 167 Brabazon 1 had flown in the previous September, the 47-ton Universal Freighter was Britain's second largest landplane and yet within four weeks all preliminary handling and control assessments, performance and load tests had been completed in 21 flights. Also, enough flying hours were completed to qualify it for participation in September's SBAC Show at Farnborough, where it dwarfed every other aircraft. It then proceeded to the A. & A.E.E., Boscombe Down, where the handling trials were completed in the unusually short time of three weeks before it went on to Abingdon where it performed with conspicuous success in competitive trials with an American Fairchild C-82 Packet which involved flying on to a rough grass strip, delivering a heavy load and flying out again. Later at Brough it lifted a 10-ton Priestman Wolf excavator and a 30-seater coach.

A Ministry of Supply order for a second prototype was announced at the SBAC Show but, since the issue of Specification C.3/46, considerable advances had been made in the technique of dropping large stores by parachute and the need for large transports able to land on small unprepared strips had receded. Proposals were therefore put to the Ministry of Supply early in 1951 for a change of power plant to the 2,850 hp Bristol Centaurus with which, carrying the same payload as in the original design, the range was trebled for an increase in all-up weight to 127,000 lb; alternatively, a load of 50,000 lb could be carried on very short flights. Corresponding changes were suggested in the shape of the rear fuselage, using clam shell doors entirely removable for dropping large stores, and for enlarging the tail boom to make it roomy enough for carrying passengers.

To assist in finalizing such drastic alterations, the Universal Mk 1 WF320 was used at Brough in May 1951 for heavy-dropping trials with the loading ramp and rear doors entirely removed, while in the following July the massive wheels were replaced by four-wheeled bogie units of the type to be used on the next machine. Thus equipped, WF320 made an impressive fully-flapped slow flypast at the Fifty Years of Flying Exhibition at Hendon on 19 July. Again piloted by H. 'Tim' Wood, it conveyed the company's Land-Rover and 22-ft caravan from Brough to Farnborough for the SBAC Show of 11–16 September 1951, and stole the show by the ease with which its vast bulk left the ground and by the shortness of its landing run. This was achieved off a fully-flapped approach by coupling the airscrew control to the equalizing beam of the bogie undercarriage so that the airscrews went automatically into reverse on touchdown. The pilot then caused considerable amusement by taxying backwards off the runway. After the Show it went to Blackburn's newly-acquired base at Holme-on-Spalding Moor for further flying in connection with the development of the Mk 2 aircraft.

Early in 1952 authorization was obtained for completing the second machine in the form suggested, and fuselage modifications were put in hand which amounted to an 80 per cent redesign. In its new configuration the machine bore the General Aircraft designation G.A.L.65 as well as a Blackburn type number B-100, and as, at this stage, Blackburn and General Aircraft Ltd hoped to sell it to civil operators, it was named the Universal Freighter Mk 2. First move in this direction was a scheme prepared for Silver City Airways for a cross-Channel car ferry version to carry six cars and five motor cycles on two decks, with up to 42 passengers in the tail boom. The project was shown in model form at the 1952 Farnborough SBAC Show in company with the Mk 1 prototype WF320, but the scheme came to nought.

Nevertheless, support for the military version came from the Ministry of Supply in the form of an order for 20 aircraft (later increased to 47) for RAF Transport Command, deliveries to commence in 1955. Allocation of the type name Beverley in December 1952 followed the usual practice of naming transport aircraft after towns and cities, the choice in this case being particularly suitable since, apart from being appropriately alliterative, it was the name of the county town of the East Riding of Yorkshire and also of the rural district in which Brough is situated.

Construction of the Mk 2 prototype proceeded quickly because a number of components made at Feltham during 1948–49 were already in existence,

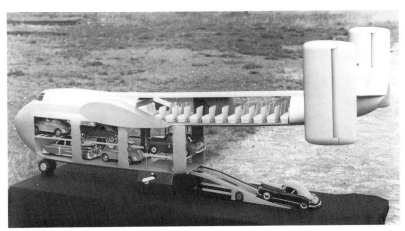

Sectional model of the Universal Freighter car ferry project prepared for Silver City Airways in 1952.

The prototype Universal Freighter Mk 2, WZ889, with rear doors removed for early dropping-trials in 1954, showing the redesigned passenger-carrying tail boom.

and the machine made a first flight of $1\frac{1}{2}$ hr duration at Brough on 14 June 1953 piloted by Wood and Brade. It carried RAF serial WZ889 and differed additionally from the Mk 1 in having $16\frac{1}{2}$-ft diameter square-tipped de Havilland Hydromatic reversible-pitch airscrews (each of which weighed more than the entire Blackburn First Monoplane) with fibre-glass spinners and integral cooling fan, inboard engines projecting 1 ft ahead of the outboard, three degrees of mainplane dihedral, increased tailplane and elevator area and Maxaret automatic braking.

Contractors trials included full-load take-off tests in December 1953 with the critical engine cut, using water ballast tanks in the main hold. Afterwards the floor was fitted with a roller conveyor, and the rear doors were removed for a demonstration over an Army dropping zone at Amesbury, Wilts., during which a support vehicle and gun, mounted on a wooden platform, descended under a cluster of six 42-ft parachutes. In silver and white, the colour scheme chosen for production aircraft, WZ889 formed a static exhibit at the SBAC Show at Farnborough in September that year, afterwards returning to Brough to be brought up to full Beverley standard, having flown 135 hr 55 min.

Beverley production

To speed deliveries to the RAF, several sub-assemblies including engine and accessory bays, undercarriage sponsons, bogie beams and clam shell doors, were made in the Dumbarton works, and the first two Beverley C. Mk 1s, XB259 and XB260, designated Blackburn B-101 and powered by four 2,850 hp Bristol Centaurus 173s, flew at Brough on 29 January and 30 March 1955 respectively. They were retained by the manufacturers for test purposes or the trial installation of modifications, and both aircraft were temporarily allotted civil markings in the following year.

The next two, XB261 and XB262, were delivered to the A. & A.E.E.,

Q   469

The first two production Beverleys, XB259 and XB260, later G-AOAI and G-AOEK, at roll out in January 1955. They had fewer tail-boom windows than the prototype.

Boscombe Down, in the following July for acceptance tests which included an investigation into their paratrooping capabilities. Flt Lt Harrison was the first man dropped, but by May 1956 more than 250 live drops had been made at Boscombe Down from the rear-fuselage floor hatch and from the side doors of the freight compartment.

XB262 was subjected to extremes of temperature, an ordeal begun on 5 August 1955 when Flt Lt Stuart Smith accompanied by Blackburn's H. 'Tim' Wood, flew it to Idris, Tripoli, to deliver a Westland Whirlwind helicopter and conduct tropical trials. Flown by a Royal Canadian Air Force crew under the command of Sqn Ldr R. H. Janzen and carrying six RAF ground technicians, XB262 left again on 4 December, for Canada. The crossing via Prestwick, Keflavik and Goose Bay to Montreal occupied 20 hr 15 min flying time and the machine arrived at Edmonton for winterization trials on 10 December. It was demonstrated at Montreal, Ottawa and Toronto by the Blackburn and General agents, Field Aviation Ltd, who also worked out a scheme for using Beverley tankers to supply Arctic outposts with fuel, up-lifting 6,000 gallons per trip. While in Canada the machine transported a 43,800 lb load of transformer equipment belonging to the Eldorado Mining & Refining Co and destined for Uranium City, and returned to Boscombe Down in June 1956 carrying a Bristol Centaurus piston engine, a Rolls-Royce Avon turbojet, and a complete Auster A.O.P.9 aircraft, WZ702, which had also been on winterization trials.

Still wearing red Arctic wing tips and the polar bear badge it had earned at the RCAF Air Material Command Central Experimental and Proving

470

Establishment at Namao, Canada, in 1955, XB262 was exhibited at the Farnborough SBAC Show two years later in September 1957.

The fifth production Beverley, XB263, was shown statically at Farnborough in September 1955 with a typical composite load consisting of three Army vehicles, 12 tons of freight in the main hold and seats for 42 passengers in the tail boom. It was one of eight aircraft completed by the end of that year, and the first delivery took place on 12 March 1956 when XB265 was handed over at Abingdon to No. 47 Squadron, a particularly appropriate choice since the squadron had been raised originally at Beverley, Yorks., in 1916. With a payload of nearly 22 tons it was the largest aircraft to enter RAF service at that time and the first specially designed for dropping heavy Army equipment.

Four others replaced Handley Page Hastings aircraft at Abingdon before the end of the month, but all five returned to Brough on 6 April when HRH Prince Philip visited the B. & G.A. factory, took the controls of one machine in flight and witnessed a supply-dropping demonstration. On 25 April this performance was repeated by one machine before West German Air Force officers at Wahn Airport, near Cologne.

During its first few months in RAF service, heavier and heavier loads were dropped with success until a maximum of 24,000 lb, suspended below eight 66-ft G.Q. parachutes, was reached in July 1956. In the same month icing trials were conducted at Luton with a 6-ft test section of Beverley mainplane flown vertically on top of the Napier Icing Research Unit's Avro Lincoln RF402 to test the thermal de-icing system, and in September's SBAC Show H. 'Tim' Wood demonstrated the 19th production aircraft XB289. With 100 fully-armed troops loaded at the double in 1 min 50 sec, he made incredibly tight circuits and dramatically short landings.

The test programme at Brough was arranged to take the Beverley to its very limits, and in the following December Wood used the first production machine, XB259, for highly-spectacular short-take-off trials using ten Napier Scarab solid fuel rocket units which reduced the unstick distance at a gross weight of 135,000 lb to that of the original Universal Freighter, viz. 400 yards. On 29 April 1957 the same pilot eclipsed even the RAF's impressive record by dropping a load of ballast exceeding 13 tons (29,120 lb) over Brough and a month later made exacting taxying tests in deep mud both at Brough and Old Sarum.

Civil use

Although the Beverley was designed for civil as well as military use, none of the airlines bought it. Nevertheless the two prototypes WF320 and WZ889 were civil-registered to the Ministry of Supply as G-AMUX and G-AMVW in November 1952 and January 1953 respectively, and the first two production machines XB259 and XB260 to Blackburn and General Aircraft Ltd as G-AOAI and G-AOEK in March and September 1955. The first three registrations were almost certainly allotted for demonstrations to potential

471

The Beverley C. Mk. 1 G-AOEK inscribed Blackburn Universal for the Umm Siad oil drilling airlift in 1955.

customers overseas but it is doubtful if the markings were ever used; in fact the Mk 1 prototype was flying in the Exeter area as WF320 on 28 April 1953, the day on which its Certificate of Airworthiness was issued and five months after civil marks were allotted.

The fourth machine, G-AOEK, was issued with a special short term C. of A., valid for four months from 22 September 1955, for a flight to the Eastern Arabian port of Umm Siad in the Qatar Peninsula. Here it was used to airlift heavy machinery to an oil drilling site, isolated by mountain ranges and formidable deserts, at Jebel Fahud, 365 miles away in the Sultanate of Muscat and Oman. This joint Blackburn and General/Hunting Clan Air Transport operation, under Grp Capt R. C. Hockey of Blackburns, was made on behalf of the Iraq Petroleum Co Ltd, and all the equipment, totalling 129 tons, including one piece 21 ft long and weighing $16\frac{1}{2}$ tons, was transported in nine flights. Each trip lasted just over two hours compared with two weeks for the sea/land alternative.

On its return the machine reverted to the manufacturers as XB260 to be used on a 500-hr intensive flying programme which included one flight of 13 hr 25 min duration. Still bearing the challenge 'Try your strength Blackburn Beverley' in Arabic over the pilots' door, the machine went to Canada in March 1957 for additional winterization trials at Namao and Edmonton, calling at Rockcliffe en route. Field Aviation Ltd were this time responsible for a project known as the Beverley Mk 2, capable of landing 160 passengers or 50,000 lb of freight at any of the 3,000-ft landing strips at remote outposts. This scheme, like the one worked out in 1955, was not proceeded with.

Service use
Nos. 47 and 53 Squadrons

On 1 July 1956, at the end of a short working-up period, No. 47 Squadron inaugurated a five-times-weekly return freight service to RAF Wildenrath, Germany, with supplies for the 2nd Tactical Air Force, a two-hour trip from Abingdon flown at 165 knots along the airways system via London and the North Foreland. As a result of this experience it became regular squadron policy to use the reversible-pitch airscrews on every landing to reduce wear and tear on tyres and brakes. Loads frequently included the Army's dismantled Bristol Sycamore and Westland Whirlwind helicopters, and later the route network was extended to include Cyprus, Malta and North Africa. At a Combined Operation staged at Farnborough on 6 Ocotber 1956, Beverley XB284 flew from Abingdon with 46 RAMC personnel and a complete field hospital weighing 9 tons. By March 1957, the squadron had moved 4,700 tons of cargo and carried 2,700 passengers, part of this total being medical supplies flown to Vienna in XB291 in November 1956 for Hungarian relief work. A large proportion resulted from British military operations at Suez where outstanding loads included a 47-ft radar scanner carried in XB267, an 18,000-lb signals vehicle, three 9,000-lb trailers and 270 tons of oil—all airlifted from Cyprus to Port Said in 21 flights.

Together with No. 53 Squadron, which re-equipped with Beverleys at Abingdon in February 1957, No. 47 bore the brunt of RAF and Army heavy-lift commitments at home and in the Near East for some years. Throughout 1957 machines of these squadrons were detached in pairs to Khormaksar, Aden, flying via Malta, Cyprus and Bahrein, to support British ground forces and those of the Sultan of Muscat and Oman. No. 47's XB268 and XB283, first to arrive at Aden on 2 February 1957, had flown 100 hr and carried 170 tons of freight by the end of March, mainly to roughly-hewn airstrips on the border of the Yemen in an area where concrete runways were unknown and servicing facilities at their most primitive.

The first pair inaugurated a system whereby Beverleys of either No. 47 or No. 53 Squadron left Abingdon after major servicing, flew to Aden with full payloads and, at the completion of their tour of duty, returned to Abingdon just as their next overhaul fell due. After an early setback when No. 53 Squadron lost XH117 in a fatal crash at Drayton, near Abingdon, on 5 March 1957, the Beverleys coped handsomely with all demands made on them in Aden. The more unusual loads included cattle for Gouraf, fire engines for Maseira and Sharjah, an 11-ton Saracen armoured car flown out of Riyad, and an adequately restrained madman from Ataq.

The Desert Mobility Trials in Cyrenaica in March 1960 represented a good example of the work of these two squadrons. Following the strategic airlift of 12 Westland Whirlwind helicopters of No. 225 Squadron from Andover in the previous month, they transported all the Land-Rovers and trailers needed during the exercise. They were joined by two Beverleys from Nos. 30 and 84

XL152 of No. 30 Squadron, MEAF, in the blue and white livery used during most of the Beverley's RAF service. (*Courtesy B. N. Stainer.*)

Squadrons of the Middle East Air Force and left El Adem every 15 min to drop 60 tons of food, water and stores daily at forward bases in the desert. Landings always resulted in self-created reverse-pitch sandstorms, but apart from clogging of the brakes serviceability was not impaired.

No. 53 Squadron was eventually disbanded and its aircraft absorbed by No. 47, but the massed Beverleys of several squadrons moved a vast quantity of essential stores from Cyprus to Amman, Jordan, in support of a Hunter squadron during the Iraqi coup. Less conventional cargoes, however, included three London buses flown to Helsinki for the British Trades Fair in 1957 and Bristol Bloodhound surface-to-air missiles conveyed from Filton to Cranwell in April 1958. In October that year Folland Gnat XN122, a spare engine and ground equipment were flown to Aden for tropical trials and afterwards reloaded for delivery to the Indian Air Force experimental establishment at Kanpur.

No. 47 Squadron's most distant assignment began in February 1966 when XB264, first of three Beverleys sent to Vietnam, arrived at the Da Nang Air Base to assist the charitable organizations in flying relief supplies to the highlands of the interior, work which continued for some 18 months.

No. 30 Squadron

The third squadron, No. 30, relinquished its Hastings aircraft in favour of Beverleys XH118–XH120, XH122–XH124, XL130 and XL131 in April 1957, and operated at Dishforth alongside No. 242 Operational Conversion Unit, which had also been issued with three Beverleys and was responsible for training all RAF Transport Command crews. XH120 was shown at the US Armed Forces Day display at Prestwick on 18 May 1957, and in February 1958 this aircraft, with four others from Nos. 47 and 53 Squadrons, airlifted 500 men, 10 tons of equipment, as well as 11 Land-Rovers and trailers, from Abingdon to Idris, Tripoli, and back during Exercise Quickstep.

All three squadrons contributed to the airlift to Cyprus during 14–19 June 1958, covering the distance in 16 hr with refuelling stops at Orange in France, and at Malta. A month later 12 Beverleys were flown to Cyprus again, to join five already there on detachment and fly the 16th Independent Parachute Brigade to Amman, Jordan, during the Iraqi revolution.

Soon afterwards No. 30 Squadron was posted to Eastleigh, Nairobi, where it played a valuable part in the drive against the Mau Mau and joined forces with Beverleys of No. 47 Squadron to fly ground crews for the Hunter squadrons to Kuwait during the emergency of July 1961. They also flew low-level food-dropping sorties to the victims of the Tana River flooding in November that year.

Early in 1963, in lighter vein, No. 30's Beverleys made the highest air drop ever recorded when building materials and parts for two new huts for the Mountain Club were parachuted to their erection sites 14,000 ft up on Mount Kenya. In more typical role, five of the squadron's Beverleys, together with an Argosy and a Shackleton, were called up at short notice on 23 January 1964 to convey two companies of the Staffordshires from Eastleigh to Entebbe during the Zanzibar revolution and army rising in Uganda, and to retrieve a third from Mombasa next day.

In May 1965, independence in Kenya compelled a move to Muharraq, Bahrein, base from which No. 30 Squadron Beverleys became the backbone of RAF transport operations in the Gulf area and ran scheduled services round the coast to Muscat, Sharjah and Masirah in support of Army units until the squadron returned to the United Kingdom in the following year.

No. 84 Squadron

In May 1958 No. 84 Squadron MEAF re-equipped with Beverleys at Aden where a detachment from Nos. 47 and 53 Squadrons had been operating for some time. It was responsible for a supply-dropping, logistic airlift in the Aden area for British and South Arabian Army units and for scheduled services as far as Bahrein in the east and Hargeisha and Eastleigh in the west. Among others it received XM106–XM112 inclusive from No. 27 MU, Shawbury, and carried many outsize and bizarre loads including a 5,000-gallon fuel storage tank flown to the 850 yard strip at Dhala in XM106 in March 1961 and a 20,000-lb gravel crusher for the new runway at Beihan, 4,000 ft above sea level, in the following August.

They played a major part during the Brunei revolt in 1962 and by July 1963, when the squadron's Beverleys had completed five years' service and flown nearly two million miles, had carried over 60,000 passengers and some 20,000 tons of freight. On 5 June 1964, XH121 was the first Beverley to land on the newly-lengthened Thumier airstrip in the Radfan Mountains during the fighting in the Aden hinterland, and in eight days during September the squadron airlifted 280,000 lb of equipment to an airfield construction squadron engaged in saving the flood-devastated Lower Aulaqi Sultanate in the South Arabian Federation, the heaviest item being a 30,000-lb tracked bulldozer which lifted the Beverley's nosewheel clear of the ground while being loaded. In 1965 and again in 1967 huge quantities of foodstuffs were flown to the civilian population cut off by flooded roads in north-east Kenya.

No. 34 Squadron

XB260, XB262, XB289 and XM104, four Beverleys forming a Flight attached to No. 48 Squadron at Singapore early in 1959, were later joined by a fifth and raised in status to form No. 34 Squadron on 10 October 1960. Based at Seletar, it was the fifth and final Beverley squadron, its main task being to fly supplies to Labuan, 850 miles distant, during the long drawn out campaign in Malaya during 1962–66.

The insignia used by the five squadrons at first took the form of the squadron number in a coloured diamond on the fin, but later No. 47 adopted a crane's head in grey on blue waves in a white circle and No. 84 a scorpion. Early in 1965 many Beverleys were flown back to the UK to be camouflaged in matt olive-green and dark sand with black under surfaces, at No. 32 MU, St Athan. On one of these positioning flights in July 1965 the veteran D.H.51 biplane VP-KAA was flown from Nairobi to Hatfield en route to the Shuttleworth Collection at Old Warden, Biggleswade.

By 1967 the end of the Beverley's useful life was in sight, a rapid phase-out began in favour of the Lockheed C-130K Hercules and during the year they were flown back in ever increasing numbers to No. 27 MU, Shawbury, where so many had commenced their Service lives. Among the first to go were XB265 of No. 242 OCU, XB263 of No. 47 Squadron and XM107 of No. 84 Squadron which passed through Abingdon en route to oblivion in March 1967. Abingdon was also the scene of an official farewell flypast staged by No. 47 Squadron on 16 September that year which culminated in a spectacular horizontal 'bomb burst' by five Beverleys which included XB286, XB290 and XL131.

Among the last of the MEAF machines to leave for the UK were XH122 and XL130 which staged through Sharjah in October, but tragically a Singapore-based Beverley crashed and was burned out in the dense jungle of Johore State, Malaysia, with the loss of six crew during a supply dropping exercise on 15 December, the very eve of its retirement. On their final day of service the last two in Britain were photographed in formation while en route to Shawbury, wearing for the last time their newly acquired RAF Air Support Command titling and the code letters F(XB269) and X(XB290).

Most of the Beverleys were then scrapped, the last (XL149) in 1977, but three have been preserved: XH124 at the RAF Museum, Hendon; XB259 (G-AOAI) by the Museum of Army Transport at Beverley, North Humberside; and XB261 by the Moat House Hotel at Southend.

476

SPECIFICATION AND DATA

Manufacturers: General Aircraft Ltd, Feltham, Middlesex, and Blackburn and General Aircraft Ltd, Brough Aerodrome, East Yorks.

Power Plants: (Universal Freighter Mk 1)
  Four 2,020 hp Bristol Hercules 730
  (Universal Freighter Mk 2)
  Four 2,840 hp Bristol Centaurus 171
  (Beverley C.Mk 1)
  Four 2,850 hp Bristol Centaurus 173

Dimensions, Weights and Performance:

	Universal Freighter Mk 1	Universal Freighter Mk 2	Beverley C. Mk 1
Span	162 ft 0 in	162 ft 0 in	162 ft 0 in
Length	99 ft 1 in	99 ft 1 in	99 ft 5 in
Height	31 ft 0 in	33 ft 0 in	38 ft 9 in
Wing area	2.916 sq ft	2,916 sq ft	2,916 sq ft
Basic weight	62,860 lb	74,030 lb	79,230 lb
Maximum load	33,600 lb	52,970 lb	55,770 lb
Maximum gross weight	105,000 lb	127,000 lb	135,000 lb
Maximum speed	242 mph	244 mph	238 mph
Recommended cruise	163 mph	169 mph	173 mph
Initial climb	830 ft/min	800 ft/min	760 ft/min
Service ceiling	16,500 ft	18,000 ft	16,000 ft

Typical range: (Universal Freighter Mk 1)
  500 miles at 163 mph at 8,000 ft with 26,000 lb load
  (Universal Freighter Mk 2)
  760 miles at 172 mph at 8,000 ft with 45,700 lb load
  (Beverley C. Mk 1)
  1,300 miles at 186 mph at 8,000 ft with 29,000 lb load or 160 miles at 170 mph at 8,000 ft with 50,000 lb load

Production:

(a) *G.A.L.60 Universal Freighter Mk 1*
  One aircraft only, constructed at Feltham, Middlesex, by General Aircraft Ltd 1948–49. Taken over by Blackburn and General Aircraft Ltd 1 January 1949 and allotted c/n 1000. Final erection at Brough, first flown as WF320 on 20 June 1950, temporarily registered to the Ministry of Supply November 1952 as G-AMUX, Certificate of Airworthiness issued 28 April 1953. Reverted to WF320, reduced to produce at Brough 1958.

(b) *G.A.L.65/B-100 Universal Freighter Mk 2*
  One aircraft only, c/n 1001, built at Brough 1952–53, first flown as WZ889 on 14 June 1953. Temporarily registered to the Ministry of Supply January 1953 as G-AMVW, reverted to WZ889 and reduced to produce at Brough 1958.

(c) *Blackburn and General B-101 Beverley C. Mk 1*

Initial order for 20 aircraft, XB259–XB269 and XB283–XB291, placed in September 1952. Certificates of Registration issued when the first two became civil, gave constructor's numbers as 1002 and 1003. The data below includes the date of first flight immediately following the RAF markings.

XB259, 29 January 1955, retained by Blackburns, temporarily civil March 1955 as G-AOAI, later to the RAE (Farnborough) as XB259; XB260, 30 March 1955, retained by Blackburns, temporarily civil September 1955 as G-AOEK, four month C. of A. issued 22 September 1955, reverted to XB260 for winterization trials in Canada March 1957, to No. 34 Sqn coded U; XB261, 5 July 1955, to A. & A.E.E. (Boscombe Down); XB262, 8 July 1955, tropical trials in Libya and winterization trials in Canada 1955, to No. 34 Sqn coded W, to No. 84 Sqn coded W; XB263, 26 August 1955, to No. 47 Sqn coded A, to No. 53 Sqn coded L, to No. 30 Sqn coded K, to No. 47 Sqn coded A, dismantled at No. 27 MU (Shawbury) 1967; XB264, 7 November 1955, to No. 53 Sqn coded C, to No. 47 Sqn coded C, to No. 34 Sqn; XB265, 26 February 1956,

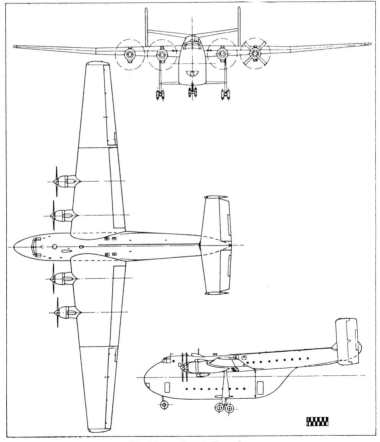

Blackburn B-101 Beverley.

first delivery to the RAF 12 March 1956, to No. 47 Sqn coded A, to No. 53 Sqn coded A, to No. 242 OCU coded W, dismantled at No. 27 MU (Shawbury) 1967; XB266, 23 November 1955, to A. & A.E.E. (Boscombe Down) for tropical trials at Idris, Tripoli June 1956–July 1956, to No. 84 Sqn coded V, to No. 30 Sqn coded E; XB267, 30 December 1955, to No. 47 Sqn coded B, to No. 53 Sqn coded B; XB268, 14 March 1956, to No. 47 Sqn coded D, crashed at El Adem 13 April 1963; XB269, 22 March 1956, to No. 47 Sqn coded F.

XB283, 17 April 1956, to No. 47 Sqn coded G, to No. 30 Sqn; XB284, 7 May 1956, to No. 47 Sqn coded H; XB285, 25 May 1956, to No. 47 Sqn coded J later C, to No. 53 Sqn coded J; XB286, 13 June 1956, to No. 47 Sqn coded S, to No. 53 Sqn coded S, to No. 242 OCU coded Z; XB287, 4 July 1956, to No. 53 Sqn coded T; XB288, 3 August 1956, to No. 53 Sqn coded U; XB289, 21 August 1956, to No. 53 Sqn coded V, to No. 34 Sqn; XB290, 7 September 1956, to No. 53 Sqn coded W, to No. 47 Sqn coded X; XB291, 3 October 1956, to No. 47 Sqn coded X, to No. 53 Sqn coded X, to No. 34 Sqn.

Further order for 27 aircraft, XH116–XH124, XL130–XL132, XL148–XL152 and XM103–XM112, placed in May 1954.

XH116, 24 October 1956, to No. 47 Sqn coded Y, to No. 53 Sqn coded Y, to No. 30 Sqn; XH117, 7 November 1956, to No. 53 Sqn coded Z, crashed near Abingdon 5 March 1957; XH118, 3 December 1956, to No. 30 Sqn coded A, crashed at Beihan, South Arabia February 1958; XH119, 3 January 1957, to No. 30 Sqn coded B, to No. 27 MU (Shawbury) 1967; XH120, 18 January 1957, to No. 30 Sqn coded C, later H; XH121, 21 February 1957, to No. 53 Sqn coded Z, to No. 84 Sqn; XH122, 13 March 1957, to No. 30 Sqn coded D; XH123, 21 March 1957, to No. 30 Sqn coded F, later C, to No. 47 Sqn 12 May 1966 coded N; XH124, 1 May 1957, to No. 30 Sqn coded G, to No. 242 OCU, camouflaged in 1965, to No. 27 MU (Shawbury) 1967.

XL130, 23 May 1957, to No. 30 Sqn coded H, to No. 242 OCU coded successively H, K and Y; XL131, 23 May 1957, to No. 30 Sqn coded J, to No. 47 Sqn coded L; XL132, 11 June 1957, to No. 242 OCU coded Z, crashed near Thorney Island 17 May 1962; XL148, 8 July 1957, to No. 242 OCU coded U, later Y; XL149, 15 July 1957, to No. 242 OCU coded X, to No. 32 MU (St Athan) for camouflage January 1965, to No. 84 Sqn via Malta 14 April 1965; XL150, 2 August 1957, to the RAE (Farnborough), to No. 47 Sqn coded K; XL151, 11 September 1957, to No. 47 Sqn coded R, to No. 53 Sqn coded R, to No. 84 Sqn coded L, crashed at Aden 11 October 1960; XL152, 27 September 1957, to No. 27 MU (Shawbury), to No. 30 Sqn coded J.

XM103, 23 October 1957, to No. 27 MU, to No. 30 Sqn coded K; XM104, 8 November 1957, to No. 27 MU, to No. 34 Sqn coded P, to No. 84 Sqn; XM105, 29 November 1957, to No. 27 MU, to No. 53 Sqn coded P, to No. 47 Sqn coded E, to No. 30 sqn coded A; XM106, 20 December 1957, to No. 27 MU, to No. 84 Sqn coded R, later X, camouflaged at No. 32 MU (St Athan) 1965, to No. 84 Sqn via Malta 14 April 1965; XM107, 3 January 1958, to No. 27 MU, to No. 84 Sqn coded S, to No. 27 MU (Shawbury) 1967; XM108, 5 February 1958, to No. 27 MU, to No. 84 Sqn coded T; XM109, 26 February 1958, to No. 27 MU, to No. 84 Sqn coded U; XM110, 19 March 1958, to No. 27 MU, to No. 84 Sqn coded V, wrecked by time bomb at Bahrein 1961; XM111, 19 April 1958, to No. 27 MU, to No. 84 Sqn coded W, to No. 30 Sqn coded D; XM112, 15 May 1958, to No. 27 MU, to No. 30 Sqn coded V, to No. 84 Sqn.

The first non-folding pre-production Blackburn, N.A.39, on an early test flight, 1958.

Blackburn B-103 Buccaneer

Advances in missile technology after the 1939–45 war gradually forced the high-flying bomber farther and farther away from its target and eventually rendered it ineffective. The least vulnerable alternative method of pressing home a successful attack, foreseen by British military strategists in the early 1950s, was to use an aircraft capable of low-level penetration at high subsonic speed below the defensive radar curtain of the enemy. The specification for such an aircraft, issued by the Admiralty in 1952 and numbered M.148T (or N.A.39), resulted in a period of fierce competitive tendering from more than a dozen firms which ended in July 1955 when Blackburn's tender, the work of chief designer B. P. Laight and his team, was accepted. The Ministry of Supply then placed an order for 20 pre-production aircraft, the first scheduled to fly in April 1958.

It was estimated that the Blackburn N.A.39 put Britain three years ahead of the rest of the world in the field of high-speed, low-level strike aircraft, with the result that security restrictions were applied very stringently and even guarded references to the project were few and far between.

First hints came in Robert Blackburn's annual report in August 1955 when he alluded to 'an important and challenging aircraft development contract' that had been placed with the company. He also revealed that enhanced lifting qualities had been obtained in boundary layer control experiments with a high-speed, thin-section swept wing which greatly improved take-off and landing. Robert Blackburn did not live to see further work on the project and the next reference came from his successor as chairman, Mr Eric Turner, who revealed in July 1956 that the company was testing a model of the new aircraft in the high-speed tunnel at RAE Bedford and was developing methods of machining major structural units from the solid.

First official admission that the aircraft under construction was a naval strike aircraft was given in February 1957 and in April the Navy Estimates referred to its ability to carry a nuclear weapon over considerable distances. Construction proceeded swiftly, and the centre section of the first machine, XK486, was removed from the jigs less than three months later on 6 July. Engine runs commenced in March 1958 and in the following month the machine, very top secret and shrouded in sheeting, left Brough on the road journey to the RAE at Thurleigh, near Bedford, for its first flight which took place, after several days delay due to a burst tyre, on 30 April, just thirty-three months after the contract was placed. With Blackburn test pilot D. J. Whitehead at the controls and the company's head of flight test B. J. Watson in the rear seat, it was a trouble-free exercise which lasted 39 minutes and included a climb to 17,000 ft.

To have met all target dates during the design and construction of so important a prototype while also engaged in erecting a supersonic wind tunnel (opened at Brough by the First Sea Lord, Earl Mountbatten, on 24 March 1958) and installing computers at the factory to assist during the years of development ahead, was a feat of which Blackburns were justly proud.

The aircraft itself was the outcome of a design study numbered B-103, an early version of which had been considered with two Armstrong Siddeley Sapphire turbine engines underslung between the legs of a wide track retractable undercarriage. Under the SBAC system it was designated Y.B.3 but more usually referred to as the Blackburn N.A.39. It was comparatively small and carried a crew of two in tandem under a sliding canopy in Martin Baker ejection seats, offset laterally to give the maximum possible view. Power was supplied by two 7,100 lb static thrust de Havilland Gyron Junior turbojets in nacelles which fitted close to the sides of the fuselage and projected well ahead of the mainplane. The aircraft sat low to the ground on a short, lever-suspension nosewheel undercarriage of Dowty manufacture, but its most striking feature was the large area-rule bulge in the rear fuselage which compensated for the loss of wing cross sectional area as the air flowed aft, delaying the drag-rise towards Mach 1 and also giving a smoother ride for the crew during low-level flight at high speed. These conditions also presented the designers with the problem of combining long fatigue life with the structural strength needed to withstand low-level turbulence. This was achieved by machining wing panels from the solid by sculptural milling, complete with integral stiffening, and the spars and ribs from single steel forgings. These measures gave the N.A.39 the same active service life as a conventional aircraft operating under less arduous conditions.

The all-metal semi-monocoque fuselage was built in three sections, nose complete with cockpit, centre portion with integral engine mountings, and the rear fuselage. It was thus a true scion of the long line of Blackburn types traceable right back to the Swift biplane of 1920, first of the three-piece fuselage designs using parts machined from the solid.

On 9 July 1958 D. J. Whitehead flew the first machine, XK486, from

Thurleigh to the old wartime airfield at Holme-on-Spalding Moor, Yorks., some 12 miles northwest of Brough, which Blackburn Aircraft Ltd had just taken over because the length of their factory runway was inadequate. Whitehead routed overhead the works to give employees a brief air display, and two months later, in September 1958, when it had flown 25 hours, the aircraft appeared at the Farnborough SBAC Show. It was the only new aeroplane present and its slow flypast caused something of a sensation. The second aircraft, XK487, flew at Holme-on-Spalding Moor on 26 August and on its second flight flew down to Farnborough to be exhibited statically to security-cleared visitors, both aircraft sporting a distinctive blue and white colour scheme. During the display it became known that the type was to be ordered in quantity for the Royal Navy.

The second and all subsequent aircraft were towed some 18 miles on their own wheels from Brough to Holme-on-Spalding Moor for final inspection and flight test, eight aircraft being completed and flown in the first 16 months in accordance with the terms of the Ministry of Supply contract drawn up some four years previously. The wisdom of placing an order for a number of pre-production aircraft in preference to the usual single prototypes was now apparent because there were sufficient trials aircraft, specially equipped and instrumented, to permit aerodynamic tests, engine development work, deck-landing trials, and the proving of all weapons, electrical and navigational systems to be programmed simultaneously. As the aircraft was supported through the Mutual Weapons Development Programme, much of the special test flight instrumentation and electronic data analysing equipment was supplied to Blackburns from America.

The first machine, XK486, was used for general handling trials; XK487 was used for flutter tests; XK489, being the first with folding wings and arrester hook, was used for preliminary trials with XK523 aboard *Victorious* in the English Channel in January 1960; XK490, first with the rotating

Line-up of test aircraft at Holme-on-Spalding Moor in 1960, with the two non-folding prototypes, XK486 and XK487, on the left.

weapons-bay was used for armament trials; XK491 for electrical tests and flight-refuelling sorties with a Canberra tanker, WH735, at Tarrant Rushton; XK524 for tests with the long-range underwing tanks; and XK525 for proving the complete weapons and electronic navigation systems.

For this work they were distributed to the RAE, Bedford, and the A. & A.E.E. Boscombe Down, or were retained at Holme-on-Spalding Moor and flown with Hawker Hunter F. Mk 4 and Gloster Meteor N.F. Mk 12 chase planes in close attendance. XK488, the first in Royal Navy colours, was handed over to the de Havilland Engine Co, manufacturers of the Gyron Juniors, for development work at Hatfield. While there it overshot on 24 July 1961 and went through greenhouses, but it was still in use by Bristol Siddeley as a test bed at Filton in 1966.

All this activity was conducted in the strictest secrecy, few were allowed to see the aircraft on the ground at close quarters and no photographs were released with personnel in the vicinity who could be scaled to reveal its dimensions. These were not disclosed until June 1959 when, as a result of a security downgrading, it was possible to inspect the fourth aircraft, XK490, first flown on 23 March 1959, at the Paris Salon.

The thin-section cantilever wing was seen to be mounted in the midwing position without dihedral and to have considerable sweepback, 40 degrees at 25 per cent chord at the root, decreasing first to 38 degrees 6 minutes and then to 30 degrees 12 minutes on the outer wing. Multi-spar construction was employed, the inner wings having a light-alloy auxiliary spar and two steel main spars which were bolted to three spar-rings in the centre fuselage. Outer wing panels were folded hydraulically, ailerons were powered by Boulton Paul duplicated tandem actuators, and trailing edge flaps were fitted inboard of the ailerons. The tip of the fin was pivoted to move with the cantilever all-moving tailplane, and the rudder and elevators were powered by the same Boulton Paul hydraulic system as the ailerons.

Super circulation, or boundary layer control, over the mainplane, flaps, ailerons and tailplane was provided by tapping approximately 10 per cent of the engine mass air flow from the final compressor stage of each Gyron Junior engine and blowing it through slits along the leading edges of wing and tailplane as well as rearwards over all control and flap surfaces. By this means the boundary layer of 'tired' air was re-energized by injecting into it a stream of high velocity air, nearly doubling the lift on the approach with flaps and ailerons drooped, and reducing the carrier approach speed by some 12 knots while retaining full lateral control. The system could also be switched to hot air to provide thermal de-icing.

Hydraulic retraction of the undercarriage folded the nosewheel backwards beneath the pilot and took the main wheels upwards into the engine air ducts. In the rear the sting-type arrester hook, also hydraulically controlled, was equipped with an anti-skid system. Integral fuel tanks were fitted in the upper part of the fuselage but there was also provision for external tanks under each wing, and a retractable probe was fitted ahead of the pilot for in-flight

Buccaneer S. Mk 1 XK531 of No. 700Z Flight preparing to land at Lossiemouth, 1961.

refuelling. The area rule bulge in the rear was used to house Ferranti navigation/attack equipment integrated with the flight instruments, autopilot, radio and radar to provide a complete control, navigation and terrain clearance system. This solved electronically the problem of navigating accurately to the target without fear of striking obstacles in the flight path while flying low at 10–12 miles a minute.

Nuclear and conventional weapons, or a reconnaissance camera pack, were carried on a large hydraulically-actuated rotating bay, or bomb door, below the fuselage. Delivery was by direct run over the target or by the newer 'toss bomb' technique whereby the pilot, approaching at zero feet, reached a pre-determined distance from his target, initiated a half loop with a roll off the top and made off without delay on a reciprocal course. The weapon was released halfway up the half loop and followed a ballistic trajectory to the target.

D. J. Whitehead, by now Blackburn's chief test pilot, and his assistant G. R. I. 'Sailor' Parker, flew the Paris Salon machine XK490 at the Farnborough SBAC Show of September 1959, but soon afterwards, on October 12, this aircraft crashed near Lyndhurst, Hants., while on test from Boscombe Down, and William Alford, test pilot of the US Office of Naval Research and his observer, John Joyce of Blackburns, lost their lives after ejecting at low altitude while the aircraft was inverted.

In January 1960 deck-landing trials were completed successfully in the English Channel on *Victorious* in a full range of weather conditions, the initial landing and launching being made by D. J. Whitehead in the seventh aircraft, XK523. It was assisted on the trials by the first fully-navalized machine, XK489, thirty take-offs and landings being completed in $3\frac{1}{2}$ days. Tests included transfer to and from the hangar deck below, for which purpose the N.A.39, to fit on a standard carrier deck lift, could be shortened by swinging the search radar nose cone sideways and by opening the hydraulically actuated sideways-hingeing air brakes in the tail.

XK489 made a slow flypast with weapons bay open during the SBAC Show in the following September; but for the second year in succession this event was followed by the loss of an aircraft, this time the prototype, XK486, from which on 5 October G. R. I. 'Sailor' Parker and his observer successfully ejected before it crashed at Little Weighton near Brough.

The 10th to 13th pre-production aircraft, XK526–XK529, were assigned to C Squadron, otherwise the Royal Naval Test Unit at the A. & A.E.E., Boscombe Down, for full carrier trials, and in January 1961 the first two went to the Mediterranean for this purpose aboard *Ark Royal*. XK526, on its return, was prepared for tropical trials and left in the following July by sea for Singapore, but XK529, in further trials aboard *Hermes* crashed in Lyme Bay, Dorset, on 31 August with the loss of Lt Cdr O. Brown and his observer.

Service use

During the proving years the N.A.39 had been nameless, but on 26 August 1960 the name Buccaneer S. Mk 1 was officially adopted, and in March 1961 No. 700Z Flight (Cdr A. J. Leahy, RN) was commissioned at Lossiemouth to undertake intensive flying trials and to clear it for naval service in readiness for the formation of the first two operational squadrons. Initially the Flight had two aircraft, XK531 and XK532, but by the end of 1961 XK533–XK535 had also arrived and later still it received the last development aircraft, XK536. The first three machines were delivered in the usual grey/white livery but the fourth, XK534, set a fashion in all-white anti-radiation paint which, by October 1961, had spread to the whole Flight, with Lossiemouth codings 680/LM–685/LM applied in pale blue. A target of 40 sorties per aircraft per month was initiated using XK531 and XK532 for airframe and

Buccaneer S. Mk 1 XN930 of No. 801 Squadron, showing the method of shortening at nose and tail to fit *Ark Royal*'s deck lift.

485

engine proving and the others for range computations from sea level to over 40,000 ft, weapons systems tests, tactical capability trials and servicing evaluation. Test sorties were also flown in the nearby Scottish Highlands with the electronic terrain clearance gear, and drills were worked out for use in case of blowing-system failure, a longer run being required for an unblown take-off coupled with a higher approach speed for landing.

Special flying by No. 700Z Flight included participation in the operational capability Exercise Shopwindow, and in September 1961 test pilots Whitehead and Parker demonstrated XK534 (already coded 683/LM but not yet delivered) at the Farnborough SBAC Show. Later in the month, accompanied by two Noratlas freighters of the West German Air Force carrying Blackburn ground equipment and technicians from Holme-on-Spalding Moor, this machine also flew to Fürstenfeldbruck near Munich to be shown off to the German authorities.

At the following SBAC Show in September 1962 No. 700Z Flight's first four Buccaneers, XK531–XK534, were chosen to perform formation aerobatics, but soon afterwards, its work complete, the unit was disbanded. The first operational squadron, No. 801 (Lt Cdr E. R. Anson, RN), was commissioned at Lossiemouth on 17 July that year with a number of Buccaneer S. Mk 1 aircraft commencing with XN925, and after the usual working-up period, embarked on *Ark Royal* in the English Channel on 20 February 1963. The aircraft were painted in the standard Navy colour scheme with grey top and white undersides and were emblazoned with *Ark Royal* codings commencing 115/R. The squadron later transferred to *Victorious* when it sailed from Portsmouth on 14 August, and on 29 January 1964, when the ship arrived at Dar es Salaam from the Far East to relieve *Centaur*, its Buccaneers were at readiness in case support was needed by ground troops dealing with East African revolts. No. 801 remained aboard *Victorious* until the ship paid off at Portsmouth in July 1965, returned to Lossiemouth and was disbanded.

To acquaint himself with the new equipment, the First Lord of the Admiralty, Lord Carrington, visited Holme-on-Spalding Moor on 16 April 1962 and flew in the all-white XN924 with D. J. Whitehead, who made two low-level, high-speed runs across the airfield, and he also inspected the 1912 Blackburn Monoplane which had been taken up by road from the Shuttleworth Trust to mark the 50th anniversary of the birth of British military aviation. The same Buccaneer was then exhibited at the Hanover Air Show, during the period 29 April–9 May 1962, for at the time the Germans were still actively interested in it.

The second Buccaneer unit, No. 809 (Lt Cdr J. F. H. C. de Winton, RN), commissioned in January 1963, was an HQ Squadron largely formed from the aircraft and crews of No. 700Z Flight, although its first aircraft was a new one, XN924, coded 220/LM. Shore-based at Lossiemouth, it continued with Buccaneer operational development until the completion of the S. Mk 1 programme in 1965. Its task over, the unit then re-formed as No. 736 Squadron to act as an operational training school for Buccaneer crews.

Buccaneer S. Mk 1 XN965 of No. 809 Squadron landing on *Eagle*, 1964.
(*Crown Copyright Reserved.*)

The third and final Buccaneer S. Mk 1 Squadron, No. 800 (Lt Cdr J. C. Mather, RN), was commissioned on 19 March 1964, took part in the Fleet Air Arm Jubilee Review at Yeovilton on 28 May and embarked for the Far East in the carrier *Eagle* on 2 December, its first aircraft XN956 bearing the code 100/E. To overcome take-off weight limitations, four Vickers Supermarine Scimitar tankers were used to fuel the Buccaneers immediately after they left the carrier. Early in 1965 the squadron took part in Exercise Showpiece Malaysia off Singapore, but from March 15, when *Eagle* took over from *Ark Royal* in the Mozambique Channel, they were employed on oil embargo-enforcement duties off Beira, seaward terminal of the oil pipeline to Rhodesia.

Four production S. Mk 1 aircraft which did not enter squadron service were the first two, XN522 and XN523, which went to Boscombe Down for acceptance tests; XN952, in which test pilot G. R. I. 'Sailor' Parker and his flight test observer G. R. C. Copeman lost their lives when it crashed at Holme-on-Spalding Moor on 19 February 1963; and XN966, which crashed at Lossiemouth on 24 January 1964 before entering squadron service.

Buccaneer S. Mk 2

After the departure of the last S. Mk 1 aircraft from Brough in December 1963, the factory began re-tooling for production of the S. Mk 2 version with 11,200 lb.s.t. Rolls-Royce Spey bypass engines to enable advantage to be taken of the development-stretch envisaged in the original design. The main airframe modification was the enlargement of the circular engine air intakes to an oval form to take the Spey's greater mass flow, but the boundary layer slits were also modified and, for the first time, blowing was applied to the inner wing. The essential advance of the new mark over the old was the 30 per cent increase in thrust which removed emergency situations such as engine failure during a full load launch or while landing-on with full BLC 'blow' selected, which had proved critical in the earlier version. The Spey's lower fuel consumption under economic cruise conditions also gave considerably greater range.

This development, first revealed in May 1961, was followed on 8 January 1962 by a Ministry of Aviation production order for the Royal Navy, i.e. before the first squadron had received the S. Mk 1. To spread the test flying, two of the early pre-production airframes, XK526 and XK527, were re-engined and modified at Brough where first engine runs were made with XK526 on 8 April 1963. Its first flight of 1 hr 10 min duration, as the prototype S. Mk 2, took place at Holme-on-Spalding Moor on 17 May piloted by D. J. Whitehead. XK527 which followed on 19 August, set a fashion for late production aircraft in having a non-retractable flight-refuelling probe.

To speed up perfection of the S. Mk 2's advanced radar systems, the second fixed-wing pre-production machine, XK487, was loaned to Ferranti Ltd and flown to Turnhouse, Edinburgh, on 8 May 1963, where Safeland arrester barriers were specially installed on the runway. The machine was maintained and flown by Ferranti until handed back at Farnborough some $3\frac{1}{2}$ years later.

In 1964, when the two modified S. Mk 1 aircraft had completed a year's development flying and full-scale fatigue tests on the Buccaneer airframe had proved the structure for a life of over 20,000 hr, the first production S. Mk 2, XN974, was ready. It was flown for the first time by D. J. Whitehead on 6 June and was used jointly with the second, XN975, for proving trials by the A. & A.E.E. and the manufacturers. The third, XN976, was shown at the Farnborough SBAC Show in the following September in full Fleet Air Arm trim, armed with two rocket pods and two Martin Bullpup air-to-surface missiles on underwing pylons. Wing tip vortex generators were also fitted.

Deck-landing and catapult trials with XN975 aboard *Ark Royal*, in the Bristol Channel and in the English Channel off Lyme Bay, by D. J. Whitehead and four pilots of the Naval Test Squadron at Boscombe Down, were completed in half the scheduled time of two weeks, 78 launches proving sufficient instead of the planned 100. The hands-off technique was used for launching with various external loads up to maximum gross weight, and automatic underwater ejection seats were fitted for the first time.

Hot-and-high trials in the USA with XK527, XN974 and XN976 involved an outward flight via Reykjavik, Goose Bay, Patuxent River and Maryland to the US Navy base at Pensacola with a supporting flight of Argosy freighters. Two aircraft which flew out on 23 July 1965 were joined by the third some three weeks later after which all three operated from the US carrier *Lexington* for four days and made 100 take-offs, equivalent to 115 hr of low-level flying in hot and turbulent conditions.

After the return of the main party, XN974 stayed behind to give displays at Elgin Air Force Base, Edwards AFB and Patuxent River Naval Air Test

Buccaneer S. Mk 2s, XV168 and XV333, of No. 801 Squadron, with *Victorious* tail crest and codings, refuelling in flight from Handley Page Victor K.1A tanker XH650, August 1967. (*Crown Copyright Reserved.*)

Centre. As a grand finale to the programme Cdr G. Higgs, RN, CO of the Naval Test Squadron at Boscombe Down, accompanied by Lt Cdr A. Taylor, RN, then flew it from Goose Bay, Labrador, to Lossiemouth, a distance of 1,950 miles in 4 hr 16 min without flight refuelling. It was the first non-stop crossing of the Atlantic by a Fleet Air Arm aircraft and 30 min fuel remained in the tanks when it landed. Later that year, a Buccaneer S. Mk 2 flew 8 hr 40 min in a 'cold soak' test which involved two in-flight refuellings from a Handley Page Victor K.1A tanker above 30,000 ft.

The engine development aircraft from this batch was XN893, delivered to Rolls-Royce Ltd at Hucknall on 23 February 1965.

Export Models

Attempts at interesting West Germany in the Buccaneer, begun when XK489 was shown to a German delegation at Dunsfold in September 1960 and continued with demonstrations by XK534 at Fürstenfeldbruck in September 1961, eventually came to nought, but on 11 October 1962 the South African Government placed an order for 16 aircraft, with an option on a further 14.

Known as the S. Mk 50, the South African Buccaneer was basically a land-based version of the S. Mk 2, without the hydraulic wing-folding gear and intended for operation over the South Atlantic and Indian Oceans. The first, serialled 411 and finished in dark sea-grey above and PRU blue below, white bordered South African Air Force emblem, and orange, white and blue fin flash, flew for the first time at Holme-on-Spalding Moor on 9 January 1965. Between the placing of the order and the first flight, opposition had grown to the supply of arms to South Africa and on 25 February 1965 the British Government announced that it would permit no more than the first order for 16 aircraft to be delivered and that the purchasers would not be allowed to take up the option.

G-2-1/411, first Buccaneer S. Mk 50 for South Africa, flying with four Nord A.S.30 missiles near Holme-on-Spalding Moor.

All 16 aircraft were completed during 1965 and 1966 but flew with Blackburn Class B registrations commencing G-2-1 through to G-2-16. For comfortable operation at high take-off weights from hot and high airfields, two retractable Bristol Siddeley B.S.605 twin-chamber rocket engines giving 8,000 lb.s.t. were installed in the S. Mk 50s immediately forward of the air brakes.

Several, including G-2-1/411, G-2-3/413 and G-2-4/414, remained at Holme-on-Spalding Moor for contractors' flying, the first with Nord A.S.30 air-to-ground missiles, but 415 and 416 were delivered to Lossiemouth to form a Buccaneer conversion unit for the South African crews. Later they were joined by several others and, on 27 October 1965, 412 to 419 inclusive all left together, flown by SAAF personnel, for the long delivery flight round 'the bulge', probably via the Canary Islands, Azores, Ascension and Luanda to Waterkloof near Pretoria. Unfortunately aircraft 419 crashed into the sea 500 miles south of the Canary Islands on 31 October, but its crew was picked up by a Dutch liner.

S. Mk 50 deliveries were completed in 1966 when the eight aircraft at Holme-on-Spalding Moor were towed back to Brough, cocooned and shipped from Hull as deck cargo. Minus their nosewheels, 421, 423, 424 and 426 were towed through the streets to the Albert Dock at 5.30 am on 27 July and from there taken by floating crane down river to King George Dock for loading aboard the *van der Stel* which sailed on 5 August. The remainder, consisting of 411, 420, 422 and 425, left in the same manner aboard the *Langkloof* on 17 October. With the seven which reached South Africa by air they formed No. 24 Squadron, SAAF, and carried two auxiliary fuel tanks on the underwing pylons when engaged on long-range reconnaissance duties, but in the strike role these were replaced by four Nord A.S.30 missiles.

490

Late in 1966 the Squadron's CO, Cmdt A. M. Muller, and his observer, Maj T. J. de Munnick, made the longest flight by a Buccaneer up to that date, covering a distance of over 5,000 miles in aircraft 414 with the aid of two in-flight refuellings from the auxiliary tanks of sister aircraft 426.

In Royal Navy service

Throughout the production programme Blackburns maintained an unbroken record of on-time deliveries, and the first Buccaneer S. Mk 2 aircraft were despatched to the Fleet Air Arm in March 1965 as planned. Following the procedure adopted when the earlier Buccaneers were introduced into service, an Intensive Flying Trials Unit, known this time as No. 700B Flight, was commissioned at Lossiemouth on 9 April 1965 and eventually received eight S. Mk 2s. Its work of proving the aircraft for Naval use occupied only a few months and it was disbanded on 30 September. As a first step in re-equipping all the Buccaneer units with the new mark, all its aircraft were transferred to No. 801 Squadron, commissioned at Lossiemouth on 14 October, and four days later the CO, Lt Cdr J. de Winton RN, made a ceremonial flypast in XN980 at 1,000 ft above Nelson's Column, in London, to mark the 160th anniversary of the Battle of Trafalgar. The wreck of its sister aircraft, XN979, first of the new type to be lost, was retrieved by Naval divers from a record depth of 60 fathoms after it had crashed into the sea off the Lizard on 9 June 1966.

In the same month the squadron embarked on *Victorious*, and working-up operations, which took place while the carrier was in the Irish Sea, included a 2,300 mile non-stop flight to Gibraltar and back by Lt K. B. Cross, RN, and his observer Lt Cdr G. Oxley, RN. The sortie also included a simulated low-level attack on the airfield at Gibraltar. *Victorious* later sailed for the Far East where it took part in an exercise with the USS *Enterprise* and gave the Buccaneer crews experience of in-flight refuelling from Douglas Skywarriors of the US Navy.

In 1967 No. 801 Squadron returned to the United Kingdom and in September two of its aircraft, XV168 and XV333, gave a flight refuelling demonstration before a military gathering at Larkhill, using a Marham-based

413, third South African S. Mk 50 at Holme-on-Spalding Moor in 1965.

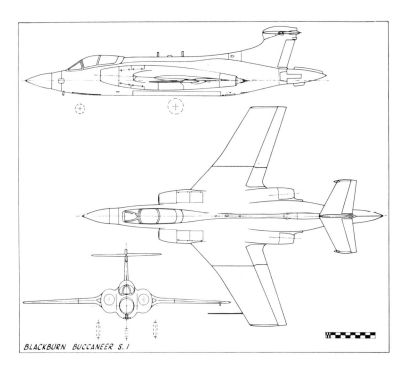

BLACKBURN BUCCANEER S. 1

Handley Page Victor K.1A tanker. A third machine was exhibited statically with Sidewinder infra-red air-to-air missiles which had been installed by the squadron. It was the first intimation that the Buccaneer was to carry this form of self-defence, although in the previous February it had been announced that one machine was to be fitted experimentally with Missile Anti-Radar Television (Martel).

The re-commissioning of No. 809 Squadron (Lt Cdr L. Middleton, RN) with Buccaneer Mk 2s took place at Lossiemouth on 27 January 1966, and in the following September it was based temporarily at Yeovilton while taking part in the mass flypast at the Farnborough SBAC Show. In 1967 it embarked on *Hermes* and patrolled off Gibraltar when restrictions were first placed on air space in the neighbourhood. Its S. Mk 1 aircraft, with those relinquished by No. 801 Squadron, formed the equipment of No. 736 Squadron, a newly-constituted Buccaneer training unit based at Lossiemouth. Operating its S. Mk 1s from Yeovilton, this unit carried out deck-landing practices aboard *Ark Royal* off South Wales in June 1966 and, soon afterwards, a number of S. Mk 2 aircraft were added to its strength.

No. 800 Squadron was also re-commissioned with S. Mk 2s later in 1966, one of its first aircraft being XV157 which formed a static exhibit in September that year at Farnborough, surrounded by a formidable array of external stores. Embarkation on *Eagle* followed, and on 11 November another of its

A Buccaneer S.2 of No. 809 Squadron unleashes a salvo of rockets during weapons practice from HMS *Ark Royal* in October 1978 near the end of the carrier's last commission.

aircraft, XN956 bearing the carrier's coding 100/E, flew in formation with the 25-year-old Blackburn-built Fairey Swordfish LS326 to mark the 26th anniversary of the crippling of the Italian Fleet at Taranto.

A very different assignment, rare in peacetime, came on 28 March 1967 when its Buccaneers, together with those of No. 736 Squadron, were ordered to destroy the tanker *Torrey Canyon* aground on the Seven Stones Reef, 16 miles off Land's End, and spreading thousands of tons of crude oil on Cornish beaches. Operating from Lossiemouth but using Brawdy as an advanced base, eight Buccaneers dropped forty-two 1,000-lb high-explosive

Bombed-up Buccaneer S.2 of No. 809 Squadron being launched from HMS *Ark Royal* in October 1978 during the ship's last commission.

One of No. 809 Squadron's Buccaneer S.2s (just visible) leaving the waist catapult of HMS *Ark Royal* while three more await their turn. Parked on the port quarter are six Phantom FG.1s of No. 892 Squadron.

bombs, 30 of which scored direct hits. Similar attacks were made on the days that followed.

On 3 July 1967 a fourth Buccaneer S.2 squadron, No. 803 (Lt Cdr M. J. A. Hornblower, RN), was formed at Lossiemouth for service in *Hermes* and the Fleet Air Arm's strike force was building up to its peak. The initial order for ten Buccaneer S.2s (XN974–XN983), placed in January 1962, had been supplemented from June 1966 by further contracts for seventy-four aircraft (XT269–XT288, DV152–XV168, XV332–XV361 and XV863–XV869), all of which were delivered on schedule, the 84th and last machine being handed over in December 1968.

In 1962 when the Buccaneer had entered operational service the Royal Navy had also obtained authorisation for the first of a new class of large (circa 50,000 tons) aircraft-carrier, designated CVA-01, and it was intended that the carrier force would continue to form the backbone of the Navy. A change of government from Conservative to Labour in 1964 brought a change in attitude to defence and the following year the Defence Minister, Mr Denis Healey, announced the cancellation of all the RAF's new aircraft programmes, including the BAC TSR-2 which, ironically, was to be replaced in part some four years later by the Buccaneer. At the same time he conducted a review of maritime tasks and concluded (erroneously) that Britain no longer needed aircraft-carriers and that in future the roles of the Navy's fixed-wing aircraft would be undertaken satisfactorily, and more cheaply, by shore-based machines of the RAF. In February 1966 the Government announced the cancellation of CVA-01 and the run-down of the existing carrier force, scheduled to be completed by the end of 1971.

No. 803 Squadron had a short life and after service in *Hermes*, from August 1968 to January 1969, disbanded at Lossiemouth on 18 December 1969. At the start of this commission four of the squadron's Buccaneer S.2s flew out from Lossiemouth via Gan in the Indian Ocean to join the carrier, which was then operating off Malaysia. In the rear seat of one of the aircraft was the First Sea Lord, Admiral Sir Michael LeFanu, who wished to visit his ships in the Far East.

The next month, September 1968, No. 809 Squadron, which had already served in *Hermes*, took part in the SBAC Display at Farnborough with its five-aircraft aerobatic team 'Phoenix Five', performing loops and rolls in close formation. During the year Buccaneers of No. 800 Squadron were detached from *Eagle* to Luqa, Malta, to take part in the NATO Exercise 'Eden Apple' and achieved a high success rate in simulated strikes on shipping. The first operational Buccaneer S.2 squadron, No. 801, whose original carrier *Victorious* had been withdrawn and scrapped in December 1967, now served at sea in *Hermes* for various periods until May 1970, when the squadron came ashore to Lossiemouth and disbanded there on 21 July 1970.

This left Nos. 800 and 809 Squadrons for, respectively, the two Fleet carriers *Eagle* and *Ark Royal*, together with No. 736 Training Squadron. In June 1970 the Conservatives returned to power and it was hoped that the decision to scrap carriers would be reversed. By October it became apparent that the new Defence Minister, Lord Carrington, had no such inclination, although some thought was given to adapting the projected anti-submarine helicopter carriers (*Invincible* class) to take Harrier V/STOL fighters as well. *Ark Royal* was to be kept in service until the late 1970s; *Eagle* was put into reserve, but promptly gutted and finally scrapped in 1978; *Hermes* was converted into a Commando carrier in 1973. As a consequence No. 800 Squadron disbanded at Lossiemouth on 23 February 1972, followed two days later by No. 736 Squadron. Of the Navy's eighty-four Buccaneer S.2s, sixty-two were to be handed over to the RAF and the remaining twenty-two would

The first RAF Buccaneer squadron was No. 12, which formed at Honington on 1 October 1969 and was equipped initially with ex-Royal Navy aircraft converted to S.2As. Note No. 12 Squadron's fox badge on the engine intakes.

The first production Buccaneer S.2Bs (XW526 nearest) went to No. 15 Squadron, RAF, which formed at Honington in October 1970 and moved to Laarbruch, Germany, in January 1971.

be used by No. 809 Squadron operating from *Ark Royal* until she was paid off.

Early in 1972 there was trouble in British Honduras, a colony that was to become the independent state of Belize and was threatened by its neighbour, Guatemala. *Ark Royal*, initially 4,000 miles away, was ordered to proceed towards Honduras and provide an 'air presence' as soon as possible. On 28 January when the ship was still 1,300 miles away, two of No. 809's Buccaneers were launched, supported by two tanker aircraft from the ship. The two Buccaneers were refuelled in the air 400 miles from *Ark Royal*, flew on to make their 'air presence' felt over Belize City, then returned and after another refuelling landed back on the carrier. The 2,600-mile nonstop round trip was accomplished in under 6 hours and won for No. 809 Squadron the Boyd Trophy for 1972. It also demonstrated most effectively the range and flexibility of Blackburn's carrier-based bomber, which could if required carry nuclear weapons. At the time No. 809 had an embarked strength of fifteen Buccaneers.

When not at sea No. 809 Squadron continued to be based at Lossiemouth until October 1972 when it moved to RAF Honington, where by now the RAF was building up its own Buccaneer force. Both Services had adopted the Hawker Siddeley Dynamics/Matra Martel air-to-surface missile, which for maritime operations gave the Buccaneer greatly enhanced anti-ship capability. Fleet Air Arm Buccaneers were now redesignated S.2C (not equipped for Martel) and S.2D (Martel-equipped). In September 1974 No. 809 Squadron embarked in *Ark Royal* equipped completely with Buccaneer S.2Ds. Four years later, in April 1978, the Buccaneers of No. 809 Squadron embarked in *Ark Royal* for their last commission. They took part in the NATO Exercise 'Northern Wedding' off Norway in September and on 27 November while *Ark Royal* was in the Mediterranean were launched for the last time to fly direct to RAF St Athan. No. 809 Squadron disbanded at Lee-on-Solent on 15

December 1978, *Ark Royal* was paid off in the same month, and most of the Navy Buccaneers were then converted to RAF equipment standards, except for XT287 and XV344 which were sent to RAE Farnborough for trials work.

Nearly two years were to elapse before the Fleet Air Arm had a carrier-based fixed-wing combat aircraft again, the British Aerospace Sea Harrier, and in this programme the Brough factory continues to play a significant part.

In Royal Air Force service

Almost from the start Blackburns had tried to interest the RAF in the Buccaneer, without success as by then the programme for the supersonic TSR-2 was under way. The second prototype Buccaneer S.1, XK487, was in fact used to aid development of the TSR-2's Ferranti radar. When the TSR-2 was cancelled in April 1965, the RAF was told that it would receive fifty General Dynamics F-111Ks instead. The order for these United States aircraft, placed in February 1966, was cancelled in January 1968.

During this period the Brough firm—now part of the Hawker Siddeley Group—renewed its efforts to fill the TSR-2 gap, offering the Buccaneer Mk.2 2-Star with more powerful Spey engines in 1965 and later the 3-Star version with reheat for its engines, capable of supersonic performance, and with a full range of TSR-2 avionics. None of these appealed but finally, following cancellation of the F-111K order, a contract was announced in July 1968 for twenty-six Buccaneer S.2Bs for the RAF (XW525–XW550). In addition, the RAF would in due course inherit some sixty-two Navy Buccaneers which, after relatively minor modification for land use, would be designated S.2As.

The S.2B version had a higher all-up weight (62,000 lb), strengthened undercarriage, could carry up to 16,000 lb of weapons, and the rotating weapons bay was enlarged, making a distinctive bulge below the fuselage, to accommodate a 425-gallon tank and increase internal fuel capacity. To avoid

No. 16 Squadron Buccaneer S.2Bs at Nellis AFB, Nevada, during the 'Red Flag' exercise in November 1981.

497

re-design the wing-folding mechanism was retained, although certain other naval features such as the catapult hold-back were deleted. Changes were made to the avionics and communications equipments to bring them into line with RAF requirements, particularly in the overland strike role, and development work in connection with the Martel missile—four of which can be carried by the Buccaneer on underwing pylons—was done at Boscombe Down on aircraft XK527, XV352 and XW529. Subsequent weapons adopted for the Buccaneer have included the PAVE-Spike 1,000-lb laser-guided bomb, British Aerospace Sea Eagle sea-skimming anti-ship missile and AIM-9 Sidewinder air-to-air missile for self-defence.

The first Buccaneer converted to RAF requirements was S.2A XV350 which made its first flight in modified form on 11 February 1969. It was later joined at Boscombe for trials work by the first production S.2B, XW525, which first flew on 8 January 1970 and was the first aircraft to incorporate the bulged bomb door fuel tank.

Buccaneer S.2B XW530 of No. 12 Squadron, RAF Lossiemouth, wearing the camouflage scheme current in 1987. The S.2B's bulged bomb bay is clearly visible in this view.

Meanwhile RAF aircrews had been converting to the Buccaneer with No. 736 Squadron at Lossiemouth and flying with No. 809 Squadron on exchange postings in *Ark Royal*. The RAF's own conversion unit, No. 237 OCU, was formed at Honington in March 1971.

The Buccaneer entered RAF front-line service on 1 October 1969 when No. 12 Squadron was re-formed at Honington under Wg Cdr G. G. Davies and equipped with ex-Navy S.2As, operating in the maritime strike role. A year later, on 1 October 1970, No. 15 Squadron (Wg Cdr D. J. H. Collins) was formed at Honington with Buccaneer S.2Bs from the first RAF production batch. Its task was low-level strike in support of NATO forces in Germany and in January 1971 No. 15 Squadron moved to its operational base, RAF Laarbruch on the Dutch/German border. RAF Germany's Buccaneer Wing was completed on 6 June 1972 when No. 16 Squadron (Wg Cdr R. A. Edwards) re-formed at Laarbuch, having previously flown Canberras.

498

During 1973 No. 12 Squadron began to receive ex-Navy S.2As that had been fully modified to S.2B standard at Brough. The next, and fourth, Buccaneer squadron was No. 208 which was officially formed at Honington on 1 July 1974 although it was not fully equipped, with S.2As, until October. Initially No. 208's role was overland strike.

In addition to service use a considerable number of Buccaneers have been used on R & D tasks and in 1976 Brough delivered three specially built S.2Bs (XW986–XW988) to the RAE for weapons trials. Supplementary contracts for seventeen aircraft (XX885–XX901), delivered between May 1974 and January 1977, and a final batch of three (XZ430–XZ432), delivered in May–October 1977, brought total Buccaneer S.2B production to forty-nine. The last Buccaneer (XZ432) was delivered to the RAF on 6 October 1977, ending a run of 19 years' continuous production during which 209 aircraft were built.

In April 1977 No. 208 sent a detachment of Buccaneers to Goose Bay, Labrador, for exercises and in August that year took part in the USAF's annual 'Red Flag' exercise, centred on Nellis AFB in the Nevada desert. There the Buccaneers performed most effectively and with their ground-hugging 100-ft 600-kt tactics earned the nickname 'dirt-eaters' from the Americans.

The fifth and final Buccaneer squadron, No. 216 (Wg Cdr P. G. Sturt) started forming at Honington on 1 July 1979. Equipped with S.2Bs for the maritime strike role, it took time to work up and did not become fully operational until 1 January 1980. No 216, however, was the first to operate the Pave-Spike laser-guided bomb.

Whereas naval Buccaneers flying fast and low over the sea had had few problems, the RAF machines, which in the overland role had to follow rugged terrain as closely as possible, were subjected to much greater stress. The first sign of a fatigue problem occurred in Germany when a Buccaneer's wing folded in flight, due it was thought to a wing bolt coming out. On 7 February 1980 a Buccaneer of No. 15 Squadron taking part in the 'Red Flag' exercise at Nellis broke up in the air. Investigation showed fatigue cracks in the wing and that the Buccaneers were now being subjected to far greater fatigue loads than those for which they had been designed. The Buccaneer fleet was immediately grounded while detailed study was made with the fatigue specimen (XN982) in the test rig at Brough. Aircraft which could not be economically repaired were scrapped and the remainder re-worked.

In the reallocation that followed No. 216 Squadron relinquished its aircraft and merged with No. 12 Squadron, which in July moved to Lossiemouth, now an RAF station. No. 216 officially ceased to exist in November. There was little change in the composition of the Buccaneer squadrons until 1983 when, with the advent of the Tornado, No. 208 Squadron was assigned to maritime strike, moving to Lossiemouth in July, and the two squadrons in Germany were run down. No 15 Squadron at Laarbruch gave up its Buccaneers on 31 October 1983 and the next day became a Tornado squadron. Its sister unit at Laarbruch, No. 16—which in 1978 and 1979 had won the Salmond Trophy—

disbanded as a Buccaneer unit on 29 February 1984, re-forming the next day on Tornadoes.

During 1983 six Buccaneer S.2Bs of Nos. 12 and 208 Squadrons were deployed to RAF Akrotiri, Cyprus, to support British troops forming part of

RAF Lossiemouth, 30 April 1988, celebrated the type's 30th birthday (first flight was 30 April 1958) by lining up thirty Buccaneers. Nearest the camera are the Station's Gate Guardian, Buccaneer S.1 XK532, and engineering trainer S.2 XT281 'ET'. The other aircraft are from Nos. 12 and 208 Squadrons and No. 237 OCU.

S.2B XZ432, the last Buccaneer built, making a slow, farewell flypast at Brough before being delivered to the RAF on 6 October 1977.

the peace-keeping force in the Lebanon. Starting on 9 September the Buccaneers made roof-top demonstration flights over Beirut but were withdrawn early the next year when it was decided to end British involvement in the crisis.

In February 1985 a programme was initiated to update sixty of the RAF's Buccaneer S.2Bs, by improving their avionics, armament and electronic counter-measures (ECM) equipment, to meet Air Staff Requirement 1012. A major element of the programme was the installation of a Ferranti FIN 1063 inertial navigation system (a derivative of the FIN 1064 used on the Jaguar). Ferranti were responsible for updating the Blue Parrot attack radar and Marconi for updating the radar warning and ECM equipment.

The RAF's two remaining Buccaneer squadrons, Nos. 12 and 208, continue to operate primarily in the maritime strike role and by 1988 crews of both squadrons had been trained in the operation of the Sea Eagle anti-ship missile which, with Martel, forms their main weapon. The Buccaneer force is now concentrated at Lossiemouth, No. 237 O.C.U. having moved there from Honington in October 1984.

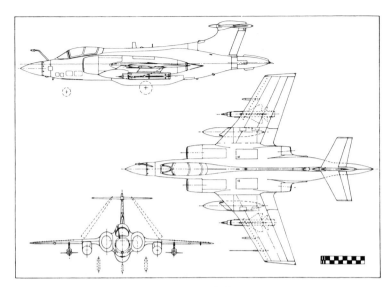

Buccaneer S.2B

SPECIFICATION AND DATA

Manufacturers: Blackburn Aircraft Ltd, Brough Aerodrome, and Holme-on-Spalding Moor Aerodrome, East Yorks.; restyled Hawker Siddeley Aviation Ltd, Brough w.e.f. 1 April 1965.

Power Plants: (Buccaneer S.1)
> Two 7,100 lb s.t. de Havilland Gyron Junior DGJ.1 (later known as the Bristol Siddeley Gyron Junior 101)

> (Buccaneer S.2)
> Two 11,100 lb s.t. Rolls-Royce R.B.168-1A Spey

> (Buccaneer S.50)
> Two 11,100 lb s.t. Rolls-Royce R.B.168 Spey and two Bristol Siddeley B.S.605 rocket engines giving 8,000 lb s.t. for 30 sec

Dimensions: Span (Buccaneer S.1) 42 ft 4 in; (Buccaneer S.2 variants) 44 ft 0 in (folded) 19 ft 11 in; length 63 ft 5 in; (folded) 51 ft 10 in; height 16 ft 3 in; wing area 514.7 sq ft

Weights: Empty 29,980 lb; loaded 45,000 lb (Buccaneer S.2B 62,000 lb)

Performance: Maximum speed at sea-level 645 mph (Mach 0.85)
> Tactical radius 500–600 miles. Range 1,730 miles (Buccaneer S.2 2,300 miles)

Armament: (Buccaneer S.1) Total warload 8,000 lb, 4,000 lb in weapons bay, 4,000 lb on underwing pylons. (Buccaneer S.2B) 16,000 lb, including sixteen 1,000 lb bombs, four in weapons bay and twelve in clusters of three on four underwing pylons. Other weapons: 1,000 lb Paveway laser-guided bombs; Martel and Sea Eagle anti-ship missiles; Sidewinders for self-defence.

502

Production:
(a) *B-103 Buccaneer pre-production*
Twenty aircraft, XK486–XK491 and XK523–XK536, ordered July 1955 to Specification
N.A.39 and produced at Brough between 30 April 1958 (first flight of XK486) and
16 December 1961
Service use: XK486–XK530, trials with manufacturers, A. & A.E.E., Boscombe Down,
and RAE Farnborough and Bedford
XK531–XK536 to No. 700Z Flight (IFTU) and later NO. 809 Squadron
Conversions to S.2 prototypes: XK526, XK527

(b) *B-103 Buccaneer S.1 production*
Forty aircraft, XN922–XN935 and XN948–XN973, delivered between 19 February 1962
and 6 February 1964
Service use: Trials with A. & A.E.E. (XN923), RAE (XN923, XN960)
736 Sqn, Lossiemouth, *eg* XN924, '950, '957, '968, '972
800 Sqn, *Eagle*, *eg* XN969, '970, '971
801 Sqn, *Victorious*, *eg* XN926, '928, '953, '957, '964
809 Sqn, Lossiemouth, *eg* XN928, '950, '960, '967

(c) *B-103 Buccaneer S.2 production*
Ten aircraft, XN974–XN983, delivered between 18 June 1964 and 29 March 1965
Service use: Trials, A. & A.E.E. (XN974), RAE (XN975), Rolls-Royce (XN983)
700B IFTU, Lossiemouth, *eg* XN977, '982
736 Sqn, Lossiemouth, *eg* XN980
800 Sqn, *Eagle*, *eg* XN982
801 Sqn, *Victorious*, *eg* XN977, '979, '980
809 Sqn, *Ark Royal*, *eg* XN977, '982
Conversions to S.2A: XN974, '975, '977, '979, '982
Service use: 12 Sqn, Honington, *eg* XN977
Conversions to S.2B: XN976, '978, '981, '983
Service use: 12 Sqn, Honington, *eg* XN976, '981, '983
15 Sqn, Laarbruch, *eg* XN977, '983
208 Sqn, Honington, *eg* XN981, '983
237 OCU, Honington, *eg* XN976, '981, '983
Twenty aircraft, XT269–XT288, delivered between 26 April 1965 and 18 February 1966
Service use: 700B IFTU Lossiemouth, *eg* XT269, '271
736 Sqn, Lossiemouth, *eg* XT275, '276
800 Sqn, *Eagle*, *eg* XT271, '277–'279, '282
801 Sqn, *Victorious*, *eg* XT269–'271
809 Sqn, *Hermes*, *eg* XT269, '275, '277–283
Conversions to S.2A: XT271, XT273–'281, '283, '284, '286
Service use: Trials with RAE (XT272)
12 Sqn, Honington, *eg* XT270, '277, '280
208 Sqn, Honington, *eg* XT271, '273, '278, '283
Conversions to S.2B: XT270, '276, '281, '288
Service use: 15 Sqn, Laarbruch, *eg* XT275
16 Sqn, Laarbruch, *eg* XT276
208 Sqn, Lossiemouth, *eg* XT270, '275, '283, '287
237 OCU Lossiemouth, *eg* XT270, '281, '283, '288
Seventeen aircraft XV152–XV168, delivered between 27 April 1966 and 13 December
1966

Service use: 800 Sqn, *Eagle, eg* XV154, '161
801 Sqn, *Victorious, eg* XV167
803 Sqn, *Hermes, eg* XV160
809 Sqn, *Hermes, eg* XV152, '154, '163
Conversions to S.2A: XV152, '154–'157, '160–'163, '165, '166–'168
Service use: 12 Sqn, Honington, *eg* XV155, '162, '165
208 Sqn, Honington, *eg* XV156, '161, '168
237 OCU Honington *eg* XV166
Conversions to S.2B: XV155, '157, '160, '162, '165, '166, '168
Service use: 12 Sqn, Honington, *eg* XV157, '160, '165, '168
16 Sqn, Laarbruch, *eg* XV166
208 Sqn, Honington and Lossiemouth *eg* XV157, '160, '163, '168
Thirty aircraft, XV332–XV361, delivered between 16 January 1967 and 2 May 1968
Service use: 800 Sqn, *Eagle, eg* XV336, '337, '343
801 Sqn, *Hermes, eg* XV334, '338
809 Sqn, Lossiemouth and *Ark Royal, eg* XV334, '339, '344, '354
Conversions to S.2A: XV332–'334, '336, '338–'342, '345, '347–'350, '352–347, '360
Service use: Trials, A. & A.E.E. (XV337, '350, '352)
12 Sqn, Honington, *eg* XV333, '347, '349, '351, '353
208 Sqn, Honington, *eg* XV342, '355, '357
Conversions to S.2B: XV332–'334, '340, '342, '347–'350, '352, '353, '359, '361
Service use: 12 Sqn, Lossiemouth, *eg* XV333, '334, '350, '359, '361
15 Sqn, Laarbruch, *eg* XV333, '334, '340, '349, '361
16 Sqn, Laarbruch, *eg* XV333, '340, '348
208 Sqn, Lossiemouth, *eg* XV332, '341, '352
237 OCU Lossiemouth, *eg* XV332, '349, '353
Seven aircraft, XV863–XV869, delivered between 25 July 1968 and 6 March 1969
Service use: 736 Sqn, Lossiemouth, *eg* XV863–'869
803 Sqn, *Hermes, eg* XV867
809 Sqn, *Ark Royal, eg* XV863, '864, '868
Conversions to S.2B: XV863–'869
Service use: 12 Sqn, Lossiemouth, *eg* XV868, '869
15 Sqn, Laarbruch, *eg* XV863
16 Sqn, Laarbruch, *eg* XV863, '864
208 Sqn, Lossiemouth, *eg* XV863, '865, '869
216 Sqn, Lossiemouth, *eg* XV865
237 OCU Lossiemouth, *eg* XV864, '867

(d) *B-103 Buccaneer S.2B production*
Twenty-six aircraft, XW525–XW550, ordered for the RAF in July 1968 and delivered between 20 January 1970 and 4 April 1973
Service use: Trials, A. & A.E.E. (XW525, '529)
12 Sqn, Lossiemouth, *eg* XW534, '539, '543, '549
15 Sqn, Honington and Laarbruch, *eg* XW526–'528, '530, '531, '540–'550
16 Sqn, Laarbruch, *eg* XW541–'545, '548, '550
208 Sqn, Lossiemouth, *eg* XW530, '533, '542, '548
216 Sqn, Honington and Lossiemouth, *eg* XW533, '540, '542, '547
237 OCU Lossiemouth, *eg* XW533, '536, '539
Three aircraft, XW986–XW988, ordered for the RAE Farnborough, and delivered between 25 January 1974 and 16 May 1974

Seventeen aircraft, XX885–XX901, ordered for the RAF and delivered between 20 May 1974 and 4 January 1977

Service use: Trials, RAE Bedford (XX897)

        12 Sqn, Lossiemouth, *eg* XX886, '889, '894, '898, '899

        15 Sqn, Laarbruch, *eg* XX885, '888, '891, '894, '899

        16 Sqn, Laarbruch, *eg* XX885–'857, '892, '893

        208 Sqn, Lossiemouth, *eg* XX886, '894, '900, '901

        216 Sqn, Honington, *eg* XX885, '886

        237 OCU Lossiemouth *eg* XX886, '899

Three aircraft, XZ430–XZ432, ordered for the RAF and delivered between 4 May 1977 and 6 October 1977

Service use: All three aircraft served with Nos. 12 and 208 Squadrons and XZ432 originally with No. 216 Squadron

(e) *B-103 Buccaneer S.2C*

This variant was a version of the S.2, modified to S.2A standard for Fleet Air Arm service, and all were conversions of S.2 airframes.

(f) *B-103 Buccaneer S.2D*

This variant was the Fleet Air Arm equivalent of the RAF's S.2B. The batch XV863–XV868 was produced to this standard (q.v.) and other aircraft were conversions of S.2 airframes.

(g) *Blackburn B-103 Buccaneer S.50*

Sixteen aircraft, 411–426, ordered by the South African Government 11 October 1962 and test flown as G-2-1 to G-2-16 respectively.

411 first flown 9 January 1965, delivered by sea ex Hull Docks 17 October 1966; 412–419 delivered by air ex Lossiemouth 27 October 1965 (419 lost at sea 500 miles south of the Canary Islands 31 October 1965); 420, 422 and 425 delivered by sea ex Hull Docks 17 October 1966; 421, 423, 424 and 426 delivered ex Hull Docks 5 August 1966.

Construction for Other Manufacturers

Faced with the urgent need for large numbers of Farnborough-designed B.E.2cs with which to equip the RFC and RNAS, the British Government placed orders in June 1914 with the Blackburn Aeroplane and Motor Co Ltd, newly formed with sizeable premises adjacent to a flying-field in Leeds, and with a number of other concerns many of which had no previous aircraft experience. The satisfactory completion of an initial batch of 12, coupled with the efficient manner in which Blackburns looked after B.E.2c production going on among local woodworking firms, brought further orders for the B.E.2c, the Sopwith Baby seaplane and eventually full responsibility for the development, navalization and production of the Sopwith Cuckoo.

Thus Blackburns emerged after the 1914–18 war with a team of specialists in the design and construction of naval aircraft but, as a result of severe economies during the between-wars period, their factory capacity was often far in excess of the work in hand. Use was twice made of it in the middle '20s for the assembly of de Havilland D.H.9A and Armstrong Whitworth Siskin IIIA aircraft, but during and after the 1939–45 war the company's factories at Leeds, Brough, Sherburn-in-Elmet and Dumbarton were fully engaged on the mammoth task of mass-producing five different aircraft types for the FAA and RAF.

History repeated itself, not only because the firm was once again responsible for supervising sub-contract work by non-aircraft firms in the Yorkshire area but also because contracts for the Supermarine Sea Otter were cancelled just as those for the Short Shirl had been a quarter of a century earlier. Coincidentally, two aircraft with experimental mainplanes followed the wars. These were the D.H.6 assembled at the Sherburn factory with the Alula high lift wing in 1920 and the Handley Page H.P.88 with scaled-down Victor mainplane built at Brough in 1951. These brought the total number of non-Blackburn aircraft built to 3,231 as under:

B.E.2c	111	Fairey Swordfish	1,700
Sopwith Baby	186	Fairey Barracuda Mk II	635
Sopwith T.1 Cuckoo	132	Short S.25 Sunderland	250
D.H.6 Alula wing	1	Percival P.40 Prentice	125
D.H.9A	18	Boulton Paul Balliol	30
A. W. Siskin IIIA	42	Handley Page H.P.88	1

Total 3,231

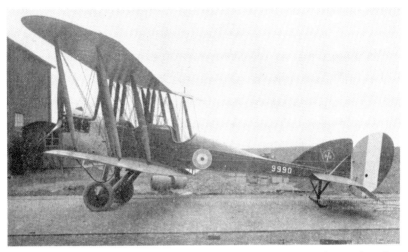

9990, a Blackburn-built B.E.2c with the famous airscrew-type badge on the tail.
(*Courtesy Royal Aeronautical Society.*)

B.E.2c

A two-seat trainer, bomber and anti-submarine aircraft of wood and fabric construction designed at the Royal Aircraft Factory, Farnborough, and first flown in 1914. Powered by the 70 hp Renault and later by the 90 hp RAF 1A, it was built in large quantities by a number of sub-contractors including the Blackburn Aeroplane and Motor Co Ltd who produced 111 for the Admiralty. The aircraft were constructed on the shop floor in the Olympia Works at Leeds, without jigs, and test flown from the nearby Soldiers' Field, Roundhay Park, by Rowland Ding. After his death, caused by the failure of an interplane strut while he was looping a new B.E.2c on its first flight, production testing was completed by R. W. Kenworthy. Surviving records show that Blackburns completed 40 by July 1915, 35 of the final batch of 50 by 29 December 1917, four more in January 1918 and five in February of that year.

Blackburn-built B.E.2cs, recognisable by the ringed airscrew motif on the fin, were used for training in the UK and on active service in every theatre during the 1914–18 war. Two aircraft, serialled 968 and 969, were shipped to the South African Aviation Corps in April 1915; 3999 was a special aircraft for Admiralty W/T experiments; 1127 was sent to Belgium in exchange for a Maurice Farman biplane; and 9969 is preserved at the Musée de l'Air, Paris.

SPECIFICATION AND DATA

Manufacturers: The Blackburn Aeroplane and Motor Co Ltd, Olympia Works, Roundhay Road, Leeds, Yorks.

Designers: The Royal Aircraft Factory, Farnborough, Hants.

Power Plants: One 70 hp Renault
One 90 hp RAF 1A

Dimensions: Span 37 ft 0 in   Length 27 ft 3 in
Height 11 ft 1½ in   Wing area 371 sq ft

Weights: Tare weight 1,370 lb   All-up weight 2,142 lb

Performance: Maximum speed 72 mph   Service ceiling 10,000 ft
Climb to 3,500 ft 6 min   Endurance 3¼ hr

Blackburn production:
(a) *With 70 hp Renault*
Thirty-seven aircraft comprising 964–975 (quantity 12); 1123–1146 (24); 3999 (1).

(b) *With 90 hp RAF 1A*
Seventy-four aircraft comprising 8606–8629 (24) under Contract C.P.60949/15; 9951–10000 (50) under Contract 132110/15.

Total: 111.

Baby seaplane N2078 from the final Blackburn batch with 130 hp Clerget engine.

Sopwith Baby

A single-seat armed reconnaissance seaplane of wood and fabric construction designed by the Sopwith Aviation Co Ltd in 1915 as a more powerful development of the Sopwith Schneider. Production for the Royal Naval Air Service was sub-contracted to the Fairey Aviation Co Ltd, Hamble, and to the

Blackburn Aeroplane and Motor Co Ltd, who were each supplied with a sample aircraft.

The Blackburn Baby seaplanes (as they were called) were built in the Olympia Works, Leeds, commencing with a prototype machine, N300, and 70 subsequent aircraft all with 110 hp Clerget air-cooled rotary engines. Ten of these, N1030-N1039, were fitted with experimental mainplanes of modified section. Later both sub-contractors were made responsible for modifying the design to take the 130 hp Clerget, after which Blackburns built 115 machines with this engine. These were in two batches, the first, N1410–N1449, being armed with Ranken anti-Zeppelin darts.

All were taken by road to be test flown from the River Humber at Brough by R. W. Kenworthy who subsequently delivered them by air to East Fortune. They operated in Palestine, as well as from seaplane carriers in the North Sea and Mediterranean, and flew fighter patrols from Dunkirk until replaced in July 1917. N1121 with 110 hp Clerget was presented to the French Government and N2121 from the final batch went to the USA in February 1918.

SPECIFICATION AND DATA

Manufacturers: The Blackburn Aeroplane and Motor Co Ltd, Olympia Works, Round-hay Road, Leeds, Yorks., and Brough Aerodrome, East Yorks.

Designers: The Sopwith Aviation Co Ltd, Canbury Park Road, Kingston-on-Thames, Surrey

Power Plants: One 110 hp Clerget
One 130 hp Clerget

A Blackburn-built Baby seaplane in Norwegian Naval Air Service colours, on a frozen fiord, 1918. (*Courtesy Old Arnesen.*)

510

Dimensions: Span 25 ft 8 in   Length 23 ft 0 in
          Height 10 ft 0 in   Wing area 240 sq ft

Weights: (130 hp Clerget) Tare weight 1,226 lb   All-up weight 1,715 lb

Performance: (130 hp Clerget) Maximum speed 100 mph
                           Climb to 10,000 ft 35 min
                           Endurance 2¼ hr

Blackburn production:
(a) *With 110 hp Clerget*
  Seventy-one aircraft comprising N300 (quantity 1); N1010–N1039 (30); N1060–N1069 (10); N1100–N1129 (30).

(b) *With 130 hp Clerget*
  One hundred and fifteen aircraft comprising N1410–N1449 (40); N2060–N2134 (75).

Total: 186.

Exports:
  In 1917 ten Blackburn Baby seaplanes were made available to the Norwegian Naval Air Service and delivered to the Naval Aircraft Factory at Horten for erection and test before issue to fighter flights at Horten, Kristiansand, Bergen, and Tromsø. They were flown off the fiords in summer and off the ice in winter and bore even serials from F.100 to F.118, but previous British naval identities have not survived.
  The date of first flight at Horten is given below, immediately after the serial:
  F.100, 13 July 1917, flown with bombs and radio, scrapped 22 December 1931, flew 76 hr 30 min; F.102, 22 October 1917, scrapped 22 December 1931, flew 111 hr 50 min; F.104, 1 November 1917, crashed 9 May 1919, flew 30 hr 30 min; F.106, 24 October 1917, scrapped 22 December 1931, flew 122 hr 50 min; F.108, 26 April 1918, scrapped 8 November 1920, flew 42 hr 10 min; F.110, 25 April 1918, crashed 1919, flew 36 hr 30 min; F.112, 27 April 1918, crashed 27 August 1927, flew 188 hr 55 min; F.114, 3 August 1918, crashed 6 September 1918; F.116, 8 August 1918, flown with bombs and radio, crashed 28 August 1919, flew 53 hr 50 min; F.118, 6 August 1918, crashed 22 August 1919, flew 72 hr 30 min.
  F.104, F.110, F.114, F.116 and F.118 were each reconstructed several times from new and salvaged Blackburn-built components held in store at Horten. F.104 was converted into a two-seat, side-by-side trainer.

Sopwith T.1 Cuckoo

  This was a single-seat, three-bay, folding-wing torpedo-carrying biplane of wood and fabric construction designed by the Sopwith Aviation Co Ltd in 1916 and powered by one 200 hp Hispano-Suiza water-cooled engine. In February 1918 the entire production was sub-contracted to three outside firms, including the Blackburn Aeroplane and Motor Co Ltd who were made responsible for developing suitable gear for carrying a standard 18-in Whitehead torpedo. As Hispano engines were all required for S.E.5As, the prototype Cuckoo, N74, was re-engined with a 200 hp Sunbeam Arab and

The fifth production Blackburn-built Cuckoo N6954 dropping a torpedo off
East Fortune 1919.

delivered to Blackburns in March 1918 as a sample aircraft. It was then
stripped and rebuilt with a divided undercarriage as a prelude to the commencement of large-scale production at Sherburn-in-Elmet, where 132
machines were built. Later versions had an enlarged rudder, first fitted to
N8005 and flown from Brough to Martlesham for test on 23 June 1920.

The prototype, N74, and the first machine of the second production batch,
N6950, were flown to the Great Yarmouth Air Station in May 1918 en route
to the Isle of Grain for performance trials, but production aircraft were test
flown at Sherburn-in-Elmet by R. W. Kenworthy and ferried to East Fortune,
80 being completed by August 1918. They equipped the Torpedo Aeroplane
School, East Fortune, and Nos. 186 and 210 Squadrons, Gosport, and the
first British aircraft carrier *Argus* embarked a full squadron on 19 October
1918.

At least eight Blackburn-built Cuckoos, N7151–N7155, N7192, N7193 and
N7999, were fitted with the 200 hp Wolseley Viper engine. N7192 and N7193,
used for tests at the Isle of Grain 1919–20, were joined on 11 September
1919 by N7990 which had been fitted with a 275 hp Rolls-Royce Falcon
engine, this machine going to Gosport on 6 December. The Cuckoo was
declared obsolete in April 1923, but six of the Viper-powered machines were
taken to Japan in 1921 by the British Air Mission to the Imperial Japanese
Navy (see page 144).

Manufacturers: The Blackburn Aeroplane and Motor Co Ltd, Olympia Works, Roundhay Road, Leeds, and Sherburn-in-Elmet, Yorks.

Designers: The Sopwith Aviation Co Ltd, Canbury Park Road, Kingston-on-Thames, Surrey

Power Plants: One 200 hp Sunbeam Arab
One 200 hp Wolseley Viper
One 275 hp Rolls-Royce Falcon

Dimensions: Span 46 ft 9 in   Length 28 ft 6 in
Height 10 ft 8 in   Wing area 566 sq ft

Weights: Tare weight 2,199 lb   All-up weight 3,883 lb

Performance: Maximum speed 103 mph   Climb to 2,000 ft 4 min
Service ceiling 12,100 ft   Endurance 4 hr

Blackburn production:
Two hundred and thirty aircraft ordered February 1918 under Contract A.S.3298/18 and comprising N6900–N6929 (quantity 30); N6950–N6999 (50*); N7150–N7199 (50); N7980–N8079 (100). Production is said to have terminated at N8011, reducing the total built to 132.

* Production rate: April 1918 (2 aircraft), May (8), June (12), July (15), August (13).

Short Shirl

A single-seat, two-bay, folding-wing torpedo-carrying biplane of wood and fabric construction powered by one 385 hp Rolls-Royce Eagle VIII water-cooled engine, built in prototype form by Short Bros Ltd at Rochester in 1918. It was contemporary with the Blackburn Blackburd, but as neither of these aircraft was an improvement on the Sopwith Cuckoo, an order for 100 Short Shirls, N7550–N7649, placed with the Blackburn Aeroplane and Motor Co Ltd, was cancelled.

De Havilland D.H.9A

A two-seat general-purpose biplane of wood and fabric construction, powered by one 400 hp Liberty water-cooled engine, evolved from the well-known D.H.9 bomber by the Westland Aircraft Works in 1917. Used in large numbers by the RAF for more than ten years, and in 1926, when a considerable number of airframes required for service in Iraq and India and stored since 1918 came up for modernization, 18 were sent to Brough to be stripped and completely rebuilt by the Blackburn Aeroplane and Motor Co Ltd. They were then re-delivered to the RAF with new serials J8208–J8225.

Blackburn-built A. W. Siskin IIIA J8901 on show at Brough beyond the Ripon II prototype, 15 May 1928. (*Aeroplane Photo.*)

Armstrong Whitworth Siskin IIIA

A single-seat fighter of fabric-covered metal construction powered by one 420 hp Armstrong Siddeley Jaguar IV air-cooled radial engine, designed by Sir W. G. Armstrong Whitworth Aircraft Ltd and first flown at Whitley in October 1925. It was the standard RAF single-seat fighter from 1927 to 1932, and over 350 were built, including 42 built at Leeds and test flown at Brough under a contract awarded to the Blackburn Aeroplane and Motor Co Ltd in June 1927.

SPECIFICATION AND DATA

Manufacturers: The Blackburn Aeroplane and Motor Co Ltd, Olympia Works, Roundhay Road, Leeds, and Brough Aerodrome, East Yorks.

Designers: Sir W. G. Armstrong Whitworth Aircraft Ltd, Parkside, Coventry

Power Plant: One 420 hp Armstrong Siddeley Jaguar IV

Dimensions: Span 33 ft 2 in Length 25 ft 4 in
Height 10 ft 2 in Wing area 293 sq ft

Weights: Tare weight 2,061 lb All-up weight 3,012 lb

Performance: Maximum speed 156 mph Climb to 5,000 ft $3\frac{1}{2}$ min
Service ceiling 27,000 ft

Blackburn production:
Forty-two aircraft, J8864–J8905, ordered June 1927 under Contract 772529/27.

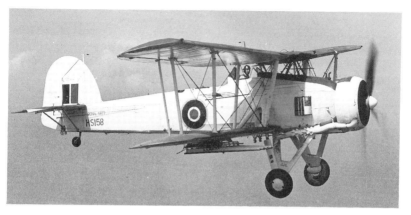

A rocket-equipped Sherburn-built Fairey Swordfish, HS158, on test flight on 28 June 1942.

Fairey Swordfish

A two/three-seat deck-landing torpedo biplane of fabric-covered metal construction powered by one 750 hp Bristol Pegasus 30 air-cooled radial engine, designed by the Fairey Aviation Co Ltd in 1934. After 1940 all production was handed over to Blackburn Aircraft Ltd who built a special factory at Sherburn-in-Elmet which produced 1,700 'Blackfish', as they came to be known, between 29 December 1940 and 18 August 1944, when test pilot H. P. Wilson cleared the last one, NS204.

The glorious operational history of the type is adequately dealt with elsewhere (Putnam: *British Naval Aircraft since 1912* by O. G. Thetford), and it is sufficient to remember here that Swordfish remained in Fleet Air Arm service throughout the 1939–45 war and that one of them made the last operational flight by a FAA biplane on 28 June 1945.

In 1967 six complete Swordfish were known to exist of which five, and almost certainly the sixth, were Blackburn-built. These were LS326, kept in flying trim by the Royal Navy at Yeovilton, home of the museum in which HS608 is suspended from the roof in the colours of V6107, the Swordfish in which Lt Cdr Esmonde, VC, led the attack on the *Scharnhorst*; NF389 preserved by the Navy at Lee-on-Solent for static exhibition; NF370 in the Imperial War Museum; NS122 in the Canadian National Aeronautical Collection at Rockcliffe, painted in RCN colours and coded TH-M; and a fabricless airframe at the Age of Flight Museum, Niagara, Canada.

The airworthy example, LS326, was flown postwar by the Fairey Aviation Co Ltd as a communications and demonstration aircraft, based at White Waltham, and in 1955 it was given temporary civil status as G-AJVH.

Manufacturers: Blackburn Aircraft Ltd, Sherburn-in-Elmet Aerodrome, Yorks.

Designers: The Fairey Aviation Co Ltd, Hayes, Middlesex

Power Plant: One 750 hp Bristol Pegasus 30

Dimensions: Span 45 ft 6 in   Length 36 ft 4 in
Height 12 ft 10 in   Wing area 607 sq ft

Weights: Tare weight 5,200 lb   All-up weight 9,250 lb

Performance: Maximum speed 139 mph   Climb to 5,000 ft 10 min
Service ceiling 10,700 ft
Range (with torpedo) 550 miles   (reconnaissance) 1,030 miles

Blackburn production:

(a) *Swordfish Mk I*
Three hundred aircraft V4288–V4337, V4360–V4399, V4411–V4455, V4481–V4525, V4551–V4600, V4621–V4655, V4685–V4719 completed between 29 December 1940 and 4 October 1941.

(b) *Swordfish Mk II with strengthened lower wing*
One hundred aircraft W5836–W5865, W5886–W5925, W5966–W5995 completed between 5 October 1941 and 27 December 1941.
One hundred aircraft DK670–DK719, DK743–DK792 completed between 27 December 1941 and 8 June 1942.
Four hundred aircraft HS154–HS196, HS208–HS231, HS254–HS299, HS312–HS346, HS361–HS410, HS424–HS471, HS484–HS519, HS533–HS561, HS579–HS625, HS637–HS678 completed between 9 June 1942 and 25 May 1943.
Two hundred and fifty aircraft LS151–LS193, LS214–LS248, LS261–LS299, LS315–LS358, LS362–LS403, LS415–LS461 completed between 26 May 1943 and 21 October 1943.
Two hundred and thirty aircraft NE858–NE906, NE920–NE957, NE970–NE999, NF113–NF161, NF175–NF217, NF230–NF250 completed between 22 October 1943 and 22 February 1944.

(c) *Swordfish Mk III with ASV scanner*
One hundred and twenty aircraft NF251–NF274, NF298–NF347, NF369–NF414 completed between 24 February 1944 and 28 April 1944.
Two hundred aircraft NR857–NR898, NR913–NR958, NR970–NR999, NS112–NS156, NS168–NS204 completed between 1 May 1944 and 18 August 1944.

Total: 1,700.

Supermarine Sea Otter

A carrier-borne or shore-based air-sea rescue and communications amphibian with metal hull and fabric-covered mainplanes designed by Vickers-Supermarine Ltd in 1938. It was powered by one 855 hp Bristol Mercury 30 air-cooled radial and carried a crew of four. An order for 190 Sea Otters BL112–BL151, BL167–BL216, BT316–BT347, BT357–BT401, BT415–BT437 placed with Blackburn Aircraft Ltd was cancelled and main production was by Saunders-Roe Ltd at Cowes 1943–46.

Brough-built Fairey Barracuda Mk II MD693.

Fairey Barracuda Mk II

A three-seat, all-metal shoulder-wing monoplane for torpedo, dive-bombing and reconnaissance duties, powered by one 1,640 hp Rolls-Royce Merlin 32 liquid-cooled engine, designed by the Fairey Aviation Co Ltd. The prototype, flown in December 1940, was followed by large-scale production by the parent company and by three sub-contractors including Blackburn Aircraft Ltd who built 635 at Brough.

From 10 January 1943, when the first Barracuda was issued to No. 827 Squadron at Stretton, until No. 815 Squadron relinquished the type in 1953, they were used in practically every carrier and at every Fleet Air Arm station. In the month of April 1944 Barracudas severely crippled the German battleship *Tirpitz* at Tromsø in northern Norway and shattered the Japanese submarine base at Sabang, Sumatra.

SPECIFICATION AND DATA

Manufacturers: Blackburn Aircraft Ltd, Brough Aerodrome, East Yorks.

Designers: The Fairey Aviation Co Ltd, Hayes, Middlesex

Power Plant: One 1,640 hp Rolls-Royce Merlin 32

Dimensions: Span 49 ft 2 in   Length 39 ft 9 in
Height 15 ft 1 in   Wing area 367 sq ft

Weights: Tare weight 9,350 lb   All-up weight 13,200 lb

Performance: Maximum speed 228 mph   Cruising speed 172 mph
Climb to 5,000 ft 6 min   Service ceiling 16,600 ft
Range (with torpedo) 690 miles   (reconnaissance) 1,150 miles

Blackburn production:
(a) *Under Contract 497/C.20B to Works Orders 3360/1 to 3360/400*
Two hundred and fifty aircraft BV660–BV707, BV721–BV766, BV788–BV834, BV847–BV885, BV898–BV922, BV937–BV981.
One hundred and fifty aircraft MD612–MD656, MD674–MD723, MD736–MD778, MD792–MD807.

(b) *Under Contract 2513/C.20B to Works Orders 3700/1 to 3700/300*
Three hundred aircraft MX535–MX576, MX591–MX638, MX652–MX696, MX709–MX753, MX767–MX808, MX820–MX864, MX877–MX907.
Note: Sixty-five aircraft MX908–MX923 and MX935–MX983 were cancelled.

Total: 635.

VB889, the last Blackburn-built Sunderland Mk V, on the Havel Lake while in service with No. 201 Squadron during the Berlin airlift in 1949. (*Crown Copyright Reserved.*)

Short S.25 Sunderland

The Sunderland was a well-armed, long-range, general reconnaissance and anti-submarine flying-boat of all-metal stressed-skin construction, powered by four 1,065 hp Bristol Pegasus 18 air-cooled radial engines. It was designed by Short Bros Ltd and built in large numbers at Rochester, where the prototype first flew in October 1937, and at Belfast.

To increase production still further, Blackburn Aircraft Ltd were awarded a contract in 1940 which kept their Clydeside works at Dumbarton fully occupied throughout the war. By 1945 Blackburns had completed 250 Sunderlands, or an average of more than 60 a year. The last 60 were Sunderland Mk Vs with four 1,200 hp Pratt & Whitney Twin Wasp R-1830 radials, and many earlier machines were re-engined to this standard. Last to leave the works was VB889 on 19 October 1945.

The ocean-going career of this famous flying-boat during and after the 1939–45 war has already been exhaustively dealt with (Putnam: *Aircraft of*

518

the R.A.F. since 1918 by O. G. Thetford; *Shorts Aircraft since 1900* by C. H. Barnes), and needs no amplification here. A number were also civilianized after the war either as Sunderland IIIs or as Sandringhams of several marks (Putnam: the author's *British Civil Aircraft 1919–1972*, Vol. 3) for BOAC, Qantas, TEAL, and for Argentine and Uruguayan operators. These included several Blackburn-built examples as indicated below.

SPECIFICATION AND DATA

Manufacturers: Blackburn Aircraft Ltd, Dumbarton Works, Dunbartonshire, Scotland

Designers: Short Bros Ltd (later Short Bros and Harland Ltd), Rochester and Belfast

Power Plants: (Sunderland Mk III) Four 1,065 hp Bristol Pegasus 18
(Sunderland Mk V) Four 1,200 hp Pratt & Whitney Twin Wasp R-1830-90B

Dimensions: Span 112 ft 9½ in   Length 85 ft 4 in
Height 32 ft 10½ in   Wing area 1,487 sq ft

Weights: (Sunderland Mk V)
Tare weight 37,000 lb   All-up weight 60,000 lb

Performance: (Sunderland Mk V)
Maximum speed 213 mph   Initial climb 840 ft/min
Service ceiling 17,900 ft   Range 2,980 miles

Blackburn production:
(a) *Sunderland Mk I*
Fifteen aircraft T9083–T9090 and T9109–T9115.

(b) *Sunderland Mk II*
Five aircraft W6000–W6004.

(c) *Sunderland Mk III*
One hundred and seventy aircraft W6005–W6016, W6026–W6033, DD828–DD867, EK572–EK596, ML835–ML884, NJ170–NJ194 and PP135–PP144.
With few exceptions, aircraft from NJ170 were converted to Sunderland Mk V.
Civil conversions as Sunderland III: DD860/G-AHEP; ML876/G-AGWX/LV-AAS; PP142/G-AHER. As Sunderland V: EK579/LV-AHG. As Sandringham 2: DD834/G-AGPT/LV-AAP; DD864/G-AGPZ/LV-AAO; ML843/G-AHRE/LV-ACT. As Sandringham 3: DD841/G-AGPY/LV-AAR. As Sandringham 4: NJ179/ZK-AME. As Sandringham 5: ML838/G-AHYY; NJ171/G-AHZB; NJ188/G-AHZF/VH-EBY. As Sandringham 7: ML840/G-AKCR/CX-ANA.
To the French Aéronavale: ML866, ML872, ML877. To the RNZAF: PP143/NZ4119.

(c) *Sunderland Mk V*
Sixty aircraft PP145-PP164, RN277-RN306 and VB880-VB889.
To the RNZAF: RN280/NZ4106; RN286/NZ4117; RN306/NZ4118; VB880/NZ4111; VB881/NZ4112; VB883/NZ4107.

Total: 250.

519

Blackburn-built Prentice VS385 in use by the RAF College, Cranwell, as a primary trainer in 1948.

Percival P.40 Prentice T. Mk 2

The Prentice was a low-wing monoplane of all-metal stressed-skin construction powered by one 250 hp de Havilland Gipsy Queen 32 inverted air-cooled engine, adopted in 1947 as the RAF's basic trainer in succession to the Tiger Moth. It accommodated pilot and pupil side by side, with a third seat in the rear.

Construction was shared between the parent company, Percival Aircraft Ltd, of Luton, and Blackburn Aircraft Ltd who built 125 Prentices commencing VS241, first flown at Brough in January 1948. The type was used at CFS, South Cerney; the RAF College, Cranwell; Flying Training Schools at Ternhill, Cottesmore and Feltwell; the Signallers' School at Swanton Morley; and for communications in the Middle East.

When withdrawn from service in 1955, 254 Prentices of mixed parentage were transferred to the British civil register, all but two under the ownership of Aviation Traders Ltd. Almost six complete registration blocks from G-AOKA to G-AOPY and several other letter sequences were reserved, but only a few machines were actually converted for civil use at Stansted and Southend.

SPECIFICATION AND DATA

Manufacturers: Blackburn Aircraft Ltd, Brough Aerodrome, East Yorks.

Designers: Percival Aircraft Ltd, Luton Airport, Beds.

Power Plant: One 250 hp de Havilland Gipsy Queen 32

Dimensions: Span 46 ft 0 in   Length 31 ft 3 in
Height 12 ft 10½ in Wing area 305 sq ft

Weights: Tare weight 3,232 lb   All-up weight 4,200 lb

Performance: Maximum speed 143 mph   Initial climb 653 ft/min
Service ceiling 18,000 ft   Range 400 miles

Blackburn production:
Twenty-five aircraft VS241–VS265 to Works Orders 5800/1–25; twenty-five aircraft VS266–VS290 to Works Orders 5810/1–25; twenty-five aircraft VS316–VS338, VS352–VS353 to Works Orders 5820/1–25; twenty-five aircraft VS354–VS378 to Works Orders 5830/1–25; twenty-five aircraft VS379–VS397, VS409–VS414 to Works Orders 5840/1–25.

Total: 125.

Note: Contracts for two further batches of twenty-five, VS415–VS439 to Works Orders 5850/1–25 and VS440–VS445, VS463–VS486 to Works Orders 5860/1–25 were cancelled.
The following Blackburn-built Prentices were fully converted for civil use: VS282/ G-APJE; VS304/G-AOMK; VS356/G-AOLU; VS374/G-AOLR; VS382/ G-AOKT; VS385/G-AOLP; VS388/G-AOLO/OO-CIM; VS397/G-AOWT/ OD-ACQ.

Blackburn-built Balliol WN522 of No. 238 OCU photographed at Colerne, Wilts., on 15 September 1950.

Boulton Paul Balliol T. Mk 2

This was a two-seat advanced trainer of all-metal stressed-skin construction designed by Boulton Paul Aircraft Ltd to replace the North American Harvard in RAF service. After the original intention to fit the Armstrong Siddeley Mamba propeller-turbine was dropped, production of the Balliol T. Mk 2 began with 1,245 hp Rolls-Royce Merlin 35 engines in 1951. A total of 183 production machines were built, including 30 by Blackburn and General Aircraft Ltd who began tooling up at Brough in August 1952.
Chief users of Blackburn-built Balliols were the RAF College, Cranwell; No. 238 OCU, Colerne; No. 3 CAACU, Exeter; and the School of Control and Reporting, Middle Wallop.

521

SPECIFICATION AND DATA

Manufacturers: Blackburn and General Aircraft Ltd, Brough Aerodrome, East Yorks.

Designers: Boulton Paul Aircraft Ltd, Wolverhampton, Staffs.

Power Plant; One 1,245 hp Rolls-Royce Merlin 35

Dimensions: Span 39 ft 4 in   Length 35 ft 1½ in
           Height 12 ft 6 in   Wing area 250 sq ft

Weights: Tare weight 6,730 lb   All-up weight 8,410 lb

Performance: Maximum speed 288 mph   Initial climb 1,790 ft/min
              Service ceiling 32,500 ft   Endurance 3 hr

Blackburn production:
Thirty aircraft, WN506–WN535. Delivery dates are given immediately after the RAF serial.
WN506, 18 May 1953, to the School of Control and Reporting, Middle Wallop; WN507, 30 June 1953, to No. 7 FTS, Cottesmore; WN508–WN510, 10 July 1953 5 August 1953 and 24 August 1953 respectively, to the School of Control and Reporting, Middle Wallop; WN511–WN535 to No. 9 MU, Cosford between 16 October 1953 and 10 May 1954.
Service use with unit code letters: No. 238 OCU, Colerne—WN511/T, WN517/Z, WN522/P, WN527/J, WN529/K, WN531/B, WN532/H. No. 3 CAACU, Exeter— WN506/K, WN508/V, WN509/Y, WN510/P. RAF College, Cranwell—WN507/CV, WN514/CE, WN515/CG, WN516/CC, WN518/CL, WN530/AW, WN533/AX, WN534/AF.

The experimental Handley Page H.P.88 at Brough in June 1951.

Handley Page H.P.88

This was a high-speed research aircraft built to enable Handley Page Ltd to study the characteristics of the tail unit and the crescent-shaped wing incorporating three different degrees of sweepback, which had been designed for their forthcoming Victor bomber. It was constructed by Blackburn and General Aircraft Ltd at Brough using the fuselage of a Vickers-Supermarine Attacker single-seat fighter mounted on a scale-model of the experimental wing but retaining its normal Rolls-Royce Nene turbojet.

Serialled VX330, and known under the SBAC designation system as the Y.B.2, the H.P.88 was first flown at Brough by Blackburn test pilot G. R. I. 'Sailor' Parker on 21 June 1951. It completed a number of test flights but disintegrated in the air over the runway at Stansted on 26 August in the same year, with the loss of the Handley Page deputy chief test pilot D. J. P. Broomfield.

No data is available, but the length of the standard Attacker with 5,100 lb.s.t. Rolls-Royce Nene 3 was 37 ft 6 in.

The Mission Symbol Designations 1918–1931

Five preliminary layouts which did not achieve the distinction of a company designation are included at the end of this appendix as a reminder that the ceaseless effort to secure production contracts which went on at Brough during the 'lean years' was not confined to the projects listed below:

Class B.T. (Bomber-Torpedo)
B.T.1   Beagle prototype 1926 to Specification 24/25.

Class C.A. (Commercial Aeroplanes)
In two series (*a*) C.A.0–C.A.05 and (*b*) C.A.2–C.A.21B (there being no surviving record of C.A.1). All were projects except C.A.15C (Monoplane/Biplane comparison) built 1931–32, C.A.18 Segrave I (also designated B-1 in the later B series), C.A.20 Segrave II, C.A.20A Segrave II (Cirrus Hermes IVAs) and C.A.21A (or H.S.T.10) later designated B-9.

C.A.0	Otherwise known as the BN-8 (or Blackburn Napier 8-seater) using Dart parts and powered by one 450 hp Napier Lion or one 350 hp Rolls-Royce Eagle VIII. With Lion: All-up weight 6,315 lb, maximum speed 117 mph, initial climb 855 ft/min, absolute ceiling 16,100 ft, range 400 miles.
C.A.01	Otherwise known as the BN-10 using Dart parts and powered by one 450 hp Napier Lion. Commercial biplane for 10 passengers and mail, all-up weight 6,966 lb, maximum speed 115 mph, initial climb 450 ft/min, service ceiling 8,500 ft, range 400 miles.
C.A.02	Long-range three-seat Cubaroo derivative powered by three 360 hp Rolls-Royce Eagle IX. All-up weight 19,985 lb, maximum speed 100 mph, absolute ceiling 14,500 ft.
C.A.03	Long-range three-seat land or seaplane similar to Blackburn Blackburn Mk. I powered by one 450 hp Napier Lion using Swift engine mounting and cowlings. All-up weight 6,852 lb, maximum speed 107 mph, absolute ceiling 13,400 ft.
C.A.04	Layout for three-engined transport for Imperial Airways dated 8 November 1924, powered by three 240 hp Armstrong Siddeley Pumas (8 or 10 passengers) or three 450 hp Napier Lions (16, 20 or 24 passengers). With Pumas: all-up weight 12,200 lb, maximum speed 106 mph, service ceiling 13,000 ft. With Lions: all-up weight 19,383 lb, maximum speed 112 mph, service ceiling 16,000 ft.
C.A.05	Four-seat touring land or seaplane, engine unspecified. As landplane: all-up weight 3,657 lb, maximum speed 115 mph, initial climb 750 ft/min, absolute ceiling 18,000 ft, endurance $3\frac{1}{2}$ hr. As seaplane: all-up weight 3,657 lb, maximum speed 110 mph, initial climb 600 ft/min, absolute ceiling 16,000 ft, endurance $3\frac{1}{2}$ hr.
C.A.1	No surviving record.
C.A.2	Three-engined eight-passenger commercial biplane with monoplane tail for an American enquirer, Montague Bradey, September 1923. All-up weight

| C.A.3 | 8,084 lb, payload 2,040 lb, maximum speed 105 mph, initial climb 750 ft/min, service ceiling 13,500 ft. |

C.A.3   Commercial land or seaplane similar to D.H.67/Gloster Survey biplane with twin-ruddered biplane tail, powered by three Bristol Jupiter engines, for the Khartoum–Kisumu route of the North Sea Aerial and General Transport Co Ltd, 1924. Intended for a maximum of 14 passengers or normally eight passengers and luggage. As landplane: span 80 ft, length 47 ft 6 in, height 18 ft 9 in, wing area 1,780 sq ft, all-up weight 16,260 lb, maximum speed 111 mph, initial climb 1,120 ft/min, service ceiling 19,500 ft. As seaplane: height 20 ft 2 in, all-up weight 15,010 lb.

C.A.4   Long-range passenger version of C.A.3 dated 8 November 1924 and powered by three Bristol Jupiter engines. All-up weight 19,200 lb, maximum speed 130 mph, service ceiling 15,300 ft, range 1,000 miles.

C.A.5   Variant of C.A.4 to carry 14 passengers and powered by three Bristol Jupiter engines. All-up weight 14,700 lb, maximum speed 137 mph, service ceiling 19,500 ft, range 500 miles.

C.A.6   Transport biplane powered by three 240 hp Armstrong Siddeley Lynx radials to carry eight passengers and two crew. All-up weight 8,400 lb, maximum speed 115 mph, initial climb 556 ft/min, service ceiling 9,000 ft, range 500 miles.

C.A.7   Long-range four-passenger biplane, similar to Bristol 110, powered by one Bristol Jupiter radial. All-up weight 6,250 lb, maximum speed 131 mph, service ceiling 19,000 ft, range 1,000 miles.

C.A.8   Four-passenger monoplane powered by one 300 hp A.D.C. Nimbus inline water-cooled engine. All-up weight 4,430 lb, maximum speed 124 mph, service ceiling 14,800 ft, range 500 miles.

C.A.9   Eight-passenger commercial biplane similar to C.A.7 dated 14 February 1928 and powered by one Bristol Jupiter radial. Span 51 ft, length 39 ft, height 12 ft 5 in. As landplane: all-up weight 6,500 lb, maximum speed 127 mph, cruising speed 107 mph, initial climb 800 ft/min, service ceiling 14,000 ft. As seaplane: all-up weight 7,000 lb, maximum speed 118 mph, cruising speed 102 mph, initial climb 630 ft/min, service ceiling 10,500 ft.

C.A.10   Three-engined commercial landplane dated 14 September 1928 for Imperial Airways in Eastern and Western versions powered by three 450 hp Bristol Jupiter IX geared radials. Eastern: span 119 ft, wing area 2,000 sq ft, all-up weight 19,670 lb, maximum speed 119 mph, initial climb 790 ft/min, service ceiling 18,000 ft. Western: span 103 ft, wing area 1,500 sq ft, all-up weight 18,800 lb, maximum speed 122 mph, initial climb 800 ft/min, service ceiling 16,000 ft.

C.A.11   Four-passenger cabin land or sea monoplane, similar to Fokker Universal, powered by one 240 hp Armstrong Siddeley Lynx IV, 220 hp Wright Whirlwind J-6, 240 hp Armstrong Siddeley Cheetah, 245 hp Bristol Titan III or 345 hp Bristol Neptune II according to employment. Span 41 ft, length 28 ft 9 in, height 10 ft. With Lynx IV as landplane: all-up weight 3,100 lb, maximum speed 123 mph, initial climb 600 ft/min, service ceiling 11,600 ft, range 370 miles. As seaplane: all-up weight 3,100 lb, maximum speed 117 mph, initial climb 490 ft/min, service ceiling 9,400 ft, range 340 miles.

C.A.11A   Six/seven-seat land or seaplane variant of C.A.11 dated 6 February 1930 and powered by three 95 hp A.D.C Cirrus IIIs, three 100 hp D.H. Gipsy Is, one 240 hp Armstrong Siddeley Lynx IV or one 345 hp Bristol Neptune II. Span 52 ft, wing area 400 sq ft. As landplane: all-up weight 4,000 lb, maximum speed 118 mph, cruising speed 100 mph, initial climb 726 ft/min, service ceiling 14,700 ft. As seaplane: all-up weight 4,290 lb, maximum speed 114 mph, cruising speed 95 mph, initial climb 585 ft/min, service ceiling 12,000 ft.

C.A.12 Four-engined, strut braced commercial land monoplane, powered by four 450 hp Bristol Jupiter IX geared radials, in four variants according to the combination of Eastern or Western layouts with wide- and narrow-chord mainplanes. Span 126 ft, length 77 ft 3 in, height 21 ft 10 in, wing area (small wings) 2,240 sq ft, (large wings) 3,000 sq ft. Eastern: two crew, one steward, 23 passengers and 3,000 lb of mail. Western: two crew, one steward and 38 passengers. All-up weight (either model, small wings) 28,000 lb, (either model, large wings) 29,500 lb.

C.A.13 Strut-braced commercial monoplane, dated 12 February 1929, for 10–12 passengers and powered by three 240 hp Armstrong Siddeley Lynx IVs or one Bristol Jupiter. In three-engined configuration the outboard engines were in underslung nacelles with the centre engine above the top centre section. Span 82 ft, length 54 ft 4½ in, height 18 ft 9 in, wing area 1,012 sq ft, tare weight 6,465 lb, all-up weight 9,800 lb, maximum speed 121 mph, cruising speed 114 mph, initial climb 630 ft/min, service ceiling 14,600 ft, range 400 miles.

C.A.14 Enlarged four-engined version of C.A.13 dated 12 February 1929 to carry 17 passengers and powered by four 240 hp Armstrong Siddeley Lynx IVs. Outer engines underslung, inner engines close together on top centre section. Span 100 ft, length 60 ft, height 23 ft 6 in, wing area 1,500 sq ft, tare weight 9,310 lb, all-up weight 14,500 lb, maximum speed 117 mph, initial climb 740 ft/min, service ceiling 16,000 ft.

C.A.15A Layouts dated 27 July 1929 for near-identical monoplane and biplane to carry 11 passengers and powered by three 240 hp Armstrong Siddeley Lynx IVs (or supercharged Lynx for use in the tropics). Monoplane: span 86 ft, wing area 1,068 sq ft, tare weight 7,150 lb, all-up weight 11,000 lb, maximum speed 121 mph, initial climb 850 ft/min, service ceiling 17,000 ft, range 400 miles. Biplane: span 64 ft, wing area 1,150 sq ft, tare weight 6,750 lb, all-up weight 10,600 lb, maximum speed 123 mph, initial climb 770 ft/min, service ceiling 14,000 ft, range 400 miles.

C.A.15B Layouts dated 4 November 1929 for nine-passenger monoplane and biplane versions of C.A.15A powered by three 240 hp Armstrong Siddeley Lynx IV supercharged radials. Monoplane: span 82 ft, length 53 ft 9 in, height 21 ft 6 in, wing area 1,008 sq ft, all-up weight 9,700 lb. Biplane: span 62 ft, length 48 ft 9 in, height 21 ft, wing area 1,075 sq ft, all-up weight 9,250 lb.

C.A.15C Twin-engined versions of C.A.15B with two 450 hp Armstrong Siddeley Jaguar IVCs built to Air Ministry Specification 6/29 and described in detail beginning page 302.

C.A.16 Layout dated 11 February 1930 for 12-passenger transport biplane with biplane tail for Imperial Airways Ltd. Powered by three Armstrong Siddeley Jaguar Major radials and similar in appearance to the Handley

526

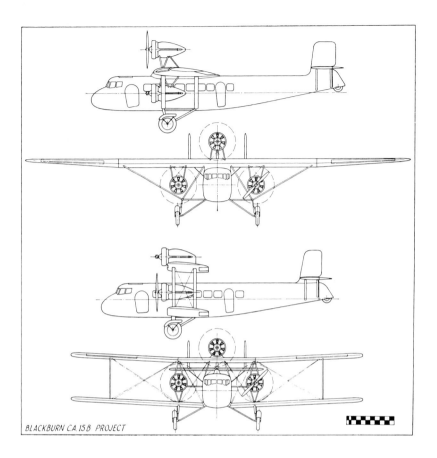

BLACKBURN C.A.15B PROJECT

Page H.P.43 with the centre engine above the top centre section. Span (upper) 100 ft (lower) 93 ft, wing area 2,816 sq ft, tare weight 12,846 lb, all-up weight 21,000 lb, maximum speed 128 mph, initial climb 820 ft/min, service ceiling 19,200 ft, range 420 miles.

C.A.17   Layout dated 11 February 1930 for nine-passenger version of C.A.16 powered by three Armstrong Siddeley Jaguar Majors. Span 82 ft, wing area 1,986 sq ft, tare weight 11,744 lb, all-up weight 17,000 lb, maximum speed 137 mph, cruising speed 110 mph, initial climb 1,080 ft/min, service ceiling 20,200 ft.

C.A.18   Blackburn B-1 Segrave I, described in detail beginning page 320.

C.A.18/1 Blackburn B-1 Segrave Ambulance powered by two 120 hp de Havilland Gipsy IIIs, tare weight 2,260 lb, payload 1,040 lb. Project only.

C.A.18A Blackburn B-1 Segrave I high-performance tourer powered by two 120 hp de Havilland Gipsy IIIs. Project only.

C.A.19   Blackburn Segrave III project, span 53 ft, length 38 ft, height 11 ft, wing area 350 sq ft. Two versions were considered: (a) eight-seater for Australia

527

resulting from discussions held at Brough 30 June 1933 between Capt Snook, Mr Lamb, and Blackburn engineers Ely and Duncanson. The design was to include a retractable undercarriage, split trailing edge flaps and two 260 hp Armstrong Siddeley Lynx Major radials. Tare weight 3,765 lb, all-up weight 6,200 lb, maximum speed 170 mph, cruising speed 150 mph, initial climb 1,000 ft/min, service ceiling 20,900 ft, range 520 miles. (b) 12-seat version to meet a specification submitted July 1933 by ex-RCAF officer L. E. Cook for a convertible land, sea or ski machine for airline service in the far north of Canada. Dimensions were the same as for the Australian version but the engines were two 174 hp Napier Javelin six-cylinder inverted inline air-cooled units.

	Landplane	Seaplane	Ski-plane
Tare weight	2,900 lb	3,300 lb	2,890 lb
Disposable load	2,700 lb	2,300 lb	2,710 lb
Maximum passengers	12	8	10
All-up weight	5,600 lb	5,600 lb	5,600 lb
Maximum speed at sea level	124 mph	134 mph	137 mph
Maximum speed at 10,000 ft	128 mph	119 mph	121 mph
Cruising speed	115 mph	110 mph	—
Initial climb	700 ft/min	640 ft/min	680 ft/min
Service ceiling	14,000 ft	12,500 ft	13,800 ft
Range (maximum passengers)	370 miles	415 miles	400 miles
Range (maximum fuel)	1,250 miles	715 miles	1,000 miles

C.A.19/1   High-speed transport similar to H.S.T.10 but with two 340 hp Armstrong Siddeley Serval radials. Span 54 ft, length 40 ft, height 11 ft 6 in, wing area 400 sq ft, tare weight 4,385 lb, all-up weight 7,200 lb, maximum speed 190 mph, cruising speed 170 mph, initial climb 1,000 ft/min.

C.A.20   Blackburn B-1 Segrave II with Duncanson wing and two 130 hp de Havilland Gipsy Majors, described in detail beginning page 325.

C.A.20A   Blackburn B-1 Segrave II with Duncanson wing and two 135 hp Cirrus Hermes IVAs. Tare weight 1,986 lb, all-up weight 3,490 lb, maximum speed 142 mph, cruising speed 120 mph, initial climb 875 ft/min, service ceiling 17,000 ft.

C.A.21   Preliminary schemes for the H.S.T.10 for pilot and eight passengers, using four 130 hp de Havilland Gipsy Majors, four 174 hp Napier Javelins or two 340 hp Armstrong Siddeley Servals. Span 57 ft, length 40 ft, height 12 ft, wing area 440 sq ft, tare weight 4,210 lb, payload 1,055 lb, all-up weight 7,410 lb, maximum speed 155 mph, cruising speed 132 mph, initial climb 670 ft/min, service ceiling 15,500 ft, range 600 miles.

C.A.21A   Blackburn B-9 (or H.S.T.10), described in detail beginning page 389.

C.A.21B   Design study based on the H.S.T.10, dated 8 January 1935 for a coastal reconnaissance/bomber transport landplane known as the H.S.B.T.10. Powered by two 390 hp Napier Rapier VIs and defended by one mid-upper and one ventral gunner. Wing area 442 sq ft, tare weight 5,156 lb, all-up weight 7,600 lb, maximum speed 180 mph, cruising speed 160 mph, initial climb 1,100 ft/min, service ceiling 23,900 ft, range 600 miles. Associated projects: (a) Long-range H.S.T.20 bomber for the RAF with two 630 hp Napier Dagger M.1s. Span 84 ft, length 63 ft, tare weight 11,275 lb, all-up weight 17,700 lb, maximum speed 206 mph, cruising speed 180 mph, initial climb 1,000 ft/min, service ceiling 22,000 ft, range 620 miles. (*b*) General purpose H.B.N.T.10 with two 500 hp Bristol Aquilas.

Class C.Bo. (*Civil Boat projects*)

C.Bo.1   Six-passenger medium-range flying-boat with one 400 hp Liberty engine and therefore known alternatively as B.L.6 (Blackburn-Liberty six-seater). Specification dated 11 April 1923 gave maximum speed 107 mph, cruising speed 85 mph, service ceiling 10,800 ft, at an all-up weight of 5,808 lb. Alternative power plants: Curtiss low-compression and Packard engines.

C.Bo.2   Medium-range five-passenger flying-boat with one 264 hp Rolls-Royce Falcon, alternative designation B.R.5. Project dated 9 July 1923, to specification issued by the Cuyaba Improvements Co of Brazil, accommodating four passengers in side-by-side pairs in an enclosed cabin (with detachable roof for fine-weather flying) and the fifth beside the pilot. Tare weight 1,500 lb, all-up weight 4,209 lb, maximum speed 101 mph, cruising speed 75 mph, initial climb 580 ft/min, service ceiling 10,900 ft, range 350 miles.

A project for a twin-engined boat with two 475 hp Napier Lions submitted to Chile 29 August 1923 was known simply as the Chilean Type A. Tare weight 7,020 lb, payload 4,427 lb, all-up weight 17,176 lb, initial climb 450 ft/min, maximum speed 103 mph.

C.Bo.3   Project for a single-engined wooden flying-boat with double-skinned mahogany hull for the West Indies Transport Co dated August 1924. Intended to carry six passengers, pilot and 190 lb of luggage on the power of one 360 hp Rolls-Royce Eagle IX and therefore also known as B.R.6. Tare weight 3,900 lb, all-up weight 6,000 lb, maximum speed 95 mph, cruising speed 80 mph.

C.Bo.4   Project for a biplane flying-boat with metal hull and powered by three 360 hp Rolls-Royce Eagles, all-up weight 17,500 lb, payload 5,590 lb, maximum speed 97 mph.

Class C.B. (*Commercial Boats*)

C.B.1   1931   Commercial project based on the Iris IV.
C.B.2   1928   Commercial Sydney project for Cobham-Blackburn Air Lines Ltd.
C.B.2F   1929   Nile in final form with Bristol Jupiter IXs.

Class D.B. (*Dive Bombers*)

D.B.1   1935   Skua I with Bristol Mercury IX.
D.B.1A   1938   Skua II with Bristol Perseus XII.

Class F. (*Fighters*)

F.1   1926   Blackcock/Turcock single-seat export fighter scheme.
2F.1   1928   Nautilus two-seat prototype to Specification O.22/26.
F.2   1928   Lincock I wooden prototype.
F.2A   1929   Lincock II all-metal prototype.
F.2B   1929   Lincock II⎫ with unspecified alternative power plants.
F.2C   1929   Lincock II⎭
F.2D   1930   Lincock III production for China and Japan.
F.2E   1931   Projected Lincock fighter for Spain.
F.3   1932   Single-seat fighter to Specification F.7/30.

Class L. (Light Aeroplanes)

L.1	1924	Bluebird I prototype for Lympne Trials.
L.1A	1927	Bluebird II production version with Armstrong Siddeley Genet II.
L.1B	1928	Bluebird III final wooden version.
L.1C	1929	Bluebird IV all-metal version for large-scale production.

Class M. (Mailplanes)

M.1	1923	Night mailplane project using Swift components.

Class R. (Reconnaissance)

R.1	1922	Blackburn Mk I production to Specification 3/21.
R.1A	1925	Blackburn Mk II production to Specification 11/23.
R.2	1925	Airedale monoplane prototypes to Specification 37/22.
R.3A	1926	Airedale alternative biplane project.

Class R.B. (Reconnaissance Boats)

R.B.1	1925	Iris I prototype to Specification R.14/24.
R.B.1A	1927	Iris II rebuild of R.B.1 Iris I with metal hull.
R.B.1B	1928	Iris III development to Specification R.31/27.
R.B.1C	1930	Iris IV experimental version with Armstrong Siddeley Leopards.
R.B.1D	1932	Iris V final variant with Rolls-Royce Buzzards.
R.B.2	1928	Sydney prototype to Specification R.5/27.
R.B.2A	1929	Sydney development project with Rolls-Royce Kestrel MS engines.
R.B.3	1933	Iris V with 37 mm C.O.W. quick-firing cannon.
R.B.3A	1933	Perth production for the RAF to Specification 20/32.

Class R.T. (Reconnaissance Torpedo)

R.T.1	1918	Kangaroo production for the RAF.

Class S. (Survey)

S.1	1927	Project dated 1 June 1927 for a survey biplane similar to the Bristol Lucifer powered by one 200 hp Armstrong Siddeley Lynx. All-up weight 2,937 lb, maximum speed 115 mph, initial climb 720 ft/min, service ceiling 13,000 ft, range 700 miles. A trainer version with Armstrong Siddeley Mongoose radial considered July 1927, span 26 ft 10 in, length 19 ft, height 7 ft 9 in.

Class T. (Torpedo)

T.1	1920	Swift I prototype for the RAF.
T.1A	1922	Swift II for Japan and Spain; Swift F for the US Navy.
T.1B	1923	Swift III amphibian project.
T.O.1	1923	Swift development for Sweden dated 19 June 1923.
T.2	1921	Dart production for the Fleet Air Arm to Specification 3/20.
T.3	1925	Velos two-seater with temperate radiator.
T.3A	1926	Velos with gun ring and tropical radiator.
T.4	1924	Cubaroo I prototypes to Specification 16/22.
T.4A	1927	Cubaroo II project with two Rolls-Royce Condor III direct drive engines.
T.4B	1927	Cubaroo III project with two Rolls-Royce Condor III geared engines.
T.4C	1927	Cubaroo IV project with lowered nacelles.

T.5	1925	Ripon I prototypes to Specification 21/23.
T.5A	1927	Ripon II production to Specification 2/29.
T.5B	1928	Ripon IIA and Ripon IIC production to Specifications 2/29 and 13/31.
T.5C	1928	Ripon project for Spain with Napier Lion or Bristol Jupiter.
T.5D	1928	Ripon IIF specimen aircraft for Finland.
T.5E	1928	Ripon III all-metal prototype.
T.5F	1929	Ripon project with Armstrong Siddeley Jaguar Major.
T.5G	1930	Ripon IV long-range bomber project.
T.5H	1931	Ripon V torpedo project.
T.5J	1932	Ripon V prototypes leading to the Baffin.
T.6	1927	Enlarged Ripon project for Japan.
T.7	1927	Second Ripon project for Japan.
T.7A	1929	Projected T.7 variant for Spain.
T.7B	1929	The 3MR4 specimen aircraft for Japan.
T.8	1933	Baffin production for the Fleet Air Arm to Specification 4/33.
T.9	1933	Shark prototype to Specification S.15/33 and Shark I production to Specification S.12/34.
T.9A	1935	Shark II production to Specification 13/35 and for Canada; Shark IIA production for Portugal.
T.9B	1937	Shark III production to Specification 19/36 and for Canada.

Class T.C. (Troop Carriers)

T.C.1	1929	Projected high-wing monoplane to Specification C.16/28 powered by three supercharged Bristol Jupiter Xs and generally similar to the C.A.10 project for Imperial Airways Ltd. Span 115 ft, length 68 ft 4½ in, height 23 ft 7½ in, wing area 2,000 sq ft, all-up weight 21,000 lb, maximum speed 122 mph, initial climb 720 ft/min, service ceiling 30,600 ft.

Class T.R. (Trainers)

T.R.1	1925	Sprat prototype to Specification 5/24.

Unclassified Design Studies

The following are typical of the countless investigations undertaken by the Blackburn design office but which did not proceed far enough for the results to reach company designation status, either under the mission symbol system or in the B series which followed. Some were purely exploratory studies made during the preparation of designs which were actually built, and others were developments of existing themes, as for example the A.39/34 layout which finds no place in any Blackburn list yet is clearly recognizable as a derivative of the B-24 Skua.

1931　Layout dated 16 March 1931 for a two-seater with 812 hp Armstrong Siddeley Leopard radial engine, designed by Maj Bumpus to the optional single- or twin-engined mailplane Specification 21/28 to carry 1,000 lb of mail 1,000 miles at better than 150 mph. Competed with the Avro 627, Gloster and other projects, the prototype contract being awarded to the twin-engined Boulton and Paul P.64 which first flew in March 1933 as G-ABYK and bore a certain resemblance to the Blackburn C.A.15C biplane G-ABKW. Span 50 ft, length 37 ft, height 15 ft 8 in, wing area 643 sq ft, all-up weight 9,650 lb.

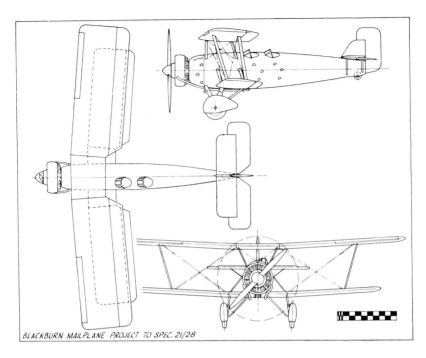

BLACKBURN MAILPLANE PROJECT TO SPEC. 21/28

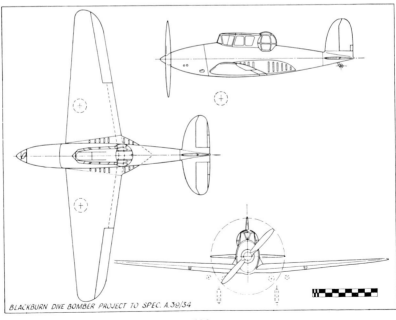

BLACKBURN DIVE BOMBER PROJECT TO SPEC. A.39/34

1934   Long-range general-purpose sesquiplane flying-boat designed by Maj J. D. Rennie to Specification R.2/33 in competition with the Short Sunderland, Saro A.33 and other projects. Powered by four steam-cooled 820 hp Rolls-Royce Kestrel XIIMS engines and fitted with wing flaps. Span (upper) 102 ft (lower) 60 ft, wing area 1,950 sq ft, tare weight 23,212 lb, military load 3,312 lb, all-up weight 41,000 lb, maximum speed 175 mph, cruising speed 148 mph, initial climb 860 ft/min, service ceiling 15,800 ft.

1935   Two-seat turret fighter to Specification A.39/34 based on the Skua and powered by one Rolls-Royce Merlin C moderately-supercharged engine. Original drawings dated 17 April 1935 and initialled by Maj Bumpus depict a machine which differed only in detail from the Roc. Probably did not go into production because Merlin engines were earmarked for the Hawker Hurricane. Span 44 ft, length 30 ft 4½ in, height 10 ft 6 in.

1936   Four-engined high-performance flying-boat to Specification R.12/35 in two versions: (a) span 82 ft, length 68 ft 6 in, height 25 ft 9 in; (b) span 76 ft, length 68 ft 6 in, height 26 ft 3 in.

1936   Five-seat naval amphibian powered by two Bristol Pegasus P.E.5m radials, all-up weight 18,500 lb, military load 3,559 lb, span 68 ft, wing area 654 sq ft, maximum speed 230 mph, cruising speed 195 mph, initial climb 1,500 ft/min, service ceiling 20,000 ft, range 1,000 miles. This project, dated 10 January 1936, also revived the old-style designation B.B.5 (Blackburn-Bristol Five-seater). A scheme to fit two Bristol Aquilas was also considered in May 1936.

The B Series

B-1	1931	Segrave four-seat twin-engined monoplane also known as C.A.20.
B-2	1931	Bluebird V, re-named B-2 Trainer.
B-3	1931	M.1/30A deck-landing torpedo-bomber.
B-4	1932	Armstrong Siddeley Tiger engined Ripon prototype ⎱ also known
B-5	1932	Bristol Pegasus engined Ripon prototype ⎰ as T.5J.
B-6	1933	Shark prototype (also known as T.9) to Specification S.15/33.
B-7	1933	Private-venture prototype to Specification G.4/31.
B-8	1934	Two-seat light aeroplane project, not built.
B-9	1935	H.S.T.10 low-wing transport also known as C.A.21A.
B-10	1935	Bluebird IV test bed for the Cirrus Minor I engine.
B-11	1936	Design study for the Blackburn Sparrowhawk. No details.

B-12 to B-19 inclusive were allocated to civil types but not used.

B-20	1937	Experimental flying-boat to Specification R.1/36 with retractable planing bottom.
B-21	1937	Torpedo-bomber-reconnaissance aircraft project to Specification S.24/37. Cancelled in favour of B-29.
B-22	1937	Fleet spotter-reconnaissance aircraft project derived from C.A.21B to Specification S.30/37 with two Bristol Aquila A.E.3m or two Napier Rapier VI in response to an Air Ministry enquiry dated 10 May 1937.
B-23	1938	Botha II private venture. Cancelled in favour of B-27.
B-24	1937	Skua I fighter/dive-bomber to Specification O.27/34.
B-25	1937	Roc I turret fighter to Specification O.30/35.
B-26	1937	Botha I torpedo-bomber production to Specification G.10/36.
B-27	1938	Botha II private-venture project with two Bristol Hercules radials.
B-28	1940	Private-venture high-speed light reconnaissance project based on the Botha with two Rolls-Royce Griffons to Specification B.3/40.

Mock-up of the Blackburn B-29 torpedo-bomber-reconnaissance type with Rolls-Royce Exe engine.

B-29	1939	Torpedo-bomber-reconnaissance monoplane with Rolls-Royce Exe engine to Specification S.24/37. Shark replacement cancelled in favour of B-36.
B-30	1939	Four-engined bomber project to Specification B.1/39.
B-31	1939	Naval fighter project with rear gun turret, to Specification N.9/39.
B-32	1939	Flying-boat project to Specification R.5/39. Cancelled in favour of B-39.
B-33	1939	Naval fighter project to Specification N.8/39.
B-34	1939	Army Co-operation aircraft project to Specification A.7/39.
B-35	1938	A scheme dated 12 October 1938 for a single-seat high-performance deck-landing amphibian powered by one 740 hp Rolls-Royce Peregrine driving the airscrew through an extension shaft designed by Rolls-Royce. Designed for the FAA at the Dumbarton works and used a retractable pontoon as on the B-20. All-up weight 8,180 lb, span 46 ft, length 39 ft, height 12 ft 6 in, wing area 303 sq ft, maximum speed 256 mph, initial climb 1,130 ft/min, range 640 miles. Also known as the B.P.1.
B-36	1938	Scheme dated 16 June 1938 for a torpedo-reconnaissance machine to Specification S.24/37.
B-37	1940	Firebrand I single-seat fighter with Sabre engine.
B-38	1940	Amphibian flying-boat project with experimental wing flaps.
B-39	1940	Long-range reconnaissance flying-boat with two Bristol Centaurus radials to Specification R.5/39.
B-40	1940	Proposals for an improved version of the B-20 with Bristol Centaurus radials.
B-41	1940	Single-seat fighter for the RAF based on the Sabre-engined B-37 Firebrand I.
B-42	1942	Design study for a Firebrand with high-lift wing.
B-43	1942	Single-seat twin-float fighter based on the B-37 Firebrand I with Sabre engine.
B-44	1943	Alternative version of B-43 designed by Maj J. D. Rennie to Specification N.2/43 and embodying a retractable pontoon. Intended for hoisting out from escort carriers out of range of shore bases and able to retract the planing bottom to lie flush with the fuselage after take-off. Stabilizing floats retracted inwards into the underside of the mainplane, and armament was four 20-mm British Hispano cannon. A mock-up was built but the machine did not go beyond the design stage. A top speed of 360 mph at 25,000 ft was expected. Span 50 ft, length 39 ft 4 in, wing area 381 sq ft, service ceiling 38,000 ft, range 1,000 miles.
B-45	1943	Firebrand T.F.III with Bristol Centaurus VII.
B-46	1945	Firebrand T.F.4, 5 and 5A.
B-47	1944	Projected dive-bomber to Specification O.5/43.
B-48	1947	Firebrand development to Specification S.28/43 built under the unofficial name Firecrest and also designated Y.A.1.
B-49	1945	The Clydesman project. This was a design study by Maj J. D. Rennie for a very large six-engined transport flying-boat outside the

Model of the Blackburn B-49 Clydesman six-engined flying-boat.

Brabazon Committee's recommendations. It was envisaged as a high-wing all-metal monoplane, 202 ft in span and 148 ft long overall with a hull and tail unit of similar outline to the Sunderland flying-boats which the firm built on the Clyde during the war. With an all-up weight of 138 tons and cruising at 270 mph at 15,000 ft, its range with 160 passengers and 30,400 lb of freight and mail would have been 2,500 miles. Alternatively with 72 passengers and 2,980 lb of freight the range was 4,375 miles. Sleeping accommodation was provided in a pressurised cabin with two decks, and there were full galley, toilet and dressing room facilities. Maximum speed 307 mph, initial climb 940 ft/min, absolute ceiling 20,000 ft.

B-50   1945   Fleet Air Arm strike aircraft project with Rolls-Royce Nene turbojet. Brochure submitted to the Air Ministry 17 February 1945 envisaged single- and twin-boom versions with tricycle undercarriage.

B-51   1945   Scheme for a five-seat postwar civil aircraft with Rolls-Royce Merlin.

B-52   1945   Advanced trainer design to Specification T.7/45 with Rolls-Royce Merlin or Bristol Perseus. Brochure submitted to the Air Ministry 10 May 1945.

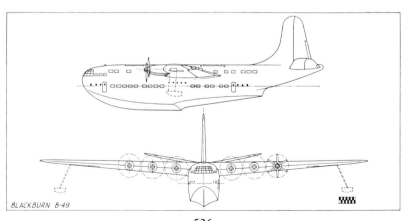

BLACKBURN B-49

B-53   1945   Zodiac torpedo research.

B-54   1945   Anti-submarine aircraft built to Specification G.R.17/45. Also designated Y.A.5.

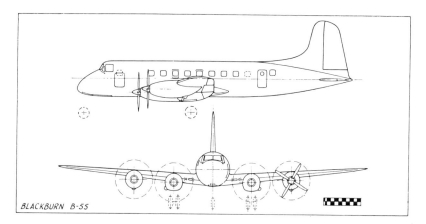

BLACKBURN B-55

B-55   1946   Layout for a 24-seat commercial aircraft with four Rolls-Royce Dart propeller-turbines. Dated 24 January 1946 and also designated Y.A.4. Span 88 ft, length 73 ft 6 in, height 26 ft 6 in, wing area 980 sq ft, all-up weight 38,500 lb.

B-56 to B-59 inclusive were not used.

B-60   1946   Design study dated 1 April 1946 for a civil transport with two Armstrong Siddeley Cheetah radials.

B-61   1946   Design study dated 1 April 1946 for a strike aircraft for the Royal Navy.

B-62   1946   Blackburn B-48 propeller-turbine conversion investigation dated 15 April 1946 with the Bristol Proteus, Rolls-Royce Clyde and Armstrong Siddeley Mamba as alternatives. Also designated Y.A.6.

B-63   1946   Layout for a high-speed transport.

B-64   1946   Preparation of drawings for the Burn torpedo 8 July 1946.

B-65   1946   Design study dated 15 July 1946 for a 20-seat civil transport with two Armstrong Siddeley Mambas. Brochure submitted to the Ministry of Aviation 1947. Span 104 ft, length 78 ft 6 in, wing area 943 sq ft, all-up weight 26,000 lb.

B-66   1946   Design study dated 10 September 1946 for a transonic delta aircraft.

B-67   1946   Proposed night fighter for the Royal Navy, brochure submitted 1947.

B-68   1946   Proposals dated 5 November 1946 for a Royal Navy fighter.

B-69   1946   Design study dated 18 November 1946 for a 64-seat civil transport with four Armstrong Siddeley Mambas, including an alternative passenger/freight version.

B-70   1947   Designs dated 29 January 1947 for a medium-range Empire transport for BOAC with four radial engines' to Specification 2/47. Tender submitted to the Ministry of Aviation 23 April 1947. Span 120 ft, length 114 ft 4 in, wing area 1,500 sq ft, all-up weight 91,500 lb.

B-71	1947	Proposals dated 30 April 1947 for an experimental naval aircraft based on the B-67 for landing on a rubber deck. Brochure submitted 19 July 1947.
B-72	1947	Designs dated 14 May 1947 for a short-range transport for British European Airways.
B-73	1947	Designs dated 14 October 1947 for a long-range Empire transport. Brochure submitted to the Ministry of Aviation 5 February 1948.

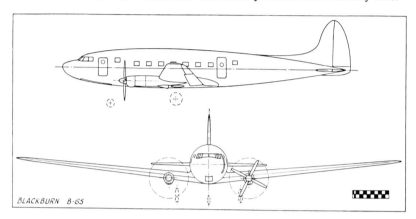

BLACKBURN B-65

B-73A	1947	Double-deck version of B-73 with Bristol Proteus engines, to carry 48 day and night passengers or 100 day passengers in the maximum seat version. Alternatively 84 day passengers in a medium-range version.
B-73B	1947	Single-deck version of B-73 with Bristol Proteus engines to carry 40 day and night passengers or 60 day passengers in the maximum seat version.
B-73C	1947	Single-deck version of B-73 with Napier Nomad engines for 32 day and night passengers.
B-74	1947	A scheme dated 15 October 1947 for a naval fighter aircraft.
B-75	1947	Designs dated 25 October 1947 for a feeder-line aircraft powered by two Cirrus Majors or Cirrus Bombardiers in two versions: (a) four–five passengers, (b) eight–ten passengers. Also designated Y.A.9.
B-76	1948	Layout dated 1 April 1948 for a commercial freight aircraft.
B-77	1948	Layout dated 13 April 1948 for a 14-seat four-engined Rapide replacement in B-77A and B-77B versions.
B-77C	1948	Twelve-seat version of B-77.
B-78	1948	Layout dated 3 December 1948 for a reconnaissance flying-boat to Specification R.2/48.
B-79	1949	Layout dated 26 January 1949 for an anti-submarine aircraft to replace B-54.
B-80	1949	Layout dated 22 February 1949 for a single-engined basic trainer to Specification T.16/48. Tender submitted 11 March 1949.
B-81	1949	Layout dated 23 February 1949 for a naval reconnaissance aircraft.
B-82	1949	Layout dated 30 March 1949 for a naval night fighter to Specification N.14/48.

| B-83 | 1949 | Layout dated 6 May 1949 for a naval reconnaissance anti-submarine aircraft with one Rolls-Royce Merlin. Brochure submitted 28 October 1949. |
| B-83A | 1949 | Alternative power plant version of B-83 with Armstrong Siddeley Mamba. |

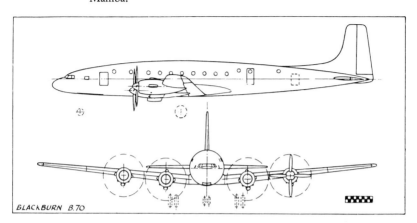

B-84	1949	Layout dated 29 August 1949 for a four-engined Rapide replacement to Specification 26/49, superseding B-77. Tender submitted to the Ministry of Aviation 28 October 1949.
B-84A	1949	18/20-seat version of B-84. Span 75 ft 4 in, length 49 ft, wing area 617 sq ft, all-up weight 12,500 lb.
B-84B	1949	12/14-seat and two-stretcher version of B-84A to Specification 26/49. Span 64 ft, length 44 ft, wing area 446 sq ft, all-up weight 9,060 lb.
B-84C	1949	17-seat version of B-84.
B-85	1950	Investigation by Mr McEwan King into composite aircraft dated 18 January 1950.
B-86	1950	Layout dated 23 May 1950 for a Coastal Command aircraft.
B-87	1950	Layout dated 23 May 1950 for a training aircraft.
B-88	1950	Anti-submarine search aircraft with Airborne Early Warning equipment to Specification G.R.17/45. Powered by one Armstrong Siddeley Double Mamba propeller-turbine and also designated Y.B.1. Brochure submitted 27 October 1950 and one prototype built.
B-89	1950	Layout dated 25 September 1950 for a naval fighter to Specification N.114T. Wind-tunnel investigation to Works Order 4761/130.
B-90	1951	Layout dated 11 January 1951 for a supersonic fighter with 60 degree sweepback to Specification ER.110T.
B-91	1951	Layout dated 12 February 1951 for a light general reconnaissance and anti-submarine aircraft.
B-92	1950	Layout dated 26 July 1951 for a jet training aircraft.
B-92A	1950	Basic trainer derived from B-92 with Armstrong Siddeley Mamba.
B-92B	1950	Twin conversion of B-92A with two Armstrong Siddeley Mamba.
B-93	1951	The Blackburn Highlander five-seat feeder-liner project dated 14 September 1951 with four Cirrus Bombardiers. Span 64 ft, wing area 446 sq ft, all-up weight 9,000 lb, cruising speed 135 m.p.h.

Model of the Blackburn and General B-84A feeder-liner. (*Courtesy P. W. Brooks.*)

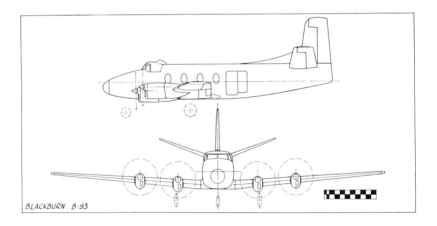

BLACKBURN B-93

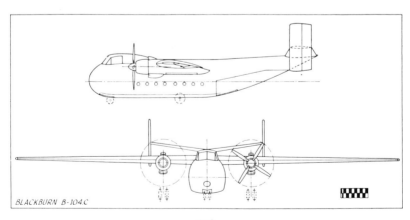

BLACKBURN B-104C

540

B-94	1951	Layout dated 21 November 1951 for an undercarriageless naval fighter.
B-95	1951	Naval fighter development.
B-96	1952	Developed Y.B.1 project with Napier E. 141.
B-97	1952	Layout dated 6 March 1952 for a naval interceptor fighter to Specification F.124T, superseded by B-99.
B-98	1952	Design study for a short-range passenger and freight aircraft in two versions: Freighter Mk 1 with Wright turbo-compound engines; Freighter Mk 2 with Napier Nomad engines.
B-99	1952	Project development dated 3 July 1952 for a naval interceptor fighter to Specification F.124T.
B-100	1952	The G.A.L.65 Universal Freighter Mk II.
B-101	1952	Beverley military freighter to Specification C.3/46.
B-102	1952	Layout dated 30 October 1952 for a naval all-weather interceptor fighter.
B-103	1952	Layout dated 1 December 1952 for a naval strike aircraft, eventually Buccaneer. Also designated Y.B.3.
B-104	1953	Initial layout dated 11 February 1953 for an RAF medium-range military transport to replace the Vickers Valetta in competition with the A.W. Argosy and Short P.D.16.
B-104A	1953	Version of B-104 with two propeller-turbines, rear loading doors, twin fins and rudders. Span 136 ft 3 in, length 92 ft 3 in, height 27 ft.
B-104B	1953	Version of B-104A with four propeller-turbines. Span 141 ft 10 in, length 92 ft 6 in, height 28 ft.
B-104C	1953	Smaller version of B-104A with high aspect ratio wing and two propeller-turbines. Span 139 ft 9 in, length 83 ft 6 in, height 28 ft.
B-105	1953	The Blackburn Baronet 18-seat Rapide replacement project. Designed for use by BEA and operators in the Caribbean, Malaya and Australia, and powered by four Bombardier engines. It was a low-wing monoplane with retractable tricycle undercarriage, and as late as September 1954 BEA were still showing active interest, and Blackburns were continually keeping the design up to date. An early arrangement with dihedral tailplane and five large oval windows had a span of 64 ft 6 in, length 47 ft 2 in, height 17 ft 6 in, wing area 555 sq ft, tare weight 8,753 lb, all-up weight 12,000 lb, cruising speed 142 mph. A later scheme had rectangular windows and a span of 75 ft 11 in and length 47 ft 6 in.
B-106	1954	A 26-seat transport with four propeller-turbines.
B-107	1956	Beverley development Stage 2. A projected tactical and strategic transport using the Beverley wing and tail unit with a completely new fuselage having a large unobstructed freight hold. STOL capability was combined with long range and high cruising speed. Powered by four 4,985 ehp Rolls-Royce Tyne R.Ty.11 propeller-turbines, it could have carried 75 parachutists, 92 stretcher cases, 108 troops, six loaded Ferret scout cars or two Prestwick Pioneers or Bristol Sycamores. Span 166 ft 8 in, length 124 ft, height 31 ft, wing area 2,916 sq ft, cruising speed 350 mph, maximum range 5,000 miles.

541

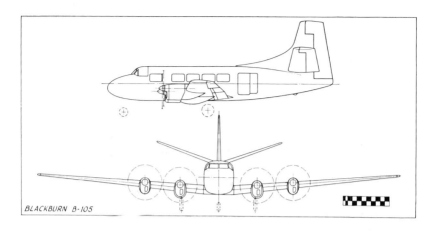

BLACKBURN B-105

B-107A 1959 Beverley development Stage 3. Differed principally from B-107 in having main loading doors at the front for direct loading and rear doors operable in flight for supply dropping. The flight deck was also moved to provide greater safety for the crew of four during small-field operations. Data as B-107. Not built.

B-108 and/or Buccaneer developments, one of them for Canada. Project/s only.
B-109

B.110 1960/61 35/38-passenger turbofan-powered low-wing project with rear-mounted engines. All-up weight about 54,000 lb. Data and drawings transferred to de Havilland.

Model of the Blackburn B-107A military freighter shown at the Farnborough SBAC Show, September 1958.

542

Blackburn Aircraft Production List from 1920

Painstaking searches among Blackburn, Ministry and other records over a period of many years have shown that Works Order numbers for many of the earlier Blackburn aircraft have now been irretrievably lost. This appendix can therefore only hint at the position of the early Dart and Blackburn Mk I and II batches and omits some more recent production runs for which this type of information is not available. In all other respects it is as complete a list as possible of the aeroplanes built in the parent factory at Brough.

Works Order	Year	Type	Qty	For	Identities
6368/1	1920	Swift	1	Air Min.	N139
	1921	Dart	3	Air Min.	N140–N142
	1922	Blackburn I	3	Air Min.	N150–N152
	1922	Swift F	2	US Navy	A-6056, A-6057
	1922	Swift II	2	Japan	1 and 2
	1922	Dart	26	FAA	N9536–N9561
	1922	Blackburn I	12	FAA	N9579–N9590
	1923	Swift II	3	Spain	M-NTBA to M-NTBC
	1923	Pellet	1	Works	G-EBHF
	1923	Blackburn I	6	FAA	N9681–N9686
	1923	Dart	20	FAA	N9620–N9629, N9687–N9696
	1924	Dart	42	FAA	N9714–N9723, N9792–N9823
	1924	Bluebird I	1	Works	G-EBKD
	1924	Blackburn I	12	FAA	N9824–N9835
	1924	Cubaroo	2	Air Min.	N166–N167
	1925	Blackburn II	24	FAA	N9978–N9989, S1046–S1057
	1925	Dart	10	FAA	N9990–N9999
	1925	Velos T.3	4	Greece	11–14 unconfirmed
8312/1–3	1925	Dart	3	North Sea	G-EBKF to G-EBKH
	1926	Dart	16	FAA	S1115–S1120, S1129–S1138
	1926	Blackburn II	5	FAA	S1154–S1158
8837/1	1926	Kangaroo	1	North Sea	G-EBMD dual conversion
8839/1	1926	Kangaroo	1	North Sea	G-EBOM dual conversion
8840/1	1926	Kangaroo	1	North Sea	G-EBPK dual conversion
	1926	Airedale	2	Air Min.	N188–N189
	1926	Iris I	1	Air Min.	N185
	1926	Ripon I	2	Air Min.	N203–N204
	1926	Sprat	1	Air Min.	N207
9593/1	1926	Velos T.3A	1	Works	G-EBWB in 1928
9725/1	1926	Turcock	1	Turkey	G-EBVP
9762/1	1927	Velos T.3	1	Works	G-AAUM in 1931
	1927	Ripon II	1	Air Min.	N231

Works Order	Year	Type	Qty	For	Identities
9803/1	1927	Bluebird I	1	Works	G-EBKD modifications
9803/2–15	1927	Bluebird II	13	Production	G-EBRE to G-EBRG; G-EBSV to G-EBTC; G-EBUH, G-EBUI; G-EBWE
	1927	Iris II	1	Air Min.	N185 conversion from Mk I
9906/1	1928	Lincock I	1	Works	G-EBVO
	1928	Beagle	1	Air Min.	N236
369/1	1928	Sydney	1	Air Min.	N241
	1928	Nile	1	Works	Unregistered
629/1	1928	Bluebird III	1	Works	G-EBWE Cirrus conversion
	1928	Ripon IIF	1	Finland	RI-121
	1928	Ripon II	7	FAA	S1265–S1271
761/1	1928	Nautilus	1	Air Min.	N234
870/1–3	1928	Iris III	3	RAF	N238, S1263, S1264
1420/1	1928	Ripon III	1	Air Min.	S1272
1430/1	1928	Bluebird IV	1	Works	G-AABV
1440/1–4	1928	Velos	4	North Sea	G-AAAW to G-AAAZ
1450/1–6	1928	Bluebird III	6	Production	G-AABB to G-AABG
1730/1–2	1928	Bluebird IV	2	Works	G-AACB, G-AACC
1850/1–13	1929	Ripon II	13	FAA	S1357–S1369
1930/1	1929	T.7B (3MR4)	1	Japan	Unregistered
2050/1	1929	Lincock II	1	Canada	G-AALH
2339/1	1929	Ripon II	1	Air Min.	N231 modifications
2485/1	1929	Iris II	1	Air Min.	N185 conversion to Mk IV
2689/1	1929	Beagle	1	Air Min.	N236 modifications
2690/1–9	1930	Ripon IIA	9	FAA	S1424–S1432
2741/1	1930	Lincock III	1	Japan	Japan 1
2780/1	1930	Monoplane	1	Air Min.	G-ABKV
2781/1	1930	Biplane	1	Air Min.	G-ABKW
2920/1–4	1930	Lincock III	4	Production	Japan 2, G-ABFK, China 1 and 2
3130/1–9	1930	Ripon IIA	9	FAA	S1465–S1473
3169/1–2	1930	Segrave I	2	Production	G-ABFP, G-ABFR
3310/1	1931	Iris III	1	RAF	S1593
3320/1–6	1931	Ripon IIA	9	FAA	S1553–S1561
3330/1–6	1931	Ripon IIA	6	FAA	S1562–S1567
3340/1–7	1931	Ripon IIA	7	FAA	S1568–S1574
3347/1–2	1931	Bluebird IV	2	Canada	CF-ALN and CF-AUP crating for shipment
3380/1	1931	M.1/30	1	Air Min.	S1640
3420/1	1931	Dart	2	FAA	N9540, N9623 reconditioning
3420/2–3	1931	Dart	2	FAA	N9823, N9692 reconditioning
3580/1	1931	B-2	1	Works	G-ABUW
3810/1–22	1931	Ripon IIC	22	FAA	S1649–S1669, S1671
3854/1	1932	Segrave II	1	Works	G-ACMI
3900/1	1932	M.1/30A	1	Air Min.	K3591
3971/1	1932	Ripon IIC	1	FAA	S1557 conversion from Mk IIA
4060/1–5	1932	Ripon IIC	4	FAA	S1670, S1672–S1674
	1932	Ripon V	2	Works	B-4 and B-5

544

Works Order	Year	Type	Qty	For	Identities
4570/1–4	1932	Ripon IIC	4	FAA	K2884–K2887
4700/1–6	1932	B-2	6	Production	G-ABWI, G-ACAH, G-ACBH to G-ACBK
4702/1	1932	Dart	1	FAA	N9723 reconditioning
4804/4	1933	Ripon IIC	1	FAA	S1366 conversion from Mk II
4970/1–2	1933	Perth	2	RAF	K3580–K3581
5060/1	1933	B-6	1	Air Min.	K4295
5093/1–6	1933	B-2	6	Production	G-ACEM to G-ACES
5120/1–14	1933	Baffin	14	FAA	K3546–K3559
5220/1	1933	Perth	1	RAF	K3582
5240/1	1934	Perth	1	RAF	K4011
5290/1–6	1933	B-2	6	Production	G-ACLC, G-ACLD, G-ACPZ, G-ACRA, G-ACUE, G-ACZH
5500/1–10	1933	Baffin	10	FAA	K4071–K4080
5568/1–2	1933	Baffin	2	Air Min.	K3589–K3590
5590/1	1933	B-7	1	Works	B-7
	1934	H.S.T.10	1	Works	B-9
5670/1–16	1934	Shark I	16	FAA	K4349–K4364
5830/1–3	1934	Baffin	3	Air Min.	K4776–K4778
5920/1–10	1935	B-2	10	Production	G-ADFN to G-ADFV G-ADLF, G-ADLG
6020/1–3	1935	Shark II	3	Air Min.	K4880–K4882
6120/1–53	1935	Shark II	53	FAA	K5607–K5659
6180/1–6	1935	Shark IIA	6	Portugal	73–78
6290/1–2	1935	Skua I	2	Air Min.	K5178–K5179
6300/1–10	1935	B-2	10	Production	G-ADZM, G-ADZN, G-AEBE to G-AEBL
6596/1–7	1935	Shark III	7	RCAF	501–507
6790/1–70	1936	Shark II	70	FAA	K8450–K8519
6795/1–3	1936	B-2	3	Air Min.	L6891–L6893
7050/1–95	1936	Shark III	95	FAA	K8891–K8935, L2337–L2386
7371/1–69	1936	Skua II	69	FAA	L2867–L2935
7375/1–21	1936	Skua II	21	FAA	L2936–L2956
7840/1–50	1936	Skua II	50	FAA	L2957–L3006
7842/1–50	1936	Skua II	50	FAA	L3007–L3056
7860/1–25	1937	Botha I	25	RAF	L6104–L6128
7862/1–25	1937	Botha I	25	RAF	L6129–L6153
7864/1–50	1937	Botha I	50	RAF	L6154–L6203
7866/1–50	1937	Botha I	50	RAF	L6204–L6253
7868/1–50	1937	Botha I	50	RAF	L6254–L6303
7870/1–42	1937	Botha I	42	RAF	L6304–L6345
8780/1–2	1937	Shark III	2	RCAF	525–526
3240/1–138	1937	Botha I	138	RAF	W5017–W5169
3360/1–400	1941	Barracuda II	400	FAA	From BV660
3380/1–9	1942	Firebrand I	9	MAP	DK363–DK371
3380/10–21	1942	Firebrand II	12	MAP	DK374–DK385
3380/22–50	1943	Firebrand III	29	MAP	DK372–DK373, DK386–DK412

Works Order	Year	Type	Qty	For	Identities
3380/51–152	1945	Firebrand 4	52	FAA	From EK601
3380/153–220	1945	Firebrand 5	68	FAA	From EK741
3700/1–300	1945	Barracuda II	300	FAA	From MX535
	1947	B-48	2	MoS	RT651, RT656
4400/1	1948	B-48	1	MoS	VF172
5800/1–25	1948	Prentice	25	RAF	VS241–VS265
5810/1–25	1948	Prentice	25	RAF	VS266–VS290
5820/1–25	1948	Prentice	25	RAF	VS316–VS338, VS352–VS353
5830/1–25	1948	Prentice	25	RAF	VS354–VS378
5840/1–25	1948	Prentice	25	RAF	VS379–VS397
	1949	B-54	2	MoS	WB781, WB788
	1950	B-88	1	MoS	WB797
c/n 1000	1950	G.A.L.60	1	MoS	WF320/G-AMUX
	1951	H.P.88	1	Handley Page	VX330
1001	1952	G.A.L.65	1	MoS	WZ889/G-AMVW
	1953	Balliol	30	RAF	WN506–WN535
1002	1955	Beverley	1	MoS	XB259/G-AOAI
1003	1955	Beverley	1	MoS	XB260/G-AOEK
	1955	Beverley	18	RAF	XB261–XB269, XB283–XB291,
	1956	Beverley	27	RAF	XH116–XH124, XL130–XL132, XL148–XL152, XM103–XM112
	1958	Buccaneer	20	FAA	XK486–XK491, XK523–XK536
	1958	Buccaneer S.1	40	FAA	XN922–XN935, XN948–XN973
	1962	Buccaneer S.50	16	SAAF	411–426
	1962	Buccaneer S.2	10	FAA	XN974–XN983
	1966	Buccaneer S.2	74	FAA	XT269–XT288, XV152–XV168, XV332–XV361, XV863–XV869
	1968	Buccaneer S.2B	26	RAF	XW525–XW550
		Buccaneer S.2B	3	RAE	XW986–XW988
		Buccaneer S.2B	17	RAF	XX885–XX901
		Buccaneer S.2B	3	RAF	XZ430–XZ432

Fleet Lists

(In order of introduction into service)

(*a*) The North Sea Aerial and General Transport Co Ltd.

Kangaroo	G-EAIT, 'IU, 'KQ, 'MJ, G-EBMD, 'OM and 'PK (see page 122).
Avro 504K	*G-EAGV, ex H6598, C. of A. issued 2 August 1919, crashed at Scarborough 3 August 1920.
	*G-EAGW, ex H6599, C. of A. issued 2 August 1919, crashed at Scarborough July 1920.
	G-EBLA, c/n R/LE/18615, C. of A. 1 July 1925, sold to A. G. Cooper April 1928.
Avro 548A	G-EBIT, c/n 5100, C. of A. issued 9 May 1924, sold to C. B. Harris February 1927.
	G-EBIU, c/n 5101, C. of A. issued 9 May 1924, sold to the Lancashire School of Flying Ltd, Squires Gate February 1928.
	G-EBIV, c/n 5102, C. of A. issued 9 May 1924, sold to Golds and Leeding July 1927.
Dart	G-EBKF, 'KG and 'KH (see page 154).
D.H.50J	G-EBOP *Pelican*, c/n 281, C. of A. issued 21 December 1926, crashed at Kisumu, Kenya 17 October 1927.
Fairey IIID	†G-EBPZ, c/n F.814 ex S1076, C. of A. issued 5 February 1927, sank in Lake Victoria 13 March 1927.
Bluebird II	G-EBTA and 'TC (see page 253).
Bluebird III	G-EBWE (see page 253).
Velos	G-EBWB, G-AAAW, 'AX, 'AY, 'AZ and 'UM (see page 179).
Bluebird IV	G-AATM, 'TS, 'UF, 'UG, 'UT, 'UW, 'TO, G-ABEU, 'VZ, 'ZX, G-AAVF, G-ABPN, G-AAUX (see page 282).
B-2	G-ABUW, 'WI, G-ACAH, 'BH to 'BK, 'EM to 'ES ,'LC, 'LD, 'UE, 'ZH, G-ADZM, G-AEBE, 'BG, 'BI, 'BK, 'BM and 'BO (see page 332).
Segrave I	G-ABFR (see page 32 and 325).

(*b*) Flying Training Ltd, Hanworth (prewar) and Brough (postwar)

B-2	G-ACEO, 'LC, 'PZ, 'RA, G-ADFN to 'FV, 'LF, 'LG, 'ZN, G-AEBF, 'BH, 'BJ, 'BL. and 'BN (see page 333).
Tiger Moth	G-AHRL, 'RM and 'RN, ex T6362, N6548 and T5841 respectively, registered to Flying Training Ltd 28 May 1946, Cs. of A. issued 14 August 1946, to Blackburn Aircraft Ltd 30 September 1947, all three sold to Universal Flying Services Ltd, Fairoaks in 1950.

* Registered to the North Sea Aerial Navigation Co Ltd.
† Registered to the Air Council.

(c) Blackburn Aircraft Ltd

Swallow II	G-AFHK to 'HM, c/n 491–493, Cs. of A. issued 17 June 1938, to London Air Park Flying Club, Hanworth February 1939.
	G-AFHN to 'HP, c/n 494–496, Cs. of A. issued 21 June 1938, to London Air Park Flying Club, Hanworth February 1939.
	G-AFHU to 'HW, c/n 497–499, Cs. of A. issued 25 June 1938, to London Air Park Flying Club, Hanworth February 1939.
	G-AFIG, c/n 472, C. of A. issued 12 August 1938, crashed at Sleaford, Lincs. 19 September 1938.
	G-AFIH, c/n 500, C. of A. issued 5 July 1938, retained by Blackburns for the Brough Flying Club postwar, to the Doncaster Ultra Light Flying Group September 1949.
	G-AFII, c/n 501, C. of A. issued 5 July 1938, to London Air Park Flying Club, Hanworth February 1939.
	G-AFIJ, c/n 502, C. of A. issued 5 July 1938, to Switzerland June 1939 as HB-AKI.
	G-AFIK and 'IL, c/n 503–504, Cs. of A. issued 11 July 1938, to Peterborough Flying Club August 1939.

(d) Communications and engine test-bed aircraft

Miles Hawk Trainer	G-AEZP, c/n 494, registered to Blackburn Aircraft Ltd 6 September 1937. Scrapped about 1943.
Percival Gull	G-ADOE, c/n D.53, registered to the North Sea Aerial and General Transport Co Ltd, C. of A. issued 29 August 1935; to Blackburn Aircraft Ltd December 1936, used throughout the war in camouflage at Brough; to Air Couriers Ltd, Filton March 1946.
Stinson Reliant	G-AFBI, c/n 5400, registered to Robert Blackburn, C. of A. issued 21 November 1937, impressed by the RAF 1 December 1939 for use by No. 1 Group Communications Flight as W5791.
Auster 5	G-AGOH, c/n 1442, registered to Blackburn Aircraft Ltd, C. of A. issued 8 October 1945, used by North Sea Air Transport Ltd from July 1946, to W. S. Shackleton Ltd December 1951.
Miles Messenger 2B	G-AGPX, c/n 6266, registered to Blackburn Aircraft Ltd, C. of A. issued 6 November 1945, to North Sea Air Transport Ltd January 1947, to W. S. Shackleton Ltd February 1951.
Miles Messenger 1	G-ALAC, ex RH420, registered to Blackburn and General Aircraft Ltd May 1948 but flew as G-2-1 as test bed for the Cirrus Bombardier 702. C. of A. issued as Messenger 5 G-ALAC 20 September 1951, wrecked at Faversham, Kent 22 September 1951.
D.H. 104 Dove 1	G-ANMJ, c/n 04006, ex VP-YES, acquired from Ferranti Ltd by Blackburn and General Aircraft Ltd October 1958, to Shackleton Aviation Ltd March 1967, to Cardinal Airways July 1967.

548

D.H.104	G-ARBE, c/n 04517, registered to Hawker Siddeley Aviation
Dove 8A	Leasing Ltd, and posted to Brough as replacement for
	G-ANMJ above.

(*e*) North Sea Air Transport Ltd

Registration and Type		c/n	In service	Disposal
G-AHLU	Rapide	6633	July 1946–Nov. 1949	To Australia as VH-AHI
G-AGOH	Auster 5	1442	July 1946–Dec. 1951	To W. S. Shackleton Ltd
G-AGPX	Messenger 2B	6266	July 1946–Feb. 1951	To W. S. Shackleton Ltd
G-AHAZ	Proctor 1	P6170	Aug. 1946–Sept. 1946	Crashed near Zürich 17 September 1946
G-AHSN	Auster J-1	2105	Aug. 1946–Apr. 1950	To Royal Naval Flying Club
G-AHSO	Auster J-1	2123	Aug. 1946–Dec. 1949	To Universal Flying Services
G-AHVG	Proctor 1	BV658	Oct. 1946–May 1952	To P. G. Lawrence, Brough
G-AIWG	Rapide	6497	Jan. 1947–Nov. 1949	To Australia as VH-AIK
G-AIWZ	Rapide	6867	Jan. 1947–July 1949	Crashed at Brough 30 July 1949
G-AISG	Aerovan 4	6405	May 1947–June 1947	Crashed at Croydon 14 June 1947
G-AIRX	Anson 1	AX232	Apr. 1948–June 1950	To Kenya as VP-KJK
G-AKEI	Gemini 1A	6470	July 1948–Oct. 1950	To R. R. Carne, Denham
G-AGBG	Lockheed 14H	1421	Oct. 1949–Mar. 1951	To Sweden as SE-BTN
G-AHAG	Rapide	6926	Oct. 1949–Apr. 1966	To Scillonia Airways
G-AHGD	Rapide	6862	Oct. 1949–Apr. 1951	To L. H. Riddell, Yeadon
G-AHTY	Rapide	6608	Oct. 1949–Sept. 1952	To France as F-BGIS
G-AHWR	Proctor 5	Ae.73	Oct. 1949–June 1954	Crashed at Baginton 18 June 1954
G-AJOG	Aerovan 4	6410	Nov. 1949–Jan. 1952	To Belgium as OO-ERY
G-AGDT	Lockheed 12A	1285	Dec. 1949–Mar. 1951	To Sweden as SE-BTO

The P.164-108, a turbofan-powered trainer study by Brough to meet AST.412.

Work of the Brough Factory 1968–1988

When Britain ordered the McDonnell Douglas Phantom in a special Rolls-Royce Spey-powered version (F-4K) for the Royal Navy in July 1964 and for the RAF as the F-4M in June 1965, it was evident that local support would be needed and Hawker Siddeley's Brough factory was appointed 'sister-design' firm, responsible for development, modification and return-to-work programmes. In all 170 Phantoms were purchased from the USA, the first arriving at Holme-on-Spalding Moor in 1968. The Navy's Phantoms, like the Buccaneers, were later transferred to the RAF, requiring further modification at Brough. In 1984 fifteen ex-US Navy F-4J Phantoms were purchased for the RAF and these too come under the Brough umbrella. To extend the lives of the Phantoms the factory is at present producing seventy-five sets of new outer wings for delivery starting in 1988.

In 1966 Brough began to share in the work of the Hawker Siddeley Harrier and since then has produced all the wings, centre fuselages and fuselage join-ups for the Kingston factory. Similar work has continued on Sea Harriers and later versions of the Harrier, currently the GR.5 for the RAF and Av-8B for the US Marine Corps.

In 1968 when Hawker Siddeley closed their Portsmouth factory work on the Trident cockpit and forward fuselage was transferred to Brough. Further airliner work came to the factory in the shape of Airbus A300 components for

The P.164-109 propeller-turbine trainer project.

assembly into wing sets at the Chester factory, starting in 1971. Similar work continues on wing ribs and fittings for the A310 and A320.

Brough continued to attract work, including the production of Nimrod pods, and in 1974 delivered the first set of wings for the Hawker Siddeley Hawk trainer to Kingston. More and more Hawk work was transferred to Brough from Kingston, culminating in 1988 with the nomination of the Yorkshire factory as the design and manufacturing authority for the type and all its variants, including the T-45A Goshawk version being produced in co-operation with McDonnell Douglas for the US Navy.

The first of thirty Pilatus PC-9 trainers for the Royal Saudi Air Force, handed over at Brough on 15 December 1986.

551

In 1977 the major part of Britian's aircraft industry was nationalised, Hawker Siddeley, the British Aircraft Corporation and Scottish Aviation being merged to form British Aerospace. Four years later it was denationalised, becoming British Aerospace plc. Brough then became an operating unit in BAe's Military Aircraft Division. Some civil work continues at Brough, however, and since 1978 the factory has been responsible for the fin, flaps and other components for the BAe 146 airliner.

By the early 1980s the RAF had a requirement, AST.412, for a new basic trainer to replace its Jet Provosts and expressed a preference for a propeller-turbine powered machine on the grounds of fuel economy. Brough produced two original designs of its own, the turbofan-powered P.164-108 and propeller-turbine P.164-109. Neither secured the interest of the Ministry of Defence, so British Aerospace joined with Pilatus to offer the Swiss company's PC-9. This too was rejected and in March 1985 a re-engined version of the Brazilian Embraer EMB-312 Tucano offered by Shorts was selected. BAe continued to have faith in the PC-9, however, marketing it as a team with the Hawk advanced trainer. They were rewarded in February 1986 when Saudi Arabia placed a contract with British Aerospace for 132 aircraft, including Tornadoes, Hawks and thirty PC-9s. Brough as the lead site for the PC-9 is responsible for any modifications required by customers and for developing a complete training system around the aircraft. The first PC-9 for the Royal Saudi Air Force was handed over at Brough on 15 December 1986, only ten months after the signing of contracts.

Today the Brough factory is the largest industrial employer on North Humberside, with more than 4,500 employees. Its most recent task is to undertake a market study among potential British operators of the Bell/Boeing V-22 Osprey tilt-rotor aircraft.

Notes on some Blackburn Monoplanes

After publication of the first edition of this book M. G. K. Byrne, then Sales & Publicity Manager, Hawker Siddeley Aviation Brough, wrote to the author stating 'We have unearthed a Blackburn sales book which contains some rather interesting information, an extract of which is attached.' He also wrote 'One item in particular interests me, namely Mr Foggin's aircraft according to the accounts was Type D, No. 776, but your book states that the plate in the cockpit at the moment [the aeroplane preserved by the Shuttleworth Trust] says Type B, No. 725.'

Because some of these questions have never been resolved, the extracts from the Blackburn sales book together with extracts from A. J. Jackson's reply to Mr Byrne are reproduced here.

Extract from Blackburn Sales Account Book

5th May, 1911	to R. J. Weiss, Blackburn Monoplane "Bleriot" type.
29th November, 1911	to Lt. Spenser D. Grey, Blackburn Military type passenger monoplane fitted with 50 h.p. Gnome motor, Type B, No. 672.
6th May, 1912	to W. Laurence, London, Blackburn Military type "all steel" monoplane two-seater.
6th September, 1912	to G. MacWilliams, Winnipeg, 1 Anzani "Bleriot" monoplane.
	to F. Jameson, Hendon, 2 "Bleriot" type monoplanes, one less engines.
31st December, 1912	to Dr. M. G. Christie, Leeds, 1 Blackburn Monoplane Type B, Single Seater fitted with 50 h.p. Gnome motor, engines No. 625 and spare motor No. 492
	This was totally wrecked on the 27th December as there is an insurance claim.
17th February, 1913	to Cyril E. Foggin, 50 h.p. Gnome Blackburn Monoplane Type D, No. 776. In April there was mention of re-building the fuselage and repairing the aircraft at Newcastle.
23rd May, 1913	there is mention of re-constructing a new machine to replace a machine damaged by Harold Blackburn.

3rd June, 1913	to Mr. M. F. Glew, Wittering, Wansford, Northants., a 50 h.p. Gnome Blackburn Monoplane, Type D, No. 776 (this was Foggin's one). There are some mentions of minor repairs to this aircraft.
19th August, 1913	to Dr. M. G. Christie, an 80 h.p. Blackburn two-seater monoplane, Type I, No. 792, less engine.
2nd September, 1913	to the Hart Engine Co., Hunslet, a 30 h.p. monoplane, Type G, No. 785.

Extract from letter of 1 January 1969 from A. J. Jackson to M. G. K. Byrne

5 May 1911	The Weiss Blériot is mentioned on page 4 line 4 of the book.
29 Nov 1911	The Spenser Grey machine is dealt with and illustrated on pages 68–69. The significance of "Type B, No. 672" is being thought about.
6 May 1912	The Lawrence machine was Type E described on pages 72–73.
6 Sept 1912	Canadian Bleriot. Have found many references to the type in Canada but none as late as 1912 and no mention of MacWilliams. Am checking with on-the-spot historians. The existence of this machine confirms the doubts I expressed on page 4 line 2, etc. The Jameson Blériots were used by the Jameson and Temple Flying School at Hendon where Temple was learning to fly on one Nov. 1912.
31 Dec 1912	As far as I can tell, this was the machine illustrated on page 65 and if so, it opens up the question of whether Christie had any financial interest in the Hendon Blackburn School. From the way in which your note on this is phrased, these recurring numbers in the 400–700 range, are serial numbers of Gnome engines.
17 Feb 1913	The discovery that Foggin's machine was Type D (and of course that Type G was for the Hart Engine Co.) is of the greatest historical importance and, had it been known in time, would have improved pages 44 and 76.
23 May 1913	The entry about re-constructing a new machine to replace that damaged by Harold Blackburn is quite sensational for it means that the present Shuttleworth aircraft is not, after all, Foggin's. "Flight" for 3 May 1913 records the trip to Harrogate on April 29 (see my book page 77) and says how he seriously damaged it there. In other words the machine

554

illustrated on page 77 (the original), is not the Shuttleworth machine shown on page 76.

The last para on page 77 about modifications is therefore not correct. The machine with straight skids and rounded wing tips was entirely new.

3 June 1913 — Type D for Glew seems to indicate that the new machine (above) had the original Foggin engine.

19 Aug 1913 — Type I for Christie—see page 81.

2 Sep 1913 — Am looking into the whole question of the Hart Engine Co's activities although the number 785 suggests Type G had a 50 h.p. Gnome. There is a contemporary reference to a 120 h.p. Hart engine but no other.

555

Index—General

(For Aircraft and Engines see p. 567)

560

Kingsley, Maj Shirley, 175
Kirbymoorside, 41
Kirkwall, 13, 14, 31, 405
Kisumu, 29–31, 271, 302
Knight, R. H. W., 286
Konigsberg, 19, 405
Korea, 284
Kuala Lumpur, 286

Laarbruch, 496, 498, 499
Labuan, 476
Laight, B. P., 24, 480
Lakes Flying Co, 86
Lancashire, 6, 160
Larkin Aircraft Supply Co, 283
Latham, Hubert, 2, 12
Lawrence, P. C., 22, 24, 35, 335, 446, 447, 452–454, 458, 459
— Lt W., 65, 66, 72, 73
Leahy, Cdr A., 485
Lebanon, The, 501
Leconfield, 404, 453
Leda, 200
Lee-on-Solent, 153, 369–372, 407, 415, 442–448, 453, 459, 496, 515
Leech, Flg Off H. H., 243
Leeds, 1, 9, 10, 21, 24, 27, 41, 43, 53, 56, 60–69, 74–77, 81–86, 115–117, 126, 155, 178, 211, 239, 254, 507, 514
Leitner-Watts airscrew, 185, 210
Lend-Lease, 40
Leuchars, 153, 154, 165, 443
Levavasseur, M., 3, 56
Leviathan, 263
Leyburn, 82
Le Bourget, 13, 191, 284
Lincolnshire, 26, 27, 332
Lindsay-Neale, R. 412
Liptrot, Capt R. N., 17
Lisbon, 201, 331, 372, 374
Livock, Wg Cdr G., 316, 317
Llandaff, 64
Locatalli, A., 13
Loch Lomond, 414
Lockheed Aircraft Co, 41
Lockspeiser, d., 26
Lodmoor, 68
Lohse, Fritz, 263
London Air Park Flying Club, 33
— & N. W. Railway, 7
Longmore, Sir Arthur, 197
Longton, Sqn Ldr W. H., 191, 192
Lord, John, 280
Lossiemouth, 485–492, 496, 498–500
Loton, A. G., 15, 28, 33, 155, 190, 239, 267, 332
Loughborough College, 391, 392
Lowdell, G. E., 16, 251, 253, 260, 280
Lowestoft, 13, 162
Lucy, Lt W. P., 405
Luton, 34, 63, 441, 442, 471, 520
Luxor, 280

Lympne, 38, 116, 117, 189–191, 251, 260, 284, 286, 446

MacGilcrist, I. C., 324
MacLaren, Maj A. S., 120
McCash, Flg Off, 156
McEwan, Lt B. S., 405
McIntosh, R. H., 323
McMullin, Capt C. R., 254
Maddocks, Cyril, 118
Malta, 153, 164, 198–203, 351–354, 406, 407, 448, 473, 475
Malton, 68
Manchester, 82, 191
Manning, W. O., ix
— Wardle & Co, 5
Marconi Co., 12, 133
Marine Acceptance Depot, 8, 28, 114
— Observers' School, 114
Marseilles, 197–201, 280, 286
Marske-by-the-Sea, 3, 53
Martlesham Heath, 6, 111–113, 131, 132, 140, 141, 150–152, 162–167, 185, 212, 216, 222, 226, 227, 235, 242, 243, 248, 259, 305–309, 321, 323, 344, 346, 350–353, 366–370, 376, 386, 387, 401–407, 412, 423, 512
Matthews, H. Grindle, 64
Maxton, Flt Lt L. B., 200, 201
Medina, River, 172, 280
Mediterranean, 152, 153, 164, 175, 197, 201, 351, 406, 485, 510
Metal Propellers, 185, 210
Middle Whitton Light Vessel, x, 14, 15
Middlesborough, 27, 251
Midland Railway, 5
Millett, P., 26
Milnathort, 448
Minehead, 64
Ministry of Aircraft Production, 43, 441, 442
— — Aviation, 488, 537–539
— — Supply, 24, 459, 467, 468, 471, 480, 482
Mitchell, L. J. C., 255
Mitsubishi Shoji Kaisha, 295–299
Mombasa, 475
Monospar wing, 18
Montreal, 262, 263, 470
Mount Batten, 15, 199–203, 313, 316, 317
Mousehold, 220, 251, 260
Moxon, G., 146
Muharraq, 475
Muir, A. F., 133
Muscat and Oman, 472, 473
Musée de l'Air, 508

Nairobi, 280, 325, 475, 476
Nakajima, 295
Napier, C. S., 18, 33, 333, 334
— D., and Son, 10, 139, 203, 441, 442, 471
Naples, 170, 197–201

562

565

Index—Aircraft and Engines

569

570